THOMAS COOK

On 5 July 1841 Thomas Cook, a 32-year-old printer from Market Harborough, in Leicestershire, England, led a party of some 500 temperance enthusiasts on a railway outing from Leicester to Loughborough which he had arranged down to the last detail. This proved to be the birth of the modern tourist industry. In the course of expanding his business, Thomas Cook and his son, John, invented many of the features of organised travel which we now take for granted. Over the next 150 years the name Thomas Cook became synonymous with world travel.

Today the Thomas Cook Group employs over 13,000 people across the globe and its Worldwide Network provides services to customers at more than 3000 locations in over 100 countries. Its activities include travel retailing, tour operating and financial services – Thomas Cook is a world leader in traveller's cheques and foreign money services.

Thomas Cook believed in the value of the printed word as an accompaniment to travel. His publication *The Excursionist* was the equivalent of both a holiday brochure and a travel magazine. Today Thomas Cook Publishing continues to issue one of the world's oldest travel books, the *Thomas Cook European Timetable,* which has been in existence since 1873. Updated every month, it remains the only definitive compendium of European railway schedules.

The *Thomas Cook Touring Handbook* series, to which this volume belongs, is a range of comprehensive guides for travellers touring regions of the world by train, car and ship. Other titles include:

Touring by train
On the Rails around France and Benelux (Published 1995)
On the Rails around the Alps (Published 1996)
On the Rails around Eastern Europe (Published 1996)
On the Rails around Europe (Third Edition Published 1998)
On the Rails around Britain and Ireland (Second Edition Published 1998)
Touring by car
On the Road around California (Second Edition Published 1996)
On the Road around Florida (Second Edition Published 1997)
On the Road around Normandy, Brittany and the Loire Valley (Published 1996)
On the Road around the Capital Region (Published 1997)
On the Road around the South of France (Published 1997)
On the Road around the Pacific Northwest (Published 1997)
On the Road around England and Wales (Published 1998)
Touring by car, train and bus
Touring Australia (Published 1997)
Touring Southern Africa (Published 1997)
Touring the Canadian Rockies (Published 1998)
Touring by ship
Greek Island Hopping (Published annually in March)
Cruising around Alaska (Published 1995)
Cruising around the Caribbean (Published 1996)

For more details of these and other Thomas Cook publications, write to Thomas Cook Publishing, at the address on the back of the title page.

TOURING

Eastern
Canada

Driving holidays
and rail journeys in
Ontario, Québec and
the Atlantic Provinces

Edited by
Stephen H. Morgan

A THOMAS COOK TOURING HANDBOOK

Published by Thomas Cook Publishing
The Thomas Cook Group Ltd
PO Box 227
Thorpe Wood
Peterborough PE3 6PU
United Kingdom

email: books@thomascook.com

Advertising sales: 01733 503568

Text:
© 1998 The Thomas Cook Group Ltd
Maps and diagrams:
© 1998 The Thomas Cook Group Ltd

ISBN 1 900341 05 0

Commissioning Editor: Deborah Parker
Project Editor: Leyla Davies
Map Editor: Bernard Horton
Route diagrams: Caroline Horton
Maps drawn by RJS Associates

Cover illustration by Tina West
Text design by Darwell Holland
Text typeset in Bembo and Gill Sans using
    QuarkXPress for Windows
Maps and diagrams created using Macromedia
    Freehand and GSP Designworks
Printed in Great Britain by Fisherprint Ltd,
    Peterborough

Written and researched by
Tom Bross
Patricia Harris and David Lyon
Lucy Izon
Barbara Radcliffe Rogers and
Stillman Rogers

Book Editor:
Stephen H.Morgan

Photographs

back cover: City Hall, Toronto: Tom Bross.
Opposite p. 32: (i) Gaspé: David Lyon; bridge: Stillman Rogers. (ii) Skyline: Tom Bross; Fort
York: Lucy Izon. (iii) Eaton Centre: Tom Bross; Niagara: Lucy Izon
Opposite p. 128: (i) and (ii) all by Lucy Izon; (iii) all by David Lyon; (iv) Skating: David Lyon;
Skis: Stillman Rogers.
Opposite p. 224: (i) Frontenac, diners: David Lyon; red restaurant: Tom Bross; (ii) David Lyon;
(iii) waterfront: Stillman Rogers; shrine: Tom Bross; (iv) Carleton; model ships: David Lyon;
Caraquet: Tom Bross.
Opposite p. 288: (i) all by Tom Bross; (ii) courtesy of Tourism Nova Scotia; (iii) coast: Tom Bross;
gardens: Stillman Rogers; (iv) all by Stillman Rogers.

ABOUT THE AUTHORS

Stephen H. Morgan, the editor of this volume and of Thomas Cook's *On the Road Around New England*, is an editor at *The Boston Globe* and former Travel Editor of the *Boston Herald*.

Tom Bross, a veteran Boston-based travel writer, contributes to a variety of newspapers, magazines and guidebook series, specialising in eastern Canada in addition to Germany, Austria and Switzerland. For this volume he covered Ottawa-Hull, Prince Edward Island and New Brunswick.

Lucy Izon, born in Ontario and based in Toronto for 27 years, is the author of the *Canadian Travellers' Trip Planner* and *Izon's Backpacker Journal*. The Ontario contributor to this volume, she has reported on Canadian travel for the Discovery Channel in Canada and writes a weekly newspaper column for young independent travellers that is syndicated in the *Los Angeles Times, Chicago Tribune* and *The Toronto Star*.

Patricia Harris and **David Lyon** have collaborated since 1981 on magazine and newspaper articles covering travel, the arts and fine dining. They are the authors of the *Compass American Guides* Boston volume and of Globe-Pequot's *Romantic Days & Nights in Boston*, and they review dining for the online guide boston.sidewalk.com. They covered Québec for this book.

Barbara Radcliffe Rogers and **Stillman Rogers**, who specialise in Atlantic Canada for guidebooks, magazines and their own newspaper column, covered Newfoundland and Labrador, Nova Scotia and part of New Brunswick for this volume. They have written guides to New Hampshire, Vermont and Rhode Island, two books on Europe, and they contribute regularly to *Yankee Magazine's Guide to New England*.

ACKNOWLEDGEMENTS

The authors and publishers would like to thank the following people and organisations for their assistance during the preparation of this book:

Ralph Johanssen, Candee Treadway and Linda Schmidtke, Canadian Consulate, Boston; Air Canada/Air Nova and Richard Griffith, Griffith Steadman & Associates; Atlantic Host Inn, Bathurst, NB; Auberge de la Pointe, Rivière-du-Loup, PQ; Auberge du Vieux-Port, Montréal; Eric Austin, Reservations Mont-Tremblant; Geraldine Beaton, Tourism Halifax; Gilles Bengle, Greater Montréal Convention and Tourism Bureau; George Bailey, Niagara Parks Commission; Nancy Bailey-Brazeau, Vintage Inns, Niagara-on-the-Lake, ON; Tom Boyd, Kelly Johnston and Judy Hammond, Ontario Tourism; Randy Brooks, Tourism Nova Scotia; Best Western Danny's Inn, Bathurst, NB; Budget Rent-a-Car; Paule Bussières, Festival d'Été, Québec City; Captain's Inn, Alma, NB; Château Laurier, Ottawa; Comfort Inns and Cindy Knaus in Brantford, Steve Robinson in Peterborough, Pam McEachern in Kingston, Julie Oakes in Brockville, Steve Carr in Huntsville, Bill Forrest in Orillia and Ken Johnston in Barrie, ON; Confederation Centre of the Arts, Charlottetown, PEI; Aiden Costello, Ferryland, NF; Country Inn & Suites, Miramichi, NB; Ann Cunningham, Greyhound Tours, Toronto; John Dunn, Le Marriott Château Champlain, Montréal; France Faucher, Association Touristique de l'Outaouais; Carol Franks, Painted Lady Inn, Kingston, ON; Richard Germain, Hotel Dominion 1912, Montréal; Gîte du Mont-Albert, Ste-Anne-des-Monts, PQ; John Hamilton, Tourism Toronto; Sandy Graham; Karen Hambrock, Quality Suites, London, ON; Hillhurst Inn, Charlottetown, PEI; Paul Holowaty, Rodeway Suites, Kitchener, ON; Carol Horne, PEI Tourism; Hôtel La Normandie, Percé, PQ; Hotel Paulin, Caraquet, NB; Hôtel Rimouski, Rimouski, PQ; Diane Houston, Ottawa Tourism; Inn on the Cove, Saint John, NB; Inns on St George, Charlottetown, PEI; Valerie Kidney, New Brunswick Tourism; Andy Kulche, Rodeway Inn & Suites, Niagara Falls, ON; Jane and Steven Locke, Lakewinds, Niagara-on-the-Lake, ON; Katherine MacDougal, Ottawa Tourism; Lori L. Malcolm, Delta London Armouries Hotel, London, ON; Percy Mallett, New Brunswick Tourism; National/Tilden Car Rental; Shailesh Patal, Quality Inn Downtown, Hamilton; Francine Patenaude, Tourisme Cantons-de-l'Est, PQ; Andrea Peddle, Newfoundland-Labrador Office of Economic Development; Serge Primeau, Manoir Labelle, Mont-Tremblant, PQ; Diane Rennie, Parks of the St Lawrence, ON; Robertson House Inn, Brockville, ON; Venicio N. Rodrigues, Manoir des Sables, Magog-Orford, PQ; Werner Sapp, Hôtel Le Château Montebello, Montebello, PQ; Eric Séguin, Tourisme Mauricie-Bois-Francs; Shipwright Inn, Charlottetown, PEI; Dorleen Sponagle, Tourism Cape Breton; Pierre Tougas, Québec Ministère du Tourisme; René Trépannier, Tourisme Bas-St-Laurent Gaspésie; Victoria Bed & Breakfast, Moncton, NB; Le Vieux Presbytére, Bouctouche, NB; John Welsh, Muskoka Sands, Gravenhurst; Woodlands Country Inn, Woodville Mills, PEI; Tara Whyte, Choice Hotels Canada; Odette Yazbeck, Shaw Festival, Niagara-on-the-Lake, ON; Amy Vreeland and Ethan Morgan.

5

CONTENTS

ROUTES AND CITIES

*In alphabetical order. For indexing purposes, routes are listed in both directions – the reverse direction
to which it appears in the book is shown in italics.
See also the Route Map, p. 8, for a diagrammatic presentation of all the routes in the book.
To look up towns and other places not listed here, see the Index, p. 348.*

6

7

REFERENCE SECTION

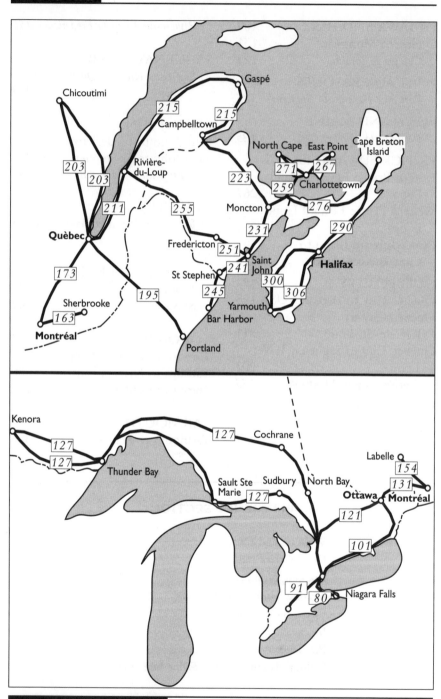

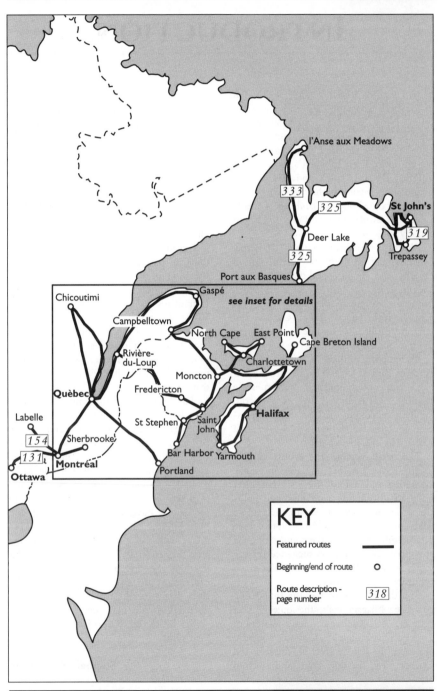

l'Anse aux Meadows

333

325

St John's

Deer Lake

319

325

Trepassey

Port aux Basques

Chicoutimi

Gaspé

see inset for details

Campbelltown

North Cape

East Point

Cape Breton Island

Rivière-du-Loup

Charlottetown

Moncton

Quèbec

Fredericton

Labelle

St Stephen

Saint John

Halifax

154

Sherbrooke

131

Bar Harbor

Yarmouth

Montréal

Portland

Ottawa

9

KEY

Featured routes	———
Beginning/end of route	O
Route description - page number	318

INTRODUCTION

Eastern Canada is not a single region but many, both geographically and culturally. From Nova Scotia's rocky shores to Québec's deep forests, from south-eastern Ontario's fertile farmland to the barren tundra up north, from Labrador's snowy peaks to Prince Edward Island's sandy beaches, the six provinces detailed in this book encompass a vast and varied physical landscape – nearly a third of Canada, the world's second largest country.

Almost as varied is the cultural landscape, which is built on the uneasy partnership of French- and English-speaking people but goes on to include Native people descended from the original inhabitants and the Scottish, Irish, Greek, Italian, German and other nationalities who came later in a quest to carve out a new homeland.

It's tempting to think of Canada as a far-northern land of ice and snow, an undeveloped and underpopulated wilderness, a country overshadowed by its powerful southern neighbour, the USA. Such impressions doubtless contain some truth – but that is only part of Canada's story.

This small volume endeavours to give readers some idea of just how accessible, interesting and unique these six provinces really are. Beginning with bustling, multi-ethnic Toronto and ending in the remote wilds of Labrador, its 39 chapters give detailed information on the major cities, the provincial capitals and on suggested driving routes between them to let you see as much as possible along the way.

And there's a lot to see: the thundering power of Niagara Falls, the quiet Amish country of Kitchener and Waterloo, Toronto's lively nightlife, Ottawa's insightful museums, the joie de vivre of Montréal and Québec City, the raw, dramatic beauty of the Saguenay Fjord and Gaspé Peninsula, the placid charm of Atlantic Canada's little villages, the rugged seascapes of Newfoundland. Historic sites and monuments – such as Cape Breton's Louisbourg fortress and Québec's Plains of Abraham – recount the colonial conflict between France and England. Scottish ceilidhs and Acadian fests keep old-country traditions alive in the hinterlands; summer fêtes celebrate music, art, film and fun in the cities.

Canada's outdoors experience is something no traveller should miss, from whale-watching in the Gulf of St Lawrence to river-rafting on the Ottawa, from skiing the Laurentians to bicycling the Cabot Trail. While this book doesn't attempt to be a guide to the great northern forests and vast back country, it does lead the traveller to some off-the-beaten-track adventures that can be had without straying too far from major routes.

This book is primarily written for British travellers and fellow Anglophones from Australia, Ireland, New Zealand, South Africa, the United States and so on, but it will serve just as well for Canadians – of English, French or any other ethnic background – hitting the road to explore their own heritage. It was researched by a team of professional travel writers from Ontario and New England, all of whom have long experience with and intimate knowledge of the areas they covered. For this volume, they hit the highways and byways of Canada's six easternmost provinces yet again, seeking the latest details on old, familiar attractions and discovering many new ones.

We invite you to tour Eastern Canada in their paths.

Stephen H. Morgan

HOW TO USE THIS BOOK

ROUTES AND CITIES

Touring Eastern Canada provides you with an expert selection of more than 30 recommended routes between key cities and attractions of Ontario, Québec, New Brunswick, Prince Edward Island, Nova Scotia and Newfoundland and Labrador, each in its own chapter. Smaller cities, towns, attractions and points of interest along each route are described in the order in which you will encounter them. Additional chapters are devoted to the major places of interest which begin and end these routes, and some circular routes explore regions of particular interest. These route and city chapters form the core of the book, from page 62 to page 343.

Where applicable, an alternative route which is more direct is also provided at the beginning of each route chapter. This will enable you to drive more quickly between the cities at the beginning and end of the route, if you do not intend to stop at any of the intermediate places. To save space, each route is described in only one direction, but you can follow it in the reverse direction, too.

The arrangement of the text consists of a chapter describing a large city or region of interest first, followed by chapters moving towards other major destinations to the east or in a circuit back to a major city. The first city to be covered is Toronto (pp.62–79), followed by Toronto to Niagara Falls (pp. 80–90) and a Toronto to London circular drive (pp. 91–100), then a route leading away from Toronto: Toronto to Ottawa (pp.101–108). Ottawa is then described in the next chapter, followed by a route that takes you back to Toronto. The routes then head east into Québec, consecutive route chapters forming a longer tour. The overall pattern of the routes runs east from Toronto in Ontario, heading into Québec to New Brunswick, with some routes turning back into Québec and others leading on into Prince Edward Island, Nova Scotia, and finally into Newfoundland and Labrador. To find the page number of any route or city chapter quickly, use either the alphabetical list on the **Contents** pages, pp. 6–7, or the master **Route Map** on pp. 8–9.

The routes are designed to be used as a kind of menu from which you can plan an itinerary, combining a number of routes which take you to the places you most want to visit.

WITHIN EACH ROUTE

Each route chapter begins with a short introduction to the route, followed by driving directions from the beginning of the route to the end, and a sketch map of the route and all the places along it which are described in the chapter. This map, intended to be used in conjunction with the driving directions, summarises the route and shows the main intermediate distances and road numbers

DIRECT ROUTE

This will be the fastest, most direct, and sometimes, predictably, least interesting drive between the beginning and end of the route, usually along major highways.

SCENIC ROUTE

This is the itinerary which takes in the most places of interest, usually using ordinary highways and minor roads. Road directions are specific; always be prepared for detours due to road construction, adverse weather conditions, etc. The driving directions are followed by sub-sections describing the main attractions and places of interest along the way. You can stop at them all or miss out the ones which do not appeal to you. Always ask at the local tourist information centre for more information on sights, lodgings and places at which to eat.

BUSES AND TRAINS

In some chapters, as an alternative to driving long distances, we give details of rail and bus travel. Information is taken from the *Thomas Cook Overseas Timetable*, and relevant table numbers are given. Details, and how to obtain a copy, can be found on p. 39 and p. 172.

 SIDE TRACK

This heading is occasionally used to indicate departures from the main route, or out-of-town trips which detour to worthwhile sights, described in full or highlighted in a paragraph or two.

CITY DESCRIPTIONS

Whether a place is given a half-page description within a route chapter or merits an entire chapter to itself, we have concentrated on practical details: local sources of tourist information; getting around in city centres (by car, by public transport or on foot as appropriate); accommodation and dining; post and phone communications; entertainment and shopping opportunities; and sightseeing, history and background interest. The largest cities have all this detail; in smaller places some categories of information are less relevant and have been omitted or summarised. Where there is a story to tell which would interrupt the flow of the main description, we have placed **feature boxes** on subjects as diverse as 'The Indians of Québec' and 'Whales and Icebergs'.

Although we mention good independently owned lodgings in many places, we always also list the hotel chains which have a property in the area, by means of code letters to save space. Many travellers prefer to stick to one or two chains with which they are familiar and which give a consistent standard of accommodation. The codes are explained on p. 346, and central booking numbers for the chains are also given there.

MAPS

In addition to the sketch map which accompanies each route, we provide maps of major cities, smaller towns, regions, national parks, and so on. At the end of the book is a section of **colour road maps** covering Eastern Canada, which is detailed enough to be used for trip planning and on the road. The **key to symbols** used on all the types of map in this book is shown on p. 13.

THE REST OF THE BOOK

The use of the **Contents** and **Route Map** pages has already been mentioned above. **Background EasternCanada** gives a concise briefing on the history and geography of this fascinating region. **Travel Essentials** is an alphabetically arranged chapter of general advice for the tourist new to Canada, covering a wide range subjects such as accommodation and safety or how much to tip. **Driving in Eastern Canada** concentrates on advice for drivers on the law, rules of the road, and so on. **Touring Itineraries** provides ideas and suggestions for putting together an itinerary of your own using the selection of routes in this book, and lists the pick of the Parks, museums and historic sites. At the back of the book, **Driving Distances** is a tabulation of distances between main places, to help in trip planning, and the **Conversion Tables** decode metric sizes and measures for those more used to imperial measures. Finally the **Index** is the quick way to look up any place or general subject. And please help us by completing and returning the **Reader Survey** at the very end of the text; we are grateful for both your views on the book and new information from your travels in Eastern Canada.

KEY TO MAP SYMBOLS

Route diagrams

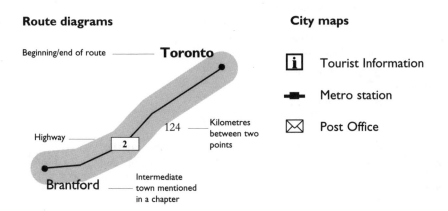

City maps

[i] Tourist Information

➡━ Metro station

✉ Post Office

13

KEY TO PRICE DESCRIPTIONS

It is impossible to keep up to date with specific tariffs for lodging and accommodation or restaurants, although we have given some general advice under 'Cost of Living' in the Travel Essentials chapter p.22). Instead, we have rated establishments in broad price categories throughout the book, as follows:

Accommodation (per room per night)
Budget	Under $50
Moderate	Under $120
Expensive	Under $200
Pricey	$200 and higher

Meal (for one person, excluding drinks, tip or tax)
Cheap	Under $7
Budget	Under $13
Moderate	Under $25
Pricey	$25 and higher

ABBREVIATIONS USED IN THE BOOK
(For hotel chains, see p. 345)

Bldg	Building (in addresses)	min(s)	minute(s)
Blvd	Boulevard	Mon, Tues	Monday, Tuesday, etc.
Ch	Chemin (French for 'road', used in Québec)	OTT	*Overseas Timetable* (see p. 39)
		Rd	Road (in addresses)
Dr.	Drive (in addresses)	Rte	Route
hr(s)	hour(s)	St	Street (in addresses)
Hwy	Highway, e.g. Hwy 1	$	Canadian Dollars
Jan, Feb	January, February, etc.	US$	US Dollars

THOMAS COOK
TOURING HANDBOOKS
The perfect companions for your holiday

These route-based guides are crammed with practical information and maps. From advice on road laws to ideas for accommodation and sightseeing, they contain all the information you need to explore the USA and Canada by car.

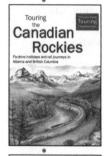

Touring the
Canadian Rockies
Fly-drive holidays and rail journeys in Alberta and British Columbia

TOURING THE
Canadian Rockies

Over 30 routes cover the Canadian Rockies. Includes full guides to Calgary, Edmonton and Vancouver, and features many other cities, towns and national parks.

PRICE
£12.95

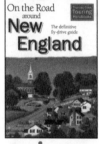

On the Road around
New England
The definitive fly-drive guide

ON THE ROAD AROUND
New England

40 routes with side-trips and scenic drives throughout this varied region. The area covered stretches from New York up to northern Maine, with side trips into Canada to visit Montreal and Quebec.

PRICE
£10.95

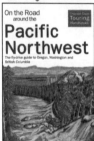

On the Road around the
Pacific Northwest
The fly-drive guide to Oregon, Washington and British Columbia

ON THE ROAD AROUND THE
Pacific North West

Award-winning guide with over 40 routes covering this stunning region. Features Oregon and Washington states, and parts of British Columbia. Includes 16 pages of colour photographs.

PRICE
£12.95

These publications are available from bookshops and Thomas Cook UK retail shops, or direct by post from Thomas Cook Publishing, Dept (OWN), PO Box 227, Thorpe Wood, Peterborough, PE3 6PU, UK.
(Extra for postage and packing.)
Tel: 01733 503571/2.
Published in the USA by Passport Books

Thomas Cook

TRAVEL ESSENTIALS

The following is an alphabetical listing of helpful tips and advice for those planning a Canadian holiday.

ACCOMMODATION

Canada offers accommodation of every price level imaginable, from five-star hotels and posh resorts to youth hostels and campsites. Local tourist offices can provide lodging lists and telephone numbers, but generally can't make bookings. Where available, lodging services are noted in the text.

Accommodation can be extremely hard to find in major tourist destinations during high season, which is usually June, July and Aug, plus weekends and major public holidays year-round in the big cities.

Thomas Cook or any other good travel agent can handle room bookings when purchasing air tickets and car or other local transportation. All-inclusive fly-drive arrangements and 'do-it-yourself packages' such as Thomas Cook Holidays' *Canada for the Independent Traveller* programme, can provide hotel coupons, exchangeable at a range of hotel chains, which guarantee a prepaid rate at participating chains, although they do not guarantee rooms – it's up to you to phone ahead as you go or take a chance on availability. It's particularly important to pre-book the first and last nights' stay to avoid problems when connecting with air flights.

Throughout the book we have indicated prices of accommodation in a comparative way by using terms such as 'moderate' and 'pricey'; see p. 13 for an explanation of what these descriptions mean in terms of Canadian dollars.

Hotels and Motels
Canadian hotel rates are quoted for single or double occupancy; children usually stay cheaply or free with parents.

Most chain hotels and motels have toll-free reservation telephone numbers than can be reached from anywhere in North America. A selection of these, along with the abbreviations used in the text of this book to indicate which chains are present in the town or city being described, is given on p. 345.

Advance bookings require a voucher or credit card number to guarantee the booking. Ask for discounts if you're disabled, a senior, a motoring club member or travelling off season. When checking in, always ask if there's a cheaper room rate than the one you pre-booked. It's often cost-effective to find lodging day by day, especially off-peak.

Motels are often the best bet. Literally 'motor hotels', motels are one- to three-storey buildings with a modest version of a hotel's accommodation. Most belong to nationwide chains which enforce service and safety standards. Independent motels may not be quite as fancy but offer even lower prices. Motels fill up fast during high season, but last-minute rooms are usually available in the off season, especially during the week. The *AAA/CAA TourBooks* for *Ontario* and for *Atlantic Provinces* and *Quebec* list thousands of motels and hotels; thousands more are just as comfortable and affordable. Check the motels that line major highways entering most cities and towns. Availability is advertised with a 'Vacancy' sign out front, changed to 'No Vacancy' when fully booked.

Budget hotels especially in cities, tend to be dim, dirty and dangerous. Look for a motel or youth hostel instead.

Inns and Bed and Breakfasts
In Canada, bed and breakfasts can be a

15

homier alternative to 'cookie-cutter' hotels and motels, and many represent almost the bargain lodging offered by their English cousins.

In country towns of New Brunswick, Nova Scotia, Prince Edward Island and Newfoundland, b & b's are typically private homes with one to four rooms available and prices on a par with budget–moderate motels; some may be cosily furnished with antiques and homespun quilts, others are plain but tidy. In big cities such as Toronto, they may offer well-kept rooms in stately Victorian or Georgian homes within walking distance of public transport, with prices in the moderate category. Facilities may be private or shared. Some owners offer guests a chance to mingle or watch television in a public parlour. Breakfast is usually the chance to interact with hosts or fellow guests; the meal itself may range from full breakfast to coffee or tea, orange juice, home-made muffins and cereal.

Country Inns

Country inns in Atlantic Canada may be historic or heritage properties, with three or more rooms and full evening meal offered, whereas an **inn** might be almost any lodging with meals available. Other types of accommodation include **cabins**, which are small free-standing units with bed-sitting room, bath and possibly kitchen facilities; **cottages**, free-standing units with multiple bedrooms, a bathroom and possibly a separate kitchen or living room; **housekeeping units**, which offer cooking facilities and utensils; **tourist/ guest/hospitality homes**, private homes with a few rooms to let and breakfast available but not included, and **resorts**, which offer extensive recreational facilities and on-site meals.

Camping

Camping means a tent or a recreational vehicle (RV) in a rural campsite. Those in provincial parks and forests are often the quietest and most primitive, with firewood available but facilities limited to pit toilets and cold showers (or coin-operated warm showers). Federal campsites similarly are outfitted for those who enjoy the outdoors experience.

Private campsites vary widely. Some cater to tenters but tolerate RVs; others resemble mini-suburbs, with laundry facilities, recreation halls and television antennas on every RV. Standard facilities include a fireplace for barbecues, tent site or electric/sewer hookups, showers and toilets.

Overnight fees range from $10–23 (depending on location and season) at private campsites, $8–14 at provincial or federal parks. Many provincial park campsites can be reserved well in advance by mail; indeed, reservations are often required in July and August.

Youth Hostels

Hostelling International Canada, *400-205 Catherine St, Ottawa, ON K2P 1C3; tel: (613) 237-7884, fax: (613) 237-7868, website: www.hostellingint.ca/english/ or email: info@hostellingint.ca,* was created for tight budgets. Most hostels provide a dormitory-style room and shared bath for $5–20 per night. Some have family rooms, all offer discounts to local attractions. The downside: there are only a handful of hostels in the Atlantic provinces. And when two or more people are travelling together and can share a room, cheap motels may be less expensive and more conveniently located.

Universities and colleges often offer dormitory rooms at inexpensive prices during summer months, particularly in Toronto and Montréal.

AIRPORTS

The major airports serving visitors to Canada are **Toronto's Pearson International Airport** (YYZ) and **Montréal's Dorval International Airport** (YUL). **Ottawa's Macdonald-Cartier International**

OUR STARS LIGHT THE WAY

Whether you are looking for a Resort or a Bed and Breakfast, you'll find the answer in our stars. Use the Canada Select Accommodations Rating Program to help you select a property that best suits your preference while enjoying Canada.

Canada Select assesses and rates properties to assure they will meet your expectations. All participating properties must meet rigorous cleanliness and maintenance standards that are uniformly administered.

Accommodations are rated within six different categories – Hotel/Motel, Inn, Bed and Breakfast, Resort, Cottage, or Hunting & Fishing Lodges. Ratings are issued and should be compared within the appropriate categories.

The Canada Select sign is your assurance of quality at more than 3,000 participating accommodations across Canada.

STAR DEFINITIONS

★
Modest accommodations meeting the Canada Select standards of cleanliness, comfort and safety.

★ ★
Moderate accommodations with additional facilities and some amenities.

★ ★ ★
Above average accommodations with a greater range of facilities, guest amenities and services available.

★ ★ ★ ★
Exceptional accommodations with an extensive range of facilities, guest amenities and services.

★ ★ ★ ★ ★
Luxurious properties. Among the very best in the country in terms of the outstanding facilities, amenities and guest services provided.

⅟
1/2 stars are awarded to properties whose overall quality of facilities exceeds their specific category star rating.

Benchmarks outlining specific facilities and services within each category star rating may be found at www.canadacoast.com/canselect or by contacting your local Canada Select office.

Canada Select

17

Airport (YOW) and **Halifax International Airport** (YHZ) in Nova Scotia also handle some international flights.

Québec City's Jean-Lesage International Airport (YQB) handles arrivals and departures to the USA and within Canada, and Montréal's Mirabel Airport (YMX) handles charter flights. Travellers can also transfer to flights into airports at many smaller cities, such as Charlottetown, Prince Edward Island; St John's, Newfoundland; and Fredericton, New Brunswick.

The major airports generally have booths that provide local tourist information (such as Travellers Aid Society booths at Toronto and Ottawa); airport information booths cover airport facilities, airport-to-city transport and local accommodation, though no bookings are made (some offer direct phone links to let you make your own bookings).

All major airports have foreign exchange and banking services and car hire facilities. Public transportation to the nearest city is usually available. Specific airport arrival information is given in the chapters dealing with the major airport cities.

Canada has two major airlines. **Air Canada**, tel: toll-free (888) 247-2262 in Canada, toll-free (800) 776-3000 in USA, 0345 1811313 in UK, serves international and US destinations and has three regional carriers in Eastern Canada: Air Ontario in Ontario and Québec; Air Alliance in Ontario, Québec and Newfoundland; Air Nova within the Atlantic provinces and to Ottawa, Montréal, Québec City, New York City and Boston. **Canadian Airlines**, tel: (800) 665-1177 in Canada, (800) 426-7000 in USA, flies to 17 countries and 105 destinations in Canada; it has partnerships with British Airways, Qantas, Air New Zealand and several small regional airlines within Eastern Canada.

BICYCLES

Cycling is popular for countryside touring in Canada. Bikes can be hired by the hour or day in most locations that cater to tourists. Biking is easier and less dangerous in slow-paced resort areas and along country roads. The use of bicycle helmets is always strongly recommended; in addition, helmets are required for all cyclists in Ontario, for all cyclists under age 18 in New Brunswick.

For serious bikers, tours are available at all levels, with accommodations arranged at campsites or posh inns and a 'sag wagon' carrying heavy gear and worn-out cyclists. Both organised and on-your-own bicycle tours are especially popular on Prince Edward Island and on Nova Scotia's Cape Breton Island, due to the scenic beauty of the countryside and the relatively short distances between towns.

BORDERS

For travellers from British Commonwealth countries, border inspections are generally routine, as long as you don't fit the 'profile' that Customs and immigration officials are trained to watch out for. Have your passport, visa, proof of support and return ticket in order. Crossings into Canada from the USA can be time-consuming if an official targets you for a car search. If you're not carrying illegal drugs, alcohol, firearms or agricultural products, and if your documents are in order, you should have no difficulty entering Canada or the USA. Carry doctors' prescriptions to prove that medications are legitimate.

BUSES

Greyhound of Canada Transportation Corp; tel: (800) 661-8747 for fares and schedules (in UK, contact **Greyhound International Travel Inc.**, West Sussex; tel: 01-342-317317, fax: 01-342-328519), provides long-distance bus service across Canada and to major US cities. There are discounts for seniors (over 65), disabled travellers and children (under 12) riding with a full-fare adult. **The International Canada Travel Pass** (for travel from Montréal westward) and **Travel Pass Plus** (which includes travel eastward to Halifax) offer continuous pre-paid bus transportation up to 60 days for travellers not resident in North America. Greyhound passes are obtainable through Thomas Cook travel shops in the UK.

Travel Pass costs $89 for 7 days up to $439 for 60 days; Travel Pass Plus costs $319 for 15 days up to $519 for 60 days (plus 7% GST added to all prices). The passes permit travel on some other bus lines, such as **Voyageur Colonial** in Ontario and Québec, **Orleans Express** from Montréal to Rivière-du-Loup, **SMT Ltd.** to Charlottetown, PEI, and Amherst, NS, and **Acadian Lines** from Amherst to Halifax.

Prices for point-to-point tickets purchased locally vary by distance travelled. The trip from Toronto to Niagara Falls costs under $40, while Halifax, NS, to London, Ontario, costs $312. Many fares and schedules are available on-line at *http://www.grey hound.ca*.

Local transportation companies listed in the telephone directory under individual cities and towns provide **local service**. Thomas Cook publishes bimonthly time-tables of North American buses in the *Thomas Cook Overseas Timetable* (see p. 39).

CAMPERS AND RVS

Fly-drive holiday packages usually offer the option of hiring an RV (recreational vehicle), caravan or motorhome. The additional cost can be offset by the economics of assured lodging for several people, space for meal preparation and eating, and the convenience of comfort items and souvenirs stored nearby.

RVs are cramped, designed to stuff you and your belongings into limited space. The economics work only if advance planning assures that the pricey spur-of-the-moment allure of a hotel shower or unplanned restaurant meal won't overcome RV campers! Factor in the cost of petrol – an RV guzzles 3–4 times more than a medium-sized car

(and remember that while Canada shares a border with the USA, it does not share its neighbour's extremely low petrol prices).

Always get operating manuals for the vehicle and all appliances before leaving the RV hire lot, and have someone demonstrate how everything works. Systems may be interdependent, or more complex than anticipated. Be prepared to pre-plan menus and allow additional time each morning and afternoon/evening to level the RV (perfect levelling is essential for correct operation of refrigerators), hook up or disconnect electricity, water and sewer hoses, and cable television plugs. As at home, some basic housecleaning must be done; also allow time for laundry at RV parks.

Technical information is available from an RV-industry organisation, **Go RVing Canada**, *670 Bloor St W, Suite 200, Toronto, ON M6G 1L2; tel: (416) 533-7800*.

Campsite directories list **private RV park** locations, directions, size, number of pitches, hook-ups, laundry, on-premises convenience stores and showers. The most comprehensive directories are *Woodall's North American Campground Directory* or the less hefty and less expensive *Woodall's Eastern Campground Directory* and *Trailer Life Campground/RV Park and Services Directory*. All include listings of RV campsites in Eastern Canada. Free information on private campsites is available from **Campgrounds Canada**, *2001 de la Metropole, Suite 200, Longueil, PQ JHG 1S9; tel: (514) 651-7396.* **Federal and provincial parks** offer listings on public campsites (see Parks Information below).

CHILDREN

Canada is ideal for travelling with children, and its many historical and natural attractions are always welcoming. From museums to transport, check for children's rates, often segmented by age, e.g., under 3 free, 6–12 years $3, 12–18 years $4. A student card must be shown to use student rates.

19

Travelling with children is never easy, but preparation helps. *Travel with Children*, by Maureen Wheeler (Lonely Planet) is filled with useful tips. Pack favourite games and books, and pick up a book of travel games. A traditional favourite is to count licence plates from all the Canadian provinces and US states. The one with the highest count – always a child – gets a special treat later in the day. If the children are old enough, suggest that they keep a detailed travel diary. It will help them focus on Canada instead of what they might be missing back home. A diary also helps them remember details later to impress friends and teachers. Collecting anything, from postcards to admission tickets, adds a new dimension to travel.

Any driving destination in Canada is equipped for children of all ages, from nappies (diapers) to video games. Most hotels and motels can arrange for babysitters, though the price may be steep. Many hotel chains allow children under 12, 14, sometimes 18, to stay free in their parents' room. A roll-away child's bed, often called a cot, usually comes at no or low cost.

Meals can be difficult, but picnic lunches offer flexibility. It's also a good idea to carry a small cooler filled with ice, cold drinks and snacks, especially in hot weather. Most towns have coffee shops with long hours, children's menus and familiar fast-food names. If the children like McDonalds at home, they'll like Big Macs in Canada – and vice versa.

CLIMATE

In general, expect short summers with warm days and cool nights and long winters with cold temperatures and heavy snow. Chilly temperatures begin in Oct, and spring stays cool into May; snow falls Nov through Apr. Rural and coastal areas are most comfortable to visit in June, July and August, consequently many accommodations in those areas are closed the rest of the year. Far northern regions may become inaccessible during winter; however, the major cities remain lively and inviting in all seasons, as do resort areas that offer skiing and other outdoor activities.

In Ontario, Toronto is quite temperate,

Average Temperatures

	Halifax	Montréal	St John's, NF	Toronto
JANUARY				
Highest	-3°C/31.5°F	-6°C/21°F	0°C/32°F	-1.1°C/30.1°F
Lowest	-8.9°C/16°F	-15°C/5°F	-7°C/19°F	-7.7°C/18.1°F
APRIL				
Highest	7.8°C/46°F	11°C/52°F	5°C/41°F	11.9°C/53.4°F
Lowest	-0.2°C/31.6°F	1.1°C/34°F	-1.1°C/30°F	3.2°C/37.8°F
JULY				
Highest	21.8°C/71.2°F	26°C/79°F	21°C/70°F	26.8°C/80.3°F
Lowest	13.1°C/55.6°F	16°C/61°F	11°C/52°F	16.1°C/62.3°
OCTOBER				
Highest	13.3°C/55.9°F	12.8°C/55°F	11°C/52°F	3.9°C/39°F
Lowest	5.2°C/41.4°F	3.9°C/39°F	3.9°C/39°F	7.1°C/44.8°F

much like New York City and Chicago, with temperatures around 27°C (80°F) in summer and at freezing or below in winter. The average annual rainfall is 68.9cm (27.25 inches), average snowfall a modest 135cm (53.2 inches). Ottawa in summer averages a few degrees cooler than Toronto and is often humid. Its winters, however, are much harsher, with heavy snowfall (average 206cm/81 inches) and Jan temperatures from a high of -6°C (21°F) to a low of -15°C (5°F).

Québec is a province of extremes, with warm (or even hot), humid summers and cold, snowy winters. Montréal averages 16°–26°C (61°–79°F) in July, with Québec City a few degrees cooler – and often more humid – and the Gaspé Peninsula cooler still at 11°–23°C (52°–73°F). Montréal average 243cm (96 inches) of snow each year, but little of it may stick in the city; whereas Québec City is often snowy (annual average 288cm/113 inches). Out in the Gaspé Peninsula, the snow lasts an average 165 days and amounts to 322cm (127 inches); the temperatures in Jan range -17° to -6°C (3°–21°F), about the same as Montréal and Québec City.

The Atlantic provinces of New Brunswick, Prince Edward Island and Nova Scotia are generally cooler than Québec or Ontario in the summer, with July temperatures averaging from 13°C (55°F) up to around 23°C (73°F) on the coast, higher inland. Expect Newfoundland to be a few degrees cooler. These provinces draw few winter tourists; they are generally cold and snowy, though more moderate in some coastal areas.

CLOTHING

Canadian summers are warm (occasionally hot) and humid, winters often bitterly cold and damp. Lightweight, summer clothing is a safe bet only in July and Aug; even then you may need to cover up sometimes for cool nights. In May, June and Sept, bring medium-weight in addition to summer clothes; nights are cool. In Oct, Nov, March and Apr, you need medium- to heavy-weight clothing; in Dec, Jan and Feb, winter clothing is needed.

In any season, take plenty of layers, from shorts for the beach to jumpers and jackets for the mountains or evenings along the shore. Cotton and wool, worn in layers, are always a safe bet. Adding and removing layers makes it easier to stay comfortable no matter how many times the weather changes in a day.

What to pack is a constant question. Except for business, Canadians dress casually. A wide range of dress is acceptable, even at the ballet or symphony in Toronto or Montréal, and only elegant restaurants require jackets and ties for men. All shops and restaurants, even at the beach, require that shirts and shoes be worn. The bottom line is: when in doubt, leave it at home. But do take good, broken-in walking shoes.

CONSULATES

Australia: *175 Bloor St E., Suites 314-316, Toronto, ON M4W 3R8; tel: (416) 323-1155. High Commission, 50 O'Conner St, Suite 710, Ottawa, ON K1P 6L2; tel: (613) 236-0841.*
New Zealand: *High Commission, Suite 727, Metropolitan House, 99 Bank St, Ottawa, ON K1P 6G3; tel: (613) 238-6097; fax: (613) 238-5707; email: nzhcott@istar.ca.*
Republic of Ireland: *Embassy, 130 Albert St, Suite 1105, Ottawa, ON K1P 5G5; tel: (613) 233-6281. Honorary Consul Craig Dobbin, St John's, NF; tel: (709) 570-0700.*
South Africa: *2 First Canadian Place, Suite 2300, Toronto, ON M5X 1E3; tel: (416) 364-0314. Suite 2615, 1 Place Ville Marie, Montreal, PQ H3B 4S3; tel: (514) 878-9217. High Commission, 15 Sussex Dr., Ottawa, ON K1M 1M8; tel: (613) 744-0330; email: safrica@ottawa.net.*
UK: *College Park, 777 Bay St, Suite 2800, Toronto, ON M5G 2G2; tel: (416) 593-*

1290; fax (416) 593-1229. 100 r. de la Gauchetiere Ouest, Suite 4200, Montréal, PQ H3B 4W5; tel: (514) 866-5863; fax: (514) 866-0202. 1 Canal St, PO Box 605, Dartmouth, NS B3Y 3Y9; tel: (902) 461-1381; fax: (902) 463-7678. 113 Topsail Rd, St John's, NF A1E 2A9; tel: (709) 579-2002; fax: (709) 579-0475. High Commission, 80 Elgin St, Ottawa, ON K1P 5K7; tel: (613) 237-1542; fax: (613) 237-7980.

USA: Cogswell Tower, Suite 910, Scotia Sq., Halifax, NS B3J 3K1; tel: (902) 429-2480. 1155 Saint Alexandre St, Montréal, PQ H2Z 1Z2; tel: (514) 398-9695. 2 Dufferin Terrace, Box 939, Quebec, PQ G1R 4T9; tel: (418) 692-2095; 360 University Ave, Toronto, ON M5G 1S4; tel: (416) 595-1700. US Embassy, 100 Wellington St, Ottawa, ON K1P 5T1; tel: (613) 238-5335.

COST OF LIVING

Canada's Goods and Services Tax of 7%, combined with provincial sales taxes of 6.5% to 10%, add up to a hefty extra charge on every purchase. In some provinces the combined levy is more than the VAT charged in most of Europe, although it is mitigated somewhat by the rebate available to visitors of tax paid on many retail purchases and accommodations (see Sales Taxes).

Petrol prices are also costly, usually $0.55–0.65 per litre – or as much as twice what you would pay just south of the border in the USA. Motel rooms cost $40–100 per night; hotels from $80 up. Restaurant meals, including soup or salad, main course, dessert, beverage and tax are about $11–30 for dinner. Most museums charge $2–10 per adult, with discounted admission fees for children, seniors, college students and others. Most federal parks charge a few dollars per car, while state parks are free.

CURRENCY

Canadian dollars are the official currency. Notes ($5, $10, $20, $50, $100) are all of the same size but different colours. There are 100 cents to the dollar: coins include the copper 1 cent piece (penny), 5 cent nickel, 10 cent dime, 25 cent quarter, 50-cent half-dollar, plus a $1 (called the 'loonie' because of the loon pictured on the front) and a $2 coin (the 'twonie', which Canadians like to joke has 'the queen on the front with a bear behind'). In this guidebook, the dollar sign ($) is used for Canadian dollars.

US dollars (US$ in this book) are widely accepted (indeed, sometimes preferred) in Canada, although occasionally 'at par', which ignores their higher value. No need to exchange money when making an excursion into the USA, as Canadian dollars are accepted in US areas near the border and can be easily exchanged in small amounts at US banks without a fee. The exchange rate fluctuates, but the Canadian dollar is usually worth 75%–80% of the US dollar.

Banks will exchange foreign currency or traveller's cheques. Better to seek out one of the **Thomas Cook bureaux de change** noted in this book. However, traveller's cheques denominated in Canadian or US dollars, from well-known issuers such as Thomas Cook, are acceptable everywhere (however, be wary of trading US cheques 'at par').

To report Thomas Cook traveller's cheque losses and thefts, call 1-800-223-7373 (toll-free, 24-hour service).

For security reasons, avoid carrying large amounts of cash. The safest forms of money are Canadian dollar traveller's cheques and credit or debit cards. Both can be used almost anywhere. If possible, bring at least one, preferably two major credit cards such as **Access (MasterCard)**, **American Express** or **Visa**. (Thomas Cook locations will offer replacement and other emergency services if you lose a MasterCard.)

Plastic is the only acceptable proof of fiscal responsibility. Car hire companies require a credit card imprint before releasing a vehicle, even if the hire has been fully prepaid. Hotels and motels also require either a credit card imprint or a cash deposit, even if the bill is to be settled in cash.

Some shops, cheaper motels, small local restaurants and low-cost petrol stations require cash. Automated teller machines, or **ATMs**, are a ubiquitous source of cash through withdrawals or cash advances authorised by debit or credit card. Cirrus, NYCE and Interbac are common systems used in Canada, but check terms, availability and PIN (personal identification number) with the card issuer before leaving home.

CUSTOMS ALLOWANCES

Personal duty-free allowances which can be taken into Canada by visitors of legal age are 1.1 litres (40 ounces) of liquor or wine, or 24 cans or bottles (each 355ml or 12 ounces) of beer or ale (by persons age 19 years or older, 18 in Quebec); 50 cigars, 200 cigarettes and 1 kg of manufactured tobacco (age 16 or older); and gifts valued no more than $60 each, excluding tobacco, alcohol and advertising materials. On your return home you will be allowed to take the following:

Australia: goods to the value of A$400 (half for those under 18) plus 250 cigarettes or 250g tobacco and 1 litre alcohol.

New Zealand: goods to the value of NZ$700. Anyone over 17 may also take 200 cigarettes or 250g tobacco or 50 cigars or a combination of tobacco products not exceeding 250g in all plus 4.5 litres of beer or wine and 1.125 litres spirits.

UK: The allowances for goods bought outside the EU and/or in EU duty-free shops are: 200 cigarettes or 50 cigars or 100 cigarillos or 250g tobacco +2 litres still table wine +1 litre spirits or 2 litres sparkling wine +50g/50 ml perfume +0.5 litre/250 ml toilet water.

USA: goods to the value of US$400 per person, provided you have been away 48 hours, or US$25 if you are away less than 48 hours or if all or part of this personal exemption has been used in the preceding 30 days. The duty-free exemption may include

one litre alcohol (for persons over age 21), 100 non-Cuban cigars and 200 cigarettes (1 carton).

DISABLED TRAVELLERS

Canada has no nationwide law requiring businesses, buildings and services used by the public to be accessible to persons with disabilities, so facilities vary between provinces. In Toronto, Montréal and the bigger provincial capitals, you can generally expect major new hotels, restaurants, museums and public buildings to have access ramps and toilets designed for wheelchairs. A few major hotel chains and resorts – especially those serving international travellers – voluntarily adopted standards set south of the border by the US Americans with Disabilities Act.

Outside the big cities, handicap amenities are sparse. And the old, historic districts and cities, such as in Québec City, are generally not accessible. Commuter airlines sometimes deny boarding to passengers with mobility problems on the grounds that they may block the narrow aisle during an emergency.

Some public telephones have special access services for the deaf and disabled. Broadcast television may be closed-captioned for the hearing impaired, indicated by a rectangle around a double cc in a corner of the screen.

UK Information: *RADAR, 12 City Forum, 250 City Rd, London, EC1V 8AF; tel: (0171) 250 3222,* publish a useful annual guide called Holidays and Travel Abroad, which gives details of facilities for the disabled in different countries.

Québec Information: *Kéroul, 4545 av Pierre-De-Coubertin, C.P. 1000, Succursale M, Montréal, PQ H1V 3R2, Canada; tel: (514) 252-3104, fax: (514) 254-0766, website: http://www.craph.org/keroul/,* advocates for the needs of people with disabilities, provides information for travellers and organises tours throughout the province.

US Information: SATH (Society for the Advancement of Travel for the

23

Handicapped), *347 Fifth Ave, Suite 610, New York, NY 10016; tel: (212) 447-7284*, provides information on Canada.

DISCOUNTS

Reductions on entrance fees and public transport for senior citizens, children, students and military personnel are common. Some proof of eligibility is usually required. For age, a passport or driving licence is sufficient. Military personnel should carry an official identification card. Students will have better luck with an International Student Identity Card (ISIC) from their local student union than with a college ID.

The most common discount is for automobile club members. Tour guides from **AAA** (Automobile Association of America) and **CAA** (Canadian Automobile Association) affiliates list hundreds of member discounts for Ontario, Québec and the Atlantic Provinces. Always ask about 'Triple A' or CAA discounts at attractions, hotels, motels and car hire counters. Most recognise reciprocal membership benefits. Some cities will send high-season discount booklets on request, good for shops, restaurants or lodging.

DRINKING

Canada taxes alcoholic beverages heavily and tightly restricts when and where they may be sold. However, drinking ages are fairly liberal: You may buy beer, wine or liquor at age 19 in Ontario and the Atlantic provinces, 18 in Québec.

Licensed establishments are called **bars, lounges, saloons, taverns, beverage rooms** or **pubs**; provinces govern hours, which vary slightly. In Ontario, for example, the hours are 1100 to 0100. In Nova Scotia, licensed dining rooms and restaurants may serve alcohol from 1100 to 0200; hours vary between types of establishments (beverage rooms, taverns, lounges and clubs), but are generally from 1000, 0100 or noon until 0100 or 0200; cabarets serve until 0330.

Provinces regulate sales of beer, wine and liquor, but the rules are similar from one province to another. Beer, wine and liquor are sold in government-owned shops (in some places in private shops as agents of the government), which are generally open Monday through Saturday, closed Sundays and public holidays.

Laws against drinking and driving are very strict and enforced with fines and imprisonment. You may be arrested for refusing to take a breathaliser test.

ELECTRICITY

Canada uses 110 volt, 60 hertz current, the same as the USA. Two- or three-pin electrical plugs are standard. Electrical gadgets from outside North America require plug and power converters. Both are difficult to obtain in Canada because local travellers don't need them.

Beware of buying electrical appliances in Canada, for the same reason. Few gadgets on the Canadian market can run on 220v, 50hz power. Exceptions are battery-operated equipment such as radios, cameras and portable computers – or a few dual-voltage models of electric shavers and hair dryers. Tape cassettes, CDs, computer programs and CD-ROMs sold in Canada can be used anywhere in the world.

Canadian and US video equipment, which use the NTSC format, are not compatible with the PAL and SECAM equipment used in most of the rest of the world. Pre-recorded video tapes sold in Canada and the USA will not work with other equipment unless specifically marked as compatible with PAL or SECAM. Blank video tapes purchased in North America, however, can be used with video recorders elsewhere in the world.

EMERGENCIES

In case of emergency in and around the big cities, such as Toronto, Montréal, etc., ring *911* from any telephone; the call is free.

Ambulance, paramedics, police, fire brigades or other public safety personnel will be dispatched immediately. See also under 'Health' below. In smaller locales, you generally dial '0' to ask the Operator to request assistance.

If you lose your Thomas Cook travellers cheques, call *1-800-223-7373* (toll-free, 24-hour service).

FOOD

Canada shares the US tradition of large breakfasts with endless refills of coffee. Eggs cooked to order (fried, scrambled, poached) come with round, thick slices of Canadian (or thin, crisp American-style) bacon and fried potatoes. Toast, a flat 'English' muffin with butter and jam, or a bagel with cream (farmer's) cheese may be served alongside. Variations include pancakes (called *crêpes* on Acadian menus), French toast (bread dipped in egg batter and lightly fried) and waffles. Fresh fruit and yoghurt, cereal and porridge are other possibilities. A 'continental breakfast' is juice, coffee or tea, and some sort of bread or pastry. In Québec, look for fresh croissants with *café-au-lait* (by the cup or bol) and *fèves au lard* (baked beans).

Menus offer similar choices for lunch and dinner, the evening meal. Dinner portions are larger and more costly. Most menus offer appetisers (starters), salads, soups, pastas, entrées (main courses) and desserts.

In Québec, the cuisine is French or hearty French provincial, with such local specialities as caribou, venison and farm-raised salmon. Cheese, made from cow, goat and sheep's milk, is abundant; roasted chicken is popular and widely available. In New Brunswick's Acadian country, try *poutine rapée* (potato and salt pork, simmered in a ball and served with brown sugar or molasses), *tourtière* (pork pie) and *fricot aux trou* (clam stew). Fiddleheads, the edible young fronds of a fern, are a common side-dish. *Poutine* (unlike *poutine rapée*) is a fast-food dish of french-fries with melted cheese and gravy.

Atlantic Canada is especially known for its fresh seafood, which is served fried (in batter) or broiled (in butter), sometimes baked, and includes locally caught cod and haddock, bluefish, tuna, Atlantic char, halibut, trout, sole and river salmon. Shellfish appearing on menus include clams, oysters, scallops and shrimp; blue mussels are a speciality. Local waters also produce lobster, which turns bright red after immersion (live) in boiling water. It is served whole (a challenge to eat without making a mess), in parts (tails and claws) or picked out of the shell for salads or sandwiches.

In Newfoundland, fried cod tongues are on every menu, sometimes well-prepared like scallops, sometimes greasy or dried out. Less common is 'fish and brewis' (pronounced brews), a sauté of salt cod and hardtack, covered with salt-pork 'cracklings'.

Ontario has fresh local fruits and vegetables and a great variety of ethnic cuisines, particularly in Toronto. The Amish country west of Toronto is known for German dishes.

For hearty eating, try a steak house where salad and baked potato accompany a thick steak. Italian restaurants serve pizza, pasta, seafood and steaks, with heavy doses of tomato and garlic. Chinese restaurants are ubiquitous in big cities, but they vary widely, from Chinese-Canadian 'chow mein' and 'chop suey' to authentic regional dishes such as spicy Szechuan or rich, meaty Mandarin. The melting pot of cuisines in major cities includes Cambodian, Caribbean, Greek, Hungarian, Indian, Japanese, Korean, Mexican, Middle Eastern, Polish, Portuguese, Thai and Vietnamese.

American-style fast food is quick, economical and impossible to miss. Outside big cities, local 'Mom and Pop' eateries offer hamburgers or fried seafood, milkshakes and soft ice-cream. McDonalds' golden arches and KFC's grinning chubby colonel are easy to spot, along with Burger King, Wendy's, Pizza Hut and Taco Bell. All are cheap.

Rotisserie St-Hubert's roasted chicken is

25

ubiquitous in Québec and Ontario, as is Dixie Lee's fried chicken everywhere else, along with Tim Horton's doughnut shops. Moose Winooski's serves steaks, salads and burgers in a log-cabin Canadian atmosphere. Swiss Chalet, with barbecued chicken, is a reliable choice; also look for Harvey's burgers and Smitty's pancake houses.

Vegetarians will have little trouble eating well, particularly if they enjoy seafood. In addition, many restaurants offer meatless choices, bountiful salad bars are common, and there are a smattering of vegetarian and macrobiotic eateries. Le Commensal is a Québec chain serving a vegetarian buffet.

In small rural towns, restaurants may close early – even by 1900 – so it's worthwhile to plan mealtimes ahead.

GAMBLING

Gambling is well on its way to being a major industry in Canada, from which the state takes its cut. Eastern Canada has casinos in Niagara Falls, Orillia, Sudbury, Thunder Bay and Windsor, Ontario; in Hull, Montréal and Pointe-au-Pic, Québec, and in Halifax and Sydney, Nova Scotia. Some are located in riverboats, others in resort hotels, complete with restaurants, bars, cabarets and stage shows; all games are represented, some casinos have high-limits areas.

HEALTH

Hospital emergency rooms are the place to go in the event of life-threatening medical problems. If a life is truly at risk, treatment will be swift and top notch, with payment problems sorted out later. For mundane problems, 24-hour walk-in health clinics are available in urban areas and some rural communities.

Payment, not care, is the problem. Some form of **health insurance** coverage is almost mandatory in order to ensure provision of health services. Coverage provided by non-Canadian national health plans is not accepted by Canadian medical providers.

The only way to ensure provision of health services is to carry some proof of valid insurance cover. Most travel agents who deal with international travel will offer travel insurance policies that cover medical costs in Canada – at least $1 million of cover is essential.

Bring enough prescription medication to last the entire trip, plus a few extra days. It's also a good idea to carry a copy of the prescription in case of emergency. Because trade names of drugs vary from country to country, be sure the prescription shows the generic (chemical) name and formulation of the drug, not just a brand name.

No inoculations are required, and Canada is basically a healthy place to visit. Common sense is enough to avoid most health problems. Eat normally (or at least sensibly) and avoid drinking water that didn't come from the tap or a bottle. Assume that most ground water in rural recreational areas, including federal and provincial parks, is contaminated with giardia ('beaver fever') and other intestinal parasites.

Sunglasses, broad-brimmed sun hats and sunscreen help prevent sunburn, sun stroke and heat prostration. Be sure to drink plenty of non-alcoholic liquids, especially in hot weather.

AIDS (Acquired Immune Deficiency Syndrome) and other sexually transmitted diseases are endemic in Canada as they are in the rest of the world. The best way to avoid sexually transmitted diseases (STDs) is to avoid promiscuous sex. In anything other than long-term, strictly monogamous relationships, they key phrase is 'safe sex'. Use condoms in any kind of sexual intercourse. Condoms can be bought in drug stores or pharmacies and from vending machines in some public toilets.

Some areas carry a risk of **Lyme disease** from ticks, which can attach themselves to humans who walk through grassy and marshy woodland areas. The disease is passed by brown, pinhead-sized deer ticks. The prevention is to wear light-coloured clothing with long sleeves and a shirt collar, long trousers tucked into socks or boots, a hat and insect repellent containing DEET. Deer ticks are most active from Apr through Oct.

HIKING

Walking is a favourite outdoor activity, especially in park areas. The same cautions that apply anywhere else are good in Canada: know the route; carry a map and basic safety gear; carry food and water. Stay on marked trails. Walking off the trail adds to erosion damage, especially in fragile forests, meadows and beaches. It can also get you lost: don't hike off the trail without telling someone, preferably a park ranger.

The most common hiking problem is **poison ivy**. The low-growing plant is difficult to identify, although its leaflets, sometimes reddish, always occur in clusters of three. Less common is **poison sumac**, identified by leaves that grow in clusters of ten (similar to, but smaller than, those of the non-poisonous sumac tree).

All parts of the plants exude a sticky sap that causes an intense allergic reaction in most people. The most common symptoms are itching, burning and weeping sores. The best way to avoid the problem is to avoid the plants. Second best is to wash skin or clothing that has come into contact with the plant immediately in hot, soapy water. Drying lotions such as calamine or products containing cortisone provide temporary relief, but time is the only cure.

Wildlife can be a problem. The presence of **mountain lions** (also called bobcats, cougars and pumas) is much rumoured but rarely seen. **Coyotes** are seen in increasing numbers in rural areas, especially in Atlantic Canada, and **foxes** are plentiful, though both species are shy of people.

Black bears are a more serious threat, and they are present in virtually all rural areas, with the exception of Prince Edward Island. They're large, strong, fast-moving, always hungry and smart enough to connect

humans with the food they carry. Bears are frequently seen mornings and evenings in public garbage dumps. Parks and campsites in bear country have detailed warnings on how to safely store food to avoid attack. When possible, hang anything ,edible (including toothpaste) in bags well above ground or store in your car. Never feed bears; they won't know when the meal is over. Unless you come between a mother and her young – or leave food or garbage out – bears generally avoid humans. Making noise usually persuades curious bears to look elsewhere for a meal.

Be on the watch for **moose** when driving, especially at night along roads marked for moose crossings, in virtually all rural areas (again, except PEI). Colliding with a moose is often fatal – for motorists as well as the animal. Be equally careful of motorists stopping suddenly when they spot one. When observing moose, stay in your vehicle; adults are enormous and their movements are unpredictable. Never get between an adult moose (or any other wild animal) and its young.

HITCHHIKING

In an earlier, more trustful era, hitchhiking was the preferred mode of transportation for budget travellers. Today, hitchhiking or picking up hitchhikers is asking for violent trouble, from theft to physical assault and murder. Don't do it.

HUNTING AND FISHING

Licences are required from each province in which you plan to hunt or fish. Check with provincial tourism offices regarding hunting seasons, bag limits, gear restrictions and where fishing and hunting licences may be purchased. In addition, federal licences (available at post offices) are required for hunting migratory game birds, and special licences are required for fishing in national parks; the latter can be obtained at any national park site.

Some firearms are restricted or prohibited

from entry into Canada; all firearms must be declared to Canada Customs. The entry of any kind of weapon is forbidden in and nearby many provincial parks and reserves.

Hikers should be extremely cautious in areas posted for hunting. Ask locally about hunting seasons for deer and other game before venturing into the woods.

INSURANCE

Experienced travellers carry insurance that covers their belongings and holiday investment as well as their bodies. Travel insurance should include provision for cancelled or delayed flights and weather problems, as well as immediate evacuation home in case of medical emergency. Thomas Cook and other travel agencies offer comprehensive policies. Medical coverage should be high – at least $1 million. Insurance for drivers is covered in more detail in the 'Driving in Eastern Canada' chapter, p. 41.

28

LANGUAGE

Officially bilingual (English and French), Canada in fact is more sharply divided over language than any other issue. In Ontario and the Atlantic provinces, English is spoken everywhere, road signs are always in English, sometimes in French as well, and all federal publications are printed in both English and French. In the province of Québec, French is spoken everywhere, and it is actually illegal for a business to put up a sign in English – even on a privately owned shop catering mostly to Anglophones – unless there is also a sign in French with letters twice as large.

Visitors will find English widely spoken along with French in Montréal, Québec City, the Eastern Townships and other major tourism areas, although not in many rural areas, where French may be the only language. New Brunswick is bilingual French and English, and there are pockets of Francophones in Acadian areas throughout the Maritimes. Native languages (Inuit, Iroquois, etc.) are heard in some areas. In the

---

How to talk Canadian

Black ice A transparent sheet of ice on the roads.
Chesterfield sofa
Chips crisps
Down East In Ontario, it means the Maritime provinces (New Brunswick, Nova Scotia and Prince Edward Island); in the Maritimes, as in New England, it means Maine.
Eh? A uniquely Canadian expression, which many English-speakers unconsciously add to nearly everything they say, as in: 'We're going to the hockey game, eh?' It defies definition.
French fries chips
Muskeg A large area of swampy, marshy land.
Pop soft drink
Resort A fancy hotel that specialises in leisure activities such as golf, tennis and swimming.
Snowbirds People who live in Canada during warm seasons, but California or Florida in the winter.

How to talk Québeçois

caisse-croute snack bar
chemin road
dépanneur convenience store
déjeuner breakfast
dîner lunch
érable maple
essence petrol or gasoline
souper supper

---

big cities, especially Toronto, recently arrived immigrants speak dozens of languages.

Canadian English is almost the same as American English, although British spellings are used and some pronunciations sound faintly Scottish. Canadian French *(Québeçois)* sometimes differs from the language in France. A selection of commonly encountered terms which may be unfamiliar or have a different meaning in Canada are set out in the box below. The next chapter, 'Driving in New England', provides a glossary of motoring terms for the non-Canadian driver.

LUGGAGE

Less is more where luggage is concerned. Porters don't exist outside the most expensive hotels, and luggage trolleys (baggage carts) are rare. Trolleys are free for international arrivals in Montréal's Mirabel airport, but they cost $1 at Pearson International Airport in Toronto. Luggage has to be light enough to carry. The normal trans-Atlantic luggage allowance is two pieces, each of 70 lb (32 kg) maximum, per person.

Luggage must also fit in the car or other form of transport around Canada. Canadians buy the same cars as the rest of the world, not the enormous American 'boats' of the 1960s. If it won't fit in the boot at home, don't count on cramming it into a car in Canada.

MAPS

The best all-round maps are produced by the **American Automobile Association**, known simply as AAA ('Triple A'), in conjunction with the Canadian Automobile Association, and distributed through their affiliates. State, regional and city maps are available free at all AAA/CAA offices, but only to members. Fortunately, most automobile clubs around the world have reciprocal agreements with AAA/CAA to provide maps and other member services. Be prepared to show a membership card to obtain service.

Rand McNally road maps and atlases are probably the best known of the ranges available outside North America, in the travel section of bookshops and more specialist outlets.

Detailed folding road maps are produced by **MapArt Corp.**, *70 Bloor St E, Oshawa, ON L1H 3M2, Canada; tel: (905) 436-2525, fax (905) 723-6677, website: www.mapart.com* and sold at booksellers and other retail outlets. Maps are also produced by **Allmaps Canada Ltd.**, *390 Steelcase Rd E, Markham, ON L3R 1G2, Canada.*

Topographical maps for back-country travel can be ordered from **Canada Map Office**, *Natural Resources Canada, 130 Bentley Ave, Nepean, Ontario K1A 0E9; tel: (800) 465-6271, fax: (800) 661-6277*, or purchased in speciality travel bookshops in Canada.

Before leaving civilisation behind, compare every available map for discrepancies, then check with national forest or park personnel. Most are experienced back-country enthusiasts themselves, and since they're responsible for lost hikers, they have a vested interest in dispensing the best possible information and advice.

OPENING HOURS

Office hours are generally Mon–Fri 0900–1700; many tourist offices also keep weekend hours in summer. Banks are usually open Mon–Fri 0900–1700; some open Sat mornings. ATMs (cash dispenser machines) are open 24 hours, and are located everywhere. Shops are generally open Mon–Fri 0900–1800, Thurs and Fri 0900–2100, Sat 0900–1700. Some small shops selling groceries and convenience items remain open evenings and Sun.

Some museums close Mondays, but most tourist attractions are open seven days a week. Almost everything closes New Year's, Thanksgiving and Christmas Day.

PARKS INFORMATION

For specific federal and provincial parks, monuments and heritage sites, see the appropriate description among the recommended routes throughout this book. For general information on national parks, historic sites, marine conservation areas and heritage exhibits, contact the appropriate regional office of **Parks Canada**: For Ontario's 32 sites, *111 Water St East, Cornwall, ON K6H 6S3; tel: (613) 938-5866.* For Québec's 32 sites, *3 Buade St, PO Box 6060, Haute-Ville, Québec, PQ G1R 4V7; tel: (800) 463-6769.* For the Atlantic provinces (eight sites in New Brunswick, 18 in Nova Scotia, five in Prince Edward Island, ten in Newfoundland), **Historic Properties**, *Halifax, NS B3J IS9; tel: (902) 426-3436.*

Parks Canada offers full information online at *http://parkscanada.pch.gc.ca.*

Campsite information in the national parks is available by region: Atlantic region, *tel: (800) 213-7275.* Québec, *tel: (800) 463-6769.* Ontario, *tel: (800) 839-8221.* For campsite information on provincial parks: Ontario, *tel: (800) 668-2746*; Québec, *tel: (800) 363-7777*; Nova Scotia, *tel: (800) 565-0000*; New Brunswick, *tel: (800) 561-0123*; Prince Edward Island, *tel: (800) 463-4734*; Newfoundland and Labrador, *tel: (800) 563-6353.*

There is a charge of $2.25–11 for entry to most national parks and sites; discounted fees often apply to seniors, disabled persons and children. If making multiple visits to national parks, monuments or historical sites for which entrance fees are charged, consider purchasing a multi-day or season pass, sold by each attraction. The **Atlantic Region Park Pass** is good for unlimited entry (mid May–mid Oct) to major parks in the Atlantic provinces and costs $30 adult, $75 family, $22.50 seniors, $15 children 6–16. Some other regional passes in Eastern Canada are also available for smaller geographical areas.

Entry to provincial parks is free.

PASSPORTS AND VISAS

A valid passport is required for entry into Canada, but no visa is required, for citizens of the Australia, New Zealand, Republic of Ireland, South Africa or the UK. If returning to the USA after a visit to Canada, check with US immigration officials that your visa, if one is required, permits your return.

US citizens and legal residents are not required to have a passport, although it is preferred. Otherwise, native-born US citizens should carry a birth certificate and picture ID; naturalised citizens should carry a naturalisation certificate and picture ID; and non-citizens who are permanent residents must bring the alien-registration card.

POLICE

To telephone police in an emergency, ring *911* in urban areas, or dial *0* for the operator in rural areas. There are many different police jurisdictions within each Canadian province, each with its own police force. **Royal Canadian Mounted Police** ('Mounties') are the national police force. Trans-Canada Highways are patrolled by Mounties, provincial roads by provincial police in Ontario and Québec, Mounties elsewhere. See also under 'Security' below and 'Police' in the next chapter.

POSTAL SERVICES

Every town has at least one post office. Hours vary, although all are open Mon–Fri, morning and afternoon. Postal Service branches may be open Saturday or (rarely) Sunday. Some big hotels sell stamps through the concierge. Stamp machines are installed in some stores. (Toronto has 40 postal outlets; many are retail franchises in stores and malls with hours influenced by the adjoining businesses.) For philatelic sales, check major city telephone directories under Canada Post.

Mail everything going overseas as Air Mail (surface mail takes weeks or even months). If posting letters near an urban area, mail should take about one week. Add a day or two if mailing from remote areas. Canada uses British-style postal codes using a combination of six letters and numbers to target specific geographic areas, not US-style zip codes.

Addresses given in this guidebook use the following **abbreviations for provinces**: ON Ontario, PQ Province Québec, NB New Brunswick, NS Nova Scotia, PEI Prince Edward Island, NF Newfoundland and Labrador. However, many Canadians prefer to write out province names in addresses.

Poste Restante is available at post offices, without charge. Mail should be addressed in block lettering to your name, Poste Restante/General Delivery, city, province, Canada, postal code. Mail is held for 15 days at the post office branch that handles General Delivery for each town or city, usually the main office.

In Toronto, Poste Restante mail is handled at *25 The Esplanade (Bay and Front Sts), M5E 1W5*; in Montréal, you can use the main post offices at *1250 r. University, H3B 3B8*, and *1250 r. Ste-Catherine Ouest, H3G 1P1*; in Halifax, the main post office is at *1680 Bedford Row, B3J 3J5*. Identification is required for mail pickup.

PUBLIC HOLIDAYS

Local celebrations, festivals, parades or neighbourhood parties can disrupt some or all activities in town. The following list of public holidays are celebrated nationally:

Canada's national holidays include New Year's (1 Jan); Good Friday (Mar or Apr); Easter Monday (Mar or Apr); Victoria Day (late May); Canada Day (1 July); Labour Day (early Sept); Thanksgiving (mid-Oct); Remembrance Day (11 Nov); Christmas (25 Dec) and Boxing Day (26 Dec).

Provincial holidays include 1 Aug (Civic Holiday in Ontario and New Brunswick Day in New Brunswick) and Saint-Jean-Baptiste Day in Québec (June 24).

Banks, post offices and government offices close on public holidays. Businesses take the day off, though some department and discount stores use the opportunity to hold sales, well advertised in local newspapers. Some petrol stations close, but those

on main highways remain open. Small shops and some grocery stores close or curtail hours, but convenience stores generally stay open.

Call in advance before visiting an attraction on a public holiday as there are frequently special hours. National and state park campsites and lodging must be reserved in advance for all holidays. Easter, Thanksgiving and Christmas are family holidays, where accommodation is available and may even be discounted. Other holidays are 'mobile' for Canadians, so book early.

SALES TAXES

Canada's federal government imposes a 7% **Goods & Services Tax** (GST) on most retail sales, restaurant meals, hotel accommodations and many consumer services such as dry cleaning and parking. In addition to GST (often called the Gouge and Screw Tax), most provinces also impose **provincial sales taxes**. Ontario has an 8% provincial sales tax on retail sales and restaurant meals, 16% on alcoholic beverages and 5% on accommodations. Québec applies a 6.5% tax to merchandise, food, liquor and accommodations; Prince Edward Island's tax is 10%.

It works differently in the provinces of New Brunswick, Nova Scotia and Newfoundland and Labrador, where both GST and provincial sales taxes have been replaced with a **Harmonised Sales Tax** (HST) of 15%.

Some provinces exempt from taxation grocery items and articles of clothing and footwear that cost less than $100 (including the 7% GST).

Visitors may apply for a **rebate** of the GST or HST paid on certain goods they remove from Canada and on lodgings of less than 30 days. To qualify for a rebate, your purchases must be for a minimum of $200 ($14 in tax), and you must show your original receipts. On the same form, visitors can apply for a rebate of Québec's 6.5% sales tax, but not provincial taxes paid to Ontario or

31

Prince Edward Island. And there's no rebate for taxes paid on tobacco, alcohol, meals, petrol or services.

The rebate application is obtained at Canadian Customs and tourism offices, department stores and hotels. Rebates are given at certain duty-free shops or by mail: **Visitor Rebate Program**, *Revenue Canada, Summerside Tax Centre, Summerside, PEI C1N 6C6 Canada; tel: (800) 66-VISIT in Canada, (902) 432-5608* outside Canada.

SECURITY

Throwing caution to the winds is foolhardy anytime, and even more so on holiday. While Canada is basically a safe place to travel, it is wise to take precautions to ensure that you don't give anyone an opportunity to make you a victim of theft or violent crime.

Millions of people travel in perfect safety each year in Canada. So can you if you take the following commonsense precautions.

Travelling Safely

Never publicly discuss travel plans or money or valuables you are carrying. Use caution in large cities, towns and rural areas. Drive, park and walk only in well-lit areas. If unsure of roads or weather ahead, stop for the evening and find secure lodging.

The best way to avoid becoming a victim of theft or bodily injury is to walk with assurance and try to give the impression that you are not worth robbing (e.g. do not wear or carry expensive jewellery or flash rolls of banknotes). Use a hidden money-belt for your valuables, travel documents and spare cash. Carrying a wallet in a back pocket or leaving a handbag open is an invitation to every pickpocket in the vicinity. In all public places, take precautions with anything that is obviously worth stealing – use a handbag with a crossed shoulder strap and a zip, wind the strap of your camera case around your chair or place your handbag firmly between your feet under the table while you eat.

Never leave luggage unattended. At air-

ports, security officials may confiscate unattended luggage as a possible bomb. In public toilets, handbags and small luggage has been snatched from hooks or from under stalls. Some airports and most bus and train stations have lockers. Most work with keys; take care to guard the key and memorise the locker number. Hotel bell staff may keep luggage for one or more days on request and for a fee – be sure to get receipts for left luggage before surrendering it.

Concealing a weapon is against the law. Some defensive products resembling tear gas are legal only for persons certified in their proper use. Mugging is a social problem in any big city around the world. If you are attacked, it is safer to let go of your bag or hand over the small amount of obvious money – as you are more likely to be attacked physically if the thief meets with resistance. Never resist. Report incidents immediately to local police, even if it is only to get a copy of their report for your insurance company.

Driving Safely

Have car hire counter personnel recommend a safe, direct route on a clear map before you leave with the vehicle. Lock all valuables and luggage in the boot or glove box so that nothing is visible to passers-by or other drivers. Don't leave maps, brochures or guidebooks in evidence – why advertise that you're a stranger in town?

Always keep car doors and windows locked. Do not venture into unlit areas,

Colour section (i): Touring Eastern Canada: a road winds around the coastline (Rte 132, Gaspé peninsula, p. 215); and a covered bridge (the world's longest, p. 257).
(ii): Toronto: (pp. 62–79) the city's skyline; Fort York (p. 78) and the CN Tower (p. 75).
(iii): The Eaton Centre, Toronto (p. 74); Niagara Falls (pp. 87–90).

SUR 5 km

TURN
ON
LIGHTS

ALLUMEZ
VOS
PHARES

HARTLAND
NEW
BRUNSWICK

ME AGAIN
ENTERING THE LONGEST
BRIDGE IN THE WORLD
282 FEET

YOU ARE
COVE

neighbourhoods that look seedy or off paved roads. *Do not stop* if told by a passing motorist that something is wrong with your car or if someone signals for help with a broken-down car. If you need to stop, do so only in well-lit areas, even if your car is bumped from behind by another vehicle. If your car breaks down, turn on the flashing emergency lights, and if it is safe to get out, raise the bonnet. Do not split passengers up. Lights on emergency vehicles are red or red and blue, so do not stop for flashing white lights or flashing headlights. Ask directions from police, at a well-lit business area or at a service station.

At night, have keys ready to unlock car doors before entering a parking lot. Check the surrounding area and inside the vehicle before entering. Never pick up hitch-hikers, and never leave the car with the engine running. Take all valuables with you.

Sleeping Safely

When sleeping rough, in any sort of dormitory, train or open campsite, the safest place for your small valuables is at the bottom of your sleeping-bag. In sleeping cars, padlock your luggage to the seat, and ask the attendant to show you how to lock a compartment door at night. If in doubt, it's best to take luggage with you.

In all lodgings, lock doors from the inside. Check that all windows are locked, including sliding glass doors. Ground-floor rooms, while convenient, mean easier access by molesters intent on breaking in. When you leave the room at night keep a light on to deter prowlers.

Use a door viewer to check before admitting anyone to your room. If someone claims to be on the hotel staff or a repair person, do not let the person in before phoning the office or front desk to verify the person's name and job. Money, cheques, credit cards, passports and keys should be with you or secured in your hotel's safe deposit box. When checking in, find the most direct route from your room to fire escapes, elevators, stairwells and the nearest telephone.

Documents

Take a few passport photos with you and photocopy the important pages and any visa stamps in your passport. Store these safely, together with a note of the numbers of your travellers cheques, credit cards and insurance documents (keep them away from the documents themselves). If you are robbed, you will at least have some identification, and replacing the documents will be easier. Apply to your nearest consulate (see Consulates above).

SHOPPING

High prices and heavy sales taxes can make Canada an expensive place to shop. The latter are mitigated somewhat for visitors, who can apply for a rebate of the 7% Goods and Services Tax and sometimes the provincial sales tax as well (see Sales Taxes).

Uniquely Canadian souvenirs include items such as T-shirts, hats and mugs emblazoned with logos of the Royal Canadian Mounted Police or stuffed bears, beaver or moose in 'Mountie' uniform. Native crafts, such as beaded jewellery and 'dreamcatchers', leather goods (moccasins, gloves, jackets) made of moose or deerskin, and Micmac soapstone carvings in PEI, make good gifts.

In Montréal, stylish clothing, particularly for winter, is a good buy; Québec City is known for French country antiques, and the Eastern Townships *(Estrie)* is a maple syrup-producing region.

In PEI, look for handmade quiltwork and wood carvings, usually on nautical theme (lighthouses, boats, etc.), and the ubiquitous dolls and other items related to *Anne of Green Gables*. The Maritimes also have Irish woollens and Scottish tartans, CDs and tapes of local musicians, such as Scottish fiddlers, good pottery and maritime and landscape paintings by local artists. Banners and emblems are good souvenirs from Acadian

33

areas. In Newfoundland, handmade knitwear is a bargain; the local rum, called 'screech' is a good souvenir item. From Ontario, try the wines of the Niagara region, or look for Inuit carvings from the north (igloo logo indicates authenticity).

Tape cassettes, blank video tapes, CDs, computer programs and CD-ROMs sold in Canada can be used anywhere in the world. For more information on electrical goods, see 'Electricity' in this chapter.

SMOKING

Lighting up is out in public buildings and public transportation. All plane flights in Canada and the USA are non-smoking, and some hire cars are designated as non-smoking. Most hotels/motels set aside non-smoking rooms or floors; bed and breakfasts are almost all non-smoking. Restaurant dining regulations vary by locality; some forbid all smoking, others permit it in the bar or lounge only, some have a percentage of the eatery devoted to smokers. Smoking is prohibited in most stores and shops. Always ask before lighting a cigarette, cigar or pipe. When in doubt, go outside to smoke.

TELEPHONES

The Canadian telephone system is largely run by Bell Canada ('Ma Bell'), although smaller phone companies operate in some locales and private carriers (such as Sprint and MCI) have begun vying for long-distance customers. Depending on the time of day and day of the week, it may be cheaper to call New York City than to call 30 miles away. After 1700 Mon–Fri and all weekend, rates are lower. Useful phone numbers are provided throughout this book.

Public telephones are everywhere, indicated by a sign with a white telephone receiver depicted on a blue field. Enclosed booths are rare; wall-mounted or free-standing machines are more commonly used. If possible, use public phones in well-lit, busy public areas. Cellular telephone use is wide-spread and rentals are available, but rates are astronomical.

Dialling instructions are in the front of the local white pages telephone directory. For all long-distance calls in North America, precede the area code with a 1. In emergencies, dial *911* for police, medical or fire brigade response. *0* reaches an operator. For local number information, dial *411*. For long-distance phone information, dial *1*, then the area code, then *555-1212*. There will be a charge for information calls.

Pay phones take coins, and a local call costs $0.25 upwards. An operator or computer voice will come on-line to ask for additional coins when needed. Most hotels and motels add a stiff surcharge to the basic cost of a call, so ask about charges before dialling or find a public telephone in the lobby.

Prepaid phone cards ($5) can be purchased in Canada. Before you travel, ask your local phone company if your phone card will work in North America. Most do, and come with a list of contact numbers. However, remember that overseas phone rates may be lower from Canada, making it cheaper to fill pay phones with quarters than to reverse charges. A credit card may be convenient, but is only economical if you pay the bill immediately.

For comparison, local call rates:
  coin $0.25
  direct dial, calling card $0.75
  operator-assisted, calling card $0.75

Most *800*-numbers and *888*-numbers are toll-free. Like all long-distance numbers the *800* or *888* area code must be preceded by a *1*, e.g. *1-800-123-4567*. Some telephone numbers are given in letters. Telephone keys have both numbers and letters, so find the corresponding letters and depress that key. A few numbers have more than seven letters to finish a business name. Not to worry, Canadian or US phone numbers never require more than seven numbers, plus three for the area code.

Numbers in the *900* area code charge the caller a fee for informational or other services; rates are often high.

Dial an international operator on *00* for enquiries or assistance.

For international dialling, dial *011-country code-city code* (omitting the first *0* if there is one)-*local number*; e.g., to call Great Britain, Inner London, from Canada, dial: *011-44-171-local number*. (Remember, you dial only 1, not 011, to call the USA.) Some country codes:

Australia 61
New Zealand 64
Republic of Ireland 353
South Africa 27
United Kingdom 44

TIME

The provinces of Quebec (except the far eastern portion) and Ontario (except the far western portion) share a time zone with the East Coast of the USA, GMT minus 5 hours, called Eastern Standard Time (EST). From the first Sunday in April until the last Sunday in October, clocks are pushed forward to Eastern Daylight Time (EDT).

The Atlantic provinces of New Brunswick, Prince Edward Island and Nova Scotia, plus Labrador, are in the Atlantic time zone, GMT minus 4 hours. Newfoundland occupies a time zone of its own, GMT minus 3½ hours.

TIPPING

Acknowledgement for good service should not be extorted. That said, tipping is a fact of life, to get, to repeat or to thank someone for service in Canada, just as in the USA.

Service charges are not customarily added to restaurant bills; the exception, when indicated, is for large groups (such as eight or more people), where experience shows that friends splitting a bill underestimate their share.

In general, tip waiters and waitresses 15% of the total bill. If you feel service was extremely good, by all means reward it by increasing the tip to 20%; you can punish truly bad service with a slightly smaller tip, but don't withhold the tip completely unless you speak to the waiter or manager, explaining the service problem and giving them the opportunity to correct it. (Poorly prepared food is the fault of the kitchen, not the waiter, and should be sent back).

In luxury restaurants, also be prepared to tip the maitre d' and sommelier a few dollars,

35

Time in Toronto and Montréal (EST)	8.00 am	12 noon	5.00 pm	12 midnight
Nova Scotia, PEI, New Brunswick and Labrador (AST)	9.00 am	1.00 pm	6.00 pm	1.00 am
Newfoundland (NST)	9.30 am	1.30 pm	6.30 pm	1.30 pm
Auckland	1.00 am	5.00 am	10.00 am	5.00 pm
Cape Town	3.00 pm	7.00 pm	12.00 am	7.00 am
Dublin	1.00 pm	5.00 pm	10.00 pm	5.00 am
London	1.00 pm	5.00 pm	10.00 pm	5.00 am
Los Angeles	5.00 am	9.00 am	2.00 pm	9.00 pm
New York	8.00 am	12.00 pm	5.00 pm	12.00 am
Perth	9.00 pm	1.00 am	6.00 pm	1.00 pm
Sydney	11.00 pm	3.00 am	8.00 pm	3.00 pm

up to 10% of the bill. Bartenders may expect the change from a drink, up to several dollars.

Doormen, bellhops and redcaps (porters) at hotels, railway stations and airports generally receive $1 per bag. Room service delivery staff should be tipped 10%–15% of the tariff, unless there's a service charge indicated on the bill. Expect to tip for most services that involve room delivery.

Some hotels will have a chambermaid name card placed in the room: it's a hint for a tip of a few dollars upon your departure, but it's never required.

Ushers in legitimate theatres, arenas and stadiums are not tipped; cinemas seldom have ushers, nor are tips expected. Tip taxi drivers, barbers and hairdressers 15%. Tip cloakroom personnel up to $1 per coat unless a service charge is posted.

TOILETS

There is nothing worse than not being able to find one. *Restroom* or *bathroom* are the common terms; *toilet* is acceptable; *W.C.* is used in some areas, as is *washroom*. Most are marked with a figure for a male or a female; *Men* and *women* are the most common terms in English-speaking areas, *hommes* and *dames* in French-speaking Québec. Occasionally a restroom may be used by both sexes (one person at a time).

Facilities may be clean and well-equipped or filthy. Most businesses, including bars and restaurants, reserve restrooms for clients. Petrol stations provide keys for customers to access restrooms. Public toilets are sporadically placed, but well-marked. Parks and roadside rest stops have toilet facilities. Carry a pack of tissues in case paper is lacking.

TOURIST INFORMATION

In Canada, each province is responsible for its own tourism promotion. Address requests for information well in advance; see p. 344 for web sites and email addresses.

Ontario Travel, *Queen's Park, Toronto,*

ON Canada M7A 2R9; tel: (416) 314-0944, fax: (416) 668-2746 or (800) ONTARIO. **Tourisme Quebec**, *C.P. 979, Montréal, PQ H3C 2W3; Canada; tel: (514) 864-3838 or (800) 363-7777.* **Tourism New Brunswick**, *PO Box 6000, Fredericton, NB E3B 5C1 Canada; tel: (800) 561-0123, fax: (506) 453-2444.* **Tourism Nova Scotia**, *PO Box 456, Halifax, NS B3J 2M7 Canada; tel: (902) 425-5781 or (800) 565-0000.* **Prince Edward Island Visitor Services**, *Box 940, Charlottetown, PEI C1A 7M5 Canada; tel: (800) 463-4734 or (888) 734-7529.* **Newfoundland and Labrador Department of Tourism, Culture and Recreation**, *P.O. Box 8730, St. John's, NF A1B 4K2 Canada; tel: (709) 729-2830 or toll-free (800) 563-6353.* **Destination Labrador**, *118 Humphrey Rd, Bruno Plaza, Labrador City, NF A2V 2J8 Canada; tel: (709) 944-7788 or (800) 563-6353.*

For US tourism information, contact the state or city you plan to visit. Parts of Maine and New York are covered in this book; contact **Maine Publicity Bureau**, *P.O. Box 2300, Hallowell, ME 04347-2300; tel: (207) 623-0363.* **New York State Department of Economic Development**, *One Commerce Plaza, Albany, NY 12245; tel: (518) 474-6950.*

Information on the six New England states is available from **Discover New England**, *56 South Park Rd, Wimbledon, London SW19 8SZ; tel: (081) 544 1000; fax: (081) 542 6556.* In the USA, the address is *21 Pearl Lane, East Falmouth, MA 02536; tel: (508) 540-8169; fax: (508) 540-8195.*

This book also gives addresses and telephone numbers of tourism offices in regions, cities and towns along specific routes.

TRAVEL ARRANGEMENTS

Given the fact that many of the world's international airlines fly into Toronto and Montréal, and given the ease of flying into smaller cities and hiring cars at airports, Eastern Canada is an ideal destination for

Train Travel

V **IA Rail Canada** is the national passenger train service in Canada; *tel: (800) 561-3949.* There is fast, frequent service along the Ontario-Québec corridor between Windsor and Québec City, including stops at London, Toronto, Niagara Falls (connecting to the USA's Amtrak system), Ottawa and Montréal. Eastern Transcontinental travel is available from Montréal to the Gaspé Peninsula and via Cambellton to Moncton, New Brunswick, and Truro and Halifax, Nova Scotia. Western Transcontinental service is available from Toronto to Vancouver, British Columbia, on Canada's west coast. From Montréal, the trains run north to Jonquière in the Saguenay area, then to Cochrane in western Québec.

Canrailpass allows unlimited rail travel in economy class for 12–15 days during a 30-day period. Adult prices are $569 for 12 days, $49 per day for 3 extra days (1 June–15 Oct), $369 for 12 days, $31 per day for 3 extra days (16 Oct–31 May). Youth rates (age 2–24) are $499/$44 and $339/$28 respectively (add 7% GST to all prices).

Information, maps and reservations are available on VIA Rail's website: *www.viarail.ca.*

Several tourist train excursions offer sightseeing opportunities through remote areas. The **Polar Bear Express** is a one-day rail excursion in northern Ontario, from Cochrane to the tip of James Bay (see Northern Ontario, p. 125). **The Hull-Chelsea-Wakefield Steam Train** chugs north from Hull, outside the capital city of Ottawa, for sightseeing excursions along the Gatineau River. **The Canadian** is VIA Rail's three-day Toronto-to-Vancouver run, departing Toronto on Tues, Thur and Sat.

independent-minded travellers. However, the many types of air ticket and the range of temporary deals available on the busy routes make it advisable to talk to your travel agent before booking, to get the best bargain.

In fact, taking a fly-drive package such as one of Thomas Cook's own, or one of the many others offered by airlines and tour operators, is usually more economical than making all your own arrangements. All include the air ticket and car hire elements; some also follow set itineraries which enables them to offer guaranteed and pre-paid en route accommodation at selected hotels. Programmes such as Thomas Cook's *Canada for the Independent Traveller* allow the flexibility of booking the airline ticket at an advantageous rate and then choosing from a 'menu' of other items, often at a discounted price, such as car hire, hotel coupons (which pre-pay accommodations but do not guarantee availability of rooms) and other extras such as excursions.

USA

All non-US citizens must have a valid full passport (not a British Visitor's Passport) and, except for Canadians, a visa, in order to enter the United States. Citizens of most countries must obtain a visa from the US Embassy in their country of residence in advance of arrival.

Citizens of Britain, New Zealand and Ireland may complete a visa waiver form, which they generally receive with their air tickets if the airline is a 'participating carrier'. Provided nothing untoward is declared, such as a previous entry refusal or a criminal conviction, which would make application for a full visa mandatory, the waiver exempts visitors from the need for a visa for stays of up to 90 days. Visitors may make a side-trip overland into Mexico or Canada for up to 30 days and return to the US.

Note: Documentation regulations change frequently and are complex for some nationalities; confirm your requirements with a good travel agent or the nearest US Embassy at least 90 days before your visit.

There is no Valued Added Tax or Goods & Services Tax in the USA. Each state imposes its own tax on sales of products and services, itemised separately on every bill. Parts of two US states are included in this book: Maine has a 6% sales tax, 7% on lodgings; New York State has a 4% sales tax, with additional local sales taxes of up to 4.5%. Items taxed by states vary; some exempt clothing, items for babies, take-away foods. State and federal taxes on petrol, cigarettes and alcoholic beverages are included in the posted price.

Officially, the USA is on the metric system, but in actual everyday usage it is not. See Weights and Measures below for conversions.

US public holidays include: New Year's (1 Jan); Martin Luther King Jr Day (third Monday in Jan); Presidents' Day (third Monday in Feb); Memorial Day (last Monday in May); US Independence Day (4 July); Labor Day (first Monday in Sept); Columbus Day (second Monday in Oct); Veterans Day (11 Nov); Thanksgiving Day (fourth Thursday in Nov); and Christmas (25 Dec).

USEFUL READING

Most British and international colour-illustrated guidebook series feature a volume on Canada as a whole; among these, the Lonely Planet guide includes coverage of remote areas that are beyond the scope of this guidebook. Several series also offer volumes on single cities, such as Toronto, Montréal or Québec City, on individual provinces or on regions, such as *Atlantic Canada Handbook* from Moon Handbooks. Michelin Guides publish detailed-oriented Canada and Québec volumes. Recreational specialities are covered in guides such as *Hiking Nova Scotia* and *Mountain Bike Nova Scotia*, from Nimbus Publishing of Halifax. Among the few books covering the entire eastern portion of the country is *Guide to Eastern Canada* by Frederick Pratson, Globe Pequot Press.

If you are arranging your own accommodations as you travel, a comprehensive guide such as the *AAA/CAA Tourbooks* for Ontario, for Atlantic Provinces and Quebec or the *Mobil Travel Guide: Northeast*, which covers Eastern Canada, New England and New York State, can often be obtained through specialist travel bookshops outside Canada.

If you are considering using bus or trains for any part of your trip, the *Thomas Cook Overseas Timetable* (published every 2 months, £8.40 per issue) is indispensable, and referred to throughout this book as the OTT. Available from any UK branch of Thomas Cook or by phoning *(01733) 503571/2*. In North America, contact the **Forsyth Travel Library Inc.**, *226 Westchester Ave, White Plains, New York 10604; tel: (800) 367 7984 (toll-free)*.

For background on history and culture before you travel, try *A Short History of Canada* by Desmond Morton, published by McClelland & Stewart, and *Culture Shock! A Guide to Customs and Etiquette: Canada* by Pang Guek Cheng and Robert Barlas, Graphic Arts Center Publishing Company of Oregon.

A comprehensive view of the geography, settlement patterns and history, including the early Norse explorations, is available in the large-format **Historical Atlas of Canada from the Beginning to 1800** from University of Toronto Press.

The local lore, anecdotes and history of Nova Scotia, New Brunswick and Prince Edward Island are lovingly told in *These are the Maritimes* by Will R. Bird, published by McGraw-Hill Ryerson Ltd. of Toronto. Visitors to Prince Edward Island will find constant references to *Anne of Green Gables*, a novel about a young orphan girl by Lucy Maude Montgomery, which gives the early flavour of the province. The English-French

cultural conflicts within Québec are examined by Mordecai Richler in *Oh, Canada! Oh, Québec!* Newfoundland's colour and hardships are told by novelist E. Annie Proulx in *The Shipping News*.

Contemporary Canadian life is also explored in the works of the late novelist, playwright and literary critic Robertson Davies; these include the *Cornish Trilogy (The Rebel Angels, What's Bred in the Bone* and *The Lyre of Orpheus); The Deptford Trilogy (Fifth Business, The Manticore* and *World of Wonders)* and *The Salterton Trilogy*, among others.

WEIGHTS AND MEASURES

Canada has partially converted to the metric system. Temperatures are given in degrees Celsius; gasoline is sold by the litre (milk and wine by the litre and millilitre) and grocery items in grams and kilograms. Clothing sizes are in centimetres, road speeds are in kilometres per hour and distances in kilometres.

WHAT TO TAKE

Absolutely everything you could ever need is available, so don't worry if you've left anything behind. Pharmacies (chemists), also called drug stores, carry a range of products, from medicine to cosmetics to beach balls. Prepare a small first aid kit before you leave home with tried and tested insect repellent, sun-screen cream, and soothing, moisturising lotion. Carry all medicines, glasses, and contraceptives with you, and keep duplicate prescriptions or a letter from your doctor to verify your need for a particular medicine.

Other useful items to bring or buy immediately upon arrival are a water-bottle, sunglasses, a hat or visor with a rim, a Swiss Army pocket knife, a torch (flashlight), a padlock for anchoring luggage, a money belt, a travel adaptor, string for a washing line, an alarm clock and a camera. Those planning to rough it should take a sleeping bag, a sheet liner, and an inflatable travel pillow. Allow a little extra space in your luggage for souvenirs.

NEW FOR 1999 !

A Brand New Series
from
Thomas Cook Publishing

Signpost Guides

Developed to meet the needs of today's tourers. Hundreds of places and attractions described in detail. The suggested routes and detours have been devised to enable travellers to get off the beaten track.

Your guide to a great driving holiday

CALIFORNIA

features include:

- ❑ Detailed road maps supported by driving directions and route suggestions
- ❑ Practical details to make the motoring easier
- ❑ Covers city sightseeing without the car
- ❑ Information on accommodation, sightseeing, dining and shopping for all main destinations

The series includes in-depth guides on :

NEW ENGLAND
CALIFORNIA
NEW ZEALAND
SCOTLAND
BRITTANY AND NORMANDY
FLORIDA
DORDOGNE AND WESTERN FRANCE
IRELAND
LANGUEDOC AND SOUTH WEST FRANCE
BAVARIA AND THE AUSTRIAN TYROL

Obtainable through Thomas Cook UK retail shops at £14.99, or by post (extra for p&p) direct from:

Thomas Cook Publishing (OWN), PO Box 227, Thorpe Wood, Peterborough, PE3 6PU, UK. Tel: 01733 503571/2

DRIVING IN
EASTERN CANADA

ACCIDENTS AND BREAKDOWNS

Holidays should be trouble-free, yet **breakdowns** can occur. Pull off to the side of the road where visibility is good and you are out of the way of traffic. Turn on hazard flashers or indicators and, if it is safe, get out and raise the bonnet. Change a tyre only out of the traffic flow.

Dial *911* (or *0* in some areas) on any telephone to reach provincial or local police, fire or medical services. Report your phone number, location, problem and need for first aid. Do not abandon your car and attempt walking for help on the Trans-Canada Highways; wait for police patrols to stop.

If involved in a **collision**, stop. Call the provincial police or Royal Canadian Mounted Police (if the accident occurs on a provincial or Trans-Canada highway), or local police if there are injuries or physical damage to either vehicle. Show the police and involved driver(s) your driver's licence, car registration, car insurance coverage, address and contact information. Other drivers should provide you with the same information.

Collisions have to be reported to your car hire company. Injuries or death must be reported to the police at the time of the accident. Collisions or accidents resulting in property damage must be reported to local police or RCMP if it's more than $700 in Ontario, $500 in Nova Scotia or Québec, $1000 in New Brunswick, Newfoundland or Prince Edward Island. Stay at the accident scene until cleared by investigating officers.

Fly-drive travellers should bear in mind the effects of **jet-lag** on driver safety. This can be a very real problem. The best way to minimise it is to spend the first night after arrival in a hotel at the airport or in the city and pick up your hire vehicle the next day, rather than take the car on the road within hours of getting off the plane.

BICYCLES

Bicyclists must follow the motor vehicle traffic laws. Use of **helmets** is encouraged everywhere, but it is *required* for all cyclists in New Brunswick, for cyclists under age 18 in Ontario and in special areas of Newfoundland.

CAR HIRE

Hiring a car or RV (camper) gives you the freedom of the road with a vehicle you can leave behind after a few weeks. Whether booking a fly-drive package with an agency or making independent arrangements, plan well in advance to ensure you get the type and size of vehicle your heart desires. Free, unlimited mileage is common with cars, less so with RVs.

Sheer volume in airport rental car turnover means that in Canada it's usually cheaper to pick up the vehicle from an airport than from a downtown site and to return it to the airport. A surcharge (called a drop fee) may be levied if you drop the car off in a different location from the place of hire. When considering an RV, ask about one-way and off-season rates.

You will need a valid credit card as security for the vehicle's value. Before you leave the hire agency, ensure that you have all documentation for the hire, that the car registration is in the glove box and that you understand how to operate the vehicle. For

41

RVs, also get instruction books and a complete demonstration of all systems and appliances and how they interconnect. Avoid hiring a car that exhibits a hire company name on a window decal, on the fender (bumper) or on licence plate frames. It is advertising for criminal attention.

Car size terminology varies, but general categories range from small and basic to all-frills posh: sub-compact, compact, economy, mid-size or intermediate, full-size or standard, and luxury. Sub-compacts are rarely available. Expect to choose between two- or four-door models. The larger the car, the faster it accelerates and consumes petrol. Some vehicles are equipped with four-wheel drive (4WD), unnecessary except for off-road driving (not covered in this book).

Standard features on Canadian hire cars usually include automatic transmission, air-conditioning and cruise control, which sets speeds for long-distance highway driving, allowing the driver to take the foot off the accelerator.

DIFFICULT DRIVING

Winter

In winter snowstorms anywhere in Canada, visibility can be nil due to high winds and blowing snow. Because of slower speed limits and slippery roads, plan on more time to get to and through areas with snow-covered streets. Local radio stations broadcast weather information.

Trans-Canada and other major highways are generally ploughed promptly and kept clear with sand and salt. In areas of Québec where skiing is a major recreational industry, secondary roads are generally cleared quickly to allow skiers to get to the slopes.

If you get stuck while driving in snow, don't spin the wheels; rock the car gently back and forward. Gently pump the brakes when slowing or stopping; if the car skids on slippery roads, turn the steering wheel in the direction of the skid. Snow chains can be useful in mountainous or remote areas, but snow tyres or regular all-season tyres are usually adequate for most winter driving conditions in well-travelled areas of Canada covered by this guidebook. Studded snow tyres are permitted in some provinces during winter months, but prohibited in others (e.g., Ontario).

Useful items are an ice scraper, a small shovel for digging out, warm sleeping bags and extra clothing in case of long delays. Keep the petrol tank at least half-filled if possible, in case of delays. If you get stuck in a snowstorm: *stay in the vehicle* until help arrives, put a red flag on the radio antenna or door handle and keep warm with blankets; run the engine and heater only until the car is warm, then turn it off. Open windows a little to give ventilation and prevent carbon monoxide poisoning. *Do not go to sleep.*

Fog and Rain

Fog can occasionally be heavy in low-lying areas and is treacherous to drive in. Turn on the headlights, but use only the low beams to prevent blinding oncoming drivers as well as yourself with reflective glare. Lower your speed; look for reflective road markings to guide you.

Heavy downpours can begin suddenly, making driving dangerous. When travelling on the Trans-Canada, it may be advisable to pull over into a rest stop until bad weather passes.

The risk of 'hydroplaning' increases on rain-slicked roads and bridges between 56–88 kph; lower your speed when roads are wet and pump your brakes gradually when slowing or stopping.

DISTANCES

In most areas covered by this guidebook, point-to-point driving distances are not great, except in northern Ontario and some rural stretches mentioned briefly as side tracks. Among the most travelled routes, Toronto to Montréal along the Trans-

Canada Highway is a 485-km drive, which takes five to six hours, depending on traffic; Montréal to Québec City is a 260-km drive, which takes about 3½ hours. Plan on 80 km per hour *direct* driving time, without stops, longer in cities and in the mountains. Use the sample driving distances and times on p. 346 as guidelines, but allow for delays and stops.

DOCUMENTATION

In Canada, your home country's driver's licence is valid for up to three or six months (varying between provinces). The minimum driving age is 16 (17 in Newfoundland). Car hire companies may have higher age requirements, typically 21 or over (with additional charges for under-25 drivers).

HEADLIGHTS

Federal law requires all autos manufactured since 1990 to have **daytime running lights**.

INFORMATION

Automobile club membership in your home country can be invaluable. Canadian Automobile Association clubs provide members of corresponding foreign clubs travelling to North America the reciprocal services that CAA members are eligible to receive abroad. Auto club services include emergency road service and towing; maps, tour guidebooks and specialist publications; touring services; road and camping information; discounts to attractions and hotels. The rule of thumb is, if it's free at home, it should be free in Canada, too.

The CAA may charge for some services, like maps and tour books. Emergency breakdown road service may not be available to some non-North American club members. For information on reciprocal clubs and services, contact your own club in advance or check the local telephone directory while travelling. Carry your own club membership card with you at all times.

MOTORCYCLES

Motorcycles provide great mobility and a sense of freedom. Luggage will be limited, however; vast distances can make for days in the saddle; and remember that potholes, gravel, poor roads, dust, smog and sun are a motorcyclist's touring companions.

Hire motorcycles locally by finding a telephone directory listing. Helmets are required by law for both driver and passenger; foreign visitors must have a valid licence to operate a motorcycle in their home country. By custom (and in some states by law), most motorcyclists turn on the headlight even in the daytime to increase their visibility. Cars can share lanes with motor cycles, though it's unsafe.

PARKING

Public parking garages are indicated by a blue sign showing 'P' with a directional arrow. Prices are posted at the entrance. Some city centre garages charge high rates, but give discounted evening parking for shoppers and theatre-goers who get their sales receipts or tickets validated. In civic centres, shopping and downtown areas and financial districts, coin-operated parking meters govern kerbside parking. The charge and time limit varies with the locality. Compare garage parking against meter charges for the most economic choice.

No parking is allowed where you obstruct a fire hydrant, a bus stop area, an intersection or crosswalk (pedestrian crossing), a loading zone for lorry deliveries, a disabled person sidewalk ramp, a fire station entrance, railway crossing or street excavation, nor is parking allowed on a sidewalk, in front of a driveway or on a bridge, in a tunnel or on a provincial or Trans-Canada highway except in emergencies. Precise parking prohibitions vary between localities, so you need to be alert to posted signs.

If you park in violation of times and areas posted on kerb signs or poles nearby, or let the parking meter expire, expect to be issued

43

with a citation – a ticket that states the violation, amount of a fine and how to pay it. If you do not pay it, the car hire company may charge the ticket amount (and any penalties) against your credit card. Fines range from a few dollars to several hundred dollars, depending on the violation and the locality.

Valet parking at garages, hotels, restaurants and events may be pricey, and the parking attendant will expect an additional tip of $1 or $2 when returning the car. Leave the car keys with the valet attendant, who will return them with the car.

PETROL

Petrol (*gas* or, in Québec, *essence*) is sold in litres. Posted prices, including tax, are shown in cents per litre. Prices can vary, depending on location and on fluctuations in the petroleum market, but are generally around $0.50–0.65 per litre. In areas with many stations there can be strong price competition. Near urban areas, prices tend to be lower. In mountain or remote rural areas, prices can be much higher. Most stations offer **self-service**; a few may offer full service – filling the petrol tank, washing the windscreen and checking motor oil.

Most cars in Canada require **unleaded** petrol; due to environmental controls, leaded is not available. The three fuel grades are regular, super and premium: use regular petrol unless the car hire company indicates otherwise. A few vehicles use diesel fuel, which is not available at all filling stations, and some use propane, which is available at some filling stations.

When petrol stations are more than a few miles apart on highways or other major routes, normally a road sign will state the distance to the next services. Open petrol stations are well lit at night; many chains stay open 24 hours. Most stations accept cash, credit cards and Canadian or US dollar traveller's cheques. Self-service stations in urban areas may require advance payment before filling the tank; many have petrol pumps with automated credit-card readers.

POLICE

Police cars signal drivers with flashing headlights and red-and-white lights, and sometimes a siren. Respond quickly, but safely, by moving to the side of the road. Roll the driver's side window down but stay in the vehicle unless asked to get out. You have the right to ask an officer – politely – for identification, though it should be shown immediately anyway. Have your driver's licence and car registration papers ready for inspection when requested. Officers normally check computer records for vehicle registration irregularities and the driver for theft, criminal record or other driving violations. If cited, do not argue with the officer, as a bad situation can only get worse.

Littering the highway is illegal, and fines can be quite costly in some provinces.

If a police officer suspects that you are intoxicated, you may be asked to take a **'breathaliser'** test to measure your alcohol level from a breathing sample. Some experts claim the tests are inaccurate and can result in a false conviction for drunken driving. Nevertheless, although you have the right to refuse to take the test, refusal will result in arrest and confiscation of your driver's licence in some localities.

You are legally drunk if your blood alcohol content is above the legal limit (generally 0.08%, although police in many provinces can suspend your licence for 24 hrs if a roadside test finds your blood alcohol is greater than 0.05%).

ROAD SIGNS

International symbols are used for directional and warning signs, but many are different from European versions, although usually the same as US signs; language signs are in English, French or both languages, depending on the locality. Signs may be white, yellow, green, brown or blue.

Stop, yield, do not enter and wrong way signs are *red* and *white*. *Yellow* is for warning or direction indicators. *Orange* is for roadworks or temporary diversions. *Green* indicates highway directions. *Brown* is an alert for parks, campsites, hiking, etc. *Blue* gives non-driving information, such as radio station frequency for traffic or park information or services in a nearby town. Speed limits and distance are primarily shown in kilometres. Speed limit signs are *white* with black letters.

Traffic lights are red, yellow and green. Yellow indicates that the light will turn red: stop, if it is safe to do so, before entering the intersection.

A growing (and highly illegal) problem in Canada is motorists who *run* the red light; that is, enter the intersection when the signal is yellow and about to turn red. Police can cite you if you enter an intersection and you will not be clear of the intersection before the light turns red; they can also cite you for **careless driving** under a variety of conditions.

Except in Québec, it is permitted to turn right at a red traffic light – after coming to a full stop – if there is no traffic coming from the left, i.e., as if it were a 'give way' sign, unless there is a sign specifically forbidding it, which is not common. 'Right turn on red' is prohibited in Québec. A green arrow showing with a red light indicates you may turn in the direction indicated; in some places, lighted arrows or X's control individual lanes of traffic.

ROAD SYSTEM

The **Trans-Canada Highway** system was built between 1948–65 to streamline transportation across the country. Federal funds maintain the highways, which vary from multi-lane, limited access expressways to two-lane, undivided roads. They are usually the straightest, least scenic, least commercialised (and sometimes the only) route from point to point. Posted signs indicate to motorists when they are travelling on the Trans-Canada system, however no special note is made in the text.

Roads called *expressway, highway* or (in Québec) *autoroute* are usually dual-carriageways with limited access.

Rest areas, commonly along highways, usually have restrooms with toilets and public telephones and are usually landscaped. Picnic tables are provided in scenic areas and rest stops of historic or geographic interest post explanatory signs and maps. Use caution when leaving your vehicle at night and carry a torch (flashlight).

Federal, provincial and local routes can range from satin-smooth to pitted, depending on local spending; some are heavily commercialised, others very scenic. Dirt roads indicated on maps or described in this text may be treacherous. Ask locally about road conditions before venturing on. Car hire companies may prohibit driving on unpaved roads.

RULES OF THE ROAD

Lanes and Overtaking

Drive on the right. Vehicles are left-hand drive. The lane on the left is fast; the right is the slowest, and cars enter or leave traffic from the right (unless otherwise indicated by signs). Overtake other vehicles on the left side. *Cars may and will pass you on both sides in a multi-lane road.* For many drivers from the UK, this is the most unexpected and confusing feature of North American roads. Use direction indicators, but don't be surprised if other drivers don't bother.

Make right turns from the right-hand lane after stopping at stop signs or traffic lights. Turn left from the most left-hand of lanes going in your direction, unless the turn is prohibited by a no-turn sign. Enter bike lanes (where they exist) only if making a right turn. Do not drive in areas marked for public transportation or pedestrians.

Overtaking on a two-way road is permitted if the yellow or white line down the centre is broken. Overtake on the left. Highways, especially in mountainous areas or on long, narrow stretches of road, have occasional overtaking areas. Overtake only when oncoming traffic is completely visible, and avoid overtaking in fog or rain. Two solid yellow or white lines means no overtaking and no turning, unless into a private driveway or for a legal U-turn. On three-lane roads, overtaking is permitted in the middle lane; signs and/or broken lines indicate in which travel direction overtaking is allowed. Driving or parking on sidewalks is illegal.

Right of Way

Main road drivers have the right of way over cars on lesser roads. At the junction of two minor roads, the car to the right has the right of way when two cars arrive at the same time. At a four-way stop, the car arriving first may go first.

School buses are painted 'National School Bus Chrome Yellow' with black markings. All vehicles in both directions must stop for school buses displaying flashing red lights. Allow emergency vehicles with sirens to get through traffic by pulling over to the right and stopping.

Drivers entering a roundabout (traffic circle) must give way to cars already in the circle.

Highway Driving

An 'exit' or 'off ramp' is the ramp (slip road) leading off the highway; an 'entrance' or 'on ramp' leads into the highway.

When highway traffic does flow, it flows smoothly and quickly. The posted speed limit, 90 or 100 kph, is widely ignored – many drivers simply use it only as a guide to how fast to drive. The safest speed: match the general traffic flow in your lane, no matter how fast or slow.

The far-left lane is for the fastest-moving traffic; stay to the right unless overtaking. Signal a lane change and move left, if

---

Some Québeçois Driving Terms

Arrêt Stop.
Arrêt d'autobus Bus stop.
Attention Danger.
Autoroute Expressway or highway.
Chemin Road.
Défense de doubler No passing.
Essence Petrol.
Feu de circulation Traffic light.
Limité de vitesse Speed limit.
Piétons Pedestrians.
Ralentir Slow down.
Rang Rural route.
Rue Street.
Stationnement Parking.
Stationnement interdit No parking.

---

it is safe to do so, to allow cars entering the highway from the 'on ramp' to merge into traffic. However, don't be surprised if other drivers don't grant the same courtesy. When entering a highway, use your signal and accelerate as you merge into the traffic flow.

Horns

Horns should be sounded only as a safety warning.

Pedestrians

Pedestrians generally have the right-of-way over vehicles. Pedestrians must cross at intersections and crosswalks (pedestrian crossings) and must wait for the 'Walk' sign at crossings governed by lights; they always have the right of way at these crossings. Some cities and towns may cite pedestrians for jaywalking.

Speed Limits

The standard speed limit is 90 kph or 100 kph on Trans-Canada highways and other major highways, 80 kph on many provincial roads, 50 kph in urban areas. Traffic may

Some Canadian Driving Terms

Big rig, 18-wheeler or tractor-trailer A large lorry, usually a tractor pulling one or more trailers.

Bumper-to-bumper Slow-moving, heavy traffic with little space between cars.

Crosswalk Pedestrian crossing.

Connector A minor road connecting two highways.

Curve Bend.

Divided highway Dual carriageway.

DWI Driving While Intoxicated, aka Drunken Driving. The blood alcohol limit in Canada is generally 0.08% (0.05% in Newfoundland) and is *very* strictly enforced.

Fender Bumper.

Garage or parking garage Car park.

Gas(oline) Petrol.

Grade Gradient, hill.

Highway, expressway, parkway Motorway.

Hit-and-run Illegally leaving the scene after being involved in a collision.

Hood Bonnet.

Motor home Motor caravan.

Pavement Road surface. A UK 'pavement' is a sidewalk.

Ramp Slip road.

Rent Hire.

Road rage Expressions of anger at other motorists through rude driving and obscene gestures; a recent phenomenon, imported from the USA and Britain.

Rubberneck(er) Slowing down to peer while driving past the scene of an accident or some unusual event.

RV (recreational vehicle) Motor caravan.

Shoulder Verge.

Sidewalk Pavement.

Speed bump A road hump intended to make motorists slow down.

(Stick)shift Gear lever.

Tailgating Driving too closely to vehicle immediately in front.

Tow truck Breakdown lorry.

Traffic cop Traffic warden.

Trailer Caravan.

Truck Lorry.

Trunk Boot.

Windshield Windscreen.

Yield Give way.

47

flow faster or slower than those limits, but provincial and local police can ticket anyone going faster than the limit. You may not see the patrols, as radar guns are used from a distance to track speeds.

The use of radar detection devices is illegal in most provinces. Mere possession of a radar detector (even if not connected) is illegal in many provinces (Ontario, Québec and New Brunswick included), and police may confiscate the device and fine you for carrying it in your car.

Seat belts

All provinces require the driver and passengers to use seat belts. Children under age 5 or weighing less than 18 kg (40 lbs) must ride in an approved child safety seat (age 6 or 51 lbs in Québec).

USA

Motorists travelling between Canada and the USA must pass through Customs at the border, which often involves a vehicle inspection for illegal firearms, drugs or agricultural materials. You will need a copy of your car hire contract showing that use of the vehicle in the USA is authorised by the hire agency.

Visitors are advised to obtain the proper automobile insurance before entering the USA. Minimum liability coverage varies between states; New York State sets a high minimum requirement of US$50,000 for death or injury to any person, US$100,000 for death or injury to more than one person and US$5000 for property damage.

Seat belt use is strongly recommended for drivers and passengers in all US states; it is required in New York, Vermont and many other states. Petrol is sold by the gallon, motor oil by the quart; petrol grades are the same as in Canada, but prices are significantly lower, sometimes half the Canadian price. Speed limits and distances are posted in miles; language signs are in English only, except in border areas near Québec.

Vehicle Insurance

Vehicle insurance is compulsory in Canada. Visitors must carry proof that they have sufficient insurance and must show proof in case of an accident. The minimum liability insurance limit is $200,000, except in Québec, where it is $50,000.

In practice, considerable more coverage is desirable, and overseas visitors hiring a car are strongly recommended to take out top-up liability cover, such as the Topguard Insurance sold by Thomas Cook in the UK, which covers liability up to US$1 million. (This is not to be confused with travel insurance, which provides cover for you own medical expenses, see p. 28.)

Car rental agencies will also ask the driver to take out collision damage waiver, or CDW (sometimes called loss damage waiver,

LDW). Refusing CDW makes the renter personally liable for damage to the vehicle. CDW is strongly recommended for drivers from outside North America and is often insisted upon as part of a fly-drive package. Sometimes it is paid for when booking the car hire abroad, sometimes it is payable locally on picking up the car. Occasionally, special car hire rates will include CDW.

US drivers using their own cars should ask their insurance company or auto club if their coverage extends to Canada and meets their minimum coverage requirements. If not, arrange for insurance before signing the car hire contract. US drivers are advised to obtain a Non-Resident Inter-Provincial Motor Vehicle Liability Insurance Card from their US insurance agent before entering Canada.

Vehicle Security

Lock it when you leave, lock it when you're inside, and don't forget the windows. Never leave keys, documents, maps, guidebooks and other tourist paraphernalia in sight. Be mindful of anyone lurking in the back seat or house part of an RV, especially at night. Watch other drivers for strange behaviour, especially if you're consistently followed. Never leave an engine running when you're not in the vehicle. Keep car keys with you at all times. And always park in well-lit areas.

BACKGROUND
EASTERN CANADA

GEOGRAPHY

Canada is the world's second-largest country (after Russia), enclosing an area of nearly 10 million square km – about 40 per cent of North America – including its off-shore islands and about 755,000 square km of inland waters. It is bordered on the east by the Atlantic Ocean and Greenland (a territory of Denmark), on the north by the Arctic Ocean and on the west by the Pacific Ocean and the US state of Alaska; to the south it shares a 8895-km border with the USA.

Canada comprises ten provinces in the more temperate south, and the Yukon, Northwest and Nunavut (created April 1999) territories in the sparsely populated north. The eastern portion detailed in this volume includes the two largest provinces, Ontario and Québec (considered to be Central Canada), and the four smallest provinces in Atlantic Canada: New Brunswick, Newfoundland and Labrador, Nova Scotia and Prince Edward Island. Although these six provinces cover a vast land area (nearly a third of Canada), most of the population – as well as roads and railroad lines – lie in a narrow corridor close to the US border.

Canada's landscape is dominated by the Canadian Shield, a huge rocky region with a landscape of low hills, valleys and glacial lakes; this geological formation circles Hudson Bay and extends southward into most of Ontario, parts of Québec north of the St Lawrence River and into Labrador. South of this region, the peninsula of south-western Ontario is mostly rolling lowland, interrupted by rocky outcroppings of the Niagara Escarpment and the Thousand Islands. To the east, the low, rounded Appalachian mountains extend north-eastward from New England into Québec's Eastern Townships and Gaspé Peninsula and across Atlantic Canada into Newfoundland.

The mighty St Lawrence River drains the five Great Lakes along Ontario's US border (as well as the Ottawa, the Saguenay and a host of smaller rivers) and bisects Québec as it flows north-eastward into the chilly Gulf of St Lawrence. Among the region's tallest peaks are Québec's Mt Jacques-Cartier (1268 m) in the Gaspé Peninsula and Mt Tremblant (1260 m) in the Laurentians, and Lewis Hill (814 m) in the Long Range Mountains of north-western Newfoundland; some peaks amid Labrador's icy fjords at the rim of the Canadian Shield top 2100 m. Coastal areas generally range from sea level to only a few hundred metres.

Canada is one of the world's most heavily forested lands. Eastern Canada has a mix of coniferous pine, cedar and hemlock with the leafy beech, oak, ash and maple – making autumn a colourful season. Northward, the thin topsoil supports a deep boreal forest of spruce and birch where logging roads, and then no roads, reach. Further north, Inuits fish and hunt in a landscape of cold and nearly barren tundra.

Although Canada is considered a far-northern country, a comparison to Europe's latitudes is surprising. Toronto, at 43° 39' N, is roughly level with Monaco. Indeed, nearly all locales covered in this book, except Labrador, are south of London. Yet, winters are predictably harsh throughout eastern Canada, with temperatures below freezing

49

and heavy snowfall the rule. Southern Ontario and Québec have hot, humid summers; all seasons are more temperate in Atlantic coastal areas (see 'Climate' in Travel Essentials, p. 20).

HISTORY

Early History

Glaciers retreated between 15,000 and 7000 years ago, and the land is believed to have become thinly inhabited by early humans who fished, hunted and gathered food. People of the Algonquian language group occupied eastern Canada as early as 5000 years ago; these Indians were living in villages and cultivating crops when Europeans first encountered them in 1535.

Prior to European exploration, Iroquoian-speaking people lived in present-day Ontario and Québec, Malecites in New Brunswick, Micmacs in Nova Scotia and Gaspé; in Newfoundland, the Beothuk people disappeared without being well documented and their relics remain a mystery. The first Europeans to visit, around AD 1000, were the Vikings, who sailed down from Greenland and built a settlement at L'Anse aux Meadows on the northern tip of Newfoundland – which went undiscovered until the 1960s. Scholars still debate whether this was the fabled 'Vinland' of Norse texts, but, in any event, the site was apparently used for only a short period, perhaps 25–50 years.

In 1497, Giovanni Caboto, a Venetian sailing under the English flag and known to history as John Cabot, landed at various points along the coast of Cape Breton Island, Nova Scotia and Newfoundland while exploring for a northern route to China. In the early 1500s, traders and fishermen came from Portugal, Spain, France and England. The Frenchman Jacques Cartier explored the Gulf of St Lawrence River and claimed its shores for France in 1534; the next year he sailed up the river to the present-day sites of

Québec and Montréal, where he first encountered the Iroquois. He called the area around present-day Québec City 'Canada' – from the Huron-Iroquois word *kanata*, meaning 'village' or 'settlement'. Later, the word Canada was used for all of New France, including areas along the St Lawrence and the Great Lakes in present-day Ontario.

France vs England

Englishman Sir Humphrey Gilbert founded a temporary settlement at St John's in 1583 – and the island of Newfoundland later became the focus of British fishing interests – but French fur traders dominated the early history of eastern Canada. They bartered with the Indians – trading tools, weapons, cloth and metal pots for fox, bear and beaver pelts, the latter fashioned in Europe into lustrous felt and beaver hats.

French navigator Samuel de Champlain, working at first for a Huguenot nobleman, the Sieur de Monts, established a settlement on an island at the mouth of the St Croix River in present-day New Brunswick. After a miserable winter, the settlers moved across the Bay of Fundy to Port Royal (now Annapolis Royal, Nova Scotia) in 1605. Although the colony lasted only a few years, this was the beginning of the French region of Acadia, which extended from Nova Scotia into Prince Edward Island, New Brunswick and Maine.

Champlain, meanwhile, moved on to the St Lawrence region, establishing Québec in 1608 at the site of the Indian village Stadacona. He delved further into present-day Ontario and along the Great Lakes, making allies of the Huron and Algonquin, who supplied furs to French traders, and enemies of the Iroquois, who traded with the Dutch in New York's Hudson River Valley.

In the beginning, the fur trade operated under monopolies granted to French companies. By 1627, the French government took a stronger hand, forming the Company of

New France (or the One Hundred Associates) to organise the trade and govern the colonies. Settlement was encouraged, though not with great success, and the *'seigneurial'* system of landholding evolved out of French feudalism. Jesuits set up missions, both to convert the Indians and to keep the colonies Catholic rather than Huguenot.

The English made inroads into the region. They controlled Canada (New France) for a few years after seizing Québec in 1629, and they ruled Acadia from 1654–70. The Hudson Bay Company managed to control trade to the north for about 30 years beginning in 1670, which squeezed French traders between their Dutch, Iroquois and English enemies. In the 1700s, the rivalry between France and England for control of the colonies heated up with a series of wars in Europe and America, whose resulting treaties repeatedly altered the colonial map. The final conflict was the French and Indian War of 1754–63, which began with a dispute over English colonists in the Ohio River valley (in present-day USA), but which raged in Europe as the Seven Years War.

Highlights of the war included the expulsion of the Acadians in 1755 and the British razing of the French fortress at Louisbourg (on Cape Breton Island) in 1758. The Canadian phase climaxed at Québec on 13 Sept 1759, as British troops outflanking French forces, climbed the city's cliffs to defeat them on the Plains of Abraham in a 15-minute skirmish that left both commanders dying. A year later Montréal fell and with it all of New France. British dominance over the North American colonies was sealed by the Treaty of Paris in 1763.

Beginnings of a Nation

Britain, establishing the province of Québec, was faced with governing a vast territory with a foreign population of French-speaking Catholics living under an alien system of land ownership. Colonial governor Guy Carleton prodded London to adopt the Québec Act of 1774, which granted religious liberty, let French civil law coexist with English criminal law, endorsed the seigneurial system and expanded Québec's area westward.

These concessions were seen as threatening by the British colonists to the south, who in 1775–76 unsuccessfully invaded Canada on the eve of the American Revolution. The Québec Act also made life difficult for the 'United Empire Loyalists' – about 6000 English colonists who had opposed independence and fled northward to the St Lawrence region after the revolution. These refugees were accustomed to simple land ownership and representative government. To satisfy them, Parliament passed the Constitutional Act of 1791, splitting the colony into Lower Canada and Upper Canada (roughly similar to Québec and Ontario today) and creating an elected assembly, while retaining rights granted to the French in 1774.

Following a period of rebellion, an attempt was made to stabilise the colonies by reuniting them in 1841 as the United Province of Canada. In 1864, the Maritime provinces of New Brunswick, Nova Scotia and Prince Edward Island began discussing unity at the Charlottetown Conference, but leaders of the United Province convinced them to wait and to join talks later that year in Québec aimed at a wider confederation of the provinces. That effort led to the establishment in 1867 of the Dominion of Canada, which included New Brunswick, Nova Scotia and the newly reconfigured provinces of Ontario and Québec.

Prince Edward Island balked, but finally joined in 1873. Canada was given full independence under Britain's 1931 Statute of Westminster and the exclusive right to amend its constitution in 1982. Today, it is officially a constitutional monarchy ruled by Queen Elizabeth II, who delegates power to the Canadian Governor General. It is also a

51

federal state with governing legislatures in each province and a democratic Parliament, which consists of an elected House of Commons and an appointed Senate modelled on Britain's House of Lords. Real power resides in the prime minister and the Cabinet.

THE PROVINCES

Ontario

More than a third (11 million) of Canada's 28.8 million people live in Ontario, but they are unevenly distributed, with about 90 per cent living on the southernmost 10 per cent of the land. Ontario is the second-largest province in area (1,068,587 square km), and its expanse is truly startling: 1600 km from the eastern border with Québec to the western border with Manitoba and 1690 km from the US border up to the Northwest Territories. That's a larger area than France and Spain combined.

There's fertile farmland in the southern peninsula along the Great Lakes and the St Lawrence River, with deep forest to the north and flat bogs and small trees in the Hudson Bay lowlands. The name Ontario derives from the Iroquois word *kanadario,* meaning 'sparkling water', and it describes the 250,000 lakes, among them the five Great Lakes, that punctuate the landscape. Up north, Hudson Bay is at sea level; Ontario's highest elevation is a modest 693 m in the Ishpatina Ridge of the Timiskaming district.

It's tempting to think of Ontario as 'English' Canada, in contrast to French Québec, but the first Europeans in the area were 17th-century *voyageurs* (French trappers and woodsmen). Champlain made the trek up the Ottawa River and along Georgian Bay during his meanderings of the 1600s. The population today is about 70 per cent English-speaking, 4 per cent French-speaking. There are large pockets of people of Italian and German origin; in all, some 60

cultures are represented, many of whom retain their own language in addition to English or French, and recent immigrants include large numbers of Asians.

Toronto, with 4.26 million people, is Canada's largest city. Ottawa, the national capital of Canada, is fourth largest at 1.01 million (including Hull, Québec, which shares the government functions). Hamilton, Mississauga and Windsor are important industrial cities, which make steel, automobiles and other metal products. But Ontario is also known for its mining of iron ore, copper, zinc, gold, silver and uranium, and its forest products in the north and agriculture in the south.

Québec

Canada's largest province in area (1,667,926 square km), Québec is second-largest in population (6.9 million). As in Ontario, most of the people live in a narrow corridor to the south. However, Québec stretches about 2000 km north from the borders of New York and Vermont to the tip of Dungava Peninsula. To the west are Ontario, James Bay and Hudson Bay; to the east are Maine, New Brunswick and Labrador – with which it shares a border fixed by Britain in 1927, but never accepted by Québec.

The St Lawrence (*Fleuve St-Laurent*) Valley is rolling farmland; to the south are the small Appalachian mountains of the *Estrie* (Eastern Townships). To the north are the higher peaks of the Laurentians (with good ski areas) and deep forests. Far north, the land turns to barren tundra. To the east, the Gaspé Peninsula curves along the south shore of the widening St Lawrence River with increasing scenic drama.

Québec City (population 168,000) is the provincial capital and the centre of French culture in Canada – as well as of separatist sentiment. Montréal, Canada's second-largest city (3.33 million), is also quite French but maintains a large population of

English-speakers and recent immigrants with a variety of tongues. Montréal, once the business and economic capital of Canada, has suffered from the separatist movement that still threatens to wrest Québec from the heart of Canada.

Québec's official motto is *Je me souviens* ('I remember'), a reference to the province's French heritage. The separatist movement harks back to the period of 1791–1841, when the Québecois essentially had their own country prior to the first attempt at confederation. But it is also driven by a sense that periods of economic success have bene-fited English-speakers more than Franco-phones. Attempts to grant Québec special status, such as the Meech Lake Accord of 1987, have failed to win nationwide approval; likewise, referendum questions on sovereignty have failed to win a majority vote within Québec. Nevertheless, the question of whether the French province will remain a part of Canada or strike out on its own remains open.

New Brunswick

New Brunswick, one of the four provinces that united to form the Dominion of Canada in 1867, is today the third smallest province in area (73,440 square km) and in population (723,900). It is roughly a rectangle, measur-ing about 340 km from the northern border with Québec to the Bay of Fundy in the south, and 300 km from its western border with Maine to the Gulf of St Lawrence. It also shares a 28-km border with Nova Scotia at the Chignecto Isthmus, and it lies across the Northumberland Strait from Prince Edward Island.

New Brunswick, Prince Edward Island and Nova Scotia together constitute the Maritime Provinces; when you include Newfoundland and Labrador, the entire region is called Atlantic Canada.

The landscape is generally rolling hills and rocky outcroppings, with Mt Carleton, in the north, the highest peak at 820 m. Forests,

mostly leaf-bearing trees, cover 90 per cent of the land, making it Canada's most heavily forested province. The best-known feature is the Bay of Fundy, which has the world's highest tides.

The original settlers were Algonquian-speaking people of the Micmac, Malecite and Passamaquoddy tribes. The land was French Acadian country beginning in the 1600s, then controlled by Britain as a part of Nova Scotia. The Acadians were expelled in 1755 during the French and Indian War, but they returned and remain a presence today. In 1780, the region still had only about 2000 Indians and 3000 White settlers, but that changed after the American Revolution, when up to 20,000 Loyalists flooded in, dominating life there. Britain created the province of New Brunswick (named after the royal House of Brunswick) to accommo-date them. In the 19th century, there was an influx of Scottish and Irish immigrants.

The provincial capital is Fredericton, named after a son of King George III, who chartered the colony, but Saint John (popu-lation 125,000), with a deep-water port at the mouth of the Saint John River, has always been the biggest and most important city. With a third of the population primar-ily French-speaking, New Brunswick is the only officially bilingual province in Canada.

Newfoundland and Labrador

Although it was the first part of Canada explored by Europeans, Newfoundland was the last to join, finally leaving the British Empire in 1949. Canada's seventh largest (405,720 square km) province, comprises two adjacent but dissimilar regions.

There's 112,790-square-km Newfound-land, an island in the Gulf of St Lawrence. Mountainous to the west, rugged and rolling to the east, it has a lively seaport city, St John's (population 172,000) as its capital. It is rimmed by fishing villages and traversed by the Trans-Canada Hwy, helping to make its far-flung attractions accessible. The

53

292,930-square-km mainland region of Labrador is a wilderness of mountains, fjords and isolated outposts connected only by small planes and coastal ferries. Outfitters help hunters and sportfishermen reach inland areas, but the only paved road is a 65-km section at the southern tip.

Europeans fished the Grand Banks before John Cabot 'discovered' the island in 1497. It was called the New Found Land, and early reports brought Portuguese, Basque, French and English fishing boats. Eventually, England came to rule the waves, but it discouraged settlement of the island to protect fishing as a mother-country rather than a colonial industry.

French and English settlers battled sporadically until 1783, when British sovereignty was secured. Voters rejected confederation with Canada in 1867, approving it narrowly, at Britain's urging, only after World War II. The ill-defined region of Labrador came under Newfoundland's jurisdiction in 1927. The province today is officially called Newfoundland and Labrador – be sure, when you say it, to put the accent on the last syllable of both names.

Newfoundland (population 568,400) has spectacular, little-touristed sights. Gros Morne National Park rewards visitors with views of dramatic scenery, migrating whales and a rare geological wonder. Nearby are the ruins of the Vikings' only known village in America. But it's not an easy province to visit by car. Distances at each end of Newfoundland are not long, but the cross-island trip is daunting and the car ferries from Cape Breton are time-consuming. It's more practical to fly up, but be wary of expensive 'drop-off' fees for a one-way trip in a hire car.

Nova Scotia

Stretching 644 km from the Gulf of Maine to the Gulf of St Lawrence, but no more than 46 km across, Nova Scotia is surrounded by water except for a 28-km border with New Brunswick. One of the Dominion of Canada's four original provinces, Nova Scotia (Latin for 'New Scotland') comprises a large mainland peninsula, 10,280-square-km Cape Breton Island, and countless small islands along the 7400-km coastline.

It is separated from Prince Edward Island by the Northumberland Strait, from Newfoundland by the Cabot Strait and from Maine by the Bay of Fundy. Car and passenger ferries ply all these waters, making Nova Scotia not only highly accessible but almost a hub for the Atlantic Canada region. At 55,490 square km, it ranks ninth in area and seventh in population (937,800).

The landscape is generally low and rocky, with the highest point at 532m on Cape Breton. It's heavily forested in some areas, windswept and craggy in others. The economy relies not only on fishing and tourism, but also agriculture, mining and some manufacturing.

Originally Micmac lands, Nova Scotia was first claimed for England. French Acadians were the first to settle, and they generally prospered throughout the Maritimes, although the orginal colony at Port Royal failed. Relations between French and English settlers alternated between conflict and cooperation, depending on the larger colonial struggle between France and England. Halifax was founded in 1749 to counter French dominance from its Louisbourg fortress on Cape Breton Island.

Today's population is a mixture of roughly one-eighth Acadian, seven-eighths English and Scottish, with a small number of Micmacs and a smattering of Irish, German, Dutch and other immigrants. Following the American Revolution, as many as 80,000 Loyalists flocked to Nova Scotia, though not all of them stayed.

Halifax, the capital (population 115,000), has museums, nightlife, historical and cultural attractions. Cape Breton provides a mix of historical attractions, such as Fortress

Louisbourg and Alexander Graham Bell's summer home, and outdoor experiences. All along the shoreline there are scenic villages and secluded spots.

Prince Edward Island

Tiny PEI, only 225 km long and from 3 to 65 km wide, is a crescent-shaped island off New Brunswick and Nova Scotia in the Gulf of St Lawrence. It is the smallest of Canada's ten provinces, both in area (5657 square km) and population (129,800).

Up until 1996, most motorists reached the province by queuing up at Cape Tormentine, New Brunswick, for the 45-min ferry ride across the Northumberland Strait. Now the 12.9-km Confederation Bridge provides quick access to and from Borden–Carleton on the island's southern coast. A second car-ferry, however, still makes a 75-min crossing from Wood Islands to Nova Scotia.

PEI's landscape is mostly one of gently rolling hills of red soil and sandstone. The seacoast is lined with high cliffs and long, sandy beaches and marked with deep inlets and bays. With only one small city, Charlottetown, the capital (population 16,000), it is a peaceful place of small villages and farms, uncrowded beaches, long vistas and simple ways.

Tourism is a major industry, yet many rural lodgings and restaurants close after the short July–August beach season. The island's most enduring attraction is a work of adolescent fiction: devoted readers come to visit the home and countryside that Lucy Maude Montgomery described in her 1908 novel, *Anne of Green Gables*. Agriculture and fishing are the main livelihoods, and PEI potatoes and Malpeque oysters are widely known.

The island was first settled by Micmacs, who called it *Abegweit,* meaning 'cradled on the waves'. It was discovered in 1534 by Cartier, claimed for France in 1603 by Champlain and colonised as Île St-Jean in 1720. Ownership flip-flopped until the 1763 Treaty of Paris placed it in British hands, at first as a part of Nova Scotia. In 1799, it was renamed after the Duke of Kent, who commanded British forces in North America.

PEI is known as the 'Cradle of Confederation' because it hosted the 1864 Charlottetown Conference. However, when the Dominion of Canada was formed PEI didn't join, instead holding out until 1873, when a political deal was struck to relieve the province's financial straits.

55

TOURING ITINERARIES

Much of the pleasure of a driving holiday lies in tailoring your itinerary to match your tastes and interests. By dividing Eastern Canada into recommended routes, this book is intended to make it easy and pleasurable to plan your ideal tour. By linking several of our routes you can create a trip that will suit your tastes, and you can be confident of following a tried and tested path that introduces you to the best that the route has to offer.

This chapter begins with some practical advice on tour planning, followed by two ready-made itineraries designed to show you as much as possible of Eastern Canada's variety in a two- or three-week trip. Feel free to vary our suggestions, using the full range of information contained in the route descriptions.

The remaining pages list features of Eastern Canada that you can use to create a self-planned 'themed' tour using the routes noted.

PRACTICAL HINTS

Here are a few tips to make practicable routes easier to plan and more fun to follow:

1. Use the most detailed maps available. The colour map section at the end of this book is useful for planning itineraries and will enable you to follow the routes while driving, but a more detailed road map will be invaluable, especially if you intend to vary the routes we have

recommended. If you haven't already acquired a good road map or atlas, stop at the nearest CAA office as soon as possible after arriving in Canada and pick up maps for the areas you will be touring. For even more detail, buy the bound or folding maps published by MapArt or Allmaps and sold at major booksellers.

2. Don't schedule too much driving each day. Allow a conservative 80 km per hour of highway driving, 64 km each hour on secondary roads to allow for stretch breaks and the inevitable unplanned stops. It's better to have more time to explore along the way than be pressed to arrive by mealtime each evening. Each route description in this book gives information not only about mileage but also likely driving times.

3. Check weather and road reports. Most paved roads are open all year, but a few secondary roads through mountain passes, such as Rte 173, which goes south from Québec City toward Maine, close in severe winter weather. Unusually heavy snows or seasonal flooding can occasionally close roads. Road construction and heavy traffic in and around large cities are the most common obstacles.

4. Unless accommodation is pre-booked, plan to arrive each night with enough time to find a place to sleep. In some areas, particularly Toronto, Montréal, Québec City and small towns with few motels, advance bookings are essential.

5. Build in time at the end of the trip to get back to the departure city (usually

Toronto or Montréal) the day before a scheduled flight home. Airlines don't hold entire planes for one carload of late arrivals, and passengers travelling on cheap fares who miss a flight may be faced with buying a new ticket home – at full price.

6. Give serendipity a chance by not planning in too much detail. Allow time to spend an extra few hours – or an extra day – in some unexpected gem of a town or to turn down an interesting side road. Anyone who wants their days preplanned in 15-min increments will be happier on a fully escorted package coach tour than a self-drive holiday.

THE BEST OF EASTERN CANADA

Eastern Canada is too large an area to cover comfortably in a single motoring trip, unless you have a minimum four to six weeks' time available. It's far better to plan to drive through a limited area, such as Ontario and Québec or the Atlantic provinces – or even to fly between 'hubs', where you can pick up rental cars or join motorcoach tours.

The following tours give examples of some reasonable ways to combine recommended routes. Suggested overnight stops are in bold type. Adapt the tours freely or use the same cut-and-paste idea to combine several routes for more personalised itineraries.

14 days

Long highway distances make it difficult to 'do' Eastern Canada in a single bout of whirlwind driving, but by breaking up your driving with a flight, you can combine the urban highlights of Ontario and Québec with some of the quieter charms of New Brunswick, Prince Edward Island and Nova Scotia.

Day 1: **Toronto** (p. 62).
Day 2: Toronto to London (p. 91) or

Niagara Falls (p. 80) and back to **Toronto**.
Day 3: Toronto to **Kingston** (Toronto to Ottawa, p. 101).
Day 4: Kingston via Thousand Islands region to **Ottawa** (Toronto to Ottawa, p. 101; Ottawa and Hull, p. 109).
Day 5: Ottawa to **Montréal** (p. 131).
Day 6: **Montréal** (p. 139).
Day 7: Montréal to **Québec City** (p. 173).
Day 8: **Québec City** (p. 184).
Day 9: Flight to Saint John, drive to **Fundy National Park** (Saint John, p. 237; Moncton to Saint John in reverse, p. 231).
Day 10: Cape Breton Island and follow Cabot Trail to **Cheticamp** or **Inverness** (Moncton to Charlottetown, p. 259; PEI to Cape Breton, p. 276; Cape Breton Island, p. 281).
Day 11: Continue Cabot Trail and visit Fortress Louisbourg, then along the lake to **Baddeck** (Cape Breton Island, p. 281–289).
Day 12: Baddeck to **Halifax** (Cape Breton to Halifax, p. 290).
Day 13: **Halifax** (p. 294).
Day 14: By air to **Toronto** or **Montréal** for homebound flight.

21 Days

Three weeks is a more realistic time frame to see most of Eastern Canada. If possible, add another week to see the remote, less travelled northern reaches of Ontario or Québec, to wander further afield in Prince Edward Island or to visit Newfoundland and Labrador.

Day 1: **Toronto** (p. 62).
Day 2: **Toronto**.
Day 3: Toronto to **London** (p. 91) or **Niagara Falls** (p. 80).
Day 4: London or Niagara via Toronto to **Kingston** (Toronto to Ottawa, p. 101).
Day 5: Kingston to **Ottawa** (Toronto to Ottawa, p. 101).
Day 6: Drive or steam train ride to Gatineau Park and back to **Ottawa** (Ottawa and Hull, p. 109).

57

Day 7:   Ottawa to **Montréal** (p. 131).

Day 8:   **Montréal** (p. 139).

Day 9:   Visit Laurentians (p. 154) or Estrie (p. 162) and return to **Montréal**.

Day 10: Montréal to **Québec City** (p. 173).

Day 11: **Québec City** (p. 184).

Day 12: Québec City to **Gaspé** or **Forillon Park** (Québec to Rivière-du-Loup, p. 211; Gaspé Peninsula, p. 215).

Day 13: Gaspé to Campbellton to **Acadian Peninsula** (Gaspé Peninsula, p. 215; Campbellton to Moncton, p. 223).

Day 14: Acadian Peninsula to Moncton to **Fundy National Park** or **St Martins** (Campbellton to Moncton, p.223; Moncton to Saint John, p. 231).

Day 15: Fundy coast to Saint John, ferry to Digby, NS, to **Annapolis Royal** (Moncton to Saint John, p. 231; Saint John, p. 237; Halifax to Yarmouth, p. 300).

Day 16: Annapolis Royal to **Halifax** (Halifax to Yarmouth in reverse, p. 300, or Yarmouth to Halifax, p. 306).

Day 17: **Halifax** (p. 294).

Day 18: Halifax to **Cape Breton Island** (Cape Breton to Halifax in reverse, p. 290; Cape Breton Island, p. 281).

Day 19: **Cape Breton Island** (p. 281).

Day 20: Cape Breton via Pictou ferry to **Charlottetown** (PEI to Cape Breton in reverse, p. 276; Eastern PEI, p. 267; Charlottetown, p. 263).

Day 21: Flight to **Toronto** or **Montréal** for homebound flight.

THE MAJOR CITIES

Toronto and Montréal are big and bustling, rich with cultural and historical attractions, and as different as the old and new worlds. But Eastern Canada's small and medium-sized cities have plenty to offer as well. They are generously sprinkled throughout the area, near to coastal, rural and wilderness experiences.

The cities are listed in alphabetical order, identifying the recommended routes from this book that lead to and from them. By studying the chapters that describe the cities in full (also cross-referenced below) and the other recommended routes, you can omit those places that don't interest you and mix in some non-city routes for a taste of forest, mountain or coastal scenery.

Charlottetown

Tiny Prince Edward Island has a proportionately small capital, population 16,000. This low-key waterfront town served as a French outpost and as host to the talks that created the Dominion of Canada. Today it's the cultural, commercial, culinary and entertainment hub of Canada's smallest province. (See Charlottetown, p. 263; Moncton to Charlottetown, p. 259; Eastern PEI Loop, p. 267; Western PEI Loops, p. 271.)

Halifax

Nova Scotia's capital, population 115,000, is compact and unpretentious, blending a sophisticated air with an unhurried pace. Quiet neighbourhoods of gracious Victorian homes surround a tidy historic centre dominated by an imposing 19th-century fortress. With fine dining and lively nightlife, Halifax wears its present as smartly as its past. (See Halifax, p. 294; Cape Breton to Halifax, p. 290; Halifax to Yarmouth, p. 300; Yarmouth to Halifax, p. 306.)

Montréal

The second largest French-speaking city in the world is decisively North American. Built on the French colonial fur trade and shipping, it is today a banking, manufacturing and software centre as well as a polyglot city of great ethnic diversity. A sophisticated centre of the arts, pop culture and fine cuisine, it is fully bilingual in French and English. (See Montréal, p. 139; Ottawa to Montréal, p. 131; Montréal to Québec City, p. 173.)

Ottawa

Once a roughneck lumberjack village,

Ottawa has grown into a bilingual mini-metropolis and a major centre of Canadian history and culture – yet it's smaller than you might expect for the capital of a vast country. The park-bordered Rideau Canal curves through the heart of the city, which shares some government functions with Hull, across the Ottawa River in Québec. A tiny taste of Canada's vast northern wilderness is available only minutes away in Gatineau Park. (See Ottawa and Hull, p. 109; Toronto to Ottawa, p. 101; Ottawa to Toronto, p. 121; Ottawa to Montréal, p. 131.)

Québec City

Within its 17th-century walls, Québec remains a picturesque low-rise city of grey stone, dominated on the bluff overlooking the St Lawrence River by the Hôtel Château Frontenac. Québec is the North American centre of French language and culture, where 95 per cent of the population speak primarily French. (See Québec City, p. 184; Montréal to Québec, p. 173; Québec to Portland, p. 195; Québec to Saguenay River Loop, p. 203; Québec to Rivière-du-Loup, p. 211.)

Saint John

Named by French explorer Samuel de Champlain and settled by Loyalists after the American Revolution, Saint John (population 125,000) was built around a natural, ice-free, deep-water harbour. Its waterfront is the centrepiece of downtown rejuvenation, with climate-controlled skywalks and pedestrian tunnels linking hotels to multi-storey shopping malls. (See Saint John, p. 237; Moncton to Saint John, p. 231; Saint John to Fredericton, p. 251; Saint John to St Stephen, p. 241.)

St John's

The capital of Newfoundland, with steep streets and a Victorian air, traces its roots to explorer John Cabot in the 1400s. Today St John's is an unpretentious, unsophisticated

and undeniably provincial seaport, filled with foreign ships and 172,000 genial, genuine and jovial residents. (See St John's, p.313; Avalon Peninsula Loop, p. 319; St John's to Port aux Basques, p. 325.)

Toronto

With its futuristic skyline and charming Victorian homes, Toronto is the financial, cultural and transportation hub of English-speaking Canada. Once stodgy, it is now vibrant, cosmopolitan and ethnically diverse. It has earned a reputation for being clean and safe and, although it's Canada's largest and most expensive city, it is known as 'New York without the Cost'. (See Toronto, p. 62; Toronto to Niagara Falls, p. 80; Toronto to London Loop, p. 91; Toronto to Ottawa, p. 101; Ottawa to Toronto, p. 121.)

TOP HISTORIC SIGHTS

Fortifications of Québec National Historic Site, *Québec City; tel: (418) 648-7016*, shows how France used the city to defend its north-eastern colonies. On the **Plains of Abraham**, the British defeated the French in 1759 to seize Québec as part of Lower Canada. The **Citadelle**, built 1820, was the eastern flank of Québec's fortress under the British and is still occupied by ceremonial troops. Various museums and interpretive centres tell the city's story. (See Québec City, p. 183.)

Fortress of Louisbourg National Historic Site, *Louisbourg, Nova Scotia; tel: (902) 733-2280*, a fortified city built by the French in the early 1700s, was blown up in 1758. Restored from utter ruin, it is now inhabited by costumed interpreters engaged in the daily life of a thriving commercial outpost. You can join them in homes, shops, gardens, bakery, tavern or guard house, sampling their foods and learning about their lives. (See Cape Breton Island, p. 280.)

Fort York, *Toronto; tel: (416) 392-6907*, is a restoration of the original settlement where Toronto was founded 1793. Staff in period dress give hourly tours as well as demonstrations of musket firing and early music. (See Toronto, p. 60.)

Halifax Citadel; *tel: (902) 426-5080,* though never attacked, is a fine example of a mid 19th-century bastioned fort. It served the British and then the Canadian Army through World War II, and serves as a repository of military and regional history. (See Halifax, p. 293.)

L'Anse aux Meadows National Historic Site, *L'Anse aux Meadows, Newfoundland; tel: (709) 623-2608,* which dates from AD 1000, is the only Viking settlement in North America yet discovered and the first known European colony in the Americas. Discovered only in the 1960s, it now includes a museum, Visitor Centre and village site, where you see foundation lines and a reconstructed sod home and workshop. (See Deer Lake to L'Anse aux Meadows, p. 333.)

Province House National Historic Site, *Charlottetown, PEI; tel: (902) 566-7626,* now the seat of PEI's provincial legislature, is the site of the 1864 Charlottetown Conference, in which representatives of New Brunswick, Nova Scotia, Ontario and Québec held talks that led to confederation under the Dominion of Canada. (See Charlottetown, p. 263.)

Upper Canada Village, *tel: (613) 543-3707,* south of Ottawa along the St Lawrence River, includes more than 40 historic buildings moved from an area flooded for the St Lawrence Seaway. Located where Loyalists settled after the American Revolution, the restored village with costumed interpreters portrays 1860s Ontario life. (Toronto to Ottawa, p. 101.)

Vieux (Old) Montréal is home to most of Montréal's historic buildings and colourful, narrow streets dating from the 17th and 18th centuries. **Vieux Port**, the area's waterfront, has a 2-mile promenade and entertainments on the old piers. (Montréal, p. 139.)

TOP MUSEUMS

Maritime Museum of the Atlantic, *Halifax; tel: (902) 424-7490,* includes items from the age of sail, steam and naval history, such as a schooner's deckhouse, Queen Victoria's barge, flotsam from the *Titanic* and memorabilia of shipping magnate Samuel Cunard. (Halifax, p. 293.)

Musée de la Civilisation, *Québec City; tel: (418) 643-2158,* has permanent exhibits that include the history of Québec and a 250-year-old boat unearthed at the museum site. Clever temporary exhibitions deal with all aspects of modern and pop culture. (Québec City, p. 184).

Musée de Québec, *Québec City; tel: (418) 643-2150,* beautifully merges the original museum building with a 19th-century prison. Some of Québec's best religious sculpture and terrific paintings by Canada's leading artists are here. (Québec City, p. 184).

The Canadian Museum of Civilization, *Ottawa; tel: (819) 776-7000,* in a century-old architectural prize, traces 1000 years of human endeavour in Canada, emphasising Native and ethnic diversity and including an enchanting Children's Museum. (Ottawa, p. 109.)

The National Gallery of Canada, *Ottawa; tel: (613) 990-1985,* the masterpiece of architect Moshe Safdie, holds collections of Canadian art, including Inuit works and superlative naturalistic paintings by the country's Group of Seven. (Ottawa, p. 109.)

The Royal Ontario Museum, *Toronto; tel: (416) 586-8000,* is Canada's largest museum, featuring archaeology and natural history and popular exhibits of Chinese and ancient Egyptian antiquities, dinosaurs and a bat cave. (Toronto, p. 62.)

The Art Gallery of Ontario, *Toronto; tel: (416) 979-6648,* features 50 galleries and 15,000 works, including many works by the Group of Seven and the largest public collection by sculptor Henry Moore. (Toronto, p. 62.)

The McCord Museum of Canadian History, *Montréal; tel: (514) 398-7100*, is the grand dame of national history museums in Canada, focusing principally on cultural history. (Montréal, p. 139.)

TOP PARKS

Algonquin Provincial Park, *tel: (705) 633-5572*, located roughly 200 km north of Toronto and 200 km west of Ottawa, covers 7600 square km of rivers, lakes and forests and is home to loons, beaver, bears and moose. A 62-km corridor is accessible by car; the rest only on foot or via 1500 km of canoe routes. (Ottawa to Toronto, p. 121.)

Cape Breton Highlands National Park, *tel: (902) 224-2306*, covers a 950 square km slice of mountain range at the northern tip of Nova Scotia. Skirted by The Cabot Trail, which brings motorists to the most dramatic scenery, it is criss-crossed with hiking trails and dotted with recreational opportunities and small villages. (Cape Breton Island, p. 281.)

Forillon National Park, *tel: (418) 892-5553*, lies at the remote and visually stunning tip of Québec's Gaspé Peninsula, incorporating mountains, cliffs and coastline. Whale-watching cruises, sea kayaking, hiking and camping are all popular activities. (Gaspé Peninsula, p. 215.)

Fundy National Park; *tel: (506) 887-6000*, covers 206 square km along New Brunswick's Bay of Fundy coast. Hills rise to a rolling plateau cut by deep valleys, streams tumble through wildflower meadows and exhibits tell the story of the Bay of Fundy's amazing tides, the world's highest. (Moncton to Saint John, p. 231.)

Gatineau Park, *tel: (819) 827-2020*, is an accessible bit of Québec wilderness, only a few minutes drive from the national capital at Ottawa. This 356-square-km realm of forests, glacial hills and a 185-km network of groomed nature trails is home to white-tailed deer, wolves, bears and beavers. It includes a former prime minister's country retreat, civilised eating places nearby and a scenic steam train ride. All this is a tiny part of south-western Québec's 33,000-square-km **Outaouais** wilderness. (Ottawa and Hull, p. 109.)

Gros Morne National Park, *tel: (709) 458-2066*, in northern Newfoundland, was named a UNESCO World Heritage Site for the Tablelands, a piece of the earth's mantle forced to the surface 450 million years ago by geological action. The park offers rare scenic beauty along Bonne Bay and views of migrating whales. (Deer Lake to L'Anse aux Meadows, p. 333.)

Parc du Saguenay; *tel: (418) 272-3008*, 85 km north-east of Québec City, covers roughly 80 km along both banks of the Saguenay Fjord, where the Saguenay River empties into the St Lawrence. Roads, hiking trails and cruise boats offer views of migrating whales and other scenic wonders. (Québec to Saguenay Loop, p. 203.)

St Lawrence Islands National Park, *tel: (613) 923-5261*, highly accessible to the average traveller, includes 21 of the famous 'Thousand Islands' (of which there are really 1800) along the US-Canadian border on the St Lawrence River. Overnight camping and day recreational activities complement river cruises among the islands. (Toronto to Ottawa, p. 101.)

TORONTO

Toronto, with its glittering office towers and charming Victorian homes, is the financial, cultural and transportation hub of English-speaking Canada. In 1788, the Mississauga Indians sold the land to the English for flannel, axes and £1700. Once thought of as stodgy, its futuristic waterfront skyline now gives way to a vibrant, cosmopolitan metropolis that was designated in 1989 by the United Nations as the world's most ethnically diverse city.

Its reputation for being clean and safe has earned it the nickname 'Toronto the Good', and although it's the largest and most expensive city in Canada, it's also been described as 'New York without the Cost'. There's an excellent public transportation system, and numerous popular sites are easy to walk to in the downtown core – many are linked by a 10-km network of underground pathways.

TOURIST INFORMATION

Tourism Toronto, *207 Queen's Quay W., Suite 590, Toronto, ON M5J 1A7, tel: (416) 203-2500* or *(800) 363-1990* (toll-free), handles written and phone enquiries. **Info TO**, *Toronto Convention Centre, 255 Front St W.; tel: (416) 869-1372*, operated by Tourism Toronto and Toronto Tours, handles walk-in enquiries. Open daily. It makes accommodation, entertainment and sporting event bookings and has maps of city and underground PATH systems, and information sheets on cycling, walking tours,

shopping, free things to do, advice for disabled visitors and gay and lesbian travellers.

Ontario Tourism, *Eaton Centre* (one level below ground), handles walk-in enquiries only, Mon–Fri 1000–2100, Sat 0930–1800, Sun 1200–1700.

WEATHER

Toronto has one of the mildest climates in Canada, thanks to the warmth of Lake Ontario and a latitude almost level with the northern border of California. Jan temperatures average -9° to -1°C, July 15°–26°C. Be prepared for extremes, though. Winter wind chill can make some days feel dramatically colder, and in summer, heat and humidity can account for two–five-day stretches of muggy weather. Late spring and early autumn offer pleasant walking weather. Oct can be brisk but refreshing, with brilliant red and orange leaves warming up the scene.

Buildings have excellent heating and air-conditioning, so walkers should wear layers that can be added or removed as needed.

If you're downtown, look to the top of the Canada Life Building, *330 University Ave (at Queen St)*, for lights that indicate the weather forecast. If the lights run up the temperature is rising; lights running down, temperature falling; lights unchanging, temperature steady; steady red light on top, overcast; flashing red light, rain; flashing white light, snow – and if it's green, expect a clear and sunny day. Major weather fronts can generally be seen approaching the city from the west.

ARRIVING AND DEPARTING

Airports
The **Lester B. Pearson International Airport** services more than 50 domestic and

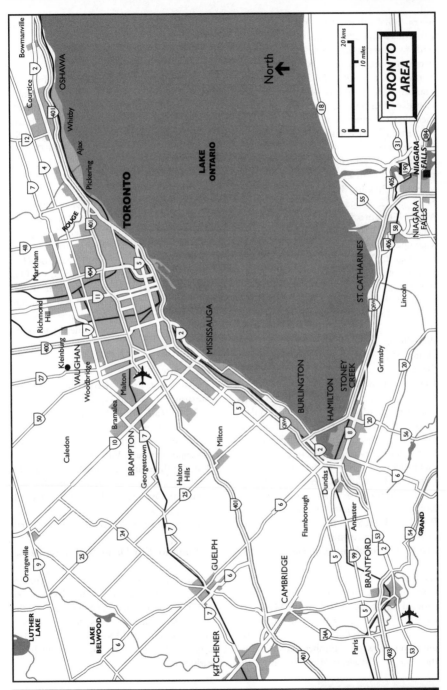

63

international airlines. Terminal 1 and 2 serve Air Canada and other airlines, tel: (905) 676-3506 for flight times, airline telephone numbers, transportation and parking information. Terminal 3, tel: (905) 612-5100, services Air France, VASP, KLM, British Airways, Canadian, Alitalia, Qantas, El Al, Continental Air Pacific, Pem Air and American. All terminals have currency exchange and food services.

Pacific Western; tel: (905) 564-3232, provides a 30-km airport–city centre bus service every 20 mins. Travel time: 30–75 mins. Stops at 12 major downtown hotels and **Metro Toronto Coach Terminal**, $12.50 one way, $21.50 return, children under 11 accompanied by adult free. It also has services to Islington, York Mills and Yorkdale subway stations every 40 mins. Fare: $6.75–8.75 one way.

Airport taxi services charge set flat rates and will often provide early morning wake-up calls if requested. For example, **Aerofleet**; tel: (416) 449-4990, does airport–Westin Harbour Castle Hotel runs for $30. See under 'Taxis' in the Yellow Pages telephone directory.

The modest **Toronto City Centre Airport**, tel: (416) 203-6942, on Hanlan's Point at the west tip of Toronto Islands, can only be reached by ferry. It handles private flights and short-haul commercial commuter flights (Air Ontario) to Montréal and to Ottawa and London, Ontario; tel: (416) 925-2311 or (800) 268-7240 (Air Canada) for reservations. A shuttle service from the Royal York Hotel to the ferry is at the foot of Bathurst St; the 2-min ferry ride to the terminal is free for airline passengers.

By Car

Coming from the west (Pearson International Airport or London) on Hwy 401, take the Hwy 427 exit south to Queen Elizabeth Way (QEW) and continue east until you cross the Humber River, where the Queen Elizabeth Way becomes the

Gardiner Expressway, and continue to the Yonge St exit. This will bring you under the Gardiner and point you north on Yonge St towards the downtown core.

From the airport or London on Hwy 401, you could also continue along the north edge of the city to the Yonge St exit and follow it south. This will be a slower, busier route to the downtown core – but good for people watching, especially south of Bloor St, where you begin to enter the area known as the Yonge St 'Strip'.

Coming from the west (Niagara) on the Queen Elizabeth Way (QEW), travel east until you cross the Humber River and the QEW becomes the Gardiner Expressway. Continue east to the Yonge St exit.

To enter Toronto from the east on Hwy 401 (from Montréal), travel west to the Don Valley Parkway and take it south to the Richmond St exit, which will lead you into the downtown core. Continue west on Richmond St and you will meet Church St, Yonge St and Bay St.

By Train

Trains arrive and depart from **Union Station**, 65 Front St W.

VIA Rail, tel: (416) 366-8411, is the national and international rail service. 'The Canadian', VIA Rail Canada's trans-Canada passenger service to Vancouver, departs from Toronto three times per week. VIA Rail also services routes between Toronto and Montréal, Ottawa, London and Niagara Falls (continuing as Amtrak to New York City), Windsor and Sarnia (continuing as Amtrak to Chicago).

Ontario Northland Rail Services, tel: (416) 314-3750 or (800) 268-9281, provides a Sun–Fri rail service north to Cochrane, connecting with the Polar Bear Express (see p.37), a one-day rail excursion 'down' the Arctic watershed by lakes, forests, muskeg and scrub brush to Moosonee on James Bay, a part of Hudson Bay. Operates late June–early Sept.

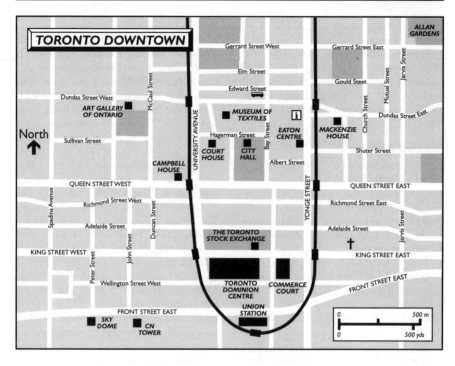

TORONTO DOWNTOWN

ALLAN GARDENS

Gerrard Street West
Gerrard Street East

Elm Street
Gould Steet
Edward Street

Dundas Street West
ART GALLERY OF ONTARIO
MUSEUM OF TEXTILES
Dundas Street East

North ↑

Sullivan Street
Hagerman Street
EATON CENTRE
MACKENZIE HOUSE

McCaul Street
UNIVERSITY AVENUE
Bay Street
Church Street
Mutual Street
Jarvis Street

COURT HOUSE
CITY HALL
CAMPBELL HOUSE
Albert Street
Shuter Street

QUEEN STREET WEST
QUEEN STREET EAST

Spadina Avenue
Richmond Street West
Duncan Street
YONGE STREET
Richmond Street East

Adelaide Street
Adelaide Street

John Street
KING STREET WEST
KING STREET EAST
Jarvis Street

Peter Street
Wellington Street West
THE TORONTO STOCK EXCHANGE

TORONTO DOMINION CENTRE
COMMERCE COURT
FRONT STREET EAST

FRONT STREET EAST
UNION STATION

SKY DOME
CN TOWER

0   500 m
0   500 yds

Go Transit, *tel: (416) 869-3200*, operating from Union Station's lower level, is a regional system of trains with connecting buses that link downtown Toronto to communities as far west as Hamilton, north to Barrie and east to Oshawa. Lakeshore westbound trains include a stop at Exhibition Place (close to Ontario Place) except during rush hours. Fares are based on distance travelled. Tickets should be retained until journey is completed.

By Bus

Metro Toronto Coach Terminal, *610 Bay (at Dundas St); tel: (416) 393-7911*, is open daily 0500–0100, telephone information daily 0730–2230. Intercity bus services connect Toronto with all of North America; **Trentway-Wagar** has services to Canadian and American destinations (with direct services to Boston and New York City); **Penatang Midland**, **Ontario Northland**,

Can-Ar and **Transtario** operate coach services within the province.

Greyhound, *tel: (416) 367-8747 or (800) 661-8747*, operates intercity transportation to Canadian and American destinations (including direct service to New York City); also sightseeing tours of Toronto and Niagara (Apr–Nov).

By Taxi

You can hail taxis from the street (the car is available if the roof light is on), call in advance (e.g. **Diamond Taxi**, *tel: (416) 366-6868)*, or look for taxis lined up near the entrance of major hotels. Meter rates start at $2.50 and rise $0.25 per 0.235 km.

By Ferry

Toronto Island Ferries (docked at foot of *Bay St* beside Westin Harbour Castle Hotel); *tel: (416) 392-8193*. Year-round transport to and from the Toronto Islands. Centre Island service every 30 mins 0800–2330 May–Sept, adults $1–4 return.

Shaker Cruise Lines; *tel: (416) 364-3938,* provides ferry service between St Catharines and Harbourfront, Toronto; $12 one way, and also hydrofoil/ferry service between Harbourfront and Niagara-On-The-Lake $20, and Lewiston, N.Y., $25.

GETTING AROUND

Toronto hugs the base of *Yonge St,* which, at 1900 km, is the longest street in the world (it's pronounced 'Young'). The city's location on the north shore of Lake Ontario evolved from its position at the beginning of a short-cut to Lake Huron, an alternative to the older canoe route.

The city is laid out in a grid pattern. *Yonge St* runs north, and streets that cross it begin their address numbers at it, always including the reference East or West. *University Ave* (which becomes *Avenue Rd* north of the Parliament Buildings) runs parallel to *Yonge St* and *Bloor St* crosses it. The city's three main subway lines run beneath these three streets. Hwy 401, on the northern edge of the city, is the second busiest highway in North America.

When walking on ground level the **CN Tower** *(301 Front St W.),* the world's tallest free-standing structure, becomes a beacon you can use to orientate yourself.

The Underground City is a 10-km system of underground walkways that connect stores, restaurants and theatres with hotels and office towers. You can explore the city without stepping outside, using this route that links the Metro Toronto Coach Terminal with the Eaton Centre, the Hockey Hall of Fame, Roy Thomson Hall, Union Station and the CN Tower Skywalk to the SkyDome. Ask Tourism Toronto for a free map and watch for posted **PATH** maps and markers along the route. Colour-coded arrows show you the direction you are heading: north is blue, east is yellow, south is red and west is orange.

Public Transport

More than 1.2 million people use the **Toronto Transit Commission (TTC)** services daily. Buses, streetcars, subways and Rapid Transit (RT) cars cover more than 6000 km of routes in the metropolitan area. The service has a reputation for being clean and modern. The subway is the heart of the system; most surface routes connect with it. Subway lines run beneath *Yonge St, University Ave* and *Bloor St,* Mon–Sat 0600–0130, Sun 0900–0130. Free maps of subway and bus routes are available at subway stations.

Drivers do not take fares or give change. Tokens can be purchased at booths in the stations, tickets are available at some convenience stores. A single fare is $2, 10 tokens $16. A Day Pass, $6.50, is valid for unlimited travel for one person on all TTC routes Mon–Sat after 0930. A $6.50 Day Pass for Sun or statutory holidays is valid for up to six people (a maximum of two adults). Tickets are valid for a single journey, including necessary transfers between buses and subways and other connecting routes. Transfers must be obtained at the beginning of a journey.

When leaving streetcars, always look to the right before stepping into the street.

For TTC information on routes and fares, *tel: (416) 393-4636.*

Driving in Toronto

Parking is very expensive in the centre of Toronto, and public transit is very good. Consider exploring by TTC. Wearing seatbelts is compulsory in Ontario. Unless indicated otherwise, you can turn right at a red light but you must come to a full stop first. Cars must stop at least 2m behind rear doors of streetcars when they are boarding or disembarking passengers. Stop for pedestrians at crosswalks, which are marked with X's on overhead yellow bars. Watch for signs indicating that road rules change during certain hours. Watch for lanes reserved for bikes, buses, taxis and cars making right turns (i.e., curb lane on *Bay St* Mon–Fri 0700–1900).

STAYING IN TORONTO

Accommodation

There are more than 32,000 hotel rooms in Metro Toronto, including 15,000 Downtown, 9000 near Pearson International Airport and another concentration in the **Parklands District** in the north-eastern section of the city (helpful if you are coming from the east, i.e., Montréal). **Tourism Toronto**, *tel: (416) 203-2500 or (800) 363-1990, fax: (416) 203-6753*, can assist with room bookings.

Most major chains are represented, either in Metro Toronto or suburban locations.

Downtown waterfront locations include the expensive–pricey **Radisson Plaza Hotel Admiral**, *249 Queen's Quay W., Toronto, ON M5J 2N5; tel: (416) 203-3333 or (800) 333-3333*, and the pricey **Westin Harbour Castle Hotel**, *1 Harbour Sq., Toronto, ON M5J 1A6; tel: (416) 869-1600 or (800) 228-3000.*

In the Theatre District, and featuring some pricey rooms with a view of the SkyDome's baseball field, is the *CP* **SkyDome Hotel**, *1 Blue Jays Way, Toronto, ON M5V 1J4; tel: (416) 341-7100 or (800) 441-1414.* For elegant old-world charm, try the pricey *CP* **Royal York Hotel**, *100 Front St W., Toronto, ON M5J 1E3; tel: (416) 368-2511 or (800) 441-1414*, and the **King Edward Hotel**, *37 King St E., Toronto, ON M5C 1E9; tel: (416) 863-9700 or (800) 225-5843.* Easier on the budget are moderate–expensive **Hotel Victoria**, *56 Yonge St, Toronto, ON M5E 1G5; tel: (416) 363-1666*, and the moderate **QI** at *111 Lombard St; tel: (416) 367-5555 or (800) 228-5151.*

In the vicinity of City Hall is the expensive–pricey **Sheraton Centre**, *123 Queen St W., Toronto, ON M5H 2M9; tel: (416) 361-1000 or (800) 325-3535*, the moderate–expensive **Toronto Marriott**, *525 Bay St, Toronto, ON M5G 2L2* (connected to the Eaton Centre); *tel: (416) 597-9200 or (800) 228-9290*, and the expensive **Colony Hotel**, *89 Chestnut St, Toronto, ON M5G 1R1; tel: (416) 977-0707 or (800) 387-8687.* Moving north, you'll find the moderate–expensive **Delta Chelsea Inn**, *33 Gerrard St W., Toronto, ON M5G 1Z4; tel: (416) 595-1975 or (800) 243-5732*, the moderate **DI** at *30 Carlton St; tel: (416) 977-6655 or (800) 325-2525*, and the elegant, pricey **Sutton Place Hotel**, *955 Bay St, Toronto, ON M5S 2A2; tel: (416) 924-9221 or (800) 268-3790.*

In the trendy upmarket *Bloor St/Yorkville* area, celebrities hide out at the pricey **Four Seasons**, *21 Avenue Rd, Toronto, ON M5R 2G1; tel: (416) 964-0411 or (800) 268-6282.* Across the road, with a popular rooftop patio, is the pricey **Park Plaza Hotel**, *4 Avenue Rd, Toronto, ON M5R 2E8, tel: (416) 924-5471 or (800) 977-4197.* Easier on the budget are the moderate **QI** at *280 Bloor St W.; tel: (416) 968-0010 or (800) 228-5151*, and **Venture Inn**, *89 Avenue Rd, Toronto, ON M5R 2G3; tel: (416) 964-3311 or (800) 387-3933.*

In Toronto, Bed and Breakfast accommodation averages $40–75 single, $55–85 double, depending on location and whether you require a private bathroom. Several associations can help you find facilities in the area and price range that you want. **Toronto Bed and Breakfast**; *tel: (416) 588-8800* (email: beds@torontobandb.com), is the oldest registry in the city with 20 locations. **Bed & Breakfast Homes of Toronto**; *tel: (416) 363-6362*, is a co-op with 18 locations. **Bed & Breakfast Guest Houses Association of Downtown Toronto**; *tel: (416) 368-1420*, has 30 locations. **Abodes of Choice B&B Homes of Toronto**; *tel: (416) 537-7629*, has 11 locations.

Female budget travellers can find economical rooms at the **YWCA Woodlawn Residence**, *80 Woodlawn Ave E., Toronto, ON M4T 1C1; tel: (416) 923-8454.* **Neill-Wycik College Hotel**, *96 Gerrard St E., Toronto, ON M5B 1G7; tel: (416) 977-2320*, offers clean, basic rooms to the public May–Aug with shared bathrooms and

67

Toronto Neighbourhoods

Two aspects of Toronto make it a unique North American city. Its cultural diversity (it's home to over 80 ethnic groups, with many neighbourhood street signs posted in English and the predominant language of the community) and the fact that downtown Toronto doesn't shut down after the business day. With the exception of the **Financial District** (the south end of *Bay St* and along neighbouring *King* and *Adelaide Sts*), residents live and play in the core of the city.

Harbourfront, once a district of waterfront warehouses, between *York St* and *Spadina Ave*, is now dominated by towering condominiums and features shops, restaurants, theatre, concerts, boat cruises, craft studios and antique sales – drawing especially large crowds on summer weekends. A 15-min ferry cruise away are the **Toronto Islands**. On **Ward's Island**, a former cottage community has become a year-round home to about 600 city residents. Visitors usually head for **Centre Island** for picnicking, cycling, in-line skating and its family amusement park.

The **Theatre District** starts on *Front St* between *Sherbourne* and *Yonge Sts*, where you'll find the **Hummingbird Centre for the Performing Arts** (ballet and opera) and the **St Lawrence Centre for the Arts and Young Peoples Theatre**. Several blocks north on *Yonge St* is the **Elgin and Winter Garden Theatre Centre** (*Joseph and His Amazing Technicolour Dreamcoat*) and **Pantages Theatre** (refurbished for the opening of *Phantom of the Opera*). Follow *King St* west across *University Ave* to **Roy Thomson Hall** (concerts), **The Royal Alexandra** (musicals and plays) and **The Princess of Wales Theatres** (built for the only full-scale *Miss Saigon* production in North America).

Queen St W., between *University Ave* and *Bathurst St*, is the heart of young Toronto – a vibrant neighbourhood with trendy cafés, restaurants, boutiques and nightclubs. **Kensington Market**, surrounding *Kensington St*, which runs north from *Dundas St* just west of *Spadina Ave*, was originally Toronto's Jewish area. Now it's a multi-cultural neighbourhood with a colourful market atmosphere – especially Sat mornings. **Chinatown**, centred on *Dundas St W.*, between *Bay St* and *Spadina Ave*, crowded with sidewalk fruit

kitchens, pleasant rooftop patio and barbecue. **HI–Toronto**, *223 Church St, Toronto, M5B 1Y7; tel: (416) 971-4440*; expect dormitory beds from $20 for members, $24 for non-members. The hostel is expected to move to a new location, so call ahead. The new **Global Village Backpackers**, *460 King St W.; tel: (416) 703-8540 or (888) 844-7875* (toll-free), is a 5-min walk from the CN Tower, Skydome and Theatre District. It offers 195 beds from $20 per night.

The closest campsite to metropolitan Toronto is the functional **Indian Line Campground**, *7625 Finch Ave W.; tel: (905) 678-1233*. Take bus 36B from Finch

subway and walk 15 mins. Direct access to Hwy 427. For a lovely setting beside hiking trails, try **Glen Rouge Park** (operated by Metro Parks), *7450 Kingston Rd E.; tel: (416) 392-2541*, on Hwy 2, 1 km east of *Port Union Rd* in Scarborough. Bus 95B or E from York Mills subway and walk 0.5 km.

Eating and Drinking

Toronto's multi-ethnic make-up has led to a wide choice of cuisines (there are more than 40 Thai restaurants alone). Budget-stretchers should be adventurous and head for the various ethnic neighbourhoods and watch for restaurants that are popular with the local residents.

and vegetable stalls, is the largest and most centrally located of three Chinese areas in the city. About 53,000 students create a youthful atmosphere surrounding the **University of Toronto** campus, which is bounded by *Spadina Ave, University Ave, Bloor* and *College Sts.*

Bloor West Village, *Bloor St* between *Jane* and *Runnymede Sts,* is a busy neighbour-hood with many restaurants and shops operated by residents from Eastern Europe. *Bloor St W.* between *Bathurst* and *Christie* is a focal point for Toronto's Korean community.

In the 1960s, **Yorkville,** north of *Bloor St* between *Bay St* and *Avenue Rd,* was the cen-tre of Toronto's hippie culture. Now its Victorian homes house trendy upmarket bou-tiques, galleries, restaurants and clubs. World leaders, film and music stars, and even a deposed duchess, stay at the neighbouring posh Four Seasons Hotel, making this an inter-esting area for celebrity sightings. The nearby **Annex** is a charming neighbourhood with Queen Anne-style residences, between *Avenue Rd* and *Bathurst, Bloor* and *Dupont Sts.* **Forest Hill** (to the north) and **Rosedale** (to the east) are upmarket residential areas with quiet streets and the beautiful homes of many wealthy and powerful Canadians.

Corso Italia, on *St Clair Ave W.* between *Bathurst St* and *Lansdowne Ave,* and **'Little Italy',** on *College St* between *Ossington* and *Euclid Ave,* are focal points for Toronto's Italian community, one of the largest outside of Italy.

East of *Yonge St,* at *Church* and *Wellesley Sts,* is the heart of Toronto's **gay commu-nity** – a neighbourhood of shops, clubs and restaurants. **Cabbagetown,** between *Wellesley* and *Dundas Sts,* east of *Sherbourne St,* was named after the crops that the early Irish immigrants planted in their yards. It's now a neighbourhood of charming restored Victorian homes that features Riverdale farm, complete with cows, in the centre of the city.

East of the downtown core, the busy area with shops, sidewalk cafés and restaurants on the Danforth (a continuation of *Bloor St),* between *Chester* and *Jones Ave,* is known as **'Greektown'.** The **Beaches,** *Queen St E.,* east of *Woodbine Ave,* was once a cottage com-munity. Its cafés, boutiques, bike paths, boardwalk and beach make it a popular family neighbourhood with a busy village atmosphere.

69

From trendy upmarket Yorkville to ethnic neighbourhoods like Greektown on the Danforth (continuation of *Bloor St E.),* summertime outdoor patios are popular for dining and people watching. In the down-town core you'll find that barbecue stands with hot dogs and sausages on buns are set up on many major street corners at noon. Chip and ice-cream trucks usually line up on *Queen St* across from City Hall.

One level below ground, along the 10-km PATH system, you'll find numerous economical fast-food services that are pop-ular with office workers during the noon hour. Toronto's Centre Island offers casual budget dining facilities as well as a terrific

skyline view for picnickers – just don't encourage the Canada Geese with scraps.

For current information on restaurants in the city, check the free *WHERE* magazine, available at major hotels. For a current list of vegetarian restaurants, contact **Toronto Vegetarian Association,** *736 Bathurst St, Toronto, ON M5S 2R4, tel: (416) 533-3897.*

Starting at the waterfront, Harbourfront offers a variety of dining opportunities from light snacks to fine dining. For casual, lake-side dining (including patios) at a moderate price there is the **Boat House Bar & Grill,** *207 Queen's Quay W.* (Queen's Quay Terminal at Harbourfront); *tel: (416) 203-6300.* The pricey **Lighthouse Restaurant,**

1 Harbour Sq. (Westin Hotel); *tel: (416) 869-1600*, revolves once an hour, offering city and lake views from a height of 37 storeys. Two km to the west at Ontario Place, with a wonderful view of the city skyline and waterfront, is the **Atlantis Complex**, *955 Lake Shore Blvd W.; tel: (416) 260-8000*, with pricey **Nemos** (continental cuisine) and moderate **Zoots** (pasta, pizza and burgers). It also features a nightclub (Deluge) and a rooftop patio.

Moving north, the most spectacular view from a dining room in the city is from atop the CN Tower at the pricey **360 Revolving Restaurant**, *301 Front St W.; tel: (416) 362-5411*. The restaurant's own elevator whisks you up 115 storeys. After dinner join regular sightseers one level below in Horizons Bar.

The area covering several blocks north from the base of the CN Tower, near SkyDome, Roy Thomson Hall and the Royal Alexandra and Princess of Wales Theatres, offers a wide variety of eating options. **Planet Hollywood**, *277 Front St W.*, tel: *(416) 596-7827*, is busy, packed, noisy, overpriced, but fun. Movie memorabilia on display includes Dan Aykroyd's foam backpack from *Ghostbusters* and John Goodman's bowling tunic from *The Flintstones*.

Hockey fans can head for **Wayne Gretzky's**, *99 Blue Jays Way; tel: (416) 979-7825*; décor includes one-of-a-kind artefacts from hockey star Gretzky's personal collection. Moderate. The **Elephant & Castle Pub & Restaurant**, *212 King St W.; tel: (416) 598-4455*, offers budget meals in a pleasant cosy atmosphere steps from the theatres. The moderate–pricey **Filet of Sole Restaurant**, *11 Duncan St; tel: (416) 598-3256*, caters to seafood lovers, while upstairs, moderate–pricey **Cha Cha Cha**, *11 Duncan St, 2nd Floor; tel: (416) 598-3538*, offers intimate dining by candlelight with a small dance floor.

For casual dining (and dancing from 2100), try the budget–moderate **Loose**

Moose Tap & Grill, *220 Adelaide St W.; tel: (416) 971-5252*. **Crocodile Rock**, *240 Adelaide St W.; tel: (416) 599-9751*, a restaurant/nightclub with pool tables and featuring contemporary and classic rock music.

John St, which links this section of the Theatre District to the *Queen St W.* area, is lined with a variety of restaurants, most with summer patios. Try moderate–pricey **Al Frisco's**, *133 John St; tel: (416) 595-8201*; **Just Desserts**, *137 John St; tel: (416) 599-0655*; or moderate **Montana**, *145 John St, tel: (416) 595-5949*, for country cuisine. In the funky *Queen St W.* area, budget–moderate **Babur**, *273 Queen St W.; tel: (416) 599-7720*, is an old Toronto favourite for tandoori cooking and other dishes from Northern India.

Amongst the office towers of the financial district, **Ruth's Chris Steak House**, *145 Richmond St W.* (Toronto Hilton Hotel); *tel: (416) 955-1455*, is known for pricey but generous portions. The **Jump Cafe & Bar**, *Commerce Court E., Court Level (Bay & Wellington Sts); tel: (416) 363-3400*, has a pricey menu and creative budget tapas in its bar. One level lower, the moderate **Soul of the Vine**, *187 Bay St; tel: (416) 368-1444*, offers more than 30 pasta dishes.

Moving toward the Hummingbird, St Lawrence Centre, Pantages and Elgin Theatres, **Marche**, *BCE Place (Yonge and Wellington Sts); tel: (416) 366-8986*, is the most casual of the popular Mövenpick restaurants, offering a market atmosphere and budget prices. Open daily 0730–0200. **Shopsy's**, *33 Yonge St; tel: (416) 365-3333*, budget, for 70 years a Toronto favourite for deli specialities – with summer sidewalk patio. Budget–moderate. **Old Spaghetti Factory**, *54 The Esplanade; tel: (416) 864-9775*, is just south of the Hummingbird Theatre.

La Maquette, *111 King St E.; tel: (416) 366-8191*, moderate–pricey, has a working fireplace and overlooks the Toronto Sculpture Gardens and St James Cathedral.

Young Thailand, *81 Church St; tel: (416) 368-1368*, offers budget all-you-can-eat lunch buffet. **Senator Steakhouse**, *253 Victoria St* (opposite Pantages Theatre); *tel: (416) 364-7517*, has steaks and lobster, pricey. Dinner Tues–Thur or Sun includes admission to Top O'The Senator Jazz Club upstairs.

Denison's Brewing Company and Restaurant, *75 Victoria St; tel: (416) 360-5877*, offers house beers on tap at three budget–moderate restaurants: **Louie's Brasserie**; *tel: (416) 360-5877*, **Conchy Joe's Oyster Bar**; *tel: (416) 360-0074*, and **Growlers Pub**; *tel: (416) 360-5836* (happy hour special – 40 items for under $5, Mon–Fri 1500–2330, Sat from 1630). **Real Jerk**, *709 Queen St E.* (a bit beyond the regular tourist track)*; tel: (416) 463-6055*, offers authentic Caribbean cuisine and music.

In the Eaton Centre, the moderate **City Grill**, *220 Yonge St; tel: (416) 598-4454*, has a peaceful pleasant summer patio. Just north, pricey **Barbarians**, *7 Elm St; tel: (416) 597-0335*, is popular a old Toronto steakhouse/tavern. Moderate–pricey **Bangkok Garden**, *18 Elm St; tel: (416) 977-6748*, is the city's best for authentic Thai food (buffet lunch available). Pricey **Bistro 990**, *990 Bay St; tel: (416) 921-9990*, is where many of the stars hang out during the Toronto International Film Festival. For a terrific view of the city, visit the moderate restaurant, bar and lounge **Panorama**, *51st Floor, 55 Bloor St W.* (Manulife Centre); *tel: (416) 967-0000*.

In trendy **Yorkville**, celebrities favour pricey **Prego della Piazza**, *150 Bloor St W.; tel: (416) 920-9900*. For a budget–moderate meal in the neighbourhood, try **Hemingways**, *142 Cumberland St; tel: (416) 968-2828*, with rooftop patio and live rock & roll after 2100. Just north, known for its romantic atmosphere and view of the city skyline, pricey **Scaramouche Restaurant/Pasta Bar**, *1 Benvenuto Pl.; tel: (416) 961-8011*, serves dinners only, Mon–Sat.

Popular with trendy Toronto, pricey **Centro**, *2472 Yonge St* (north of Eglinton subway); *tel: (416) 483-2211*, and **North 44**, *2537 Yonge St; tel: (416) 487-4897*, both have a restaurant and wine bar.

The **Old Mill**, *21 Old Mill Rd; tel: (416) 236-2641*, is a historic Tudor-style mansion with landscaped gardens. Afternoon teas, buffets at lunch Sun–Fri and Sun evening, moderate. Mon–Sat à la carte pricey – with ballroom dancing and a live band.

Communications

The area code in downtown Toronto is 416. The *905* code is used (usually without dialling *1* because it's not long distance) for many of the surrounding areas, including Mississauga.

There is no single central post office in Toronto. There are now more than 40 postal outlets – many are retail franchises in stores and malls and their hours are influenced by the adjoining businesses. For example, at *First Canadian Place, lower level*, a postal outlet is open Mon–Fri 1000–1800. An outlet in the lower level of The Bay, *Yonge and Richmond Sts*, extends its hours to include Sat. For closest outlet and hours, call **Canada Post**; *tel: (416) 979-8822*. Mail sent poste restante can be picked up Mon–Fri 0730–1745 at *25 The Esplanade (Bay and Front Sts), M5E 1W5*.

Money

Thomas Cook bureaux de change are located downtown at *55 Bloor St W.* (Manulife Centre); *tel: (416) 961-9822; 10 King St E.; tel: (416) 863-1611; 9 Bloor St W.; tel: (416) 923-6549* and *123 Queen St W.* (Sheraton Centre); *tel: (416) 363-4867*. Surrounding areas: *1 Yorkdale Rd* (Yorkdale Shopping Centre); *tel: (416) 789-1827; 100 City Centre Dr., Mississauga* (Square One Shopping Centre); *tel: (905) 276-3341; 655 Dixon Rd* (International Plaza Hotel); *tel: (416) 247-4600, 300 Borough Dr.* (Scarborough Town Centre); *tel: (416) 296-*

1544, and *Lester B. Pearson Airport, Terminal 3, tel: (905) 673-7607.*

ENTERTAINMENT

Featuring more than 40 theatres, Toronto follows London and New York with the third largest theatrical industry in the English-speaking world. Tickets average $8–40, dinner theatre $30–75, blockbuster musicals $38–91.

T.O. TIX (Toronto's half-price ticket centre), *208 Yonge St* (at the Eaton Centre); *tel: (416) 596-6468*, sells discounted tickets for same-day performances. Tickets must be purchased in person Tues–Sat 1200–1930. Call for listings of available shows. Tickets for next day out-of-town events may also be available. You can arrange tickets to popular shows before you arrive in Toronto through **Edwards & Edwards**, *tel: (914) 328 2150* or *(800) 223-6108.*

Three daily newspapers cover entertainment information: *The Toronto Star* (see *What's On* section on Thur), the *Globe & Mail* (see *The Arts* on Sat), and the *Toronto Sun*. For extensive restaurant listings, check *WHERE* magazine, published monthly and available free at hotels. Watch street racks for free weekly tabloids – *NOW* and *eye* (major focus on entertainment) – and *City Parent*, *The Metro Word* (Black culture), plus *XTRA* (gay and lesbian scene).

Musicians on TTC property (subway buskers) have auditioned for their position. Each summer at the Canadian National Exhibition 150–200 musicians compete for 70 licences.

Theatres

Toronto's refurbished grand old theatres that feature major productions include: the **Royal Alexandra Theatre**, *260 King St W.* (subway: *St Andrew); tel: (416) 872-1212;* **Pantages Theatre**, *263 Yonge St* (subway: *Dundas); tel: (416) 872-2222;* and the world's last operating double-decker theatre, the **Elgin and Winter Garden Theatres**,

189 Yonge St (subway: *Queen); tel: (416) 872-5555.*

The **Hummingbird Centre for the Performing Arts** (formally O'Keefe Centre), *1 Front St E.* (subway: *King); tel: (416) 872-2262,* is home to the **Canadian Opera Company** and the **National Ballet of Canada**. When rush seats are available, they go on sale at 1100 at the box office the day of the performance.

The **St Lawrence Centre for the Arts**, *27 Front St E.* (subway: *King); tel: (416) 366-7723,* houses both the 850-seat Bluma Appel Theatre and the 480-seat Jane Mallett Theatre. The **Ford Centre for the Performing Arts**, *5040 Yonge St* (subway: *Sheppard); tel: (416) 395-7425,* has housed musicals from *Showboat* to *Ragtime.* **Atlantis Theatre**, *955 Lake Shore Blvd W.* (at Ontario Place); *tel: (416) 260-8000,* is a 450-seat theatre in a giant pod above Lake Ontario.

The **Premiere Dance Theatre**, *Queen's Quay Terminal, 207 Queens Quay W.* (at Harbourfront); *tel: (416) 973-4000,* is the only theatre in Canada devoted entirely to dance. Tiny **Toronto Truck Theatre**, *94 Belmont St; tel: (416) 922-0084* (near Yorkville), is home to the longest running play in Canada, Agatha Christie's *The Mousetrap.* A family favourite – **Famous People Players**, *110 Sudbury St; tel: (416) 532-1137* – has life-size characters of famous personalities becoming animated through the use of black light. Dinner packages are available.

The non-profit **Young Peoples Theatre**, *165 Front St E.; tel: (416) 862-2222,* is Canada's largest professional Children's Theatre. Some productions are suitable for children as young as two. The Canadian Stage Company; *tel: (416) 367-8243,* presents **Shakespeare in the Park**, in High Park near Grenadire Pond, evenings Tues–Sun (July–Aug); pay-what-you-can.

Music

Roy Thomson Hall, *60 Simcoe St* (subway:

St Andrew); tel: (416) 593-4828, is home to the Toronto Symphony Orchestra Sept–June. Rush seats sold 1100 weekdays, 1300 Sat. Call one hour ahead for availability (limit two tickets per person). **Massey Hall**, *178 Victoria St* (subway: *Queen); tel: (416) 593-4828,* is a 19th-century concert hall favoured for its acoustics and named after the family of actor Raymond Massey.

Jazz
Montreal Bistro/Jazz Club, *65 Sherbourne St; tel: (416) 363-0179.* **Top O'The Senator**, *253 Victoria St; tel: (416) 364-7517.*

Dinner Theatre
La Cage Dinner Theatre, *279 Yonge St, 2nd Floor* (subway: *Dundas); tel: (416) 364-5200.* **Mysteriously Yours**, *100 Front St W.* (Royal York Hotel, subway: *Union); tel: (416) 486-7469* or *(800) NOT-DEAD,* interactive murder mystery. **Limelight Dinner Theatre**, *2026 Yonge St* (subway: *Eglinton); tel: (416) 482-5200.* **Medieval Times Dinner & Tournament**, *Lake Shore Blvd W.* (Exhibition Place); *tel: (416) 260-1234* or *(800) 563-1190.* **Stage West Theatre Restaurant**, *5400 Dixie Rd, Mississauga; tel: (905) 238-0042.*

Comedy
Second City, *56 Blue Jays Way* (subway: *St Andrew); tel: (416) 863-1111;* alumni include Dan Aykroyd, Martin Short, Mike Myers, Andrea Martin and the late John Candy. Student concessions and free improv after regular show. **The Laugh Resort**, *26 Lombard St; tel: (416) 364-5233,* has stand-up comedy. **Yuk Yuk's Comedy Club**, *2335 Yonge St* (subway: *Eglinton); tel: (416) 967-6425,* has stand-up comedy; alumni include Jim Carrey and Howie Mandel.

Clubs
Bear in mind the legal age for purchasing and consuming alcohol in Ontario is 19. The area west of *University Ave* along *Queen St W.* and in former warehouses for several blocks south contains a variety of clubs frequented by a young crowd, such as **Whiskey Saigon**, *250 Richmond St W.; tel: (416) 593-4646.* **Deluge**, in the Atlantis Complex at Ontario Place; *tel: (416) 260-8000,* sets the scene with 10-m floor-to-ceiling windows, indoor pyrotechnics and a rooftop patio.

Events
The multi-cultural make-up of Toronto is celebrated for eight days in mid June with the **Metro International Caravan**, which features the food, music, dance and crafts of 40 nationalities at pavilions scattered around city. The **Downtown Jazz Festival** includes free and ticketed events for 10 days in late June. **Symphony of Fire** international fireworks competition is featured at Ontario Place, Sat and Wed, mid June–early July.

In late July, during Toronto's largest spectator sporting event, the **Molson Indy**, a special race course is set up through Exhibition Place and along *Lake Shore Blvd.* **Caribana**, a two-week West Indian festival on Toronto Islands late July–Aug, concludes with a parade on *Lakeshore Blvd* that draws over one million spectators. The **Canadian National Exhibition**, known simply as 'the Ex' (and held at Exhibition Place, late Aug–Sept), is the world's oldest and largest annual agricultural fair. It features games and rides and concludes early Sept with the world's largest air show.

The **Festival of Festivals**, the second largest film festival in the world, is held for 10 days in early Sept at various theatres. The **Royal Agricultural Winter Fair** is featured at Exhibition Place, mid Nov for 10 days.

Sports
The **SkyDome** stadium, *One Blue Jays Way* (subway: *St Andrew),* is home to two Toronto sports teams. For baseball, **Toronto**

73

Blue Jays, *tel: (416) 341-1111,* Apr–Sept or Oct, $4–25; Canadian-style football **Toronto Argonauts**; *tel: (416) 341-1234,* June–Nov, $10–35. Beginning in 1999, two teams play at **Air Canada Centre**, *40 Bay St.* Toronto's National Hockey League team, the **Toronto Maple Leafs**; *tel: (416) 872-5000,* Oct–Apr, $23.50–92.50; basketball **Toronto Raptors**; *tel: (416) 872-5000,* Oct–Apr, $5–99.

Thoroughbred horse-racing with pari-mutuel betting is held at **Woodbine Racetrack**, *555 Rexdale Blvd (at Hwy 27); tel: (416) 675-7223,* Thur–Mon year round.

SHOPPING

The three-block long **Eaton Centre**, *290 Yonge St* (subway: *Queen* or *Dundas),* draws more than one million visitors per week to its 350 shops, restaurants and services. In general, the higher the level, the more expensive the retailer. Linked to the south end is **The Bay** department store, a branch of Canada's oldest retailer (established 1670). The entire complex is connected to the subway *(Queen* and *Dundas* stops) and the 10-km underground PATH walkway system. Mon–Fri 1000–2100, Sat 0930–1800, Sun 1200–1700.

The **Bloor St/Yorkville** area is the centre for upmarket shopping. Shops along *Bloor St* between *Yonge St* and *Avenue Rd* include: **Tiffany & Co.**, **Chanel**, **Montblanc's**, **William Ashley** (china, crystal and silver) and **Holt Renfrew** (ladies high fashion). For several blocks north, on *Cumberland, Yorkville* and *Bellair Sts,* Victorian buildings have been renovated into trendy boutiques and sidewalk cafés. **Lundstrom**, *136 Cumberland St,* is an award-winning Canadian designer, the **Guild Shop**, *118 Cumberland St,* is the oldest dealer of Inuit and Native art in Toronto.

Newcourt Centre (formerly Queen's Quay Terminal), *207 Queen's Quay W.* (at *Harbourfront),* houses more than 100 shops, galleries and restaurants, including **Tilley Endurables** (Canadian adventure clothing),

Oh Yes Toronto (quality Toronto T-shirts) and **Arctic Canada** (Inuit and Dene fine arts, crafts, clothing and carvings), Mon–Sat 1000–2100, Sun 1000–1800.

Harbourfront Antique Market, *390 Queen's Quay W.,* is the largest permanent antique market in Canada, open Tues–Fri 1100–1700, Sat–Sun 1000–1800. **Eskimo Art Gallery**, *12 Queen's Quay W.* (across from the Westin Harbour Castle Hotel) features Toronto's largest selection of Inuit sculpture.

Queen Street W. (between *University* and *Bathurst Sts)* offers a youthful funky atmosphere, featuring bookstores, T-shirt and jewellery vendors, cafés and trendy boutiques, such as **GAP** and **Roots** (Canadian casual clothing). Toronto's **Fashion District** for wholesale prices and discounted designer clothing is on *Spadina Ave* between *Queen St* and *College St.* Quality outdoor equipment stores, such as **Europe Bound**, **Trail Head** and **Mountain Equipment Co-op**, line *Front St,* just east of *Yonge St.*

Bargain hunters can scour **Honest Ed's**, *581 Bloor St W.,* then relax around the corner on *Markham St* (the first street west) in **Mirvish Village**, where Victorian homes now house antiques shops, bookstores and restaurants.

Visitors from outside Canada may claim a refund of the 7 per cent goods and services tax (GST); see p. 31. Refund forms can be picked up at the Ontario Travel Information Centres (Eaton Centre).

SIGHTSEEING

Grey Line Toronto offers the 2-hr Greater Toronto Tour, $25, daily Apr–Nov, Greater Toronto including CN Tower, $39, daily Apr–Nov, and Greater Toronto including Casa Loma, $35, daily June–Sept; *tel: (416) 594-3310.* Departures from major hotels and the Metropolitan Toronto Coach Terminal, *610 Bay St.* Senior, child and family concessions available. **Olde Town Toronto Tours** operate year-round hop-on, hop-off

74

narrated trolley and double-decker bus tours. The route includes 18 stops at sites and attractions, tickets valid for 24 hrs, $12–25; *tel: (416) 798-2424.*

The **Toronto Historical Board** provides free 90-min city walking tours most Sun early May–early Oct; *tel: (416) 392-6827.* Free **University of Toronto Campus Tours** depart from the Map Room, Hart House, 7 *Hart House Circle; tel: (416) 978-5000,* Mon–Fri June–Aug.

A variety of boat tours of the Toronto Islands and harbour depart from Harbourfront (beside Queen's Quay Terminal) Apr–Oct, including 1-hr **Toronto Harbour Tours**, *145 Queen's Quay W., Pier 6* (the foot of *York St),* $9.75–15.75. Daily departures every 30 mins; *tel: (416) 869-1372.*

On the Waterfront

Harbourfront, *410 Queens Quay W.* (take the Light Rapid Transit (LRT) streetcar from Union Station to *York St); tel: (416) 973-3000,* is a ten-acre site featuring the Premier Dance Theatre, Power Plant Art Gallery, multi-cultural festivals, marine activities and marine museum, crafts (glass blowing, metal working and ceramics workshops), community and cultural events, restaurants and shops and Molson Place open-air stage. Many events and activities are free. In winter it features the largest artificial ice rink in North America. For ticketed events, *tel: (416) 973-4000.*

Running through Harbourfront and stretching for 22 km between the Beaches and the Humber River is the **Martin Goodman Trail**; watch for joggers, cyclists and rollerbladers. From beside the Westin Harbour Castle Hotel, take a 15-min, $4 ferry ride to **Centre Island**, where you'll find a 15-acre family amusement park (May–Sept), a great view of the city skyline, picnic and barbecue facilities and plenty of trails for cycling and rollerblading (equipment rentals also available). No cars are permitted.

Ontario Place, *955 Lakeshore Blvd* (2 km west of Harbourfront adjoining Exhibition Place); *tel: (416) 314-9900,* is a 56-acre waterfront park on three artificial islands, with a marina, restaurants, picnic areas, children's village and waterplay. Admission $10. For additional fees, or $20 play-all-day-pass, enjoy pedal boats, water rides, miniature golf and visit retired Canadian warship **H.M.C.S. Haida**. Separate admission to the **Cinesphere** theatre, with six-storey IMAX screen and **Molson Amphitheatre** (topline entertainment); *tel: (416) 870-8000* for tickets. Grounds open May–Sept. Atlantis theatre, restaurant and nightclub complex open year-round.

Downtown

At 553.3m, the **CN Tower**, *301 Front St W.* (just west of *University Ave;* subway: *Union* or *St Andrew),* is the world's tallest free-standing structure; *tel: (416) 868-6937.* At the observation deck level, admission $8–12, you can see the mist from Niagara Falls 100 km away on a clear day, and you can stand on a patch of glass floor 336m above the ground.

You'll also find a restaurant, bar and EcoDeck (an interactive attraction focusing on environmental issues). To visit Space Deck, 33 storeys higher, costs an additional $4. Open daily 0900–2200, Fri and Sat 0800–2300, weather dependent.

The **SkyDome Tour**, *Gate 2, One Blue Jays Way* (subway: *Union* or *St Andrew); tel: (416) 341-2770,* shows off the world's only stadium with a fully retractable roof (opens or closes in 20 mins at a cost of $500). The stadium also has an on-site hotel and restaurants, including Hard Rock Cafe. Tours $6–9.50.

Across the road, the **Canadian Broadcasting Centre**, *255 Front St W.,* has a small free broadcast museum off the lobby, open Mon–Fri 0900–1700. For information on free guided tours (reservations required), *tel: (416) 205-8605.* For information on

75

audience seats at live recordings, *tel: (416) 205-3700.*

The **Toronto Stock Exchange**, *2 First Canadian Pl.* (subway: *St Andrew); tel: (416) 947-4700,* has an information centre on the main floor, open Mon–Fri 0900–1630, $3–5. The **Design Exchange**, *234 Bay St; tel: (416) 216-2160,* is a non-profit centre promoting Canadian design and innovation. Located in former Toronto Stock Exchange, open Tues–Fri 1000–1800, Sat–Sun 1200–1700. Exhibition Hall $3.50–5.

The **Elgin and Winter Garden Theatres**, *189 Yonge St* (subway: *Queen); tel: (416) 314-2871,* form one of the few remaining 'stacked' (one on top of the other) theatre complexes in the world. Now owned and operated by the Ontario Heritage Foundation, guided tours are available Thur 1700, Sat 1100 (year round), Sun 1100 (July–Aug), $3–4. The **St Lawrence Market**, *92 Front St E.* (at *Jarvis)* is located in Toronto's first City Hall. Open Tues–Sat, but liveliest Sat morning with lots of fresh produce, street performers, etc.

Toronto City Hall, *Queen at Bay St* (subway: *Queen* or *Osgoode); tel: (416) 392-7341,* features **Nathan Phillips Square** in the front, which is a venue for free art shows, concerts and community festivals. In the centre is a reflecting pond, which in winter becomes a popular skating rink. The square also features a sculpture by Henry Moore, popularly known as *The Archer.* Inside City Hall (enter under the area that looks like a space ship), you can pick up a booklet for a free self-guided tour, Mon–Fri 0830–1630. The **Ontario Legislative Buildings**, *University and College Sts* (subway: *College); tel: (416) 325-7500,* offer free tours daily (mid May–early Sept), Mon–Fri (early Sept–mid May).

Architecture

In the downtown core, wander into **Union Station**, *65 Front St W.* (subway: *Union),* for a look at the enormous grand hall,

constructed in 1924. Across the road at the **Royal Bank Plaza**, *200 Bay St,* the windows glint with the reflection of 2500 ounces of real gold embedded into the panes to enhance insulation. **BCE Place**, *42 Yonge St* (at *Wellington),* has a fascinating six-storey Galleria. The **Gooderham Building**, *Front and Wellington Sts at Church St,* was originally called the coffin box building and is now referred to as the Flat Iron Building. It's one of the most photographed sights in the city.

Osgoode Hall, *130 Queen St W.* (beside City Hall, subway: *Osgoode); tel: (416) 947-4041,* has been the home of the Law Society since 1832 and is now also home to the Supreme Court of Ontario. It's still surrounded by a black iron fence, with doors designed to prevent cows from wandering in. Free tours Mon–Fri 1315 (July–Aug).

Parks

High Park, located between *Queensway* and *Bloor St W.,* west of *Parkside Dr.* (subway: *High Park); tel: (416) 392-1111.* Hiking trails, gardens, historic Colborne Lodge, animal paddock, trackless train concession and Shakespeare in the Park summer theatrical productions. Open daily all year. Some streets close intermittently to vehicle traffic. Call for map or pick up at park.

Allan Gardens, south side of *Carlton,* between *Jarvis* and *Sherbourne Sts* (subway: *Carlton); tel: (416) 392-7288.* Victorian glass greenhouses, built in 1909, house tropical plants. Free admission; open Mon–Fri 0900–1600, Sat–Sun and holidays 1000–1700.

Museums and Historic Sites

The **Royal Ontario Museum**, *100 Queen's Park* (subway: *Museum); tel: (416) 586-8000,* is Canada's largest museum. It features archaeology and natural history and includes popular exhibits of Chinese and ancient Egyptian antiquities, dinosaurs and a bat cave. Open Mon–Sat 1000–1800, Tues 1000–2000, Sun 1100–1800. $5–$10. Pay what you can after 1630 Tues. ROM Shops

The Group of Seven

Even the most casual browser in Canadian art museums will soon become aware of the Group of Seven, a circle of artists in the early 20th century who strove to break from traditional forms and to define a uniquely Canadian style of art.

The group, who became friendly in Toronto between 1911–13, consisted of Franklin Carmichael, Lawren Harris, Alexander Y. Jackson, Franz Johnston, Arthur Lismer, J.E.H. MacDonald and Fred Varley. An eighth member, Tom Thomson, strongly influenced the others through his use of vivid colours and thick brushstrokes, as well as by his back-woods Canadian lifestyle – he worked as a guide and fire ranger in northern Ontario's Algonquin Park, where he found inspiration for his paintings – but Thomson drowned before the group began exhibiting together.

The first Group of Seven exhibition was in 1920 at the Art Gallery of Toronto. Because they shunned the conservative style of the time and prided themselves as Canada's 'national school' of painting, they angered the art establishment. However, the National Gallery of Canada acquired their works, and their influence grew in the 1920s. Canadian landscapes were prominent among their subjects, but the group's key artistic goal was to redefine the relationship between art and nature, giving up the attempt to imitate nature and instead expressing their feelings about it. Critics derided their work as 'rough, splashy, meaningless, blatant plastering and massing of unpleasant colours in weird landscapes'.

By 1933, some members had left the group, new ones were invited to join and the name was changed to **Canadian Group of Painters**. Today, most art museums in eastern Canada show some works by the Group of Seven; one of the best displays is in Kleinburg, outside Toronto, at the **McMichael Canadian Art Collection**, which was founded to house their works.

include reproductions inspired by collections and a Museum Toy Shop.

Visit the **Bata Shoe Museum**, *327 Bloor St W.* (subway: *St George); tel: (416) 979-7799,* to discover the history of footwear. Ten thousand piece collection, from Napoleon's socks to John Lennon's boots. Open Tues–Sat 1000–1700, Thur 1000–2000, Sun 1200–1700, $4–6, $12 families. Free first Tues each month.

The **Art Gallery of Ontario**, *317 Dundas St W.* (three blocks west of *St Patrick* subway); *tel: 416 979-6648,* features 50 galleries and houses 15,000 works, including many works by the Group of Seven and the largest public collection of work by sculptor Henry Moore. Open Wed–Fri 1200–2100, Sat–Sun 1000–1730. Open Tues mid May–early Oct. Suggested admission $5. Extensive Gallery Shop.

The Grange, *317 Dundas St W.* (entrance is through the AGO and included in admission); *tel: (416) 979-6648,* was once the centre of social and political life in Upper Canada. This 'Gentleman's House' was built in 1817 and is the oldest remaining brick house in Toronto. Open Thur–Sun 1200–1600, Wed 1200–2100.

George R. Gardiner Museum, *111 Queen's Park* (subway: *Museum); tel: (416) 586-8080.* The only museum in North America specialising in ceramics. It features pre-Columbian pottery and one of the world's great collections of 15th–19th-century European ceramics. Some exhibits date back 3000 years. Mon–Sat 1000–1700, Tues 1000–2000, Sun 1100–1700; $3–5.

Campbell House, *160 Queen St W.* (subway: *Osgoode); tel: (416) 597-0227,* was built in 1822 and served as the residence of

Sir William Campbell, an early chief justice of Upper Canada. Open Mon–Fri 0930–1630 (year-round), plus Sat–Sun 1200–1630 (mid May–mid Oct), $2–3.50.

Casa Loma, *1 Austin Terrace* (subway: *Dupont*, and a good uphill walk); *tel: (416) 923-1171*, is a 98-room castle in the centre of the city, built by Sir Henry Pellatt in 1911–14 with bricks shipped from Scotland. Turrets, hidden passageways, suits of armour and a 240-m tunnel to the stables. Self-guided audio tours (in seven languages) included with admission. Open daily 0930–1600. Admission $5–9.

Fort York, *100 Garrison Rd* (off *Fleet St* just east of *Strachan Ave*, east of the CNE grounds); *tel: (416) 392-6907*, is a restoration of the original settlement where Toronto was founded in 1793. Tours with staff in period dress are given on the hour, demonstrations (such as musket firing and music) on the half-hour. Open weekdays 1000–1600, weekends 1000–1700. Admission $3.25–5.

Collborne Lodge, *One Colborne Lodge Dr.* (south end of High Park); *tel: (416) 392-6916*, is the 1837 residence of John George Howard, who owned the land that became High Park. Interpretation by costumed staff and mid 19th-century watercolours of Toronto in the parlour. Open Tues–Sun 1200–1700 (May–Sept), weekends only (Sept–May), $2.50–3.50.

Museum for Textiles, *55 Centre Ave* (subway: *St Patrick*, attached to the Metropolitan Hotel); *tel: (416) 599-5515*, features two floors of contemporary and historic exhibits from around the world. Open Tues–Fri 1100–1700, Wed 1100–2000 (after 1700 pay what you can), Sat–Sun 1200–1700, $4–5.

Market Gallery, *2nd Floor, 95 Front St E.* (South St Lawrence Market); *tel: (416) 392-7604*, is an exhibition facility for the City of Toronto archives – from fine arts to photography. Open Wed–Fri 1000–1600, Sat 0900–1600, Sun 1200–1600, admission free. Closed Mon, Tues.

Thomson Gallery, *176 Yonge St* (9th floor of The Bay, subway: *Queen); tel: (416) 861-4571*, displays pieces from the collection of Lord Kenneth Thomson of Fleet, featuring works by 19th- and 20th-century Canadian artists. Open Mon–Sat 1100–1700, $2.50.

Canada's Sports Hall of Fame, *Exhibition Place* (north side of stadium); *tel: (416) 260-6789*, honours outstanding achievements by Canada's sportsmen and women with three storeys of memorabilia from a variety of sports, rotating exhibits and 6-ft silver Wrigley Trophy. Open Mon–Fri 1000–1630. Admission free.

At the **Hockey Hall of Fame**, *30 Yonge St, lower level* (BCE Place, subway: *Union); tel: (416) 360-7765*, interactive displays and memorabilia trace the history of hockey. Take your best shot at a computer-generated goalie. Exhibits include the Stanley Cup, the oldest trophy in the world for which professional sports teams still compete – stored in a walk-in vault of the beautifully restored former Bank of Montréal (built in 1885). Open Mon–Fri 1000–1700, Sat 0930–1800, Sun 1030–1700. During school holiday periods open Mon–Sat 0930–1800 and Sun 1000–1800. $5.50–9.50.

The Victorian home of William Lyon Mackenzie, who was elected Toronto's first mayor in 1834 and who led an armed Rebellion against the government in 1837, is preserved at **Mackenzie House**, *82 Bond St; tel: (416) 392-6915*. Open Tues–Sun 1200–1700 (May–Aug), for other months call for hours. $2.50–3.50.

Metropolitan Toronto Police Museum, *40 College St* (entrance off the lobby of police station); *tel: (416) 808-7020*, has interactive displays and exhibits from major crime investigations. Open daily 0900–2100, free but donation requested.

Spadina House, *285 Spadina Rd; tel: (416) 392-6910*, is the 1866 mansion built by James Austin, founder of the Dominion Bank. It includes six acres of Victorian gardens. Open Tues–Sun 1200–1700 (May–Sept), slightly different hours other months; $3–5.

Enoch Turner Schoolhouse, *106 Trinity St* (one block east of Parliament, south of *King St); tel: (416) 863-0010*, is Toronto's oldest schoolhouse, dating back to 1848. Open Mon–Fri 1000–1600. Call before coming, sometimes closed for private programmes.

Ontario Science Centre, *770 Don Mills Rd; tel: (416) 696-3127*, is a 'hands-on' science museum with more than 800 interactive exhibits. Includes Omnimax Theatre (domed screen with wrap-around digital sound). Open daily 1000–2000 (June–Aug), otherwise daily 1000–1700, Wed to 2000, Fri to 2100. Admission $6–10, by donation Wed evening; Omnimax Theatre $5.50–8.50; combination ticket $9–22.

OUT OF TOWN

The **Kortright Centre for Conservation**, *Pine Valley Dr. (south of Major Mackenzie Dr., west of Hwy 400), Kleinburg; tel: (905) 832-2289*, is Canada's largest environmental awareness/education facility, offering guided walks on 15 km of trails, talks and activities. Open daily 1000–1600, guided programme 1300 daily, $3–5.

A 30-min ride from downtown Toronto is **Paramount Canada's Wonderland**, *9580 Jane St, Vaughan; tel: (905) 832-7000*, a 300-acre theme park with eight theme areas, 160 attractions, 50 thrill rides, live shows, Canada's largest outdoor wave pool and children's interactive water play area. Open 1000–2000 or 2200 (mid May–early Sept), weekends 1000–2200 (May and Sept–mid Oct). Day pass $37.95 includes all rides. Off Hwy 400, 10 mins north of Hwy 401, exit at *Rutherford Rd.* Buses from Yorkdale and York Mills subway stations; *tel: (416) 869-3200*, for schedule information.

Black Creek Pioneer Village, *Jane St at Steeles Ave W., N. York; tel: (416) 736-1733*, is a working mid 19th-century village, which

forms an outdoor museum with 35 authentically restored buildings and staff in period costume. Open Mon–Fri 0930–1630, Sat–Sun 1000–1700 (May–June); daily 1000–1700 (July–Sept); Mon–Fri 0930-1600, Sat–Sun 1000–1630 (Oct–Nov); admission $4–8.

The **David Dunlap Observatory** in Richmond Hill (3 km north of Hwy 7, enter off *Bayview Ave); tel: (905) 884-2112*, is a research centre and home of Canada's largest telescope. Tours Wed morning year round, Sat half-hour after sunset mid Apr–late Sept. Reservations required, three weeks in advance suggested. No children under seven. $1.25–4. Phone ahead for directions.

Located in a log building in a lovely setting 30 km north of downtown Toronto, **McMichael Canadian Art Collection**, *10365 Islington Ave, Kleinburg; tel: (905) 893-1121*, houses landscape paintings by Canada's Group of Seven, plus First Nations, Inuit and contemporary works of art. Open daily 1000–1700 (May–Oct), Tues–Sat 1000–1600, Sun and holidays 1000–1700 (Nov–Mar); $4–7, families $15, parking $3. Take Hwy 400 north and exit at *Major Mackenzie Dr.*, go west 1 km, turn right on *Islington Ave.*

In the vicinity is the **Doctor's House**, *21 Nashville Rd, Kleinburg; tel: (416) 234-8080*. Originally built in 1867, the Doctor's House and Livery was restored and expanded in 1993. Its dining facilities feature old Canadian furnishings and medical memorabilia. Lunch, dinner and Sunday brunch served. Piano Fri–Sat evenings.

Metro Toronto Zoo, *Meadowvale Rd, Scarborough; tel: (416) 392-5900*, includes more than 5000 animals on 710 acres. Open daily 0930–1630, closing varies 1630–1930 (June–Sept). $7–12, parking $5 (Mar–Sept). Zoomobile (open-sided train) $2.50 per ride. Located 20 km east of Don Valley Parkway, just north of Hwy 401 – take exit 389. For TTC service to front door, take bus route 86A from *Kennedy* subway station.

79

TORONTO– NIAGARA FALLS

The drive from Toronto to Niagara Falls takes you around the west end of Lake Ontario (an area known as the Golden Horseshoe) and past the vineyards and orchards of the Niagara Peninsula. As you pass Hamilton's steel mills and harbour and enter Niagara, the right-hand side of the route is dominated by the Niagara Escarpment. Ten thousand years ago this imposing ridge was the shoreline of glacier-carved Lake Iroquois. You continue to the Welland Canal, the eight-lock international shipping link between Lake Ontario and Lake Erie, and on to Niagara Falls.

Without traffic tie-ups the 128-km direct route can take as little as 90 minutes; however, if you hit holiday traffic it could easily take two or three hours. The scenic 185-km drive includes smaller port communities along the north shore of Lake Ontario, the Wine Route through Niagara's vineyards and one of the prettiest cities in Canada, Niagara-on-the-Lake.

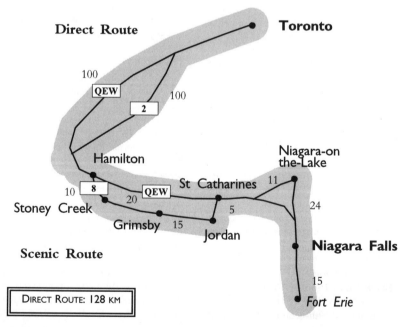

ROUTES

DIRECT ROUTE

➡️ Exit Toronto westbound on the Gardiner Expressway, which becomes the *Queen Elizabeth Way (QEW)* at the Humber River. At the west end of Lake Ontario, the *QEW* leads across the Burlington Skyway and into the Niagara region; you then cross the Garden City Skyway, which is built over the Welland Canal. There is an **Ontario Travel Information Centre** at the base of Garden City Skyway Bridge. Continue on the *QEW* and take exit 420 into Niagara Falls.

Avoid departing Toronto during rush hour, and keep in mind that bad weather and especially high winds can slow down and occasionally close traffic on the Burlington Skyway.

SCENIC ROUTE

➡️ From the *Queen Elizabeth Way*, go south at *Winston Churchill Blvd* to Hwy 2 and turn right. This will lead you through the lakeside communities of **Oakville**, **Bronte** and **Burlington**, passing through some lovely old residential areas. Between Burlington and **Hamilton** Hwy 2 goes under the *QEW* and becomes *North Shore Blvd*. In less than 1 km, it bears to the right and becomes *King Rd*. When you reach *Plains Rd,* turn left. In about 4 km, you'll pass by the 2700-acre **Royal Botanical Gardens**.

Depart Hamilton on *Main St E.,* which becomes *Queenston Rd* and Hwy 8 as it approaches **Stoney Creek**. When you reach **Grimsby**, Hwy 8 becomes Regional Rd 81. You are now on what is known as Niagara's **Wine Route**. The microclimate created by Lakes Erie and Ontario and the protection of the Niagara Escarpment have created similar conditions to the wine regions of Germany and of Champagne and Burgundy in France. Royal blue signs with white grapes on them will lead you along Regional Rd 81 through

Lincoln and **Jordan**. As you approach **St Catharines**, at *Fifth St,* go south to Pelham (Rd 69), and then east to Glendale (Rd 89); watch for Rd 89 to jog to the left at *Merritt St*. You'll cross the **Welland Canal** and go under the *QEW*. At York (Rd 81), go right to St David's, then left on *Four Mile Creek Rd* (Rd 100) to Virgil.

At Virgil, right turn onto Hwy 55 to go directly into **Niagara-on-the-Lake**, or turn left to continue meandering along the Wine Route for another 20 km before arriving there. From Niagara-on-the-Lake the scenic **Niagara Parkway** runs for 24 km, hugging the shoulder of the mighty **Niagara River** and passing through historic **Queenston**, before entering **Niagara Falls, Ontario**.

Niagara Falls, New York, can be reached by crossing the Rainbow Bridge by foot or by car (you must clear Canadian and US Customs). There is a $1.25 toll for cars. For a side track to **Fort Erie**, continue south on the Niagara Parkway for 15 km.

BUSES AND TRAINS

Trentway-Wagar and Greyhound Lines of Canada operate a regular bus service from Toronto to Niagara Falls. See OTT table 182.

GOTransit and Greyhound Lines of Canada run a local and train and bus service to Hamilton (OTT tables 16, 26 and 190). Trentway-Wagar operate from Hamilton to Niagara Falls – see OTT table 184.

OAKVILLE TO HAMILTON

From Hwy 2 in Oakville, detour north for 4 km on *Dorval Dr.* to visit the **Canadian Golf Hall of Fame Museum** at the famous **Glen Abbey Golf Club**; *1333 Dorval Dr.; tel: (905) 849-9700,* designed by Jack Nicklaus and home of the Canadian Open; open daily 1000–1800 (Apr–Oct), 1000–1700 (Nov–Mar), $2–4. The course is open to the public May–Oct. Greens fees are expensive; reduced rates after 1400 Sat. Dining facilities available.

As you pass into Burlington, there is a **Tourist Office**: *1340 Lakeshore Rd; tel: (905) 634-5594.* Several hundred metres further on is the **Joseph Brant Museum**, *1240 North Shore Blvd E.; tel: (905) 634-3556.* Brant was a Mohawk chief and this reconstruction of his circa 1800 home features pioneer implements, artefacts and period costumes, open Tues–Fri 1000–1600, Sun 1300–1600. Admission $1.50–2.75.

The **Royal Botanical Gardens**, *680 Plains Rd W.; tel: (905) 527-1158,* cover 2700-acre areas and include six main viewing areas, each with parking. The gardens include the world's largest lilac collection, an acre of irises, two acres of roses and 125,000 spring bulbs. There is a natural wildlife sanctuary, nature trails and a Mediterranean Garden greenhouse. It's a lovely spot to picnic. Open daily 0900–1800, $2–7.

HAMILTON

Tourist Information: Greater Hamilton Economic Development, *127 King St E.; tel: (905) 546-2666* or *(800) 263-8590* (toll-free). Information on accommodation (including a list of Bed and Breakfasts), restaurants, entertainment and tourist activities. Open daily 0900–1700 (July–Sept), closed Sun (Sept–July).

Hamilton, at the western end of Lake Ontario, is quickly identified by its steel factories, but it's also within easy reach of the rugged beauty of the Niagara Escarpment and the Royal Botanical Gardens. Be prepared for one-way streets. Note that most addresses are numbered east or west from *James St N.* There is metered parking downtown.

ACCOMMODATION

The *QI* is a 2-min walk from Hess Village. Also downtown are *CI, HJ* and *Sh*. Further out are *CI, DI* and *Hd*. For budget travellers there's a centrally located **YWCA**, *75 MacNab St S.; tel: (905) 522-9922,* and **YMCA**, *79 James St S.; tel: (905) 529-7102.*

EATING AND DRINKING

Your best option for dining is **Hess Village**, *on Hess St, between King and Main Sts,* a little neighbourhood with a variety of restaurants and shops in restored 19th-century buildings. Many of the bistros have outdoor patios and menus are posted. Some feature late evening music, especially on weekends. For picnic supplies, from fresh fruit to baked goods, try the **Hamilton Farmer's Market**, *55 York Blvd; tel: (905) 546-2096,* open Tues–Thur 0700–1800, Fri 0900–1800, Sat 0600–1800.

ENTERTAINMENT

In addition to Hess Village, check with **Hamilton Place**, *10 MacNab St; tel: (905) 546-3100,* home of Opera Hamilton and venue for top-line entertainers such as Tony Bennett and Roger Whittaker.

SIGHTSEEING

As you enter Hamilton, you pass **Dundurn Castle**, *610 York Blvd; tel: (905) 546-2872,* a 35-room, 19th-century Italianate villa, which was the home of Sir Allan Napier MacNab, prime minister of the United Provinces of Canada from 1854–56. Frequent guided tours are given by staff and children volunteers in period costume, open daily 1000–1600 (June–early Sept), Tues–Sun and holiday Mon 1200–1600 (early Sept–June), $2.50–6. There is a covered picnic area, gift shop and tea room with traditional Victorian fare. Dundurn admission includes entrance to the adjoining **Hamilton Military Museum**; *tel: (905) 546-4974,* which features artefacts from the War of 1812 to World War I, plus an interesting exhibit on two American warships which still rest in the depths of Lake Ontario, open daily 1100–1700 (mid June–early Sept), 1300–1700 (mid Sept–mid June), closed non-holiday Mon.

Downtown you can visit the **Art Gallery of Hamilton**, *123 King St W.; tel: (905) 527-6610,* open Wed–Sat 1000–1700, Thur 1000–2100, Sun 1300–1700, year round,

$3–4. It's home to a comprehensive Canadian art collection and has strong British, American and European holdings. The **Canadian Football Hall of Fame**, *58 Jackson St W.; tel: (905) 528-7566*, covers the history of Canadian football, open year round Mon–Sat 0930–1630, plus 1200–1630 Sun and holidays (May–Nov), $1.50–3. Directly across the road is **Whitehern**, *41 Jackson St W.*, the residence from 1852–1968 of the McQuesten family, who founded the Royal Botanical Gardens. It is now a National Historic Site, open daily 1100–1600 (June–early Sept), 1300–1600 (Sept–May), closed 25 Dec–1 Jan; admission $2.50–3.50.

A Hamilton highlight, and well worth the 13-km drive out on Hwy 6, is the **Canadian Warplane Heritage Museum**, *Hangar 4, Hamilton Airport, 9280 Airport Rd, Mount Hope; tel: (905) 679-4183*. The collection of World War II aircraft includes one of only two Lancaster bombers left in the world that can still fly, open daily 0900–1700, Thur to 2000 year round, $4–7. Heading towards Niagara you'll find the **Children's Museum**, *1072 Main St E.; tel: (905) 546-4848*, in a park-like setting. It's designed for kids aged 2–13. Open Tues–Sat 1000–1600, Sun 1300–1600, closed Sept and Jan, $1–2.50.

STONEY CREEK TO GRIMSBY

Exiting Hamilton, you'll enter Stoney Creek, where each June hundreds camp in period costume and participate in a re-enactment of the 1813 Battle of Stoney Creek at the **Battlefield House Museum**, *77 King St W.* (from Hwy 8 turn right at Hwy 20 and left at *King St); tel: (905) 662-8458*. Museum open Tues–Sun and holiday Mon 1000–1600 (July–early Sept); Sun, holiday Mon and Tues–Fri 1300–1600 (mid May–June); $1.50–2.75.

In the Grimsby area, signs lead to **wineries**. Many offer tastings, tours and shops; some also have restaurants. Ask at any for the free Wine Route Map by the **Ontario Wine Council**, *110 Hanover Dr., Suite B205, St Catharines, ON L2W 1A4 tel: (905) 684-8070, fax: 684-2993*, which describes 31 Niagara locations.

After the **Grimsby Museum**, *6 Murray St; tel: (905) 945-5292*, which details the town's Loyalist history, turn right onto *Mountain St* and climb the escarpment to *Ridge Rd*, which leads to the **Beamer Memorial Conservation Area**. There's a 25-min, 900-m walk to the lookout point; from early Mar–mid May this is a popular spot to watch for migrating hawks. The best hours for sightings are 1000–1500. As you pass through **Lincoln**, Rd 24 on your right leads to **Balls Falls Conservation Area**, which has two waterfalls, two pioneer homes, a church, picnic facilities and nature trails, $1.75–2.75.

JORDAN

Return to Rd 81 and **Jordan**, a tiny village that offers shopping, tea rooms, fine dining and accommodation, ranging from the budget–moderate **Vintage House Bed and Breakfast**, *3853 Main St; tel: (905) 562-3441*, an 1840s home, to expensive–pricey **Vintners Inn**, *3845 Main St, Jordan, ON L0R 1S0; tel: (905) 562-5336 or (800) 701-8074*, with rooms featuring fireplaces, lofts and Jacuzzis; reservations recommended. There's camping at **Jordan Valley Campground**, *3058 21st St, tel: (905) 562-7816*, 0.5 km from the centre of town, on a river with canoe rentals.

The restaurant **On The Twenty**, *3836 Main St; tel: (905) 562-7313*, is well-known for innovative cuisine using local produce (moderate–pricey), and its special moderately priced Winemakers Luncheon, reservations recommended. **Cave Spring Cellars**, *3836 Main St; tel: (905) 562-3581*, offers wine tastings and free tours daily at 1100 or 1500.

The **Jordan Historical Museum of the Twenty**, *3802 Main St; tel: (905) 562-5242*, features historic buildings, including an 1815 pioneer home, an 1859 stone schoolhouse,

83

a giant fruit press, crafts and antiques; open Mon–Fri 1000–1600, Sat–Sun 1300–1600 (late May–early Sept), $1–3. A variety of quality boutiques, antique stores and specialty shops line *Main St*, including **Ninavik– The Native Arts Place**, *3845 Main St, tel: (905) 562-8888,* which features Inuit and Aboriginal art, open daily 1000–1700.

ST CATHARINES TO NIAGARA-ON-THE-LAKE

St Catharines, the largest city in the region, celebrates the grape harvest every Sept with the **Niagara Grape and Wine Festival**, *tel: (905) 688-0212.* You'll find tourist information at the **Lock 3 Viewing Complex and Museum**, *1932 Government Rd; tel: (905) 984-8880* or *(800) 305-5134,* from Rd 89 *(Glendale Ave),* turn left at the Welland Canal. Here you can watch international ships pass through the lock system Mar–Dec. The museum has a relief map of the canal systems, Niagara River and Niagara Falls, a free 12-min video of the history of the canal, a gift shop and a restaurant. Open 0900–2100 (late May–early Sept), 0900–1700 (Sept–late May), $1–2.40.

Port Dalhousie, a charming lakeside town with two lighthouses, a beach, craft shops, restaurants and an antique carousel ($0.05), is just a 15-min detour from the Lock 3 Viewing Complex. Go north on *Government Rd,* west on *Lakeshore Rd.* Here the 300-passenger **Shaker Cruise Line**; *tel: (905) 934-2375,* provides a 90-min ferry service to Toronto (multiple trips daily, no cars), $12.50 one way, and 90-min cruises up the Niagara River, $7.50.

Brock University, *500 Glenridge Ave, St Catharines, ON L2S 3A1; tel: (905) 688-5550, ext. 3369, fax: (905) 688-2110,* offers budget accommodation for the public May–Aug (from Rd 89/*Glendale Ave,* turn right at *Glenridge Ave*).

An **Ontario Travel Information Centre** is located at *QEW at Glendale Ave; tel: (905) 684-6354* or *(800) ONTARIO,* open daily 0800–2000 (mid May–early Sept), 0830–1800 (Apr–mid May and early Sept–mid Oct), 0830–1630 (mid Oct–Apr). It has a currency exchange.

Blink and you'll miss **St Davids**. From Rd 81 *(York Rd),* turn right at *Four Mile Creek Rd* for several antique stores, turn left to continue the Wine Route (Rd 100) to **Virgil**. At Virgil a right turn onto Hwy 55 leads into Niagara-on-the-Lake; a left turn takes you along the Wine Route for another 20 km, first passing **Hillebrand Estate Winery**, *Hwy 55; tel: (905) 468-7123* or *(800) 582-8412.* Daily tours on the hour 1000–1800, tastings, a wine store and 2½-hr vineyard bicycle tours (call to reserve). Try the Icewine, made from grapes harvested in Jan.

The rest of the Wine Route to Niagara-on-the-Lake is well-marked with the exception of a necessary right turn at *Stewart St,* beyond **Stonechurch Vineyards**.

NIAGARA-ON-THE-LAKE

Tourist Information: Niagara-on-the-Lake Chamber of Commerce, *153 King St, Box 1043, Niagara-on-the-Lake, ON L0S 1J0; tel: (905) 468-4263,* offers a free reservation service for hotels, inns and Bed and Breakfast homes. Also maps for self-guided walking tours plus information on activities in the area.

Niagara-on-the-Lake, founded in 1792 as a British military site, originally served as the capital of Upper Canada. It's a charming historic village of quaint shops, old inns and lovely parks – but it's known for its outstanding summer theatre series, the **Shaw Festival**. The majority of shops, theatres and restaurants are within an easy stroll along *Queen St.*

ACCOMMODATION

There are 213 Bed and Breakfasts in the Niagara region. Circa-1880 **Lakewinds**, *328 Queen St, Box 1483, Niagara-on-the-Lake, ON L0S 1J0; tel: (905) 468-1888,* moderate–expensive, has a heated swimming pool. The five-room **Olde Angel Inn**, *224 Regent St, Box 1603, Niagara-on-the-Lake, ON L0S 1J0; tel: (905) 468-3411,* is the town's oldest inn, circa 1789. It's said that in 1792 when the Assembly passed an act outlawing slavery – the first passed anywhere in the world – the legislators celebrated at the inn. It's centrally located with pub meals and a wine bar, moderate–expensive. It also has two 2-bedroom cottages, expensive–pricey. Hotel rooms are $90–350 per night, many offer theatre packages.

Three luxury hotels are jointly owned; guests can use the facilities at any of them and charge the fees to their room bill: **Pillar and Post Inn–Spa and Conference Centre**, *48 John St, Box 1011, Niagara-on-the-Lake, ON L0S 1J0; tel: (905) 468-2123 or (800) 361-6788,* **Queen's Landing Inn**, *Byron and Melville Sts, Box 1180; tel: (905) 468-2195 or (800) 361-6645,* and the historic, centrally located **Prince of Wales Hotel**, *6 Picton St, Box 46; tel: (905) 468-3246 or (800) 236-2452.* All expensive– pricey.

Camping is 9 km south at **Shalamar Lake Trailer and Family Park**, *Niagara Parkway and Line 8, Box 100, Queenston, ON L0S 1L0; tel: (905) 262-4895.* Pool, store, laundry, tent and trailer sites are all available.

EATING AND DRINKING

Stroll along *Queen St* and browse the posted menus. The **Shaw Cafe and Wine Bar**, *92 Queen St; tel: (905) 468-4772,* is centrally located with a patio overlooking the main street. The **Olde Angel Inn** has after-theatre food service, budget–moderate. The **Vineyard Cafe**, *Hwy 55; tel: (905) 468-2444 or (800) 582-8412,* at Hillebrand Estates Winery, serves Niagara cuisine lunch and dinner daily in the dining room or patio with vineyard view. Moderate–pricey. **Donna's Old Towne Ice Cream Shoppe & Restaurant**, *61-63 Queen St; tel: (905) 468-2532,* has good breakfast specials, from 0700.

ENTERTAINMENT

The **Shaw Festival Theatre**, the **Court House Theatre** and the **Royal George Theatre** present the works of George Bernard Shaw and his contemporaries, Apr–Oct. Performances cost $22–65. **Shaw Festival Box Offices**, *Box 774, Niagara-on-the-Lake, ON L0S 1J0; tel: (905) 468-2172 or (800) 511-7429, fax: (905) 468-3804.* Rush seats (discounted 20%, further discounts for seniors and students) may be available daily starting at 0900 at the Festival Theatre Box Office. There are also noon-hour short plays and readings at the Royal George Theatre, $7–15.

SHOPPING

Queen St is lined with boutiques, many featuring quality Canadian products. For example, **Angie Strauss Fashions and Gifts**, *125 Queen St; tel: (905) 468-2570,* sells casual clothing with designs by Angie Strauss; her Art Gallery is next door and she has a discount outlet at *183 Victoria St.*

SIGHTSEEING

The romantic way to view the village would be in a horse-drawn **Sentineal Carriage**; *tel: (905) 468-4943,* which can be booked where they park beside the Prince of Wales Hotel. Tours cost from $45.

Ontario's first historical museum, the **Niagara Historical Museum**, *43 Castlereagh St; tel: (905) 468-3912,* open daily 1000–1700 (May–Oct), daily 1300–1700 (Nov–Dec and Mar–Apr), Sat–Sun 1300–1700 (Jan–Feb), has exhibits from the United Empire Loyalists, the War of 1812 and the Victorian period; $1–2.50. The storefront **Apothecary Museum**, *5 Queen St,* is an authentic restoration of an 1866 pharmacy, open daily 1200–1800, free admission.

Thrill seekers can head for **Whirlpool Jet Boat Tours**, *61 Melville St; tel: (905) 468-4800,* for one-hour tours of Niagara River and rapids, $48. The 1790s **Fort George**,

Queens Parade; tel: (905) 468-4263, was built by the British to guard the mouth of the Niagara River. It's a National Historic Park with costumed staff re-enacting daily life prior to 1812, open daily 0930–1630 (Apr–late June and Sept–late Oct), daily 1000–1700 (July–early Sept), weekdays 0900–1600 (Nov–Apr), $4–6.

NIAGARA-ON-THE-LAKE TO NIAGARA FALLS

Winston Churchill called the Niagara Parkway 'the prettiest Sunday afternoon drive in the world'. It's a former military trail which begins at Niagara-on-the-Lake and follows the shoulder of the Niagara River and Gorge south for 56 km through Niagara Falls to historic **Fort Erie**. The route features spectacular views, historic sites, fruit markets, wineries, picnic facilities and a variety of attractions operated by the **Niagara Parks Commission**, *tel: (905) 356-2241,* a self-funded agency of the Ontario government. A recreational trail for cyclists, joggers, walkers and in-line skaters runs parallel to the road.

The first 7 km includes **McFarland House**; *tel: (905) 468-3322,* a historic home that served as a hospital during the War of 1812. Costumed staff provide guided tours daily and serve tea on the tiny patio, daily 1100–1600 (mid May–June), 1000–1700 (July–early Sept), $1–1.75. **Kurtz Orchards Country Market**; *tel: (905) 468-2937,* is a good place to pick up picnic supplies, open daily 0900–1800 Apr–Dec; call in advance for orchard tours. The **Reif Estate Winery**; *tel: (905) 468-7738,* offers tours at 1330 May–Sept, and opens year round. **Inniskillin Wines**; *tel: (905) 468-3554,* with a shop and art gallery, is also open year round, with five daily tours Mon–Fri, Sat–Sun 1030 and 1430 (June–Oct).

Eleven km from Niagara-on-the-Lake, the parkway leads through **Queenston**, location of the **Laura Secord Homestead**, *Partition Rd; tel: (905) 684-1227* Sept–May,

(905) 262-4851 June–Aug. Laura walked 32 km to warn the British of a surprise American attack in 1813. Open daily 1000–1700 (mid May–early Sept), $1. The adjoining shop is a good stop for ice-cream. The **Mackenzie Heritage Printery**, *1 Queenston St; tel: (905) 262-5676,* features antique printing presses in the home of William Lyon Mackenzie, who was the first mayor of Toronto and a leader of an 1837 rebellion, open daily 1100–1700 (mid May–early June), 1000–1700 (early June–early Sept), closed Mon (Sept–June), $1–1.50.

As the Niagara Parkway climbs to **Queenston Heights, Brock's Monument** comes into view. Sir Isaac Brock, a British War of 1812 hero, was killed here in battle. There are picnic sites, good views of the Niagara River, and indoor and patio dining at the **Queenston Heights Restaurant**, *tel: (905) 262-4276.* There are free concerts Sun at 1500 and 1700 (mid June–late Sept). Queenston is where Niagara Falls originated when glaciers receded 12,000 years ago; erosion has since moved them 11 km upstream. It is also the starting point of Ontario's oldest and most popular long-distance footpath, the **Bruce Trail**, which ends in Tobermory, 323 km north-west of Toronto.

After the parkway passes under the **Queenston-Lewiston Bridge** (taking car traffic to the USA), you come to the 12.2-m diameter **Floral Clock** (formed from 15,000 plants), a popular tourist photo stop, and the **Centennial Lilac Gardens** (best viewed late May), which adjoin the **Sir Adam Beck Power Plant**. Most of the Canadian generating station is under the parkway so you can't see it, but if you look across the river you can see the American version – the Robert Moses Generating Station.

In less than 1 km, on the right, is the **Niagara Parks Botanical Gardens**, which now includes the **Butterfly Conservatory**; *tel: (905) 356-8119.* Walk among 2000 free-flying butterflies in a rain forest setting, open daily 0900–1800 year round, $3.50–7. Across the parkway is the **Niagara Glen Nature Reserve**. Trails lead down to the river. Maps at the gift shop sell for $1. Free guided tours daily Thur–Mon (late June–early Sept).

Next on your right is the **Whirlpool Public Golf Course**; *tel: (905) 356-1140*, with a public restaurant and fully licenced lounge. On the riverside you'll pass **Thompsons Point**, a lookout over the Whirlpool Rapids. You can see the **Spanish Aero Car**, *tel: (905) 354-5711*. Rides in the suspended cable car operate from 1 km further south, mid Mar–late Nov (weather permitting), $2.50–5. Less than 1 km further on is the **Great Gorge Adventure Trip**. An elevator descends to a 205-m boardwalk, where you can enjoy a pleasant stroll alongside the raging Whirlpool Rapids, open Mon–Fri 0900–1700, Sat–Sun 0900–1800 (May), 0900–2000 (June–Aug), 0900–1700 (Sept–Oct), $2.40–4.75. You'll now pass under **Whirlpool Rapids Bridge** and into downtown Niagara Falls. The Falls are about 4 km further on.

NIAGARA FALLS

Tourist Information: Ontario Travel Information Centre, *5355 Stanley Ave; tel: (905) 358-3221 or (800) ONTARIO*, open daily 0800–2000 (mid May–early Sept), Fri–Sat 0830–1800 (early Sept–mid Oct, Apr–mid May), Fri–Sat 0830–1800 (mid Oct–Apr). It has a currency exchange. **Niagara Visitor and Convention Bureau**, *5115 Stanley Ave, Niagara Falls, ON L2G 3X4, tel: (905) 356-6061 or (800) 56-FALLS*. Accommodation referrals but no bookings, open daily 0800–2000 (mid May–mid Oct), Mon–Fri 0800–1800 (mid Oct–mid May). Seasonal **Government Information Centres** at **Table Rock**; *tel: (905) 356-7944*, **Rapids View**; *tel: (905) 354-6266*, and **Fort George**; *tel: (905) 468-4263*.

Thomas Cook bureau de change: *5986 Lundy's Lane; tel: (905) 374-3325*.

As you enter Niagara Falls, on your left you will first see the **American Falls**, then the smaller **Bridal Veil Falls** and ahead, to the right, the larger **Horseshoe Falls**, which are in Canada. This is the most visited scenic attraction in North America and one of the world's great natural wonders. Daredevils, sightseers and honeymooners (a trend started by Napoleon's brother) have all been drawn to watch the awesome power of the foaming water as it thunders 52m into the Niagara River.

GETTING AROUND

The **People Mover**; *tel: (905) 357-9340*, is a system of green air-conditioned motorcoaches travelling a 30-km circular route from just above the Falls (Rapids View parking lot) to Queenston Heights. Operates approximately every 20 mins, with stops at all major sites. Unlimited travel day ticket $2.25–4.25, open late Apr–mid Oct.

ACCOMMODATION

Chain hotels include *BI, BW, Ch, Hd, QI, Rm, Ro, S8* and *Sh*. Hotels with 'Falls view' rooms include: **Michael's Inn**, *5599 River Rd, L2E 3H3; tel: (905) 354-2727 or (800) 263-9390*, moderate–expensive, the **Skyline Brock Hotel**, *5685 Falls Ave, L2E 6W7; tel: (905) 374-4444*, and the **Skyline Foxhead Hotel**, *5875 Falls Ave, L2E 6W7; tel: (905) 374-4444*, both moderate–pricey. Rates drop as you move away from the river.

The Niagara Parkway *(River Rd)* is lined with Bed and Breakfasts as you enter the city. **Butterfly Manor**, *4917 River Rd, L2E 3G5; tel/fax: (905) 358-8988*, moderate–expensive, operates a booking service for others. The budget **HI Niagara Falls**, *4549 Cataract Ave; tel: (905) 357-0770 or (888) 749-0058* (toll-free), is a 25-min walk to the Falls, but it's also on the People Mover system. Bike rentals available. Rooms shared by 2–6 people.

Budget rooms (doubles and 4-bed dormitories) are also available at **Niagara Falls**

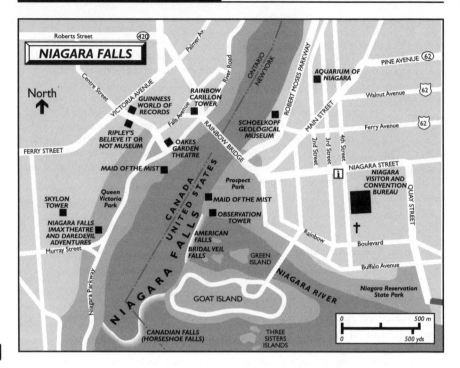

Guest House, *4487 John St, L2E 1A4; tel: (905) 356-9037,* one block from the casino. The closest campsite to the Falls is **Glen-View**, *3950 Victoria Ave; tel: (905) 358-8689,* on the People Mover system, with a large swimming pool. During the day helicopters land across the street.

EATING AND DRINKING

Sky-high dining is available at the **Skylon Tower**, *5200 Robinson St; tel: (905) 356-2651* (the dining room revolves once an hour 232m above the Falls), and the **Minolta Tower**, *6732 Oakes Dr.; tel: (905) 356-1501,* 157m above the Falls. Both moderate–pricey. **Table Rock Restaurant**, *6650 Niagara Parkway, tel: (905) 354-3631,* has a terrific view from beside the Horseshoe Falls. Budget fast food with a great view is available at the **Maid of the Mist Fast Food Restaurant**, *Maid of the Mist Plaza.* The quirky side of Niagara Falls is reflected

in the **Flying Saucer Restaurant**, *6768 Lundy's Lane; tel: (905) 356-4553,* shaped like a flying saucer, open 0600–0300, and known for $0.99-breakfasts. Niagara Falls also has a large Italian population; the **Capri Restaurant & Lounge**, *5438 Ferry St; tel: (905) 354-7519,* is a local award-winner.

ENTERTAINMENT

The falls are illuminated nightly. Times vary according to light conditions. There are free fireworks displays at the Falls Fri 2200 (late May–Sept) and on July 1.

Oakes Garden Theatre is an outdoor amphitheatre at the foot of *Clifton Hill,* with free live entertainment, 1900–2100 (mid June–Sept). **Oh Canada, Eh?**, *Pyramid Pl., 5400 Robinson St; tel: (905) 374-1995,* is a fun dinner-theatre musical celebration of Canada, with log cabin and wilderness décor. $48 at 2000, $43 at 1600 (early bird show Thur only).

Casino Niagara, *5705 Falls Ave* (temporary home); *tel: (905) 374-3598 or (888) WINDFALL (946-3255)*, features 3000 slot machines, 123 gaming tables, snack and restaurant facilities. Open daily 24 hrs year round. Minimum age 19.

SHOPPING

Souvenirs are available at all key tourist sites and in shops along *Clifton Hill*. One of the most unique shops is **Sgt Preston's Outpost**, *5685 Falls Ave, (street level, Skyline Brock Hotel); tel: (905) 374-2288,* which sells Royal Canadian Mounted Police gifts, souvenirs, clothing and accessories. An RCMP officer can often be seen on duty during busy periods at the Table Rock Complex or Maid of the Mist Plaza.

SIGHTSEEING

For more than 150 years visitors have cruised to the foot of the Falls on the **Maid of the Mist** excursion, *5920 River Rd; tel: (905) 358-5781.* Rain gear provided, operating late Apr–late Oct (weather permitting), $6.25–10.10. Raincoats are also provided for **Journey Behind the Falls**, *Table Rock Complex,* in which elevators descend 38 m for a self-guided tour behind Horseshoe Falls, open from 0900 year round, $2.90–5.75. Falls observation decks are located at the **Skylon Tower**, *5200 Robinson St,* from 0900 until illumination shuts off, $3.95–7.50, and at the **Minolta Tower**, *6732 Oakes Dr.,* open daily 0900–2300, $4.95–6.

The **IMAX Theatre and Daredevil Museum**, *Pyramid Pl., 5400 Robinson; tel: (905) 374-4629,* presents the history of the Falls from Native legends to modern-day daredevils on a six-storey-high screen, $5.50–7.50. Nature lovers enjoy **Niagara Parks Greenhouses**, *Niagara Parkway, south of Horseshoe Falls; tel: (905) 356-2241,* open from 0930, free admission. Less than 1 km south are the **Dufferin Islands**, where you can enjoy some short nature trails.

Most family amusements and quirky museums are on **Clifton Hill**, including **Ripley's Believe It or Not Museum** and the **Guinness Museum of World Records**. The **Niagara Falls Museum**, *5651 River Rd; tel: (905) 356-2151,* North America's oldest museum (established in 1827), has an interesting Egyptian collection. Open 0900–2300 (May–Sept), 1000–1700 (Oct–Apr), $3.95–6.95.

Lundy's Lane Historical Museum, *5810 Ferry St; tel: (905) 358-5082,* covers the history of Niagara Falls and the War of 1812, open daily 0900–1600 (May–Nov), Mon–Fri 1200-1600 (Dec–Apr), $1–1.60. **Marineland** (with a deer-petting park) is at *7657 Portage Rd; tel: (905) 356-9565,* south of downtown, open daily mid Apr–late Oct, $19.95–22.95, under 5 free, parking free.

NIAGARA FALLS, NY (USA)

Tourist Information: Niagara Falls Convention & Visitors Bureau, *310 4th St, Niagara Falls, NY 14303 USA; tel: (800) 338-7890,* for a free guide. **Orin Leham Visitor Centre**, *Niagara Reservation State Park; tel: (716) 278-1796,* open daily 0800–2215. Both give accommodation information but do not make bookings. **Thomas Cook bureau de change**: *Rainbow Centre Mall; tel: (716) 284-0642.*

The *BW* **Inn on the River** is the only waterfront hotel. *CI* **The Pointe** is the closest to the Falls. You'll also find *DI, EL, Hd, HJ, QI, Rd* and *Rm*. The budget **HI** hostel, *1100 Ferry Ave; tel: (716) 282-3700,* is in a Victorian house several kilometres from the Falls. It's closed 0930–1600. The NFCVB can supply a list of Bed and Breakfasts.

Most of the area near the river and around the American Falls is part of the **Niagara Reservation State Park** (immediate right turn from the Rainbow Bridge); *tel: (716) 278-1770.* It's America's oldest state park. Open daily from sunrise–2300, US$4 parking. You can travel for three miles around the park in the **Viewmobile**, stopping at six scenic points. Day pass US$3.50–4.50. One of the most popular activities is **Cave of the Winds**; *tel: (716) 278-1730,* a walk along the base of the falls; raincoats and footwear provided, open daily 1000–1900, US$5–5.50. From **Prospect Point Observation Tower**, you can see the view from above the Gorge and take an elevator down to the base of the American Falls, daily 0800–2300, US$0.50. The **Maid of the Mist** one-hour cruise costs US$4.50–8. North of the Rainbow Bridge is the **Aquarium of Niagara**, US$4.25–6.25.

⬏ SIDE TRACK TO FORT ERIE

Fort Erie, at the union of the Niagara River and Lake Erie, is a pleasant 15-km drive south along the Niagara Parkway. Named after a fort established in 1764, it serves as a link to Buffalo, NY, via the International Peace Bridge. Several popular historic sites are located 8–10 km from the town centre, so plan a whole day if you want to include them all.

90

   Tourist Information: Ontario Travel Information Centre, *100 Goderich St (near the Peace Bridge); tel: (905) 871-3505* or *(800) ONTARIO,* open daily 0800–2000 (mid May–early Sept), 0830–1630 (early Sept–mid May). Currency exchange and reservations for hotels, motels and Bed and Breakfasts.

ACCOMMODATION

There's an *S8*. Hotels, motels and Bed and Breakfasts are all moderate, most are independently owned. Camping is available at **Riverside Park Motel & Campground**, *13541 Niagara River Parkway (12 km north of Fort Erie); tel: (905) 382-2204,* has a pool and view of Niagara River, budget motel rates.

ENTERTAINMENT

The **Royal Canadian Legion** performs at Historic Fort Erie Sun at 1400 and 1600 July–Aug. Thoroughbred racing is held at **Fort Erie Racetrack**, *Bertie St; tel: (905) 871-3200,* Sat–Tues (mid May–mid Sept), free admission and parking.

SIGHTSEEING

Centrally located sites include: **Mildred M. Mahoney Dolls' House Gallery**, *657 Niagara Blvd; tel: (905) 871-5833.* This historic hall, used by the underground railroad for smuggling slaves into Canada, now houses the world's largest collection of doll houses, open daily 1000–1600 (May–Dec), call for winter hours, $2–3. **Fort Erie Firefighting Museum**, *118 Concession Rd; tel: (905) 871-1271,* is a fire hall with antique firefighting equipment, open Wed–Sun and holiday Mon 1000–1700 (July–early Sept), free. **Fort Erie Railroad Museum**, *Central Ave; tel: (905) 871-1412,* features the last steam engine to transport passengers in Canada, open daily 1000–1700 (mid May–early Sept), Sat–Sun (early Sept–mid Oct). $2.

   Historic Fort Erie, *Niagara Parkway (Lakeshore Rd, 1.5 km south of Peace Bridge); tel: (905) 871-0540,* was built in 1764, captured by Americans in the War of 1812 and later abandoned. Guided tours of the restored fort by staff in period costume are conducted on the hour. Snacks and gift shop. Open daily (mid May–late Sept), $3–5.

   About 8 km west of downtown, is the **Ridgeway Battlefield Museum**, *Garrison Rd (Hwy 3); tel: (905) 894-5322.* This log house museum is on the site of the Fenian Raids of 1866 (Civil War soldiers who wanted to force Britain to free Ireland). About 2 km south, in a former town hall, is the **Fort Erie Historical Museum**, *402 Ridge Rd, Ridgeway: tel: (905) 894-5322,* which covers the early settlement of the area and includes an interesting series of oils painted during the Fenian Raids, open daily 0900–1700 (mid June–early Sept), $0.50–1.50. ⬏

TORONTO–LONDON LOOP

With little traffic you can travel 122 km directly to London in about two hours. Or this scenic loop can easily be stretched over four or five days, taking you through some of the richest agricultural land in the province. Roads between villages meander through rolling green countryside, with farm signs that beckon you to stop to purchase maple syrup, fresh strawberries and Mennonite quilts. Some roads have extra wide shoulders to accommodate the horse and buggy vehicles still favoured by the Mennonites of the area. This route takes in farmers' markets, excellent craft shopping and two major summer music festivals.

From Brantford, you can go on to Hamilton to link up with the Niagara route, either returning to Toronto or going south-west to Niagara's vineyards and famous falls.

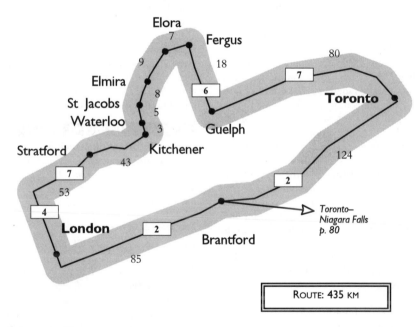

ROUTE: 435 KM

91

Depart Toronto westbound on either Hwy 401 or *Queen Elizabeth Way*. Exit at *Mississauga Rd* and go north to Hwy 7, following it west through the rolling Halton Hills and the villages of Norval, Georgetown (with its strip malls), tiny Acton, and on into the city of **Guelph**.

From Guelph, follow Hwy 6 north 18 km to **Fergus**; then Regional Rd 18 another 7 km to **Elora**. From there, take Rd 21 south (it becomes Rd 23); at the junction of Rd 86, turn right and continue to **Elmira**, a total of 35 km. You exit Elmira on Rd 21, which becomes Hwy 86, and go south for 8 km to **St Jacobs**, then continue south on Rd 8 until it becomes *Weber St*; 4 km from there it leads into **Waterloo**. *Weber St* continues south into the twin city of **Kitchener**.

Then, from Waterloo, take Rd 9 *(Erb St)* to Rd 12 at **St Agatha**. Go south on Rd 12 to Rd 1 and turn west (right). Continue through Baden and New Hamburg and you'll rejoin Hwy 7, which leads through the hamlet of Shakespeare and on to the theatre festival town of **Stratford**. From Stratford take Hwy 7; 12 km later, there's a right-hand turn into **St Marys** on Rd 28. From St Marys you can rejoin Hwy 7 by exiting on *Water St*. Continue south on Hwy 7. As you approach Lucan, turn left at Hwy 4 and go south for 17 km to **London**.

From London, you could choose to head west on Hwy 401 all the way to Windsor and the US border crossing into Detroit. Or, continue our scenic loop eastbound on Hwy 2 for an 85-km trip to **Brantford**, passing through **Woodstock** and the edge of Paris, where Hwy 2 bears to the right.

Exit Brantford on Hwy 2. If you continue straight, Hwy 2 you will take you into **Hamilton**, where you can link up with the Niagara scenic tour, either continuing on Hwy 2 to Toronto, or by making a right turn at *Main St* (Hwy 8) and heading out into **Niagara**.

BUSES AND TRAINS

Greyhound Lines of Canada operate 15 buses a day, two of which go via Kitchener. Journey time: 3¼ hrs. See OTT table 190.

VIA Rail run two trains daily (except Sat) via Kitchener. Journey time: 3 hrs. See OTT table 17.

TORONTO TO GUELPH

At the turn of the century, the village of **Acton** was home to the one-million-square-ft Beardmore Tannery. As you cross the railroad tracks on your left you'll see **The Olde Hide House**, *49 Eastern Ave; tel: (519) 853-1031*. Originally a warehouse for the tannery, it's now a huge leather goods retail outlet, open Sat–Thur 1000–1800, Fri 1000–2100. Across the road, the **TimBri Tea-house**, *40 Eastern Ave*, formerly the mayor's house, serves budget sandwiches and desserts and is licensed for beer and wine, open Mon–Fri 1100–1600, Sat–Sun 1100–1700. Around the corner is **Wetherby's**, *149 Church St E.*, which sells British products and acts as the local tourist information office.

Exit Acton by taking *Mill St* west to *Main St* and turning right. In less than 1 km, Hwy 7 continues on your left – it's 23 km to Guelph. About halfway there, just past Rockwood, is **Rockwood Conservation Area**. This would be an ideal stop for a picnic, swim or to camp for the night. Day entry $1.75–3.25, campsites $9–12. Food concessions and canoe rentals are available.

GUELPH

Tourist Information: Guelph Visitor & Convention Services, *55 Wyndham St N.* (in Eaton Centre), *Guelph, ON N1H 7T8; tel: (519) 837 1335, fax: (519) 837-1527,* open Mon–Sat 1000–1730.

ACCOMMODATION

Guelph has a *BW, Ch, CI, DI, Hd* and *S8*, plus four budget–moderate Bed and Breakfasts, including **Willow Manor**, *408 Willow Rd (off Hwy 6), Guelph, ON N1H 6S5; tel: (519) 763-3574,* an 1860 manor house with lush gardens and a swimming pool, moderate. Try **Summer Hostel Accommodation**, *Gordon St and College Ave, University of Guelph, Guelph, ON N1G 2W1; tel: (519) 824-4120,* for budget single or twin rooms (shared washrooms) (early May–mid Aug).

ENTERTAINMENT

Guelph is a university town that prides itself on its artistic and cultural community. The new **River Run Centre**, *35 Woolwich St; tel: (519) 763-3000*, features theatre, contemporary music, symphony and ballet.

The three-day **Hillside Festival**; *tel: (519) 763-6396*, at Guelph Lake Conservation Area in late July includes music, crafts, international food and a kids' programme. The **Guelph Jazz Festival**; *tel: (519) 763-4952*, focuses on local and national artists and is held at various locations in early Sept.

SIGHTSEEING

Local history is examined at the **Guelph Civic Museum**, *6 Dublin St S. (at Waterloo Ave); tel: (519) 836-1221*, open daily 1300–1700 (June–Aug), Sun–Fri 1300–1700 (Sept–May), closed holidays, $2–3. **McCrae House**, *108 Water St; tel: (519) 836-1482*, a National Historic Site, is the 19th-century home of John McCrae, a professor of medicine who is best remembered as the author of the poem *In Flanders Fields*. Open daily 1300–1700 (June–Aug), Sun–Fri 1300–1700 (Sept–Dec and Apr–May), Mon–Fri 1300–1700 (Jan–Mar), $2–3.

One of Guelph's unique sites is the 37-m **Lattice Covered Footbridge**, *Gordon St* at the Speed River, constructed by 400 timber framers during a single week in 1992. It's one of only two covered bridges in Ontario.

The **Arboretum**, *Arboretum Rd; tel: (519) 824-4120, ext 2113*, at the University of Guelph (turn east off *East Ring Rd* on to *Arboretum Rd*), features interpretive nature trails with plant collections and 2900 types of trees and shrubs on 165 hectares, open all year, free. The **MacDonald Stewart Art Centre**, *358 Gordon St (at College Ave, north of University of Guelph campus); tel: (519) 837-0010*, features historical and contemporary Canadian art in a three-storey turn-of-the-century building, open Tues–Sun 1200–1700. Donations accepted.

FERGUS

Tourist Information: Information Fergus, *Fergus Market Building, 100 Queen St (Box 3, Fergus, ON N1M 2W7); tel: (519) 843-5140*, open daily, can provide details on about 20 moderate Bed and Breakfasts in the area.

The **Breadalbane Inn**, *487 St Andrew St W., Fergus, ON N1M 1P2; tel: (519) 843-4770*, in a large 1860 stone house, serves lunches and dinners in a Victorian garden, dining room and Scottish pub, Tues–Sun. There are seven guest rooms, including a cottage with private patio, fireplace and Jacuzzi, moderate–expensive.

The town, which straddles the Grand River, is known for its historic limestone buildings and its annual mid Aug Scottish heritage celebration – the **Fergus Scottish Festival and Highland Games**, *P.O. Box 25, Fergus, ON N1M 2W7; tel: (519) 787-0099*.

Fergus Market, *100 Queen St; tel: (519) 843-5221*, is a mixture of a flea market plus produce, baked goods and some crafts, open Sat 0800–1700, Sun 0900–1700. The Tourist Office is on the second floor, along with the **Heather and Hearth** Scottish shop and **Bedded Down**, featuring Ontario's largest bed and bathroom store. The adjoining **River's Edge Cafe**; *tel: 519 787-9303* (at the footbridge which crosses the river from the Market parking lot) offers budget meals overlooking the water.

Professional summer theatre is presented July–Sept at **Theatre on the Grand**, *244 St Andrew St, P.O. Box 449, Fergus, ON N1M 3E2; tel: (519) 787-1981*. Perched on a hill overlooking *County Rd 18*, midway between Fergus and Elora, is **Wellington County Museum and Archives**, a National Historic Site. It's open Mon–Fri 0930–1630, Sat–Sun and holidays 1300–1700, $0.50–3.

ELORA

Tourist Information: Village of Elora Information Centre, *1 MacDonald Sq., Box*

93

814, Elora, ON N0B 1S0; tel: (519) 846-9841.

ACCOMMODATION

There are 19 Bed and Breakfasts in the area, budget–expensive. Centrally located in a 'century home' (more than 100 years old) is moderate–expensive **Gingerbread House**, *22 Metcalfe St S.; tel: (519) 846-0521.* For budget travellers there is **Hornsby Home**, *231 Queen St, Elora, ON N0B 1S0; tel: (519) 846-9763*, a clean little bungalow (look for the sign that says 'Lew & Ethel's').

On the bank of the Grand River, **The Elora Mill Inn**, *77 Mill St W.; tel: (519) 846-5356*, is one of the very few early Ontario five-storey grist mills still in existence. It has 32 moderate–pricey rooms. You can view the falls and beginning of the gorge from the dining room, budget–pricey, and there's a special Sunday brunch. The **Bed and Breakfast Inn**, *9 Bridge St., W. Montrose N0B 2V0; tel: (519) 669-2112*, beside the 'Kissing Bridge' (see below), is a century house with six suites, operated by a family of Mennonite descent, moderate–expensive.

EATING AND DRINKING

Dining opportunities range from budget pub lunches on *Mill St* and cheap vegetarian fare at **The Desert Rose Cafe**, *130 Metcalfe St; tel: (519) 846 0433*, to the moderately priced **La Cachette**, *13 Mill St; tel: (519) 846-8346*, which has a riverside dining room and patio.

ENTERTAINMENT

The mid July–early Aug **Elora Festival** (mailing address: *33 Henderson St, P.O. Box 990, Elora, ON N0B 1S0; tel: (519) 846-0331*), presents contemporary and classical music in unique locations, including a barn, a natural amphitheatre in the Elora Quarry and a church, $15–75. Classic and international films are featured at the **George Cinema**, *43 Mill St.*

SHOPPING

Mill St and *Metcalfe St* are lined with more than 50 shops, dining establishments and artists' studios. Antiques, original jewellery designs, handmade pottery and clothing are all featured.

SIGHTSEEING

Elora is a charming village perched on the banks of the Grand River where the quiet waters – popular for fly fishing – drop down for a rugged 4-km ride through the **Elora Gorge**. The village is known for historic churches and artists' studios.

As you approach Elora from Fergus, the **Elora Quarry**, on the left along County Rd 18, is an ideal stop for a picnic, hike or swim. The popular 'old swimming hole' is a former limestone quarry with a 0.8-hectare pond encircled by 12-m cliffs. $1.75–3.25. You can stop for a look for no charge.

The **Elora Gorge Conservation Area**, *County Rd 21* (less than 1 km west of Elora)*; tel: (519) 846-9742*, covers 250 hectares with trails to lookouts over the 25-m cliffs of the Elora Gorge, a lake, playground, picnic sites and camping, open 1000–dusk (May–mid Oct), 1000–1700 (Jan–Mar), $1.75–3.25. Camping $9–13, plus $6 reservation fee.

ELORA TO ELMIRA

After exiting Elora via Regional Rd 21 (past the Elora Gorge Conservation Area), the road becomes Rd 23. When you reach the junction of Rd 86 turn right, and then left in less than 1 km in the direction of West Montrose. Almost immediately you will come to the **Covered Bridge**, also known as the 'Kissing Bridge'. It was built in 1881 and is the last remaining traditional covered bridge in Ontario. Next to the entrance is a craft shop (selling ice-cream) and a Bed and Breakfast Inn; on the other side are some picnic facilities.

As you backtrack to Rd 86 and continue towards Elmira, the shoulders of the road are exceptionally wide to accommodate the

Mennonite horse and buggies in this region. Pass them with caution; the horses are familiar with road traffic but can be startled by noise or stones tossed up by tyres.

ELMIRA

Tourist Information: Elmira & Woolwich Chamber of Commerce, *5 First St E., Elmira, ON N3B 2E3; tel: (519) 669-2605.* You'll have to drive clear through town to reach the office.

This village, 6 km from West Montrose, was settled by Mennonites from Pennsylvania and is well known for its one-day spring **Maple Sugar Festival**, held the first Sat in Apr (unless it conflicts with Easter). There is a craft market at the **Elmira Olde Town Village**, *10 Church St W.;* Mon–Sat 0930–1800, Thur–Fri 0930–2100. Budget–moderate country cuisine is served up at the **Stone Crock Restaurant**, *59 Church St W.; tel: (519) 669-1521.*

ST JACOBS

Tourist Information: The Visitor Centre, *33 King St, Box 411, St Jacobs, ON N0B 2N0; tel: (519) 664-3518 or (800) 265-3353.*

ACCOMMODATION AND FOOD

St Jacobs and Area Bed and Breakfast Association, *Box 500, St Jacobs, ON N0B 2N0; tel: (519) 664-2622,* has eight members, moderate; a board with photos and information sits on *King St* in the village centre. The centrally located, 12-room **Jakobstettel Guest House**, *16 Isabella, tel: (519) 664-2208,* has a pool and a five-acre yard; expensive, breakfast included. The 1852 **Benjamin's Restaurant and Inn**, *17 King St S.; tel: (519) 664-3731,* has nine rooms and outdoor patio, moderate. Dining room open daily 1130–2100, reservations recommended.

SIGHTSEEING

St Jacobs is home to one of the world's largest Mennonite populations, and it's the location of one of the largest authentic farmers' markets in North America. Travellers also stop for the more than 100 one-of-a-kind shops and the market's adjoining factory outlet mall.

The **Visitor Centre**, in the village centre, gives information on Mennonite history, lifestyle and beliefs. The multimedia presentation includes a 15-min video, *Mennonites of Ontario.* Mon–Fri 1100–1700, Sat 1000–1700, Sun 1330–1700 (May–Oct); Sat 1100–1630, Sun 1400–1630 (Nov–Apr). Suggested donation $2–3.

Lining *King St* are antiques shops, restaurants and historic buildings filled with the works of local artists, including handmade brooms, leatherwork, pottery, quilts and the products of glass blowers and a master blacksmith. Inside the **Old Factory Antique Market**, *Spring St*, is the **Maple Syrup Museum of Ontario**, open Mon–Sat 1000–1700, Sun 1230–1700 year round, closed Mon (Jan–mid Mar). Free.

Two km south of St Jacobs, the **St Jacobs Farmers Market and Flea Market**, *Farmer's Market Rd at King and Weber Sts; tel: (519) 747-1830,* features hundreds of vendors, including local Mennonite farmers. There's fresh produce, baked goods, arts, crafts, clothing, furniture and a food fair. Open Tues 0800–1500, Thur and Sat 0700–1530. Next to the Farmers Market is **St Jacobs Factory Outlet Mall** with 30 stores. Open Mon–Fri 0930–2100, Sat 0830–1800, Sun 1200–1700 year round, open most holidays. Between the two is the **Log Cabin**, a quilt and craft store, and home base for **Country Livery Services**, which offers farm tours by horse-drawn trolley, $6–10.

KITCHENER AND WATERLOO

Tourist Information: Kitchener-Waterloo Area Visitor & Convention Bureau, *2848 King St E., Kitchener, ON N2A 1A5;*

95

tel: (519) 748-0800 or *(800) 265-6959,* open Mon–Wed 0900–1700, Thur–Fri 0900–1900, Sat–Sun 1000– 1600 (summer).

ACCOMMODATION AND FOOD

Chains include *BW, Ch, CI, HI, HJ, Ro, Sh* and *TL.* **Kitchener/Waterloo and Area Bed & Breakfast Association;** *tel: (519) 743 4557,* includes 18 homes with budget–moderate rooms.

The **University of Waterloo,** *200 University Ave; tel: (519) 888-4567, ext 3614,* offers budget rooms with shared washrooms. Camping is available at **Green Acre Park,** *580 Beaver Creek Rd, Waterloo, ON N2J 3Z4; tel: (519) 885-1758.*

The Swiss Castle Inn, *1508 King St E., Kitchener; tel: (519) 744-2391,* is a local landmark, built 1929, with a colourful history that includes rumours of bootlegging during Prohibition. At one time it had its own chocolate factory, now reflected in the dessert special – chocolate pecan pie. They also have a very large collection of antique Swiss cow bells. The owner speaks five languages. Budget–moderate.

For upmarket casual dining, try **Krebs Restaurant,** *130 King St S., Waterloo; tel: (519) 886-2550,* and **20 King Restaurant,** *20 King St E., tel: (519) 745-8939,* which offers fine dining and pizza in a wood-fire oven, moderate–pricey.

SIGHTSEEING

Coming from St Jacobs, you first enter Waterloo. The University of Waterloo has several on-campus museums, including the **Brubacher House Museum,** *North campus* (off *Columbia St W.); tel: (519) 886-3855,* a Mennonite home built in 1850, open Wed–Sat 1400–1700 (May–Oct), $1, and the **Museum and Archive of Games,** *Bert Matthews Hall (Columbia St entrance); tel: (519) 888-4424,* open Tues–Fri 1200–1700 year round.

The **Waterloo–St Jacobs Railway Ltd;** *tel: (519) 746-1950,* offers travel with a

1950s atmosphere between Waterloo and St Jacobs. Departs Waterloo Station daily (July–mid Oct) and weekends (mid Oct–late Nov), $5.50–8.50 for a day pass.

You'll hardly notice leaving one city to enter the other. Kitchener, which was originally named Berlin, was the boyhood home of Mackenzie King, the tenth prime minister of Canada. The city is now the location of the second largest **Oktoberfest** in the world, held annually for nine days (late Sept–early Oct).

In the town centre, the 125-year-old **Kitchener Farmers' Market,** *49 Frederick St* (corner of *Duke St); tel: (519) 741-2287,* has 150 vendors with fresh produce, Mennonite baking and crafts, open Sat 0600–1400, all year. The **Joseph Schneider Haus,** *466 Queen St S.; tel: (519) 742-7752,* is a Mennonite home restored to depict the mid 1850s, open Mon–Sat 1000–1700 and Sun 1300–1700 (mid May–early Sept), Wed–Sat 1000–1700, Sun 1300–1700 rest of year, $1.50–2.25.

Center in the Square, *101 Queen St N.; tel: (519) 578-1660* or *(800) 265-8977* for tickets, is a 2016-seat performing arts centre that has featured the Kitchener-Waterloo Symphony, Bill Cosby and Anne Murray. Most shows cost $20–50.

Woodside National Historic Site, *528 Wellington St N.; tel: (519) 571-5684,* was the boyhood home of William Lyon Mackenzie King. It has a quiet setting, surrounded by five wooded hectares of parkland with picnic facilities. The staff is in period costume, open daily 1000–1700 (mid May–Dec), closed 11 Nov, $1.50–2.50.

Doon Heritage Crossroads, *Homer Watson Blvd; tel: (519) 748-1914,* depicts an historic rural village of the 1800s, with 20 buildings, two farms and costumed interpreters, open daily 1000–1630 (May–early Sept), Mon–Fri 1000–1630 (Sept–Dec), $2–5. Two km away is **Homer Watson House and Gallery,** *1754 Old Mill Rd* (follow signs); *tel: (519) 748-4377,* formerly the home of this internationally renowned land-scape artist (1883–1936). It features traditional and contemporary art exhibits, open Tues–Sun and holiday Mon 1200–1630, Thur–2000 (Apr–mid Oct), $2 donation.

WATERLOO TO STRATFORD

Following Regional Rd 9 *(Erbs Rd W.)* west, a good stop is **Angie's Kitchen**, *85 Erbs Rd W., St Agatha; tel: (519) 747-1700,* a family-run licensed restaurant (in a building that served as a hotel in 1839), with home-style cooking and fresh baking. There is a craft shop out back, open Tues–Sun. Budget–moderate.

From St Agatha, take Regional Rd 12 south to Rd 1 and go west (right) to Baden for **Castle Kilbride**, *60 Snyder's Rd W., Baden; tel: (519) 634-8444.* This Italianate Victorian mansion is now a National Historic Site, open Tues–Sun 1300–1600 year round, $3–5. Continue west through New Hamburg to Hwy 7, and go west through the hamlet of Shakespeare (known for its antiques shops) to Stratford.

STRATFORD

Tourist Information: Tourism Stratford, *88 Wellington St, Stratford, ON N5A SW1; tel: (519) 271-5140 or (800) 561-SWAN, ext. 12.* There's a summer booth at *41 York St* (beside Avon River or Lake Victoria); *tel: (519) 273-3352,* open Tues–Sat 0900–2000, Sun–Mon 0900–1700 (June–Aug), where you can browse through books showing accommodation facilities and use the telephones.

Ask for your free **Parking Pass**, which can be used for one day of your visit. Free guided **Heritage Walks** depart from the *York St* office Mon–Sat at 0930 (July–Sept), weather permitting, and there are maps for do-it-yourself tours. Canoes and paddle boats can be rented downstairs.

ACCOMMODATION

The 30-room, 145-year-old **Queen's Inn**,

161 Ontario St, Stratford, ON N5A 3H3; tel: (519) 271-1400 or (800) 461-6450, is located on the edge of the prime shopping area, moderate–expensive.

The **B & B House**, *14 Caledonia St, Stratford, ON N5A 5W5; tel: (519) 272-1908,* is a Queen Anne Revival home (built 1905), within walking distance of the theatres, low moderate. In nearby St Marys (a 20-min drive out on *Erie St* and Hwy 7), a beautiful greystone 1867 manor house, the **Westover Inn**, *300 Thomas St, P.O. Box 280, St Marys, ON N4X 1B1; tel: (519) 284-2977,* has been favoured by well known actors such as Christopher Plummer, moderate–expensive.

For those on tight budgets, **Stratford General Hospital Residence**, *130 Young St, Stratford, ON N5A 1J7; tel: (519) 271-5084, fax (519) 272-8221,* has single and twin rooms (separate floors for men and women), with lounges, kitchenettes and a swimming pool. Lakeside camping is available at **Wildwood Conservation Area**, *Hwy 7* (as you approach St Marys); *tel: (519) 284-2931.*

EATING AND DRINKING

A unique dining opportunity is moderate–pricey **Church Restaurant**, *70 Brunswick St: tel: (519) 273-3424.* It's a beautifully restored 121-year-old church, behind the Avon Theatre. Reservations recommended. For a comfortable budget–moderate meal, afternoon tea or after-theatre dining in wing-back chairs before a fireplace, try **Mrs Carter's Restaurant**, *116 Downie St; tel: (519) 271-9200.*

ENTERTAINMENT

Half a million theatre-goers each year flock to picturesque riverside Stratford (mid May–early Nov) to enjoy the works of William Shakespeare, contemporary drama and musical theatre.

There are three venues: the **Festival Theatre**, *55 Queen St,* in Queen's Park; the

97

Avon Theatre, *99 Downie St,* and the **Tom Patterson Theatre**, *Lakeside Dr.* Tickets average $26–67. A special rate is available to full-time students under 30 for all performances, and there are also special discounted student and seniors' mid-week matinee performances. For tickets contact **Stratford Festival**, *55 Queen St, Box 520 Stratford, ON N5A 6V2; tel: (519) 273-1600* or *(800) 567-1600.*

Art in the Park presents works by local artists on Wed, Sat and Sun, weather permitting (June–late Sept); from the tourist information kiosk continue along *Lakeside Dr.* to *Front St.* **Jazz on the River** (free concerts from a small floating stage) is presented Tues, Fri, Sat and some Sun 1815–2000 (mid June–mid Sept).

SHOPPING

Entering Stratford on Hwy 7 *(Ontario St),* you will pass the **Samsonite Factory Outlet**, *753 Ontario St,* on your left, which sells luggage.

98

LONDON

Tourist Information: Tourism London, *300 Dufferin Ave, London, ON N6B 1Z3; tel: (519) 661-5000* or *(800) 265-2602, fax: (519) 661-2366.* London has lovely tree-lined streets with large Victorian homes, and a youthful atmosphere due to a large university population.

ACCOMMODATION

Chain hotels include *BW, Ch, CI, DI, EL, Hd, HJ, QI, QS, Rm* and *TL.* One unique accommodation is **Delta London Armouries Hotel**, *325 Dundas St, London, ON N6B 1T9; tel: (519) 679-6111* or *(800) 668-9999.* Modern luxury has been incorporated into the historic 1905 hotel, including former messes turned into period suites, some with turrets.

London and Area Bed and Breakfasts; *tel: (519) 641-0467, fax: (519) 641-1258,* has information on 20 budget–low

moderate Bed and Breakfasts. Lakeside camping is available at **Fanshawe Conservation Area**, *1424 Clarke Rd, London, ON N5V 5B9; tel: (519) 451-2800,* from early May–mid Oct.

EATING AND DRINKING

Richmond St, near the Grand Theatre, is a popular area for dining. Moderate **Garlic's Restaurant**, *481 Richmond St; tel: (519) 432-4092,* is open Mon–Sat. Some non-garlic items are available. The **Mongolian Grill**, *645 Richmond St; tel: 519 645-6400,* creates customised stir-fries. Moderate. At **Horse and Hound**, *1269 Hyde Park Rd, tel: (519) 472-6801,* a countryside Victorian mansion has been turned into a dining establishment with outdoor patio. Live easy listening music Fri–Sat at 2030. Budget–pricey.

There's excellent dining at **Lakeview Cafe**, *85 Main St, Grand Bend* (at Lake Huron); *tel: (519) 238-2622,* a 70-km jaunt from downtown, but convenient for playhouse patrons. Budget–pricey. Reservations recommended. You may catch one of this area's great sunsets along the lakeside's beautiful beach.

ENTERTAINMENT

Free evening concerts are conducted (May–Sept) at the **Victoria Park** bandshell. The 839-seat Victorian **Grand Theatre**, *471 Richmond St; tel: (519) 672-8800,* offers contemporary comedy, romance and drama Sept–May, $23–43.

The Western Fairgrounds on *Dundas St* (Hwy 2) is the site of a large 10-day annual **country fair** (early Sept), and location of the **Western Fair Imax Theatre**; *tel: (519) 438-4629,* with its five-storey high screen.

In a 648-seat barn-style venue 70 km north-west of London, **Huron Country Playhouse**; *tel: (519) 238-6000* or *(800) 706-6665,* presents family-oriented professional entertainment (mid June–late Aug). Take Hwy 81 towards the village of Grand Bend on the shore of Lake Huron. You'll see a sign to turn right 2 km before Grand Bend. For dining visit the village.

SIGHTSEEING

Double Decker Tour of London, *300 Dufferin Ave; tel: (519) 661-5000 or (800) 265-2602*, offers city tours from **City Hall**, *Dufferin Ave and Wellington St.* Departures daily 1000 and 1400 (July–early Sept), $3–7.50.

London Museum of Archaeology and Lawson Prehistoric Indian Village, *1600 Attawandaron Rd; tel: (519) 473-1360*, includes gallery exhibits on the 11,000-year history of South-western Ontario. The gift shop offers native arts and crafts, open Tues–Sun and holiday Mon 1000–1700 (May–Sept); Wed–Sun 1000–1700 (Sept–mid Dec); Wed–Sun 1300–1600 (Jan–Apr). On the same property is an archaeological site showing the partial reconstruction of a 500-year-old village longhouse. Digging continues, so watch for archaeological students at work. Open Tues–Sun and holiday Mon 1000–1700 (May–Sept). Donation.

Memorabilia of London's most famous band leader is collected at the tiny **Guy Lombardo Museum**, *205 Wonderland Rd S.; tel: (519) 473-9003*, open daily 1100–1700 (mid May–early Sept), $2. The **Banting Museum**, *442 Adelaide St N.; tel: (519) 673-1752*, focuses on the life of Nobel-prize winner Sir Frederick G. Banting (1891–1941), co-discoverer of insulin, open Tues–Sat 1200–1630 year round, $1.50–3.

Along with the history of the regiment formed in 1883, the **Royal Canadian Regiment Museum**, *Wolseley Barracks, Oxford and Elizabeth Sts; tel: (519) 660-5102*, includes a simulated World War I trench system, a Korean War command post and a Boer War battle relief model, open Tues–Fri 1000–1600, Sat–Sun 1200–1600 year round. **Fanshawe Pioneer Village**, *Fanshawe Conservation Area; tel: (519) 457-1296*, includes 22 restored heritage buildings, costumed interpreters and a tea room, open Wed–Sun

1000–1630 May–Nov, $3–5. The surrounding park is a good place for a picnic or swim.

Storybook Gardens, *Springbank Park (off Wonderland Rd); tel: (519) 661-5770*, is a good-value children's theme park featuring animals, live entertainment and a miniature train, open daily 1000–2000 (early May–early Sept), Mon–Fri 1000–1700 and Sat and Sun 1000–1800 (Sept–Oct), $3–5. **London Princess Tours**; *tel: (519) 473-0363*, offers afternoon (45 mins, $4.95–6.95), dinner (Wed–Sun) and Sun brunch cruises on Thames River from Storybook Landing in **Springbank Park**.

OUT OF TOWN

If you want to continue from London to Windsor and on across the US border to Detroit, take Hwy 2 west. On your way, 32 km from London (5 km west of the village of Delaware) on Hwy 2, is **Longwoods Road Conservation Area** and **Ska-Nah-Doht Iroquoian Village and Museum**; *tel: (519) 264-2420*, a fascinating re-creation of Iroquoian life 1000 years ago. There's a resource centre with audio-visual shows, open daily 0900–1630 (July–early Sept), Mon–Fri 0900–1630 (early Sept–July). The grounds are open 0900–sunset all year, $2–2.75.

BRANTFORD

Tourism Information: Tourism Brantford, *1 Sherwood Dr., Brantford, ON N3T 1N3; tel: (519) 751-9900 or (800) 265-6299.* Ask for the new self-guided garden tour brochure.

ACCOMMODATION AND FOOD

There are *BW, CI, DI,* and 35 Bed and Breakfasts in the area. The **Grand Bed & Breakfast**, *119 Tutela Heights Rd, Brantford, ON N3T 5L6; tel (519) 752-2972*, is a century home with a wonderful view of the countryside, just 800m from the Bell Homestead.

Moose Winooski's, *45 King George Rd;*

99

tel: (519) 751-4042, a fun, lively Canadian-themed restaurant that looks like a large log cabin, is just a quick dash across the street from *CI*. As you drive in from London, 5 km past Paris and 2 km before Brantford, **The Olde School Restaurant**, *Hwy 2 and Powerline Rd; tel: (519) 753-3131,* a school in the 1870s, is now a good stop for a moderate–pricey lunch or dinner. There's a piano bar, and reservations are recommended.

SIGHTSEEING

Brantford is named for the famous Mohawk leader, Joseph Brant, who earned the rank of captain as a British soldier and brought the Six Nations Confederacy here from Upper New York State after the American Revolution.

The **Bell Homestead**, *94 Tutela Heights Rd; tel: (519) 756-6220,* is where Alexander Graham Bell lived with his parents from 1870–81, and where he conceived the idea for the telephone in 1874. The house is furnished as it was when his family lived here. There is a 20-min audio-visual presentation, a tea room and picnic grounds, open Tues–Sun 0930–1630 all year (closed Tues following Mon holidays), $1.50–2.50.

On the site of the original Mohawk Village stands **Her Majesty's Royal Chapel of the Mohawks**, *291 Mohawk St; tel: (519) 758-5444,* the first Protestant church in Ontario and the only Royal Chapel in the world belonging to Native people. Wander in for a look at the stained-glass windows depicting the history of Six Nations people. There is usually someone from the community present to explain the history, open Wed–Sun 1300–1730 (mid May–June), daily 1000–1800 (July–early Sept), Sat–Sun 1300–1700 (early Sept–mid Oct). Donations accepted.

Down the road, the **Woodland Cultural Centre**, *184 Mohawk St; tel: (519) 759-2650,* focuses on the aboriginal culture and heritage of the First Nations of the Eastern Woodland area, open Mon–Fri 0830–1600, Sat–Sun 1000– 1700, closed 21 June (First Nations Solidarity Day), Labour Day and Thanksgiving, $1–3. A third site in this area of *Mohawk St,* **Kanata** (a Mohawk word for village), is due to open fall 1998. It will be an authentically recreated Iroquois village with three longhouses.

In a large yellow building of the Greenwich Industrial site is the **Canadian Military Heritage Museum**, *347 Greenwich St* (it branches off *Mohawk St); tel: (519) 759-1313.* Exhibits cover Canada's military heritage from the 18th century to modern day, and include four life-size World War I aircraft reproductions by Canadian high school students. Within the museum is a collection of vintage motorcycles, open Tues–Sun and holiday Mon 1030–1630 (Apr–mid Oct), Fri–Sun 1030–1630 (mid Oct–Apr), $1–3.

In a park-like setting is the **Glenhyrst Art Gallery**, *20 Ava Rd; tel: (519) 756-5932,* whose **Gardener's Cottage**; *tel: (519) 758-9512,* is a delightful place for a light lunch or dessert. They will even prepare a picnic. Reservations recommended, open Mon–Fri (May–Oct). The Art Gallery is free.

OUT OF TOWN

About 13 km east of Brantford in Ohsweken is **ODrohekta – The Gathering Place**, *Hwy Regional Rd 254 (formerly Hwy 54) and Chiefswood Rd; tel: (519) 758-5444.* A cultural centre provides information on Six Nations history, crafts and tourist information. During the fourth weekend of July, the **Grand River Powwow** is presented. It's an open-air event on the grounds of the former estate of the Canadian Mohawk poetess, E. Pauline Johnson. It features dancers and singers representing every major North American native cultural group dressed in their regalia, plus arts and crafts and Canadian and Native foods. Admission $6.

TORONTO–OTTAWA

This drive from Canada's biggest metropolis to its seat of government begins with apple orchards and quiet bird-watching spots along the shores of Lake Ontario. Then it crosses Prince Edward County, an island in the lake, as it follows the path of early settlers along The Loyalist Parkway, now an area popular for crafts and antiques shopping. At historic Kingston you can experience the military life of 1867 at Fort Henry, then continue north along the shore of the mighty St Lawrence by the spectacular Thousand Islands (which actually number around 1800). Finally, the route turns inland for either an hour's ride on the highway or a leisurely countryside ramble to the nation's capital.

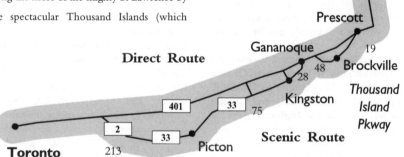

101

ROUTES

DIRECT ROUTE: 445 KM

DIRECT ROUTE

➡ Hwy 401 east to **Prescott** then Hwy 16 north to **Ottawa** is one of the fastest ways from Toronto to Ottawa, covering 445 km.

SCENIC ROUTE

▪▪▶ This scenic version runs parallel to the Direct Route most of the way, allowing you to move over to Hwy 401 for faster travel, or to short cut to Ottawa on Hwy 16.

Exit Toronto on Hwy 401 eastbound.

After 45 km, exit onto Hwy 12 for a stopover in **Whitby**. Another 21 km on Hwy 401 brings you to **Bowmanville**, where you exit at *Liberty St* and go north, then east on Hwy 2 for a nice countryside ride, eventually turning down to Lake Ontario at **Port Hope** and on to **Cobourg**. Continue along the shore of Lake Ontario 12 km to **Grafton**, 10 km to **Colbourne** (the Apple Route) and 12 km further to **Brighton**. In Brighton centre, turn right onto County Rd 64 and stick with it across the Murray Canal and into **Prince Edward County** as far as **Carrying Place**, where you turn right onto Hwy 33 – **The Loyalist Parkway**. This leads through the villages of **Hillier**, **Wellington** and **Bloomfield** and on to **Picton**. Continue east on Hwy 33 across the Glenora ferry and then 75 km through farming country, past antique shops, shore-side picnicking and swim areas to **Kingston**.

Exit Kingston on Hwy 2 east across the La Salle Causeway, which is the beginning of the **Rideau Canal**, to **Gananoque**, then another 37 km east along the **Thousand Island Parkway** (after 1 km a Parks of the St Lawrence information board details the camping, scenic stops, grocery stores, boat and bike rentals, accommodation, etc.). The parkway leads past several small villages and the Hill Island Bridge to the USA, and merges with Hwy 401. After 1 km, rejoin Hwy 2 east for a 10-km trip into **Brockville**.

Exit Brockville on Hwy 2 east for the 19-km trip to **Prescott**, where a 96-km short cut north on Hwy 16 brings you to Ottawa. Or continue on Hwy 2 through **Cardinal**, **Iroquois**, **Morrisburg** and **Upper Canada Village**. Two km past **Ingleside**, turn left onto Rd 14 north, then onto Rte 12, a two-lane country road that leads through **Finch**, **Berwick** and **Crysler**, where it becomes Rd 5. Continue north to Limoges and follow the multi-lane Hwy 417 westbound 35 km into Ottawa. (Eastbound Hwy 417 is the Ottawa to Montréal route, see p. 131.)

Another option at Prescott is to continue 105 km east on Hwy 401, then about 70 km on Hwy 20 to Montréal, see p. 131.

BUSES AND TRAINS

Trentway-Wager and Voyageur Colonial operate a twice-weekly bus service, changing at Brockville (4-hr wait). See OTT tables 188–204. Alternatively, you could change at Kingston and continue the journey via Smiths Falls (4 trips daily). Journey time: 6 hrs plus change time. OTT table 188/208.

VIA Rail operate two trains daily and three others on various days of the week. Reservation required. Journey time: 4 hrs. See OTT table 21.

TORONTO TO PRINCE EDWARD COUNTY

From Hwy 401, exit onto Hwy 12 *(Brock St)* and go north 7 km through Whitby to visit **Cullen Gardens and Miniature Village**, *300 Taunton Rd, W. Whitby, ON L1N 5R5; tel: (905) 668-6606 or (800) 461-1821* (toll-free), whose 26 acres are covered with spectacular gardens and 160 waist-high miniatures of Ontario buildings – including farming communities, cottage country and a country fair. There's a splash pool for kids and a pleasant restaurant with garden view at the entrance, open daily 0900–2100 (late June–Sept), slightly different hours other seasons, $5–10, family $30.

In **Cobourg**, founded in 1798 by United Empire Loyalists, **Dressler House**, *212 King St W.; tel: (905) 372-5831,* free, was the birthplace of 1930s Hollywood actress Marie Dressler. The house has two rooms of memorabilia and houses the Chamber of Commerce, which has tourist information on the region. Both are open Mon–Sat 0900–1700, Sun 1100–1700 (July–Aug), Mon–Fri 0900–1700, Sat 0900–1400 (Sept–June). Also in Cobourg, the 1860 **Victoria Hall**, *55 King St W., tel: (905) 372-4301,* houses a gallery of Canadian, European and Inuit art and a concert hall. Behind the hall, a **Farmer's Market** is held Sat 0700–1200 (May–Oct), Tues (July–Aug). **Victoria Park** has a white sand beach and a floral clock 30 ft in diameter with 3000 plants.

On the way into **Grafton**, a village with antique stores and cafés, is **Barnum House Museum**, *Hwy 2; tel: (905) 349-2656.* Built in 1819 and now operated by the Ontario Heritage Foundation, there are short walking trails, and a tea room is open on the second floor, Thur–Mon 1000–1700 (June–early Sept), $2–2.50. North of town is **Ste**

Anne's Country Inn and Spa, *RR1 Grafton, ON K0K 2G0; tel: (905) 349-2493 or (888) 346-6772*, a lovely stone mansion with ten antique-filled guest rooms and a swimming pool on a 560-acre estate, expensive–pricey.

The village of **Colborne**, with its murals and antique shops, begins the **Apple Route**, lined with highway fruit stands and orchards inviting customers to pick their own. In **Brighton**, you can turn off onto Rd 66 for **Presqu'ile Provincial Park**, *R.R. 4 Brighton, ON K0K 1H0; tel: (613) 475-2204*, a favourite with birders during spring and fall migration periods. At least 312 species of birds have been spotted here, and there are 4 km of sand beaches and 394 campsites. The Visitor Centre is open daily Apr–mid Oct, camping $17.75–16.75, day use $7 per vehicle.

PRINCE EDWARD COUNTY

Tourist Information: Prince Edward County Chamber of Tourism and Commerce, *116 Main St, P.O. Box 50, Picton, ON K0K 2T0; tel: (613) 476-2421, fax: (613) 476-7461.*

ACCOMMODATION AND FOOD

Mallory House Bed and Breakfast, *Hwy 33 at Mallory Rd, R.R. 1, Bloomfield, ON K0K 1G0; tel: (613) 393-3458*, 6 km before Picton, is a nicely restored 1850 farmhouse, open late May–early Sept, budget–moderate.

Timm's Grandview Manor, *Hwy 49, RR 2, Picton, ON K0K 2T0; tel: (613) 476-8875*, built in the 1930s in the Loyalist style, is 3 km north of town, with three acres of grounds on Picton Bay, moderate; there is a two night minimum stay Sat–Sun in July and Aug. The distinctive 14-room **Merrill Inn**, *P.O. Box 1318, 343 Main St E., Picton, ON K0K 2T0; tel: (613) 476-7451 or (800) 567-5969*, built circa 1878 with narrow windows and tall gables, has a pub. Rooms are moderate, breakfast included.

On the way to Glenora Ferry (on Rd 7,

2 km off Hwy 33), the historic, family-run **Lake on the Mountain Resort and Inn**, *RR 9, Picton, ON K0K 2T0; tel: (613) 476-1321*, has self-catering cottages and two tiny log cabins (with modern interior), moderate, and a stone restaurant with patio. Reservations are recommended for dinner Sat–Sun (Apr–Nov), budget–moderate.

SIGHTSEEING

Named after the father of Queen Victoria, Ontario's only island county is also called Quinte's Isle, or simply The County. Hwy 33, which stretches for 94 km to Kingston, is also called **The Loyalist Parkway** because it winds through land settled by the United Empire Loyalists, who fled the USA following the 1776–83 War of Independence and were given land parcels because of their loyalty to the British Crown.

The village of **Wellington**, population 2500, originally a port and mill town, is now popular for trout and salmon fishing. Amid the lovely tree-lined streets and Victorian homes along Hwy 33 is the area's original **Quaker Meeting House**, open Sat–Sun 1000–1600.

Bloomfield is a charming small village of craft shops, artisan galleries (including glassworks, woodcrafts, jewellery and pottery), tea rooms and Bed and Breakfasts. Here you can turn off for **Sandbanks Provincial Park**, *tel: (613) 393-3319*, which is known for its 25-m high sand dunes and long sandy beaches. There's camping, $7.50–20.75 (reservations recommended in summer; *tel: 969-8368*) and guided hikes; day visits $3.75–8 per vehicle.

The heart of Prince Edward County is **Picton**, population 4500, where Canada's first prime minister, Sir John A. Macdonald, grew up and began his law career. His father owned the stone mills at Glenora ferry dock.

The Tourist Office provides information for self-guided walking tours of the town's many historic buildings, including the refurbished 1830 **Regent Theatre**, *Main St*

103

(Hwy 33); tel: (613) 476-8416 or *(800) 667-1244*, which served as a 1920s vaudeville venue. Now it presents films, live productions (plays, ballet, etc.), and the **Quinte Summer Music Festival** in early Aug.

On the way to Glenora Ferry and adjoining the resort and inn of the same name, **Lake on the Mountain Provincial Park** is a good place for a picnic overlooking Picton Bay, if it's not windy. The lake is 62m higher than the neighbouring Bay of Quinte. The Mohawks called it *Onokenoga*, or 'Lake of the Gods', and believed that spirits lived in its waters. Early settlers believed the lake was bottomless; a more recent myth is that it's fed underground by Niagara Falls.

Glenora Ferry provides free service daily 0600–0130, every 15–30 mins.

KINGSTON

Tourist Information: Kingston Area Economic Development Commission, *209 Ontario St, Kingston, ON K7L 2Z1; tel: (613) 548-4415, fax: (613) 546-2882*, located in a former rail station by the waterfront.

ACCOMMODATION AND FOOD

Chains include *BW* (all rooms with fireplaces), *CI, DI, Hd, HJ, QI, Rm* and *TL*. Also *HI; tel: (613) 531-8237*.

The **Alexander Henry**, *55 Ontario St, Kingston, ON K7L 2Y2; tel: (613) 542-2261*, is a 64-m Canadian Coast Guard Ship moored at the Marine Museum of the Great Lakes, which offers Bed and Breakfast in officers and crew quarters (with lots of chipped deck paint) (mid May–mid Oct), budget–moderate. The **Painted Lady Inn**, *181 William St, Kingston, ON K7L 2E1; tel: (613) 545-0422*, is a centrally located Victorian home decorated with antiques, moderate. Rooms have fireplaces and Jacuzzis. The 1880s **Hochelaga Inn**, *24 Sydenham St S., Kingston, ON K7L 3G9; tel/fax: (613) 549-5534*, has 24 rooms, gardens and a verandah.

Take the ferry for budget–moderate rooms at **General Wolfe Hotel**, *Wolfe Island, ON K0H 2Y0; tel: (613) 385-2611* or *(800) 353-1098*. It has pricey gourmet dining and a second restaurant for light casual meals.

On the waterfront at Kingston's west end is 34-acre **Lake Ontario Park Campground**; *King St W.* (mailing address: *City Hall, 216 Ontario St, K7L 2Z3); tel: (613) 542-6574.*

Chez Piggy, *68R Princess St; tel: (613) 549-7673*, is owned by Zal Yanovsky, a former member of the 1960s band 'The Lovin' Spoonful'. It has a courtyard patio and serves vintage wines and microbrewery beers.

Curry Village, *169A Princess St; tel: (613) 542-5010*, serves excellent budget–moderate Indian cuisine and budget lunch specials.

Fort Henry, *at Fort Henry; tel: (613) 530-2550*, offers candlelight dining served by costumed staff, Thur–Sat 1730–2300, cheap–budget. English country brunch Sun 1030–1430. *Ontario St* is lined with restaurants, pubs and patios.

ENTERTAINMENT

The **Grand Theatre**, *218 Princess St; tel: (613) 530-2050* or *(800) 615-5666*, presents music, comedy and theatre. **Tir Nan Òg** *200 Ontario St; tel: (613) 544-7474*, is an authentic Irish pub (hand-crafted in Ireland) that features live entertainment. The four-day **Limestone City Blues Festival**; *tel: (613) 548-4415*, is held mid–late Aug.

SIGHTSEEING

Settled by fur traders in the 17th century and named capital of the United Provinces of Canada (Ontario and Québec) in 1841, Kingston today has more museums per capita than any other city in Ontario. It sits at the base of the **Rideau Canal**, a 202-km waterway with 47 locks and 24 dams that was begun shortly after the War of 1812 as a supply route to Ottawa in case of a US invasion. It's the start of the Thousand Islands region.

The **Confederation Tour Trolley**, *209 Ontario St; tel: (613) 548-4453*, departs

Boldt Castle

The story of Boldt Castle amounts to a turn-of-the-century fairy-tale. After arriving in America as a poor immigrant from Prussia, George C. Boldt worked his way from dishwasher all the way up to manager and millionaire proprietor of the world famous **Waldorf Astoria Hotel** in New York City.

Along the way, he met and married Louise Kehrer, and after the two paid a visit to the Thousand Islands, he purchased one of the smaller islands to create a tribute to her. The island, originally known as Hart, was renamed **Heart**, and he even had it re-shaped to look like one. Having seen the fabulous castles on the Rhine as a youth, he began to build one on it for Louise in 1900. For four years, more than 300 stonemasons, artists and carpenters worked on the six-storey, 120-room castle. Suddenly, in 1904 tragedy stuck – Louise fell ill and unexpectedly died. The broken-hearted Boldt ordered all work on the castle stopped, and he never returned to the island. The castle fell to neglect and remained vacant for 73 years.

Now, after restoration work, it's open to the public, operated by the Thousand Islands Bridge Authority. It is accessible by private boat, water taxi or tour. Some tours circle the castle while others allow you the opportunity to get off for several hours. The island is technically part of the USA, so foreign visitors need a visa to disembark. For current details, check with US immigration.

From Heart Island it's only a short shuttle hop to the **Yacht House**. Looking like a castle itself, the slips for boats stretch 128 ft. The current exhibit of antique boats includes three that were once owned by George C. Boldt.

105

hourly from the Tourist Office for 50-min trips past the Royal Military College, Fort Henry, Olympic Harbour, Bellevue House, Queen's University and the penitentiaries. Runs daily mid May–Sept, Sat–Sun (Sept–Oct), $6–8.

The **Maritime Museum**, *55 Ontario St; tel: (613) 542-2261,* a National Historic Site, focuses on the history of Great Lakes shipping from the 17th century, open daily 1000–1700 (May–Nov), 1000–1600 Nov–May, $3.45–4, family $8.75.

Fort Henry, *Hwy 2 at Hwy 15; tel: (613) 542-7388* or *(800) 437-2233,* was built 1832–37, where Lake Ontario meets the St Lawrence River, to protect from possible American invasion. Costumed staff present garrison life in 1867, and there are guided tours, drills and parades, open daily 1000–1700 (mid May–late Sept), $4.65–8.75, family $23.70. There's a free shuttle from the Tourist Office.

Bellevue House National Historic Site, *35 Centre St, Kingston; tel: (613) 545-8666,* is an 1840s Italianate villa that was once a home of Sir John A. Macdonald, Canada's first prime minister, open daily 0900–1800 (June–early Sept), 1000–1700 (Apr–June, early Sept–Oct), $1.40–2.75.

Correctional Service of Canada Museum, *555 King St W., tel: (613) 530-3122,* located in the former residence of the warden of Kingston Penitentiary, displays early punishment and restraint equipment, contraband weapons, escape paraphernalia and other artefacts dating to the early 1800s, open Wed–Fri 0900–1600, Sat–Sun 1000–1600 (mid May–early Sept), free.

River Cruises

An economical way to view the waterfront is on **Wolfe Island Ferry**. The 25-min ride (cars included), hourly 0545–2430, free, provides views of Fort Henry, the Royal

Military College and the sailing site from the 1976 Olympics. The island has bike rentals and camping.

Kingston 1000 Island Cruises, *1 Brock St; tel: (613) 549-5544*, operate 1-hr and 3-hr riverboat cruises, $12–17, (mid May–mid Oct), plus lunch $29.50, dinner $42, Sun dinner theatre (in Gananoque), $59.50.

GANANOQUE

Tourist Information: Thousand Islands Gananoque Chamber of Commerce, *2 King St E., Gananoque, ON K7G 1E6; tel: (613) 382-3250* or *(800) 561-1595*.

ACCOMMODATION AND FOOD

Chains include *BW* (with a log cabin at regular room rate), *DI*, *QI* and *TL*. The **Victoria Rose Inn**, *279 King St W., Gananoque, ON K7G 2G7; tel: (613) 382-3368*, offers moderate–expensive guest rooms with private bathrooms, a licenced dining room and lunch, tea or dinner on the verandah (open to non-guests Wed–Sun, moderate). **The Gananoque Inn**, *550 Stone St S., Gananoque, ON K7G 2A8; tel: (613) 382-2165* or *(800) 465-3101*, is centrally located on the waterfront with river view dining and a licenced patio. Rooms moderate–pricey, dining pricey.

In a historical limestone house, the **Golden Apple Restaurant**, *45 King St W.; tel: (613) 382-3300*, serves lunch, dinner and afternoon tea. For regional Canadian cuisine, **Cook Not Mad**, *110 Clarence St; tel: (613) 382-4361*, pricey, is open for dinner only.

SIGHTSEEING

MacLachlan Woodworking Museum, *Hwy 2; tel: (613) 542-0543*, is a two-storey log house with a 5000-piece collection of antique woodworking tools, open Wed–Sun 1000–1700 (late May–early Sept), 1200–1600 (Mar–May, Sept–Nov), $1–3.25.

Gananoque Boat Line, *Gananoque waterfront; tel: (613) 382-2144*, offers 1-hr and 3-hr cruises (300–500 passengers) of the St

Lawrence River. The 3-hr trips stop at **Boldt Castle**, a turreted stone castle built by the owner of New York's Waldorf Astoria Hotel (whose chef created Thousand Island salad dressing). You can get off at the castle, but it's US territory, so passport and visa restrictions apply. Numerous departures daily May–mid Oct, 1 hr $6–11, 3 hrs $6–16. Dockside is the historic **Thousand Islands Village**, a Heritage Centre with shops and exhibits.

Thousand Islands Playhouse; *tel: (613) 382-7020*, is a rustic turn-of-the-century building on the waterfront that presents summer theatre Tues–Sun (May–Oct), $20.

THOUSAND ISLANDS PARKWAY

From Gananoque the **Thousand Islands Parkway** stretches 37 km, lined with campsites, picnic areas, beaches and a bike trail. About 16 km from Gananoque is the village of **Ivy Lea**, where you can board one-hour cruises on **Gananoque Boat Line**, *tel: (613) 382-2146*, which go past Boldt Castle, $11. Dockside there is a restaurant, lounge and patio. Multi-language commentary. A popular camping area on the parkway is **Ivy Lea Campsite**; *tel: (613) 659-3057* or *(800) 437-2233*, operated by Parks of the St Lawrence. Across from the camping is a seasonal **Ontario East Welcome Centre** office with currency exchange.

At the **Hill Island Bridge** (to USA) you can visit 1000 Islands Skydeck, *Hill Island; tel: (613) 659-2335*. It's before the American border. On a clear day, from 121 m above the St Lawrence, you can see from Kingston to Brockville. There is a restaurant, open daily year round, $3.95–6.95.

The next village is **Rockport** where you can stop at the **Boathouse Country Inn**, *19 Front St, Rockport, ON K0E 1V0; tel: (613) 659-2348* or *(800) 584-2592*, which has a restaurant and waterside patio (pies a speciality). Eight motel-style rooms are available, moderate. **Heritage Boat Tours**, *tel: (613) 659-3151*, depart from here every

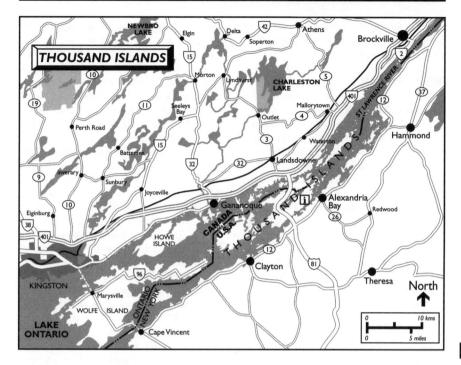

30 mins. The service acts as a shuttle to Boldt Castle, $8–11. Next door, **Rockport Boat Line**; *tel: (613) 659-3402 or (800) 563-8687,* provides 1-hr cruises and a separate shuttle to the castle. There's a restaurant, patio, gift shop and dive centre (mid May–mid Oct), $7–11. Shuttle $7–10, Sat–Sun only (Sept–mid Oct) .

Stop at **St Lawrence Islands National Park**, *tel: (613) 923-5261,* for a swim and picnic and information on island campsites. Entry $5 per vehicle. Among the Thousand Islands are 21 that form St Lawrence Islands National Park. On these islands are 72 campsites, which are accessible by boat. The islands also have day-use picnic facilities, but you must arrange transportation. Day use $5–12 per boat. Island camping $10.

BROCKVILLE

Tourist Information: Brockville Tourism, *P.O. Box 5000, 1 King St W.,* *Brockville, ON K6V 7A5; tel: (613) 342-8772, ext 430.*

Brockville is Ontario's oldest incorporated municipality and the eastern gateway to the Thousand Islands. The focal point of the city, which was founded in 1765, is its 1842 **Court House Square**. The area is accented murals and patterned tiled roofs. Ocean-going vessels can be spotted from the historic waterfront.

ACCOMMODATION AND FOOD

There's *BW, CI, DI* and *S8.* The **Royal Brock Hotel Spa and Sports Club**, *100 Stuart St (Hwy 29); tel: (800) 267-4428,* moderate–expensive, is known for its wine list, and has live entertainment nightly in the lounge. **Robertson House Inn Bed and Breakfast**, *10 Broad St, Brockville, ON K6V 4T7; tel: (613) 345-7378,* is a stone home that has been designated a historic landmark. Its dining room chef formerly prepared catering for Japan's prime minister. The owner also has a dive shop. Lodging moderate, dining moderate–pricey.

SIGHTSEEING

Also down by the historic waterfront is the **Brockville Museum**, *5 Henry St; tel: (613) 342-4397*, in one of the city's oldest homes, which illustrates the town's history, open Mon–Sat 1000–1700, Sun 1300–1700 (mid May–mid Oct), Mon–Fri 1000–1630 (mid Oct–mid May), $0.75–2. Canada's oldest underground railway tunnel (built in 1854) is the **Brockville Railway Tunnel** in Armagh Sefton Price Park, overlooking the St Lawrence, south of *Market St,* open mid June–early Sept, free. **Thousand Islands and Seaway Cruises**, *Blockhouse Island; tel: (613) 345-7333*, operate 1- and 3-hr cruises (May–late Dec), $8–17.

A popular stop is **Fulford Place**, *287 King St E.; tel: (613) 498-3003*, an Edwardian mansion built in 1899 by Senator George Taylor Fulford from money earned from his cure-all remedy, Pink Pills for Pale People, open Wed–Sun 1100–1600 (June–mid Oct), Sat–Sun 1100–1600 (mid Oct–late May), $3–4.

On Tues, Thur and Sat, a **Farmers Market** is held beside City Hall 0700–1300. In late June, the ten-day **Riverfest** is celebrated with fireworks and street entertainment.

BROCKVILLE TO OTTAWA

At the east end of Prescott, **Fort Wellington National Historic Site**, *370 Van-Koughnet St; tel: (613) 925-2896*, restored to 1840s-style, is staffed by costumed interpreters, open daily 1000–1700 (mid May–late Sept), $1.50–3. About 2 km further east on Hwy 2 is **Windmill Point**, a stone windmill that is a National Historic Site.

From **Iroquois**, where there is a viewing deck beside the lock, it's 13 km to **Morrisburg**, home of **Upper Canada Playhouse**, *Hwy 2, Box 852, Morrisburg, ON K0C 1X0, tel: (613) 543-3713*, a theatre in an old

toothbrush factory, open July–Sept, $7–16. About 9 km east of Morrisburg, is **Prehistoric World**, *Hwy 2; tel: (613) 543-2503*, where brothers Paul and Serge Dupuis have spent 20 years creating 40 life-size dinosaurs, which are displayed along nature trails through the forest, open daily 1000–1600 (late May–early Sept), Sat only (early Sept–mid Oct), $3–6.

About 2 km further east is **Upper Canada Village**, *Hwy 2, tel: (613) 543-3704*, one of Ontario's most popular tourist sites. More than 40 historic buildings threatened by flooding for the St Lawrence Seaway were moved, creating a village with costumed interpreters who role-play Ontario life of the mid 19th century. You can smell bread baking, see a class in session at a one-room school house, listen to a speaker advocating temperance and enjoy a period meal at the local hotel, open daily mid May–mid Oct, $6–12.75; dining, a large craft souvenir shop and tourist information are on site.

At **Ingleside**, about 19 km from Morrisburg, you can turn north for Ottawa. **Upper Canada Migratory Bird Sanctuary**, *Hwy 2, Ingleside; tel: (613) 537-2024*, has 3500 acres of hiking trails through wetlands and woodlands, plus public nature programmes. Sanctuary open year round, nature programmes May–Oct, $2.50; watch for thousands of ducks and geese mid Sept–early Oct.

Ingleside is also located at the beginning of the **Long Sault Parkway**, a 10-km scenic drive on causeways and bridges that link 11 islands that were created during the development of the St Lawrence Seaway and Power Project, $1.75–2.25.

As you travel north on Rd 14 then Rd 12, the **MacLeod House Bed & Breakfast and Cafe**, *32 Front St, Finch, ON K0C 1K0; tel: (613) 984-0101*, makes a good stop. Formerly the home of the village doctor and decorated with antiques, it offers two homely rooms, full breakfast included, budget. The Bed and Breakfast is open year round; the café closes late Dec–early Feb.

OTTAWA AND HULL

Despite being the capital of a vast ocean-to-ocean country, Ottawa is much smaller – and comparatively less-visited by travellers from abroad – than Toronto and nearby Montréal. However, the city has considerable appeal as a major centre of Canadian history and culture along with its worldly political stature.

Three rivers converge north-east of downtown, and the park-bordered Rideau Canal curves 7.8 km right through the heart of Ottawa. Those waterways were strategic when Queen Victoria ruled Britannia. Hence her decision, in 1857, to make what was then a roughneck lumberjack village capital of the empire's Upper and Lower Canada (Ontario and Québec provinces). Since then, a bilingual governmental mini-metropolis has evolved.

Most parliamentary doings chug along in Ottawa, Ontario. Some offices and ministries, however, function across the Ottawa (French: Outaouais) River in francophone Hull, Québec. So welcome to what's called, collectively, Canada's Capital Region; Ottawa has 317,000 citizens, Hull 61,000.

TOURIST INFORMATION

Ottawa Tourism & Convention Authority, *130 Albert St, Suite 1800, Ottawa, ON K1P 5G4; tel: (613) 237-5150 or (800) 363-4465* (toll-free), can provide brochures, maps and other materials.

The National Capital Commission's **Infocentre**, *90 Wellington St; tel: (613) 239-5000 or (800) 465-1867,* open daily 0830–2100 (mid May–early Sept), 0900–1700 (early Sept–mid May), with its 16 TouchNet computer/video terminals, is an excellent information and reservations resource covering the entire Capital Region.

Association touristique de l'Outaouais, *103 r. Laurier, Hull PQ, J8X 3V8; tel: (819) 778-2222 or (800) 265-7822,* open Mon–Fri 0830–2000, Sat–Sun 0900–1700 (mid June–early Sept), Mon–Fri 0830–1700, Sat–Sun 0900–1600 (early Sept–mid June), can be contacted for in-depth information about Hull as well as Québec province's outdoorsy Outaouais tourist region.

WEATHER

Discounting nature's variables, the mid-summer climate tends to be hot and sometimes humid, with temperatures apt to reach 29°–32°C. Springtime is ordinarily brief but flowery and delightful, in the 10°–13°C range; nippier autumn temperatures bring crisp air and gorgeous foliage, with the first frost usually coming in early Oct. If you like snow, ice and deep-down thermometer readings, you'll love a winter visit to the capital. For daily weather reports; *tel: (613) 998-3439.*

ARRIVING AND DEPARTING

Airport
Macdonald-Cartier International Airport; *tel: (613) 998-1427,* handles non-stop flights from and to Montréal, Québec City and Toronto, plus Newark, Boston, Washington and Chicago in the USA. Direct service is also available between London in the UK and Ottawa, usually entailing flight connections in Montréal or New York. Air

Canada, however, operates a non-stop London–Ottawa service during the summer season commencing in June. Shuttle-bus service costs $9 to ten downtown hotels, $14 returning to the airport. Taxicab fare for the 20-min drive averages $20–25.

By Bus
For information about **Voyageur Colonial** bus service; *tel: (613) 238-5000* or *(613) 238-6668* in Ottawa, *(819) 771-2442* in Hull. Voyageur motorcoaches make numerous daily runs between Ottawa/Hull and Montréal (175 km) and Toronto (349 km).

By Rail
Ottawa is on the Canadian **VIA Rail** network, with frequent service between the capital and major cities in Ontario and Québec. The train station is east of the city centre at *200 Tremblay Rd; tel: (613) 244-8289.*

GETTING AROUND

Public Transport
Hop aboard **OC Transpo** buses for exact-change $1.85 adult fare; *tel: (613) 741-4390.* On Hull's side of the river, **STO** buses provide a comparably efficient service; exact-change adult fare, $2.60; *tel: (819) 770-3242.*

Driving in Ottawa and Hull
A grid pattern makes city-centre streets reasonably easy to navigate. White-on-blue pictogram signs guide motorists towards key landmarks, and four bridges connect Ottawa and Hull. Parking meters in both locales gobble $0.25 coins at the rate of one per 15 mins during weekdays, and on-street overnight parking is prohibited during wintertime. So avoid undue stress by leaving your car at a public garage for full-day cost of about $6–10.
    Validate vouchers at the Infocentre for free one-hour parking in the **World Exchange Plaza's underground garage**,

between Albert and Metcalfe Sts. At the above-indicated 'La Maison du tourisme' office on Hull's *r. Laurier*, ask for a visitor's parking pass, valid for one full day in Hull.
    Primary Canadian motorways into the metro area are Hwy 417 (westward from Montréal and Québec City, eastward from Toronto), and Hwy 148 from the direction of Montréal and Québec City.

Bicycles
A parkland greenbelt and lanes alongside the Rideau Canal amount to a metropolitan network of more than 150 km – terrific landscape for outings on both sides of the Ottawa River. During 'Sunday Bikedays', mid May–Aug, the entire 7.6-km length of Ottawa's **Colonel By Drive** stays wondrously free of motor-vehicle traffic, 0900–1300. Two-wheelers are available May–Oct at **Rent-a-Bike**, *1 Rideau St (behind the Château Laurier); tel: (613) 241-4140.* Bikes can be rented year round at another downtown location: **Sunshine Bicycles**, *161 Laurier Ave W.; tel: (613) 230-1845.* For rentals in Hull, contact **Cycle Bertrand**, *136 r. Eddy; (819) 771-6858.*

STAYING IN OTTAWA

Accommodation
In-town hotel chains include *BW, CI, De, DI, HJ, Nv, Rd, Rm, Sh, Su, S8, TL* and *We* – along with the grand-luxe *CP* **Château Laurier**, *1 Rideau St, Ottawa, ON K1N 8S7; tel: (613) 241-1414* or *(800) 441-1414.*
    Moderate–expensive accommodations consisting of suites with kitchenettes are plentiful. For example, **Minto Place Suite Hotel**, *433 Laurier Ave W., Ottawa, ON K1R 7Y1; tel: (613) 232-2200* or *(800) 267-3377.* Another is **Les Suites Hotel**, *130 Besserer St, Ottawa, ON K1N 9M9; tel: (613) 232-2000* or *(800) 267-1989.* Also, the **Albert at Bay Suite Hotel**, *435 Albert St, Ottawa, ON K1R 7X4; tel: (613) 238-8858* or *(800) 267-6644*; **Capital Hill Hotel &**

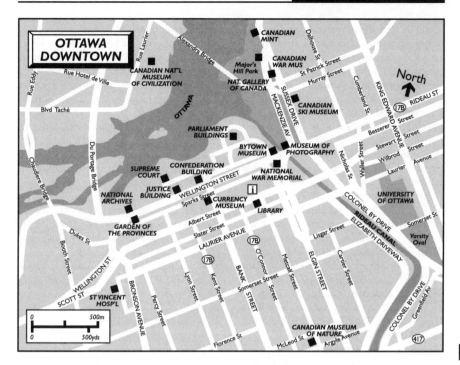

OTTAWA
DOWNTOWN

North ↑

CANADIAN MINT
CANADIAN WAR MUS
Major's Hill Park
St Patrick Street
Murray Street
Cumberland St.
KING EDWARD AVENUE
RIDEAU ST
CANADIAN NAT'L MUSEUM OF CIVILIZATION
NAT. GALLERY OF CANADA
SUSSEX DRIVE
MACKENZIE AV
CANADIAN SKI MUSEUM
Besserer Street
Stewart Street
Wilbrod Street
Laurier Avenue
Rue Laurier
Alexandra Bridge
Rue Hotel de Ville
Rue Eddy
Blvd Taché
PARLIAMENT BUILDINGS
OTTAWA
BYTOWN MUSEUM
MUSEUM OF PHOTOGRAPHY
SUPREME COURT
CONFEDERATION BUILDING
NATIONAL WAR MEMORIAL
JUSTICE BUILDING
WELLINGTON STREET
Sparks Street
CURRENCY MUSEUM
LIBRARY
NATIONAL ARCHIVES
GARDEN OF THE PROVINCES
Albert Street
Slater Street
LAURIER AVENUE
Nicholas St.
Waller Street
COLONEL BY DRIVE
UNIVERSITY OF OTTAWA
Lisgar Street
RIDEAU CANAL
ELIZABETH DRIVEWAY
Somerset St
Varsity Oval
Du Portage Bridge
Chaudiere Bridge
Dukes St
Booth Street
WELLINGTON ST.
SCOTT ST
ST VINCENT HOSP'L
BRONSON AVENUE
Percy Street
Lyon Street
Kent Street
BANK STREET
Somerset Street
O'Connor Street
Metcalf Street
ELGIN STREET
Cartier Street
COLONEL BY DRIVE
Greenfield Av
CANADIAN MUSEUM OF NATURE
Florence St
McLeod St
Argyle Avenue
417

0   500m
0   500yds

111

Suites, *88 Albert St, Ottawa, ON K1P 5E9; tel: (613) 235-6047 or (800) 463-7705.*

A stalwart city landmark since opening in 1941, the genteel **Lord Elgin**, *100 Elgin St, Ottawa, ON K1P 5K8; tel: (613) 235-3333 or (800) 267-4298*, combines moderate room rates with an all-purpose location. For a similar price range but more of a modern business/convention alternative, consider the **Citadel Ottawa**, *101 Lyon St, Ottawa, ON K1R 5T9; tel: (613) 237-3600 or (800) 567-3600*. The ten-room **Carmichael**, *46 Cartier St, Ottawa, ON K2P 1J3; tel: (613) 236-4667*, is a pricey, posh, inn and health spa. Kids under 12 stay and eat free at the moderate, few-frills **Market Square Inn**, *350 Dalhousie St, Ottawa, ON K1N 7E9; tel: (613) 241-1000 or (800) 341-2210*, in the heart-of-town Byward Market district.

Three moderate Bed and Breakfasts are in officially designated 'heritage' dwellings: **Albert House Inn**, *478 Albert St, Ottawa,*

ON K1R 5B5; tel: (613) 236-4479 or (800) 267-1982; **Olde Bytowne Bed and Breakfast,** *459 Laurier Ave E., Ottawa, ON K1N 6R4; tel: (613) 565-7939;* gemütlich **Gasthaus Switzerland**, *89 Daly Ave, Ottawa, ON K1N 6E6; tel: (613) 237-0335 or (800) 267-8788.*

The closest May–Oct camping place is **Ottawa-Nepean Municipal Campsite**, *411 Corkstown Rd, Nepean, ON K2G 5K7; tel: (613) 828-6632, (613) 727-6610* off season – a 20–30-min drive south-west of downtown, in a wooded section of the regional greenbelt. A gaol for 104 years now exists more benignly as the **Ottawa International Hostel**, *75 Nicholas St, Ottawa, ON K1N 7B9; tel: (613) 235-2595.*

Eating and Drinking

Inherently multicultural to start with, Ottawa has, at last count, 111 foreign embassies and missions. There's your basic explanation for the restaurant scene's zest and variety. Visitors can 'go ethnic' in any number of exotic directions, either spending a bundle whilst doing so or contentedly scrutinising money-saver menus.

For French haute cuisine, take your pick between **Le Jardin**, *127 York St; tel: (613) 241-1828,* or **Wilfrid's** in the Château Laurier, *1 Rideau St; tel: (613) 241-1414.* A moderate–pricey steak or seafood meal served out on its namesake courtyard is delightful at a stone heritage building, the **Courtyard Restaurant**, *21 George St; tel: (613) 241-1516.* Looking for something ethnic and moderate? Ponder **Silk Roads Café** (Afghan), *47 William St; tel: (613) 241-4254;* **Casablanca Resto** (Moroccan), *41 Clarence St; tel: (613) 789-7855;* **Café Shafali** (Indian), *308 Dalhousie St; tel: (613) 789-9188;* **Polonus** (Polish), *87 George St; tel: (613) 241-6143;* **Suisha Gardens** (Japanese); *208 Slater St; tel: (613) 236-9602;* **Don Alfonso** (Spanish); *434 Bank St; tel: (613) 236-7750;* **Pancho Villa** (Mexican/Tex-Mex); *361 Elgin St; tel: (613) 234-8872;* **New Dubrovnik Dining Lounge** (Croatian); *1170 Carling Ave; tel: (613) 722-1490;* **Fairouz** (Lebanese); *343 Somerset St W.; tel: (613) 233-1536;* and **Korea Garden**, *470 Rideau St; tel: (613) 789-5496.* **Santé**, *45 Rideau St; tel: (613) 241-7113,* cooks up Caribbean–Mediterranean–Thai fusion dishes in an art-gallery setting. For pricey continental cuisine: **Noah's**, *407 Laurier Ave W.; tel: (613) 782-2422,* or the **Euro Café House**, *499 Sussex Dr.; tel: (613) 241-2412.* Also pricey is **Hy's**, a top-notch steak house, *170 Queen St; tel: (613) 234-4545.* Moderate–pricey **La Ronde**, atop the Radisson Hotel; *tel: (613) 783-4212,* is Ottawa's only high-altitude revolving restaurant.

The Old Fish Market can't be beaten for inexpensive seafood, *54 York St; tel: (613) 241-3474.* You'll spend somewhat more for Louisiana-style Cajun catfish and blackened alligator(!) at **Big Daddy's Crab Shack**

and Oyster Bar, *339 Elgin St; tel: (613) 569-5200.* Paying for lunch or dinner won't break the bank at **Major's Brew House**, *453 Sussex Dr.; tel: (613) 789-7405.*

Two choices for moderate–expensive Canadian specialities are **The Marble Works**, *14 Waller St; tel: (613) 241-6764,* and **Le Café** in the National Arts Centre; *tel: (613) 594-5127.* A light meal's bonus extra at the **Plaza Café**, *101 Sparks St; tel: (613) 563-0636,* is a knockout view of Parliament Hill's Peace Tower, and a jazz combo entertains on Fri and Sat evenings. Thin-crust gourmet pizzas are shovelled out of a wood-burning oven at **Oscar's**, *123 Queen St; tel: (613) 234-9699,* a moderate California-Italian grill with an upstairs pub.

If you're on a budget, **Dunn's**, *57 Bank St; tel: (613) 230-4005,* typifies all that's expected of a Jewish-Canadian deli, and **Nickels**, *128 George St; tel: (613) 562-9865,* is a burger-fries-milkshake eatery loaded with retro-1950s pop-cultural miscellanea.

Budget–moderate city-centre trattorias, both tomato-sauce-traditional and *nuovo*, are ubiquitous. Or delve instead into Ottawa's 'Corso Italia' neighbourhood to eat at **Trattoria Italia Dining Lounge & Caffé**, *228 Preston St; tel: (613) 236-1081.*

The western stretch of *Somerset St* runs through **Chinatown**, lately multiplied by culinary Vietnamese incursions. A particularly good Cantonese-Szechuan choice would be **Fuliwah**, *691 Somerset St W.; tel: (613) 233-2552.* For an 'Oriental difference': **Viet Nam Palace**, *819 Somerset St W.; tel: (613) 238-6758.* The décor and chef's specials are both sensational at **Maplelawn Café**, *529 Richmond Rd; tel: (613) 722-5118,* occupying a restored 1831 Georgian mansion in the West End.

STAYING IN HULL

Accommodation
Central Hull's three chain hotels are *BW, Cr* and *Hd.* West of town, near riverside

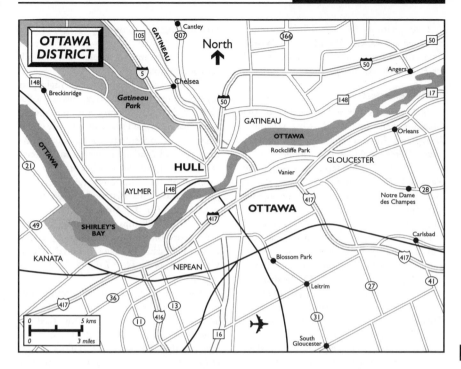

Aylmer, is the sprawling, pricey **Château Cartier Sheraton Hotel and Golf Resort**, *110 Aylmer Rd, Aylmer, PQ J9H 5E1; tel: (819) 777-1088 or (800) 807-1088.*

Forty-two guest rooms are in architecturally rakish moderate–expensive **Auberge de la Gare**, *205 blvd St-Joseph, Hull, PQ J8Y 3X3; tel: (819) 778-8085 or (800) 361-6162.* Two of several budget–moderate Bed and Breakfasts are **Au Versant de la Montagne**, *19 r. Du Versant, Hull, PQ J8Z 2T8; tel: (819) 776-3760,* and **La Maison Sanche**, *245 Papineau St, Hull, PQ J8X 1W9; tel: (819) 595-0095.*

Eating and Drinking

Hull's francophone essence accounts for its proportionate number of French restaurants. **Café Henry Burger**, *69 r. Laurier; tel: (819) 777-5646,* qualifies as the best-known and longest-established. Another, with a garden patio and featuring extensive *table d'hôte*

selections, is pricey **Le Tartuffe**, *133 r. Notre-Dame; tel: (819) 776-6424.*

Daily *table d'hôte* offerings are also on the menu in a petite cottage with side patio: **La Soupiére**, *53 r. Kent; tel: (819) 771-6256,* moderate–expensive. Same cost category, plus Parisian bonhomie is available at **Le Pied de Cochon**, *248 r. Montcalm; tel: (819) 777-5808.* Gallic, too, **L'Aubry Café**, *5 pl. Aubry; tel: (819) 777-3700,* occupies a brick townhouse overlooking a little plaza sporting a cast-iron fountain, moderate.

If you'd prefer a casual budget–moderate bistro for unassuming but hearty French-Canadian fare and micro-brewed beers, **Le Twist Café-Bar**, *88 r. Montcalm; tel: (819) 777-8886,* would fit the bill.

Communications and Money

You'll find a **central post office** at the corner of *Elgin and Sparks Sts; tel: (613) 844-1545.*

Two handy facilities for currency exchange are **ACCU-RATE** in the **World Exchange Plaza**, *Albert and Metcalfe* Sts, and the **Royal Bank**, *90 Sparks St.*

ENTERTAINMENT

Each Thursday's *Going Out* section of the *Ottawa Citizen* updates showbiz schedules throughout the area. Another such guide is Ottawa's free weekly *X Press* tabloid.

The city's modernistic, canalside **National Arts Centre**, *53 Elgin St; tel: (613) 947-7000,* is Canada's most prestigious performing arts venue, encompassing three stages for English and French theatre, in addition to ballet, musicals and international pop star and variety shows. For classical music enthusiasts, English maestro Trevor Pinnock conducts the **NAC Orchestra**; the centre is also home of **Opera Lyra Ottawa**.

Elsewhere, the **Great Canadian Theatre Company**, *910 Gladstone Ave; tel: (613) 236-5196,* focuses on Canadian playwrights as well as Shakespearean comedies. The **Ottawa Little Theatre**, *400 King Edward Ave; tel: (613) 233-8948,* presents popular works. For avant-garde productions on an open-air stage in Strathcoma Park, there's the summer season's **Odyssey Theatre**, *2 Daly Ave; tel: (613) 232-8407.*

Orchestre de chambre de Hull, *tel: (819) 595-0265,* performs chamber music in a Canadian Museum of Civilization theatre. Also in this museum: the **Cinéplus**, *tel: (819) 776-7010,* a hemispheric dome for a sensual barrage of cinema-watching on its IMAX-OMNIMAX wraparound screen.

High-wattage glitz and glamour pervades **Casino de Hull**, *1 blvd du Casino; tel: (819) 772-2100 or (800) 665-2274,* opened in 1996, just 4 km from city-centre Ottawa, open daily 1100–0300. Along with 45 gaming tables and 1250 slot machines, this perpetually hyperactive complex includes bars, lounges and buffet and gourmet restaurants. The dress code, perhaps surprisingly, is 'tastefully casual' rather than jacket-and-neck tie.

Free parking if you come by car. Otherwise, a complimentary shuttle-bus service is available from and to several (but not all) downtown hotels.

Ottawa has an abundance of nightspots reverberating to rock, jazz, blues, folk/Celtic and twangy country stuff, plus discos, a few piano bars and stand-up comedy clubs. The thickest concentration is around the historic Byward Market, as well as on the city centre's *Elgin* and *Rideau Elgin* Sts.

One of the consistently grooviest jazz joints is **Maxwell's Bistro**, *340 Elgin St; tel: (613) 232-5771.* **Le Bop**, *9 pl. Aubry; tel: (819) 777-3700,* tops a smattering of Hull dance bars that jump 'til 0300. Near the Byward Market, Ottawa's **Hard Rock Café**, *73 York St; tel: (613) 241-2442,* packs 'em in.

Brit-style Ottawan pubs offering live entertainment as well as elemental victuals and import brews include **The Earl of Sussex**, *431 Sussex Dr.; tel: (613) 562-5544,* and **Double Deckers**, *62 William St; tel: (613) 241-0066.* For a Guinness and folk songs in an Irish pub, head for **Molly McGuire's**, *130 George St; (613) 241-1972,* or the **Heart & Crown**, *67 Clarence St; tel: (613) 5562-0674.* **BJ's Boom Boom Saloon**, *200 Rideau St; tel: (613) 562-2512,* along with being Ottawa's biggest dance club, has five bars and 15 billiard tables.

Special summertime 'happenings' cover a broad musical spectrum: July's **Bluesfest** and the **Ottawa International Jazz Festival**, the July–Aug **Ottawa Chamber Music Festival** and the **Ottawa Folk Festival** in Aug.

Spectator Sports

The **Ottawa Senators** skate against National Hockey League opponents Sept–Apr in the new **Corel Centre**, *1000 Palladium Dr.; tel: (613) 599-0250,* in west-suburban Kanata. (The 18,500-seat arena hosts other sports events along with ice shows and celebrity-superstar concert appearances.)

The **Ottawa Lynx**, a farm team of major league baseball's Montréal Expos, play Apr–Sept in fan-friendly **Jetform Park** stadium, *300 Coventry Rd; tel: (613) 749-9947.*

Harness-style horse-racing is featured afternoons and evenings May–Nov at southeast suburban Gloucester's **Rideau Carleton Raceway**, *4837 Albion Rd; tel: (613) 822-2211.*

Events

The Capital Region buzzes with an all-seasons succession of festivals. **Winterlude**, on three consecutive Fri–Sun weekends in Feb, has become one of the world's most exuberant cold-weather celebrations since its inaugural in 1979. Primary attractions are skating on the frozen-over Rideau Canal and ice-sculpturing competitions.

Dutch citizens have been donating tulip bulbs to Ottawa annually since 1945, their gesture of appreciation for refuge provided to Princess Juliana and her family during World War II. That, in turn, inspired May's week-long **Canadian Tulip Festival**, an explosion of colour when some 3 million of the springtime flowers are in full bloom. (A 10-km 'Tulip Route' follows the Rideau Canal.)

Le Festival Franco-ontarien in June highlights French-Canadian cuisine, artists, craftspeople and street performers. Staunchly francophone Hull whoops it up during Québec province's big annual bash, **La Fête de Saint-Jean-Baptiste**, each 24 June, concluding with after-dark bonfires. Then comes 1 July's **Canada Day**, commemorating the country's becoming a full-fledged Confederation in 1867. The grand finale is a razzle-dazzle fireworks display above Parliament Hill.

Taste of Ottawa, four days in late July–early Aug, is a massive outdoor food-a-rama accompanied by music and entertainment. In Lansdowne Park, mid Aug's **Central Canada Exhibition** – which is locally called the 'Ex' – is an old-fashioned country fair with agricultural pavilions, a carnival midway, thrill rides and humongous gobs of food. Earlier that month, **Fête Caribe** enlivens downtown with nine days of Caribbean parades and partying.

Gatineau, a Québec community adjacent to Hull, puts on Canada's biggest **Hot Air Balloon Festival** in La Baie Park during the last weekend of Aug. For a month spanning early Dec to early Jan, **Christmas Lights Across Canada** sets Parliament Hill and four dozen other sites throughout the capital ablaze with 200,000 tiny lights in a myriad of colours.

Recreation

With 40 courses in the Ottawa/Hull area, it shouldn't be difficult to fit a game of golf into your stay. For 'where', ask at the Infocentre or call the **National Golf Course Owners' Association**; *tel: (613) 826-1046* or *(800) 660-0091.*

Whitewater rafting on the Ottawa River is another choice. Two sources are situated west of town: **Esprit Rafting**, *Pembroke, ON K8A 6X7; tel: (819) 683-3241* or *(800) 596-RAFT,* and **OWL Rafting**, *Foresters Falls, ON K0J 1V0; tel: (613) 238-7238* or *(800) 461-7238.* The Canada Capital Region's biggest and best 'urban beach' isn't far from central Hull, on the shore of **Leamy Lake**, *Leamy Lake Rd.*

Downtown's **Rideau Centre** is an urban mega-mall chock full of 200-plus retail establishments. Contrast that with the nearby, mid 19th-century **Byward Market**, now mostly occupied by vendors of artsy-craftsy items.

Along the four-block **Sparks Street Mall**, Canada's earliest auto-free urban corridor, storefronts flank rock gardens, fountains and benches for a congenial shopping environment. You'll find a **Marks & Spencer** branch and high-fashion **Holt**

Renfrew. Two stores specialising in Canadian and native Indian/Inuit crafts are also in this pedestrian zone: **Canada's Four Corners**, *93 Sparks St; tel: (613) 233-2322,* and **The Snow Goose**, *83 Sparks St; tel: (613) 232-2213.*

Another tempting window-shopping area is called the **Bank Street Promenade**: a 15-block stretch of north-south *Bank St,* from *Wellington St* to *Gladstone Ave.* An assortment of little boutiques are inside downtown's **World Exchange Plaza** and equally slick **Place de Ville**. For an offbeat alternative, go further south on *Bank St* to a neighbourhood, weirdly known as the **Glebe**, to browse an eclectic batch of speciality shops. If you're passionate about collectables, 50 independent dealers display their wares in the **Ottawa Antique Market**, *1179-A Bank St; tel: (613) 730-6000,* open daily 1000–1800.

Sales Taxes

Since you'll quite likely be going back and forth between two provinces during your stay in Canada's Capital Region, be mindful of the taxation differences. Ontario's retail sales tax is 8% – plus 8% restaurant taxation on food, a hefty 16% on alcoholic beverages and 5% on accommodation. In Québec, a 6.5% tax is slapped onto merchandise, food, liquor and accommodation. Also factor in the 7% national Goods and Services Tax (GST), which Canadians lovingly nickname their 'Gouge and Screw Tax'. Non-residents can apply for **rebates** (see Travel Essentials, p. 31).

SIGHTSEEING

By Bus

Capital Trolley Tours; *tel: (613) 729-6888,* enable riders to step off, then afterwards reboard another jaunty trolley bus, thus combining narrated sightseeing with self-guided looking-around. The 90-min tours operate mid May–mid Nov, $13–16.

By Foot

Meandering, professionally guided **Ottawa Walks** tours; *tel: (613) 692-3571,* provide citywide close-ups and insights. Year round, $4.50–6. For self-guided touring opening onto sensational views of the Ottawa River and Parliament Hill, follow maple-leaf signposts and colourful banners that distinguish **Confederation Boulevard**, a walkable 2-km loop interconnecting *Wellington St*, Pont du Portage Bridge, *r. Laurier* in Hull and Pont Alexandra Bridge.

By Boat

Two vessels operated by **Ottawa Riverboat Company**; *tel: (613) 562-4888,* take passengers on 90-min riverine excursions for skyline panoramics of Ottawa and Hull, including dinner and brunch cruises; early May–late Nov, $10–12. During the same seasons, **Paul's Boat Lines**; *tel: (613) 225-6781,* operate smooth Rideau Canal cruises (75 mins), as well as breezier Ottawa River outings (90 mins), $10–12.

Architecture

Nothing evokes prideful Canadian nationhood with greater visual impact than the ensemble of monumental buildings spread over **Parliament Hill**, a craggy 46-m escarpment on the Ottawa River's south bank. 'The Hill' consists primarily of three neo-Gothic structures: East Block, West Block and Centre Block, the latter with rearend, circular **Library of Parliament** attachment, and topped for all to see by the 89-m **Peace Tower** – Ottawa's Big Ben – with its clock, 53-bell carillon and, inside, the Hall of Honour in remembrance of Canada's war dead. Free daily Centre Block tours are conducted year round; East Block early July–early Sept. A white **Infotent** situated between Centre and West Blocks is staffed to provide full details, mid May–early Sept.

Changing the Guard, a ceremonial crowd-pleaser on the front lawn, entails the Governor General's Foot Guards' and

Canadian Grenadier Guards' drill routines and martial band music; daily (weather permitting) 1000–1030, late June–late Aug. But that stirringly traditional pomp is outdone by a patriotic showstopper entitled *Reflections of Canada: A Symphony of Sound and Light* – the national saga set to words, music, film and multicoloured laser images projected giant-size onto Parliament Hill's buildings; nightly (weather permitting) 2130 and 2230 (one 45-min show in English, one in French), mid May–early Sept.

Canada's **National War Memorial**, a granite arch dedicated by King George VI in 1939, dominates **Confederation Square**, a traffic roundabout where *Wellington, Sparks* and *Elgin Sts* converge to become 'Confusion Square' in honour of Ottawa's mild version of vehicular rush hour. A much newer (1992) **National Reconciliation Monument**, *Sussex Dr. and St Patrick St,* with sculpted figures atop knife-like edges of limestone, is dedicated to modern-day Canadian peacekeepers who have served in zones of conflict around the world.

Completed in 1858, **Notre-Dame Cathedral-Basilica**, *385 Sussex Dr.; tel: (613) 241-7496,* is Ottawa's oldest church, featuring painted and carved woodwork, an opulent main altar, stained-glass windows and twin steeples surrounding gilded Madonna and Child statues. Montréal and Québec City have nothing on the capital city when it comes to prominent statues of explorer-discoverer Samuel de Champlain. Ottawa's version, holding a navigational astrolabe, stands high atop **Nepean Point**, near the southern end of the Pont Alexandra Bridge.

Celebrity architect Moshe Safdie created additions to the **Ottawa City Hall**, *11 Sussex Dr.; tel: (613) 244-5464,* in futuristic love-it-or-hate-it style. Judge for yourself by observing the impressive Green Island site. Hull's city hall, **La Maison du Citoyen**, *25 r. Laurier; tel: (819) 595-7175,* makes nearly as radical a design statement and includes a library, art gallery and fitness centre along with the requisite municipal offices.

Historic Houses

A grandiose 1838 mansion on a garden estate, **Rideau Hall**, *1 Sussex Dr.; tel: (613) 998-7113,* is home of the Governor General, British royalty's official representative in the Dominion, open Sat–Sun 1000–1600 (mid May–late June), daily 1000–1600 (late Aug–1 Sept), Sat–Sun 1200–1500 (early Sept–mid Oct), free. The ceremonial 'Relief of the Sentries' takes place each hour 1000–1800 daily (late June–late Aug).

Laurier House, *335 Laurier Ave E.; tel: (613) 992-8142,* was the residence of prime ministers Sir Wilfred Laurier and William Lyon Mackenzie King, who, according to legend, communed with the ghost of his dear departed mother in the third-storey study, open Tues–Sat 0900–1700, Sun 1400–1700 (early Apr–late Sept), $2.75. The **Billings Estate**, *2100 Cabot St; tel: (613) 247-4830,* dating from 1812, was originally the home of a pioneering family and includes heritage plantings, picnic grounds and English summertime refreshments served at the Tea-on-the-Lawn, open Sun–Thur 1200–1700 (early May–late Oct), $2.50.

Parks

Downtown's **Major's Hill Park**, the oldest segment of the capital region's contiguous public greenspace, was developed in 1874 and couldn't be more advantageously situated for skyline, river and canal panoramics. Even more central, **Confederation Park**, *Elgin St and Laurier Ave,* is a natural for festive events and noteworthy, moreover, because its fountain once splashed in London's Trafalgar Square.

Not surprising, numerous ambassadorial residences grace an upper-crust neighbourhood fringing **Rockcliffe Park** (*OC Transpo line 4),* with an Ottawa River Belvédère lookout and **Rockcliffe Rookeries**, abloom with spring and fall flowers.

117

Another flowery spread is **Commissioners Park** *(Queen Elizabeth Driveway, OC Transpo lines 3 and 85)* alongside Dows Lake, surrounded by scenic pathways; Dows Lake Pavilion has three informal restaurants and a summer terrace, as well as facilities for canoe, pedal-boat, rollerblade and ice-skate rentals.

Walk east through the elegant Sandy Hill residential district on *Laurier Ave* (or take *OC Transpo line 5*) to reach **Strathcona Park**, shaded by old trees and a haven for swans paddling on the Rideau River. An attractively landscaped little park overlooking **Hog's Back Falls** *(OC Transpo lines 3 and 111)* is a rocky vantage point where the Rideau Canal meets the cascading Rideau River. That same waterway crashes louder and falls further whilst thundering 9 m down into the Ottawa River, hence the **Rideau Falls**, approached through a close-to-downtown park on *Sussex Dr.* at *Stanley Ave*, directly across from City Hall.

Hull's most noticeable riverside greenery is hilly **Parc Jacques Cartier**, at the northern end of the Pont Alexandra Bridge, turned into a children's snow kingdom during Winterlude and, at any time of year, great for towards-Ottawa views of Parliament Hill.

Museums

Learn about the epic 1826–32 digging of the 202-km waterway, connecting Ottawa with Kingston on Lake Ontario, at the eight **Rideau Canal entrance locks** located between Parliament Hill and the Château Laurier. Interpretive exhibits are on-site in the stone Commissariat building's **Bytown Museum**; *tel: (613) 283-5170*, open Mon–Fri 1000–1600 (early Apr–mid May and mid Oct–late Nov), Mon–Sat 1000–1700, Sun 1300–1700 (mid May–mid Oct), $2.50.

A few steps from there, the **Canadian Museum of Contemporary Photography** is ingeniously ensconced in an ex-railroad tunnel; *1 Rideau Canal; tel: (613) 990-8257*, open daily 1100–1700, Wed 1600–2000

(early May–early Sept), Wed and Fri–Sun 1100–1700, Thur to 2000 (early Sept–late Apr), free.

The **Canadian War Museum**, *330 Sussex Dr.; tel: (819) 776-8600*, focuses on two centuries of national military history, with huge emphasis on World War I campaigns and World War II's Normandy D-Day landings, open daily 0930–1700, Thur to 2000 (early May–mid Oct), slightly different times (mid Oct–late Apr), $3.50.

Biggest of its kind in Canada, the **National Museum of Science & Technology**, *1867 St Laurent Blvd; tel: (613) 991-3044*, covers all manner of sci-tech stuff, from hatching chicks and home cooking to steam engines and orbiting satellites, open daily 0900–1800, Fri to 2100 (early May–early Sept), Tues–Sun 0900–1700 (early Sept–late Apr), $6. The vast Dominion's environmental realm of creatures, plants and minerals is what the **Canadian Museum of Nature** is all about, *Metcalfe at McLeod Sts, OC Transpo lines 14 and 99; tel: (613) 566-4700*, open daily 0900–1700, Thur to 2000 (early May–early Sept), slightly different times (early Sept–late Apr), $4 but Thur 1000–1700 half-price, Thur 1700–2000 free.

Ottawa also has a small but comprehensive **Canadian Ski Museum**, *457-A Sussex Dr.; tel: (613) 241-5832*, open daily except Mon 1200–1600 (early Oct–late Apr), 1100–1600 (early May–late Sept), 1200–1600 (early Oct–late Apr), $1.

Rickety early-century flying machines and a World War II Spitfire are amongst 118 aircraft on display in the **National Aviation Museum**, *Rockliffe Airport, OC Transpo line 198; tel: (613) 993-2010*, open daily 0900–1700, Thur to 2100 (early May–early Sept), daily 1000–1700 (early Sept–early May), $5 but Thur 1700–2100 free.

Visitors gape at over $100 million worth of gold bullion and see how coins and medals are produced at the **Royal Canadian Mint**, *320 Sussex Dr.; tel: (613) 991-8990*, open

Mon–Fri 0900–1600, Sat–Sun 1000–1700, $2. Also money-wise: the National Bank of Canada's **Currency Museum**, downtown at *245 Sparks St; tel: (613) 782-8914,* open Tues–Fri 1200–1900, Sat–Sun 1200–1700 (Sept–May), Tues–Sun 1200–1800 (June–Aug), free.

A curvilinear architectural blockbuster a decade old in 1999, the **Canadian Museum of Civilization**, *100 r. Laurier; tel: (819) 776-7000,* traces 1000 years of human endeavour in Canada, emphasising native and ethnic diversity, and including a downright enchanting **Children's Museum** along with special-attraction theatres and performances, open daily 0900–1400, Thur to 2100 (early May–late June), daily 0900–1800, Thur–Fri to 2100 (early July–early Sept), daily 0900–1800, Thur to 2100 (early Sept–mid Oct), Tues–Sun 0900–1700, Thur to 2100 (mid Oct–late Apr). Children's Museum open daily 0900–1800 (early May–mid Oct), 0900–1700 (rest of year), adults $5, children (2–12) $3, families $15.

Ottawa's **Central Experimental Farm**, *accessed via Prince of Wales Dr.,* or *OC Transpo line 3; tel: (613) 991-3044,* truly *is* a working in-town farm; ornamental gardens and an arboretum, too, open daily 0900–1700 (Mar–Nov), daily 0900–1600 (Dec–Feb), free. The Farm's **Agricultural Museum** opens daily 0900–1700 (Mar–Nov), adults $3, children (3-15) $2, family $7.

Galleries

Opened a year earlier than Hull's auspicious museum, the **National Gallery of Canada**, *380 Sussex Dr.; tel: (613) 990-1985,* is the bravura masterpiece of architect Moshe Safdie, who also designed the Ottawa City Hall additions (see p. 117). Its vaulted tower, made of blue honeycomb glass, glows like a mammoth civic night light. Collections of Canadian art – including Inuit works and naturalistic paintings by the country's 'Group of Seven' (see p. 77) – are superlative.

Prominent, too: the reconstructed 19th-century Rideau Street Convent Chapel with its fan-vaulted ceiling, open daily 1000–1800, Thur to (early May–early Sept), daily 1000–1700 (early Sept–early May), free.

The municipal **Ottawa Art Gallery**, in the city's former provincial courthouse, *2 Daly Ave; tel: (613) 233-8699,* offers another opportunity to admire works of the 'Group of Seven' along with changing exhibitions of contemporary art, open Tues–Fri 1000–1700, Thur to 2000, Sat–Sun 1200–1700, free.

Hull's municipal counterpart is **Galerie Montcalm** in *Maison du Citoyen, 25 r. Laurier; tel: (819) 595-7488,* concentrating on modern art, mostly local and regional, open Tues–Fri, 1000–1700, Thur 1000–2000, Sat–Sun 1200–1700, free.

OUT OF TOWN

Gatineau Park

Tourist Information: Visitor Centre, *318 Meech Lake Rd, Chelsea, PQ J0X 1N0; tel: (819) 827-2020,* open daily 0900–1800 (mid May–early Sept), Mon–Fri 0930–1630, Sat–Sun 900–1700 (early Sept–mid May).

From slightly north of Ottawa's city centre, cross the Macdonald Cartier Bridge to take Hwy 5 through Hull, then exit 12 onto *Old Chelsea Rd* for a 1.2-km drive to the Visitor Centre. Gatineau Park is even closer to Hull. From that city, go westbound on *blvd Alexandre-Taché* (Hwy 148), then turn right while following Gatineau Parkway signs.

In addition to living in a city surrounded by a greenbelt, Ottawa's fortunate citizens have nearby access to this 356-square-km Québec realm of forests, glacial hills, hundreds of tent pitches, a 185-km network of groomed nature trails (one of North America's most extensive) for hiking, biking, cross-country skiing and snow-shoeing, plus some four dozen pristine lakes. There's wildlife, too – including white-tailed deer, wolves and bears, 216 species of birds and more beavers than any other park in the world.

If you plan on hiking or mountain-biking, consider purchasing a $3 *Summer Trails* map. For balmy weather enjoyment, two of the lakes, **Lac Philipe** and **Lac la Pêche**, feature fine sandy beaches and boat rental facilities. During autumn, parkland foliage ordinarily reaches peak colours between late Sept–mid Oct.

Covering 231 hectares inside Gatineau Park, the 1920s **Mackenzie King Estate**, *Barnes Rd, Chelsea/Aylmer; tel: (819) 827-2020*, was the tenth Canadian prime minister's country retreat. In addition to the prime ministers Kingswood and Moorside 'cottages', the wooded property is a showpiece of Victorian garden landscaping; light meals are served in the Moorside Tea Room, open Wed–Sun 1100–1700 (mid May–mid June), daily 1100–1700 (mid June–mid Oct), $6 per vehicle.

If you crave food before or after exploring the park, two restaurants in charming Old Chelsea village near the Visitor Centre are recommended. A budget café, **Gerry & Isobel's Country Pleasures**, *14 Scott Rd; tel: (819) 827-4341*, brews herbal teas and cappuccino to go with breakfasts and soup-salad-sandwich luncheons. *Table d'hôte* fixed-price specials are moderate at French-influenced **L'Orée du Bois**, *Kingsmere Rd; tel: (819) 827-0332*.

Pulled by a 1907 locomotive, the **Hull-Chelsea-Wakefield Steam Train**, *tel: (819) 778-7246*, clickety-clacks 32 km alongside Gatineau Park's eastern flank and the Gatineau River, with narration and entertainment during the 80-min round-trip excursion that includes a leisurely Wakefield stopover. Various departure days/times mid May–Oct from Hull's station, adults $26, children (12 and under) $12, families

$68. The line's gastronomic **Sunset Dinner Train** runs Fri 1830–2200 (June–Aug), $58. Enquire about bicycle/rail and train/Gatineau boat-cruise packages.

The Outaouais

Gatineau Park, despite its impressive size, takes up a minuscule one-tenth of this 33,000-square-km region of south-western Québec province.

Early in the 19th century, the Outaouais became known as 'Great Britain's wood-yard', because its forests (mostly sturdy red and white pine along with 'trademark' Canadian maple trees) supplied timber for shipbuilding during the Napoleonic wars. Saw mills and paper mills are important income-producers today, but so is eco-tourism as enjoyed by city escapees seeking close-to-nature recreation and fresh-air serenity.

They have 20,000 lakes and dozens of rivers at their disposal; **Papineau-Labelle** is an immense 1628-square-km wildlife pre-serve (see also Laurentians, p. 162). A good number of towns depend upon the four-sea-sons vacation trade, especially those situated west and east from Hull along the Ottawa River, and north beyond Gatineau Park via Hwy 105 following the Gatineau River. (Be mindful that French – rather, the French-Canadian *patois* – is spoken almost exclu-sively the further you venture from Hull.)

In addition to that city, these Outaouais communities' Tourist Offices stay open year round: Gracefield, Grand-Remous, Mani-waki and Montebello. Tourist Offices in the following towns are open mid June–early Sept: Aylmer, Chénéville, Plaisance, Pontiac, Rapides-des-Joachims, Ripon and Shawville. Ask for specifics at Hull's La Maison du tourisme. As you'd expect, camp-sites are plentiful throughout the region; so are outfitters for all manner of activities and rustic accommodation.

OTTAWA-TORONTO

This northerly route between the big cities leads through the rolling countryside of the Ottawa Valley, by log buildings constructed by early settlers and, for a taste of Canadian wilderness, through the southern section of Algonquin Park. Travelling south from Huntsville you'll pass through the Muskoka Lakes, a popular region for Canadian cottagers.

Sticking to the main highways, the trip east to Huntsville is 352 km and south to Toronto another 225 km.

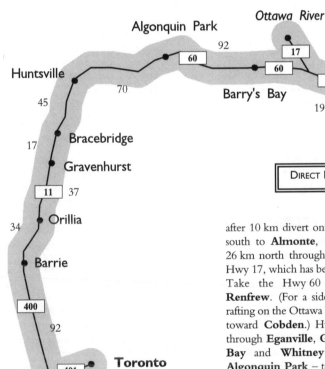

121

DIRECT ROUTE: 577 KM

ROUTE

Depart Ottawa via Hwy 417 to Exit 145, then turn onto Hwy 17 (Trans-Canada) westbound. To enjoy some countryside,

after 10 km divert onto Hwy 44 for 16 km south to **Almonte**, then Hwy 15 another 26 km north through **Pakenham** to rejoin Hwy 17, which has become a two-lane road. Take the Hwy 60 exit, 3 km east of **Renfrew**. (For a side track, instead, to go rafting on the Ottawa River, stay on Hwy 17 toward **Cobden**.) Hwy 60 continues west through **Eganville**, **Golden Lake**, **Barry's Bay** and **Whitney** – where it crosses Algonquin Park – to **Huntsville**.

From Huntsville, Hwy 11 is the fastest route south. But a diversion on side roads allows a closer glimpse of Canadian cottage country. After 16 km south on Hwy 11, take Hwy 141 west to **Ullswater**, then Regional Road 24 south 5 km to Rd 4. Continue south to Rd 25, turn right onto Hwy 118 and go 3 km to visit **Port Carling**. Backtrack on Hwy 118 eastbound 35 km to **Bracebridge**.

From there, you can fast-forward south on Hwy 11, or follow Rd 4 south 3 km, then turn right onto Rd 17 and go 8 km along a winding two-lane road with a forest canopy to the Muskoka Sands Resort, and another 5 km into **Gravenhurst**. Follow Hwy 11 south 37 km to **Orillia** and another 34 km to **Barrie**.

Toronto is 92 km south of Barrie via the multi-lane Hwy 400. For a more pleasant trip, depart Barrie via *Dunlop St*, which merges into Hwy 90 west, then Hwy 27 south through rolling countryside and the villages of **Thorton, Cookstown, Bond Head** and **Nobelton**. Take the east (left) cut-off at *Islington Ave* for the charming village of **Kleinburg**, then *Major MacKenzie* east to rejoin Hwy 400 into Toronto.

BUSES

Ontario Northland operate four bus trips a day from Ottawa to Huntsville. Journey time: 3¾ hrs. See OTT table 201. From Huntsville, there are plenty of local services to Barrie.

OTTAWA TO BARRY'S BAY

Straddling Ontario's Mississippi River 48 km south-west of Ottawa, the village of **Almonte**, a former textile centre, was one of the first settlements in the Ottawa Valley. A historical plaque on Hwy 15 marks the site of the home of Dr James Naismith, who invented the sport of basketball while working in the USA at Springfield, Mass. In **Pakenham**, the General Store (and bakery) sells picnic supplies, and you can find riverside tables 500 m further on the right.

SIDE TRACK
TO OTTAWA RIVER

Leading up to Cobden, Hwy 17 begins to cut through the pink and grey granite of the Canadian Shield. Shortly before Cobden there is a roadside restaurant built to resemble Noah's Ark and signs leading 15 km through the village of Foresters Falls.

Six companies offer rafting here on the Ottawa River. **Wilderness Tours**, *Box 89, Beachburg, ON K0J 1C; tel: (613) 646-2241*, pioneered the sport in this area. One- and two-day rafting trips range from gentle paddling to high adventure, May–Sept. Full day $85–102, gentle adventures for families with children 8–12, $34–54.

The company's lakeside base has camping (with small tents for rent), cabins, a restaurant and lounge, volleyball and bungee-jumping. Also kayaking lessons, voyager canoe excursions, horseback riding and mountain bike rentals. Reservations are advised.

Rather than backtracking, return to Hwy 17 and follow Regional Rd 8 to Hwy 60. ◩

As you enter **Eganville**, look for the seasonal **tourist information office**, *tel: (613) 628-1594*, in a log cabin on the left side of Hwy 60. **Bonnechere Caves**, *off Rd 39 about 9 km from town; tel: (613) 628-2283*, feature fossils from sea creatures that lived 450–500 million years ago, open daily 1000–1600 (late May, June and Sept), 1000–1700 (July–Aug). Guided tours, $4.50–7.50.

At **Golden Lake**, turn left at the Snowbird gift shop to enter the Golden Lake Reservation; it's about 1 km to **Algonquin Indian Heritage Centre**; *tel: (613) 625-2823*, a small log cabin museum and craft shop. More craft shops are located along the road up the hill. Reserve members hold a **Pow Wow** in mid Aug; the public is invited for traditional drumming, dancing, crafts and food.

Approaching the village of **Wilno**, look behind you for splendid views of the Ottawa Valley. The tiny **Wilno Tea Room** serves lunch daily, cheap–budget, with fresh sourdough bread. Across the road, local artisans are featured at the **Wilno Craft Gallery**, open daily (late May–Christmas).

BARRY'S BAY

Tourist Information: Barry's Bay Visitor Centre, *15 Opeongo Line W., Box 940, Barry's Bay, ON K0J 1B0; tel: (613) 756-0974*, is located in an old Canadian National railway station, open daily 1000–1700, Mon and Fri 0900–1900 (July–Aug), Thur–Sat 0900–1600 (early Sept–mid Oct).

Barry's Bay Bed and Breakfast, *29 Sandhill Dr., Barry's Bay, ON K0J 1B0; tel: (613) 756-1023*, is homely, and the owners are avid gardeners. Budget–moderate. **Pinewood Inn**, *Hwy 62 S., P.O. Box 760, Barry's Bay, ON K0J 1B0; tel: (613) 756-2646*, a moderate motel-style lodging, is 1 km south of Hwy 60 and a 5-min walk from Lake Kamaniskeg, where you can find public swimming, picnicking and barbecues. It also features **Fortune's Restaurant**; *tel: (613) 756-9014*, for budget casual meals and moderate fireside fine dining.

Follow *Dunn St* 14.4 km south for **Madawaska River Family Float Trips**, *Box 635, Barry's Bay, ON K0J 1B0; tel: (613) 756-3620, (613) 238-7238 (Sept–mid May)*. On 2-hr family float trips (age 2 and older), $20–25, passengers don't paddle. Reservations are necessary. It's located on the Madawaska River at **Madawaska Kanu Centre**, a whitewater school for kayaking and canoeing, which offers weekend and five-day courses.

ALGONQUIN PARK

Tourist Information: Ministry of Natural Resources, *Whitney, ON K0J 1M0; tel: (705) 633-5572* for park information, *(705) 633-5538/5725* for camping reservations.

Hwy 60 cuts 62 km through the southern section of the park. This section of road is called 'the corridor', and all literature gives directions in kilometres from the western gate. At the east entrance (km 62), you can get details on park programmes and purchase car permits ($10) that allow stops at all sites in the corridor.

ACCOMMODATION AND FOOD

Algonquin Park operates eight campsites ($15–21) and a new type of permanent tent on a wooden deck with barbecue called **Habitat**. Each habitat accommodates up to six people and costs $40 per night. You must supply bedding. Open May–mid Oct; Mew Lake campsite is open year-round.

Three expensive–pricey lodges have dining rooms open to the public; bring your own wine. **Arowhon Pines**, *Box 10001, Huntsville, ON P1H 2G5; tel: (705) 633-5661*, 8 km into the park on Little Joe Lake, is popular for its log dining room and fine food. Rates include all meals and activities, such as tennis, canoeing and sailing, open June–mid Oct. **Bartlett Lodge**, *P.O. 10004, Huntsville, ON P1H 2G8; tel: (705) 633-5543*, is a 5-min shuttleboat ride from Hwy 60. **Killarney Lodge**, *Box 10005, Huntsville, ON P1H 2G9; tel: (705) 633-5551*, just off Hwy 60, a 5-min drive from the Visitor Centre, has log cabins, each with canoe, open May–Oct. Ask for a room facing away from the highway.

SIGHTSEEING

With 7600 square km of rivers, lakes and forests, Algonquin Park is home to loons, beaver, more than 2000 bears, and it's one of the best places in North America to view moose. Open year round, it offers the best wildlife sightings in spring; fishing, camping and canoeing in summer; colourful scenery in early autumn; and cross-country skiing, snowshoeing, dogsledding and camping in winter. Most of the park is accessible only by foot or by using the 1500 km of canoe routes.

Along Hwy 60 are 13 accessible, short (0.8–11 km) hiking trails, plus bike trails, beaches, campsites, lodges and outfitters. At

123

km 54.5 is the **Logging Museum**, which features a video and 1.5-km trail with 19 exhibits on the logging history of the region, open daily 1000–1800 (mid May–mid Oct). At km 43 is the **Algonquin Park Visitor Centre**, with exhibits, audio-visual presentations, a restaurant, gift shop and wildlife viewing balcony, open daily (mid Apr–Nov), Sat–Sun (Nov–mid Apr). The **Algonquin Gallery**, at km 20, displays a wildlife art (June–late Oct), $3–5. It also has a small patio with light snacks at the front.

Spring is prime time to see moose, attracted by salty water beside the highway. (Drive carefully; collision with a moose can severely damage your car and injure or kill its occupants, not to mention the moose.) One of the most popular public park programs is the **Wolf Howl**, often held Thur nights in Aug. If the staff can locate a wolf pack, as many as 1500 people gather at the appointed place to hear the eerie calls. To enquire if a Wolf Howl is being held, *tel: (613) 637-2828.*

Voyageur Quest, *tel: (416) 486-3605,* provides full-day guided canoe trips for $69. Guided excursions and equipment for self-guided adventures are available through park outfitters: **Portage Store**, *Box 10009, Canoe Lake, Algonquin Park, Huntsville, ON P1H 2H4;* *tel: (705) 633-5622,* and **Opeonogo Algonquin**, *c/o Algonquin Outfitters, RR No 1, Dwight, ON P0A 1H0; tel: (613) 637-2075.*

HUNTSVILLE

Tourist Information: Huntsville Chamber of Commerce, *8 West St N, Box 1470, Huntsville, ON P1H 2B6; tel: (705) 789-4771.* **Muskoka Tourism Information**; *tel: (800) 267-9700* (toll-free), has information on Bed and Breakfasts.

ACCOMMODATION AND FOOD

CI is centrally located, *BW* is at Hidden Valley, 10 mins east of Huntsville. You'll find riverside restaurants on *John St.*

Rustic lodging and fine dining are available at the **Norsemen Restaurant and Resort**, *Limberlost Rd, Walker Lake (mail address: RR 4, Huntsville, ON P1H 2J6); tel: (705) 635-2473,* moderate. This taste of old Muskoka offers very simple lakeside cabins with barbecues and kitchenettes, a small beach and a quiet lake a 10-min drive east of Huntsville. The pricey dining room is open for dinner only, Tues–Sun in summer, Thur–Sun in winter. **Deerhurst Resort**, *1235 Deerhurst Dr., Huntsville, ON P1H 2E8; tel: (705) 789-6411,* on Peninsula Lake, moderate–pricey, features two 18-hole golf courses, tennis, watersports, horseback riding, a spa, cross-country skiing, snowmobiling and a Maple Syrup Festival.

SIGHTSEEING

Muskoka Pioneer Village, *88 Brunel Rd; tel: (705) 789-7576,* is a reconstructed 1890s village with costumed interpreters. Museum open daily 1100–1600 year round, village open daily 1100–1600 (July–late Sept), Sat–Sun 1100–1600 (mid May–July), $4–6.

HUNTSVILLE TO BRACEBRIDGE

Windermere House, *Windermere, ON P0B 1P0; tel: (705) 769-3611,* a sparkling white resort hotel on Lake Rousseau, has welcomed visitors since 1870. Originally guests arrived by boat, so the resort faces the water – car drivers enter from the back. Devastated by fire in 1996 during the making of a feature film and now fully reconstructed, it has a pub, patio, dining room and golf. Expensive.

The village of **Port Carling** surrounds the locks that link Lake Muskoka and Lake Rosseau. It features craft and souvenir shops and cafés. Its **Muskoka Lakes Museum**, *tel: (705) 645-5367,* is housed in a squared-timbered 1875 log home beside the lock. It features artefacts of early settlers, antique Muskoka boats, a Victorian era room, plus farming, lumber and woodworking artefacts, open Mon–Sat 1000–1700, Sun 1200–1600 (July–Aug), closed Mon (June–mid Oct), $1.25–$2.25.

BRACEBRIDGE

Tourist Information: Chamber of Commerce, *1 Manitoba St, Bracebridge, ON P1L 1S4; tel: (705) 645-8121, fax: (705) 645-7592.*

Victorian **Inn At The Falls**, *17 Dominion St, P.O. Box 1139, Bracebridge, ON P1L 1V3: tel: (705) 645-2245*, offers rooms overlooking Muskoka River and a street of quaint cottages, moderate–pricey. Many rooms have fireplaces and Jacuzzis. There's an English pub (budget), pool and riverview patio and fine dining room (moderate).

Lady Muskoka Cruises, *Muskoka Riverside Inn, 300 Ecclestone Dr., Bracebridge; tel: (705) 646-2628*, navigate visitors past the cottages of Canadian millionaires on a triple-deck, 200-passenger ship, daily 1100 and 1415 (July–Aug), call for times Sept and Oct, $7–14.

GRAVENHURST

Tourist Information: Gravenhurst Chamber of Commerce, *685-2 Muskoka Rd N., Gravenhurst, ON P1P 1N5; tel: (705) 687-4432.*

ACCOMMODATION AND FOOD

Gravenhurst has *HJ.* **Muskoka Sands Resort**, *Muskoka Beach Rd, Gravenhurst, Muskoka, ON P1P 1R1; tel: (800) 461-0236*, is a year-round resort and conference centre on Lake Muskoka with indoor and outdoor pools, tennis and water sports rentals. Many of the suites and cottage condominiums have lake views and fireplaces.

Cunninghams Bed & Breakfast, *175 Clairmont Rd, Gravenhurst, ON P1P 1H9; tel: (705) 687-4511*, is a 5-min walk from the Segwun dock. Budget–moderate.

SIGHTSEEING

A popular tourist activity in Muskoka is the 99-passenger **RMS Segwun Steamship Cruises**, *820 Bay St, Muskoka Bay; tel: (705) 687-6667*. Built in 1887, it is the oldest operating coal-fired steamship in North America. Cruises daily (June–mid Oct), 2 hrs $6–18, 4 hrs $25–31, 7 hrs $39–50 (lunch extra), breakfast $11.45–20, dinner $48. Reservations recommended. The *Segwun* is docked beside the 1915 *Wanda III*, the former private yacht of Mrs Timothy Eaton of Eaton Department Stores. The dockside ticket office, formerly the 1895 Grand Trunk train station, is also the **Segwun Heritage Centre**, with a museum that covers the historic steamship era and grand hotels of the Muskoka Lakes.

Bethune Memorial House, *235 John St N.; tel: (705) 687-4261*, was the birthplace of Dr Norman Bethune, a field surgeon in China who invented many widely used surgical instruments, open daily 1000–1200 and 1300–1700 (mid May–mid Oct), closed Sat–Sun (mid Oct–May), $1.25–2.25.

The 350-seat **Gravenhurst Opera House**, *295 Muskoka Rd S., Gravenhurst; tel: (705) 687-4432*, a Heritage building built in 1901, presents amateur and professional productions year round, $5–30.

ORILLIA

Tourist Information: Orillia and District Chamber of Commerce, *150 Front St S., Orillia, ON L3V 4S7; tel: (705) 326-4424*, is located in a former CN Rail station, which still serves as a bus terminal.

ACCOMMODATION AND FOOD

Orillia has *CI.* Off Hwy 11 at the Severn River Bridge is the historic, ten-room **Severn River Inn**, *Box 100 Cowbell Lane, Severn Bridge, ON P0E 1N0; tel: (705) 689-6333*, moderate. There's a pub for light meals, cheap–budget, and a Victorian-style dining room and patio, moderate. Dining reservations recommended for weekends. **Betty and Tony's Bed & Breakfast**, *677 Broadview Ave, Orillia, ON L3V 6P1; tel:*

(705) 326-1125, moderate, backs onto a canal that leads into Lake Couchiching. Guests have use of a paddle boat.

Enjoy a meal down at the waterfront in fully restored, turn-of-the-century railway dining cars at **Ossawippi Express Dining Cars,** *210 Mississaga St E.; tel: (705) 329-0001,* budget–moderate. For a fast snack, nearby in Couchiching Beach Park, **French's Stand** has been serving take-away fare since 1920.

SIGHTSEEING

Decorated with Aboriginal art on the exterior, **Casino Rama,** *Rama Rd; tel: (705) 329-3325,* is on the **Rama Indian Reservation.** Canada's largest casino, it is open 24 hours and features more than 100 gaming tables, 2000 slot machines, an entertainment lounge and three restaurants, ranging from deli snacks to a Chinese buffet. Three km north on *Rama Rd* is the **Rama Moccasin and Craft Shop,** *tel: (705) 325-5041,* selling native crafts and souvenirs, including moccasins, mukluks, jewellery, original art, Indian dolls and clothes.

The **Stephen Leacock Museum,** *50 Museum Dr.; tel: (705) 329-1908,* a lakeside National Historic Site, was the summer home of Canada's most famous humourist, open daily 1000–1900 (mid June–early Sept), Mon–Fri (early Sept–mid June), $1–7. Afternoon tea is served on the terrace, July–Aug.

Island Princess Boat Cruises, *tel: (705) 325-2628,* offer sightseeing and dinner cruises on Lake Couchiching aboard a 200-passenger paddle-wheeler (mid May–mid Oct), $10–$30. **Orillia Opera House,** *corner of Mississaga and West Sts; tel: (705) 326-8011,* presents classics in the Sunshine Festival Theatre May–Sept, $14–17.

BARRIE

Tourist Information: Barrie Visitor and Convention Bureau, *205 Lakeshore Dr., Barrie, ON L4N 7Y9; tel: (705) 739-9444* or *(800) 668-9100,* is on the waterfront.

ACCOMMODATION AND FOOD

Barrie has *BW, CI, HI* and *TL.* Circa 1911 **Richmond Manor Bed & Breakfast,** *16 Blake St, Barrie, ON L4M 1J6; tel: (705) 726-7103,* moderate, is the former home of a Barrie mayor and a local judge. Nicely decorated with folk art painted by the present owner, it's a short walk from the waterfront.

Many restaurants and stores line the strip of *Bayfield St* north of Hwy 400. **Las Angela's,** *168 Dunlop St E.; tel: (705) 728-5899,* down by the waterfront with a view of Lake Simcoe, features Italian and Mediterranean cuisine, with fireplaces, a patio and a cigar lounge. Budget–pricey.

SIGHTSEEING

The city of Barrie, 90 km north of Toronto, is the gateway to the Lake Simcoe resort region. With three ski resorts in the area, it's a year-round destination. **Serendipity Princess Cruises,** *Barrie City Dock; tel: (705) 835-3011,* operates morning and afternoon cruises of Lake Simcoe on a triple deck paddle-wheeler (late May–late Sept). Reservations required for lunch and dinner cruises, $7–12, lunch $20, dinner $29. About 8 km north of the city (take Hwy 27 to Hwy 26 and go west 1 km) is the **Simcoe County Museum,** *tel: (705) 728-3721,* a 16-acre site with five galleries, covering the Victorian era, an aboriginal long house and quilt making among others. There are also 18 outdoor displays, including pioneer buildings.

BARRIE TO TORONTO

The village of **Cookstown**, at the junction of Hwy 27 and Hwy 89, is known for its antique shops. **Cookstown Antique Market**; *tel: (705) 458-1275,* has a 6000-square-ft barn full of items, open daily 1000–1730 (Apr–Dec), 1200–1730 (Jan–mid Mar).

At Kleinburg you can branch off to the east at *Islington Ave* to visit the **McMichael Art Gallery**, **Kortwright Centre** and **Canada's Wonderland** (see p. 79).

NORTHERN ONTARIO

The *voyageurs* (traders and explorers) opened this region in the late 1700s, transporting their furs down lakes and rivers by canoe. Today, modern highways wind through rugged terrain, linking gold, silver and lumbering communities. Hiking, fishing and canoeing draw visitors in the summer; early autumn brings a blaze of colour as leaves begin to fall; and in winter, ice fishing, snowmobiling and skiing are popular. The distances will be your greatest challenge. Ontario is immense. Toronto to the Manitoba border is a 1902-km trip, just 38 km less than driving to Florida.

TOURIST INFORMATION

Ontario Tourism, *Eaton Centre, Level 1 Below, Toronto; tel: (416) 314-0944,* handles walk-in enquiries and operates welcome centres at **Fort Frances, Sault Ste Marie, Kenora, Rainy River** and **Pigeon River.** They are generally open daily 0800–2000 mid May–early Sept. Fort Frances and Sault Ste Marie locations are also open 0830–1630 Sept–mid May.

In addition, regional chambers of commerce or tourism bureaus run visitor information offices at **North Bay**, *tel: (705) 474-6634;* **Sudbury**, *tel: (705) 522-0104;* **Sault Ste Marie**, *tel: (705) 254-4293;* **Thunder Bay**, *tel: (807) 626-9420;* **Kenora**, *tel: (807) 468-5853;* and **Cochrane**, *tel: (800) 354-9948.*

WEATHER

In Sudbury, the hub of the north, the daily temperature in July averages a comfortable 14°–25°C; by Feb it drops to between -10° and -20°C. Temperatures are 3°–5° warmer closer to the large lakes. Northern summers are short. Extreme cold and heavy snow is possible mid Oct–early May.

ARRIVING AND DEPARTING

By Air
Air Canada, *tel: (800) 268-7240* (toll-free), has jet service to Timmins; its connector service, **Air Ontario**, *tel: (519) 453-8440,* flies from Toronto's Island Airport into North Bay, Sault Ste Marie and Sudbury. **Canadian Regional Airlines**, a partner of Canadian Airlines; *tel: (416) 798-2211* or *(800) 665-1177,* connects from Toronto International Airport to Sudbury, Sault Ste Marie, Thunder Bay and Dryden. **Air Creebec Inc**, *tel: (705) 264-9521,* provides service from Timmins to James Bay, including Moosonee. **Bearskin Airlines**, *tel: (807) 737-3473,* based in Sioux Lookout, services most major communities in Northern Ontario. **Pem Air Ltd**, *tel: (613) 687-5579,* flies from Pembroke to Toronto International Airport and services northern communities, including Elliot Lake, Kirkland Lake and Wawa.

By Bus
Greyhound Lines of Canada; *tel: (416) 367-8747,* provide services from Toronto to Manitoba, a 28-hour trip that follows Hwy 17 around Lake Superior. **Ontario Northland**; *tel: (416) 393-7911,* provide services from Toronto to communities in the northeast, including Sudbury, North Bay, Timmins and Hearst.

By Rail
Three times per week, transcontinental trains

of **VIA Rail**, *tel: (416) 366-8411*, pass through Sudbury and Sioux Lookout on their 28-hour journey from Toronto to Manitoba. **Ontario Northland Rail**, *tel: (416) 314-3750*, departs Toronto for North Bay and Cochrane via Temagami with bus connections to Timmins and Hearst. This company also operates the popular **Polar Bear Express** (see below). **Algoma Central Railway**, *tel: (705) 946-7300*, provides service between Sault Ste Marie and Hearst.

By Car
Distances between the larger communities are substantial, but there are good automobile and food services along the major highways. The southerly route on Hwy 17 is the most popular and scenic; the northern route along Hwy 11 offers drivers with trailers fewer hills and transport trucks. Both are the Trans-Canada Hwy.

Southerly Route
Hwy 400 north to Hwy 69 is the most convenient route from Toronto to **Sudbury**, a 400-km trip. From Ottawa Hwy 17 brings you through the popular fishing centre of **North Bay** past Lake Nipissing to **Sudbury**, a 490-km trip. Then it's 296 km to **Sault Ste Marie**, one of the world's busiest waterways. From 'the soo', Hwy 17 follows the shore of Lake Superior north 266 km to **Wawa**, then over the next 467 km detours around **Pukaskwa National Park**, passes through **White River**, rejoins the shore of Lake Superior at **Marathon** and continues to **Thunder Bay** – one of the world's largest grain ports.

From Thunder Bay take Hwy 11 335 km past **Quetico Provincial Park** to **Fort Frances**; after another 41 km you have a choice of continuing west 94 km to the US border crossing into Minnesota at **Rainy River**, or taking Hwy 71 north for 157 km to rejoin Hwy 17, and continue 19 km into **Kenora**.

Northerly Route
Hwy 11 will take you 341 km from Toronto to **North Bay**, then 369 km north through **Temagami**, known for its old growth forest and 2560 km of canoe routes, to **Cochrane** (with cut-offs to the mining communities of **Kirkland Lake** and **Timmins**). From Cochrane, Hwy 11 continues west though **Kapuskasing**, **Hearst** and **Thunder Bay**. Then from Thunder Bay, Hwy 17 takes the northern route 490 km through **Dryden** to **Kenora**, popular for trophy fishing. From Kenora it's 48 km to the **Manitoba** border.

STAYING IN NORTHERN ONTARIO

Accommodation
Accommodation ranges from chain hotels and motels in major centres to campsites, cabins, houseboats, full service resorts and fly-in fishing lodges. **Tourism Ontario**, *tel: (800) ONTARIO*, offers information and makes reservations. For **Provincial Park** summer campsite vacancy information, *tel: (416) 314-0998*. Reservations for many private campsites can be made through the **Ontario Private Campground Association**, *tel: (800) 353-4313*.

Hotel chains in North Bay include *BW*, *HJ* and *Ve*; in Sudbury, *HJ*, *QI*, *Rm* and *Ve*; in Sault Ste Marie, *Ch*, *CI*, *Hd*, *QI*, *Rm* and *S8*; in Timmins, *BW*, in Kirkland Lake, *Ve*; in Marathon, *BW*; in Dryden, *BW* and *CI*; in Kenora, *BW* and *TL*.

Colour section (i): Boldt Castle Boathouse (p. 105); a wintry view of Parliament Hill, Ottawa (p. 116).

(ii): The *Segwum* at Port Carling (see p. 124); cross-country skiing at Gatineau (p. 132); inset: canoeing in Algonquin Park (p. 123).

(iii): Montréal (pp. 139–153): Basilique Notre-Dame; Marché Atwater.

(iv): Skating against the backdrop of Vieux Montréal (p. 152); Ski Village in Mont Tremblant (p. 159).

Backpacker Hostels Canada, *1594 Lakeshore Dr., Longhouse Village, P.O. Box 10-1, RR 13, Thunder Bay, ON P7B 5E4; tel: (807) 983-2042*, offers budget accommodation and is a good source of information on independent hostels throughout Canada.

ENTERTAINMENT

Events

Major summer celebrations include Sudbury's three-day **Northern Lights Festival** in early July and the two-day **Ojibwa Keeshigun** festival of aboriginal culture at Old Fort William in mid Aug. In late Aug, White River recognises former resident Winnie the Pooh with the **Winnie Hometown Festival**. Sault Ste Marie presents the 16-day **Algoma Fall Festival** starting late Aug and one of Canada's largest winter carnivals, **Bon Soo**, early Jan–early Feb. **North Bay's** Winter Carnival is celebrated with a French flavour the second week in Feb.

Parks and Recreation

Northern Ontario has more than 60 provincial parks including: **Quetico Provincial Park**, 161 km west of Thunder Bay on Hwy 11, known for 1500 km of canoe routes and 30 aboriginal pictographs on sheer cliff walls; **Killarney Provincial Park,** on the shore of Georgian Bay 100 km south-west of Sudbury – its rugged beauty was a favourite subject for painter A. Y. Jackson of the Group of Seven (see p. 77); and **Lake Superior Provincial Park**, Ontario's largest, known for its scenic shoreline.

Pukaskwa National Park, on the north-east corner of Lake Superior, is Canada's largest national park, a wilderness area featuring camping, canoe routes and a coastal hiking trail.

Outfitters operate out of many communities, including Thunder Bay, Killarney Provincial Park, Temagami and Wawa. Fly-in outfitters take you to lodges from Timmins, Cochrane, Hearst, Matheson, Kapuskasing, Goama, Elk Lake and Foleyet. **The Northern Ontario Tourist Outfitters Association**, *269 Main St W., Suite 408, North Bay, ON P1B 2T8; tel: (705) 472-5552, fax: (705) 472-0621*, can assist with information.

SIGHTSEEING

Southerly Route

Sudbury's **Science North**, *Ramsey Lake Rd and Paris St; tel: (705) 522-3701*, is the most popular tourist attraction in Northern Ontario. This snowflake-shaped centre specialises in hands-on exhibits. Learn about space, pet a beaver, or take in a 3D film and laser show in a 200-seat theatre blasted out of Canadian Shield rock, open daily 0900–1800 (mid June–early Sept), 0900–1700 (May–mid June), 1000–1600 (mid Oct–Apr), $7–10. Adjoining buildings house an **IMAX theatre**; *tel: (705) 523-4629*, $6–8.50, and Virtual Voyages Adventure rides.

Affiliated with Science North is the **Big Nickel Mine Underground Tour**, *5 km west of downtown at Regional Rd 55 and Big Nickel Mine R; tel: (705) 522-3701*, offering 30-min tours in a safe underground environment, open daily 0900–1700 or 1800 (May–mid Oct), $7–$10. Closed all winter.

At Espanola, 85 km west of Sudbury, Hwy 6 cuts off to the south and leads 53 km to **Manitoulin Island**, the world's largest freshwater island.

From **Sault Ste Marie** you can board the **Agawa Canyon – Wilderness by Rail Tour**, *Algoma Central Railway Depot, 129 Bay St; tel: (705) 946-7300*. This one-day rail excursion covers 183 km of wilderness with views of waterfalls, rivers and gorges and a two-hour picnic/hiking stop in Agawa Canyon Wilderness Park. Departs daily at 0800 (June–mid Oct). Mid Sept–mid Oct is best for fall foliage, $16–52. The Snow Train tour operates Sat–Sun (late Dec–mid Mar), $27–53. Tickets: **Passenger Sales Depot**,

129

P.O. Box 130, 129 Bay St, Sault Ste Marie, ON P6A 6Y2.

Also in Sault Ste Marie, **Lock Tours Canada** at St. Mary's River *(next to Holiday Inn); tel: (705) 253-9850,* operates cruises through the locks of one the world's busiest canal systems, open daily June–mid Oct, $8.50–17. At the Sault Lock, *Bay St,* is the **Canadian Heritage Bushplane Heritage Centre**, open daily 1000–1600 or 1900, $4.50–5.

White River, a lumbering community, is the birthplace of the bear that inspired the 'Winnie the Pooh' stories by A.A. Milne. During World War I a Canadian soldier brought the bear from here to London, England, naming it Winnie after his home town of Winnipeg. A statue of the bear stands at White River's Visitor Park.

In **Thunder Bay**, a city known for hosting world ski jumping competitions, **Old Fort William**, *Broadway Ave off Hwy 61 S.; tel: (807) 473-2344,* is a reconstruction of the Northwest Company Fort of 1815. There are 42 rebuilt historic buildings on the 125-acre site with costumed interpreters, $8–10.

From **Kenora** you can cruise Lake of the Woods on **M.S. Kenora Cruises**, *Kenora harbourfront; tel: (807) 468-9124.* The 2-hour 30-km cruises operate daily mid May–mid Sept, $7–13.50.

Northerly Route

From **North Bay**, the **Chief Commanda II**, *Government Dock off Memorial Dr.; tel: (705) 494-8167,* provides 90-min to 5-hr cruises on triple-deck boats following routes carved by the *voyageurs.* Daily mid June–early Sept, $8–20. Also in North Bay is the home of the world's first surviving identical quintuplets. The **Dionne Quints Museum**, *Seymour St at Hwys 11 and 17; tel: (705) 472-8480,* is open daily 0900–1700 or 1900 (mid May–mid Oct), $1.50–2.75. On the same property, in two renovated boxcars, is the **Model Railroad Exhibit**, open daily 0900–1700 July–Aug, $2.

In **Kirkland Lake**, the **Museum of Northern History** at the **Sir Harry Oakes Chateau**, *2 Chateau Dr.; tel: (705) 568-8800,* features exhibits on Northern Ontario history from mining to personalities like local mining magnate Sir Harry Oakes, who died mysteriously in the Bahamas, open Mon–Sat 1000–1600, Sun and holidays 1200–1600 year round, $1–3.

In Timmins, on the **Timmins Underground Gold Mine Tour**, *Hollinger site of Royal Oak Mines, James Reid Rd off Moneta Ave; tel: (705) 267-6222,* you'll be supplied with a hard hat, protective clothing and safety glasses for the underground adventure, open daily mid May–late Oct. Surface tour $5–7, underground tour $15–17.

From **Cochrane**, the **Polar Bear Express** departs for a 300-km, 4-hr wilderness rail journey north to **Moosonee**, where you can take a 15-min boat ride to **Moose Factory** – Ontario's oldest permanent settlement, the site of the original Hudson Bay post, open Sat–Thur (late June–early Sept), $48. One-, three- and four-day excursions available. Reservations are essential; contact **Ontario Northland Rail**, *65 Front St W., Union Station, Toronto ON M5J 1E6; tel: (416) 314-3750 or (800) 268-9281.*

From Moosonee, **Wilderness Excursion**, *River Rd; tel: (705) 336-2944,* operates 6-hr tours of Moose River at the southern tip of James Bay on the *M.V. Polar Princess.* Sun–Fri (late June–early Sept), $23–46, box lunches provided. The **Fossil Island** tour is a 3-hr trip by large freighter canoe 10 km south to Fossil Island, site of 350-million-year-old fossils, Sat–Thur at 1430, $8.50–17.

Hwy 11 and 17 merge at Nipigon on the north shore of Lake Superior; 56 km before **Thunder Bay** is the largest amethyst mine in North America. **Amethyst Mine Panorama** is open to the public with guided and self-guided tours, plus a pick-your-own amethyst adventure ($1 per lb), daily 1000–1900 (July–Aug), 1000–1700 (May–July and Sept–mid Oct), $1–3.

OTTAWA–MONTRÉAL

The routes that link Ottawa, the national political capital, and Montréal, the economic capital of French Canada, represent extremes. The direct route follows major highways through eastern Ontario into Québec across long expanses of empty territory, complicated only by the tangle of routes at the urban ends. The scenic route, on the other hand, follows the St Lawrence River *(Fleuve St-Laurent)* on its Québec bank, essentially paralleling the settlement of Lower Canada via the river.

The communities along the route remain agricultural, as they have been since the 17th century. The area was severely depopulated in the late 19th century with the abolition of the old French seigneurie farming system, but has rebounded since World War II with the boom of tourism oriented to outdoor activities. Although a slow drive, this route weaves through stunning orchard country and flirts continuously with scenic views of the St Lawrence.

Scenic Route

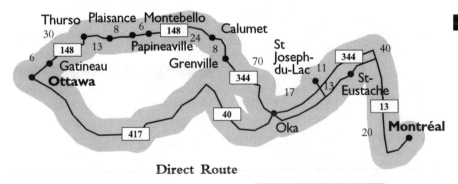

131

Direct Route

DIRECT ROUTE: 202 KM

DIRECT ROUTE

From Capitol Hill in Ottawa, turn east onto Rte 417, *King Edward St,* and follow Rte 417 signs as it leaves the city at the Queensway. Rte 417 becomes Hwy 40 when it rejoins the Ottawa River, just west of the Québec border. Approaching Montréal, turn off to Hwy 13 south, which ends at

Hwy 20. Take Hwy 20 east, following the signs for 'Centre-Ville' or 'Vieux Port'. Driving time is approximately 2½ hrs.

SCENIC ROUTE

From just north of Ottawa's city centre, cross the Macdonald Cartier Bridge into Hull and follow signs to Hwy 5, taking the turn-off for Rte 148 east to **Gatineau**. Continue 16 km to Masson-Anger. Turn right and follow Rte 309 for 2 km to Hwy 148, also known as the 'Route Outauoais'. This road follows the *Rivière Outauoais* (Ottawa River) through the towns of **Thurso**, **Plaisance**, **Papineauville**, **Montebello**, **Fassett** and **Calumet** before veering inland.

Approximately 3 km outside Calumet, turn right onto Rte 344 toward **Grenville**. Rte 344 follows the bends in the river, but often out of sight of the water. Continue 23 km to **Carillon**, then another 47 km to **Oka**. Continue east on Rte 344 for approximately 6 km, watching carefully for a left turn to **St-Joseph-du-Lac**. This 11-km loop on *r. Principale* or *ch. Principal* crosses high hills and orchards before rejoining Rte 344 for 5 km to the village of **Ste-Marthe-sur-le-Lac**, another 4 km to Deux-Montagnes and another 2 km to the more substantial town of **Ste-Eustache**. Follow Rte 344 east approximately 3 km to Hwy 13, which you will follow south to its conclusion (22 km). Turn east on Hwy 20 *(blvd Ste-Anne)* to reach downtown Montréal. Driving time is approximately 5 hours.

This route passes through two tourist districts within Québec, with separate offices and publications: the *Outaouais* and the Laurentians *(Laurentides)*. For information and assistance with reservations west of Montebello, contact **Association touristique de l'Outaouais**, *103 r. Laurier, Hull, PQ J8X 3VB; tel: (819) 778-2222 or (800) 265-7822* (toll-free). For information and reservations from Grenville eastward, contact **Association touristique des Laurentides**, *14 142 r. de la Chapelle, RR1, St-Jérôme, PQ J7Z 5T4; tel: (514) 436-8532* for information, *tel: (800) 561-6673* for reservations.

BUSES AND TRAINS

Voyageur Colonial operate an hourly bus service, from 0700–2200. Journey time: 2 hrs 10 mins. They also run two trips a day which go via Montebello. Journey time: 4 hrs 15 mins. See OTT tables 213 and 210.

VIA Rail have four daily services Mon–Fri, three services at weekends. Journey time: 2 hrs. See OTT table 20.

GATINEAU TO THURSO

For westbound travellers, Gatineau is considered the gateway to the Capital District – a sprawling suburb rapidly becoming urbanised. The eastbound traveller experiences precisely the opposite. Even the highway strip malls on the outskirts of Gatineau begin to suggest the broader open spaces of the Rivière des Outaouais floodplain. The landscape around the highway begins to open up into farmland at the municipality of Masson-Angers, and as the vistas broaden, the highway narrows, ultimately varying between one and two lanes in each direction at Thurso.

The payoff for the poorer road comes in improved views of the river, which at places can reach nearly to the road during the spring flooding. This is a broad river, almost lake-like, with reeds and patches of wild rice growing in its marshy edges.

PLAISANCE

Tourist Information: Association touristique de l'Outaouais, *276 r. Desjardins; tel: (819) 427-6400,* open daily 0900–1700 (mid June–early Sept).

La Réserve Faunique de Plaisance, *Rte 148; tel: (819) 771-4840,* open late Apr–mid Oct, is a wildlife preserve, principally of habitat for waterfowl and other creatures who dwell in the interstices of river and bank. The preserve encompasses 27 km along the Rivière des Outaouais, and three portions are open for recreational use. The kilometre-long *'Zizanie-des-marais'* consists of a wooden boardwalk above the marshes with interpretive plaques. The *'Baladeurs'* trails, both along the river and through nearby fields, are excellent spots for both casual hiking or mountain biking. The sector of the preserve called *Presque des Iles* also has tent and RV pitches (call the general information number for prices and availability).

Some 5 km north of Rte 148 are the **Chutes de Plaisance**, *Rang Malo,* an historic site of rustic scenery and long, cascading falls that drop 75 m over about a kilometre. The falls parking lot is open late June–early Sept with minimal fee, but is free at other times. Paths follow the bubbling river, making this a good spot to stretch your legs and have a picnic. The falls played a decisive role in the founding of the village of North Nation Mills here in the early 19th century.

Archaeological excavations at the site led to the creation of the Plaisance Heritage Centre (see below). During peak usage times, horses may be available for rides on the paths along the river. For availability and rates, call **Centre d'Équitation des Chutes de la Pétite-Nation**; *tel: (819) 985-3137.*

The **Plaisance Heritage Centre**, *Rte 148, next to the church; tel: (819) 427-6400,* open late June–early Sept, adults $2.50, delves into the history of the immediate region with an exhibition of three villages – the original Amerindian settlement, the small North Nations Mills logging community and the present town of Plaisance. Excavated artefacts from the earlier communities help bring them alive.

Stop at **Fromage Bar Laitier**, *222 r. Principale (Rte 148),* for cheeses from the factory behind the dairy bar and store. While these are not the artesanal cheeses of Oka, say, they are sturdy and very fresh Canadian versions of mild cheddars, offered at very economical prices – just the ticket for a picnic. The store also sells fresh cheese curds, a peculiarly Québecois snack food found throughout dairy country at every little store and *dépanneur* and often served on *poutine,* another local specialty consisting of fried potatoes topped with brown gravy.

PAPINEAUVILLE

Sugar maple trees stand in the low hills north of the Rivière des Outaouais, and just before entering the picturesque village of Papineauville, you'll see signs pointing up a narrow road to sugar shacks. **Cabane à sucre Brazau**, *316 St-Charles; tel: (819) 427-5611,* is open Feb–Apr. **Cabane à sucre Chez Ti-Mousse**, *442 St-Charles; tel: (819) 427-5413,* is open all year. During the winter, both establishments offer sleigh rides as well as demonstrations of the process of making maple syrup from raw maple sap.

MONTEBELLO

Tourist Information: Association touristique de l'Outaouais, *502-A r. Nôtre-Dame (Rte 148); tel: (819) 423-5602,* open daily 0900–1800 (mid June–early Sept), 1000–1700 (rest of year).

Situated almost exactly halfway between Ottawa and Montréal, Montebello has developed into a bona fide country riverside resort, worth visiting by bus if you are not driving. Originally the administrative centre of the Petite-Nation seigneurie of Louis-Joseph Papineau (one of the leaders of francophone Lower Canada and a supporter of the Patriotes Rebellion), Montebello's Château Montebello resort made the municipality a vacation retreat for residents of Canadian capital district and of Montréal.

Smaller hotels and Bed and Breakfast operations have sprung up in the district for vacationers who wish to avail themselves of the same striking scenery and opportunities for outdoor activities but cannot or do not wish to pay resort prices for lodging.

GETTING AROUND

Bus service from Montréal is via **Aérocar Murray Hill**; *tel: (514) 585-1210,* **Gray Line**; *tel: (514) 934-1222,* or **Autobus Larose**; *tel: (514) 472-2901.* Bus service from Ottawa is via **Ottawa Valley Tours**; *tel: (613) 725-3045,* or **Leduc Bus Lines**; *tel: (613) 679-2595.*

ACCOMMODATION

Hotel Le Château Montebello, *392*

133

r. Nôtre-Dame (Rte 148), Montebello, PQ J0V 1L0; tel: (819) 423-6341 or (800) 268-9411, is pricey but enquire about special promotional and package rates. Built in the 1930s as a private club, this huge dwelling consists of a large central hall with several spokes of guest rooms extending outward, thus providing each room with maximum window light.

As the world's largest log structure, it is testament to the extent of Québec's vast forests and the size of its trees. The resort either owns or has exclusive access to 65,000 acres of recreational land. Both indoor and outdoor pools and a fitness centre are available at the lodging itself.

Additional recreational activities include cycling, hiking, horseback riding, squash, lawn games and canoeing. During the winter, the resort focuses on cross country skiing, curling, dogsledding, ice fishing, ice skating and snowshoeing.

Perhaps the greatest single draw during snow-free periods is **Le Château Montebello golf course** (green fees $39–55). This course was designed by legendary golf course landscape architect Stanley Thompson to capture the natural flow and beauty of the rolling countryside. As such, it feels like a much older style of golf course, without the artificial constrictions usually imposed by adjoining development.

Another resort choice is **Auberge Suisse Montevilla**, *P.O. Box 309, Montebello PQ J0V 1L0; tel: (819) 423-6692 or (800) 363-0061,* pricey, located about 4 km north of Montebello village off Rte 148. In contrast to the hotel-style Château Montebello, the auberge consists of 18 cottages in the Swiss-chalet style; 13 of these are fully 'winterised' and feature fireplaces and full kitchens for self-catering. They will sleep four to eight people comfortably.

Summer activities at the auberge include fishing, tennis, hiking, canoeing and swimming on the property's own natural beach. During the winter, it is most popular for skating and snowmobiling, a sport for which

The Rise and Fall of the Seigneurie

Under French rule from 1630–1763, agricultural land grants in Québec followed the French *seigneurie* system of a feudal lord (who often stayed in France) holding title to the lands and the serfs (colonists) working the property in exchange for payments to the lord.

In Québec, most lands were divided into long narrow strips perpendicular to rivers or lakes to guarantee everyone access to the water. Because the population was sparse and the territory vast, most early settlers profited handsomely. But when British law came into effect, foreign lords no longer received payments, and the British crown finally abolished the system altogether in 1854.

Ironically, this led to the subdivision of land into parcels so small that families could not survive, and approximately 750,000 French Canadians emigrated to the USA between 1840 and 1930, effectively devastating Québec's agricultural economy. The hardest hit area was the valley of Fleuve St-Laurent.

the Québecois have a particular passion, since they invented it.

For accommodation without resort facilities, the best buy in town is **Motel du Manoir Montebello**, *676 r. Nôtre-Dame (Rte 148), Montebello PQ J0V 1L0; tel: (819) 423-6000,* moderate.

EATING AND DRINKING

Most visitors to Montebello are either daytrippers or are staying in – and dining at – the resort dining rooms. Among these, the most notable is the elegant and pricey restaurant **Aux Chantignoles**, *Le Château Montebello, 392 r. Nôtre-Dame; tel: (819) 423-6341,* which specialises in continental and Asian cuisine. Views are extraordinary – both inside and out. Tables overlook the Fleuve St Laurent, and the room is decorated with souvenirs of *seigneurial* era.

Much more casual meals – crêpes and the like – are available at **Le Mar-Lyn**, *527 r. Nôtre-Dame; tel: (819) 423-1122*, budget–moderate. For a simple French country meal, try **Le Pot au Feu**, *489 r. Nôtre-Dame; tel: (819) 423-6901*, moderate.

SIGHTSEEING

One key to understanding the cultural and political history of this intensely French segment of Québec is the **Manoir-Papineau National Historic Site**, *500 r. Notre-Dame (access from tourist information centre at train station); tel: (819) 423-6965*, open daily 1000–1800 (mid June–early Sept), Wed–Sun 1000–1700 (mid May–mid June and early Sept–mid Oct), Sat–Sun 1000–1700 (mid Oct–mid Nov), adults $3.50.

Louis-Joseph Papineau was a major political figure in Lower Canada in the early 19th century. After the failure of the Patriotes Rebellion, he fled to the USA and France for six years before returning to the seigneurie of Petite-Nation. Here he began to build the splendid manor house, using his land revenues and the back salary owed to him as the Speaker of House of Assembly. Several of his heirs lived on the property, but in 1929 it passed to the private Seigniory Club, the group that built Le Château Montebello.

The exemplar of the majesty of a seigneurial manor house, the property is believed by many French separatists to express Papineau's creativity. An English-speaking visitor is more likely impressed by the poignancy of the country retreat of a failed rebel. Papineau's memory is still invoked a century and a half after his heyday because, as the first influential leader to insist on French Canadian rights, he stands for the cause of peaceful revolution to create a separate French Canada.

Be sure to get your bag of carrots at the gate of **Le Parc Oméga**, *ch. 323; tel: (819) 423-5487* or *(888) 423-5487*, open daily 1000–one hour before sunset, adults $8, children $4, higher in July–Aug. This unusual animal park encompasses 1500 acres of lakes, meadows, valleys and hillsides through which you drive in your car to see European red deer, wapiti elk, white-tailed deer, black bear, wild boar, bison, ibex and Corsican moufflon. The park also offers hiking along two nature interpretation trails as well as limited dining at the interpretation centre.

The municipality of Montebello joined with private landowners to assemble a network of more than 30 km of **mountain biking trails**, all of which are maintained and well-signed. Trail maps are available at tourist locations in town and trails are blazed by colour to indicate level of difficulty.

CALUMET

On Rte 148, shortly before entering Calumet, a road to the left marked *chemin de Rivière Rouge* is the access road for active sports facilities that include river-rafting expeditions of 4–5 hrs. The Rouge River is one of the most interesting and competitive rafting rivers in Québec.

Chief outfitters are: **Aventure en eau vive**; *tel: (800) 567-6881* or *(819) 242-6084*, which also offers kayaking and paintball games; **Aventure W3 Viking**; *tel: (514) 334-0889*, which offers kayaking lessons and rafting; **Nouveau Monde**; *tel: (819) 242-7238* or *(800) 361-5033*, which offers river expeditions and bungee-jumping; and **Propulsion excursions en rivière**; *tel: (514) 229-6620* or *(800) 461-3300*, which offers rafting, kayaking and hydroluge expeditions.

GRENVILLE TO OKA

Tourist Information: Association touristique des Laurentides, *12 r. des Érables, Grenville; tel: (819) 242-2432*; open daily 1000–1800 (24 June–early Sept).

The drive along this stretch of Rte 344 begins to lose sight of the river, even as it

135

The Indians of Québec

About 60,000 members of 11 Native nations dwell in Québec, the majority in the north. Colonists and Indians rarely fought in early Québec, and many tribes supported the French cause against the English. But European diseases and war between Iroquois and Algonquian peoples decimated the original populations. The most traditional communities are those who pursue a hunting-based economy in the far north, notably the Inuit and the Cree. Several more assimilated Native communities are found along the St. Lawrence River.

The **Mohawks** were stranded in Québec by the French-British colonial wars. Numbering about 12,000, they live mostly in three communities: Kahnawake (near Montréal), Kanasatake (west of Montréal on Lac-de-Deux-Montagnes), and in the south-west corner of Québec on lands overlapping New York and Ontario. They are members of the Iroquois culture and many of the elder tribe members still speak the Mohawk language.

The **Wendat-Huron**, also an Iroquoian Nation, originated in Ontario but fled to Québec in 1657 to escape an epidemic, eventually settling north-east of Québec in 1697, where the village of Wendake now sits. They produce moccasins, canoes and snowshoes that they sell around the world. Their language is considered extinct in Québec.

The **Abenaki** nation originated in Maine but fled to Québec in 1675 after the failure of a general Algonquian Confederation uprising aimed at rooting out English colonists from New England. About 1600 Abenaki still live in Québec, mostly in the villages of Odanak and Wôlinak. Their language has virtually disappeared.

The **Micmac** nation was the first to encounter the French, as their ancestral home is the Gaspé peninsula. About 4000 Micmacs live in the villages of Restigouche and Gesgapegiag in the Gaspésie, and many more live throughout Québec and northern New England. Although integrated into modern society, many Micmacs still speak their ancestral language, and schools in the two main villages teach in both French and Micmac.

136

passes by a number of fine houses (products of the lucrative 19th-century lumber business) intermixed with humbler dwellings. Consider stopping for a 75-min tour of the **hydroelectric plant at Carillon**; *tel: (800) 365-5229*, which produces more than 654,000 kilowatts of electricity. A huge plant by standards elsewhere in the world, it is relatively small in a province that earns substantial incomes by selling electricity to adjacent New York and New England.

Carillon, formerly known as Long-Sault, was the site of a famous stand by 18 French soldiers in 1660 that helped prevent the Iroquois allies of the British from taking Montréal during the Anglo-French wars over this part of Canada. The charmingly quaint village, with its well-preserved houses

in the French colonial style of the region, also holds a pleasantly local museum, **Musée de la Société d'Histoire d'Argenteuil**, *50 r. Principale; tel: (514) 537-3861*, open Tues–Sun 1100–1700 (mid May–mid Oct), $2.50. The stone building was erected as an inn in 1836, only to become a military barracks when British soldiers arrived a year later to put down the Patriotes insurrection.

OKA

Tourist Information: Association touristique des Laurentides, *quai municipal; tel: (514) 479-8389*, open daily 1000–1800 (24 June–early Sept).

The Sulpicians settled here in 1721 on this point on Lac de Deux-Montagnes called Oka, meaning 'golden fish', as they sought to convert the Mohawk, Algonquin and Huron tribes who were allied with the French. (The Iroquois from New York decimated these tribes at the end of the 18th century in what the British and Americans called the French and Indian Wars.) The Mohawk, however, persist as a recognisable tribal unit and recently renamed their reserve lands *Kanesatake*, a place name seen along Rte 344 west of Oka village, which is the French settlement.

The **Abbaye Cistercienne**, *1600 ch. Oka (Rte 344); tel: (514) 479-8361*, resulted from a Sulpician land grant to Cistercian brothers from France in 1881. This religious community, locally nicknamed 'La Trappe', is particularly famed for its Oka cheese – a semi-soft, rind-ripened variety made nowhere else. Along with locally produced chocolate and maple syrup, this cheese is available in pieces and in wheels of differing sizes in **Le Magasin de l'Abbaye**; *tel: (514) 479-6170*, open Mon 1000–1200 and 1230–1630, Tues–Fri 0930–1200 and 1230–1630, and Sat 0930–1600. It is also worth a quick visit to the Abbey's **Romanesque Revival chapel**, open Mon–Sat 0400–2100.

The **Parc d'Oka**, *2020 ch. d'Oka (Rte 344); tel: (514) 479-8365*, admission $2, is one of the larger recreation and outdoor activity areas between Ottawa and Montréal. Well developed facilities managed by the provincial department of the environment include beaches suitable for swimming, 45 km of trails for summer hiking and cycling and winter cross-country skiing, an observation tower, floating walkways along fragile marsh environments and paths to the 168-m **Colline d'Oka**, a summit with a panoramic view.

One path crosses the oldest **outdoor stations of the cross** in North America, established by the Sulpicians in 1740. From early May–mid Sept, the park also offers 800 pitches for tents and caravans, with rates from $17.75–24, depending on facilities and proximity to the beach. For reservations; *tel: (514) 479-8337*.

◤ SIDE TRACK TO HUDSON

French-speaking Oka is connected to Hudson, its English-speaking cousin across the St Lawrence River, by the **Oka–Hudson ferry service**, *Oka quai; tel: (514) 458-4732*, which operates every 15 mins late Apr–mid Nov; variable hours, car and driver $5, each additional passenger $0.25. Although this floating platform under tow by a motorboat looks precarious, the 5-min trip is a safe and quick way to pop over to Hudson, an Anglophone town in Québec of considerable charm that is otherwise a one-hour remove by road.

Although Hudson has a number of tiny homestay lodgings, the best bet for an overnight is the handsomely appointed **Willow Place Inn**, *208 ch. Main, Hudson, PQ J0P 1H0; tel: (514) 458-7006*, moderate, which sits directly on the St Lawrence River looking across to the Oka monastery. Both its public areas and nine rooms are richly finished with Canadian antique furnishings. The dining room, which is open to the public, serves dinner daily, lunch Mon–Sat and Sun brunch at bargain rates. During warm weather there is additional patio seating.

More casual dining, especially at lunchtime, is available in the village centre at **Strudels Boulangerie and Patisserie**, *429 ch. Main; tel: (514) 458-2122*. To get a sample of some of the elegant New French provincial cooking sweeping parts of the province, try **Clémentine**, *398 ch. Main; tel: (514) 458-8181*, moderate. Hudson's centre boasts a concentrated shopping area that serves both local residents and the considerable number of day-trippers from Montréal. Two of the better shops for housewares and home decorating are **Pickering**, *407 ch. Main*, and, across the street, **Cornell Trading Ltd.** ◤

137

ST-JOSEPH-DU-LAC

This diffuse village of fewer than 5000 people is spread over a large area of rolling hills. St-Joseph is known for its apples, strawberries, raspberries, maple syrup and honey. Many farm stands offer these products in season at the side of the road. For outstanding *tarte au sucre* – the Québec brown sugar pie – stop at **Verger des Musiques**, *854 r. Principale; tel: (514) 623-4889*. Some of these farm operations offer pick-your-own fruit (strawberries June–July, raspberries July–Aug, apples Sept) and offer picnic grounds, tractor rides and other entertainment.

ST-EUSTACHE

Tourist Information: Bureau touristique région de Deux-Montagnes, *600 r. Dubois; tel: (514) 472-5825*, open daily 1000–1800 (24 June–early Sept).

St-Eustache has a special place in the hearts of Québecois because 250 of the valiant warriors of the Francophone Patriotes Rebellion against British rule made their last stand at the church here on 14 Dec 1837. The British leader bombarded the church, leaving only its walls standing at the end of the battle. The troops then burned most houses in the village to the ground. To this day, the residents of St-Eustache remain resistant to the English language. (The rebellion reverberates down to the present in modern sentiment for Québec's secession from English-speaking Canada.)

The walls of **Église de St-Eustache**, *r. St-Louis*, still bear the marks of the British cannon from the fateful day of 14 Dec 1837, when 1600 British soldiers crushed the 250 Patriotes. Since 1980, the Montréal Symphony has made its recordings here to take advantage of the superb acoustics. The church is open for viewing Tues 1300–1700, Wed–Fri 0900–1200 and 1300–1700, Sat 0900–1200 and Sun 1300–1700.

St-Eustache was part of the seigneurie of Rivière-du-Chêne, and the last seigneur, Charles-Auguste-Maximilien Globensky,

built himself a suitably grand home in 1863. The seigneurie system had been officially abolished in 1854, but the townsfolk still called it the *manoir*, and so it remains today **Manoir Globensky**, *235 r. St-Eustache; tel: (514) 974-5055*, open Mon–Fri 0900–1700. Ironically, the manoir is now the town hall, and the French architecture lies buried by a plantation-style Greek Revival renovation from 1902, making the building resemble a stage set from *Gone With the Wind*. The front room alone, however, speaks volumes about a country squire's life with its rich furnishings and expensive books.

Across the street is the **Moulin Légaré**, built in 1762–63 and one of the oldest grain mills still standing in Canada. A fine park makes strolling along the millstream a pleasure. The mill is open (free) Mon–Fri 0900–1200 and 1300–1700 and, June–Aug only, also Sat–Sun 1230–1630. An explanatory tour is available and the mill shop sells flour ground at the mill, local bread made from the flour and Oka cheese.

Guided walking tours of St-Eustache (in French only) concentrate on the history and development of the village. They are available daily at 1400 (late June–early Sept) from Manoir Globensky, adults $2.50, students and seniors $2.

Consider stopping for a French country lunch at **Restaurant Au Biniou**, situated in the centre of town in the historic **La Maison Plessis-Belair**, *163 r. St Eustache*. Au Biniou specialises in Breton crêpes, but also offers chicken and lobster dishes.

From mid Feb–end Apr, the town's 'sugar shacks' are busily boiling maple sap down into maple syrup. At least a half dozen along Rte 148 and the roads crossing it sell maple products ranging from maple syrup to maple sugar to 'sugar on snow' – literally the hot sap caramelised by dropping onto fresh snow. The regional cuisine association especially recommends **Cabane à Sucre Constantin**, *1054 blvd Arthur-Sauvé; tel: (514) 473-2374*.

MONTRÉAL

Although it is the second largest French-speaking city in the world, Montréal is as decisively North American as it is Francophone. Its early fortunes were made in furs and shipping as the most inland navigable port on the St Lawrence River, but today Montréal is a banking, manufacturing, software and world trade centre. It emerged as an international city with the Expo 67 world fair, which created the Métro system and Underground City as well as harbour islands as recreational and exposition resources.

The 1976 summer Olympiad prompted massive public works to create open spaces and the Olympic Park. Through the 1970s and 1980s, Montréal was an economic dynamo and served as an immigration magnet for French-speakers from around the globe, creating a polyglot city of great ethnic diversity. Perhaps no industry has so benefited from this immigration as food service. It is hard to find a better place to eat in all of North America.

Most younger Montréalers are fully bilingual in French, the language of their collective past, and English, the language of international commerce and pop culture. Throughout the Canadian constitutional crisis over the status of Québec province, Montréal has steadfastly and overwhelmingly favoured continued union.

TOURIST INFORMATION

Greater Montréal Convention and Tourism Bureau, *1555 r. Peel, Bureau 600, Montréal, PQ H3A 1X6; tel: (514) 844-5400,* produces superb maps and brochures available at the main **Infotouriste Centre**, *1001 r. du sq.-Dorchester* (Métro: Peel); *tel: (514) 873-2015;* open daily 0830–1930 (June–early Sept), daily 0900–1800 (early Sept–May). An additional centre with more variable hours is located at *174 r. Nôtre-Dame est.* Various ticket offices and reservation systems share quarters with the main Infotouriste Centre. **Montréal Reservation Centre;** *tel: (514) 284-2277* or *(800) 567-8687* (toll-free), handles event and tours reservations. **Hospitalité Canada Tours**; *tel: (514) 393-9049* or *(800) 665-1528,* offers tickets to most major attractions as well as complete packages that include hotels; the desk also makes hotel reservations free of charge.

139

WEATHER

July–Aug are humid and can be hot (up to 30°C). Winter is cold and snowy; the average Jan high is -8°C, and overnight lows in Feb can plummet to -25°C. May–June and Sept are nearly perfect, with daytime highs 18°–22°C and nighttime lows 10°–12°C.

ARRIVING AND DEPARTING

By Air

Montréal International Airport (Aéroport de Dorval) is the chief national and international airport, handling scheduled commercial flights from the USA, Canada and Europe; *tel: (514) 633-3105.* It is 20 km from downtown Montréal.

There is a **Thomas Cook Foreign Exchange** office at Dorval Airport, in the Arrivals level Customs hall.

Connaisseur Bus Company; *tel: (514) 934-1222,* provides service to downtown Montréal; Mon–Fri every 30 mins 0700–0800 and 2300–0130, every 20 mins 0800–2300; every 30 mins Sat–Sun 0700–0130. The bus stops at a few downtown hotels, the central rail station and the Voyageur Bus Terminal; $9, $17 return. Taxi approximately $28. Although travel time is longer, a public bus also services Dorval. From the terminal, take bus 204 going east to the Dorval terminus, then bus 211 going east to the Lionel-Groulx Métro station.

Montréal International Airport (Aéroport de Mirabel), about 50 km north-west of the city, handles charter, freight and private aircraft. Taxi fare to Montréal is approximately $65.

By Car

From Ottawa, see Ottawa to Montréal chapter, p. 131. From Québec City, either take Hwy 20 west to the Pont Champlain, then Hwy 10 (Autoroute Bonaventure) directly Downtown, or take Hwy 40 west to Hwy 15 south (Autoroute Décarie) and follow signs for 'Centre-Ville'. From the USA, via either Hwy 10 or Hwy 15, cross the Pont Champlain to Hwy 10 directly downtown.

By Rail

VIA Rail, *Gare Central, 895 r. de la Gauchetière Ouest (beneath Hotel La Reine Elizabeth* – Métro: *Bonaventure); tel: (514) 989-2626* or *(800) 361-5390,* connects daily to Ottawa, Toronto and Québec and frequently to Atlantic Canada and Vancouver. **Amtrak,** *tel: (800) 835-8725,* connects to New York City.

By Bus

All buses use **Terminus Voyageurs,** *505 blvd de Maisonneuve Est* (Métro: *Berri-UQAM); tel: (514) 842-2281.* **Orleans Express Coach Lines** connects to Québec City and elsewhere in the province. **Voyageur Colonial** connects to Atlantic

Canada and Ontario. **Adirondack Trailways** provides bus service between Montréal and New York City.

GETTING AROUND

The island of Montréal is large – 32 km at its longest point and 16 km at the widest, with 28 different municipalities – but the areas of most interest to visitors are on the south and east sides of the mountain that gave the city its name. Within each district, attractions are easy walking distance, and excellent public transit via an extensive network of subway trains and buses makes it very easy to hop between districts.

Vieux Montréal has most of the historic buildings and colourful, narrow streets dating from the 17th and 18th centuries. (Remnants of the 1642 town lie beneath the Point-à-Callière museum.) **Vieux Port,** the waterfront area of Vieux Montréal, has been recently redeveloped to create a 2-mile promenade and entertainments on the old piers. Former warehouses and chandleries on the surrounding streets are blossoming as art galleries, restaurants and boutique lodgings.

The definition of **Downtown** varies, but covers the business and shopping district from *av. St-Laurent* west to *r. du Fort,* from *r. Sherbrooke Ouest* down to Vieux Montréal. It contains many museums, all of the major shopping centres and most of the large hotels. **Av. St-Laurent** bisects the city: cross streets are numbered east or west. *Av. St-Laurent* and the nearby parallel **av. St-Denis** are the most lively streets in Montréal for restaurants, nightlife and boutique shopping, particularly in the district above *Sherbrooke* now generally called **Plateau Mont-Royal** or, more commonly, 'Le Plateau'. **Maisonneuve,** in the east end of the city, is predominantly residential but includes the complex of attractions around the Olympic Park and Botanical Gardens.

The **Underground City** is a 29-km network of underground passageways linked to the Métro system. Construction began in the

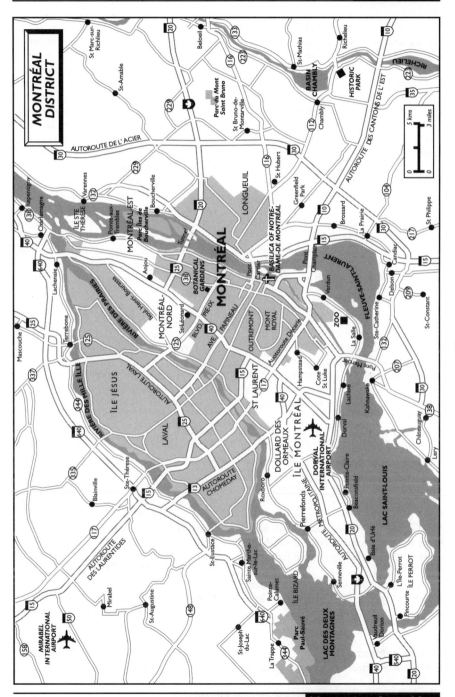

MONTRÉAL DISTRICT

141

1960s, and the underground continues to expand, now providing access to 1700 boutiques, department stores, restaurants, movie houses, theatres and seven major hotels. It is entirely possible – and in the coldest parts of Jan and Feb, often desirable – to spend several days in Montréal seeing the sights without ever stepping out of doors. City maps are free at the Infotouriste Centre, and Métro maps are available at most Métro stations.

Public Transport

The extensive network of bus and Métro (subway) lines that covers the city is operated by **Société de transport de la Communauté urbaine de Montréal**; *tel: (514) 288-6287.* Métro stations are identified by a blue sign with a downward-pointing arrow and the word Métro. Trains run every few minutes 0530–0100.

Bus stops are indicated by blue and white signs, and are usually found on street corners. Tickets for bus or Métro are $1.85 (or six for $8, 12 for $16). *La Carte touristique* provides unlimited travel for one day for $5, for three consecutive days for $12; available at the Infotouriste Centres and the Berri-UQAM Métro station. Buses also take exact change in coins.

To transfer from one bus to another, ask the driver of the first bus for a transfer when boarding. If transferring from a Métro line to a bus, take a transfer from the automated machine before leaving the station. Timetables for buses are available at the Métro stations where they stop. In general, Métro travel is safe at all hours, and the stations are clean and well policed. Neither the Métro nor the buses are fully accessible for persons with disabilities.

Passenger and bicycle ferry service between Vieux Port *(Quai Jacques-Cartier)* and Île Ste-Hélène runs late May–early Oct; $3.75; *tel: (514) 281-8000.*

Driving in Montréal

Driving in Montréal follows the aggressive

North American style, although it begins to approach the extremes of, say, Rome during the annual Grand Prix in mid June. Québec law prohibits turns from a red light. Seatbelts must be worn in both front and back seats. Most foreign drivers' licences are honoured in Québec for up to six months after arrival. Note that in Montréal, traffic lights are often located on the far side of intersections but that drivers are expected to stop at the white line before the intersection.

Limited parking is available at street meters ($1.50 per hour), but most visitors park at the plentiful garages for $7–20 per day. Montréal police ticket illegally parked cars aggressively, and tickets are expensive. On certain thoroughfares, parked vehicles are towed during rush hour. In addition, most rental car agencies impose a substantial surcharge ($20 or more) on parking tickets.

Car rental companies require that you be at least 21 years of age with at least one year's driving experience; a cash deposit of $500 or more may be required unless you rent with a credit card.

For a report in French on road conditions, particularly as they might be affected by weather; *tel: (514) 873-4121.*

Bicycles

Bicycling is an excellent way to see much of Montréal, with the exception of the crowded streets of the Downtown. A bicycle path network covers the island; ask for a map at the Infotouriste Centre. Bicycles may be taken on the Métro except during rush hours. Helmets are optional, but are strongly recommended.

STAYING IN MONTRÉAL

Accommodation

Lodging is available at every price range in Montréal, although budget accommodation is in short supply July–Aug, when rooms are expensive. Over all, hotels in Montréal are comparable in price to those in Toronto and

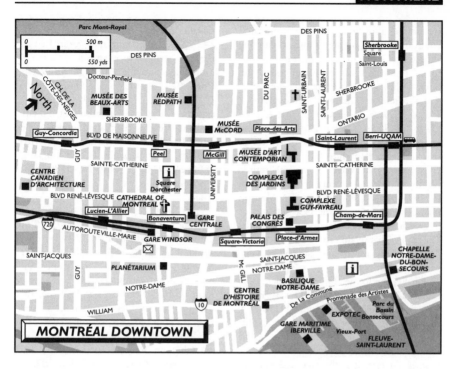

more expensive than in the rest of Québec. During the Grand Prix races in mid June and the Festival du Jazz in late June–early July, rooms are hard to find at any price and should be reserved well in advance.

Because Montréal is a business centre, rooms at hotels, in particular, tend to be less expensive on weekends. All room rates are subject to the 7% federal Goods and Services Tax and the 6.5% Québec provincial Services Tax, both of which are refundable to non-residents of Canada. A credit card is essential for making summer reservations, as many lodgings require prepayment of the first night. Within the city itself, motels are rare but hotels and Bed and Breakfast accommodations abound. Camping is not permitted anywhere on the island of Montréal.

Hotel chains include *BW, CP, De, DI, Hd, HJ, Hn, Ic, Ke, Ma, Nv, QI, Rd, RI, Rm, Sh, TL, We.*

Four notable Downtown hotels also serve as important meeting places and lodgings for celebrities as well as lesser-known visitors. The largest, and in many ways still the grandest, is **Hôtel La Reine Elizabeth**, *900 blvd René-Lévesque Ouest, Montréal, PQ H3B 4A5; tel: (514) 861-3511* or *(800) 441-1414,* which underwent extensive renovation in 1996. The 'Queen' serves as a social, business and political centre in Montréal, and its lobby is a supreme expression of traditional Canadian luxury. Its location above the train station and Bonaventure Métro station also make this CP hotel conveniently situated. Although stated room rates are expensive–pricey, packages and promotions often bring them down to the middle of the moderate range.

The **Ritz Carlton Kempinski Montréal**, *1228 r. Sherbrooke Ouest, Montréal, PQ H3G 1H6; tel: (514) 842-4212* or *(800) 363-0366,* remains a social centre for a significant portion of the Montréal elite and a favourite for visiting film and television production companies. Its rooms are furnished with fine antiques and the marbled bathrooms contribute to an air of luxury. Pricey room rates often decline Dec–Apr to merely expensive. **Le Marriott Château Champlain**, *1 Place du Canada, Montréal, PQ H3B 439; tel: (514) 878-9000 or (800) 228-9290*, is also known by locals as 'the cheese grater' for its unique landmark architecture. Owned by a consortium that includes several retired hockey stars, it underwent major renovations in 1995–97 and emerged under Marriott management as one of the best hotels in its price range. The sport world has made the Château Champlain its favoured hotel. Moderate–expensive rates are often mitigated by promotions.

Finally, the former Hôtel Meridien, now called **Hôtel du Complexe Desjardins**; *4 Complexe Desjardins, Montréal, PQ H5B 1E5; tel: (514) 285-1450 or (800) 361-8234*, is literally steps from Place des Arts and the Musée d'Art Contemporain. During the Festival du Jazz, it is the favoured hotel of musicians, many of whom can be found jamming at the bar long after the outdoor concerts have concluded. Rates range from expensive on weekdays and during the Festival du Jazz to moderate on weekends.

Many good business hotels also offer deep discounts on weekends and shoulder seasons, including the moderate–expensive **Hôtel Novôtel**, *1180 r. de la Montagne, Montréal, PQ H3G 1Z1; tel: (514) 861-6000 or (800) 668-6835*, the expensive–pricey **Hôtel Inter-Continental**, *360 r. St-Antoine Ouest, Montréal, PQ H2Y 3X4; tel: (514) 987-9900 or (800) 361-3600*, and the pricey but strikingly modern and elegant **Loews Hôtel Vogue**, *1425 r. de la Montagne, Montréal, PQ H3G 1Z3; tel: (514) 285-5555 or (800) 465-6654*.

For accommodation with a combination of outstanding hospitality, elegant design and unbeatable Old Montréal location, try **Les Passants du Sans Soucy**, *171 r. St-Paul*

Ouest, Montréal, PQ H2Y 1Z5; tel: (514) 842-2634, a moderate nine-room Bed and Breakfast attached to an art gallery, or the 27-room, non-smoking **Auberge du Vieux-Port**, *97 r. de la Commune Ouest, Montréal, PQ H2Y 1J1; tel: (514) 876-0081;* moderate–expensive. The most extensive of the city's Bed and Breakfast reservation services is **Bed and Breakfast Downtown Network**, *3458 av. Laval, Montréal, PQ H2X 3C8; tel: (514) 289-9749 or (800) 267-5180*, which represents properties in the mid–high budget range.

The least costly (low moderate) self-catering option Downtown is **La Tour Centre-Ville**, *400 blvd René-Levesque Ouest, Montréal, PQ H2Z 1V5; tel: (514) 866-8861 or (800) 361-2790*. La Tour Centre-Ville offers a swimming pool, sauna and exercise room and is located close to Place des Arts, making it a convenient location for the summer outdoor concert season. Two other moderate self-catering options Downtown are **Château Royal Hotel Suites**, *1420 r. Crescent, Montréal, PQ H3G 2B7; tel: (514) 848-0999 or (800) 363-0335*, and **L'Appartement-in-Montréal**, *455 r. Sherbrooke Ouest, Montréal, PQ H3A 1B7; tel: (514) 284-3634 or (800) 363-3010*. More luxurious and expensive self-catering suites are available at the **Marriott-Residence Inn Montréal**, *2045 r. Peel, H3A 1T6; tel: (514) 982-6064 or (800) 999-9494*, which was virtually rebuilt in a sweeping renovation in 1997.

The least expensive (budget–moderate) small hotels lie on *r. St-Hubert* uphill from the bus station, including the cozy **Hotel Bon Accueil**, *1601 r. St-Hubert, Montréal, PQ H2L 3Z1; tel: (514) 527-9655*, and the classier **Hotel L'Emérillon**, *1600 r. St-Hubert, Montréal, PQ H2L 3Z3; tel: (514) 849-3214 or (800) 613-3383*.

The **HI: Montréal Youth Hostel**, *1030 r. Mackay* (Métro: *Lucien-L'Allier); tel: (514) 843-3317*, is close to the Downtown in a pleasant residential neighbourhood; budget.

Rather rudimentary but exceptionally clean are the dormitory-style beds in **Auberge Alternative**, *358 r. St-Pierre, Montréal, PQ H2Y 2M1; tel: (514) 282-8069*, in Old Montréal; budget. Men, women and children are all welcome to the small rooms, each with one or two beds, at the Downtown **YMCA**, *1450 r. Stanley, Montréal, PQ H3A 2W6; tel: (514) 849-8393*, budget. From mid May–mid Oct, budget rentals are available in the 1100 two-bed rooms of the residence halls of **McGill University**, *550 r. Sherbrooke Ouest, West Tower, Suite 490, Montréal, PQ H3A 1B9; tel: (514) 398-3770; email: Reserve@ Residences.Ian.Mcgill.ca.*

Eating and Drinking
More than 5000 restaurants dot Montréal, and dining is a leading form of entertainment. French and North American cuisines dominate, followed closely by cuisines from Indochina, West Africa, Lebanon and Central Europe. Two local specialities are roast chicken dinners as pioneered in 1936 by **Rôtisserie Laurier**, *381 r. Laurier Ouest; tel: (514) 273-3671*, and 'smoked meat', a pickled-smoked brisket introduced in 1908 at **Ben's Delicatessen**, *990 blvd de Maisonneuve Ouest; tel: (514) 844-1000*.

To dine well but economically, choose the fixed midday menu and forgo the overpriced wine (provincial taxes seem designed to stamp out inebriation by making it unaffordable). Traditional French-Canadian dishes are seen less and less often but are found chiefly in cheap–budget neighbourhood restaurants. Some Québecois specialities you may encounter are *binnes* (beans), also known as *fèves au lard; la tourtière* (a meat pie) and *le cipaille*, a layered pie with different types of meat.

In the Downtown area near the hotels, many restaurants on *Crescent, Bishop* and *de la Montagne Sts* are overblown pubs, but the exceptions are truly exceptional. The best French meal in Downtown is at **Les Halles**,

1450 r. Crescent; tel: (514) 844-2328; pricey, and worth it. Excellent French provincial fare in a charming old house set among skyscrapers near McGill College is the order at **Le Caveau**, *2063 r. Victoria; tel: (514) 844-1624*; moderate. For haute cuisine where the food matches the legend, try **The Beaver Club** at the Queen Elizabeth Hotel, *900 blvd René-Lévesque Ouest; tel: (514) 861-3511*. A surprisingly excellent steak-frites meal is the only menu item at **L'Entrecôte St-Jean**, *2022 r. Peel; tel: (514) 281-6492*; moderate.

Affable and popular, **L'Actuel**, *1194 r. Peel; tel: (514) 866-1537*, was the pioneer Belgian restaurant in Montréal, specialising in mussels; moderate. Old-fashioned French restaurants have come and gone, but the great survivor – perhaps because it offers good food at good prices in a friendly atmosphere and has never changed its look – is **Le Paris**, *1812 r. Ste-Catherine Ouest; tel: (514) 937-4898*.

Visitors with access to self-catering will find many *dépanneurs*, or convenience stores, but few good markets near their lodgings. Two good options, however, are found west of Downtown. In addition to a mostly ethnic food court (budget), **Le Faubourg shopping centre**, *1616 r. Ste-Catherine Ouest* (Métro: *Guy-Concordia*), proffers a wide selection of fresh fruit, fish, meat, cheeses, beverages, ethnic foods and sundry snacks. Serious food shoppers and gourmets, however, should hop the Métro orange line (toward *Côte Vertu* from Downtown) to the *Atwater* stop and head directly to the **Marché Atwater**, *138 av. Atwater*. Growers from the countryside sell their produce from outdoor stalls. The interior is filled with purveyors of local meats, fish, breads and cheeses.

Québec produces more than 70 cheeses, and more than 50 of the artesanal cheeses from cow's, sheep's and goat's milk are offered at very good prices by **La Fromagérie du Marché Atwater**; *tel: (514) 932-4653*. Proprietor Gilles Jourdenais will also vacuum-pack and ship Québec cheeses.

145

Look also for the handmade chocolates at **Boulangerie Première Moison**; *tel: (514) 932-0328.*

The restaurants of Vieux Montréal tend to fall in extremes of the fast-food *terrasses* of *Place Jacques-Cartier* and wonderful provincial French spots like the masterful and eponymous **Claude Postel**, *443 r. St-Vincent; tel: (514) 875-5067*, pricey, and the charmingly bourgeois **Bonaparte**, *443 r. François-Zavier; tel: (514) 844-4368.*

Even amid the hamburger-fries hubbub of *Place Jacques-Cartier* there are some notable exceptions for both quality and value. **Le Jardin Nelson**, *407 Place Jacques-Cartier; tel: (514) 861-5731*, specialises in excellent Breton crêpes, served during warm weather in two large outdoor gardens as a chamber music group (weekdays) or a jazz combo (weekends) plays; budget–moderate.

Directly across a little square from the Centre d'Histoire de Montréal is the *très charmant* and extremely reasonable **Le Gargote**, *351 Place d'Youville; tel: (514) 844-1428*, which offers two choices of traditional French cuisine each night with complete meals at budget prices. A Montréal institution for Polish cuisine at budget–moderate prices reopened two blocks away in Vieux Port after its old spot next to the Notre-Dame basilica suffered a disastrous fire: **Stash's Café Bazar**, *200 r. St-Paul; (514) 845-6611.*

As in most cities with a substantial Chinese population, a vast number of tiny, mostly budget restaurants dot Montréal's Chinatown, which is located between Old Montréal and Downtown, principally on *r. de la Gauchetière* between *av. St-Urbain* and *blvd St-Laurent*. Unlike Toronto, with its large Cantonese population, spicy Szechuan cuisine dominates in Montréal. By and large, you get what you pay for,' with the exception of the exquisite and authentic Szechuan dishes at **Hun Dao**, *1065 blvd St-Laurent; tel: (514) 874-0093*, which prepares a memorable spicy salt-and-pepper squid; budget.

The liveliest and most diverse dining in the city is found on the *Plateau Mont-Royal*, mostly along *avs St-Denis* and *St-Laurent* and their cross streets. This neighbourhood has absorbed successive waves of immigration from Central Europe and Italy earlier in the century, and from Portugal, West Africa, North Africa and Latin America in more recent years. St-Laurent features the cuisines of Central Europe and speciality stores that proffer sausages, spices and other imports. St-Denis is action-central for sidewalk dining and young chefs' own restaurants, of which the brightest star is Normand Laprise at the eccentric and witty **Toqué**, *3842 r. St-Denis; tel: (514) 499-2084;* moderate–pricey.

A locally rooted version of traditional French cuisine shows up at **Allumette**, *3434 r. St-Denis; tel: (514) 284-4239*, moderate–pricey. For a good buy on French bistro fare in small and friendly surroundings, try **Persil Fou**, *4669 r. St-Denis; tel: (514) 284-3130*, moderate.

For cheesy Swiss dishes, visit the old house converted into **Fondue Mentale**, *4325 r. St-Denis; tel: (514) 499-1446*, moderate. Among the budget options on the Plateau are the Belgian fries-and-sausage restaurant known as **Frite Alors**, *433 r. Rachel; tel: (514) 843-2490;* the simple food in an aluminum-and-neon structure at **Galaxie Diner**, *4801 r. St-Denis; tel: (514) 499-9711*, and the strikingly excellent French-Algerian fare (couscous, lamb kebab) on the *terrasse* at **Bistro Méditerranéen**, *3857 r. St-Denis; tel: (514) 843-5028.*

St-Denis is also the home of many other often-excellent ethnic eateries from Ethiopian to Cambodian and Thai. They are typically budget–moderate.

Communications

Canada Post offices are open Mon–Fri 0800–1745. The two main offices are at *1250 r. University; tel: (514) 395-4909*, and *1250 r. Ste-Catherine Ouest; tel: (514) 522-5191.*

The area code for all of Montréal is *514*. Pay phones are much cheaper than in Europe and easy to use. All machines accept coins of $0.05, $0.10 and $0.25 and many accept credit cards. Local calls cost $0.25, but it is wise to have a roll or two of $0.25 pieces (called quarters in English or *trente sous* in colloquial French), available at banks.

Money

The proliferation of automatic teller machines (ATMs) that accept both bank cards and international credit cards threatens to put currency exchange offices out of business in Montréal, as an ATM may be found on virtually every corner in the shopping and entertainment districts. Royal Bank and Caisse Popular Desjardins have the largest number of outlets. Automated currency exchange machines are available 0600–0200 daily at Complexe Desjardins on *r. Ste-Catherine* between *r. Jeanne-Mance* and *r. St-Urbain,* and at Dorval airport. These machines will convert most major currencies into Canadian money and will convert Canadian bills into American dollars or French francs.

Consulates

Belgium: *999 blvd de Maisonneuve Ouest, Suite 850* (Métro: *Peel).*
Germany: *1250 blvd René-Levesque Ouest, Suite 4315* (Métro: *Bonaventure).*
The Netherlands: *1002 r. Sherbrooke Ouest* (Métro: *Peel).*
UK: *1155 r. University* (Métro: *McGill).*
USA: *Place Félix-Martin, 1155 r. St-Alexandre* (Métro: *Place des Arts).*

ENTERTAINMENT

English-language schedules of performances, exhibitions, club dates and movies appear in the Friday edition of *Gazette.* Performances are also listed in the free (and widely available) weekly newspapers, *The Mirror, Voir* and *Hour.*

Gay entertainment is especially well served by three telephone lines that detail activities and diversions: **The Gay Line**; *tel: (514) 990-1414* in English, **Gai Écoute**; *tel: (514) 521-1508* in French, and **Gai-Info**; *tel: (514) 768-0199,* which is bilingual.

Centre Info-Arts Bell, *Places-des-Arts; tel: (514) 790-ARTS,* provides information about all arts activities Mon–Sat 1100–2000, Sun 1200–1700. Three ticket agencies sell admission to concerts, shows and other events over the telephone, adding service charges: **Admission**; *tel: (514) 790-1245* or *(800) 361-4595;* **Telspec**; *tel: (514) 790-2222;* and **Billetterie Articulé**; *tel: (514) 844-2172.*

Bars, Cafés and Clubs

Montréal is a sociable city, and Montréalers consider entertainment to be incomplete without the addition of good conversation and drink – either alcohol or strong coffee. Distinctions among bars, clubs, discos, cafés and restaurants are consequently very blurred.

Interest in jazz has blossomed in Montréal in recent years. The two well-established clubs are **L'Air du Temps**, *194 r. St-Paul Ouest* in the Old Port, and **Biddles**, *2060 r. Aylmer,* Downtown, near McGill and Concordia Universities, where bassist Charles Biddle is on hand most nights. Also Downtown is **Upstairs**, *1254 r. Mackay,* which features jazz and blues shows every night. Despite the name, a casual and relaxed jazz scene reigns at **Club Chaos**, *1635 r. St-Denis,* while the drinks are cheap and the jazz always interesting at **Le Central**, *4479 r. St-Denis.*

Good local blues can be heard at **Inspecteur Épingle**, *4051 r. St-Hubert.* The dance-till-you-drop crowd frequents **Dogue**, *4177 r. St-Denis,* while alternative rock is the beat at the youngish **Les Foufs** discotheque, *87 r. Ste-Catherine Est,* something of a pick-up joint.

French-speaking tourists throng to sing along with Québec variety singers at **Aux**

147

Deux Pierrots, *104 r. St-Paul Ouest*. Celtic music rings out at **Hurley's Irish Pub**, *1225 r. Crescent*, **Pub le Vieux-Dublin**, *1219 r. University*, and **Finnigan's**, *79 r. Prince-Arthur Est*. The leading African nightclub in Montréal is the smoky and packed **Le Balattou**, *4372 blvd St-Laurent*, which presents live music during the week only (prices vary), but is a popular meeting spot at weekends ($7 cover charge, including one drink).

Gay and Lesbian Nightlife

The principal gay district of Montréal is **The Village**, which centres on *r. Ste-Catherine Est*, between *r. Amherst* and *r. Papineau*.

The transvestite shows of **Cabaret l'Entre-Peau**, *1115 r. Ste-Catherine Est*, attract a mixed and lively crowd, while the quiet piano bar of **Club Date**, *1218 r. Ste-Catherine Est*, is predominantly patronised by well-dressed older men. Young men seem to prefer the **Katacombes** and **Home** nightclubs of **Station C**, *1450 r. Ste-Catherine Est*, a complex that also includes the lesbian disco **Sisters** and the mixed-crowd **K.O.X.**

Women looking for a quiet spot to converse often choose **O'Side**, *4075A r. St-Denis*. The busiest gay bar in Montréal is the refined **Sky Pub**, *1474 r. Ste-Catherine Est*, which has a youthful techno-pop alter ego called **Sky** located upstairs.

Performing Arts

Locally based performing arts groups that appear in the five theatres of Place des Arts include **Orchestre Symphonique de Montréal**; *tel: (514) 842-9951;* **Les Grands Ballets Canadiens**; *tel: (514) 849-8681;* and **Le Opéra de Montréal**; *tel: (514) 985-2258*. The box office number for Place des Arts; *tel: (514) 842-2112*.

Centaur Theatre, *453 r. St-François-Xavier;* *tel: (514) 288-3161*, presents an extensive season of live theatre in English. Free open-air shows of French-language theatre are presented by **Théâtre de Verdure**; *tel: (514) 872-2644*, in Parc Lafontaine.

Amusements

The **Casino de Montréal**; *tel: (514) 392-2746*, open daily 0900–0500, occupies the former French and Québec pavilions from Expo 67 on Île Notre-Dame. With 100 gaming tables and more than 2700 slot machines (and a separate non-smoking section), the Casino is one of the ten largest in the world. It cultivates decorum through a dress code banning casual attire. The cabaret shows featuring Las Vegas headliners also draw a crowd. Free casino shuttle bus departs *sq.-Dorchester* (near Infotouriste Centre) on the hour 1100–1800. By public transit: Métro: *Île Ste-Hélène* and Bus 167.

Although the **Cirque du Soleil**, *Vieux Port; tel: (514) 790-1245*, is based in Montréal, it performs its elaborate shows of acrobatics and mime only on even-numbered years at *Quai Jacques-Cartier*. The **École Nationale de Cirque**, *417 r. Berri; tel: (514) 982-0859*, is one of only five independent schools in the world that trains circus performers. Its highly entertaining graduation show plays for 10 days in late May to packed houses in its headquarters in a former train station on the east end of Old Montréal.

La Ronde amusement park, *Île Ste-Hélène* (Métro: *Île Ste-Hélène*/Bus 167 or Métro: *Papineau*/Bus 169); *tel: (514) 872-6100*, open late May–early Sept, is the largest of its kind in the region; day pass $18.87. La Ronde hosts the annual fireworks festival on Sat and Sun nights June–July.

Movie Theatres

Two major downtown theatres show films exclusively in English: **Égyptien**, *Cours Mont-Royal, 145 r. Peel; (514) 849-3456*, and **Loews**, *954 r. Ste-Catherine Ouest; tel: (514) 861-7437*. **Cinéma du Parc**, *3575 av. du Parc; tel: (514) 287-7272*, shows repertory English-language films or films dubbed or subtitled in English.

Office National du Film Montréal, *1564 r. St-Denis; tel: (514) 283-4823*, has movie and video theatres as well as 21 cinescope stations to view Canadian and Québecois films. **IMAX**, *Quai King-Edward, Vieux Port; tel: (514) 496-4629,* is Montréal's version of the 7-storey-high cinema screen.

Sporting Events

In 1997, the **Montréal Canadiens** professional hockey team moved its operations to the *Centre Molson, 1250 r. de la Gauchetière; tel: (514) 989-2841*. The 42 games of the regular season begin in Oct, but play off season stretches into May. The team has won the Stanley Cup 24 times. The **Montréal Expos** professional baseball team plays Apr–Sept at **Olympic Stadium**, *4549 av. Pierre-de-Coubertin; tel: (514) 846-3976*.

Some 45,000 cyclists pedal 65 km around the island of Montréal in early June each year in the **Tour de l'Île**. Registration begins in April; for forms, contact *Tour de l'Île de Montréal, 1251 r. Rachel Est, Montréal, PQ H2J 2J9; tel: (514) 847-8356*. Race car aficionados descend on Montréal from all over the world in mid June for the three days of **Grand Prix Player's du Canada**, held on Île Notre-Dame. To reserve seats; *tel: (514) 350-0000*.

Outdoor Sports

With many trails set up in the parks and along even major thoroughfares, bicycling is a popular outdoor activity. Up-to-date information on bike paths and trails, as well as information on rentals, are available by visiting **La Maison de Cyclistes**, *1251 r. Rachel Est; tel: (514) 521-8356,* open daily 0900–1700.

Cyclepop, *978 r. Rachel Est; tel: (514) 524-7102,* rents bicycles at rates beginning at $25 for the first day and $12 for additional days. Rate includes delivery and pick up at your hotel. Similar deals may be struck with **La Cordée**, *2159 r. Ste-Catherine Est; tel: (514) 524-1515,* which charges $35 per day but includes insurance. **Vélo-Aventure** in the Vieux Port also rents bicycles by the

hour, half day and full day, with rates changing with the season.

The bicycle paths of the Vieux Port around Canal Lachine are particularly scenic, if sometimes crowded, on weekends. Parc LaFontaine, where the Maison des Cyclistes is located, offers broader, leafier paths and less bicycle traffic, as it lies in a residential neighbourhood.

The artificial lake of **Parc LaFontaine** (Métro: *Sherbrooke)* turns into one of the city's best outdoor ice-skating rinks in the winter. Other outstanding public rinks, where skates are usually available for rental, include **Bonsecours Basin** on the waterfront at Promenade du Vieux Port (Métro: *Champs-de-Mars);* **Lac aux Castors** at the summit of Mont-Royal Park (Métro: *Mont-Royal,* bus 11); **Parc Maisonneuve**, *4601 r. Sherbrooke Est,* across from Olympic Stadium. (Métro: *Pié-IX* or *Viau);* and the **Olympic Rowing Basin** on Île Notre-Dame, near the Montréal Casino (Métro: *Parc-des-Îles).* **Indoor ice skating** is available all year at **Bell Amphitheatre**, *1000 de la Gauchetière Ouest; tel: (514) 395-0555.*

Events

Montréal celebrates a festival with the slightest provocation. The **Festival International de Jazz de Montréal**, late June–early July, is one of the five largest jazz festivals in the world with more than 350 shows, including several nights of outdoor concerts at Place des Arts. The **Festival Juste Pour Rire** (mid July–end July), with more than 300 shows in both indoor and outdoor venues – some in French, some in English – is the world's largest festival of humour.

Le Concours Internationale d'Art Pyrotechnique (mid June–late July), the world's largest fireworks competition, takes place at La Ronde amusement park on Île Ste-Helène, but can be viewed for free from the Pont Jacques-Cartier. **La Fête de St-Jean-Baptiste**, 24 June, is Québec

149

province's 'national' day and is celebrated in Montréal with non-stop parties in the streets, homes and bars.

For 10 days at the end of July and beginning of Aug, the city buzzes with concerts by musical artists from throughout the French-speaking world (Europe, Africa, the French Antilles, Québec and other Francophone parts of Canada) in the **FrancoFolies**; *tel: (514) 871-1881*. In late Aug–early Sept, the city's theatres are filled 0900–2400 with the **Festival International des Films du Monde**; *tel: (514) 848-3883*.

Cold weather doesn't deter Montréal from celebrations. The **Fête des Neiges** takes place on Île Notre-Dame late Jan–early Feb, with ice-skating, giant toboggans and snowmobile and ice-boat racing.

Old Montréal is rife with souvenir shops. The western edge of the **Old Port** district, between *Point-à-Callière* and *Place d'Youville*, is in an interesting bohemian flux, with new art galleries featuring young artists opening at a steady pace. Although portions have become seedy, *r. Ste-Catherine Ouest* is the traditional shopping street, with the grand old department stores and entrances to many of the shopping centres that also link to the Underground City.

Perhaps the most extensive bookstore (about three-quarters in English) is **Chapters**, *1171 r. Ste-Catherine Ouest*. The three largest shopping centres in the city are along *r. Ste-Catherine* (Métro: *McGill*): **Place Montréal Trust** and **Le Centre Eaton de Montréal**, both at the corners with *r. McGill College*, and **Les Promenades de la Cathédrale**, a half-block west. (The most important shopping centres of the Underground not directly on *r. Ste-Catherine* are **Place Ville-Marie** and **Place Bonaventure**.)

Montréal is arguably the best place in North America to buy stylish clothes for cold weather. Québec designers are featured at

Artefact, *4117 r. St-Denis*, and **Revenge**, *3852 r. St-Denis*. Locally designed and produced winter outerwear is a specialty of **Kanuk**, *485 r. Rachel Est*. Montréal's original *raison d'être* was the fur trade; two fine furriers in the Downtown are **Desjardins Fourrure**, *325 blvd René-Lévesque Est; tel: (514) 288-4151*, and **McComber**, *440 blvd de Maisonneuve Ouest; tel: (514) 845-1167*.

The stretch of *r. Notre-Dame Ouest* around the 1800 block is known as '*rue des antiquaires*' because more than 45 dealers in antiques and collectables line the street. Among them is a charming combination antiques shop and tearoom, **Ambiance**, *1874 r. Notre-Dame Ouest; tel: (514) 939-2609*. Dozens of other dealers in used, collectable and antique goods occupy the hangar-like building of **Marché aux Puces** (or Flea Market) on *Quai King-Edward* in the Old Port. **Davidoff**, *1452 r. Sherbrooke Ouest; tel: (514) 289-9118*, carries fine Cuban cigars.

Several galleries featuring graphic arts, painting and crafts lie on *r. Sherbrooke Ouest* in the two blocks west of the Musée des Beaux-Arts. For 10 days in Dec, **Québec Arts and Crafts Show** at Place Bonaventure features the work of studio craft artists of the province. Year-round outlets for Canadian, Québec, Inuit and Amerindian crafts and arts include the **Guild Canadienne des Métiers d'Arts**, *2025 r. Peel; tel: (514) 849-6091*, and **Le Chariot**, *446 Place Jacques-Cartier; tel: (514) 875-6134*, which focuses on Inuit and Amerindian work.

By Bus

Bus tours leave from Infotouriste Centre, *1001 r. sq.-Dorchester;* tickets sold at centre and many hotels; $23.50–25. Several bus tours allow reboarding (late June–early Oct), including **Murray Hill Trolley Bus**; *tel: (514) 871-4733*, and **Royal City Tour**;

tel: (514) 871-4733. **Amphi-Bus Tour**; *tel: (514) 849-5181*, leaves from *Quai King-Edward* (junction of r. *de la Commune* and r. *St-Laurent*), Vieux Port, to tour city and adjacent river in an amphibious vehicle; reservations required; (May–Oct), adults $18.

By Boat

Closest Métro for all boat tours: *Champs-de-Mars*. **Le Bateau-Mouche**, *Quai Jacques-Cartier, Vieux Port; tel: (514) 849-9952*, modeled on the Parisian tour ships, cruises upstream through ancient locks, under bridges and around the islands of Expo 67, May–Oct; adults $21.95 for 1½-hr scenic cruise, $62.75 for 3-hr dinner cruise; weekday 1000 tours, children under 12 free with adult. **Croisières du Port de Montréal**, *Quai Victoria, Vieux Port; tel: (514) 842-3871* or *(800) 667-3131*, cruises 2 hrs around Vieux Port and nearby islands, including Île Ste-Hélène (mid May–early Oct); adults $21.75. **Croisières Nouvelle Orléans**, *Quai Jacques-Cartier, Vieux Port; tel: (514) 842-7655* or *(800) 667-3131*, offers a 1½-hr cruise on a replica of a Mississippi riverboat (mid May–early Oct); adults $16.75. **Saute moutons Jet St-Laurent**, *Quai de l'Horologe, Vieux Port; tel: (514) 284-9607*, shoots the Lachine rapids upstream twice on a jet boat with passengers riding back down on rafts; adults $48.

Walks and Rides

Ask at the main Infotouriste Centre for various walking tours, including the detailed booklet, *Old Montreal: A Walking Tour*, which pokes into obvious and less obvious corners of Vieux Montréal. High points for many visitors are the Nôtre-Dame church and a *calèche* (horse-drawn carriage) tour ($30 for half an hour, $50 for an hour).

Less documented but fascinating in its own right is the **Vieux Port**; *tel: (514) 496-PORT*, which was reclaimed as a recreational area in time for the 350th anniversary

in 1992. The piers have many entertainments, but the highlight is the green promenade from the *Quai de l'Horologe*, or Clocktower, lookout westward to the old lock system.

Heritage Montréal; *tel: (514) 875-2985*, offers 2-hr **Architectural Walking Tours** of Downtown Montréal (June–mid Oct) daily at 1400 from the kiosk on *sq.-Dorchester* opposite the Infotouriste office. Tickets must be purchased in advance from the Ulysse bookstore inside the Infotouriste Centre; $8.

A tour of city highlights by bicycle can be arranged with **Vélo-Tour Montréal**; *tel: (514) 236-8356*. The $25 package includes guide, bicycle and free transportation to the top of Mont-Royal, where the tour begins.

Parks

The vast green space of **Parc du Mont-Royal** in the centre of the island was designed by Frederick Law Olmsted (best known for Central Park in New York City and for Boston's 'Emerald Necklace' of parks) and has been a recreational resource since the 1870s. Footpaths and bicycle paths become cross-country ski trails in winter. Lac aux Castors at the west end of the park becomes a skating rink.

Parc des Îles (Métro: *Île Ste-Hélène*), in the middle of the St Lawrence River, comprises the natural island of Île Ste-Hélène and the man-made Île Notre-Dame. The islands were developed for Expo 67, and the city has made adaptive reuse of the site for La Ronde amusement park, the Casino de Montréal, and **La Biosphère**, *160 Tour d'Isle, Île Ste-Hélène* (Métro: *Île Ste-Hélène*); *tel: (514) 283-5000*, open daily 1000–2000 (early June–Sept), 0900–1800 (Oct–May), adults $7.50. Occupying Buckminster Fuller's landmark geodesic dome, which was the USA pavilion at Expo 67, La Biosphère is an environmental educational centre about the St Lawrence River and the Great Lakes.

The park's beach and swimming pools are

MONTRÉAL

popular in the summer. In winter, it has toboggan slides and 14 km of cross-country ski trails. The former Olympic rowing basin becomes a 2-km-long skating rink. **Olympic Park** (Métro: *Viau*) dates from the 1976 summer Olympiad. **La Tour de Montréal** arches above the stadium and provides a panoramic view of the city and St Lawrence valley, open Mon 1200–2100, Tues–Thur 1000–2100, Fri–Sun 1000–2300 (mid June–early Sept), Mon 1200–1800 and Tues–Sun 1000–1800 (early Sept–mid June), adults $8.25.

Olympic Stadium is home to the Montréal Expos baseball team. At its base is the Sports Centre, with pools where visitors may train, swim, dive, scuba dive or work out. Tours of the stadium cost $6. The nearby **Jardins Botaniques** and **Insectarium**, *4101 r. Sherbrooke Est; tel: (514) 872-1400,* open daily 0900–1700 (Sept–late June), 0800–2000 (late June–Aug), adults $8.75 ($14.75 with Biodôme), are beautiful and creepy, respectively.

Biodôme de Montréal, *4777 r. Pierre-de-Coubertin (Métro: Viau); tel: (514) 868-3000,* open daily 0900–1800 (Sept–late June), 0900–2000 (late June–Aug) adults $9.50 ($14.75 with Jardins Botaniques and Insectarium), contains four distinct environments – the tropical rain forest, the temperate Laurentian forest, the St-Laurent marine environment and the polar world – complete with flora and fauna.

Museums and Historic Sites
The **Montréal Museums Pass**, available at Infotouriste Centre and most participating museums, provides entrance to 19 museums: one day costs $18 (family $35), three days $30 (family $65).

Downtown
Musée des Beaux-Arts, *1379 r. Sherbrooke Ouest* (Métro: *Peel* or *Guy-Concordia); tel: (514) 285-1600,* open Tues–Sun 1100–1800, Wed 1100–2100, free, has superb

collections of Canadian and Arctic art. Touring exhibitions often unseen elsewhere in North America cost $10. In a striking new facility inaugurated in mid 1997, the **Musée des Arts Decoratifs**, *2200 r. Crescent* (Métro: *Peel); tel: (514) 259-2575,* open Tues–Sun 1100–1800, Wed 1100–2100, adults $6, emphasises decorative art and industrial design from 1935 to the present day. It is known around the world for its stunning collection of modern jewellery. **Centre Canadien d'Architecture**, *1920 r. Baile* (Métro: *Atwater* or *Guy-Concordia); tel: (514) 939-7026,* open Wed and Fri 1100–1700, Thur 1100–2000, Sat–Sun 1100–1700 (Oct–May), Tues–Sun 1100–1800, Thur 1100–2100 (June–Sept), $6, is devoted to great architecture all over the world, with particular emphasis on Montréal. **Musée d'Art Contemporain de Montréal**, *185 r. Ste-Catherine* (Métro: *Place-des-Arts); tel: (514) 847-6212,* emphasises Québec and international art after 1940 with excellent guided tours; open Tues–Sun 1100–1800, Wed 1100–2000, $6, free Wed evenings.

The **McCord Museum of Canadian History**, *690 r. Sherbrooke Ouest* (Métro: *McGill*/Bus 24); *tel: (514) 398-7100,* open Tues–Fri 1000–1800, Sat–Sun 1000–1700, $7 but free Sat 1000–1200, is the grand dame of national history museums in Canada, and since its mid 1990s renovation has focused principally on cultural history.

Musée Juste Pour Rire, *2111 blvd St-Laurent* (Métro: *St-Laurent); tel: (514) 845-4000,* open Tues–Sun 1300–2000, adults $11, is about humour – as well as spectacle, sensation and a peculiarly French-Canadian take on cinema.

Vieux Montréal
Pointe-à-Callière, Montréal Museum of Archaeology and History, *350 Place Royale* (Métro: *Place d'Armes*/Bus 26); *tel: (514) 872-9150,* open Tues–Fri 1000–1700, Sat–Sun 1100–1700 (July–Aug weekends

until 1800), $8, stands on the site of the original city settlement and brilliantly relates land, trade, culture and language. Clever interactive exhibits tell the more conventional tale of civic growth at the **Centre d'Histoire de Montréal**, *335 place d'Youville* (Métro: *sq.-Victoria); tel: (514) 872-3207,* open daily 0900–1700 (early May–mid June), daily 1000–1800 (mid June–early Sept), Tues–Sun 1000–1700 (early Sept–mid Dec), non-resident adults $5.

A feel for Montréal's role as the economic and political centre of Canada in the 19th century comes through at the **Sir George-Étienne Cartier National Historic Site**, *458 r. Notre-Dame Est* (Métro: *Champs-de-Mars); tel: (514) 283-2282,* open Wed–Sun 1000–1700 (Sept–mid May), daily 0900–1700 (mid May–Aug), adults $4. **Basilique Notre-Dame**, *110 r. Notre-Dame Ouest; tel: (514) 842-2925,* open daily 0700–1800 (early Sept–late June), daily 0700–2000 (late June–early Sept), is a masterpiece of neo-Gothic architecture constructed 1824–1829. **Musée des Hospitalières de l'Hôtel de Montréal**, *201 av. des Pins Ouest* (Métro: *Sherbrooke/Bus 144); tel: (514) 849-2919,* open Tues–Fri 1000–1700 and Sat–Sun 1300–1700 (mid June–mid Oct), Wed–Sun 1300–1700 (mid Oct–mid June), adults $5, relates the tale of a key influence in Montréal history, the Hospitalières de St-Joseph, who first arrived in 1659.

The Islands
David M. Stewart Museum, Museum of Discoveries, *Le Fort, Île Ste-Hélène* (Métro: *Île Ste-Hélène); tel: (514) 861-6701,* open daily 1000–1800 (late June–early Sept), Wed–Mon 1000–1700 (early Sept–late June), adults $5, is a repository of early maps and documents of exploration. In recent years, it has also featured costumed interpreters suggesting life at the fort, built in the 1770s to guard against an invasion by the Americans. Both the skirling bagpipes and tartans of the Olde 78th Fraser Highlanders and the blue-and-grey of La Compagnie Franche de la Marine add to the spectacle.

OUT OF TOWN
Laval, Québec's second largest city, is reached by any of four bridges via Hwys 15, 19 or 25, or by Rte 335. Although it is contiguous with Montréal, Laval claims its own tourist district.

Tourist Information: Maison du Tourisme, *2900 blvd St-Martin Ouest, Laval, PQ H7T 2J2; tel: (514) 682-5522 or (800) 463-3765,* open Mon–Fri 0900–1700, extended hours July–Aug.

The Cosmodôme and Space Camp Canada, *2150 autoroute des Laurentides (Hwy 15), St-Martin Ouest exit; tel: (514) 978-3600 or (800) 565-CAMP,* isn't exactly NASA, but it does offer an excellent introduction to the exploration of outer space and Canada's role in that great human endeavour. Space Camp offers half-day programmes for elementary and secondary school students. The multimedia exhibition on space exploration is open to all. It is open daily 1000–1800 (late June–Aug), Tues–Sun 1000–1800 (Sept–late June), adults $8.75, children 6–12 $5, family $22.

The **Parc de la rivière des Mille-Îles**, *345 blvd Ste-Rose; tel: (514) 622-1020,* serves as the departure for eco-excursions by canoe, kayak and pedal-boat. It is open Mon–Fri 0900–1800 and Sat–Sun 0900–2000 (mid May–Sept). The interpretation centre and equipment rentals are open only late June–Aug. Park admission is free. Pedal boats and rowboats rent for $7 an hour or $35 a day, canoes for $7 an hour or $30 a day, kayaks for $6 an hour or $25 a day.

Laval has two public golf courses: **Club de Golf Le Cardinal**, *1000 ch. St-Antoine; tel: (514) 627-3077;* and **Golf St-François**, *3000 blvd des Mille-Îles; tel: (514) 666-4958.*

LAURENTIANS

The *Laurentides* (Laurentians in English) are among the world's oldest mountains, ground down by glaciers into sandy soil. They were almost unpopulated until a century ago, when an effort to sustain Québec's population made land available here to impoverished farm families along the St-Laurent valley. But sandy soil and a short growing season made the district ill-suited to farming. Those who settled in the Pays d'en Hautes soon found that summer farming had to be supplemented with winter woodcutting – hardly a lucrative occupation. Not until the development of the ski industry after World War II and the more recent boom in ecotourism has the district enjoyed a sound economic footing.

The *Laurentides* are now Montréal's premier outdoor playground – a land of mountains and alpine lakes, where downhill skiing reigns supreme in the winter (supplemented by both cross-country skiing and snowmobiling) and cycling and canoeing provide summer recreation.

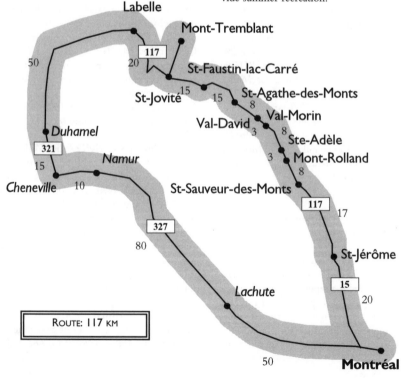

ROUTE

From downtown Montréal, take *r. Sherbrooke Ouest* (Rte 138 Ouest) through the suburb of **Westmount** for 5 km to the junction with Hwy 15 north. Hwy 15 joins Hwy 40 – watch signs carefully for appropriate lanes to stay on Hwy 15 north toward **St-Jérôme**. In 55 km, turn off on exit 43-E for St-Jérôme and Rte 117. Continue on Rte 117, with jogs off side roads to reach individual villages, to **St-Jovité**, another 130 km. Turn right onto Rte 327 north and 4 km further to reach **Mont-Tremblant**.

For a speedy return to Montréal, retrace your route to Hwy 15. Die-hard scenery watchers can loop back toward Montréal via a side track on poor roads through small villages and the **Papineau–Labelle Wildlife Reserve**.

TOURIST INFORMATION

For tourist information in advance, write to **Association touristique des Laurentides**, *14 142 rue de la Chapelle, RR#1, St-Jérôme, PQ J7Z 5T4; tel: (514) 436-8532 or (800) 561-6673* (toll-free); available by telephone daily 0900–1700. For free central reservation assistance; *tel: (800) 561-6673.* For information in person: **La Maison du Tourisme des Laurentides**, *Hwy 15, exit 39;* open daily 0830–2030 (late June–early Sept), daily 0900–1700, Fri 0900–1900 (rest of year).

ST-JÉRÔME

Between 1880 and 1895, the St-Jérôme parish priest, Curé Antoine Labelle, launched his efforts to colonise the Laurentides area, reasoning that the impoverished workers who were emigrating to work in the mills of New England would stay in Québec if they only had their own land to farm.

This town is sometimes called the 'Gateway to the North' because it sits where the St-Laurent valley begins to rise into the low Laurentian mountains. The Cathédral was built as a simple parish church in 1899, but the archdiocese saw fit to honour the

town's importance as the source of the colonisation of the upper Laurentides by erecting the immense Roman-Byzantine edifice. Alfred Laliberté's bronze statue of Curé Labelle stands out front.

Across *r. de-la-Palais* stands the **Centre d'Exposition du Vieux Palais**; *tel: (514) 432-7171,* open Tues–Sun afternoons, adults $3.50. This former courthouse now houses expositions of contemporary art. St-Jérôme also marks the beginning of the **Parc Linéare Le P'tit Train du Nord**, a 200-km ribbon along rivers and lakes to Mont-Laurier. The park follows the right-of-way of the tourist train which opened the ski villages of the Laurentians in the 1920s–1940s. It now serves as a bicycle path in summer, with quick access to villages along the route, and as either cross-country ski or snowmobile trails in winter. As the trail follows river valleys, the average inclination is only 2 degrees, ascending as you ride northward.

ST-JÉRÔME TO ST-SAUVEUR-DES-MONTS

Continue north on Rte 117, passing into the village of **Prévost**, a destination for antiques-hunters from Montréal. Shops line both sides of the highway. Prévost had the first commercial downhill ski trails in the Laurentides in 1932. The skiers soon tired of walking back up; in 1933 Prévost installed the first mechanical chairlift in North America. This original slope has long since been overshadowed by more ambitious ski areas nearby.

ST-SAUVEUR-DES-MONTS

Tourist Information: Bureau touristique des Pays-d'en-Haut, *100 r. Guindon, Building M at Factoreries St-Sauveur; tel: (514) 227-2564,* open daily 0900–1700.

St-Sauveur was the first area in the Laurentides to develop as a ski resort, and has a kind of sprawling charm. Like water seeking a low spot, the village has settled into a valley surrounded by five ski mountains with 84 trails and 32 ski lifts. It claims to have the longest skiing season in eastern Canada and the largest night skiing area in the world. At some level, such hyperbole is really secondary to the fact that St-Sauveur is a wildly popular ski area less than an hours' drive from Montréal.

ACCOMMODATION

The sweet little **Aux Petits Oiseaux B&B**, *342 r. Principale, St-Sauveur-des-Monts, PQ J0R 1R0; tel: (514) 227-6116,* offers two rooms that share baths and a suite with private bath, all with full breakfast and hospitality; moderate. **Motel des Pentes**, *12 r. Lanning, St-Sauveur-des-Monts, PQ J0R 1R0; tel: (514) 227-5351,* offers a variety of rooms, some with whirlpool baths and working fireplaces at rates that top out at $75.

Somewhat more elegant rooms are available in the Bed and Breakfast-style hotel **Relais St-Denis**, *61 r. St-Denis; St-Sauveur-des-Monts, PQ J0R 1R0; tel: (514) 227-4766;* high moderate. The condo-apartments of **Manoir St-Sauveur**, *246 ch. de Lac Millette, St-Sauveur-des-Monts, PQ J0R 1R0; tel: (514) 227-1811,* offers a selection of rooms, some with self-catering, all with access to indoor and outdoor pools and tennis courts.

EATING AND DRINKING

Most people come to St-Sauveur for outdoor activities, and they tend to work up quite an appetite. Not surprisingly, the main street is literally lined with dining choices, many of them selling more alcoholic beverages than food. But it's also possible to dine well at moderate prices.

Wherever there's a ski mountain in the world, there's bound to be a Swiss restaurant. St-Sauveur's is **La Raclette Kindli**, *22 Lafleur N.; tel: (514) 227-2229;* budget–moderate. For Provençal cuisine, it's worth making a reservation at **Restaurant des Oliviers**, *239 r. Principale; tel: (514) 227-2110.* A heartier bistro style – complete with wood-grilled entrées – prevails at **La Marmite**, *314 r. Principale; tel: (514) 227-1554.*

For a lighter French bistro style crossed with Canadian health food, **La Mère Miche**, *259 r. Principale; tel: (514) 227-6811,* is hard to beat. In winter, aim for a table near the wood-burning hearth; in summer opt for the delightful outdoor terrace. If you're more interested in speed and French–Canadian casual cuisine, visit **Chez Jules**, *26 r. Principale, no phone,* for hot dogs, hamburgers and several variations on the French–Canadian dish called 'poutine', which consists of fried string potatoes topped with a generic brown gravy and often with other items more commonly found on a pizza crust; budget.

OUTDOOR ACTIVITIES

The all-purpose outdoor equipment rental operation in town is called **Performance**, *333A r. Principale; tel: (514) 227-2082,* where mountain bikes rent for $25 per day.

Alpine Skiing

One-day lift tickets near St-Saveur range from $17–34 per day. **Mont Avila**, *350 St-Denis, St-Sauveur-des-Monts; tel: (514) 227-4671 or (800) 363-2426,* has 11 trails and a vertical drop of 185 m. **Mont St-Sauveur**, *350 St-Denis, St-Sauveur-des-Monts; tel: (514) 227-4671 or (800) 363-2426,* has 28 trails and a vertical drop of 213 m. **Mont Habitant**, *12 blvd des skieurs, St-Sauveur-des-Monts; tel: (514) 227-2637,* has 8 trails and a vertical drop of 200 m. **Mont Christie**, *Côte St-Gabriel Est, St-Sauveur-des-Monts; tel: (514) 226-2412,* has 12 trails and a vertical drop of 170 m. **Mont Olympia**, *330 ch. de-la-Montagne, Piedmont; tel: (514) 227-3523 or (800) 363-3696,* has 22 trails and a vertical drop of 197 m. **Ski Morin Heights**, *Morin Heights; tel: (514) 227-2020 or (800) 661-3535,* has 22 trails and a vertical drop of 200 m.

Slides

Not everyone goes downhill standing on skinny boards. Sliding over the snow on inner tubes is a peculiarly Québecois pastime that turns out to be exhilarating. One area on Mont Avila is devoted exclusively to this activity: **Glissades des Pays-d'en-Haut**, *440 ch. Avila, Piedmont; tel: (514) 224-4014.* The operation maintains 26 different trails serviced by chairlifts ($17). During the summer, waterslides operate in the same area.

An even more substantial water park operates on Mont St-Sauveur: **Parc aquatique Mont St-Sauveur**, *exit 58/60 Hwy 15; tel: (514) 227-4671, 871-0101 or (800) 363-2426;* admission varies by height from $6 to $22. Among the attractions is a giant wave pool (which mimics the wave action of an ocean beach), two high-speed water slides, and six giant spiral water slides.

MONT-ROLLAND

Alpine skiing at **Mont Gabriel**; *tel: (514) 227-1100 or (800) 363-2426,* includes 12 slopes with a vertical drop of 200 m, lift tickets $20–29. **Hotel Mont-Gabriel Resort & Country Club**, *1699 ch. Montée Gabriel, Mont-Rolland, PQ J0R 1G0; tel: (514) 229-3547 or (800) 668-5253,* offers a number of winter ski packages and summer tennis and golf packages; moderate–expensive.

STE-ADÈLE

The **Musée Village de Seraphin**, *Montée à Seraphin; tel: (514) 229-4777,* open daily 1000–1700 late May–mid Oct, adults $8.50, is a replica of the early days of the colony. The attraction grew out of the set for a movie and television series based on Claude-Henri Grignon's novel *Un homme et son péché (A Man and His Sin),* which concentrated relentlessly on the wretchedness of life in the early days of the Laurentians. Through media exposure, this era somehow came to be romanticised – hence the popularity of the 20-building museum.

Martin-le-Pêcheur, *265 av. Canadienne; tel: (514) 229-7020,* offers year-round recreational fishing as well as smoked trout, trout sausage and trout mousse.

Ski Chantecler, *ch. Chantecler; tel: (514) 229-3555 or (514) 393-8884,* offers 22 trails with a vertical drop of 201 m; lift ticket $17–23.

VAL-MORIN

Hôtel Far Hills Inn, *ch. Lac Lasalle, Val-Morin, PQ J0T 2R0; tel: (819) 322-2014,* is an idyllic small resort (72 rooms) on a private lake, with one of the finest cross-country ski centres in eastern Canada. Moderate rates include breakfast and dinner, with special packages tailored to seasonal activities. **Les Circuits Val-Va**, *5285 blvd Labelle (Rte 117); tel: (514) 229-4133,* is an all-season motorised sports centre. The summer activities include go-carts, speed boats and kiddy rides from mid Apr–mid Nov. In the winter, the activities become rather more traditional: 500 luges, 200 bobsleds, 1000 large inner tubes for sliding, mechanical lifts. The site also offers a track for snowmobiling and another track for snowboards, open for winter activities mid Dec–mid Apr.

One of the original golf courses of the Laurentians, founded in 1922, is also found here: the **Club de golf Val-Morin**, *4500 av. 5e; tel: (819) 322-7183,* greens fees $40.

VAL-DAVID

Tourist Information: Bureau Touristique de Val-David, *2501 r. de l'Église; tel: (819) 322-2900, ext. 235,* open daily 0900–1900 (mid June–early Sept), Thur–Mon 1000–1600 (early Sept–mid June).

Rock climbing started in Québec in this funky and artistic village about halfway between St-Sauveur and Mont-Tremblant. The centre of the village has several art galleries and shops featuring the work of local artisans working in pewter and other media.

ACCOMMODATION

Val-David has a *CI*. Built of logs, **Hôtel La Sapinière**, *1244 ch. de-la-Sapinière, Val-David, PQ J0T 2N0; tel: (819) 322-2020,* has a lakeside location and recently renovated rooms to offer a mini-resort retreat experience at a moderate rate. The **Auberge du Vieux Foyer**, *3167 1er Rang Doncaster, Val-David, PQ J0T 2N0; tel: (819) 322-2686 or (800) 567-8327*, moderate, is a Swiss-style lake and mountain chalet situated near the P'tit Nation bicycle trail; the inn loans bicycles to guests.

For sparkling motel accommodation rather than lodge rooms, **Motel des Pays-d'en-Haute**, *1140 Rte 117, Val-David, PQ J0T 2N0; tel: (819) 322-2032*, offers good value at budget–moderate rates. **Le Rouet**, *1288 r. Lavoie, Val-David, PQ J0T 2N0; tel: (819) 322-3221*, is a hotel geared for families with a wide range of rather sparsely furnished rooms, shared bathrooms and a full meal package; budget–moderate.

The budget youth hostel, **Le Chalet Beaumont**, *1451 r. Beaumont, Val-David, PQ J0T 2N0; tel: (819) 322-1972*, is constructed of logs and features two fireplaces; budget. **Camping Laurentien**, *Rte 117, Val-David, PQ J0T 2N0; tel: (819) 322-2281*, offers 86 pitches with water, electric and sewage hook-ups optional.

158

EATING AND DRINKING

For game specialities prepared in a style evocative of the chef's native Toulouse (France), try **Restaurant-Crêperie La Toupie**, *2367 r. de l'Église; tel: (819) 322-7833*; budget–moderate. In the middle of **Les Jardins de Rocailles** – a beautifully landscaped rock garden property featuring more than 300 varieties of trees, shrubs and plants – is a fine restaurant featuring pasta, vegetarian dishes and a variety of light meals: **Restaurant/bistro des Jardins**, *1319 r. Lavoie; tel: (819) 322-6193*, moderate.

OUTDOOR ACTIVITIES

Val-David is the perfect place to get an introduction to rock-climbing, or to tackle difficult ascents if you are an experienced climber. **Passe-Montagne**, *1760 2e rang; tel: (819) 322-2123 or (800) 465-2123*,

available Apr–Oct, offers programmes for three to six climbers per instructor, who demonstrate security measures and proper technique. Call for rates and times.

Pause Plein Air, *1293C r. Dufresne; tel: (819) 324-0798*, rents canoes (paddles and life jackets included) for a 2-hr trip down Rivière du Nord to Lac Raymond; $25 per canoe. The company also rents bicycles for $5 per hour or $15 per day for use in the Linear Parc 'Le P'tit Train du Nord'. **Boutique Phénix**, *2444 r. de l'Église; tel: (819) 322-5475*, also rents canoes for the same route at the same price, and bicycles for $5 per hour, $15 for 4 hours and $20 per day.

In the winter, Phénix becomes **Ski se loue** and rents cross-country ski equipment, kicksleds, skating skis, snowshoes and skates from a location in the heart of an 80-km trail network that is also adjacent to the 45-km section of the Linear Parc that permits cross-country skiing. Call for rates.

Alpine skiing is available at **Mont-Alta**, *Rte 117; tel: (819) 322-3206*, with 2 trails and a vertical drop of 178m, and at **Valée-Bleue**, *1418 ch. Valée-Bleue; tel: (819) 322-3427*, with 16 trails and a vertical drop of 111m. Lift tickets at both sites range $12–22.

ST-AGATHE-DES-MONTS

Tourist Information: Bureau Touristique de Ste-Agathe-des-Monts, *190 r. Principale, Ste-Agathe-des-Monts, PQ J8C 1K3; tel: (819) 326-0457*.

The centrepiece of this year-round recreation centre is the **Lac du Sables**, which is popular during warm weather for canoeing, sailing and swimming at the three municipal beaches and for skating in winter.

ACCOMMODATION AND FOOD

Auberge du Lac des Sables, *230 r. St-Venant, Ste-Agathe-des-Monts, PQ J8C 2Z7; tel: (819) 326-3994*, moderate, offers 19 small but nicely furnished rooms near the beaches and cross-country trails; two-night minimum stay.

Domaine de Lausanne, *150 Rte 117; St-Agathe-des-Monts, PQ J8C 2Z8; tel: (819) 326-3550*, offers 180 tent pitches. **Parc des Campeurs de Ste-Agathe-des-Monts**, *50 r. Sant-Joseph, Ste-Agathe-des-Monts, PQ J8C 1M9; tel: (819) 324-0482*, has 556 tent pitches in a veritable camping community.

For good casual meals, **Crêperie la Quimperlaise**, *11 ch. de la Tour-du-Lac; tel: (819) 326-1776*, has seafood crêpes as well as steaks, brochettes and salads at budget–moderate prices. **Chalet Vienna**, *6 r. Ste-Lucie; tel: (819) 826-1485*, is known for its Austrian and game specialities, moderate–pricey; closed Nov and Apr.

SIGHTSEEING

During the ice-free weather mid May–late Oct, plan on a 50-min sightseeing cruise on Lac des Sables aboard **Bateaux Alouette**, *r. Principale dock; tel: (819) 326-3656*, adults $11. In winter, **Randonneige**, *25 Brissette; tel: (819) 326-0642*, rents new snowmobiles and can arrange guided snowmobile touring.

ST-FAUSTIN-LAC-CARRÉ

The recreational village of St-Faustin has evolved as something of a suburb of Mont-Tremblant – an option for skiers who wish to escape the crowds. Alpine skiing at **Mont–Blanc**, *Rte 117; tel: (819) 688-2444*, offers 35 slopes with a 300m vertical drop; lift tickets $20–30.

During Mar and Apr, visit the local institution of **Cabane à Sucre Millette**, *1357 r. St-Faustin; tel: (819) 688-2101*, for a demonstration of the manufacture of maple syrup or to purchase maple products. For summer outings, one of the most beautiful golf courses in Québec is the 18-hole par 71 **Club de golf Royal Laurentien**, *2237 ch. Lac Nantel; tel: (819) 326-2347 or (800) GOLF-ROYAL;* greens fees $30–38

ST-JOVITÉ

A convenient campsite for RVs near Mont-Tremblant is **Camping de la Diable**, *140*

r. Régimbald, St-Jovité, PQ J0T 2H0; tel: (819) 425-5501, a mobile home park with facilities for temporary hook-ups and a separate section of tent pitches.

MONT-TREMBLANT

Tourist Information: Bureau Touristique de Mont-Tremblant, *140 r. de la Convent, Mont-Tremblant, PQ J0T 1Z0; tel: (819) 425-2434*, open daily 0900–2000, Fri 0900–2100 (June–Sept), Mon–Fri 0830–1700 rest of year. For hotel and condominium central reservations, **Mont-Tremblant Réservations**; *2001 ch. Principal, C.P. 240, Mont-Tremblant, PQ J0T 1Z0; tel: (819) 425-8681 or (800) 567-6760*.

The ski mountain at Mont-Tremblant is the most dramatic in the Laurentians, and development of the area around the mountain has proceeded at a breathtaking pace since 1991, the investment of more than $350 million resulting in an entirely new community at the base of the mountain known (confusingly) simply as Tremblant. (The original village a few kilometres away is called Mont-Tremblant.)

It took more than a half century for this peak to become a ski centre. Skiing pioneer Joe Ryan first climbed the peak in Feb 1938, hiking up the mountain with sealskin furs strapped to his skis. Legend has it that he commented that the only thing wrong with the mountain was that it was too hard to climb – so he began planning a lift. The original cabins of the ski resort have been restored as 'Vieux Tremblant', although new condo construction stands next door, inviting some confusion about what's old and what's new. Cycling, in-line skating and cross-country skiing are free for guests and residents of the Tremblant resort condo-hotels. Visitors may purchase an activity pass (rate varies with season) at the Tremblant Resort Association kiosk at St-Bernard.

ACCOMMODATION

Chateau Mont-Tremblant, *3045 ch.*

Principale, Mont-Tremblant, PQ J0T 1Z0; tel: (819) 681-7000, is the *CP* Hotels resort that dominates Place-Bernard in Tremblant Village, the area at the base of the mountain; expensive.

Another excellent option, moderate–expensive, is **Manoir Labelle–Marriott Residence Inn**, *170 ch. Curé-Deslauriers, Mont-Tremblant, PQ J0T 1Z0; tel: (819) 681-4000 or (888) 272-4000,* where the rooms are all set up for self catering. The **Auberge de Coq de Montagne**, *2151 ch. Principal, Mont-Tremblant, PQ J0T 1Z0; tel: (819) 425-3380 or (800) 895-3380,* is a family-run lodge of 16 rooms with a private sandy beach in the older part of the resort area, about a 5-min drive from the ski mountain; moderate. **Auberge la Porte Rouge**, *1874 ch. Principal, Mont-Tremblant, PQ J0T 1Z0; tel: (819) 425-3505 or (800) 665-3505,* offers 22 rooms in the centre of the original town of Mont-Tremblant; moderate.

Directly on the cross–country ski trails that stretch 90 km around the mountain base, **Le Lupin Bed & Breakfast**, *127 Pinoteau, Mont-Tremblant, PQ J0T 1Z0; tel: (819) 425-5474,* is a cosy log home option if you prefer the genial camaraderie of fellow visitors.

EATING AND DRINKING

In the Tremblant resort, the most dramatic spot for fine dining is **La Légende**; *peak Mont-Tremblant; tel: (819) 681-5500,* reached by a 9-min ride on a bubble-enclosed chair-lift; moderate–pricey. **Aux Truffes**, *le St-Bernard; tel: (819) 681-4544,* serves creative French cuisine; moderate–pricey. You will probably find the cuisine of **Coco Pazzo**, *le Deslauriers; tel: (819) 681-4774,* by following your nose for classical Italian preparations of excellent Québec salmon and veal along with the usual pastas; moderate–pricey.

La Savoie, *Vieux Tremblant; tel: (819) 681-4573,* specialises in raclette, fondue and other authentic Swiss cuisine; moderate. **Microbrasserie la Diable**, *Vieux-Tremblant;*

tel: (819) 681-4546, has pub grub with a Germanic twist (sausages, *sauerkraut)* and six of its own brews, ranging from pale to red to porter.

In the old town of Mont-Tremblant: **Abbé du Nord**, *112 r. Deslauriers; tel: (819 425-8394,* serves fine Italian cuisine in a for-mer presbytery; moderate; and **Restaurant La Hutte**, *1918 ch. Principal; tel: (819) 425-5193,* established in 1930 as a pioneer in the village, offers soups, salads, pastas and – in season – its own venison and home-smoked salmon; moderate.

Some 12 km from Mont-Tremblant in Lac Duhamel on Rte 117 is a landmark of Québecois cuisine, **La Table Enchantée**, *600 Rte 177, Lac Duhamel; tel: (819) 425-7113,* pricey, known for such specialities as caribou, game pie and fiddlehead soup.

SIGHTSEEING

Aviation Wheel Air, *Lake Ouimet, Mont-Tremblant; tel: (819) 425-5662; postal address: C.P. 1454 St-Jovité, PQ J0T 2H0,* offers panoramic sightseeing of the Laurentian region on pontoons in the summer and wheels and skis in the winter. Rates vary.

Outdoor Activities

Mont-Tremblant is the king of the hills in the Laurentians, and **Tremblant Ski Area** has more trails (74), more lifts (ten; six of them high speed lifts), more terrain (500 acres) and a longer vertical drop (649m) than any other place in the mountain range. The longest run is the 6-km Nansen, which has a gentle grade suitable for novice skiers, while the steepest is Dynamite, with a 42-degree pitch. Advanced skiers enjoy the variable contours of Le Géant, while expert skiers who enjoy moguls opt for the Expo. Lift rates are $46 per day, although sleep-and-ski packages are available.

Cross-country skiing near Mont-Tremblant is nearly as well established as alpine skiing. The **Maple Leaf Trail** between Tremblant and the foot of the

Laurentians was opened in the 1940s, and additional trails have been added almost each year, bringing the complete network to more than 110 km, with terrain suitable for novice to expert skiers. Trail maps and tickets are available at the **Tremblant Resort Association kiosk**, *le St-Bernard*. An additional 200 km of trails lace adjacent Parc du Mont-Tremblant.

Golf course construction continues at a manic pace near Mont-Tremblant, with more than 90 holes available within a 5-km radius. Tremblant Resort's **Le Géant** course was built in 1995 to integrate harmoniously with the surrounding environment. The 18-hole par 72 course is ranked in Canada's top ten and provides striking views of the mountains and the resort village. A second 18-hole course opened in early 1998. Most players stay at one of the resort hotels, and greens fees are rarely quoted because they are usually bundled into a golf-lodging package. For tee reservations and information: *tel: (819) 681-2000.* The older course in Mont-Tremblant is **Club de Golf Gray Rocks**, *525 ch. Principal; tel: (819) 425-2771 or (800) 567-6744,* although the club opened a second 18-hole course in mid 1998.

Occupying a broad basin among the Mont-Tremblant hotels, a new **Aquapark** that opened at the end of 1997 features three indoor pools and one outdoor pool. More than 20 km of **mountain bike trails** snake through the Tremblant resort properties. A 10-km in-line skating track circles Le Géant golf course.

Equipment Rentals
The following shops rent ski equipment in the winter, and bicycles and/or canoes and kayaks during the summer: **Magasin de la Place**, *le St-Bernard, Tremblant; tel: (819) 681-4502;* **Tommy & Lefebvre**, *le Johannsen, Tremblant; tel: (819) 425-3013,* and **Yves & Yves Sports**, *1908 ch. Principal, Mont-Tremblant Village; tel: (819) 425-1377.*

Parc du Mont-Tremblant
At nearly 1500 square km, Parc du Mont-Tremblant is the largest of Québec's provincial parks, encompassing 400 lakes and seven rivers. It is a major outdoor sporting destination in both summer and winter. Summer activities include swimming, fishing, mountain biking, horseback riding, canoeing and kayaking, canoe-camping, mountain climbing, hiking, and camping with and without services. Winter activities include snowshoeing, cross-country skiing, ice fishing and winter camping. There is no admission charge, but there are fees for some activities.

Three information centres serve the park at its different access points, with **Centre de Services du Lac-Monroe**; *tel: (819) 688-2281,* being the closest to the village of Mont-Tremblant. Written information is available from **Parc du Mont-Tremblant Administration**, *731 ch. de la Pisciculture, C.P. 129, St-Faustin, PQ J0T 2G0; tel: (819) 688-2336.*

Camping ranges from primitive pitches ($12) in backwoods areas to campsites that supply simple pitches without services ($15) to those with water, electric and septic ($20). Log cabins are also available on the east end of the park; reservations must be made less than 45 days before arrival with **Société des établissements de plein air du Québec**, *801 ch. St-Louis, Suite 180, Québec, PQ G1S 1C1; tel: (418) 890-6527 or (800) 665-6527.* Fishing permits cost $11.41–22.82 per day; reservations required two days in advance; *tel: (418) 890-6527 or (800) 665-6527.*

161

⤴ SIDE TRACK
FROM MONT-TREMBLANT
A side track through extremely rural scenery (and unrelieved woodlands with deeply rutted dirt roads) brings intrepid travellers back toward Montréal without retracing their route on the highway.

To press on, continue north on Rte 117 for 33 km to **Labelle**. In another 4 km, turn left onto an unnumbered road called *ch. de-la-Minerve*. In 16 km you will encounter the **Réserve Faunique de Papineau-Labelle** information booth. Continue across the intersection onto what is known as (but rarely marked as) Road #6 for 46 km through forest to an intersection with *ch. Lac-du-Gagnon*, following signs to **Duhamel** (expect detours around washouts or fallen trees).

At Duhamel, turn onto Rte 321 south and proceed 19 km to **Chénéville**, where you will turn left onto Rte 315 north toward Namur. Rte 315 ends in 9 km, but pretend that it doesn't and proceed across the intersection to the dirt road that leads 13 km to **Boileau**. At Boileau, turn right onto *ch. Maskinongé* toward **Lachute**. In 25 km, turn onto Rte 327 Sud, proceeding 28 km to Rte 148 Est toward **St-Eustache**.

In another 41 km, pick up Hwy 640 east, taking Hwy 13 Sud in 4 km toward Montréal. Six km later, exit to Hwy 15 Sud. In another 6 km, take exit 63 Est for Hwy 720 Est, following signs to Centre-Ville.

LABELLE

Tourist Information: Bureau touristique de Labelle, *7404 blvd du Curé-Labelle, Labelle, PQ J0T 1H0; tel: (819) 686-2606*, open daily 0900–2000, Fri to 2100 (June–Sept), daily 0900-1600 (rest of year).

Founded in 1880 by Curé Labelle, the town has a well-preserved train station and the **Soeurs Ste-Croix** convent as sights, but most people visit either for winter snowmobiling or to purchase petrol before the long drives to the wildlife preserves of Rouge-Matawin, Papineau-Labelle or Mont-Tremblant.

RÉSERVE FAUNIQUE DE PAPINEAU-LABELLE

This immense (1628 square km) wildlife preserve does not require permits for picnicking, mountain biking, hiking or canoeing. Permits for fishing, hunting, camping and canoe-camping must be purchased at the **Centre d'Information de Minerve**; *tel: (819) 454-2013* or *(800) 665-6527*, during its limited opening hours: 0700–1000 and 1400–1600 (15 May–22 June and 18 Aug–14 Sept), 0700–1100 and 1300–1800 (23 June–17 Aug), and 0700–1000 and 1400–1800 (19–28 Sept). The drive through the park is especially stunning in mid Sept, when foliage is at peak colour of luminescent yellows of birch, larch and aspen and fiery reds and oranges of various maple trees.

DUHAMEL

Some years ago, residents of Duhamel began feeding the white-tailed deer in the area, encouraging their proliferation and inhibiting their otherwise cautious fear of humankind. The herd now numbers about 3000, and a 26-km trail, the **Sentier d'Interpretation du Cerf de Virginie**, criss-crosses the roads. The trail is open to hikers, snowshoers and cross-country skiers.

DUHAMEL TO LACHUTE

Descending from Duhamel, the landscape flattens out into broad plains, some of it farmland, the rest overgrown with scrub trees. This area is especially popular with snowmobilers in winter and dirt-bikers in summer; be wary of excessively exuberant riders crossing roads without warning.

LACHUTE

Lachute is an excellent spot to refill the petrol *(essence)* tank and purchase something from one of the *dépanneurs* to eat in the car. About 3 km east of town on Rte 148 is **Ferme Grand Duc**, *165 ch. St. Jérusalem, Lachute; tel: (514) 562-6641*. This farm, one of the participants in reviving the North American bison herds, offers tours and sells bison products. ◪

EASTERN TOWNSHIPS

The Eastern Townships *(Estrie,* in French) represent the British overhaul of municipal government in Québec, replacing the French *seigneuries* with an English township system. The region is full of English names (even in French-speaking towns), and the more English townships often flout Québec's language laws requiring principal signage in French.

This route encompasses the orchard and vineyard country of the south-western portion of the Eastern Townships, where one also finds the mountain resorts and ski areas near the Vermont border, and the lakes country to the east. Pick-your-own fruit operations line the roads beginning with strawberries and raspberries in mid June, followed by apples in August and September and pears through November. Domestic architecture has its roots in the English country home, with a strong infusion of Greek Revival imported from New England. Estrie has many working artists and craftspeople, many of whom hold open studios in September and October.

163

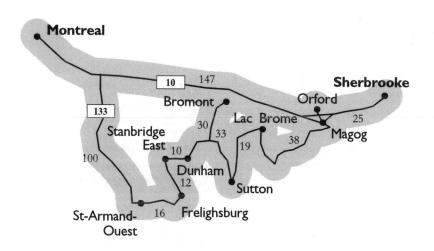

ROUTE

From Montréal city centre, follow *r. University* toward the river, following signs for Pont Champlain and Hwy 10 Est. Continue for 33 km to exit 29, getting on Rte 133 Sud toward Philipsburg and the US border. In 45 km, detour briefly toward the left to Notre-Dame-de-Stanbridge, and on to Mystic. Return to Rte 133 Sud, and continue 10 km to a left turn for **St-Armand-Ouest**. Continue 20 km through Pigeon Hill to **Frelighsburg** to Rte 237 Nord 12 km toward **Stanbridge East**. Turn right on Rte 202 for 10 km toward **Dunham**. Continue 10 km to **Cowansville**, taking Rte 104 east for 4 km. Turn left onto Rte 241 Nord 16 km toward **Bromont**. Backtrack to Rte 104 Est for 3 km to Rte 139 Sud 14 km through Brome Ouest to **Sutton**.

At Sutton, take Rte 215 Nord 13 km through **Brome** to Rte 104 Est for 6 km to the **Lac Brome** village of Knowlton. From Lac Brome, drive east on Rte 243 to South Bolton, then north 5 km on Rte 245, looking for signs to **St-Benoit-du-Lac**. This unnumbered road, known variously as *ch. Bolton-Est, Rte de la Baie Sergent* and *ch. du Lac* continues 5 km into Austin, where a 1-km access road leads to the Abbaye de St-Benoit-du-Lac.

Return to *ch. du Lac,* turning right and following the road along **Lake Memphrémagog** for about 15 km to a junction with Rte 112 east. In Magog, turn left onto Rte 141 Nord *(r. Merry Nord)* to **Orford** and Parc du Mont-Orford. Return to Hwy 112 Est for 25 km to **Sherbrooke**. At Sherbrooke, follow *blvd Portland Est* to Hwy 410 north to Hwy 10 east for the return to Montréal, or follow Hwy 10 north to join the Montréal to Québec City route at **Drummondville**.

TOURIST INFORMATION

Tourist Information district-wide: **Tourisme Cantons-de-l'Est**, *20 r. Don-*

Bosco sud, Sherbrooke, PQ J1L 1W4; tel: (819) 820-2020 or *(800) 355-5755* (toll-free). The Eastern Townships boast nine golf courses within a 45-km radius and many lodgings offer special golf packages that include greens fees, lodging and sometimes meals; *tel: (800) 263-1068* for information. The alpine ski centres of the Eastern Townships offer an interchangeable lift ticket and cooperative packages with several lodgings; call **Ski Eastern Townships**; *tel: (800) 355-5755.*

MONTRÉAL TO ST-ARMAND-OUEST

Once you leave Hwy 10, you will motor through tidy farm country. Covered bridges cross many small streams, but most are located on back roads. Watch for the detour sign to the **covered bridge** at **Notre-Dame-de-Stanbridge**. Continue about 5 km to Mystic, passing on the left the 12-sided **Wallbridge Barn**, an adaptation of Shaker influence. (The Shakers, a religious sect, believed the circle was a symbol of perfection and that 12 sides approximated a circle. Well, the town *is* called 'mystic'.)

Return to Rte 133 Sud and drive toward Philipsburg and St-Armand-Ouest, which are only a few kilometres from the US border.

SIDE TRACK TO VERMONT

To visit **Burlington, Vt**, continue on Rte 133 Sud without making any turns. At the US border it becomes I-89, connecting to the US Interstate system.

ST-ARMAND-OUEST TO FRELIGHSBURG

In approximately 3 km after the bridge turnout at St-Armand-Ouest, turn left onto *ch. Bedford,* follow it to the end, and turn right to see one of the oldest **covered bridges** in Québec. Cross the bridge and turn right onto *ch. Pigeon Hill,* continuing to the end, where you turn left toward

Frelighsburg. The village of **Pigeon Hill** is a holdout from hippie days – a peace-loving community of farmers and artisans. During the summer, signs will direct you to studios.

FRELIGHSBURG

Tourist Information: Tourisme Cantons-de-l'Est, *1 Pl. de l'Hôtel de Ville; tel: (514) 298-5630,* open daily 1000–1800 (June–early Sept), variable hours off season. If nothing else, Frelighsburg has character. Its **General Store**, open Tues–Sun; sells what many claim to be the best maple syrup pie in Québec. It also sells a wide variety of maple products.

Lodging opportunities include **Camping des Chutes Hunter**, *18 ch. des Chutes, Frelighsburg , PQ J0J 1C0; tel: (514) 298-5005* or *(888) 486-8737,* open May–Oct, 150 pitches with complete services; budget. For clothing-optional camping or motel, **Centre Nudiste Vallée Rustique**, *40 ch. des Bouleaux, Frelighsburg, PQ J0J 1C0; tel: (514) 298-5372* or *(888) NUDISTE,* offers more than 180 pitches with services and motel rooms with or without meals; budget. **Les Services de la Montagne**; *tel: (514) 538-1787,* 8.3 km from the centre of the village on Rte 252, offers winter sleigh rides ($10 per adult) and tours of a sugaring operation Feb–Apr ($16 per adult).

STANBRIDGE EAST

The **Musée de Missisquoi**, *2 r. River; tel: (514) 248-3153,* open daily 1000–1700 late May–mid Oct, adults $3, relates local history with artefacts in a cluster of buildings, including an historical mill. Another museum structure, **Bill's Barn**, houses antique automobiles.

ROUTE DU VIN (STANBRIDGE EAST TO DUNHAM)

Rte 202 weaves through a section of orchard country that, beginning in the 1980s, has evolved as a wine-growing region. Nearby rivers and lakes temper the microclimate sufficiently to just barely make it possible to grow noble wine grapes.

Although some of the vineyards produce wine from French-American hybrids, such as Maréchal Foch and Chancellor (both red types), wine production concentrates on the whites, Seyval Blanc and Vidal Blanc. Vineyard owners sometimes have to resort to wind machines or helicopters to keep the grapes from freezing before they ripen, and adding sweeteners to the must is a common practice here. Nonetheless, the best of the wines are well-made, crisp, and acidic enough to complement food well. Production is small and is sold entirely at farm winery stores, with most bottles ranging $12–17.

Vignobles de l'Orpailleur, *1086 Rte 202, Dunham; tel: (514) 295-2763,* is open daily 0900–1600 (mid Apr–Dec) and Sat–Sun 1000–1200 and 1300–1700 (Jan–mid Apr), tours $4. From June through mid Oct, the winery's terrace restaurant (moderate) is open for lunch and dinner. In addition to table wines, l'Orpailleur also produces a *methode champenoise* and an aromatic apéritif of slightly fermented must.

Fleurs de Pommiers, *1047 Rte 202, Dunham; tel: (514) 295-2223,* offers sweet, fermented and fortified apple ciders. **Les Blancs Coteaux**, *1046 Rte 202, Dunham; tel: (514) 295-3503,* open Mon–Wed by reservation, Thur–Sun 1000–1700, tours $4, produces a dry white and an apple apéritif. The tour includes wine tasting with local cheeses. **Vignoble Domaine des Côtes d'Ardoise**, *879 r. Bruce, Dunham; tel: (514) 295-2020,* open daily 1000–1700 (June–Oct), Sat–Sun 1000–1800 (Apr–May and Nov–Dec), pioneered winemaking in the area, making its first plantings in 1980. In addition to the hybrid grape varieties, Côtes d'Ardoise also grows a limited production of Riesling. Light meals are offered on the terrace outside the wine boutique June–Oct.

165

Vignoble Les Trois Clochers, *341 r. Bruce, Dunham; tel: (514) 295-2034*, produces white wine as well as a strawberry liqueur.

Slightly off the *route du vin* – about 2 km south of Dunham centre – **Vignoble Les Arpents de Neige**, *4042 r. Principale, Dunham; tel: (514) 295-3383*, open daily 0900–2100 June–Oct, hours vary out of season, produces two white wines and a rosé, as well as an aperitif wine of Seyval Blanc fermented with maple syrup. One option for lodging in the orchard and vineyard country is **Paradis des Fruits**, *519 Rte 202, Dunham, PQ J0E 1M0; tel: (514) 295-2667*. This Bed and Breakfast offers three bedrooms in the middle of orchards and encourages guests to pick their own fruit; budget–moderate.

DUNHAM TO BROMONT

Rte 202 concludes in Cowansville. Follow Rte 104 east for 5 km to the swimming beach called **Plage du Lac Davignon**. Continue on Rte 104 east for 1 km to Rte 241 north to Bromont. Cowansville has a DI.

BROMONT

Tourist Information: Tourist Office of Bromont, *83 blvd Bromont, C.P. 666, Bromont, PQ J0E 1L0; tel: (514) 534-2006*, open Mon–Fri 0900–1700, Sat–Sun 1000–1700.

Although vestiges of a sleepy village remain, Bromont is more a scene than a place. As a four-season outdoor resort literally minutes off Hwy 10 and quickly accessible from Montréal, Bromont sprawls with condominium complexes that tend to be self-contained communities. The social centre is not the village square or even a shopping district, but the ski mountain and outdoor centres.

ACCOMMODATION

At this major four-season resort, lodging

ranges from campsites to condos adjacent to the ski mountain. **Le Château Bromont Hôtel**, *90 r. Stanstead, Bromont, PQ J0E 1L0; tel: (819) 534-3433 or (800) 304-3433*, is a sumptuous resort at the base of the ski mountain with special packages for skiing and golf; expensive. **La Chambrière**, *12 r. du Chevreuil, Bromont, PQ J0E 1L0; tel: (514) 266-1240*, offers packages that include horseback riding at the centre where equestrian events were staged during the 1976 Olympic Games; moderate.

Close to the ski mountain is **Hôtel Le Menhir**, *125 blvd de Bromont, Bromont, PQ J0E 1L0; tel: (514) 534-3790 or (800) 461-3790*; moderate. A smaller property close to cross-country ski trails is **La Petite Auberge**, *360 blvd Pierre Laporte, Bromont, PQ J0E 1L0; tel: (514) 534-2707*; moderate. An older-style hotel in the village centre is **Auberge de Vieux Manoir**, *871 r. Shefford, Bromont, PQ J0E 1L0; tel: (514) 534-2502*; moderate.

Camping options include **Camping Carousel**, *1617 r. Shefford, Bromont, PQ J0E 1L0; tel: (514) 534-2404* (which has an artificial lake with a beach), and **Camping Parc Bromont**, *24 r. Lafontain, Bromont, PQ J0E 1L0; tel: (514) 534-2712*; both budget.

EATING AND DRINKING

Restaurant options in Bromont run to extremes – from chain restaurants offering roast chicken to gourmet restaurants at the pricey end with sweetbreads and wild game. The first category is well represented by **Rôtisserie St-Hubert**, *8 blvd Bromont; tel: (514) 534-0223*, while the upmarket **Les Quartre Canards** at the Château Bromont resort is among the finer of the haute cuisine options. The **Musée du Chocolat**, *679 r. Shefford; tel: (514) 534-3893*, also serves light meals, assuming your appetite is still intact after sampling the house specialities.

SIGHTSEEING

Bromont is connected to several surrounding

communities via 65 km of **reserved bicycle paths**, mostly along abandoned railroad rights of way. A cycling guide and trail map is available from the tourist information centre. **Jardin Marisol**, *1 r. Marisol; tel: (514) 534-4515*, is a landscaped park of more than 10 km of paths and a 3-acre wildflower garden. Admission is $4. Horses with full tack may be rented at **Equitation Lombart**, *37 Pierre Laporte; tel: (514) 534-2084*, for $12–15 per hour daily 0900–1800. The property includes 250 acres laced with bridle paths. Mountain bikes may be rented from **Sports Bromont Ski-Vélo**, *58 blvd Bromont; tel: (514) 534-5858*. Rates range from $20 to $30 per day.

Outdoor Activities

Centre de Plein Air, *319 r. du Lac Gale; tel: (514) 534-2277 or (800) 363-8952*, is nestled on the banks of Lake Gale. Admission is $7 per day. During the summer, the centre offers horseback riding, mountain biking, 22 km of walking trails, canoeing, pedal boating and sail boarding. In the winter, it offers hillside sliding on large inner tubes with a mechanical lift, skating and 22 km of groomed cross-country ski trails. Equipment rental is available on site.

Le club de Golf et Auberge Bromont, *95 r. de Montmorency; tel: (514) 534-1199 or (888) BROMONT*, is an 18-hole course built in 1969 and ranked among Québec's best public courses. Treat yourself to a Rolls Royce golf cart furnished with television, radio and ice maker. Greens fees range $18–33; reservations required. Moderate packages are available with golf and lodging at a 50-room auberge on the course.

Le parcours du Vieux Village Bromont, *50 r. de Bourgmestre; tel: (514) 534-1166*, also offers 18 holes with a par 72. Greens fees range $26.50–32.50, reservations required. **Ski Bromont**, *150 r. Champlain; tel: (514) 534-2200*, offers 22 trails of skiing on two mountains with a 405-m vertical drop. The centre has six lifts, including one high-speed quad chair and three-quarters of the trails are lit for night skiing. In addition, Ski Bromont offers 57 km of cross-country ski trails, 18 km of skating trails and innertube sliding. Lift rates range $20–32; cross-country trail pass is $8.50. During the summer, Ski Bromont offers 100 km of mountain biking trails and an aquatic park with pools and slides; rates vary with season, $16–21.50.

BROMONT TO SUTTON

About halfway between Bromont and Sutton is the blink-and-you'll-miss-it village of **Brome Ouest**, halfway between the two ski areas. **Auberge West Brome**, *128 Rte 139, West Brome, PQ J0E 2P0; tel: (514) 266-7552*; moderate, is a good choice for self-catering and also has a pleasant dining room serving simple Canadian cuisine; moderate, with occasional budget specials.

SUTTON

Tourist Information: Tourist Office of Sutton, *11-B Main St Sud; tel: (514) 538-8455 or (800) 565-8455*, open daily 1000–1800 (June–Sept), daily 0900–1700 (Oct–May).

Sutton was established in 1793, although a 19th-century fire wiped out all traces of the older town. Despite an early jump on developing its ski area, Sutton remains a charming country village with a ski area attached rather than a ski area with a ghost of a village on its outskirts. Although technically a Francophone community, Sutton flouts Québec language laws with extensive English signage.

ACCOMMODATION

Sutton offers two centralised reservation services for all levels of lodging from simple homestays to chalet rentals: **Sutton Accommodation**, *10-2 Main St North, P.O. Box 418, Sutton, PQ J0E 2K0; tel: (514) 538-2646 or (800) 663-0214*, and

Mont-Sutton Reservations, *582 Maple St., P.O. Box 600, Sutton, PQ J0E 2K0; tel: (800) 363-1226.*

Two moderate Bed and Breakfast options in the village are **Gîte Vert le Mont**, *18 r. Maple, C.P. 415, Sutton, PQ JOE 2K0; tel: (514) 538-3227,* with some shared baths; and **Le St-Amour**, *1 r. Pleasant, Sutton, PQ J0E 2K0; tel: (514) 538-6188,* all rooms with private baths. Closer to the ski mountain but still moderate is the **Auberge des Appalaches**, *234 ch. Maple, Sutton, PQ J0E 2K0; tel: (514) 538-5799,* all rooms with private bath.

Right at the entrance to the ski mountain is the **Auberge La Paimpolaise**, *615 ch. Maple, C.P. 548, Sutton, PQ JOE 2K0; tel: (514) 538-3213.* Rooms are modest, but the reception area is warm and handsome. Rates begin at the top end of the moderate category, but excellent packages with lift tickets are available.

OUTDOOR ACTIVITIES

Alpine skiing is available on **Mont Sutton**, *671 ch. Maple; tel: (514) 538-2545,* situated in the middle of a natural snow belt. Its 53 slopes are served by eight chairlifts and the 460-m vertical drop is one of the longest in Québec. Daily lift rates range $26–39.

Set high in the mountains south of Sutton near the US border, **Au Diable Vert Station de Montagne**, *168 ch. Staines, Glen Sutton, PQ J0E 1X0; tel: (514) 538-5639* or *(888) 779-9090,* offers guided excursions for biking, mountain biking, hiking, canoeing, off-trail skiing, snowshoeing and fly-fishing. The centre also teaches beginner's courses in outdoor activities, including lessons on map and compass orientation and hunting with bow and arrow. Chalet lodging and extremely primitive wilderness camping are available.

Les Rochers Bleus, *Rte 139; tel: (514) 538-2324,* offers an 18-hole, rolling par 72 golf course with on-site lodging; expensive. Greens fees range $26–32.

Au Diable Vert offers use of its trail system for mountain biking. Sutton is linked to 75 km of cycling trails, including an 11.6-km spur leading to the US border and further networks of American cycling trails. Local cyclists organise 50- and 100-km weekend outings from Sutton; for information call the Sutton tourist information office.

> **SIDE TRACK**
> **FROM SUTTON**
>
> From Sutton, continue south on Rte 101 for 11 km to the US border. The crossing continues to **Richford, Vt**, with Rte 105 leading to St Albans on the way to **Burlington.**

SUTTON TO LAC BROME

The route passes through Brome, home of the **Brome Fair**, a quintessential country agricultural fair held every Labour Day weekend (first weekend after first Mon in Sept) since 1856; *tel: (514) 242-3976.*

LAC BROME

Brome Lake, as the Anglophone residents call it (and there are plenty of them), takes in several villages surrounding the lake. The most interesting for sightseeing is Knowlton, which offers the only easy public access to a **swimming beach** on this small jewel of a lake, 1 km east of the village centre on Lakeside.

Like several of the Eastern Townships, Brome Lake owes its existence to Loyalists from the American colonies who opted to remain as British citizens by re-settling in Canada. Those sympathies are part of the local mindset, and give the village a more British character than most settlements in Québec. The lake is widely known in gastronomic circles for the quality of the ducks produced here, and local restaurants and farmers celebrate the **Brome Lake Duckling Festival** mid Oct–mid Nov.

Knowlton is one of the few towns in the

region with a concentration of boutiques and posh shops, and has an Anglophone summer theatre, **Théâtre du lac Brome**, 267 r. Knowlton; tel: (514) 242-2270 or (514) 242-1395.

ACCOMMODATION

Within Knowlton, the **Lake View House**, 50 Victoria St., Knowlton, Brome Lake, PQ J0E 1V0; tel: (514) 243-6183 or (800) 661-6183; expensive, is an historic inn dating from 1874 and completely restored in 1986. Its continental dining room features Brome Lake duck in many forms and has an excellent wine cellar.

Far more modest, the bright and clean **Motel Cyprès**, 592 Lakeside, Lac Brome, PQ J0E 1R0; tel: (514) 243-0363, offers use of private docks on the lake; budget–moderate. Camping is available on the west side of the lake (with docks and swimming beach) at **Camping Domaine des Érables**, 688 r. Bondville, Lac Brome, PQ J0E 1R0; tel: (514) 242-8888, budget.

OUTDOOR ACTIVITIES

Alpine skiing is available on 26 trails at **Ski Mont Glen**, ch. Glen; tel: (514) 243-6142, on a total vertical drop of 335 m. This modest ski area offers two chair lifts and 2 T-bars. Lift tickets range $15–25. **Pleins Air Mont-Écho**, 2651 ch. Mont-Écho (off Rte 243); tel: (514) 243-6843, offers 11 cross-country ski trails that total 53 km. During the summer, the operation switches to mountain bike trails. Trail fee $10.

Marina Quai-7 Rentals, 77 Benoit St, Knowlton; tel: (514) 243-5453, rents fishing boats with small trolling motors ($18 per hr, $40 half day), canoes and pedal boats ($10 per hr, $20 half day) for use on Lac Brome. Lac Brome is home to two golf courses – the 1997 course at the intersections of Rtes 215 and 243 called **Club de golf du Lac Brome**, and the better established 18-hole, par 71 **Golf Inverness**, 511 ch. Bondville; tel: (514) 242-1595, greens fees $25–32.

LAC BROME TO MAGOG

The drive from Brome Lake crosses high country past Mont-Glen to reach the western bank of the mighty Lac Memphrémagog, a long and deep body of water comparable to some of the Scottish lochs, complete with its own legendary serpent-like creature first spotted more than 200 years ago. The US-Canadian border divides the lake in half.

Along this route is the **Abbaye de St-Benoit-du-Lac**, where Benedictine monks have lived the contemplative life since 1912. The stately buildings blend conventions of religious architecture with the geometric thrust of 20th-century design. Daily mass at 1100 and vespers at 1700 (at 1900 on Thur all year and on Tues in July–Aug) are celebrated in Gregorian chant. The abbey **boutique**; tel: (819) 843-4080, open Mon–Sat 0900–1045 and 1400–1630, sells religious articles, recordings of the chanting and the farm products produced at the abbey – outstanding blue cheeses made from goat and cow milks, a strong cheddar and a mild fresh ricotta. Also available are sparkling hard ciders produced at the abbey.

MAGOG-ORFORD

Tourist Information: Tourist Office of Magog-Orford, 55 r. Cabana (off Rte 112); Magog, PQ J1X 2C4; tel: (819) 843-2744, open daily 1000–1800 (June–Sept), daily 0900–1700 (Oct–May).

At the head of Lac Memphrémagog, Magog is the beach town and nerve centre for the lakes region of the Eastern Townships. It is generally mentioned in the same breath with its northern neighbouring township of Orford, which consists of wide open spaces kept that way by the provincial Parc du Mont-Orford. The friendly and sociable Magog and the strong and silent Orford make a good team, with one offering most of the accommodation, dining and shopping and the other the lion's share of the wilderness.

169

ACCOMMODATION

The **Auberge l'Étoile-sur-le-lac**, *1150 r. Principale Ouest, Magog, PQ J1X 2B8; tel: (819) 843-6521* or *(800) 567-2727*, moderate–expensive, offers views of Lac Memphrémagog.

An outstanding example of new construction is the **Manoir des Sables Hôtel & Golf**, *90 av. des Jardins, Magog-Orford, PQ J1X 3W3; tel: (819) 847-4747* or *(800) 567-3514*, expensive–pricey, but with many discounted golf packages.

A simpler motel right at the edge of the park is **Auberge du Parc**, *1259 ch. de la Montagne, R.R. 2, Magog-Orford, PQ J1X 3W3; tel: (819) 843-8887* or *(800) 567-3475*, moderate. **IYH hostel: Auberge La Grande Fuge**, *Parc du Mont-Orford (Rte 141), C.P. 280, Magog, PQ J1X 3W8; tel: (819) 843-8595* or *(800) 567-6155* May–Oct; budget, is located within the park's arts centre and extensively used by the summer music school.

Within Magog village are several good but small Bed and Breakfast operations, all of them moderate. The best camping in the region is through **Parc du Mont-Orford**, with two different areas of wooded camping adjacent to lakes. Pitches vary from primitive tent pitches to sophisticated caravan parking with full services. Prices depend on type of pitch, type of camping gear (caravan, tent, etc.) and number of people. Reservations are essential; *tel: (819) 843-9855*.

EATING AND DRINKING

The village centre in Magog abounds with inexpensive pub dining where you get what you pay for. However, **Chat Noir**, *266 r. Principale Ouest; tel: (819) 843-4337*, offers a relaxed bistro menu along with nightly jazz and a dance orchestra on weekends; moderate. For lunches, excellent coffees and pastries, try **Caffuccino**, *219 r. Principale Ouest; tel: (819) 868-2225*, budget–moderate.

Roast chicken with chips and gravy constitutes the Québec national meal, and a budget spot to enjoy it is **Rôtisserie Orford**, *196 r. Sherbrooke; tel: (819) 843-6833*. For a gourmet French meal with fresh herbs and vegetables from the restaurant's garden, book a reservation at **La Merise**, *2329 ch. du Parc, Orford; tel: (819) 843-6288*, moderate–expensive.

SIGHTSEEING

Croisières Memphrémagog, *quai Federal; tel: (819) 843-8068*, offers several daily cruises of 1 hr 45 mins on Lac Memphrémagog from mid May–mid Oct, adults $12.

Parc du Mont-Orford, a provincial park 4 km north of Magog, offers hiking, cycling and cross-country ski trails, beaches for swimming and water sports, an 18-hole golf course and a downhill ski area. Admission to the park is $3.50 per adult per day, with an additional charge of $2.60–12 per vehicle, depending on size.

At the beaches on Lakes Stukely and Fraser, it is possible to rent mountain bikes, canoes and small boats ($9.50 per hr, $20 half day, $25 day) as well as windsurfing boards ($11 per hr, $25 half day, $40 day).

Centre d'Arts Orford, *3165 ch. du Parc, Parc Mont-Orford; tel: (800) 567-6155* or *(819) 843-3981*, was founded in 1951 as a summer music school. Set in stunning modern buildings within the Parc du Mont-Orford, the school is one of the venues for the **Festival Orford**. From early July to mid Aug master musicians perform classical music concerts each Friday and Saturday while students perform free concerts on Thur and Sun. For more information, contact the arts centre.

Outdoor Activities

Station Touristique du Mont-Orford, *C.P. 248, Magog-Orford; tel: (819) 843-6548* or *(800) 361-6548*, is a major ski centre within Parc du Mont-Orford. The 540-m vertical drop is the steepest in the Eastern Townships, and skiing is available on 43 trails (many of them wooded) on four mountains serviced by six chair lifts. The area also has a large skating rink and 650-m tube slide. Passes are available for the day or in blocks of 2 and 3½ hrs, with free skiing under age 5 or over age 70.

In summer, the lifts provide panoramic views and access to alpine hiking trails. Master hikers may wish to tackle the **Sentier des Crotes**, a trail from the summit of Mont-Orford. The lift rates are $32.75 per day.

Club de golf de Venise, *1519 ch. de la Rivière, Canton Magog; tel: (819) 864-9891*, has two 18-hole courses, one a par 72 the other a par 71; greens fees $21–35. **Golf du Mont-Orford**, *ch. de Parc, Orford; tel: (819) 843-5688* or *(800) 567-2772*, offers an 18 hole par 72; greens fees $26–34. **Golf Manoir des Sables**, *90 av. des Jardins, Orford; tel: (819) 847-4299*, has both 18-hole par 71 and 9-hole par 27 courses; greens fees for 9 holes $8–10, for 18 holes $25–29.

Magog has two swimming beaches on Lac Memphrémagog just off Hwy 112: the **Plage du parc de la Baie-de-Magog** (adjacent to the Tourist Information centre) and the **Plage du parc de la Pointe Merry** (adjacent to the 800-m in-line skate park on Hwy 141 one block south of Magog centre). Admission to the beaches is free, but a parking fee is charged. **Laby Rouly**; *tel: (819) 868-4188,* admission $7.75, is a labyrinth at the parc de la Baie-de-Magog for in-line skaters; walkers are also admitted.

Equipment Rentals

Voile Magog, *at the municipal beach; tel: (819) 847-3181,* rents pedal boats, kayaks and canoes ($10 per hr, $8 each additional hr), windsurfers ($12/$9), and small sailboats ($18/$12 and $25/$20). **Bombardier Guy Bicycles,** *2301 route 112, Magog; tel: (819) 843-8356,* rents a wide variety of road and mountain bikes in several sizes. A hybrid bike rents for $12.50 for 2 hrs, $17 half day, $22 full day. **Locavelo**, *101 DuMoulin,*

Magog; tel: (819) 843-1191, rents bicycles at similar rates and offers guided excursions. **Zig-Zag**, *ch. Principale Ouest* (behind Rossy), rents hybrid and mountain bikes at the same rates, as well as kayaks for $20 for 2 hrs, $25 half day, $35 full day.

SHERBROOKE

Tourist Information: Tourist Office of Sherbrooke Region, *48 r. Dépôt, Sherbrooke; tel: (819) 820-1919* or *(800) 561-8331;* open daily 1000–1800 (June–Sept), 0900–1700 (Oct–May).

As the regional capital of the Eastern Townships, Sherbrooke is a centre for education and the arts, with a distinct taste for outdoor activities.

ACCOMMODATION

Sherbrooke has three chain hotels: *CI, De, HG.*

SIGHTSEEING

Sherbrooke Historical Society, *275 Dufferin St; tel: (819) 821-5406,* open Tues–Fri 0900–1200 and 1300–1700, Sat–Sun 1300–1700, adults $3, students $1.50, contains two exhibit rooms on Eastern Townships history. The genealogical library is a particularly good resource both for the area and other parts of Canada and the USA. The Society also produces audio tapes in French and English for a 2-hr historic walking tour of Old Sherbrooke; tape rental is $6.

Musée du Seminaire de Sherbrooke, *22 Frontenac St; tel: (819) 564-3200,* open daily 1000–1700 (late June–Aug), Tues–Sun 1230–1600 (Sept–late June), adults $4, ranks among Canada's oldest natural history museums. The permanent exhibits in the tower show specimens of minerals, plants, birds and, set in realistic tableaux, animals. The larger exposition centre holds temporary exhibits with many interactive opportunities for children.

Musée des beaux-arts de Sherbrooke, *241 Dufferin St; tel: (819) 821-2115,* open

Tues–Sun 1300–1700 except Wed 1300–2100, opens 2 hrs earlier (late June–early Sept), adults $2.50, focuses on art from the Eastern Townships (where several members of the Group of Seven painted) and on naive and folk art. It occupies a stately former bank building in Old Sherbrooke.

Centrale Frontenac, *Frontenac St; tel: (819) 821-5406,* free, open Wed–Sun 0930–1630 late June–Aug, is the oldest operating hydroelectric plant in Québec. Situated in the middle of the dramatic Magog River gorge, the station presents an informative tour of how electricity is generated. You may picnic on the terrace behind the plant.

Outdoor Activities

Magog River Gorge cuts through Sherbrooke. Free guided tours of the steep river banks are available Tues–Sun at 1030 and 1430 late June–Aug, departing from the Centrale Frontenac.

Blanchard Park follows along the Magog River with 18 km of cycling and walking trails and a pontoon extension onto the river itself. It is possible to rent pedal boats, bicycles and rowboats at **La Maison de l'eau**, *755 r. Cabana; tel: (819) 821-5893.* Blanchard Park is also one of the access points to the **Grande-Fourches cycle trail network**, a 75-km trail that takes in several natural and historic attractions in the Sherbrooke region. It follows the banks of the Magog, St Francis and Massawippi rivers, passing through covered bridges and crossing wildflower meadows.

During the winter, both alpine and cross-country skiing are available at **Mont-Bellevue**, *r. Jogues; tel: (819) 821-5872,* a modest mountain with an 81-m vertical drop and two rope tows. Lift fee is $12; cross-country skiing is free. There is skating on the rink at **Les Jardins du Domaine Howard**, *1350 blvd de Portland.* Predictably, the town has its 18-hole, par 71 **Club de golf de Sherbrooke**, *r. Musset; tel: (819) 563-4987.*

172

The Thomas Cook

OVERSEAS
TIMETABLE

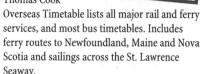

♦ Updated bi-monthly

♦ Summary maps and a comprehensive index allow easy reference

♦ Includes bus and ferry services

♦ Covers the entire world outside Europe

Perfect for advance planning or en route reference, the Thomas Cook Overseas Timetable lists all major rail and ferry services, and most bus timetables. Includes ferry routes to Newfoundland, Maine and Nova Scotia and sailings across the St. Lawrence Seaway.

Obtainable through Thomas Cook UK retail shops at £8.99, or by post (extra for p&p) direct from:

Thomas Cook Publishing (OWN), PO Box 227, Thorpe Wood, Peterborough, PE3 6PU, UK.
Tel: 01733 503571/2

Available in the US from Forsyth Travel Library Inc., 226 Westchester Ave, White Plains, New York 10604
Tel: 800 367 7984 or 914 681 7250

MONTRÉAL– QUÉBEC CITY

These routes essentially parallel the settlement patterns of the heart of Québec province, flowing along both sides of the *Fleuve St-Laurent* (St Lawrence River). Just as the great river links the two communities, it also divides the roads and, to a great extent, the cultures of north and south shores.

While both shores are still extensively agricultural, the north shore developed a strong industrial base in the pulp and paper industry that has only recently been displaced by other types of manufacturing. Wheat is still grown along the north shore, and the rivers and streams that drain into the St-Laurent on both shores have powered a number of grain and sawmills over the years. Many of these historic mills survive on both routes.

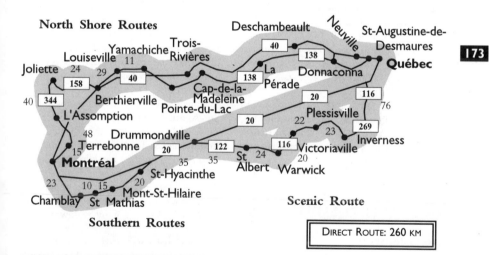

173

DIRECT ROUTE: 260 KM

NORTH SHORE ROUTES

DIRECT ROUTE

From Downtown Montréal proceed east on *r. Sherbrooke* for 4–5 km to a left onto *blvd Pié-IX,* which is Rte 125. Take exit for Hwy 40 Est toward Québec and continue to downtown Québec. (Hwy 40

becomes Hwy 440 and then *blvd Charest* in the central city.) Total distance is approximately 260 km, driving time approximately 3½ hrs, but the route plays tag with the scenic route, making it easy to pick and choose between sightseeing stops along the way.

SCENIC ROUTE

From Downtown Montréal proceed east on *r. Sherbrooke* for 4–5 km to a left onto *blvd Pié-IX*, which is Rte 125. In 4 km this becomes Hwy 25. Take exit 22 for **Terrebonne**, making a right at the first light and a left at the T-intersection to reach Rte 344 Est. Continue on 344 Est to **L'Assomption**, then turn left onto Rte 344 Nord to **St-Paul-de-Joliette** and **Joliette**. At Joliette, pick up Rte 158 Est to **Berthierville**, where it joins Rte 138 Est, the so-called *'Chemin du Roy'*, or *King's Rd*. With small turn outs into villages, you will follow this road all the way to Québec City.

TOURIST INFORMATION

This route crosses three regional tourist areas. For advance information and assistance with reservations through Berthierville, contact **Association Touristique de Lanaudière**, *3643, r. Queen, C.P. 1210, Rawdon, PQ J0K 1S0*; tel: *(514) 834-8100*. From Maskinogé through Ste-Anne-de-la-Pérade, contact **Association Touristique de Mauricie–Bois-Francs**, *1180 r. Royale, 2 étage, Trois-Rivières, PQ G9A 4J1*; tel: *(819) 375-1222* or *(800) 567-7603* (toll-free). From Grondines to Ste-Augustin-De-Desmaures, contact **Office du Tourisme et des Congrès de la Communauté Urbaine de Québec**, *835 av. Wilfrid-Laurier, Québec, PQ G1R 2L3*; tel: *(418) 649-2608*.

SOUTHERN ROUTES

DIRECT ROUTE

From Downtown Montréal proceed east on *r. Sherbrooke* for 4–5 km to a left onto *blvd Pié-IX*, which is Rte 125. Take exit for Hwy 40 Est toward Québec and continue for 2 km to exit for Hwy 20 Est toward Québec. As you approach Québec, take the Pont (bridge) Pierre-Laporte exit. Across the bridge, *blvd Laurier* continues into Québec city, becoming *Grand Allée Est* as it enters the

downtown area. This route hugs the scenic route up to Drummondville, then loosely parallels it the rest of the way, making some sightseeing stopovers possible. Total distance is approximately 260 km, driving time approximately 3¼ hrs.

SCENIC ROUTE

From the Montréal waterfront, cross the Pont Champlain to Hwy 10 as far as exit 29. Follow Rte 133 Nord to Rte 122 Ouest (toward Montréal) to **Chamblay**. Return to Rte 133 Nord and to **St-Mathias** and on to **Mont-St-Hilaire**. Turn onto Rte 116 Est to **St-Hyacinthe**. Get on Hwy 20 Est to **Drummondville**. In Drummondville, take Rte 122 Ouest toward **St-Cyrille-de-Wendover**. Continue about 20 km to the village of **St-Albert** and turn right on the road to **Warwick**. At Warwick, rejoin Rte 116 (left turn) toward Victoriaville and on to **Plessisville**.

From Rte 116 outside of Plessisville, watch carefully for a right turn toward **Inverness**; the road is Rte 267 but is poorly marked. In the village centre, make a left onto Rte 218. Do not despair when the pavement turns to dirt. Keep going toward **Ste-Agathe**, then on to the end of Rte 218. Turn right onto Rte 269 through **St-Étienne** and **St-Rédempteur**, turning right onto Rte 116 Est for a few kilometres before joining Hwy 20. Take the Pont (bridge) Pierre-Laporte exit. Across the bridge, *blvd Laurier* continues into Québec city, becoming *Grand Allée Est* as it enters downtown.

TOURIST INFORMATION

This route crosses three regional tourist areas. For advance information and assistance with reservations through St-Hyacinthe, contact **Association Touristique de Montérégie**, *989 r. Pierre-Dupuy, Longueil, PQ J4K 1A1*; tel: *(514) 674-5555*.

From Drummondville through Inverness, contact **Association Touristique de Mauricie-Bois-Francs**, *1180 r. Royale, 2* *étage, Trois-Rivières, PQ G9A 4J1; tel: (819) 375-1222 or (800) 567-7603.* From Ste-Agathe through St-Rédempteur, contact **Association Touristique de Chaudière-Appalaches**, *800 Autoroute Jean-Lesage, Bernières, PQ G7A 1C9; tel: (418) 831-4411.*

BUSES

Orleans Express run hourly express services from 0600–2200. Journey time: 3 hrs. Two of those services (at 0800 and 1315) stop at Trois-Rivières. Journey time: 3½ hrs. See OTT table 215.

TERREBONNE

Founded in 1707, the seigneurie of Terrebonne soon grew prosperous on the strength of its mills and its superb location as a base for fur-trading forays. The concentration of old mills and other buildings from the 19th century at **Îles des Moulins**, *Parc des Îles des Moulins; tel: (514) 471-0619,* open Tues–Sun 1000–2000 (late June–early Sept), free, presents a striking picture of pre-industrial life in Québec. The complex includes grain and sawmills, an 1850 woollen fabric mill and the province's first large-scale bakery, which produced cookies and crackers for the voyageurs to take on their fur-trading trips.

L'ASSOMPTION

This town grew up along a portage route of voyageurs. Around 1800, when tensions were still high between native French settlers and British interlopers, the women of the village invented a special wool sash to be worn by French-Canadian fur traders to differentiate themselves from the Scottish traders employed by the Nordwest Company. This was the birth of the V-shaped sash, the famous *ceinture fléchée,* that became a symbol of the province. Between 1800 and 1825, L'Assomption had the monopoly on manufacturing these sashes. The store that sold them, **Magasin Le Roux**, still stands at *195 r. du Portage.*

ST-PAUL-DE-JOLIETTE

Stop briefly in this tiny village to examine the village church, **Église St-Paul**, *8 blvd Brassard; tel: (514) 756-2791.* Designed by Pierre Conefroy de Boucherville and inaugurated in 1804, its austere elegance guided church design throughout the province for the next half century – coincidentally the period during which about half of Québec's parish churches were built.

JOLIETTE

Tourist Information: Office du Tourisme et des Congrès de la Région de Joliette, *500 r. Dollard, Joliette, PQ J6E 4M4; tel: (514) 759-5013 or (800) 363-1775.*

Born in 1823 as a sawmill town to carve up the great forests to the north, Joliette has become a cultural and economic centre of the Lanaudière region. It is worth visiting just to see the **Musée d'Art de Joliette**, *145 r. Wilfrid-Corbeil; tel: (514) 756-0311,* open Tues–Sun 1200–1800 (late June–early Sept), Wed–Sun 1200–1700 (early Sept–late June), adults $4.50. The clerics of St-Viateur, the most powerful Catholic order in Joliette, amassed a striking art collection during the 1940s, now displayed in this rather severe building. Sections of the collection are devoted to religious art of the medieval period, Québec religious art (a soulfully expressive, sometimes maudlin tradition) and – surprisingly – a great deal of striking modern art by Canadian, American and European artists, including Emily Carr, Jean-Paul Riopelle and Henry Moore.

From early July through early Aug, symphonic orchestras, opera singers and baroque ensembles perform in the 2000-seat outdoor **Amphithéâtre de Lanaudière**, *1500 ch. Base-de-Roc; tel: (514) 759-7636,* in the **Festival International de Lanaudière**.

BERTHIERVILLE

This village had the distinction of becoming perhaps the first personal vacation getaway in

175

the province. Founded in 1637, it passed through many hands before being acquired after the British Conquest (as *les Québecois* call it) by James Cuthbery – an aide de camp of General Wolfe, commander at the battle on the Plains of Abraham – who developed the riverfront property as a summer retreat from the city for himself and his friends.

Fortunately, Cuthbert did not raze the **Église Ste-Geneviève**, *780 r. Montcalm*, a 1781 structure with an especially rich interior, including several major religious paintings. He did, however, build the province's first Protestant church, **Chapelle des Cuthbert**, *r. de Bienville; tel: (514) 836-7336*, open daily 1000–1800 June–early Sept, free.

The town also claims to have the only museum dedicated to a racing driver, **Musée Gilles-Villeneuve**, *960 av. Gilles-Villeneuve; tel: (514) 836-2714*, open daily 1000–1700 June–Aug, adults $5. A local boy and championship driver, Villeneuve hit the wall and died in a fiery crash during the 1982 qualifying trials for the Grand-Prix du Belgique.

LOUISEVILLE

Founded in 1665, Louiseville was renamed in the 19th century in honour of one of Queen Victoria's daughters when it became the administrative centre for the area around Lac St-Pierre, a basin within the St. Lawrence River. Historically a farming town, each year in early Oct it celebrates the 10-day **Festival de la Galette de Sarrazin** (Buckwheat Pancake Festival) with parades, auctions, shows and folklore productions. For information; *tel: (819) 228-9993*.

Gîte de la Seigneurie, *480 ch. du Golf; tel: (819) 228-8224*, features three acres of old-time gardens, including a rose garden with 15 heirloom varieties, open daily 1000–1700 (mid June–early Sept), adults $6.

For guided nature tours in all seasons on the 'lake', contact **La Domaine du lac St-Pierre**, *75 Lac St-Pierre Est; tel: (819) 228-8819*. Naturalist tours of the ecosystem and

natural history of Lac St-Pierre – part of the St. Lawrence River – and its archipelago and marshes depart daily at 1030. Tours are by motorboat in spring, summer and fall, and by a woodstove-heated sleigh pulled by a snowmobile in winter. Prices vary.

YAMACHICHE

The farming community of Yamachiche sits slightly inland from Lac St-Pierre. Its weeklong **Festival de Ste-Anne**; *tel: (819) 296-3289*, in late July follows the Latin tradition of honouring a local patron saint with a blend of religious observances (a novena, organ concert, high mass) and celebratory activities (fireworks, craft exhibitions, family picnics).

POINTE-DU-LAC

In recent years Pointe-du-Lac has become a windsurfer's mecca, but the sailors were here first and they still dominate this north-east corner of Lac St-Pierre. It's possible to take sailing lessons or rent boats for your own tour of the lake at **Centre Nautique de Francheville**, *3751 r. Notre-Dame; tel: (819) 377-5454*, open daily (May–Sept). Tent pitches and dormitory housing are available should you decide to spend all day sailing.

The **Moulin Seigneurial**, *2930 r. Notre-Dame; tel: (819) 377-1396*, open Tues–Sun 1200–1730 (late June–early Sept), adults $2, a 1721 flour mill, was classified as an historical monument in 1975. The guided tour includes a milling demonstration. **Cabane-à-Sucre Chez Danny**, *195 de la Sablière; tel: (819) 370-4769*, is one of the area's few maple sugar houses open all year.

TROIS-RIVIÈRES

Tourist Information: Office du tourisme et des congrès de Trois-Rivières, *1457 r. Notre-Dame, Trois-Rivières, PQ G9A 4X4; tel: (819) 375-1122*, open daily 0900–1700.

Situated almost exactly halfway between Montréal and Québec, Trois-Rivières makes

The Coming Battle

As you approach Québec, consider the bright, young man James Wolfe, at the age of 32 already a major general in His Majesty's Army, as he approached the city in June 1759. The French and English were locked in a struggle for North America, and Wolfe's counterpart, the equally brilliant Brigadier General Louis Joseph de Montcalm-Gozon, had secured New France on every frontier but one. With the aid of American colonials from Massachusetts and Connecticut, British forces took Fortress Louisbourg on Cape Breton, opening the St Lawrence River. Under Wolfe's leadership, a fleet of 9000 soldiers sailed up the river to lay siege to Québec, the nerve centre of New France.

But Montcalm held the high ground, bombarding the British ships from both sides of the river, and while British cannon dropped 40,000 cannonballs on Québec City, the siege held. By September, Wolfe was faced with the coming winter, when ice would immobilise his troops and they would be sitting ducks. Hatching a plan of near-suicidal desperation, Wolfe ordered his men to scale the Cap Diamant escarpment by night, taking position by dawn in the fields of Abraham Martin behind the French citadelle on 13 Sept 1759.

Faced with this bold move, Montcalm threw his troops and their Indian allies into pitched hand-to-hand combat. Within quarter of an hour, the bloody battle was over, the British were victorious, and the brave and brilliant Wolfe and Montcalm were both mortally wounded. Wolfe died the next day, Montcalm on the battlefield. Told of the severity of his wound, Montcalm is said to have replied: 'Thank God! I shall not live to see the surrender of Quebec'.

The war would drag on another four years, but New France was lost. The generals are remembered fondly even today in a dance tune, Wolfe and Montcalm, played by Anglophone and Francophone fiddlers alike.

177

a good overnight stop if you're making the inter-urban journey at a measured pace. Until recently, Trois-Rivières was primarily a pulp-and-paper processing town, but now with strict environmental constraints on air pollution and the cessation of logging on the city's tributary rivers, it has built a more diversified economy and has found itself as a tourist destination with a generous offering of restaurants, art galleries, festivals and sporting events.

Trois-Rivières lacks a colonial core because the old town, with the exception of a few stone buildings, burned to the ground in 1908. It sits at a dramatic point, where the three-forked Mauricie River (hence the name) meets the St Lawrence. The graceful, arching span of Pont LaViolette is the only bridge across the St Lawrence between Montréal and Québec.

ACCOMMODATION

Hotel chains in Trois-Rivières and adjoining Trois-Rivières-Ouest include *De* and *HG*.

Easily the highest quality for the best price in the Trois-Rivières area is **Les Suites de LaViolette**, *7201 r. Notre-Dame, Trois-Rivières-Ouest, PQ G9B 1W2; tel: (819) 377-4747 or (800) 567-4747*, which offers large, modern and very comfortable rooms at moderate rates. On-site breakfast is cheap and generous.

Other lodgings tend to be either over-the-hill budget motels or quite charming, low-moderate Bed and Breakfast operations, where an ability to speak French will be useful. Two of the better among these are **La Gîte Loiselle**, *836 r. des Ursulines, Trois-Rivières, PQ G9A 1T5; tel: (819) 375-2121*, and **L'Emerillon**, *890 Terasse Turcotte*,

Trois-Rivières, PQ G9A 1T5; tel: (819) 375-1010. Both establishments offer three guest rooms, each with private bath.

EATING AND DRINKING

As a former loggers' town, Trois-Rivières has no shortage of bars, and its outskirts boast a plentiful supply of Québecois fast-food – i.e. in addition to the usual North American chains, a plethora of dairy bars that offer *poutine* and a large number of chicken roasters.

Fortunately, there are two excellent, semi-formal French restaurants in the district: **Gaspard**, *475 r. des Forges; tel: (819) 691-0680*, in Vieux Trois-Rivières, moderate, and **Chez Claude in Le Castel des Prés**, *5800 blvd Royal; tel: (819) 375-4921*, in Trois-Rivières-Ouest, moderate–pricey. Chez Claude shares the building with a wine bar, **L'Etiquette**, that offers an Italian-French light menu and several wines by the glass; budget–moderate. **La Becquée**, *4970 blvd des Forges; tel: (819) 372-1881*, specialises in Québec cuisine, offering a four-course dinner with wine for two for about $50.

ENTERTAINMENT

Downtown Trois-Rivières has a concentration of clubs and bars on *r. Notre-Dame* and *r. Laviolette*. English is rarely a first language here (although many people speak it), so cinemas show all movies in French. Most local residents find their entertainment outdoors with windsurfing, sailing and cycling in the summer and snowmobiling in the winter.

For golf enthusiasts, **Club de golf Ki-8-Eb**, *8200 blvd des Forges; tel: (819) 375-8918*, has both a par 72 18-hole course and a par 27 9-hole course; green fees $33–35 for 18 holes. **Club de golf Les Vielles Forges**, *1975 rue Grimard; tel: (819) 379-7477*, has an 18-hole, par 70 course; green fees $23–28.

Events

The **Trois-Rivières International Vocal Arts Festival**, late June, celebrates religious, lyric, popular, ethnic and traditional song

with concerts in the streets and public parks; *tel: (819) 372-4635*. **Trois-Rivières Agricultural Exhibition**, 10 days in early July, is a traditional fair with livestock and produce judging, a circus, concerts and rides; *tel: (819) 374-2714*. On the first weekend in Aug, the streets roar with race cars and fireworks light the sky as the city hosts the annual **Player's Grand Prix of Trois-Rivières**; *tel: (819) 3733-9912* for tickets, *tel: (819) 380-9797 or (800) 363-5051*. For 10 days in early Oct, the city celebrates French verse with the **Trois-Rivières International Poetry Festival**; activities include concerts, exhibitions, films and more than 100 public readings; *tel: (819) 379-9813*.

SIGHTSEEING

The city Tourist Office sponsors a guided walking tour through Vieux Trois-Rivières on request. The same office also provides a map of the 300 permanent panels with excerpts of love poems (in French, of course): **Promenade de la poésie**. Cruises along the St Lawrence and Mauricie rivers are available daily May–Sept from **Croisières** *M/S Jacques-Cartier, 1515 r. de la Fleuve; tel: (819) 375-3000*, adults $11.

Before the invention of the wood-pulp paper industry in the mid 19th century, Trois-Rivières was already a major industrial centre courtesy of its ironworks, which were established in 1730 and operated for more than 150 years. The site was destroyed after the 1908 fire, when townspeople dismantled the buildings for materials to reconstruct their homes.

In 1973, however, the Canadian government began archaeological excavations at the site, and in 1975 opened it as a national historic site: **Forges du St-Mauricie**, *10000 blvd des Forges; tel: (819) 378-5116 or (800) 463-6769*, open daily 0930–1730 (May–early Sept), 0930–1630 (early Sept–mid Oct), adults $4. Animated and exceptionally well-trained guides demonstrate the technology of the blast furnace (partially restored) and relate the iron-working village life during three eras. Also on the site is the 'devil's fountain', a natural outlet of methane claimed by local Indians as a sacred fire.

In 1997, Trois-Rivières inaugurated a new 'national' (meaning Québec) museum that dramatically captures common life in the province over the years: **Musée des Arts et Traditions Populaires du Québec**, *200 r. Laviolette; tel: (819) 372-0406, open Tues–Sun 1000–1700 (May–late June, early Sept–mid Oct), daily 1000–1900 (late June–early Sept)*, adults $6. Housed in an elegantly modern building next to the old jail, the museum touts itself as a 'visit to the house of Québec', detailing the lives of the first settlers who arrived via the Bering Straits after the last glaciation and continuing through French settlement, British Conquest and modern Canadian eras.

Changing exhibitions highlight such areas as folk medicine, hand tools and toys. The collection grew from the private collections of a local historian/folklorist who spent two decades collecting regional folk art, farm machinery and other items of everyday Québec life. Superb interpretation and well-curated collections make this museum a must-see.

CAP-DE-LA-MADELEINE

This town is primarily a suburb of Trois-Rivières, but it is best known throughout Québec for its shrine: **Sanctuaire Notre-Dame-du-Cap**, *626 r. Notre-Dame, Cap-de-la-Madeleine; tel: (819) 374-2441*. In March 1879, the parish decided to build a new church, intending to carry the necessary stones from across the river. But it had been a warm winter and the river was not frozen. Prayers and rosaries were directed to the parish's statue of the Virgin and 'by miracle' an ice bridge formed and the stones were transported in a week. The old church, built 1714–17, is preserved as a sanctuary devoted to the Virgin, and several other minor miracles are attributed to the spot, thereby drawing hundreds of thousands of pilgrims each year.

Pilgrims needed a bigger place to worship, so in the mid 1950s, the enormous **Basilique Notre-Dame-du-Rosaire** was built. It so dwarfs everything else in the village that it looks like a movie set for a biblical epic.

CAP-DE-LA-MADELEINE TO STE-ANNE-DE-LA-PÉRADE

The road east of Trois-Rivières soon flattens out into broad, rich bottomlands along the Fleuve St-Laurent, lined on both sides with extensive farms that raise truck vegetables and grains, especially oats and wheat. (The extraordinary quality of Québec croissants results from the local wheat, a heritage strain from France, and local butter.)

At Champlain, pull over on the left at a little garden and look out across from the Romanesque church. This pleasant roadside rest stop celebrates the village's reputation for its fine floral displays. The sign reads 'Champ plein de fleurs'. For a taste of the wood-carving tradition of the St Lawrence valley, visit the workshop at **La Paysanne de Champlain**, *607 r. Notre-Dame; tel: (819) 295-3888*. The next village, **Batiscan**, has a small museum of 18th- and 19th-century Québecois furniture in the **Vieux Presbytère de Batiscan**, *340 r. Principale; tel: (418) 362-2051, open daily 1000–1700 early June–late Oct*, adults $3.

STE-ANNE-DE-LA-PÉRADE

Tourist Information: Information Touristique, *21 blvd Lanadière (in person only), open 0900–1700 late June–early Sept*.

This tiny village (population 2400) at the confluence of the Ste-Anne and St-Laurent rivers is picturesque enough in warm weather, when its orchards are either in bloom or heavy with fruit, but it is transformed once the weather turns cold enough to freeze the Fleuve Ste-Anne. Thousands of people suddenly arrive and put up shacks on the ice to fish for tom cod. The village capitalises on this influx with a six-week festival beginning immediately after Christmas that features ice sculptures, fishing competitions and gastronomic events. Fishing cabins and all the necessary gear may be rented from $20 per person and up from the river's management committee, **Comité de Gestion de la Rivière Ste-Anne**; *tel: (418) 325-2475.*

DESCHAMBEAULT

Tourist Information: Bureau Régional d'Information Touristique, *12 r. des Pins, Deschambeault* (no mail enquiries); *tel: (418) 285-4616,* open daily 0900–1700.

The **Moulin de la Chevrotière**, *109 r. de Chavigny (within sight of Rte 138 and well-signed); tel: (418) 286-6862,* open 0900–1700 June–Sept, free, contains art exhibits and offers a small nature trail beside its mill stream. The mill dates from 1802; the rough building behind it, built in 1766, was the original mill but was converted to a forge.

In the village, the **Vieux Presbytère**, *117 r. St-Joseph; tel: (418) 286-6891,* is a picturesque structure on the top of a high bluff with excellent scenic views. Built in 1815, it was rescued from decay by an antiques dealer in 1955 and is now the pride and joy of a local preservation association. The exhibition within focuses on archaeological relics of the Indians in the area circa AD 1450. It is open daily 0900–1700 (June–Aug), Sat–Sun 1000–1700 (May and Sept–Oct); adults $1.50.

CAP-SANTÉ

The tiny village of Cap-Santé has been often called the most picturesque in Québec. That accepted wisdom is a bit of a stretch, but the **Vieux Chemin** (watch for signs on Rte 138) is lined with a large number of 18th-century homes facing the river, and its majestic **Église de la Ste-Famille**, *r. du Quai,* is perhaps the largest and one of the last parish churches built under the French

regime. Three striking wooden statues stand in alcoves on the façade; amazingly, they have survived in place since 1775.

DONNACONNA

Signs along Rte 138 in Donnaconna will direct you about 3 km off the main route to the **fish ladder**, established in 1979 to help restore Atlantic salmon to the Rivière Jacques-Cartier, where they had been wiped out by logging on the river by 1910. The effort has been extremely successful and salmon fishing is permitted July–Sept, with fishing permits available at the site. (Salmon permits run $30–70 above and beyond a provincial fishing licence for non-residents of Québec.)

NEUVILLE

A vein of limestone runs through Neuville, so the early inhabitants built many of their homes from blocks of stone rather than the plentiful timber used elsewhere in Québec. A surprising number of these structures built between 1785 and 1825 still survive and several are classified as historical monuments. Shortly after seeing the 'Neuville' sign on the road, watch on the left for *r. des Érables,* a 5 km detour through the village that rejoins Rte 138.

STE-AUGUSTIN-DE-DESMAURES

The parish of this small town on the outskirts of Québec dates from 1691, and the church of the same name as the town was restored to its 1809–16 condition in celebration of the tricentennial. It contains some of the best Québecois religious art outside a museum in the province. The cemetery around the church is watched over by two handsome stone owls, a Québec symbol for guardians of the night.

CHAMBLAY

Chamblay occupies a strategic point on the Rivière Richelieu, which was the chief transportation route between Montréal and New York and New England in the 17th and 18th centuries. The first fort was built here in 1665 to protect Montréal from Iroquois attacks, and subsequent forts played important roles in the struggle between the French and British and then the British and the Americans. Today it is the **Lieu Historique National du Fort-Chamblay**, *2 r. Richelieu; tel: (514) 658-1585,* open daily 0930–1800 (late June– Aug), variable days and hours but always on Sat–Sun 1030–1700 (Feb–late June and Sept–Oct), admission $3.50. The interpretation centre explains the role of the fort in different eras, and during July–Aug the 'Compaignes Franches de la Marine' perform manoeuvres in full regalia.

ST-MATHIAS

Now a peaceful suburban village, St-Mathias was once torn with factionalism. A Vermont military group, Ethan Allen and his Green Mountain Boys, took over the village during the American revolution to try to convince the inhabitants to join the United States. And during the Patriotes Rebellion of 1837–38, it was a rebel stronghold. If the church happens to be open, peek into **Église St-Mathias** to see the master altar and pulpit sculpted in the Louis XV style in 1795.

MONT-ST-HILAIRE

This mountain town has spawned several Québec landscape painters, and its bucolic charm persists – as does one of the last untouched blocks of mature forest. In 1978, UNESCO designated this area as the first Biosphere Reserve in Canada, now designated the **Centre de Conservations de la Nature du Mont-St-Hilaire**, *422 ch. Des Moulins; tel: (514) 467-1755,* open daily all year 0800 to one hour before sunset, adults $4. Hiking trails lead to three hilltops with panoramic lookouts. Concerts are given July–Aug, Sun only. Skating, sledding and cross-country skiing are permitted but no equipment is provided.

ST-HYACINTHE

This capital of the truck farm industry is surrounded by agricultural science institutions and stunning farms. Be sure to visit the landscaped gardens (including water gardens, rock gardens, a Zen garden and several formal gardens) of **Jardins Daniel A. Séguin**, *3215 r. Sicotte; tel: (514) 778-0372,* open Tues–Sun 1100–1830 (late June–Aug), Sat–Sun 1100–1630 (Sept), adults $5. The town has been known for its pipe organs since 1878. **Ex Arte bookstore**, *12790 r. Yamaska,* is dedicated strictly to music for the organ and harpsichord.

DRUMMONDVILLE

Tourist Information: Office du Tourisme et des Congrès de Drummondville, *1350 r. Michaud; tel: (819) 477-5529,* open daily 0900–1700 (late June–Aug), Mon–Fri 0900–1700 (Sept–late June).

Spread out over a broad area where Hwy 20, Hwy 55 and several secondary routes all cross, Drummondville is more a convenience for the traveller than a destination – except during its annual international festival. Prices for petrol *(essence* in Québec) are lower here than elsewhere in Québec and fast-food operations abound in the strip malls. Yet Drummondville is also central for forays to surrounding towns and villages with fewer tourist services and, because it lies roughly halfway between Montréal and Québec, it makes a good base for slow exploration between the two urban centres.

ACCOMMODATION

Drummondville has a *CI*. Three other good options, all moderately priced, are the **Auberge Universel**, *915 r. Hains, Drummondville, PQ J2C 3A1; tel: (819) 478-4791* or *(800) 668-3521;* **Hôtellerie Le Dauphin**, *600 blvd St-Joseph, Drummondville, PQ J2C 2C1; tel: (819) 478-4141 or (800) 567-0995;* and **Motel Blanchet**, *225 blvd St-Joseph Ouest, Drummondville, PQ J2E 1A9; tel: (819) 477-0222 or (800) 567-3823.*

181

Camping des Voltigeurs, *C.P. 878, Hwy 20, exit 181, Drummondville, PQ J2B 6X1; tel: (819) 477-1360 or (418) 686-4875* (off season), is the official name for the 270 pitches available at Parc des Voltigeurs (see below) at $23 per night, open late May–early Sept. This unusually nice campsite has full services and offers a variety of recreational activities.

Parc des Voltigeurs, *C.P. 878, Hwy 20, exit 181, Drummondville, PQ J2B 6X1; tel: (819) 477-1360 or (418) 686-4875* (off season), open end of May–early Sept. Located on the banks of the St-François River, the park is named after the Québec regiment that defeated US invaders in the War of 1812. Now a recreational site with hiking trails, picnic tables and soccer field, the park also has camping. Admission to the park and use of trails is free.

Within the park is the Trent Estate, which houses the **Musée de la Cuisine**, which tries to elucidate the origins and development of Québec cuisine, open late June–Aug. Near the park is the living history museum, **Le Village Québecois d'Antan**, *1425 r. Montplaisir; tel: (819) 478-1441,* open daily 1000–1700 (June–early Sept), Sat–Sun through end of Sept, adults $10. Historic re-enactors in 70 buildings demonstrate Québec life from 1810 to 1910. Craftspeople demonstrate candle-making, wool carding and preparation of vegetable dyes. Horse-drawn wagon rides cost $2.

The largest rose-grower in Québec, **Rose Drummond**, *210 blvd Lemire Ouest; tel: (819) 478-0245,* offers tours of its 930-square-m garden under glass throughout the year with advance registration, adults $3.50. In the winter, **Cité des Loisirs**, *950 r. Hemming (4 km from downtown Drummondville); tel: (819) 478-5475,* offers facilities and equipment rentals for cross-country skiing, skating, sliding and snowshoeing. Rates vary with activity.

Drummondville assumes centre stage in eastern Canada during early–mid July each year with its 10-day **Festival Mondiale de Folklore**; *tel: (819) 472-1184 or (800) 265-5412.* The festival features musicians and dancers, usually from about a dozen countries, as well as storytellers, temporary restaurants, artisans in various craft media and an international marketplace selling folk art, fabrics, carvings and other traditional expressions of the participating countries. Admission is $8 per day or $12 for a pass good throughout the festival.

Duffers will also find the **Club de Golf de Drummondville**, *400 ch. de Golf; tel: (819) 478-0494,* a handsome 18-hole par 72 course, greens fees $25–30.

WARWICK

Small as it is, Warwick is central to much of the Québec cheese industry and hosts the **Festival de Fromage**; *tel: (819) 358-4316,* each year (mid June), complete with tastings and cheese and wine pairings, $12 at the door. It is also home to **Club de Golf Canton**, *5 Rte 166 Ouest; tel: (888) 287-2874* (toll-free), an 18-hole, par 71 course; green fees $20–25.

The **Parc Linéaire des Bois-Francs** begins here. This 71-km cycling trail built along abandoned railways stretches through Victoriaville and Plessisville. Outside the urban areas, the park becomes a snowmobile trail in winter.

VICTORIAVILLE

Tourist Information: Chambre des Commerce, *122 r. Aqueduc, C.P. 641, Victoriaville, PQ G6P 6V7; tel: (819) 758-6371.*

Formed by the amalgamation of several smaller communities during the 1990s, Victoriaville is the *de facto* economic capital of the Bois-Francs region. The original village was founded in 1861 and named after Britain's (and Canada's) queen at the time. It's worth turning off the road into town just to drive by a number of fine Victorian homes.

The chief attraction is the **Musée Laurier**, *16 r. Laurier Ouest; tel: (819) 357-8655*, open Mon–Fri 0900–1800, Sat–Sun 1300–1700 (June–Aug), closed 1200–1300 (Sept–May), adults $3.50. This blocky mansion was built in 1876 for Sir Wilfrid Laurier, the first French-Canadian to become prime minister of Canada. It became a museum in 1929, featuring furniture and memorabilia, but was substantially upgraded in 1996 to include changing exhibitions of political figures and themes in both Québec and Canada. A free park with extraordinary scenic outlooks lines the slopes of Mont St-Michel on *blvd Bois-Francs Sud*. It's easy to find – just look for the 24-m high cross on a hilltop.

Club de Golf Victoriaville Itée, *223 r. Perreault; tel: (819) 752-2133*, has an 18-hole par 72 course; greens fees $25–29.

In the middle of May each year, Victoriaville hosts the two-week **Festival de Musique Actuelle**; *tel: (819) 758-9451*. English-language literature about this event is a bit misleading, describing it as 'new music', which is literally true but not what most fans of new music would expect. It is, instead, a festival of New Age music, complete with ethereal synthesisers and plaintive lyrics.

PLESSISVILLE

Tourist Information: Information Touristique, *355 blvd Baril Ouest* (in person only), open daily 0900–1700 late June–early Sept.

Plessisville claims to be the world capital of maple *(érable)* products – it certainly has some of the largest factories processing syrup and about half the province's exports of maple products bear the town name. Plessisville holds a three-day **Festival de l'Érable**; *tel: (819) 362-9292* or *(800) ERABLE-0*, each year on the first weekend in May.

Club de Golf Plessisville 1990 Inc., *328 Rang de Golf; tel: (819) 362-3387*, is an 18-hole, par 72 course; greens fees $20–23.

INVERNESS

The countryside drive around Inverness offers a particularly good snapshot of the hillside dairy farming for which the Bois-Francs area is known. Inverness stands out for its Scottish heritage and its preponderance of artists. In recent years it has become a centre for sculptors working in bronze, and the old Methodist church has been converted to a bronze foundry, casting work by Alfred Laliberté and other well-known Québec sculptors.

This flurry of activity has spawned the **Musée du Bronze d'Inverness**, *1760 r. Dublin; tel: (418) 453-2101*, within a few metres of the only intersection in the village. You will receive a glove as you enter to permit you to experience the castings by running your hand over them. The museum is open daily 1000–1700 (late June–Aug), Sat–Sun 1000–1700 (May– mid June and Sept–mid Oct), adults $6.

INVERNESS TO QUÉBEC

The drive from Inverness into the city passes first through woodlands, where you will go through the **covered bridge** at **Ste-Agathe Falls Park**, before emerging into the open farmland of the St-Laurent plain, following in a general way the course of the Rivière Beaurivage, a timber river until the early 19th century, when the trees gave out and the farmers moved in. Several horse-breeding farms are visible along the route, as is an ostrich farm at **St-Étienne-de-Lauzon**.

As you get within 40 km of Québec, the farms are suddenly cut up into house lots, where a substantial portion of the urban workforce lives. Consequently, avoid rush hours on these roads built for tractors and wagons but now subjected to suburban traffic.

QUÉBEC CITY

Perched atop an escarpment over the Fleuve St-Laurent (St Lawrence River), the fortified city of Québec was the first North American site chosen for the UNESCO World Heritage list. Within its 17th-century walls, Québec remains a picturesque city built chiefly of local grey stone, dominated on the bluff overlooking the river by the Loire Valley-style Hôtel Château Frontenac. The vigorous industrial city outside the walls is less unusual, although the wooden homes of the residential districts are tended with obvious pride.

Besieged six times since its founding in 1608, Québec fell twice to the British – temporarily in 1629 and decisively in 1759. But the French won the peace; Québec is the North American centre of French language and culture. Some 95 per cent of the population speak French as their primary language.

With the rise of the separatist Parti Québecois in the mid 1990s, Québec has taken greater pride than ever in its French heritage. At the same time, hostility toward monolingual English speakers has been replaced with an amused pity that they are missing out on the riches of French culture. A few French phrases, however ineptly pronounced, go a long way toward eliciting help.

A city of only 570,000 residents, Québec receives more than 4 million visitors each year, making the tourist service industries among the largest in the city. It is also noted for its low crime rate.

TOURIST INFORMATION

Greater Québec Area Tourism and Convention Bureau, 835 av. Wilfrid-Laurier, Québec, PQ G1R 2L3; tel: (418) 649-2608, provides a superb tourist guide and fairly detailed map of Québec City and the surrounding region. The **Maison du Tourisme de Québec**, 12 r. Ste-Anne, across from Château Frontenac; tel: (418) 873-2015 or (800) 363-7777 (toll-free), open daily 0830–1930 (late June–early Sept), daily 0900–1700 (early Sept–late June), has an automated banking machine, a bureau de change and stations for car hire and hotel reservations, in addition to literature and kiosks where you can book various bus and walking tours. It also has excellent public restrooms.

WEATHER

July–Aug are humid and can be hot (up to 30°C), although the average daily temperature in July is 19°C. Winter is cold and snowy; the average Jan daily is -12°C and overnight lows in Feb can plummet to -30°C. May–June and Sept are nearly perfect, with daytime highs of 18°–22°C and nighttime lows of 9°–10°C.

ARRIVING AND DEPARTING

By Air

Jean–Lesage International Airport; tel: (418) 874-8333, in Ste-Foy, 16 km from downtown, is served by Air Canada/Air Alliance; tel: (418) 692-0770 or (800) 361-8620, and Inter-Canadian/Canadian International; tel: (418) 692-1031 or (800)

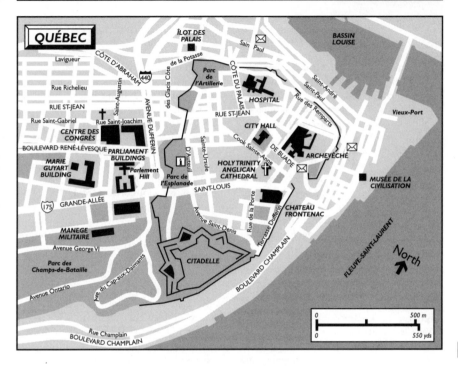

665-1177. A taxi to downtown is fixed by local ordinance at $22. Airport shuttle service is $9 one way or $17 round trip. Shuttles run about every 2½ hours Mon–Fri 0845–2145, Sat–Sun 0900–2000. Local bus service, designed principally for the convenience of airport workers, is limited to trips at 0800 and 1700.

By Rail

VIA Rail; *tel: (418) 692-3940,* offers a daily service between Montréal and Québec, arriving at **Gare du Palais**, *450 r. de la Gare-du-Palais; tel: (418) 524-4161,* and at **Gare de Ste-Foy**, *3255 ch. de las Gare; tel: (418) 658-8792.*

By Bus

Orleans Express Coach Lines (connecting to other major Canadian cities) and **Intercar Côte-Nord** (provincial transport) also use the Gare du Palais, but a different

entrance, *320 r. Abraham-Martin; tel: (418) 525-3000.*

GETTING AROUND

Although it has developed above and below a cliff, Québec remains principally a walking city. The easiest way to negotiate this precipitous division is by riding the **Funiculaire**, $1, a small rail car, from the Terrasse Dufferin to Le Quartier Petit Champlain. (When the funiculaire is under repair, shuttle vans make the same trip for the same price.)

Many visitors to Québec City never venture more than 1 km outside the old walls, content with the venerable (and considerable) pleasures of **Vieux (Old) Québec**. The old city is generally defined in terms of inside and outside the walls. West of the walls are **Parlement Hill**, seat of provincial government (though the government refers to itself as a 'national' assembly), and **Place**

d'Youville, the de facto central gathering place for outdoor concerts and rallies and the centre-point of the city bus system. Just west of Parlement Hill is **av. Grand-Allée**, the 'petit Champs-Élysée' of Québec with its strip of outdoor restaurants. West of *Place d'Youville* is the bohemian and immigrant neighbourhood of **St-Jean-Baptiste**.

South-east of the walls is the **Vieux Port** district, which encompasses the quickly gentrifying area between the Port of Québec and *Place Royale,* where Québec began in 1608. The area immediately below the bluff is **Le Quartier Petit-Champlain** – the shopping and dining district reached by funiculaire, shuttle bus or a steep and twisting staircase.

Public Transport

City buses cost $1.85 in change or $1.50 with the purchase of tickets from **Tabagie Giguere**, *61 r. Baude,* or from the *Place d'Youville* bus station. For information; *tel: (418) 627-2511;* or enquire at the Maison du Tourisme. Buses to suburban shopping and sights use *Place d'Youville* as a main terminus.

Driving in Québec City

Driving is awkward in Vieux Québec, and on-street parking is sparse. Meters are $1.25 per hour and take $0.25 and $1 coins. Maximum parking is two hours. Park at an underground lot when you arrive and use your car only for excursions. Even many small hotels have parking, and those outside the walls generally have their own garages or lots or an arrangement with one of the commercial car parks. Motorcycles are prohibited within the walls of Vieux Québec, and few bicycles are seen because the terrain is so steep.

STAYING IN QUÉBEC CITY

Accommodation

Accommodation is widely available in all but the least expensive categories, with camping at a substantial remove from the city. A resurgence of tourist interest in Québec City in the last decade has stimulated the renovation of many older hotels and the construction of several new ones inside historic buildings. Immediately west of Parlement Hill are several large hotels (moderate–expensive) constructed in the 1960s and renovated in recent years. Many boutique hotels in the moderate–expensive range have opened in the Vieux Port district.

Hotel chains include *CP, Ra, Rm. Hn* and **Loews Concorde Hotel**, *1225 Place Montcalm; tel: (418) 647-2222,* have tower hotels just outside the city walls with remarkable views. Chains in neighbouring Ste-Foy include *BW, DI, HI.*

Le Château Frontenac, *1 r. des Carrières, Québec, PQ G1R 4P5; tel: (418) 692-3861,* the most prominent site in the old city, celebrated its 100th anniversary in 1993; pricey. If you can't afford to stay, take a guided tour of the hotel, which will show you the public areas and some of the more expensive rooms–daily 1000–1800 (May–mid Oct), Sat–Sun 1230–1700 (mid Oct–Apr), $5.50.

Inside the Walls

Three properties stand out in the moderate–expensive range. The art nouveau **Hôtel Clarendon**, *57 r. Ste-Anne, Québec, PQ G1R 3X4; tel: (418) 692-2480,* sports an excellent jazz bar. The beaux-arts exterior of the **Hôtel du Théâtre Capitole**, *972 r. St-Jean, Québec, PQ G1R 1R5; tel: (418) 694-4040* or *(800) 363-4040,* hides a contemporary interpretation of art deco inside. The Capitole is popular with performers visiting to give outdoor concerts, as it stands just steps from *Place d'Youville.* The **Hôtel Manoir Victoria**, *44 Côte du Palais, Québec, PQ G1R 4H8; tel: (418) 692-1030,* offers 145 recently spruced-up rooms in what passes as Victorian décor in French Canada, though Anglophiles might deem it rather more Third Empire. Set up equally for business and pleasure travellers, this hotel offers eminently comfortable rooms and suites beginning in the moderate range and rising to pricey for the multi-bedroom suites. Moderately priced lodgings inside the city fortifications are surprisingly common. Two directly behind the Frontenac are the **Château Bellevue**, *16 r. Laporte, Québec, PQ G1R 4M9; tel: (418) 692-2573*, a handsome stone building where the spare and modern interior doesn't quite match the exterior, but the prices are good and the location is quiet yet convenient, and the **Hôtel au Jardin du Gouverneur**, *16 r. Mont-Carmel, Québec, PQ G1R 4A3; tel: (418) 692-1704*. The **Cap Diamant Maison de Touristes**, *39 av Ste-Geneviève, Québec, PQ G1R 4B3; tel: (418) 694-0313*, is hidden away on a quiet street, while the **Auberge La Caravelle**, *68½ r. St-Louis, Québec, PQ G1R 3Z3; tel: (418) 694-0656 or (800) 267-0656*, is set in the thick of things on the street that connects *av. Grand-Allée* to the Château Frontenac.

The historic **Hôtel Marie-Rollet**, *81 r. Ste-Anne, Québec, PQ G1R 3X4; tel: (418) 694-9271*, occupies an 1876 greystone building constructed by the Ursuline order. Its ten rooms (a few of which are extremely small), include two with fireplaces; moderate. If you would like an historic lodging truly in the centre of the action, literally hanging above *r. de Petit Champlain*, then investigate the **Gîte Côte de la Montagne**, *54 Côte de la Montagne, Québec, PQ G1K 4E2; tel: (418) 694-0740*, situated in a 1722 building. There are only three rooms, but the moderate rate includes what the Québécois refer to as a 'gastronomic breakfast' – a substantial meal encompassing every major food group.

Rue Ste-Ursule, the second street inside the walls from Parlement Hill, has evolved as a district offering a range of comparatively inexpensive lodging, with most rooms in the $60–80 range for two persons, some with shared baths. Some excellent options in this price range include 3-star **Hôtel L'Ermitage**, *60 r. Ste-Ursule, Québec, PQ G1R 4E6; tel: (418) 694-0968*, where all rooms have private baths and small refrigerators; **La Maison Ste-Ursule**, *40 r. Ste-Ursule, Québec, PQ G1R 4E2; tel: (418) 694-9794*, which has a lovely tree-shaded courtyard; and the small **Hôtel La Maison Demers**, *68 r. Ste-Ursule, Québec, PQ G1R 4E6; tel: (418) 692-2487 or (800) 692-2487*, where rates drop into the bargain category Sept–May.

Outside the Walls (Grand-Allée)

Château Laurier, *695 r. Grand-Allée Est, Québec, PQ G1R 2K4; tel: (418) 522-8108*, offers 57 rooms, some of them rather small but furnished in a classical French style; moderate. The back of this five-storey hotel near the city walls overlooks the Plains of Abraham. **Hôtel Le Manoir Lafayette**, *661 r. Grand-Allée Est, Québec, PQ G1R 2K4; tel: (418) 522-2652*, has 67 pleasant rooms in a nicely restored Victorian greystone a short distance outside the city walls; moderate.

Vieux Port

The Vieux Port district, already rife with artists and antique dealers, recently began to come into its own as a lodging district with the conversion of once decrepit buildings into stylish hotels, most moderate–expensive. A pioneer in this movement was the contemporary-chic **Le Priori**, *5 r. Sault-au-Matelot, Québec, PQ G1K 3Y7; tel: (418) 692-3992*, moderate–expensive. Its rival, especially in the contemporary reinterpretation of art deco stylings, is the 40-room **Hotel Dominion 1912**, *128 r. St-Pierre, Québec, PQ G1K 4A8; tel: (418) 692-2224 or (888) 833-5253 (toll-free)*, moderate–expensive. Half the rooms in this eight-storey hotel in a former warehouse overlook the river, the other half the city fortifications. Even-numbered floors are non-smoking.

Somewhat more modest in ambition, but

187

smartly styled on more of a budget, is the **Hôtel St-Paul**, *229½ r. St-Paul, Québec, PQ G1K 3W3; tel: (418) 694-4414*, moderate. The **Auberge St-Pierre**, *79 r. St-Pierre, Québec, PQ G1K 4A3; tel: (418) 694-7981* or *(888) 268-1017*, occupies the building of North America's first insurance company. Striking architectural details and drop-dead design make each of the 24 rooms and eight suites spread out on four floors unique; moderate–expensive.

Centre International de Séjour de Québec (HI), *19 r. Ste-Ursule, Québec, PQ G1R 4E1; tel: (418) 694-0755*, is the city's youth hostel; membership (available on site) mandatory for non-Canadian visitors.

Out of Town

Le Château Bonne Entemps, *3400 Chemin Ste-Foy, Ste-Foy, PQ G1X 1S6; tel: (418) 653-5221* or *(800) 463-4390*, lies at the suburban edge of the city on the bus line and just off a major highway exit. The hotel also provides free shuttle service to the heart of Vieux Québec. Main hotel rooms are expensive–pricey, but the cabins (with full self-catering) are moderate; guests also have access to health club and spa facilities.

Nearest campsite is **Camping Municipal de Beauport**, *95 r. Sérénité, Beauport, PQ G13 3L1; tel: (418) 666-2228*, about 20 mins from downtown and close to Montmorency Falls.

Eating and Drinking

Despite what you learned in French class, Québec meals consist of *déjeuner* (breakfast), *dîner* (lunch) and *souper* (supper), coming in that order, though often punctuated by *un café* or *une bière*. (Despite protests to the contrary, the Québecois are true Canadians in their devotion to malt beverages.) Midday *table d'hôte* meals Mon–Fri are usually the best value, frequently offering full meals at less than half the cost of the evening equivalents.

During the growing season, essentially Mar–Nov, farmers from around the region sell their produce at the **Marché du Vieux-Port**, *169 r. St-André; tel: (418) 692-2517*, near the rail station on the waterfront. Good picnic and self-catering supplies may be had here. A broader range of supplies, including cooked deli meats and fine cheeses, may be found at **Marché Richelieu Je-An-Dre**, *1097 r. St-Jean; tel: (418) 692-3647*, and (a more limited choice) **Épicerie Richard**, *42 r. des Jardins; tel: (418) 692-1207*, which also sells a good variety of pre-made sandwiches.

Inside the Walls

The restaurants of the Château Frontenac are predictably dependable and pricey. **Café de la Terrasse** emphasises grilled meats and bistro plates, along with noon and evening buffets. It also serves tea, beginning at 1500, and an à la carte menu at 1800. Offering a moderate and elegant Sun brunch buffet as well as dinner nightly, **Le Champlain** is the more formal and traditionally French of the Frontenac's restaurants, as well as one of the priciest in the city. Its match might be found at **Le Charles Baillairgé** at the Hôtel Clarendon, *57 r. Ste-Anne; tel: (418) 692-2480*, where the cuisine is more contemporary, the décor more deco, and the piano music more classical.

Famous in the tourist trade, **Restaurant Aux Anciens Canadiens**, *34 r. St-Louis; tel: (418) 692-1627*, provides an upmarket treatment to traditional Québecois dishes that have largely vanished from other restaurants' menus; moderate–pricey. **A la Table de Serge Bruyère**, *1200 r. St-Jean; tel: (418) 694-0618*, pioneered serious modern cuisine in Québec and still sets the local standard. Its main dining room is elegant and pricey, but the establishment also has a bistro-style room, moderate, a budget priced café, and a pub, **Falstaff**; budget.

A retractable roof over the central garden is one of the pleasures of dining at **Restaurant Le Saint Amour**, *48 r. Ste-Ursule; tel: (418) 694-0667*; the others are the remarkable creations of chef de la cuisine Jean-Luc Boulay; budget–moderate. **Café de la Paix**, *44 Des Jardins; tel: (418) 692-1430*, is a longtime favourite traditional French restaurant with an excellent moderate *table d'hôte* with several options for a main course. A comparably priced spot with a similar menu – but, alas, not serving lunch – is **Restaurant Café d'Europe**, *27 r. Ste-Angèle; tel: (418) 692-3835*, moderate.

Rôtisserie Ste-Angèle, *32 r. St-Angèle; tel: (418) 694-3339*, offers Québec's favourite bird (the chicken) in many forms (along with other casual grill food) in a small dining room or a charming terrace; bargain. Homesick Brits might be amused by **Saint Alexandre Pub**, *1087 r. St-Jean; tel: (418) 694-0015*, budget, where one can order steak and kidney pie and such 'English' fare as *sauerkraut* and sausages in this 'typical London public house'. There are 20 beers on tap and another 180 in bottles or cans (all served with a distinct North American chill) and some 40 single malt whiskeys available. (As English-speaking Canadians would say, 'Not so bad, eh?')

The budget traveller need not despair of a good, protein-packed meal. Steak-frites is often the sole menu option at **L'Entrecôte St-Jean**, *1011 r. St-Jean; tel: (418) 694-0234*, budget; sometimes a veal dish is also offered. Coffee in Québec has always been better than in most of Eastern Canada (probably the French taste); **Brûlerie Tatum Café**, *1084 r. St-Jean; tel: (418) 692-3900*, cheap, brews the best java in Québec City.

Outside the Walls

In the Bas Ville (lower city) in the Quartier Petit-Champlain, many comparatively inexpensive restaurants vie for travellers' dollars with casual fare. A longtime favourite here – in no small part for its indulgent desserts – has been **Le Cochon Dingue** (the Pink Pig), *46 blvd Champlain; tel: (418) 692-2013*, moderate. If the entrée interests you more than the sweets, try the bistro-style charm of **Le Lapin Sauté**, *52 r. Petit-Champlain; tel: (418) 692-5325.*

Av. Grand-Allée, between *George V* and *Place Montcalm*, is blessed with broad terraces and a wide variety of good dining, although prices reflect the *bon vivant* quality of the neighbourhood. Bistro-like and très français is **Le Paris-Brest Restaurant Française**, *590 Grand-Allée Est; tel: (418) 529-2243*; moderate.

The **Bar-Restaurant Rotatif L'Astral** at the Loews Concorde Hotel, *1225 Place Montcalm; tel: (418) 647-2222*, has a splendid view of the Plains of Abraham and the old walled city, moderate–pricey. Its modestly priced Sun brunch buffet is a local institution. **La Strada**, *690 av. Grand-Allée Est; tel: (418) 529-6237*, serves the northern Italian style cuisine sweeping North America, with a speciality of grilled pizzas; moderate.

The student-oriented St-Jean-Baptiste neighbourhood, also the centre of gay life in Québec, offers many reasonably priced small restaurants, including a number of very inexpensive Indian and Pakistani shops. It also has a particularly good example of the Québec chain of vegetarian buffet restaurants, **Le Commensal**, *860 r. St-Jean; tel: (418) 647-3733*; budget–moderate.

Vieux Port

The renaissance of the Vieux Port, due in large part to rehabilitation of the waterfront and the construction of the Musée de la Civilisation, has been accompanied by a boom in excellent dining with a contemporary feel. One of the neighbourhood pioneers was **Môss Bistro Belge**, *255 r. St-Paul; tel: (418) 692-0233*, which serves wonderful local mussels; moderate.

All day (and evening) long, **Café Restaurant Le Péché Véniel** (Venial Sin), *233 r. St-Paul; tel: (418) 692-5642*, offers bistro-grill fare such as *moules-frites*, steak-frites and hamburgers at budget prices in a smartly contemporary setting, with enough bustle to be lively and not so many customers as to be crowded. More restrained, more refined and more expensive are the light dishes of **Mistral Gagnant Salon de Thé Provençal**, *160 r. St-Paul,; tel: (418) 692-4260,* moderate, where the proprietors are a Provençal woman furnituremaker (she made most of the furnishings) and her Québecois husband.

The streets of *r. St-Paul, r. St-Pierre* and *r. du Sault-au-Matelot* all converge on a square dominated by a large fountain with a contemporary sculpture of a woman holding sheaves of grain. Each of the streets running into this square has several small restaurants that spill out onto the sidewalks at the first sign of warm weather and don't retreat until the snow flies.

One of the first was **Restaurant Asia**, *89 r. du Sault-au-Matelot; tel: (418) 692-3799,* which exemplifies colonial French cuisine with its refined Indochinese menu (grilled shrimp at lunch, for example, more exotic Vietnamese entrées at night) at refined prices; moderate–pricey. At the other end of the same block is the nouvelle French cuisine of **L'Échaude**, *73 r. du Sault-au-Matelot; tel: (418) 692-1299;* moderate–pricey. French comfort food – *cassoulet,* duck, *bouillabaisse* – can be found at **Café Le St-Malo**, *75 r. St-Paul; tel: (418) 692-2004;* moderate. Close by is the venerable **Buffet de l'Antiquaire**, *95 r. St-Paul; tel: (418) 692-2661,* a favourite in the antiques district for its prices; budget–moderate.

Along the waterfront, **Bistro Restaurant Café du Monde**, *57 r. Dalhousie; tel: (418) 692-4455,* offers a Parisian-style menu at Québec-style prices, budget–moderate. **Poisson d'Avril**, *115 r. St-André; tel: (418) 692-1010,* is sandwiched between the Vieux Port produce market and the yacht basin. Open all year, it is best known for offering an all-you-can-eat *moules-frites* (mussels and chips) plate; moderate.

Communications

Canada Post offices are open Mon–Fri

0800–1745. The main Post Office is located at *300 r. St-Paul; tel: (418) 694-6176;* the upper city office is at *3 r. Buade; tel: (418) 694-6102.*

Money

Automatic banking machines are plentiful within the walls of Vieux Québec, with stations owned by the Royal Bank being the most plentiful. Few such machines are found outside the walls, however. Perhaps the most convenient and secure is the one inside the Maison du Tourisme, *12 r. Ste-Anne.*

ENTERTAINMENT

Some of Québec's best entertainment is free – its world-class street performers. Musicians, acrobats and quirky circus acts congregate at the *Terrasse Dufferin,* the *Place d'Armes* and the tattoo-and-nose-ring end of *r. St-Jean* near Porte St-Jean. Parks and amphitheatres often have free evening performances of musical programmes. The *Québec Chronicle-Telegraph,* the Wednesday English-language newspaper, carries listings. Extensive listings also appear in the local French-language dailies *Le Soleil* and *Le Journal de Québec.*

The **Québec Symphony Orchestra**, the oldest in Canada, performs at the **Grand Théâtre de Québec**, *269 blvd René-Lévesque Est; tel: (418) 643-8131.* The theatre is also a venue for other music, variety shows, dance and theatre (**Le Thèâtre du Trident**). Theatrical productions – almost exclusively in French – and other entertainments are also found at **Le Capitole**, *Place d'Youville; tel: (418) 694-4444,* and **Palais Montcalm**, *995 Place d'Youville; tel: (418) 670-9011.*

Many churches offer concerts of both sacred and secular music, including the Anglican **Cathedral of the Holy Trinity**, *31 r. des Jardins; tel: (418) 692-2193;* the **Église St-Jean-Baptiste**, *490 r. St-Jean (corner of r. de Ligny); tel: (418) 525-7188,* and the historic **Chapelle Bon-Pasteur**, *1080 r. de la Chevrotière; tel: (418) 648-9710.* Best bet

190

for jazz buffs are performances at **l'Emprise at the Hotel Clarendon**, *57 r. Ste-Anne; tel: (418) 692-2480;* no cover, one drink minimum. Local singer-songwriters and Québecois folksingers hold forth at **La Boîte aux Chansons Chez son Père**, *24 r. Stanislas; tel: (418) 692-5308.*

Spectator Sports

The International Hockey League team, **Le Club de Hockey Les Rafales**, play mid Sept–Apr at the **Colisée de Québec**, *2205 av. du Colisée, Parc de l'Exposition, Québec, PQ G1L 4W7; tel: (418) 691-7211 or (800) 900-SHOW;* bus lines 4 and 12.

Harness-racing takes place all year at the **Hippodrome de Québec**, *C.P. 2053, Parc de l'Exposition, Québec, PQ G1K 7M9; tel: (418) 524-5283;* bus lines 4 and 12. General admission is $1.

Outdoor Sports

A 1.3-km paved trail for **in-line skating** winds through the Plains of Abraham, where skates and bicycles may be rented from **Vélo Passe-Sport Plein Air**; *tel: (418) 692-3643.* The same concession rents ice-skates and snowboards in the winter. Ice-skating is also available next to the Château Frontenac at the **Glissades de la Terrasse**; *tel: (418) 692-2955 or (418) 694-9487.*

Events

Two ten-day seasonal events celebrate Québec's position as the standard-bearer of French culture in North America. **Festival d'Été International de Québec**, early–mid July, is the summer party. At the centre of this celebration is a non-stop concert schedule, principally of Francophone musicians from Québec, France, the West Indies and Africa. Four daily outdoor concerts (admission by inexpensive pass) are performed, along with four to six smaller events in clubs and performance halls (individual admissions). While the emphasis is on contemporary pop music, each day features at least one performance each of classical music and jazz.

Carnaval d'Hiver, early–mid Feb, marks the distinctly Québecois love for their intense winter with a variety of outdoor competitions, hearty foods and a general madcap air in the streets.

SHOPPING

Shopping is one of Québec City's principal forms of entertainment. The most interesting goods are those produced by local artisans, as well as some French imports generally unavailable elsewhere in North America.

In the Quartier Petit-Champlain, **Verrerie La Mailloche**, *58 r. Sous-le-Fort; tel: (418) 694-0445*, at the foot of the Escalier Casse-Cou, demonstrates glass blowing daily 0900–2200 (late June–early Oct), daily 0930–1730 (early Oct–late June). **La Dentellière**, *56 r. Champlain; tel: (418) 692-2807*, sells excellent French lacework for curtains and domestic applications. Nearby, **Boutique Métiers d'Arts**, *29 r. Notre-Dame; tel: (418) 694-0267*, shows the work of Québec artists, including the imaginative and innovative stonework of Richard Haché, who applies unusual stones and fossils to his jewellery. **Galerie d'art et d'artisant les Trois Columbes**, *46 r. St-Louis; tel: (418) 694-1114*, features Québec and Canadian crafts as well as Inuit sculptures and Amerindian graphic art.

Within the walls of the upper city, **Atelier Plein-Air**, *between r. du Trésor and the Episcopal cathedral*, features a variety of artisans in jewellery, wood, ceramics, leather and textiles in an open-air market. **Rue du Trésor**, really a small alley, is lined with graphic artists selling their landscapes and portraits. **Claude Berry**, *6 Côte de la Fabrique; tel: (418) 692-2628*, sells a great deal of imported French porcelain, including carved *santones* from Provence, as well as the Québec adaptations of this tradition by Madeleine Robillard. Among the galleries featuring Inuit and Amerindian art are

Canadeau, *1124 r. St-Jean; tel: (418) 692-4850,* and **Aux Multiples Collections**, *69 r. Ste-Anne; tel: (418) 692-1230.*

The Vieux Port has a longstanding residential community of artists. As the district becomes more gentrified, the number of art galleries and studios seems to multiply exponentially. **L'Eau Vive Gallerie de Art**, *21 r. du Sault-au-Matelot; tel: (418) 692-2499,* not only carries some charming paintings and watercolours, but also the bizarre musical instruments of Michel Fafard. Self-taught leather worker and sculptor **Guy Levesque**, *79 r. du Sault-au-Matelot; tel: (418) 694-1298,* makes extraordinary leather masks modelled on the figures of the '*commedia dell'arte*', as well as crafting some strikingly modern furniture.

Also in the Vieux Port, *r. St-Paul* between *r. Rioux* and *r. au Sault-au-Matelot,* has developed as Québec's primary district for antiques shopping, with more than 20 shops. Québec's largest shopping centre, **Place Laurier**, is in Ste-Foy, a 10-min ride on the Route 800 bus from *Place d'Youville.*

SIGHTSEEING

For a sweeping vantage of Québec City from the St Lawrence River, take the **Lévis ferry**, $1.75 each way June–Sept, $1.50 Sept–May, from the terminal opposite *Place Royale.* For a bird's-eye view, visit the free art gallery and observation deck on the 31st floor of a government building: **Anima G**, *Édifice Marie-Guyart, 1037 r. de la Chevrotière,* open Mon–Fri 1000–1600, Sat–Sun 1300–1700, closed mid Dec–mid Jan.

The classic tour of Vieux Québec is by *calèche* (horse-drawn carriage). The price of $50 (plus $7 tax) is set by the city. Rides last a minimum of 35 mins and may be hailed at *Place d'Armes* or along *r. d'Auteuil.* Several companies offer bus tours of the city and countryside; information is available from kiosks in the Maison du Tourisme.

You can get on and off all day from the narrated trolley city tour: **Maple Leaf**

Sightseeing Tours & Dupont, *36½ r. St-Louis; tel: (418) 649-9226* or *(800) 267-0616,* $19.95. Tours leave from *Place d'Armes.* The **Ligue de Taxis Québec**; *tel: (418) 648-9199,* has certified 125 drivers as tour guides after they completed 105 hours of courses; rates vary. Several sightseeing boats offer cruises of 1–1½ hours from the Vieux Port to Montmorency Falls and back; $15–20. Rather more unusual is a 2-hr cruise aboard **La Goélette** *Marie-Clarisse,* a 100-passenger schooner berthed May–Oct at *Quai 19* in the Vieux Port. Cruises depart daily at 1000, 1300, 1600 and 2000, adults $25.

The best way to see Vieux Québec, providing you can muster the stamina, is on foot. Guided walking tours in French or English are given daily at 0930, 1330 and 1600 (late June–Sept), and at 1000 and 1400 (Oct–late June) by **Les Tours Adlard**; *tel: (418) 692-2358.* Tours, which cost $10, depart from the Maison du Tourisme. **Audio-Guide**, also in the Maison du Tourisme, rents audio tours of Vieux Québec, Parlement Hill and Artillery Park. The packages, which range up to $24 for two people, provide a portable CD player, a CD in English or French, and an illustrated guidebook; equipment deposit required.

Québec's walls are the physical manifestation of the civic spirit as defender of the French faith, and strolling the ramparts is the best way to begin to comprehend the city and its moods. Without doubt, Québec is most charming on the **Terrasse Dufferin**, a wooden boardwalk next to the Château Frontenac overlooking the Fleuve St-Laurent. Québecois and visitors alike are drawn to promenade amid musicians and performers.

Historic Sites

Nestled between the Cap Diamant escarpment and the St Lawrence River, **Place Royale** is where, in 1608, Samuel de Champlain began the fortified fur-trading post that would become Québec. Restored to reveal the 17th- and 18th-century city, the district bustles with modern commerce amid interpretive sites. The **Information Centre**, *215 Marché Finley; tel: (418) 643-6631*, open daily 1000–1800 early May–Sept, has slide shows in French and English that trace Québec history from the Native period to present. Guided tours of the area leave from the centre.

At the **Living Heritage Workshop**, *42 r. Notre-Dame; tel: (418) 647-1598*, artisans and craftspeople in period dress demonstrate their trades, music and dance. Admission to the centre and workshop are free. The multimedia sound and light show of **Explore–Sound and Light**, *63 r. Dalhousie; tel: (418) 692-2063*, recounts the events that led to the founding of Québec in a 30-min show; daily 1000–1800 May–Aug, adults $5.50.

Colonial powers fought over Québec because it was a strategic shipping point, and **Le Centre d'Interprétation du Vieux Port de Québec**, *100 r. St-André; tel: (418) 648-3300*, open daily 1000–1700, $2.75 adults, $1.50 children 6–16, does a dynamic job of telling the port's tale with interactive exhibits and costumed interpreters giving demonstrations to background music of sea shanties sung in Québecois French. The roofdeck has a good view of today's working port.

Atop Cap Diamant, the **Citadelle**; *tel: (418) 648-3563*, was the eastern flank of Québec's fortress under the British. Built in 1820, it is the largest group of fortified buildings in North America still occupied by troops, though their tasks are largely ceremonial. Guided tours – on the hour 0900–1800 daily late June–Aug, shorter hours in May and Sept–Oct, $5 – include the **Royal 22nd Regiment Museum**, and, when timing is right, **Changing of the Guard** or **Beating of Retreat**.

For deeper understanding of Québec's original fortifications, visit the **Artillery National Historic Park**, *2 r. d'Auteuil; tel:*

(418) 648-4205, open daily 1000–1700 Mar–Oct, $3. The buildings have been recently restored. Among the chief attractions are a scale model of the fortifications created 1806–08 and the foundry building, where cannon were cast for the British throughout eastern North America.

Near the St-Louis gate is the old powder magazine building, now the visitors' centre for the **Fortifications of Québec National Historic Site**, *100 r. St-Louis; tel: (418) 648-7016*, open daily 1000–1700, $2.75. Guided tours of the ramparts can be arranged here. The **National Battlefields Park Interpretation Centre**, *Musée du Québec, Baillairgé Building, level 1; tel: (418) 648-5641*, open daily 1000–1700, $2 basic admission, extra for multimedia shows and driving tour, explains the **Plains of Abraham**, where the British conquered the French to seize Québec as part of Lower Canada (the 13 Sept 1759 battle lasted only 15 mins and left both British General Wolfe and French General Montcalm mortally wounded). Or simply walk the rolling 250-acre battlefield above the river and read the plaques and statues.

Québec's complex politics is embodied in **Hôtel du Parlement**, *av. Honoré-Mercier and av. Grand-Allée Est; tel: (418) 643-7239*, a 100-metre-square French Renaissance revival structure, housing a British form of government conducted in French. Half-hour free guided tours in French and English depart from Door 3 daily 0900–1630 (late June–Aug), Mon–Fri 0900–1630 (Sept–late June).

Religious History

Religious orders have played central roles in Québec's story, and the Roman Catholic Church still has a looming presence. The richly decorated **Basilique-cathédrale Notre-Dame-de-Québec**, *16 r. Buade; tel: (418) 692-2533* or *(418) 694-0665*, open daily 0730–1630, dates from 1650. The basilica also runs a sound-and-light show ($8)

193

on French missions in North America. Guided tours of the basilica and crypt are given Mon–Sat 0900–1630, Sun 1230–1630 (May–Oct) by the **Corporation of Religious Tourism**; *tel: (418) 694-0665;* the corporation can also arrange tours to other churches, convents and the Québec seminary.

The **Musée des Ursulines**, *12 r. Donnacona; tel: (418) 694-0694,* open Tues–Sat 0930–1200 and 1300–1630, Sun 1230–1700 (closed Dec–Jan), $3, outlines this cloistered teaching order's history in Québec. The adjacent chapel, open Sun 1330–1630, Tues–Fri 1000–1130 and 1330–1630, maintains the interior décor of its 1723 predecessor. It features a great deal of 18th-century art and General Montcalm's crypt.

As you pass churches, peek in if they're open. **Église Notre-Dame-des-Victoires**, *Place Royale,* dating from 1688, has a magnificent high altar sculpted in the form of a castle. The original was virtually destroyed by shellfire in 1759 and has been restored twice. Unless a wedding, funeral or christening is scheduled (and many are), the church is open daily 0900–1630. Guided tours in French and English are given (May–mid Oct) on request.

Art and Culture

The **Musée de la Civilisation**, *85 r. Dalhousie; tel: (418) 643-2158,* open daily 1000–1900 (late June–early Sept), Tues–Sun 1000–1700 (early Sept–late June), $7, Tues free except summer, has permanent exhibits that include the history of Québec and a 250-year-old boat unearthed at the museum site. Clever temporary exhibitions deal with all aspects of modern and pop culture. The outdoor terrace and indoor café are splendid places to rest – as a sign invites: 'All summer long the splendid view and rest area of the museum's terrace offer you a welcome break'.

The 1992 complete overhaul of the **Musée de Québec**, *Parc des Champs-de-Bataille; tel: (418) 643-2150,* open daily 1000–1745, Wed 1000–2145 (June–early Sept); Tues–Sun 1100–1745, Wed 1100–2045 (early Sept–May), $6.50, beautifully merged the original museum building with a 19th-century prison (a youth hostel in the 1970s). Similar imagination informs the exhibitions. Some of Québec's best religious sculpture is here, and some terrific paintings by Canada's leading artists.

OUT OF TOWN

Montmorency Falls is an 83-m natural waterfall (1½ times the height of Niagara Falls but not as dramatic) a few kilometres east of the city. The falls have always been a popular natural wonder – recently developed to create a genuine attraction.

Pick up Autoroute Dufferin just outside the walls of the city in front of *Place Québec,* veering left at the major interchange to Rte 175 (Autoroute Laurentienne). At the cloverleaf interchange, take Rte 138 east about 15 km to Parc de la Chute-Montmorency parking lot. Or take the Number 800 bus, with a change at Terminus Beauport to Rte 50.

Most scenic tours also include the falls. A cable car ($6 round trip) running every few minutes connects the lower falls with the upper cliffs, where the **Manoir Montmorency** stands. Once the home of the Duke of Kent, the restaurant complex is the region's favourite spot for wedding receptions. A narrow footbridge crosses the falls to steps down the cliffs of the eastern side through the mists to the parking area.

Just 1 km back toward Québec City along Rte 138 is the bridge to the **Île d'Orleans**, known for its fruit and vegetable production and handcrafts. Rte 368 circles the perimeter of the island, passing through the six villages separated by large tracts of agricultural land. It makes a pleasant afternoon drive punctuated by stops at roadside farm stands and visits to the 18th-century stone churches in **St-Jean**, **Ste-Famille** and **St-Pierre**.

QUÉBEC CITY TO PORTLAND

The *Rivière Chaudière* connected Québec and New England in the early days of European settlement, and the construction of the Kennebec Rd around 1820 cemented the trade and military route between the regions. This tour follows that historic path over the US border all the way to Portland. Because the route crosses the Appalachian Mountain chain to follow river valleys, portions may be closed during severe winter weather.

Portland is Maine's cultural and financial hub, with fewer than 65,000 inhabitants, but offering the amenities of places thrice its size. The architectural remains of the city's Victorian heyday as a shipping and shipbuilding centre have been salvaged, and a recent influx of young professionals has transformed the once rather dreary downtown and port districts into a lively, engaging city. Portland is central to good beaches and islands and only minutes from Maine's woodlands.

Québec City

73
181
173
Jackman
31
201
The Forks
Carrabasset Valley
23
Kingfield
27
27
16
61
Farmington
27
95
82
295
Portland

195

DIRECT ROUTE: 503 KM / 314 MILES

ROUTE

From Québec City, take Hwy 73 across the Pont (bridge) Pierre-Laporte, continuing 51 km to Scott (exit 131) and Rte 173. Rte 173 continues past **Vallée-Jonction** for 38 km as a secondary road to St-Joseph-de-Beauce, where it continues as improved highway for 63 km to the Canada-US border. The US road is called Rte 201 and continues 18 miles into **Jackman**.

Follow Rte 201 south another 31 miles to **The Forks** (population 30), where the road parallels the Kennebec River. In 34 miles, cross the river to Rte 201A, and in 11 more miles, turn right on Rte 16 west for 16 miles to **Kingfield**. A 23-mile side track on Rte 16 west reaches the ski area of **Carrabasset Valley**. From Kingfield, follow Rte 27 south for 27 miles to **Farmington**, then another 26 miles to Belgrade Lakes. Follow Rte 27 another 16 miles to I-95 South for 36 miles to I-295, then 4 miles to **Portland**.

TOURIST INFORMATION

For general tourist information on the route, contact **Association Touristique Chaudière-Appalaches**, *800 Autoroute Jean-Lesage, St-Nicolas, PQ G7A 1C9; tel: (418) 831-4411.* For the Maine portion, contact the **Maine Publicity Bureau**, *PO Box 2300, Hallowell, ME 04347-2300 USA; tel: (207) 623-0363.*

QUÉBEC TO JACKMAN

The road passes through some of the oldest villages of the Chaudière valley. In Ste-Marie, the family home of the Vachon clan is an interesting interpretive centre for the snack-cake giant Vachon Foods. **Maison J.-A.-Vachon**, *383 r. de la Coopérative, Ste-Marie; tel: (418) 387-4052,* is open 0900–1600 Mon–Fri (Apr–Oct), daily (July–Aug); house tour costs $3.50, house and factory $6.95. Snack cake samples are provided; among the exhibits is the world's largest wedding cake.

The **Vallée-Jonction Railway Interpretation Centre**, *397 r. Rousseau, Vallée-Jonction; tel: (418) 253-6449,* displays photographs and artefacts to conjure up the heyday of railroading here, when the village was the junction of railroads linking Québec City to the Eastern Townships and to New England. Open Tues–Sun 0900–1700 (June–Aug), Sat–Sun (Sept), this museum of the Québec Central Railway charges $3.50.

In the former convent of the Sisters of Charity in St-Joseph, the **Musée Marius-Barbeau**, *139 r. Ste-Christine, St-Joseph; tel: (418) 397-4039,* is the chief history museum of the Chaudière valley, located improbably in a village that has flooded every spring since 1737. The museum is open Mon–Fri 0830–1800 and Sat–Sun 1000–1800 (June–Sept) and Mon–Fri 0830–1600 and Sat–Sun 0830–1600 (Oct–May), $3.75.

JACKMAN

Tourist Information: Jackman Chamber of Commerce, *Main St, PO Box 368, Jackman, ME 04945-0637; tel: (207) 668-4171,* open Wed–Sun 1000–1800 (mid June–early Sept).

Jackman thrives on wilderness camping, hunting and fishing. **Sally Mountain Cabins**, *Box 50, Jackman, ME 04945; tel: (207) 668-5621,* handles everything from lodging to licences; budget.

THE FORKS

This village is the best place to put in a raft or kayak for Class II–III whitewater down a 12-mile gorge on the Kennebec River. The outfitter, **Northern Outdoors**, *Rte 201, P.O. Box 100, The Forks, ME 04985; tel: (800) 765-RAFT,* is located on the spot.

KINGFIELD

The Stanley Museum, *School St; tel: (207) 265-2769,* open Tues–Sun 1300–1600, is filled with memorabilia of the brothers who invented the Stanley Steamer automobile, as well as extraordinary turn-of-the-century photography by their talented sister Chansonetta; US$3. **The Inn on Winter's Hill**, *Winter Hill Rd, RR1, Box 1272, Kingfield, ME 04947; tel: (800) 233-WNTR,* moderate–expensive, has cross-country ski trails and is also the site of **Julia's**; *tel: (207) 265-5426,* for fine dining, moderate–pricey.

SIDE TRACK TO CARRABASSETT VALLEY

Tourist Information: (by mail) **Sugarloaf Area Chamber of Commerce**, *RR#1, Box 2151, Carrabassett Valley, ME 04947.* **Lodging information** (telephone only); *tel: (800) THE-AREA.* **Sugarloaf/USA**; *tel: (207) 235-2100,* is the ski mecca of Maine with 45 miles of trails, which become mountain bike trails during the summer and fall.

FARMINGTON TO PORTLAND

Farmington was a wealthy lumber and farming community and has a legacy of grand old homes. The drive through the summer cabin communities of the Belgrade Lakes is a breather before the interstate highway to Portland.

PORTLAND

Tourist Information: Convention and Visitors Bureau of Greater Portland (CVB), *305 Commercial St, Portland, ME 04101; tel: (207) 772-4994,* is a resource for advance materials.

The **Visitor Information Center of Greater Portland**, at the same address, open Mon–Fri 0800–1700, Sat–Sun and holidays 1000–1500, with extended hours in the summer, tracks availability of rooms of CVB members during high season and provides a telephone for direct contact. The centre also sells inexpensive but excellent architectural walking tour booklets. A smaller centre at the **Portland Jetport** provides the same services during the same hours.

WEATHER

The sea tempers Portland's climate, making for mild winters and cool summer breezes. Temperatures range from daytime summer highs of 60°–85°F to daytime winter highs of 20°–40°F. Winter snowfall in Casco Bay tends to be the heaviest on the New England coast, with storms dumping from 4 inches to 1 ft.

ARRIVING AND DEPARTING

Airport

Portland International Jetport, *tel: (207) 874-8300,* is 10 mins from downtown Portland in South Portland. Taxi to downtown, US$14. METRO bus service to downtown, US$1.25. **Mid-Coast Limo**, *44 Elm St, Camden ME 04843; tel: (207) 236-2424,* provides daily van service between the Portland Jetport bus station and midcoast towns that lie north of the city between Brunswick and Camden.

By Ferry

Prince of Fundy Cruises, *International Marine Terminal, 468 Commercial St, Portland, ME 04101; tel: (207) 775-5616 or (800) 482-0955,* sails daily (early May–late Oct) between Portland and Yarmouth, Nova Scotia (p. 307). The trip takes approximately 11 hours; many travellers spend the time in the on-board casino. Package options include non-stop 23-hour return-trip cruises, or one or two nights in Nova Scotia before return. For fares and sailing times, see p. 308.

By Bus

Vermont Transit Lines, *950 Congress St; tel: (207) 772-6587,* and **Concord Trailways**, *100 Sewall St; tel: (207) 828-1151 or (800) 639-3317,* provide services to Boston, Bangor and a daily round-trip service through the coastal Maine towns. Concord Trailways also connects to Boston. The **Shuttle Bus**, *tel: (207) 282-5408,* provides daily service between Portland and Biddeford/Saco.

GETTING AROUND

City maps and bus routes are available free at the Visitors Information Centre. Most attractions are concentrated in the downtown and Old Port areas, where it's easiest to park at a

197

peripheral lot or garage and navigate on foot. But even some of the in-town attractions are a bit of a hike in the city's hilly terrain, and recent highway construction has effectively separated the waterfront and residential sections of the city, making a private automobile highly desirable for thorough touring.

Public Transport

Greater Portland Transit District (METRO), *114 Valley St; tel: (207) 774-0351,* buses run daily. All METRO lines provide service from Mon–Sat 0600–1800 except some holidays, with some routes running until midnight. Exact change of US$1.25 required; discount passes available. Contrary to the system name, these are *not* trains.

STAYING IN PORTLAND

Accommodation

Hotel chains in Portland include *ES, Hd, HJ, Rm, Su;* South Portland also has *BW, CI, HJ, Ma, Sh. HI* is open summer only.

Portland Regency, *20 Milk St, Portland, ME 04101; tel: (207) 774-4200 or (800) 727-3436,* in an historic armoury building in the centre of the Old Port is posh but not unreasonable; expensive. For a treat, try one of the several grand Bed and Breakfasts in the posh West End: the moderate **Inn on Carleton**, *46 Carleton, Portland, ME 04102; tel: (207) 775-1910,* or the moderate–expensive **Pomegranate Inn**, *49 Neal St, Portland, ME 04102; tel: (207) 772-1006,* or **West End Inn**, *146 Pine St, Portland, ME 04102; tel: (207) 772-1377.*

Other Bed and Breakfasts are scattered throughout the city in gracious older homes; prices decline with distance from the downtown and waterfront. A superb choice is the moderate **Andrews Lodging**, *417 Auburn St (Rte 26), Portland, ME 04103; tel: (207) 797-9167,* with shared cooking and limited laundry facilities.

Nearest campsites for tent, trailer and RV

camping are **Wassamki Springs**, *855 Saco St, Westbrook, ME 04092; tel: (207) 839-4276,* on a private 30-acre lake, open May–mid Oct, and **Bailey's Pine Point**, *Rte 9, Pine Point, W. Scarborough, ME 04074; tel: (207) 883-6043,* with shuttle bus to beaches.

IYHF: *Portland Hall, University of Southern Maine, 645 Congress St, Portland, ME 04101; tel: (207) 874-3281, (207) 731-8096* (off season), open June–Aug. The Portland Summer Hostel offers double rooms with private bath; budget.

Eating and Drinking

With more than 100 restaurants, Portland is neither a capital of haute cuisine nor a wasteland of fast food. Local seafood – especially shellfish – is almost uniformly good if steamed, less dependable if fried. A broad variety of restaurants and cafés cluster in the Old Port, spilling over into downtown. Restaurants with serious culinary aspirations almost always require reservations.

Two spots stand out for romantic, elegant meals. **Back Bay Grill**, *65 Portland St; tel: (207) 772-8833,* specialises in seafood and grilled meats complemented by an extensive wine list. It's smoke-free and expensive.

One good bet for informed, often elegant cooking in the moderate range is **Street & Company**, *33 Wharf St; tel: (207) 775-0887,* which prepares fish in any number of creative, innovative ways and matches the plates with a cosy atmosphere and friendly, helpful service. It's also smoke-free, but it can be a long wait for a table. **Fore Street**, *288 Fore St; tel: (207) 775-2717,* changes its offerings of spit and wood-oven roasted, applewood grilled or braised entrées daily. Be sure to reserve: chef Sam Hayward's straightforward bistro fare has been discovered by the international press and tables are hard to get; expensive. Food in a similar vein without the wait can be found at **Zephyr Grill**, *653 Congress St; tel: (207) 828-4033,* which also features several vegetarian dishes

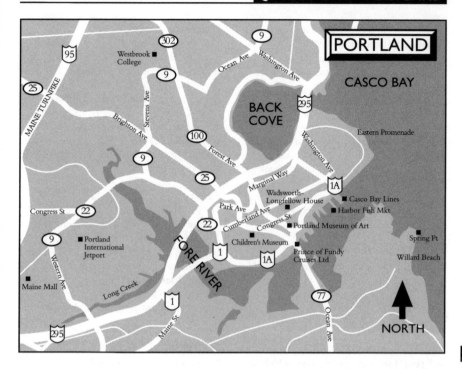

in addition to grilled meats and fish; moderate–expensive. Vegetarians might also check out **The Pepperclub**, *78 Middle St; tel: (207) 772-0521,* budget.

Portland has been a leader in New England in the 'real ale' movement, first with Geary's Pale Ale, then with **Gritty McDuff's**, *396 Fore St; tel: (207) 772-BREW,* which offers budget English pub fare and some good fried fish. It has been so successful that it has spawned a host of similar brewpubs, including **Stone Coast**, *14 York St; tel: (207) 773-2337,* which offers a smoke-free bar downstairs and a cigar-friendly bar upstairs.

Portland *is* Maine, and at mealtime, Maine means fish. On the casual side, **The Village Café**, *112 Newbury St; tel: (207) 772-5320,* consistently wins local polls for best fried clams, while **Gilbert's Chowder House**, *92 Commercial St; tel: (207) 871-5636,* right near the fish docks is a good

choice for chowder and baked fish as well as a broad selection of draft beers and ales. If you have cooking facilities, the city's best fishmonger is **Harbor Fish Market** on Custom House Wharf. (Walk down this street for local colour, whether or not you're buying.) Dining literally on the water makes an institution of **DeMillo's Floating Restaurant**, *25 Long Wharf; tel: (207) 772-2216.*

Old-time New England cooking has its good points, as you might discover over a lunchtime plate of meatloaf and mashed potatoes at the **Miss Portland Diner**, *49 Marginal Way; tel: (207) 773-3246,* open daily for breakfast and lunch and Sat for brunch; budget. This meticulously maintained Worcester Diner from 1949 made a cameo appearance in the Mel Gibson film, *Man Without a Face.* **Katahdin**, *106 High St; tel: (207) 774-1740,* brings New England cooking to the brink of the 21st century in a funky, eclectic décor that attracts Portland's upmarket Bohemians as well as many of its 'foodies'; moderate. You can't go wrong with the roasted pork with pineapple conserves or the pan-fried oysters.

Fresh Market Pasta, *43 Exchange St/60 Market St; tel: (207) 773-7156,* has the best deal on a meal to eat in or take away; budget. To assemble your own gourmet picnic (perhaps to eat on the overlooks at Eastern or Western Promenade), head to the back of **The Whip and Spoon**, *161 Commercial St; tel: (207) 774-6262.* This cooking utensil and appliance store stocks excellent wine, cheese and caviar for take-away.

ENTERTAINMENT

Pick up a copy of the free *Casco Bay Weekly* or *Go,* a Thur supplement to the *Portland Press Herald,* for complete listings of stage, concerts, clubs, galleries, dance, film, performing arts, comedy, etc.

The hippest night spots in town are alleged to be **Gritty McDuff's**, *396 Fore St,* and **Java Joe's**, *29 Exchange St,* which has live music and poetry in addition to various caffeinated beverages. The **Portland Performing Arts Center**, *25A Forest Ave; tel: (207) 774-0465,* hosts performances by the **Portland Stage Company**, the largest professional theatre company in northern New England, and other performing groups. The **Portland Symphony Orchestra**, *30 Myrtle St; tel: (207) 773-8191,* performs classical, pop and chamber concerts in the City Hall Auditorium.

From late June–early Aug, the city sponsors free outdoor band concerts on Tues evenings at **Deering Oaks Park** – a beautifully landscaped park (bounded by *Forest, Park* and *Brighton aves)* with duck pond and playgrounds. The city also sponsors free folk concerts Wed evenings at Western Promenade. **Nickelodeon** cinema complex, *Temple and Middle Sts; tel: (207) 772-9751,* shows current films on six screens at half of standard ticket prices.

Spectator Sports

The **Portland Sea Dogs**, a minor-league baseball affiliate of the Florida Marlins, play at 6000-seat **Hadlock Stadium**, *271 Park Ave; tel: (207) 874-9300,* from early Apr–early Sept. The **Portland Pirates**, *One Civic Center Sq., tel: (207) 828-4665,* a minor-league hockey team affiliated with the Washington Capitals, play early Oct–early Apr at the **Cumberland County Civic Center** on *Spring St.*

Events

For ten days spread across the middle weekends of March, Portland goes nautical with **Aucocisco**, a festival that celebrates Casco Bay with events emphasising local history, environmental concerns, arts and food. The **Maine Boatbuilders Show**, on the second weekend, attracts so many people that lodging can be almost as tight as during the summer high season.

SHOPPING

Most of the best shops, galleries and boutiques are found in the Old Port area bounded by *Commercial, Franklin, Congress* and *Union Sts.* **Emerson Booksellers**, *420 Fore St; tel: (207) 874-2665,* is notable for antique prints, especially marine charts. Portland's best known product today is the Shaker-influenced furniture designed and made by **Thomas Moser Cabinetmaker**, whose elegant showroom can be visited at *415 Cumberland Ave; tel: (207) 774-3791.*

Maine's famous outdoors gear retailer, **L.L. Bean**, operates a factory store at *542 Congress St; tel: (207) 865-4761.* The original store, open around the clock, lies 20 miles north in Freeport.

Portland is rich in fine crafts. Two superb galleries with all media are **Nancy Margolis Gallery**, *367 Fore St; tel: (207) 775-3822,* and **Abacus**, *44 Exchange St; tel: (207) 772-4880.* **Stein Gallery**, *20 Milk St; tel: (207) 772-9072,* represents 65 of the best US glass artists. **Maine Potters Market**, *376 Fore St;*

200

tel: (207) 774-1633, is a cooperative gallery of the state's ceramic artists.

A 3.5-million karat find of the pink and green semi-precious stone, tourmaline, in 1972, has made it the gem of choice for Maine jewellers. An especially good selection is available weekdays only at **Cross Jewelers**, *570 Congress St; tel: (207) 773-3107.* Less precious but still very local are the Maine-only products at **Just Me.**, *510 Congress St; (207) 775-4860,* including canned chowders and bisques, clam spread, crab dip and almost anything that can be made from blueberries. In South Portland, **The Maine Mall** (exit 7 off Maine Turnpike or exits 2 and 3 off I-295) has about the same number of shops in one place as all of Portland.

SIGHTSEEING

Inexpensive brochures of self-guided architectural tours of four Portland neighbourhoods are available from the Visitor Information Center. The **Western Promenade** highlights the architecture of one of America's best-preserved Victorian residential neighbourhoods. The Promenade itself, a public walk 175 ft above sea level, offers views to the White Mountains and beyond. The **State Street** tour emphasises architecture of the Federal period and Greek revival mansions, including the grandest dame of all, Victoria Mansion.

Congress St is the commercial and transportation spine of the Portland peninsula, and this tour continues from the shops and civic buildings eastward to the Portland Observatory lookout and the city's oldest graveyard. The **Old Port Exchange** brochure is especially worth picking up, since you'll probably shop and dine in the district. The tour highlights architecture and history in this neighbourhood; Old Port is the oldest part of the city, but was largely destroyed by British bombardment during the American Revolution and again by the Great Fire of 1866. Although it was immediately

rebuilt, the district had declined by the 1960s but was redeveloped in the 1970s.

Although there's no brochure, the **waterfront** holds equal interest if less distinguished architecture. Be sure to walk Custom House Wharf (directly across from the Portland Regency Hotel) to see a working fishing port in action. There's also a public fish auction Mon–Thur at 1300 on Portland Fish Pier.

Casco Bay Lines ferries depart from Casco Bay Ferry Terminal, *Commercial and Franklin Sts; tel: (207) 774-7871,* with many scenic rides at various times. Two scenic routes are offered in all seasons: the Mail Boat Run (the longest operating service of its kind in the USA) stops at the islands of Cliff, Chebeague, Long, and Little and Great Diamond. Ferries depart 1000 and 1400 (mid June–Labour Day), 1000 and 1445 the rest of the year; adult fare is US$10. The Sunset Run follows the same route, departing daily all year at 1745; adult fare is US$10.

There is also a regular round-trip ferry service to Peaks Island (US$3), a Portland bedroom island community with a good beach.

The 58-ft sailing yacht *Palawan, tel: (207) 773-2163,* sails from Old Port for morning, afternoon or day-long sails; from US$20; minimum number required. **Eagle Tours**, *tel: (207) 774-6498,* does harbour sightseeing and seal-watching cruises from Long Wharf; US$5–15. **Olde Port Mariner Fleet**, *tel: (207) 775-0727* or *(800) 437-3270,* offers fishing, whale-watching, harbour cruises and lobster trap hauls, also from Long Wharf.

Most museums in Portland charge US$5 admission. The **Portland Museum of Art**, *7 Congress Sq.; tel: (207) 775-6148,* open Tues–Sat 1000–1700, Thur 1000–2100, Sun 1200–1700, closed Mon, occupies an award-winning building erected in 1983. The American galleries have works by Winslow Homer, Andrew and N.C. Wyeth, Edward Hopper, Rockwell Kent and other American notables, as well as an excellent

201

collection of 19th-century American commercial glass. The prize collection of Homer watercolours tend only to be on view in the summer.

Next door, **The Children's Museum**, *142 Free St; tel: (207) 828-1234,* is open Mon, Wed, Thur and Sat 1000–1700, Tues and Sun 1200–1700, Fri 1000–2000, with extended summer hours. It's a must-see if you have small children in town and the weather's too damp for the beach. Most amazing exhibit? The camera obscura offers a panoramic view of Portland rooftops.

The **Wadsworth–Longfellow House**, *485–489 Congress St; tel: (207) 879-0427,* was the childhood home of poet, scholar and translator Henry Wadsworth Longfellow, open Tues–Sun 1000–1600 (June–Oct), limited Sat hours (Jan–May). Built in 1786 of brick, it represented the outskirts of town. Volunteer guides vary in their ability to interpret the site.

The most visited house in Maine is **Victoria Mansion**, *109 Danforth St; tel: (207) 772-4841.* Built 1858–62 by one of the first Mainers to go out into the wide world and make a fortune, this Italianate villa has its original over-the-top interiors and ornate furnishings created by an operatic set designer, open Tues–Sat 1000–1600, Sun 1300–1700 (late May–early Sept), Sat 1000–1600 and Sun 1300–1700 (early Sept–mid Oct).

The **Maine Narrow Gauge Railroad Company and Museum**, *58 Fore St; tel: (207) 828-0814,* open daily 1000–1600, tells the story of Maine's five lines of 2-ft railroads that operated 1870s–1940s. The narrow gauge allowed the lines to penetrate countryside inaccessible for standard-gauge railroads. Engines and many of the cars were built in the museum building. Admission is free, but a half-mile ride along the waterfront costs US$5.

202

OUT OF TOWN

Portland's lighthouses and beaches are actually not in Portland at all, but in the communities of Cape Elizabeth and Scarborough south of the city.

Some maps give directions that only locals can follow. Instead, take Rte 77 south from the waterfront. After crossing the bridge to South Portland, follow the left arrow toward Cape Elizabeth. Turn right at the first traffic light onto *Ocean Rd,* which is also Rte 77. In about three miles, turn left onto *Shore Rd,* following the signs to **Portland Head Light**. One of the most photographed lighthouses in the world, Portland Head has a lighthouse and historical museum (US$2); open Sat–Sun 1000–1600 (Apr–May), daily 1000–1600 (June–Oct). The park – the Revolutionary War **Fort Williams** – has grand views out to sea and is perfect for flying kites.

Retrace *Shore Rd* back to Rte 77, turn left, and continue 1.6 miles to left turn to **Two Lights State Park**. The park is a knobby lookout, but the lighthouses of its name are a mile further down the road, with the **Lobster Shack Restaurant** between them on the dunes.

Another mile south on Rte 77 is **Crescent State Beach**, considered Portland's finest, but often very crowded. Another 3 miles brings you to the less-cramped **Higgins Beach**, a rocky shore with a sandy beach and only limited parking.

For a final view of more cragged glory, continue south on Rte 77 to the junction of Rtes 207, 1 and 9. Turn left onto Rte 207 south, also known as *Black Point Rd.* This route passes **Scarborough Beach**, most favoured sun spot for the young and hip, en route to Prout's Neck. The view is breathtaking, but private property laws have made it virtually impossible to park to enjoy them unless you're pretending to buy real estate.

QUÉBEC CITY–
SAGUENAY RIVER LOOP

This drive leaves Québec City for the wilderness parklands of the Rivière Jacques-Cartier due north of the city en route to the northern communities along the dramatic fjord of the Saguenay River. It returns to Québec through the picturesque fishing villages of the tidal section of the *Fleuve St-Laurent* (St Lawrence River) in the district of Charlevoix before reaching the Côte-de-Beaupré just east of the city.

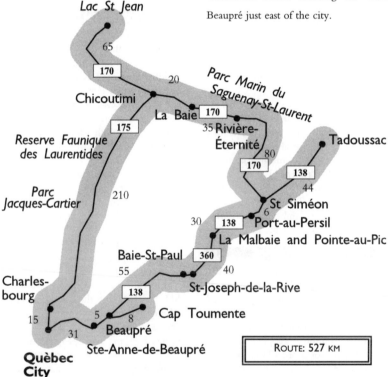

Lac St Jean
65
170
20
Parc Marin du Saguenay-St-Laurent
Chicoutimi
La Baie **170**
175
35 Rivière-Éternité
Reserve Faunique des Laurentides
Tadoussac
80
170
138
44
Parc Jacques-Cartier
210
St Siméon
6
30
138 Port-au-Persil
La Malbaie and Pointe-au-Pic
Baie-St-Paul **360**
55
40
Charles-bourg
138 St-Joseph-de-la-Rive
15
5
8 Cap Toumente
31
Beaupré
Ste-Anne-de-Beaupré
Quèbec City

203

ROUTE: 527 KM

ROUTE

From downtown Québec, take Hwy 73 north to **Charlesbourg** and the **Parc Jacques-Cartier**. Stay on the road as it turns into Rte 175 and cuts through the **Réserve Faunique des Laurentides**, following it all the way into **Chicoutimi**, about 225 km, a 3-hr drive without stopping.

From Chicoutimi, choose Rte 170 Ouest for a side track to Lac St-Jean or take Rte 170 Est along the south shore of the

Saguenay fjord to **La Baie**, **St-Félix-d'Otis**, **Rivière-Éternité** and **Petit-Saguenay**, then inland to **St-Siméon**. From there, an optional side track leads up Rte 138 Nord (a left turn) to the astonishing landscape of **Parc Marin du Saguenay–St-Laurent** accessed from **Tadoussac**, and on to the rugged and sparsely populated Côte-Nord.

The main route continues south on Rte 138 (with a turnout for **Port-au-Persil**) about 36 km as far as **La Malbaie** and **Pointe-au-Pic**, where it turns left onto Rte 360 after crossing the bridge (follow signs toward Charlevoix Casino). In about 40 km, Rte 360 rejoins Rte 138 at **Baie-St-Paul** for the 91-km drive to Québec City. When approaching the city, follow signs for Centre-Ville (Autoroute Dufferin).

BUSES

Intercar run four bus trips a day from Québec to Chicoutimi, taking 3 hrs. See OTT table 222. There is also a service from Chicoutimi to Tadoussac, running up to the north end of the St Lawrence River. Journey time: 1 hr 40 mins. OTT table 226. Two daily bus services run along the St Lawrence to St Simeon (2½ hrs) and on to Tadoussac (another hour). See OTT table 228.

CHARLESBOURG

About 15 km north of Québec take exit 154, turning right to visit **Jardin Zoologique du Québec**, *9300 av. du zoo; tel: 622-0312*, open daily 0900–1700, adults $8 (Metrobus 801 from downtown Québec City also goes to the zoo). The Jardin Zoologique has more than 600 creatures of about 125 species from around the world. An internal river separated into basins by waterfalls segregates predators from prey in natural exhibits.

Some 6 km in the other direction from the exit is the **Wendake Amerindian Reserve**. In the heart of the village, the **Maison Aroüanne**, *10 r. Chef-Alexandre-Duchesneau; tel: (418) 845-1241* (July–Aug)

or *(418) 843-3767* (Sept–June); open daily 1000–1800 (July–Aug), Mon–Fri 0800–1600 (Sept–June), free, relates the history of the Huron tribe, which was forced off its land by the Iroquois and re-settled in 1700 in a place the French called *Jeune-Lorette,* later granted as a reserve.

Nearby is the recreation of a traditional village, **Onhoüa Chetek8e** (pronounced *On-HOO-ah she-TEK-wheet-ay), 575 r. Stanslas-Koska; tel: (418) 842-4308,* open daily 0900–1800 (May–Oct), 0900–1700 (Nov–Apr), adults $5.

PARC JACQUES-CARTIER

One of Québec City's favourite outdoor playgrounds, this park 40 km north of downtown, occupies a corner of the Laurentian Wildlife Preserve (see p. 162). Admission is free, but certain activities require a fee; open late May–mid Oct. **Camping** is available, both as primitive (outhouse) for $17.50 per tent pitch, or with water, shower and flush toilet for $19.95. During July–Aug, reserve in advance; *tel: (418) 848-7272.*

Canoes, kayaks and small rafts are available at rates beginning at $12 per hr to $36 per day. During the early summer, wet suits may be rented for $14 to avoid hypothermia if you go overboard. (The water can be 1°–2°C well into June.) Transport to other parts of the park (so you can paddle back to your car) can be arranged.

Bicycles and helmets are available from $11–30. Although the fishing is better elsewhere, it is possible to purchase either a 3-day ($22.35) or all-year ($51.50) provincial license here and pay a $13 daily access fee to angle for trout. The interpretive centre at **Secteur la Vallée** (the first entrance) sells detailed park maps ($2) that show elevation changes and the 100-km trail network.

RÉSERVE FAUNIQUE DES LAURENTIDES

This reserve of 8000 square km offers access to a vast network of wilderness trails, rivers and streams and several large lakes through eight points of entry. Activities require registration at **accueil Mercier**, *Rte 175; tel: (418) 686-1717* or *(800) 848-2422* (toll-free). Canoe-camping and fishing dominate in the summer (although some hunting for black bear is permitted), and cross-country skiing in the winter. Simple access for hiking is $11.41 per person. Day fishing costs $29.18 for one, $40.59 for two and $52 for three people. Each canoe or boat is charged $17.77. Fishing season extends from late May into Oct, depending on species, although most people fish for rainbow trout, for which the season ends 1 Sept. Access is limited, so reserve at least two days in advance with a credit card by calling; *tel: (418) 890-6527* or *(800) 665-6527* between 1800–2030, Eastern time.

Cabin accommodation with kitchen and full plumbing ($17–40 per person per day) can be reserved at the same number. Reservations not required for camping. Fees range from $12.29–20.18 per pitch per day.

CHICOUTIMI

Tourist Information: Association Touristique du Saguenay–Lac-St-Jean, *198 r. Racine Est, Bureau 210, Chicoutimi, PQ G7H 1R9; tel: (418) 543-9778* or *(800) 463-9651*, open Mon–Fri 0830–1200 and 1330–1630. Also in person or by phone: **Office du Tourisme et des Congrès de Chicoutimi**, *2525 blvd Talbot, C.P. 1023, Chicoutimi, PQ G7H 5G4; tel: (418) 698-3167*, open Mon–Fri 0830–1200 and 1330–1630.

At the head of the Saguenay fjord, Chicoutimi is the furthest inland navigable port of the region. Nomadic Amerindian peoples used the spot for meetings and trading more than 1000 years before the French established a fur-trading post in 1676, which remained active into the mid 19th century, when industrialisation brought a sudden influx of population. Many French-speaking people with English surnames live in this district – a situation unique to the northern frontier country of Québec.

ACCOMMODATION

All lodging falls within the moderate range, with small *gîtes* at the low end, a few motels in the middle and large hotels outside of town running somewhat higher (few exceed $100). Chicoutimi has both *DI* and *HG*.

Among the nicer hotels is the 117-room **La Nouvel Hôtel La Saguenéenne**; *250 r. des Saguenéens, Chicoutimi, PQ G7H 3A4; tel: (418) 545-8326* or *(800) 461-8390*, which has a central glassed-in pool and a Parisian Folies-style show in the summer.

Other choices include the 307-room **Le Montagnais**, *1080 blvd Talbot, Chicoutimi, PQ G7H 5B6; tel: (418) 543-1521* or *(800) 463-9160*, which has a nightly musical spectacle (mid June–Aug); the downtown **Hotel Chicoutimi**, *460 r. Racine Est, Chicoutimi, PQ G7H 1T7; tel: (418) 549-7111* or *(800) 463-7930*, with excellent views of the Saguenay River; and a modest, three-level motel on the shore of the Saguenay fjord, **Motel Panoramique**, *1303 blvd Saguenay Ouest, Chicoutimi, PQ G7J 1A1; tel: (418) 549-7102* or *(800) 463-9164*.

Bed and Breakfast operations include **Gîte de Beauvoir**, *149 r. Beauvoir, Chicoutimi, PQ G7G 2M2; tel: (418) 549-9165*; and **Gîte de la Promenade**, *782 blvd Saguenay Est, Chicoutimi, PQ G7H 1L3; tel: (418) 543-9997*. Each has three non-smoking rooms, with three bathrooms outside the guest rooms. Neither accepts credit cards.

EATING AND DRINKING

Like many restaurants in the far north, those in Chicoutimi emphasise quantity over culinary finesse. Most visitors settle for a fast-food chain (all here, including Québec's own Rôtisserie St-Hubert), hotel restaurants or pubs with the usual grilled meats and pastas. For a good French meal featuring regional seafood, book a table at **La Bourgresse**, *260 Riverin; tel: (418) 543-3178; moderate.*

205

ENTERTAINMENT

Massive spectacles are favoured in Chicoutimi and the surrounding region. **Paris Folies à Chicoutimi** is a song and dance (especially dance, with 35 showgirls in lots of feathers and a little fabric) production that plays mid June–Aug in the **Caberet du Complex La Saguenéenne**, *250 r. des Saguenéens; tel: (800) 461-8390*, $22–35.

Summer Sports

Chicoutimi has 5 km of **mountain bike trails**; *tel: (418) 698-3167*. Bicycles for road touring may be rented through the **Office du tourisme**, *2525 blvd Talbot; tel: (418) 698-3167*.

Guide Aventure, *1069 r. Nil-Tremblay; tel: (418) 545-2268*, offers guided sea kayak expeditions of 5–7 days. **Parcours Aventures**, *1668 Rang St-Joseph; tel: (418) 698-6673*, rents sea kayaks and river canoes by the day or week and provides shuttle service. **Passion Québec**, *2071 Place Belvédere; tel: (418) 690-0066*, organises outdoor excursions for small groups, with travel by canoe, kayak and off-road vehicles.

Winter Sports

The Saguenay–Lac-St-Jean region has more than 3000 km of snowmobile *(motoneige)* trails and the **Association Touristique du Saguenay–Lac-St-Jean** provides a snowmobile trail map as well as information on lodging–dining–snowmobiling packages; *tel: (418) 543-9778* or *(800) 463-9651*. Three companies in Chicoutimi offer snowmobile rentals: **Passion Québec**, *2071 Place Belvédere; tel: (418) 690-0066;* **Location Centre Nautique St-Martin**, *2781 Rang St-Martin; tel: (418) 549-8206*, and **Loisir Techno Sport**, *1539 blvd Tadoussac; tel: (418) 690-3313*.

Events

During the second week of Feb, townspeople turn the clock back to the 1890s to celebrate **Carnaval-Souvenir**; *tel: (418)*

543-4438, with traditional meals, *bals*, operettas and dramas.

SIGHTSEEING

The **Office du Tourisme**, *2525 blvd Talbot; tel: (418) 698-3167*, arranges guided walking tours of Chicoutimi on request. The **Old Port** area, rehabilitated in 1992, has a promenade by the Fleuve Saguenay and boutique shopping in the old train station and old public market. Calèches (horse-drawn carriages) are out in force July–Aug ($30–50) and painters set up their easels all along the river.

From late June–Aug, cruises of the fjord are available from **Croisières La Marjolaine** and its subsidiary, **Croisières de la Baie**; *tel: (418) 543-7630* or *(800) 363-7248*. This activity is particularly popular for families with young children because it is a relatively simple way to see dramatic landscape. The 400-passenger *La Marjolaine* cruises with narration for 4½ hrs to Ste-Rose-du-Nord, returning by bus after a 2-hr stopover. Departures are daily at 0830; adults $30, under 14 $15.

The 152-passenger *Le Bagotville II* makes three 2-hr trips a day between Chicoutimi and La Baie and around the upper reaches of the fjord, departing at 0930, 1330 and 1600; adults $20, under 14 $10. **Croisières sur la Gaïa**; *tel: (418) 696-1248* or *(800) 267-9265*, collects natural specimens aboard a robust open–ocean ship that can carry 60 passengers. Departures for the 3-hr trip are at 1300 from Chicoutimi Yacht Club; adults $20, under 14 $10.

Chicoutimi initially flourished as a paper-making town, and **La Pulperie** (the Old Papermill) represents the first French-Canadian industrial complex. The five remaining buildings at *300 r. Dubuc; tel: (418) 698-3100*, now house a permanent exhibition on the Chicoutimi Pulp Mill Company and a local history museum, **Le Musée du Saguenay–Lac-St-Jean**. In 1994, **La Maison-Musée du Peintre Arthur-Villeneuve** was also moved to the site. This self-taught primitive artist frescoed the walls of his house in 1957–58 and went on to produce more than 4000 paintings with a certain naive charm before his death in 1990. The site is open daily 0900–1800 (mid May–mid Oct), until 2000 in July and 1200–1600 (mid Oct–Nov). Admission is $8.50.

⇄ SIDE TRACK TO LAC ST JEAN

At Chicoutimi, turn west on Rte 170 toward Hébertville to pick up Rte 169, which follows the shores of **Lac St-Jean** in a mostly paved 250-km loop through tiny villages and rugged back country.

The district was heavily damaged in the 1996 floods, but its appeal as wilderness persists. Among the attractions are the granite cave, **Trou de la Fée**, *ch. du Trou de la Fée, Desbiens; tel: (418) 346-5632*, open daily variable hours mid June–Aug, entry fee $6.50. Also, an excellent history museum covers early contact between European and Amerindian peoples: **Centre d'Histoire et d'Archéologie de la Métabetchousane**, *243 r. Hébert; tel: (418) 346-5341*, open daily 0900–1700 (late June–Aug), Mon–Fri 0900–1700 (Sept–late June), $3.50.

Mashteuiatsh, the only Amerindian reservation in the region, has a newly renovated **Musée Amérindien**, *1787 r. Amisk; tel: (418) 275-4842*, open variable hours (mid May–Aug), $3.50. The reserve also offers one of the finest unobstructed views of Lac St-Jean.

One other excellent lake access is at **Parc de la Pointe-Taillon**, *825 3e Rang, St-Henri-de-Taillon*, open daily (late June–mid Sept), basic admission free. Rentals available for canoes, kayaks and bicycles to explore the lake or 32 km of trails. Wilderness camping may also be available, pending trail repairs. ▧

LA BAIE

The town's name refers to the **Baie des Ha! Ha!**, locally called 'the sea'. In addition to outdoor sports, La Baie is a major port for the paper and aluminum industries. (With both a plentiful supply of bauxite ore and the electricity to smelt it, La Baie was a natural for aluminum.) In winter, the bay freezes over and a community of more than 800 ice-fishing cabins springs up.

Mountains rise abruptly just south of the fjord at La Baie. The **Centre Plein Air Bec-Scie**, *7400 ch. des Chutes; tel: (418) 697-5132*, open daily 0900–1700, provides an impressive view of the **Rivière-à-Mars**, a 20-m waterfall that crashes down in a 1-km-deep canyon. 'La Deluge' of 1996 struck the region as a flood of biblical proportion, tumbling house-sized boulders along the path of the rushing water, destroying roads and rerouting rivers. A small interpretive display at the centre (which was hit hard) explains the damage in geological and meteorological terms. The centre also rents bicycles ($5–30) to explore 90 km of mountain bike paths and provides shuttle service to the canyon walls.

Musée du Fjord, *3356 blvd de la Grande-Baie Sud; (418) 697-5077*, open Mon–Fri 0900–1800 and Sat–Sun 1000–1800 (late June–early Sept), Mon–Fri 0830–1200, 1330–1700 and Sat–Sun 1300–1700 (early Sept–late June), adults $3.50, is dedicated to the natural history of the Saguenay fjord and relates the tale of the local populace – including the socioeconomic side of 'La Deluge'.

Besides its natural attractions, La Baie is known for its summer pageants, *'Les Grands Spectacles'*. From late June–early Aug, **La Fabuleuse Histoire d'un Royaume** (200 performers and 1500 costumes) illustrates local history, complete with an assortment of animals and vehicles. **Le Tour du Monde de Jos Maquillon** rolls out large-scale choreography, a veritable cavalry of horses, a 60-ft rotating stage and fireworks through the remainder of Aug. **Les Spectacles** take

207

place Wed–Sat at the **Théâtre du Palais Municipal**, *591 r. 5e; tel: (418) 697-5151 or (800) 667-4582*, adults $27.

LA BAIE TO RIVIÈRE-ÉTERNITÉ

Fiction brings fact alive (or history, at least) at the **Site de Tournage 'Robe-Noire'**, *Du Vieux Chemin, St-Félix-d'Otis; tel: (418) 544-8027*. The sets left behind from filming *The Robe*, a movie about a missionary in the Québec wilderness, actually make Samuel de Champlain's Québec of 1634 seem tangible through rustic dwellings, an Iroquois village and trading camps. The site is 8 km off the main route and is open daily 0900–1700 (late June–Aug). The 1¼-hr guided tour costs $7.

RIVIÈRE-ÉTERNITÉ

The town with the poetic name ('River of Eternity') has one of the key access points to the **Parc du Saguenay**; *tel: (418) 272-3008*, reached by a well-marked turn-off a few kilometres before the village. Drive 7 km down to the **Centre d'Interprétation du Fjord du Saguenay**, open mid May–mid Oct, for permits, maps and an explanation of how the fjord was formed by a crack in the earth's crust further gouged by glaciers.

Hiking trails are free, as is parking except late June–Aug, when a fee of $7.75 is charged. Rustic tent camping costs $14 for two people, except on Les Caps trail, where it costs $16 per person to camp in this environmentally sensitive area. Fishing access (mostly salmon) is available for $13 per day or $70 for a week. Hiking maps cost $2 each (the park is so big that there are two).

One of the most popular hikes is a 3.5-km trek to the statue of **Notre-Dame-de-Saguenay** atop a 180-m bluff overlooking the fjord (about 3-hr return trip). Hour-long interpretive cruises of the fjord are offered here ($15.50) leaving at 1100 and 1430 (late May–June and Sept), with a 1300 departure added July–Aug.

RIVIÈRE-ÉTERNITÉ TO ST-SIMÉON

The village of **L'Anse-St-Jean** became an official municipal monarchy in 1997 with the installation of His Majesty King Denys the First of the Cove – consider this free-wheeling recreational village a sort of Margaritaville of the Far North. Hiking and bridle trails cross it, but the most telling attraction is the microbrewery **Les Brasseurs de L'Anse**; *tel: (418) 272-3234*. Within the municipality of Petit-Saguenay is **La Réserve Faunique de la Rivière Petit-Saguenay**, which offers salmon fishing, cottage rentals and canoe expeditions. See Réserve Faunique des Laurentides, p. 162, for reservation information.

ST-SIMÉON

Roads from the Saguenay district, the Côte-Nord and Québec City all meet here, where travellers can cross to the south shore of the St-Laurent by ferry to Rivière-du-Loup (see p.214). Frequent daily sailings (late Mar–early Dec) can carry 100 vehicles and 446 passengers. Fare per person is $9.80, per car or van $24.85, per bicycle $3.50.

If you're driving on but need a break, stop at **La Domaine Récréo-Touristique Les Pallisades**; *tel: (418) 638-2442*, for a picnic or hike on short forested trails, open mid May–early Oct, admission by donation.

 **SIDE TRACK TO PARC MARIN DU SAGUENAY–ST-LAURENT**

At St-Siméon, turn left on Rte 138 Est to drive 32 km to **Baie-Ste-Catherine**, a village at the mouth of Saguenay River with sandy beaches and many artists and studio craftsmen. This is the gateway to **Parc Marin du Saguenay–St-Laurent**, created to protect the marine ecosystem at the confluence of the Saguenay River and the St-Laurent estuary.

Comparatively warm river water overlays brutally cold ocean water, creating a rich bloom of life that attracts immense blue whales and white beluga whales rarely seen outside the Arctic. Many boats offer **whale-watching cruises** from Baie-Ste-Catherine, Grands-Bergeronnes and Tadoussac at rates from $24–36. Some operators use small inflatable boats to get closer to the whales – a practice of dubious environmental sensitivity.

The **Pointe-Noire Interpretation and Observation Centre**, *Rte 138, 1.6 km south of Tadoussac ferry terminal, Baie-Ste-Catherine; tel: (418) 237-4383,* offers striking views of the mouth of the fjord, often with whales in the distance. The centre is open at no charge daily 0900–1800 (mid June–early Sept), Fri–Sun 0900–1700 (early Sept–mid Oct) – the season when the whales are visiting.

To cross the fjord, take the 10-min free ferry ride; *tel: (418) 235-4395,* to **Tadoussac**. Continue 18 km to the **Cap-de-Bon-Désir Interpretation and Observation Centre**; *tel: (418) 232-6751.* Rte 138 continues another 640 km along a rugged coast with its own quieter attractions to Havre St-Pierre. For more information, request the **Côte-Nord Tourist Guide** from Tourisme Québec (see Travel Essentials, p. 36).

PORT-AU-PERSIL

This picturesque artists' village, reached by a turnout that reconnects to Rte 138, clings to its harbour. The **Port-au-Persil Pottery**, *Rte 138; tel: (418) 638-2349,* is famous for its glazes made from local materials, including ash from algae and hay, and stone and sand from the harbour. Workshops are offered (late June–mid Aug), and a gallery sells the work of many Québec master potters. The gallery/boutique is open daily 0900–1800 (late May–Sept).

Galerie d'Art Nicole Deschênes, *30 Port-au-Persil; tel: (418) 638-5315,* shows the work of about 40 painters as well as Charlevoix studio craft artists, open Sat–Sun

1000–1800 (May–June and early–mid Oct) and daily 0900–1800 (July–Sept).

LA MALBAIE AND POINTE-AU-PIC

Tourist Information: Association Touristique Régionale de Charlevoix, *630 blvd de Comporté, C.P. 275, La Malbaie, PQ G5A 1T8; tel: (418) 665-4454 or (800) 667-2276,* open daily 0900–2100 (mid June–early Sept), daily 0900–1630 (early Sept–mid June).

Pointe-au-Pic was the birthplace of Québec tourism as a stopover for the ocean liners and private yachts that sailed the St-Laurent from the 19th century until the Depression. The cream of society stayed at **Manoir Richelieu**, now gorgeously restored, at *181 av. Richelieu, Pointe-au-Pic, PQ G0T 1M0; tel: (418) 665-3703 or (888) 270-0111* (toll-free). Rooms range from moderate–pricey, depending on season.

Behind the Richelieu is the small, rather elegant **Casino de Charlevoix**; *tel: (418) 665-5300 or (800) 665-2274,* where well-dressed patrons can play at 15 gaming tables or feed coins into about 300 slot machines. Admission, parking and coat check are free; patrons must be 18 years or older.

POINTE-AU-PIC TO ST-JOSEPH-DE-LA-RIVE

The drive down into **Ste-Irénée** provides dazzling views of a village set into a hillside. **Le Domaine Forget**, *388 ch. des Bains; tel: (418) 452-8111,* runs a famous international classical music festival on Sat and Sun evenings (July–Aug). Admissions vary. The village of **Les Éboulements** was named for the huge landslide here after the earthquake of 1663, the strongest ever recorded in eastern North America.

ST-JOSEPH-DE-LA-RIVE

A secondary road spirals down a hillside into this one-time shipbuilding community turned vacation escape. A small museum next to three beached schooners, **Exposition Maritime**, *305 place d'Église; tel: (418) 635-1131*, recounts the history of the St-Joseph *goelettes* (schooners), $2. A free ferry departs here to **Île aux Coudres**, a historic island with an excellent local and natural history museum, **Musée de l'Isle-aux-Coudres**, *231 ch. des Coudriers; tel: (418) 438-2753*, open daily 0800–1900 (July–Aug), 0830–1830 (May–June, Sept–Oct), $3.50.

BAIE-ST-PAUL

Tourist Information: Belvédere Baie-St-Paul, *444 blvd Msgr-De Laval (Rte 138); tel: (418) 435-4160*, open daily 0900–2100 (mid June–early Sept), daily 0900–1630 (early Sept–mid June). Also mid June–early Sept: **Centre d'Art**, *4 r. Fafard, Baie-St-Paul, PQ G0A 1B0; tel: (418) 435-5795*.

The narrow river valley opening on the St-Laurent at Baie-St-Paul has inspired generations of Canadian painters, and the town is laced with art galleries and boutiques.

In addition to the many galleries, two art centres in the same complex are worth visiting: **Centre d'Art de Baie-St-Paul**, *4 r. Ambroise-Fafard; tel: (418) 435-3681*, open 0900–1900 (late June–early Sept), 0900–1700 (early Sept–late June), free; and **Centre d'Exposition de Baie-St-Paul**, *23 r. Ambroise-Fafard*, same phone number and hours, $3. A few kilometres outside town, **Domaine Charlevoix**, *Rte 362; tel: (418) 435-2626*, is a family recreation centre with extraordinary scenic overlooks and a hiking trail suitable for all ages that passes five waterfalls. It is open 0930–2300 (mid June–early Oct), adults $8, children 8–12 $4.

BEAUPRÉ

Station Mont-Ste-Anne; *tel: (418) 827-4561* for snow conditions (in French); or *(418) 827-4579*, has alpine skiing with 51 slopes and a vertical drop of 625 m, one of the steepest in Québec. Lift ticket costs $45, in part because this is the best skiing close to Québec city.

In the summer, gondolas give access to mountain hiking trails ($9). Admission to the park and use of cycling and hiking trails are free. The park is open daily dawn–dusk.

> **SIDE TRACK**
> **FROM BEAUPRÉ**

CAP TOURMENTE

Réserve Nationale de Faun du Cap-Tourmente; *tel: (418) 827-4591*, reached by an 8-km access road from Rte 360, is a bird-watcher's nirvana. As many as 325,000 snow geese at a time stop on their migrations in Apr and Oct. The trail-laced marshlands also host 250 other bird species. The preserve is open at all times, the wildlife centre and parking lot daily 0900–1700 (May–Sept) and Sat–Sun 0730–1800 (first three weeks of Oct). Admission is $5.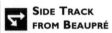

STE-ANNE-DE-BEAUPRÉ

More than one million visitors make the pilgrimage to the shrine of Ste-Anne, leaving behind their crutches in the basilica and their money in the souvenir shops on *av. Royale*. Miraculous cures were reported soon after the first church on the site was built in 1658.

The **Basilique Ste-Anne-de-Beaupré**, *10018 av. Royale; tel: (418) 827-3781*, has daily masses at varying hours. The information booth on the south-east side of the basilica is open daily 0830–1700 (early May–mid Sept). The present basilica was built in 1922 after a fire to replace the 1872 original. It is beautifully lit by more than 200 stained-glass windows and contains an impressive collection of religious art. The 'Great Relic', set off in its own niche, is a piece of Saint Anne's forearm sent over from the San Paolo Fuori le Mura in Rome.

Also on the site are the striking **Way of the Cross**, a group of life-size bronzes, and the **Musée de Ste-Anne-de-Beaupré**; *tel: (418) 827-6873*, open daily 0900–1900 (June–Oct), adults $6.

QUÉBEC CITY– RIVIÈRE-DU-LOUP

The southern coast of the Fleuve St-Laurent (St Lawrence River) is a rich agricultural land with spectacular views of the ever-widening river. Locally grown strawberries and raspberries are sold in roadside stands in June and July, and wildflowers cover the terrain.

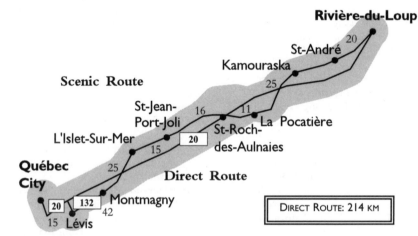

DIRECT ROUTE: 214 KM

211

ROUTES

DIRECT ROUTE

From Québec City, take Hwy 73 across the Pont (bridge) Pierre-Laporte. Fifteen km from downtown Québec, take the Hwy 20 Est exit. Continue on Hwy 20 for 199 km to **Rivière-du-Loup**. Exits to seaside villages are scattered liberally along the route.

SCENIC ROUTE

Follow the direct route out of Québec City. After 11 km on Hwy 20 Est, take exit 325N to **Lévis Centre-Ville**, picking up Rte 132 Est. This road continues to Rivière-du-Loup, about 210 km. All attractions, except where noted, lie along Rte 132 or between the road and the St-Laurent. Do not be lured by road signs into turning right to enter villages.

TOURIST INFORMATION

This route crosses two tourist districts. For information on the route from Lévis to St-Roche-des-Aulnaies, contact **Association Touristique Chaudière Appalaches**, *800 Autoroute Jean-Lesage, St-Nicolas, PQ G7A 1C9; tel: (418) 831-4411*. For the remainder, contact **Association Touristique du Bas–St–Laurent**, *189 r. Hôtel-de-Ville, Rivière-du-Loup, PQ G5R 5C4; tel: (418) 867-3015 or (800) 563-5268*.

BUSES AND TRAINS

Orleans Express operate seven buses daily from Québec to Rivière-du-Loup, some stop at Montmagny. Journey time: 2½ hrs. See OTT Table 224.

VIA Rail operate a service from Lévis to Rivière-du-Loup every day except Tues at 2235. Journey time: 2 hrs. OTT table 24.

LÉVIS

Tourist Information: in person only: **Association Touristique Chaudière-Appalaches**, 7 *Monseigneur Gosselin (Hwy 20 exit 325N – in library at Collège de Lévis); tel: (418) 838-4126*, open Tues–Wed 1100–1730, Thur–Sun 1000–1900.

This dormitory community is connected to Québec by a ferry and two bridges. The town has a **tourist shuttle**, Wed–Sun 0900–1700 hourly (late June–Aug), adults $3 or $5 with return-fare ferry ticket; *tel: (418) 833-2181*. Walking maps also cover this route.

Lévis offers splendid views of Québec, the best from **Lévis Terrace**, *r. William-Tremblay*. Inaugurated in 1939 by King George VI and Queen Elizabeth, this park becomes a winter skating oval. **Fort No.1 at Pointe-Lévy National Historic Site**, *41 ch. du Gouvernement; tel: (418) 835-5182 or (800) 463-6769,* is the vestige of a fort system built 1865–72 to protect Québec from the Americans, who never attacked. Costumed re-enactors show how the fort was manned, but its chief attraction is the wooded parkland. Open Sun–Fri 0900–1600 (mid May–mid June), daily 1000–1700 (mid June–Aug), Sun 1200–1600 (Sept–late Oct), $2.75.

LÉVIS TO MONTMAGNY

Rolling farmland and small villages line the south shore of the St-Laurent. In **Beaumont**, notable largely for its French-era architecture, the **Moulin de Beaumont**, *2 r. du Fleuve; tel: (418) 833-1867,* open Sat–Sun 1000–1630 (May–late June and Sept–Oct), Tues–Sun 1000–1630 (late June–Aug), $5, demonstrates old-fashioned flour-milling

and sells fresh baked goods and stoneground whole wheat flour.

Intimate **St-Michel-de-Bellechasse** is nicknamed the 'town of maples' – practically the only kind of tree in town. A chapel replicates Lourdes, but the village is best known for sea kayaking. Kayaks may be rented or guided tours arranged at the *quai* with **Explore Kayak de Mer**; *tel: (418) 884-2441 or (888) 839-7567* (toll-free). An introductory trip costs $25–35 per person, longer trips up to $69.

St-Vallier marks the beginning of the snow goose migration territory, and the village is popular with hunters and birdwatchers in the fall. The bakeshop, **La Levée du Jour**, *344 r. Principale; tel: (418) 884-2715,* specialises in gourmet breads and pastries. This is the last touch of sophisticated cuisine for many kilometres. The **Musée des Calèches**, *Rte 132; tel: (418) 884-2238,* open daily 0900–1800 (June–Aug) and Sat–Sun 0900–1800 (Sept), $3, has a collection of 65 horse-drawn carriages, including both summer and winter models.

Berthier-sur-Mer is called 'the sailing capital', in large part for its cruise boats to Grosse-Île and the Île-aux-Grues in an archipelago in the St-Laurent. From 1832–1937, Grosse-Île was the main quarantine station in Canada for 4 million immigrants arriving by boat from Europe. Between 1845–47, thousands of Irish famine refugees stopped at Grosse-Île, and many died there. A memorial was erected to their memory in 1997.

Les Croisières Lachance, *110 r. de-la-Marina; tel: (418) 259-2140 or (888) 476-7734,* offers a variety of boat tours, from a guided visit to Grosse-Île to a visit followed by a cruise of other islands, rates $22–32. The same company also offers return-trip ferry service for bicyclists to Île-aux-Grues, $19.50. More information about Grosse-Île may be obtained from **Grosse-Île National Historic Site**, *2 r. d'Auteuil, PO Box 2474 Postal Station, Québec, PQ G1K 7R3; tel: (418) 563-4009 or (800) 463-6769.*

MONTMAGNY

Tourist Information: (in person or by telephone only) **Office du Tourisme de Côte-du-Sud**, *45 av. du Quai; tel: (418) 248-9196 or (800) 463-5643,* open daily 0800–2000 (July–Aug).

Montmagny has several disparate passions, including the snow goose (for which they hold a festival during each fall migration) and the accordion (honoured with a world festival late each Aug). It is also a major departure point for the Île-aux-Grues archipelago. **Montmagny–Île-aux-Grues ferry service**, *Quai de Montmagny; tel: (418) 248-3549,* operates Apr–Nov, for autos and bicycles ($4) and pedestrians ($1). **Croisières Taxi des Îles**, *Quai de Montmagny; tel: (418) 248-2818,* offers several packages related to Île-aux-Grues, with transportation by boat or air (any combination) and bicycle or kayak on the island. These range from $24 for a half day with bicycle to a three-day overnight with kayak and bicycle for $235. **Le Centre Éducatif des Migrations**, *53 r. du Bassin Nord; tel: (418) 248-4565,* began as a centre to elucidate the migration habits of snow geese, but has expanded to also address human migrations through a multimedia show on the history of Grosse-Île, open daily 0930–1730 (late Apr–mid Nov), $6.

If the strains of *'Lady of Spain'* float through the air, you are approaching **L'Économusée de l'Accordéon**, *301 blvd Taché Est; tel: (418) 249-7927,* open Mon–Fri 0900–1700 and Sat–Sun 1000–1600 (mid May–Aug), Mon–Fri 0900–1700 (Sept–Oct), Tues–Fri 0900–1700 (Nov–mid May), $2. Exhibits show the history of the accordion and artisans assemble instruments, which are for sale.

L'ISLET-SUR-MER

A true seafaring village, L'Islet-sur-Mer's crowning jewel is **Musée Maritime Bernier**, *55 r. des Pionniers Est; tel: (418) 247-5001,* open daily 0900–1800 (mid May–late Oct) and Tues–Fri 0900–1200, 1330–1700

(late Oct–mid May); $4.50–7, depending on activities. Prominent Arctic explorer Joseph-Elzéar Bernier was born in L'Islet-sur-Mer, and the museum named after him is dedicated to preserving the maritime heritage of the saltwater sailors of the St-Laurent.

ST-JEAN-PORT-JOLI

Woodcarving is a venerable Québec folk art, and St-Jean-Port-Joli is the provincial capital of the activity. Many roadside carving shops are evident on the road from L'Islet-sur-Mer, and they proliferate as one approaches St-Jean-Port-Joli.

Maison Médard Bourgault, *322 av. de Gaspé Ouest (Rte 132); tel: (418) 598-3880,* open mid June–mid Aug, honours the memory of the carver who launched the tradition in the town, $2. Other members of the family have carried on the carving tradition (Médard died in 1967). One of the town's best shops was founded by André Bourgault in 1936, **Centre d'Artisant**, *334 av. de Gaspé Ouest; tel: (418) 598-6162.* Next door is the **Musée des Anciens Canadiens**, *332 av. de Gaspé Ouest; tel: (418) 598-3392.*

St-Jean-Port-Joli also serves as a gateway to lakes and rivers of the interior for fishing. One guide based here offers trips for non-residents of Québec for $70 per day, minimum party of two, including provincial permit. For reservations: **Guide Accompagnateur d'Excursions de Pêche Sébatien Lord Enr**, *1 r. des Pionniers Est, St-Jean-Port-Joli, PQ G03 3G0; tel: (418) 598-7267.*

ST-ROCH-DES-AULNAIES

Seigneurie des Aulnaies, *525 r. de la Seigneurie; tel: (418) 354-2800,* open daily 0900–1800 (mid June–early Sept), daily 1000–1600 (early Sept–mid Oct), $5, is a comprehensive interpretive centre on seigneurial life in Québec. Costumed interpreters bring back the mid 19th-century manor house and grain mill. Asked if all tours were in French, staff replied *(en français)* 'Who else would care?' Actually, it's quite interesting.

213

LA POCATIÈRE TO KAMOURASKA

Tourist Information: (in person) **Maison Touristique du Bas-St-Laurent**, *Hwy 20, exit 439; tel: (418) 856-5040*, open daily 0900–2000 (late June–Aug), daily 0900–1700 (late May–late June, Sept–mid Oct).

The river broadens and becomes tidal along this stretch, known as the Kamouraska area, an Algonquin word meaning 'where bullrushes meet the water'. In **La Pocatière**, the main factory of the Bombardier company manufactures subway cars for New York, Montréal and other cities. Kamouraska's shallow waters leave 2 km of mudflats at low tide, exposing the poles of fishing weirs. Kamouraska also has a traditional eel fishery, elucidated in the **Site d'Interprétation de l'Anguille de Kamouraska**, *205 av. Morel; tel: (418) 492-3935*, open daily 0900–1800 (mid May–Oct), adults $3.

ST-ANDRÉ

214

Halte écologique des Battures deu Kamouraska, *Rte 132; tel: (418) 493-2604*, is a roadside pullout with nature trails, scenic outlooks, bird-watching, an obstacle course and picnic area, open Mon–Fri 1000–1800, Sat–Sun 0930–2000 (late June–Aug), $3.

RIVIÈRE-DU-LOUP

Tourist Information: Association Touristique du Bas-St-Laurent, *189 r. Hôtel-de-Ville, Rivière-du-Loup, PQ G5R 5C4; tel: (418) 867-3015 or (800) 563-5268*, open daily 0830–2030 (late June–Aug) and Mon–Fri 0830–1700 (Sept–late June).

Perhaps named for the seals *(loups-marin)* that used to live in its harbour, Rivière-du-Loup is the hub where land roads to Québec, the Gaspé and New Brunswick meet the sea road: the ferry to St-Siméon that links the north and south shores of the St-Laurent.

ACCOMMODATION

Chain hotels include *CI* and *DI*. **Hotel Levesque**, *171 r. Fraser, Rivière-du-Loup, PQ*

G5R 1E2; tel: (418) 862-6927, is an in-town, two-storey motel with saunas, whirlpool, swimming pool; moderate. **Auberge de la Pointe**, *10 blvd Cartier, Rivière-du-Loup, PQ G5R 3Y7; tel: (418) 862-3514*, is located on the outskirts of town overlooking the river. A self-contained resort, it offers a health club, swimming pool, lawn games and summer theatre; moderate. For more modest lodgings, **Service du Logement**, *Cégep de Riviere-du-Loup, 325 r. St-Pierre, Rivière-du-Loup, PQ G5R 1R1; tel: (418) 862-6903, ext 297*, supplies bargain college dormitory rooms (mid May–mid Aug) by the day or week. **Camping Municipal de la Pointe**, *Rte 132, Rivière-du-Loup, PQ G5R 3Y7; tel: (418) 862-4281 (summer), (418) 862-8293 (winter)*, open mid May–late Sept, adjacent to the Auberge de la Pointe resort, has walking trails along the river, scenic overlooks, bicycle rental and volleyball; budget.

EATING AND DRINKING

Auberge de la Pointe's restaurant is contemporary Canadian; moderate–expensive. **Rôtisserie St-Hubert**, *80 blvd Cartier; tel: (418) 867-3008*, an interesting variation on the ubiquitous Québec chain, is in a complex with a motel and the Musée de Bateaux Miniatures ('museum' of miniature boats); budget. Several moderate restaurants and bars line *r. Fraser*, including **Café Bistro le Novello**, *169 r. Fraser; tel: (418) 862-9895*, with upmarket pizza and contemporary Italian dishes. **Restaurant Chez Antoine**, *433 r. LaFontaine; tel: (418) 862-6936*, specialises in French bistro dishes with a strong component of local produce and fish.

SIGHTSEEING

The **Club de Golf de Rivière-du-Loup**, *Rte 132; tel: (418) 862-7745*, is a full-service 18-hole, par 72 course; greens fees $31.05.

Croisières Navimex, *200 r. Hayward; tel: (418) 867-3361*, runs whale-watching cruises on a 250-passenger boat, daily 0900 and 1300 late June–mid Sept; adults $35.

GASPÉ PENINSULA

This drive up the southern bank of the *Fleuve St-Laurent* (St Lawrence River) around the perimeter of the Gaspé peninsula encompasses some of eastern Canada's most spectacular coastal scenery. Through Rimouski the route skims along tidal marshes teeming with shorebirds, but the landscape becomes abruptly more harsh at Ste-Flavie, where the first of the Gaspé's great salmon rivers empties.

In the Gaspé, the Appalachian mountain chain reaches its northern terminus, crashing into the sea with *Götterdämmerung* histrionics. Because the Gaspé has been physically and (until satellite television) culturally isolated, the Québecois hold a special fondness for it as symbolic of both the wilderness of Québec and old-time French ways that have faded elsewhere.

Ste-Anne-Des-Monts

Matane

85

132

299   40   132   222

Rimouski   30

Forillon
National Park

St-Fabien 10   Ste-Flavie

Parc de la
Gaspésie

68

20

20 30   Bic

Trois-Pistoles   132

Gaspé

31 L'île-Verte

95

Rivière-du-Loup   160

Maria

Pointe-à-la Croix

6   60   30

Campbellton   Carleton

20   Bonaventure   Percé

ROUTE: 1145 KM

*Campbellton–
Moncton
p. 223*

132   90

27   New Carlisle

215

ROUTE

From Rivière-du-Loup continue on Rte 132 east, being careful to take the left fork of that road at **Ste-Flavie**. (The right fork makes a 165-km shortcut to Campbellton, but skips the Gaspé's scenic attractions.) At **Ste-Anne-des-Monts**, 153 km from Ste-Flavie, turn right on Rte 299 to side-track 40 km to the **Parc de la Gaspésie**, returning by the same road. Continue east on Rte 132,

which encircles the peninsula as Rte 132 Est to **Gaspé**, where it becomes Rte 132 Ouest. **Pointe-à-la-Croixe** and the crossing to New Brunswick lie 328 km further on.

TOURIST INFORMATION

This route crosses two regional tourist areas. For information from Rivière-du-Loup through Rimouski, contact the

Association Touristique du Bas-St-Laurent, *189 r. Hôtel-de-Ville, Rivière-du-Loup, PQ G5R 5C4; tel: (418) 867-3015 or (800) 563-5268* (toll-free). For Ste-Flavie through Point-à-la-Croixe, contact the **Association Touristique de Gaspésie**, *357 rte de la Mer, St-Flavie, PQ G0J 2L0; tel: (418) 775-2234.*

L'ÎLE-VERTE

Fish smokers dominate L'Île-Verte, lending the whole town a distinctive aroma. Access to the island, the only one in this region inhabited all year, and a prime whale-watching spot on its north shore, is via ferry: **Société Inter-Rives de L'Île-Verte**, *Île-Verte Quai; tel: (418) 898-2843;* $5 non-residents, $20 per vehicle. The 1809 light-house is the oldest on the St-Laurent.

TROIS-PISTOLES

Tourist Information: Bureau Régional d'Information Touristique, *Rte 132; tel: (418) 763-5832,* open daily 0800–2000 (mid June–early Sept).

ACCOMMODATION

Camping Plage Trois-Pistoles, *Rte 132, C.P. 3110, Trois-Pistoles PQ G0L 4K0; tel: (418) 851-2403,* offers 150 pitches along the St-Laurent.

SIGHTSEEING

Trois-Pistoles (a 17th-century French sailor lost a silver mug here worth three *pistoles)* is notable for its string of sandy beaches and access to Île-aux-Basques, 5 km from shore, which was a base for Basque fishermen as early as 1580 and is now a nature sanctuary. **Excursions à l'Île aux Basques**, *Marina de Trois-Pistoles; tel: (418) 851-1202,* $12 (early June–mid Oct), will get you there. **Parc de l'Aventure Basque**, *66 r. du Parc; tel: (514) 851-1556,* open daily 1000–1700 (late June–mid July), 1000–2000 (mid July–mid Aug), 1000–1700 (mid Aug–early Sept), $5, interprets the island's long history.

Ferry service across the St-Laurent to the village of Les Ecoumins is available from the town quai: **La Compagnie de Navigation des Basques, Inc.**; *tel: (418) 851-4676,* $7.45 return trip.

ST-FABIEN, BIC AND PARC DU BIC

Tourist Information: Comité de Development Bic/St-Fabien, *33 Rte 132 Ouest, St-Fabien, PQ G0L 2Z0; tel: (418) 869-331,* open daily 0900–1900 (mid May–mid Oct), Mon–Fri 0900–1200 and 1300–1630 (mid Oct–mid May). **Parc du Bic Visitors Centre**; *tel: (418) 869-3502,* open daily 0900–1700 (mid June–Sept).

ACCOMMODATION

Camping du Bic, *Rte 132, Bic, PQ G0L 1B0; tel: (418) 736-4711,* offers 140 pitches for tents, trailers and RVs.

SIGHTSEEING

The 33-square-km Parc du Bic – a coastal park with islets, shoals and headlands jutting into the St-Laurent – is one of Québec's loveliest, most accessible parks. The towns of St-Fabien and Bic are gateways to the park, which has three entrances on Rte 132: Cap-à-l'Orignal (main entrance with visitors centre and interpretation centre), Rivière-du-Sud-Ouest (campsite) and Havre-du-Bic (moorings and boat ramp).

Excursions to Parc du Bic depart from the St-Fabien tourist centre; *tel: (418) 869-3333.* Among the options are a 2-hr trolley tour ($12.50) and a shuttle to the 346-m summit of Pic Champlain ($4). Both operate daily (early July–late Aug), weekends only (late June, early Sept), Sun only (Sept–mid Oct). Admission to the park is otherwise free, and a network of easy hiking and cycling trails winds through wild roses to offer panoramic views and excellent birding. Grey seals often cavort off l'Anse à l'Orignal. Kayak and boat tours are available July–Aug at **Marina du Bic**, *tel: (418) 736-5252.*

RIMOUSKI

Tourist Information: Office du Tourisme et des Congrès de Rimouski, *50 r. St-Germain Ouest, Rimouski, PQ G5L 4B5; tel: (418) 723-2322 or (800) 746-6875,* open daily 0830–2000 (late June–mid Sept), 0900–1700 (late May–late June), Mon–Fri 0900–1700 (mid Oct–late May).

ACCOMMODATION AND FOOD

Rimouski has *CI* and *HG* chains. **Hôtel Rimouski,** *225 blvd Réné-Lepage Est, Rimouski, PQ G5L 1P2; tel: (418) 725-5000 or (800) 463-0755,* offers good summer packages from $79 for a family of four. *R. St-Germain* in the heart of town is a very good street for bistro dining.

SIGHTSEEING

Musée Régional de Rimouski, *35 r. Saint-Germain Ouest; tel: (418) 724-2272,* open Wed–Sat 1000–2100 and Sun–Tues 1000–1800 (late June–Aug), Wed–Sun 1200–1700 (Sept–late June), $4, is housed in Rimouski's oldest stone church. The museum combines contemporary art, local history and oceanographic science.

STE-FLAVIE

Tourist Information: Association Touristique de Gaspésie, *357 rte de la Mer, St-Flavie, PQ G0J 2L0; tel: (418) 775-2234,* open daily 0800–2000 (mid June–early Sept), Mon–Fri 0830–1700 (early Sept–mid June).

Ste-Flavie shows great originality with its souvenir shops, most notably **Centre Chouiñart Le Pêcheur,** *710 rte de la Mer; tel: (418) 775-7813,* daily 0900–1900 June–early Sept, $4, a regional craft shop with attractions related to seafaring life and seafood products; and **Centre d'Art Marcel Gagnon,** *564 rte de la Mer; tel: (418) 775-2829,* open daily 0800–2300 (Apr–mid Oct) daily 0800–2100 (mid Oct–Mar), free, displaying the work of artist Marcel Gagnon, with a restaurant and an outdoor exhibition of statues and rafts floating on the St-Laurent.

The **Centre d'Interprétation de Saumon Atlantique,** *900 rte de la Mer; tel: (418) 775-2969,* open daily 0900–1700 (mid June–Oct), $6, explains the life cycle of the most important fish of the Gaspé.

GRAND-MÉTIS

Les Jardins de Métis, *242 Mont-Joli; tel: (514) 775-2221,* open daily 0830–1830 June–mid Oct, $7, has more than 40 acres of beautifully landscaped display gardens as well as a boutique, café and garden shop.

MATANE

Tourist Information: Bureau Régional d'Information Touristique, *968 av. du Phare Ouest, Matane, PQ G4W 395; tel: (418) 562-1065,* open daily 0800–2000 (mid June–early Sept), Mon–Fri 0830–1700 (early Sept–mid June). This Tourist Office occupies a working lighthouse.

Promenade des Capitaines along the Matane River has signage in French about the riverboat captains from Matane. Salmon fishermen ply the river; the walk concludes at a fish ladder observation post at **Mathieu-D'Amours** dam, open daily 0700–2100 (June–mid Oct).

Société des Traversiers du Québec, *1410 r. de Matane-sur-Mer; tel: (418) 562-2500,* offers ferry crossings to the remote Côte-Nord communities of Baie-Comeau and Godbout, one-way adults $10.90, car $26.50, bicycle free.

STE-ANNE-DES-MONTS

Tourist Information: Bureau Régional d'Information Touristique, *Rte 132; tel: (418) 763-5832,* open daily 0800–2000 (mid June–early Sept).

The cross-peninsula road, Rte 299, meets the north coast here, making Ste-Anne a base for forays to the Parc de la Gaspésie. Two good moderate lodgings are **Motel à la Brunante,** *94 blvd Ste-Anne, Ste-Anne-des-Monts, PQ G0E 2G0; tel: (418) 763-3366 or (800) 463-0828;* and **Riotel Monaco des**

217

Monts, *90 blvd Ste-Anne, Ste-Anne-des-Monts, PQ G0E 2G0; tel: (418) 763-3321.*

> **SIDE TRACK**
> **TO PARC DE LA GASPÉSIE**
> Tourist Information: Centre d'Inter-prétation, *Rte 299; tel: (418) 763-7811*, open daily 0900–1700 early June–mid Oct.
>
> Some 850 square km of mountainous terrain in the centre of the Gaspé peninsula was set aside in 1937 to conserve this habitat, where deer, moose and caribou live side by side (about two moose per square km) and boreal forest meets arctic tundra. Superb free hiking trails lace the park, and wilderness camping is permitted June–Aug in limited areas. Admission is free, but fees are assessed for camping and fishing. A **shuttle bus** from the interpretation centre to the trailhead to ascend Mont Jacques-Cartier (1268 m) leaves 1000–1600, $12. The ascent and return require 3–4 hrs.
>
> **Gîte du Mont-Albert**, *C.P. 1150 (Rte 299), Ste-Anne-des-Monts, PQ G0E 2G0; tel: (418) 763-2288 or (888) 270-4483* (toll-free), is a gîte (Bed and Breakfast) in name only. This comfortable resort hotel with full restaurant is open mid Feb–early Nov and mid Dec–early Jan; expensive–pricey, including breakfast and dinner. Other accommodation is mostly primitive at park campsites (June–mid Oct); *tel: (418) 763-7811.* ◪

STE-ANNE-DES-MONTS TO FORILLON NATIONAL PARK

One of eastern North America's most scenic drives follows the cliffs of the shore through small villages along the south shore of the Fleuve St-Laurent as it opens into the Gulf of St Lawrence. Several segments veer so close to the water that high waves sometimes wash over the road. As the route approaches the end of the peninsula, the road cuts across mountains.

Some 27 km past Ste-Anne, **La Martre** marks the beginning of the rugged coastline. Its **Centre d'Interprétation des Phares et Balises**, *10 av. du Phare; tel: (418) 288-5698*, open daily 0900–1700, $3, provides exhibits on the role of the Gaspé lighthouses and beacons, housed in a small building next to the landmark red lighthouse that faces a white church, both on a bluff over the ocean.

In another 30 km, **Mont-St-Pierre** appears suddenly as a deep cove. This hang-gliding capital of eastern Canada is also a prime staging ground for hikes into the Parc de Gaspésie. **Carrefour Aventure**, *Rte 132; tel: (418) 797-5033 or (800) 463-2210*, can arrange all activities and provide necessary gear. Hang-gliding (which could last 5–45 mins) costs $100; two-person sea kayaks rent for $10 per hr; a guide for hiking or back-country fishing starts at $30 for two people.

In late July–early Aug, the town hosts the annual hang-gliding event, **Fête du Vol Libre**; *tel: (418) 797-2222.*

Excellent tent pitches are available at the shore: **Camping Municipal Mont-St-Pierre**; *tel: (418) 797-2250.* There are also several budget–moderate motels lining the shore: **Motel Les Flots Bleus**, *18 r. Prudent-Cloutier, Mont-St-Pierre, PQ G0E 1V0; tel: (418) 797-2860;* **Motel Mont-St-Pierre**, *60 r. Prudent-Cloutier, Mont-St-Pierre, PQ G0E 1V0; tel: (418) 797-2202;* and **Motel Au Délice**, *100 r. Prudent-Cloutier, Mont-St-Pierre, PQ G0E 1V0; tel: (418) 797-2850.*

Tiny **Madeleine**, set on high bluffs where the salmon river of the same name joins the St-Laurent, has a picturesque lighthouse (tours $1) and an adjacent souvenir and bakeshop where the keeper's wife sells cakes and biscuits (cookies). As Rte 132 leaves town, it leaves the coast as a twisting road through mixed forest on the coastal mountains, with occasional glimpses of the sea for the next 40 km before descending to water's edge highway again at **Canton**

Cloridorme, where a narrow, stony beach is marked with a line of turquoise pavilions.

Cap-Des-Rosiers (Cape of Roses) earned its sobriquet from the wild roses that once covered its headlands. Treacherous rocks lurk just offshore, and the Cape saw many early shipwrecks as captains came too close. The 37-m high lighthouse, a national historic monument built in 1858, is Canada's tallest. Cap-des-Rosiers is the gateway to Forillon National Park.

FORILLON NATIONAL PARK

Tourist Information: Forillon Interpretation Centre, *ch. du Portage, Forillon, PQ G0E 1J0; tel: (418) 892-5553*, open daily 0900–1700 (early June–mid Oct).

A stunning coastal park incorporating mountains, cliffs and coastline, Forillon was established as a national park in 1970. Daily admission is $3.50. Fees are charged for cross-country skiing, camping, use of tennis courts or boat moorings, and certain activities such as sea kayaking and cruising. The park is open year round, but camping is limited to the June–mid Oct period.

Camping is available at four areas, $15.50–19 per night: *tel: (418) 368-6050*. Telephone reservations are accepted (mid May–early Aug). Reservations by mail must arrive by early May: *Reservations Dept, Forillon National Park, P.O. Box 1220, Gaspé, PQ G0C 1R0*, with a non-refundable $5 deposit per night.

Eight well-maintained trails, ranging from 0.6 km to 9.1 km, cross varied terrain for casual and serious hikers. One of the finest is **Les Graves**, a 7.8-km (return trip) route that follows high bluffs above the sea to the top of Cap-Gaspé.

Croisière aux Baleines Forillon, *Grande-Grave; tel: (418) 892-5500*, offers daily whale-watching cruises to see as many as seven species; adults $32. **Bonaventure Destination Aventure**, *Petit-Gaspé; tel: (418) 892-5088*, offers two-hour sea kayaking tours of the Forillon coast from the

Grande-Grave fishing harbour, daily at 1730; adults $34.

GASPÉ

Tourist Information: Bureau Régional d'Information Touristique, *Rte 132, Gaspé, PQ G0C 1R0; tel: (418) 368-6335*, open daily 0800–2000 (mid June–early Sept).

Gaspé is served by **VIA Rail** (Sun, Wed, Fri from Montréal); *tel: (418) 368-4313;* by **Inter-Canadian Airline**; *tel: (800) 665-1177*, and **Air Alliance**; *tel: (800) 361-8620*; and by **Orleans-Express** bus; *tel: (418) 368-1888*.

ACCOMMODATION

Gaspé has a *QI*, which overlooks the harbour. Two moderate motel options are **Motel Plante**, *137 r. Jacques-Cartier, Gaspé, PQ G0C 1R0; tel: (418) 368-2254 or (888) 368-2254*, and **Motel Adams**, *2 r. Adams, Gaspé, PQ G0C 1R0; tel: (418) 368-2244 or (800) 463-4242*.

SIGHTSEEING

Gaspé is the administrative centre of the eastern peninsula, but less a destination in itself than surrounding communities are. The leading attraction is the **Musée de la Gaspésie**, *80 blvd. Gaspé; tel: (418) 368-1534*, adults $4, which chronicles the inhabitation of this remote peninsula with exhibits in both French and English. In front stands the **Jacques Cartier Monument National Historic Site**, which commemorates the explorer's planting a cross here on 24 July 1524 to claim Canada for France. The **Site historique Micmac de Gespeg**, *783 blvd Pointe-Navarre, Fontanelle, Gaspé; tel: (418) 368-6005*, is a replica of a 16th-century Micmac Amerindian village, open June–Sept; adults $3.

GASPÉ TO PERCÉ

The 77 km between these two centres detours briefly onto Rte 198E before rejoining Rte 132; simply follow signs to Percé. In

219

Douglastown, 25 km from Gaspé, is **La Ferme Chimo**, *1705 blvd Douglas; tel: (418) 368-4102*, where the farm store sells bread, honey, maple products and cheese and yogurt made from goats' milk. Guided visits with tastings are offered mid June–Aug, $1.

Twelve km further is **Fort-Prével**, a fort converted to a resort community with a 9-hole, par 36 golf course with striking views of the ocean: **Club de Golf Auberge Fort-Prével**, *2053 blvd Douglas, St-George-de-Malbaie; tel: (418) 368-6957*, greens fees $20.

In another 25 km is the small English-speaking village of **Coin-du-Banc**, settled by Irish immigrants in the mid 19th century. Just before reaching Percé, **Plongée Pointe St-Pierre**, *1377 r. Belle Anse, Barachois; tel: (418) 645-3927*, offers wet-suit scuba diving and snorkeling expeditions of varying lengths and prices.

PERCÉ

Tourist Information: Bureau Régional d'Information Touristique, *Rte 132, Percé, PQ G0C 2L0; tel: (418) 782-5448*, open daily 0800–2000 (mid June–early Sept).

Percé is perhaps the premier destination on the Gaspé peninsula and has the most tourist amenities. Unlike most places in the Gaspé, Percé is functionally bilingual in French and English. It is named for the island, Rocher Percé or 'pierced rock', just offshore with an arch cut through it by wind and waves.

ACCOMMODATION

Percé has the greatest concentration of lodging on the peninsula, including several good hotels and motels. **Hôtel La Normandie**, *221 Rte 132 Ouest, Percé, PQ G0C 2L0; tel: (418) 782-2112 or (800) 463-0820*, moderate–expensive, offers exceptional value with a direct view of Rocher Percé. Other excellent choices include **Riôtel Percé**, *10 r. de l'Auberge, Percé, PQ G0C 2L0; tel: (418) 782-5535 or (800) 463-7468*, moderate; **Au Pic de l'Aurore Village**

Chalets, *1 Rte 132 Ouest, Percé, PQ G0C 2L0; tel: (418) 782-2166 or (800) 463-4212*, which has a hilltop panoramic view, moderate; **Auberge et Motel Les Trois Soeurs**, *77 Rte 132 Ouest, Percé, PQ G0C 2L0; tel: (418) 782-2183*, moderate; **Hotel-Motel Manoir Percé**, *212 Rte 132, Percé, PQ G0C 2L0; tel: (418) 782-2022 or (800) 463-0858*, moderate–expensive; **Motel Bellevue**, *183 Rte 132, Percé, PQ G0C 2L0; tel: (418) 782-2182*, moderate.

Camping Le Phare de Côte Surprise, *385 Rte 132, Percé, PQ G0C 2L0; tel: (418) 782-5588*, has a magnificent hilltop view of Percé Rock. **Camping Baie-de-Percé**, *Rte 132, Percé, PQ G0C 2L0; tel: (418) 782-2846*, offers 162 pitches in the centre of the village.

EATING AND DRINKING

The centre of Percé village is lined with small eateries, including a complex of fast-food shops across the street from the main *quai*. In addition, most hotels also have dining rooms. **Hôtel La Normandie** offers classic afternoon tea in addition to all other meals. **La Maison du Pecheur**, *155 Place du Quai; tel: (418) 782-5624*, has both an elegant dining room upstairs (moderate–expensive) and a casual bistro-bar downstairs (moderate). For good local pastries, visit **Do-Ré-Mie Boulangerie Patisserie**, *9 r. Ste-Anne; tel: (418) 782-2780*.

SIGHTSEEING

Several **whale-watch boats** leave from the main *quai*, with rates varying $25–33. Up to a dozen boat captains also offer sightseeing boat cruises to Rocher Percé and Île Bonaventure, with optional drop-offs at Bonaventure, $10–11. Kiosks offering both kinds of tours line Rte 132 in the centre of town.

Parc de l'Île-Bonaventure-et-du-Rocher-Percé, *4 r. du Quai; tel: (418) 782-2240*, free admission. Bonaventure Island is a nature preserve of rare beauty, covered with wildflowers and arctic-alpine plants. Quarter of a million birds nest on the island, declared an ornithological sanctuary in 1919, including 70,000 gannets. Boat trips drop visitors off on one side of the island, then pick them up on the other side. Bring water, as none is available on the island. Bonaventure is open for visiting (early June–mid Oct).

Rocher Percé is best seen from a boat, but it is also possible to walk to the rock at low tide. The **Centre d'Interprétation**, *Rang d'Irlande; tel: (418) 782-2721,* on the mainland, provides a good overview of the park, open 0900–1700 daily (early June–mid Oct).

Musée Chafaud, *145 Rte 132; tel: (418) 782-5100,* open daily 1000–2200 June–Sept, is dedicated to various artistic representations of Rocher Percé over the years. In addition to paintings and sculpture, the museum also exhibits fossils, furniture, historic photographs and furniture; adults $3.

PERCÉ TO BONAVENTURE

Rte 132 stays within continuous sight of the ocean through this stretch, passing directly through the middle of villages rather than around the edges. **Ste-Thérese**, still a true fishing village, is covered with racks for sun-drying the codfish catch. Other towns along the route – Chandler, for example – derive their livings from timber. In **Newport**, which remains a commercial fishing centre, **Site Mary Travers dite 'La Bolduc'**, *124 Rte 132; tel: (418) 774-2401,* was inspired by the life and work of folk-singer Madame Bolduc. Celebrating the folklore and traditional music of the Gaspé, the site is open daily 1000–1700 (June, Sept, Oct) and 0800–1800 (July–Aug); adults $3.

After Newport, the road follows the north shore of the **Baie des Chaleurs**, a region settled alternately by English Loyalists and Acadian refugees. The bay is comparatively warm (hence its name, 'bay of warmth') and swimming beaches abound. Seas are calm and the shoreline consists of red clay and sandstone banks. The roadsides are covered with wildflowers, especially roses and the purple-pink spikes of wild lupine.

In the town of **Paspébiac**, 113 km from Percé, the marine heritage of the region is well interpreted at **Site Historique du Banc-de-Paspébiac**, *r. 3e, route du Quai; tel: (418) 752-6229.* The buildings hark back to the company town run by the Robin and LeBoutillier companies from Jersey, which held the concession to process and ship codfish from this region. The site is open daily 0900–1800 (mid June–Aug) and 0915–1600 (Sept–Oct), adults $5.

BONAVENTURE

Tourist Information: Bureau Régional d'Information Touristique, *Rte 132; tel: (418) 534-4014,* open daily 0800–2000 mid June–early Sept.

An Acadian stronghold, Bonaventure developed as an agricultural centre rather than a fishing town, so its prosperity has survived the closing of the fishing banks.

ACCOMMODATION

Riôtel Le Château Blanc, *98 av. Port-Royal, Bonaventure, PQ G0C 1E0; tel: (418) 534-3336* or *(800) 463-7468,* offers a good private swimming beach, moderate. A large campsite in the middle of town at the main beach is **Camping Plage Beaubassin**, *av. Beaubassin, Bonaventure, PQ G0C 1E0; tel: (418) 534-3246.*

SIGHTSEEING

Musée Acadien du Québec, *95 av. Port-Royal; tel: (418) 534-4000,* interprets the history and culture of Acadian habitation in Québec. Open daily 0900–2000 (late June–Aug), 0900–1700 (Sept–mid Oct), Mon–Fri 0900–1200 and 1300–1700, Sat-Sun 1300–1700 (mid Oct–late June), adults $3.50.

Plage de Bonaventure, the city beach, is free. Heaped with piles of driftwood and littered with tiny periwinkle shells, it is one of the best swimming beaches on the Gaspé, featuring warm water with very light waves.

221

BONAVENTURE TO CARLETON

Rte 132 continues to follow the Baie-des-Chaleurs shoreline, with several picture-postcard *'haltes routières'*, or roadside stops with picnic tables, large clean restrooms and excellent views. In **New Richmond**, a Loyalist town, the **Centre de l'Héritage Britannique de las Gaspésie**, *351 blvd Perron Ouest; tel: (418) 392-4487*, proudly celebrates the English-speaking heritage (in French). It is open daily 0900–1800 (early June–Aug), adults $5. Rte 299 meets Rte 132 again here – it is 83 km to the **Parc de Gaspésie**. The Micmac population of **Maria** worships at a church built in the shape of a wigwam.

CARLETON

Tourist Information: Bureau Régional d'Information Touristique, *Rte 132; tel: (418) 364-3544*, open daily 0800–2000 (mid June–early Sept).

Protected by a sandbar that provides a warm-water lagoon in lieu of a harbour, Carleton has developed as a sea-and-mountain vacation getaway.

ACCOMMODATION

Three moderate options for motels are **Le Thermôtel**, *895 blvd Perron, Carleton, PQ G0C 1J0; tel: (418) 364-7055 or (800) 463-0867*; **Hostellerie Baie Bleue**, *482 blvd Perron, Carleton, PQ G0C 1J0; tel: (418) 364-3355 or (800) 463-9099*; and **Manoir Belle Plage**, *474 blvd Perron, Carleton, PQ G0C 1J0; tel: (418) 364-3388 or (800) 463-0780*. Extraordinary camping with more than 200 pitches is offered on the sandbar: **Camping Carleton**, *Banc de Larocque, Carleton, PQ G0C 1J0; tel: (418) 364-3992*.

SIGHTSEEING

The tidal lagoon is especially good for watching shorebirds, notably herons, grebes and terns. The slate and agates found on the beach resemble modern art. **Parc de la**

Point Tracadigash occupies the far end of the sandbar with an excellent shallow swimming beach and a picturesque lighthouse. From Rte 132, a 4.9-km road winds back and forth to ascend 582 m to the top of Mont-St-Joseph (there are also hiking trails up the mountain) for extraordinary panoramic views of the shore and surrounding farmland. **Oratoire Notre-Dame-du-Mont-St-Joseph**; *tel: (418) 364-3723*, at the summit, features stained-glass windows and striking mosaics. It is open daily 0800–2000 (late May–Aug), 0900–1700 (Sept).

PARC DE MIGUASHA

Sixteen km after leaving Carleton, follow the signs (a left turn) for 7 km to the provincial **Parc de Miguasha**, *232 rte de Miguasha Ouest; tel: (418) 794-2475*. The fossil banks along the Miguasha River have been important to biologists and paleontologists since their discovery in 1880. The exhibit halls of the park are some of the most impressive interpretations of the fossil records outside the Smithsonian Institution or the British Museum. Plan on a visit of at least 2 hrs if you also tour the fossil banks. The park is open daily 0900–1800 (June–Aug), reduced hours Sept–mid Oct, free. A few hundred metres down the road is the **ferry** to **Dalhousie, New Brunswick**, $3.50 per person, $16 automobile.

POINTE-À-LA-CROIXE

Unlike all surrounding towns, Pointe-à-La-Croixe is on Atlantic Standard Time – proof of its close economic and social links with Campbellton, NB, across the bridge on Rte 11. The **Battle of Ristigouche National Historic Site**, *Rte 132; tel: (418) 788-5676*, relates the perilous (and unsuccessful) journey of the supply fleet sent to rescue New France in 1760, but sunk here by the British Navy. The interpretive centre exhibits many objects from and portions of the vessel *Le Machault*. The site is open daily 0900–1700 (early June–mid Oct).

CAMPBELLTON- MONCTON

Your north–south journey along New Brunswick's Acadian Coastal Drive covers 465–500 km, depending on how many diversions you take. Except for a short, final stretch from Shediac inland to Moncton, you'll see water to the left and terra firma on your right throughout the scenic route.

Dozens of place names reflect the predominance of French settlement in shoreline locales. But the English, Scottish and Irish have a stake in east coast New Brunswick's cultural history, too.

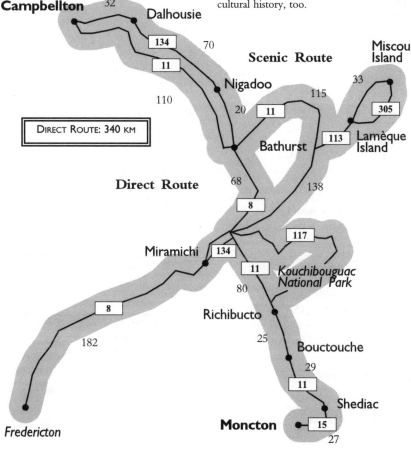

Campbellton   32   Dalhousie

134   70   **Scenic Route**   Miscou Island

11

Nigadoo   33

110   115

20   11   305

DIRECT ROUTE: 340 KM   223

113   Lamèque Island

Bathurst

Direct Route   68   138

8

117

Miramichi   134

11   Kouchibouguac National Park

80

8

Richibucto

182   25   Bouctouche

29

11

Shediac

Moncton   15

Fredericton   27

ROUTES

DIRECT ROUTE

➡ From **Campbellton**, on New Brunswick's side of the Restigouche River, follow Rte 11 signs about 110 km as far as **Bathurst**. Bypass the Acadian Peninsula by following Hwy 8 then Rte 134, a total of 68 km, to **Miramichi**, where you return to Rte 11 for a final 130 km to **Shediac**. Bear right onto Rte 15 to **Moncton** after another 27 km. Quickest access to downtown comes at the Moncton Centre/Rte 106 exit.

SCENIC ROUTE

➡ Forgo Rte 11 in favour of Rte 134 upon leaving Campbellton. It follows 114 km of Chaleur Bay's shoreline as you go through **Dalhousie, Jacquet River, Petit-Rocher** and **Bathurst**. On the outskirts of that fairly populous city, get onto Rte 11, which becomes a *very scenic* coast road curving east to south around the **Acadian Peninsula**. For more maritime vistas, turn left onto Rte 113, bringing you to **Shippagan**, followed by bridge crossings to **Lamèque** and **Miscou Islands**. Backtrack via Rte 305 through Lamèque's tiny **Pigeon Hill** and **Saint-Marie-Saint-Raphaël** for your return to Rte 113, then connect back onto Rte 11 at **Pokemouche**.

After crossing the Centennial Bridge in **Miramichi**, switch to Rte 117 through **Baie-Saint-Anne** and **Kouchibouguac National Park** before resuming your southward Rte 11 drive to Shediac.

Alternatively, from Miramichi, you can side-track 182 km on Rte 8 through splendid fishing country, ending up in the provincial capital of **Fredericton** (see p. 252) instead of Moncton.

BUSES AND TRAINS

SMT have one daily bus service from Campbellton to Moncton via Bathurst, which takes 5½ hrs. (See OTT table 239.) There are also two daily buses from Fredericton to Moncton. Journey time: 3 hrs. (OTT table 235.)

A VIA Rail service from Montréal to Halifax (daily except Wed) calls at Campbellton (0700), Miramichi (0924) and Moncton (1105). See OTT table 24.

CAMPBELLTON

Tourist Information: Provincial Visitor Information Centre, *56 Salmon Blvd, Campbellton, NB E3N 3P1; tel: (506) 789-2367*, open daily 0800–2100 (mid June–early Sept), 0900–1800 (early–late Sept), 1000–1800 (late Sept–mid Oct).

The Charlo/Campbellton airport offers connections via **Canadian Airlines** from Montréal, Toronto and Ottawa. Car rentals are available. Campbellton is on **VIA Rail's** Eastern Transcontinental line.

ACCOMMODATION AND FOOD

Campbellton has *CI* and *HJ*, the latter on the riverfront and attached to the City Centre Mall. Nothing's fancy up this way, so most visitors wind up dining in hotel restaurants, if only to find substitutes for the local fried-chicken joint and Atlantic Canada's omnipresent Dixie Lee fast-food chain. Two alternatives are **Something Else**, *55 Water St; tel: (506) 753-7744*, for moderate home cooking, including shrimp and scallop brochette, and budget **Soup 'n' Sweets**, *33 Pleasant St; tel: (506) 753-4040*.

SIGHTSEEING

Salmon Plaza is an attractive waterfront park, dominated by 'Restigouche Sam', an

---

Colour section (i): Québec City (pp. 184–194); Château Frontenac; inset, dining out in the city. (ii): Canada's tallest lighthouse, Gaspé (p. 219). (iii): Miramichi waterfront (p. 226); inset, shrine on Miscou Island (p. 226). (iv): A view of Carleton (p. 222); fishing boats in Caraquet's harbour (p. 226); inset, model ships for sale on the roadside, Gaspé peninsula (pp. 215–222).

8.5-m statue of a leaping Atlantic salmon. Late June's **Campbellton Salmon Festival** includes a beauty pageant, pancake breakfasts, horseshoe-tossing tournament, horsehauling contest, road race and other activities along with, naturally, salmon suppers.

At 283-m altitude, **Sugarloaf Mountain** provides panoramics of Campbellton, the river and Bay of Chaleur, northern Appalachian ranges and, across the water, Gaspé's hills. The mountain is in **Sugarloaf Provincial Park**, *C.P. 629, Atholville, NB E0K 1A0; tel: (506) 789-366*, with campsites, a summit-viewing platform reached by chairlift, Prichard Lake, Atlantic Canada's only alpine slides, plus 22 km of hiking trails (fine for wintertime sports, too). Mountain bike, rollerblade and paddle boat rentals available.

DALHOUSIE TO BATHURST

Tourist Information: Dalhousie Area Visitor Information, *Inch Arron Park, P.O. Box 250, Dalhousie, NB E0K 1B0; tel: (506) 684-7363*, open daily 0830–2200 (mid June–mid Sept).

Dalhousie, on high ground overlooking Baie des Chaleurs (Bay of Warmth, apt terminology for the warmest saltwater north of Virginia), was named in 1826 after the Earl of Dalhousie, at that time governor of Upper and Lower Canada. **Eel River Bar**, one of the world's longest barrier sand-bars, is washed by tepid saltwater on one side, colder freshwater on the other. It's part of **Chaleur Beach Park**, midway between Dalhousie and Charlo along Rte 134. **Charlo** features 12 km of beachfront and, in-town and beyond, 27 km of groomed cross-country ski trails. Passengers aboard the *Chaleur Phantom* cruise from Dalhousie's wharf to Heron Island, the Bon Ami Rocks and Miguaska, Québec; *tel: (506) 684-4722*.

ACCOMMODATION AND FOOD

Dalhousie's *BW* is subtitled **Manoir Adelaïde**. Lodgings are moderate, French-accented dinners moderate–pricey at

Auberge d'Anjou, *587 r. Principale, Petit-Rocher, NB E0B 2E0; tel: (506) 783-0587*.

Similar cost combination for accommodation and Gallic cuisine (bouillabaisse, crêpes, brochettes) at bayside **La Fin Grobe Sur-Mer**, *Rte 134, Nigadoo, NB E0B 2A0; tel: (506) 783-3138*. Proximity to beaches and Heron Island Nature Park makes **Auberge Blue Heron** another appealing Bed & Breakfast, *Box 10, New Mills, NB E0B 1M0; tel: (506) 237-5560*.

SIGHTSEEING

Dalhousie's **Restigouche Regional Museum**, *437 r. George; tel: (506) 684-4685*, traces that town's fisheries and paper-mill livelihoods, open Mon–Fri 0900–2100, Sat–Sun 0900–1700 (June–Aug), Mon–Fri 0900–1700 (Sept–Dec), free. Mining is another enterprise in this part of the province, hence Petit-Rocher's **New Brunswick Mining & Mineral Interpretive Centre**, *Rte 134; tel: (506) 783-0824*, with its simulated descent into a mine shaft, open daily 1000–1730 (June–Aug), \$4.50.

BATHURST

Tourist Information: Bathurst Chamber of Commerce, *275 Main St, Bathurst, NB EZA 1A9; tel: (506) 548-8498*. The local **Tourist Information Centre**, *Vanier Blvd exit off Rte 11, tel: (506) 545-6375*, opens daily 0900–2100 (June–Aug).

Bathurst's airport offers connections via **Air Nov** from Fredericton, Montréal, Québec City, Toronto, Boston and New York; car rentals are available. Bathurst is on **VIA Rail's** line.

ACCOMMODATION AND FOOD

BW (in suburban Beresford) and *CI* are here. So are **Atlantic Host Inn**, *Vanier Blvd, Bathurst, NB E2A 3Y8; tel: (506) 548-3335*, and **Country Inn & Suites**, *777 St Peter Ave, Bathurst, NB E2A 2Y9; tel: (506) 548-4949 or (800) 456-4000* (toll-free). Conveniently located downtown: **Keddy's Le**

225

Chateau Hotel, *80 Main St, Bathurst, NB E2A 1A3; tel: (506) 546-6691 or (800) 561-7666.* All three are moderate.

Deli-type food and outdoor summer entertainment make moderate **Montréal Café** Bathurst's hippest eatery, *129 Main St; tel: (506) 546-6664.* Budget–moderate **Au Café Gourmet**, *210 King Ave; tel: (506) 545-6754,* opens onto a patio. Two farmers' markets enliven Sat mornings – at *150 Main St* and adjacent to Coronation Park.

SIGHTSEEING

Harbourview Park is another urban green space. The Nepisiguit River's **Pabineau Falls**, tumbling through three stages of black granite, isn't far from downtown, nor are marshland trails winding through **Daly Point Reserve**. Swimmers dip into Nepisiguit Bay at **Youghall Beach Park** ($2 parking fee).

ACADIAN PENINSULA

226

Tourist Information: Information Touristique, *51 blvd Saint-Pierre Oest, Caraquet, NB E1W 1B6; tel: (506) 726-2676.* Open daily 0900–2100 (mid June–mid Sept). While skirting the peninsula's coastline, watch for '?' signs, leading to other such facilities with summer-season hours – in Bertrand, Grande-Anse, Tracadie-Sheila, Shippagan and Néguac. For pre-trip planning: **Acadian Tourism Association**, *P.O. Box 1010, Shippagan, NB E0B 2T0; tel: (506) 336-8831.*

ACCOMMODATION AND FOOD

Moderate **Hôtel Paulin**, *143 blvd Saint-Pierre Oest, Caraquet, NB E1W 1B6; tel: (506) 727-9981,* dates from 1891 and is an 'in' place for moderate–pricey dinners. Motor hotels, plentiful along the peninsular shores, are invariably moderate. For instance, **Auberge de la Baie**, *139 blvd Saint-Pierre Oest, Caraquet, NB E0B 1K0; tel: (506) 727-3485,* **Motel Brise Marine**, *Shippagan, NB E0B 2P0; tel: (506) 336-2276,* and **Motel**

Beausejour, *Néguac, NB E0C 1S0; tel: (506) 776-8718.*

Here in New Brunswick's *Acadie*, you're seldom far from a chatty place to eat. Two such Caraquet establishments, both moderate and specialising in *fruits de mer* (seafood), are **Le Caraquette**, *89 blvd Saint-Pierre Est; tel: (506) 727-6009,* and, in Carrefour de la Mer waterfront park, **Le Poisson d'Or**, *tel: (506) 727-0004.* Likewise moderate: Shippagan's **L'Abri des Flots**, *Centre Marin; tel: (506) 336-0909.*

Menu choices are all-Acadian at Bertrand's moderate **Restaurant la Pantrie**, *170 blvd des Acadiens (Rte 325); tel: (506) 764-3019.* For pricier, epicurean dining, make a reservation at **La Poissonniere**, *484 r. Acadie; tel: (506) 732-2000,* in Grande-Anse. **Brasserie Deauville**, *3494 r. Principale; tel: (506) 395-2346,* with sidewalk terrace and sports bar, is a favourite gathering place in Tracadie-Sheila, moderate. Best locally for romantic ambience: **Maison de la Fondue**, *3613 r. Luce; tel: (506) 393-1100;* moderate–pricey.

SIGHTSEEING

Tricolour Acadian flags outnumber Canadian maple-leaf banners on this sizeable point of land, with farms in its interior and two bridge-connected islands forming the north-easterly tip. French is spoken much more than English in everyday conversation. The commercial fishing-boat harbours in Caraquet and Shippagan are among the Atlantic Canadian provinces' biggest and busiest.

Bay meadows, shingle-sided barns and sandstone bluffs come into view during your eastward coastal drive from Bathurst. Approaching **Pokeshaw**, *do not bypass* this village's **Community Park**, overlooking Île aux Oiseaux (Bird Island), an offshore sea stack. Covered up top with dead tree trunks and branches, it's a nesting and roosting place for hundreds of black-breasted cormorants. Park opens daily at 0830 (late June–early Sept), $1 per car.

Its founding in 1758 qualifies Caraquet as northern New Brunswick's oldest French-Canadian community and the region's Acadian cultural capital. The patriotic faithful flock to **Village Historique Acadien**, *Rte 11 at Rivière-du-Nord, 15 km west of Caraquet; tel: (506) 726-2600*, which recalls 'marsh settler' folkways, circa 1770–1890, open daily 1000–1800 (June–early Oct), $8, $20 family rate. The peninsula's French-influenced history is chronicled in Caraquet's **Acadian Museum**, *blvd Saint-Pierre Est; tel: (506) 727-1713*, open Mon–Sat 1000–2000, Sun 1300–1800 (June–Sept), $3. Among the highlights of the ten-day **Acadian Festival**, *tel: (506) 727-2787*, each Aug is a Sun-morning blessing of Caraquet's fishing fleet.

In Caraquet, **Une-Mer-d'Adventures**, *tel: (506) 727-2727*, operates whale-watching cruises (seals and porpoises, too). Shippagan has a noteworthy attraction: its modernistic **Aquarium and Marine Centre**, *off Rte 113; tel: (506) 336-3013*, complete with seal pool and hands-on trawler wheelhouse, open daily 1000–1800 (mid May–late Aug), $5. The peninsula's prevailing Roman Catholicism is exemplified by **Sainte-Anne-du-Bocage pilgrimage shrine**, *Rte 11, Caraquet*. In Grande-Anse, **The Pope's Museum**, *184 r. Acadie; tel: (506) 732-3003*, includes a papal portrait gallery and scale model of St Peter's Basilica, open daily 1000–1730 (June–Sept), $5.

SIGHTSEEING

Amongst numerous opportunities for swimming and beachcombing, the strand at **Maisonnette Park**, *Rte 303 off Rte 11*, consists of a sand-bar, 2.4-km long, extending halfway across the mouth of Caraquet Bay. Paddle boats and bicycles can be rented at **Shippagan Park**. Toward the Acadian Peninsula's southeastern edge, drive across a causeway to **Néguac Park**, *3 km off Rte 11*, for the pleasures of an uncrowded beach, picnic tables and a marshland nature trail.

In Caraquet, arrange sea kayaking at

Tours Kayaket Ltée, *51 blvd Saint-Pierre Est; tel: (506) 727-6309*. Abandoned railway lines are being cleared and resurfaced for **Sentiers Péninsule acadienne** – a network of biking-hiking trails on the peninsula. Bicycle equipment/rental shops are in Caraquet and Tracadie-Sheila.

LAMÈQUE AND MISCOU ISLANDS

Staunchly francophone, the islands separate placid Baie des Chaleurs from the Gulf of St Lawrence's shipping lanes. Prior to completion of a 500-m long bridge in 1996, outermost Miscou was reachable only by boat. Peat bogs cover much of that island. They're barren but profitable, thanks to the production of widely marketed peat moss.

If needed, get petrol and provender in **Miscou Centre**. Six km further north, you'll spot the island's **Bog Trail**, a half-hour boardwalk loop with interpretive signs explaining the boggy, marshy ecosystem. Visitors climb the spiral stairway inside **Miscou Lighthouse**, blinking since 1856, daily 0900–1900 (July–Aug), $1.

Rte 305 passes bogs, scrub pines and tide flats to reach the harbour at **Pigeon Hill** on Lamèque's eastern shore. On that island's opposite coast, your Rte 113 drive includes **Petit-Rivière-de-l'Île**. *Do not bypass* the village's white, twin-steepled **Saint-Cécile Church**. Every nook and cranny of its interior has been hand-painted in a wild green-yellow-orange-blue-red kaleidoscope – where colour and sound harmonise during the **Lamèque International Baroque Music Festival** each July.

MIRAMICHI

Tourist Information: Miramichi City Tourism, *141 Henry St, Miramichi, NB E1V 2N5; tel: (506) 623-2150*. A seasonal resource on *Ritchie Wharf, tel: (506) 622-9100*, in former Newcastle opens daily 0900–2100 (mid May–early Sept). A visitors centre across Miramichi Bay, in what used to

227

be Chatham, *Rte 11; tel: (506) 778-8444*, opens 0900–2100 (mid May–early Oct).

In 1995, two cities (Chatham and Newcastle) and three villages were amalgamated into a single 'new city', Miramichi (population 22,000). The officially non-existent old place names still appear on most maps; even the locals remain befuddled.

ACCOMMODATION

Several moderate lodgings, including *CI*, are on Newcastle's side of the Miramichi River, such as **Wharf Inn**, *1 Jane St, Miramichi, NB E1V 3M6; tel: (506) 622-0302* or *(800) 563-2489*, and **Country Inn & Suites**, *333 King George Hwy, Miramichi, NB E1V 1L2; tel: (506) 627-1999* or *(800) 456-4000*. In Chatham centre on the other side, is newer **Rodd Miramichi River Lodge**, *1809 Water St, Miramichi, NB E1N 1B2; tel: (506) 773-3111* or *(800) 565-7633*; moderate–expensive.

EATING AND DRINKING

Linger over something light and refreshing at Ritchie Wharf's waterview **Boardwalk Café & Tea Room**, *tel: (506) 622-6124*, budget. For full-course dining: **Ranchers' Steak House**, *390 Pleasant St; tel: (506) 627-0096*, moderate; and **Keystone Kelly's** grill and taproom, moderate, downtown at *124 Newcastle Blvd; tel: (506) 627-0809*.

EVENTS

What's promoted as Canada's biggest multi-attraction **Irish Festival** covers a four-day weekend in mid July. Vocalists, stepdancers, fiddle players and other performers do their thing early Aug during the **Folksong Festival**.

SIGHTSEEING

Joseph Cunard of Atlantic Canada's ship-building Cunard family is a famous native son. Equally so, Max Aitken, aka Lord Beaverbrook, London newspaper tycoon and Winston Churchill's World War II minister of war production. His Lordship's

boyhood home, **Beaverbrook House**, *22 Mary St (Newcastle); tel: (506) 622-7832*, dates from 1877, open Tues–Thur, 1200–1600 (July–Aug). Scottish immigrant Alexander MacDonald's rural 18th-century family homestead has become the **MacDonald Farm Historic Site**, *Rte 11; tel: (506) 778-6085*, 30 km north of Miramichi in Bartibog Bridge, open 0930–1630 (June–Aug), \$2.50.

> **SIDE TRACK**
> **FROM MIRAMICHI**

You'll delve into New Brunswick's river-valley midsection by heading south on Rte 8 from Miramichi. Staying on that two-lane road's full distance to **Fredericton** (see p.252) amounts to 182 km. This is bait'n'tackle back country, renowned for Atlantic salmon fishing. Lumberyard and sawmill territory, too, with stands of cedar, poplar, birch, fir and white spruce seen throughout your journey. **Boiestown** is at the province's precise geographic centre point.

Tourist Information: Blackville Chamber of Commerce, *Box 38, Blackville, NB E0C 1C0; tel: (506) 843-2288*, open daily 0900–1800 (June–Oct). The Tourist Offices in Miramichi are equally helpful.

ACCOMMODATION AND FOOD

Built of blond cedar logs, **The Ledges**, *30 Ledges Inn Lane, Doaktown, NB E0C 1G0; tel: (506) 365-1820*, fits its surroundings overlooking the Miramichi River. The lodge's bicycles and canoes are available to guests, along with hearty dinners, moderate. Same cost category for two comfy Bed and Breakfasts: **Victoria's Cottage**, *289 Main St, Doaktown, NB E0C 1G0; tel: (800) 563-8724*, and **Dunvargen Manor**, *45 Alcorn Dr., Blackville, NB E0C 1C0; tel: (506) 843-6312*. Well maintained campsites are in **Red Pines Park**, *Rte 8, Boiestown, NB E0H 1A0; tel: (506) 369-2393*.

228

A Rocky Brook fishburger at budget **Flip's**, *Rte 8, Boiestown; tel: (506) 369-1915*, the very essence of a gossipy diner. Moderate **Village Family Restaurant**, *Doaktown; tel: (506) 365-4301*, offering good home-made desserts, is 25 km further down the same road.

SIGHTSEEING

Browse through **McCloskey's**, *Rte 8, Boiestown; tel: (506) 369-2282*, an old-time general store, where the proprietors somehow keep track of groceries, liquor, dry goods, hardware and plumbing supplies, hunting and fishing gear, paints, crockery, stationery and who knows what else. Watch for a sign barely 1 km west from Doaktown, leading you to the Nelson Hollow **covered bridge**, New Brunswick's oldest (1870).

A suspended footbridge connects two unassuming villages, **McNamee** and **Priceville**. It spans the Miramichi River, about 4 km off the highway, midway between **New Bandon** and **Ludlow**. You can also stretch your legs by taking a 0.5-km hike beside Dunbar Stream and its waterfall, accessed from Rte 8 at a speck of a hamlet called **Durham Bridge**. Flowing through a verdant valley, all of the Nashwaak River is public water for trout and salmon angling. Rows of look-alike brick cottages downhill from an 1880s cotton mill identify **Marysville**, 4–5 km from Fredericton, as originally a company town. **Boiestown** hosts a late-July country fair. Doaktown's **Old Mill Pond Golf & Country Club**, *tel: (506) 365-7584*, invites non-members onto its nine-hole course.

The **Miramichi Salmon Museum**, *267 Main St, Doaktown; tel: (506) 365-7787*, open daily 0900–1700 (June–Sept), $3, a veritable Hall of Fame for the area's premier game fish, covers sportsmanship aspects along with ongoing conservation measures; an aquarium familiarises visitors with Atlantic salmon's development and life cycle in its natural habitat. A steam-powered sawmill, lumber-camp cookhouse and bunkhouse, restored trapper's cabin, lumberjack equipment and vintage photos are features of the **Central New Brunswick Woodmen's Museum**, *Rte 8, Boiestown; tel: (506) 369-7214*, open daily 0930–1730 (May–Sept), $5.

KOUCHIBOUGUAC NATIONAL PARK

What nearly everyone has trouble pronouncing is a native-Canadian Micmac word meaning 'river of long tides'. Established in 1969, the park has 32 km of bikeways (groomed in winter for cross-country skiers), 48 km of woodland trails, eight 'flat-water' canoeing rivers, campsites and – on its 238-km Kouchibouguac Bay coastline – 25 km of protected sand dunes.

You'll find a snacks-and-drinks canteen and picnic tables at Kellys Beach. Some 225 bird species have been recorded amidst wildlife preserves. A rental concession inside the park supplies bikes, boats, canoes and kayaks. **Kouchibouguac National Park**, *tel: (506) 876-2443*, is open year round. Day pass $3.50.

For an overnight stay and German/Austrian cooking on the park's southern perimeter, pull into **Kouchibouguac Restaurant & Motel**, *Rte 134, Saint-Louis-de-Kent, NB E0A 2Z0; tel: (506) 876-4317*.

RICHIBUCTO AND BOUCTOUCHE

Tourist Information: Kent County Tourist Association, *21 Main St, Richibucto, NB E0A 2M0; tel: (506) 523-4547*, open daily 0900–2100 (June–Aug).

Barrier dunes sheltering the Acadian Peninsula, then seen along the national park's beachfront, remain part of the seascape as you reach the Northumberland Strait's shoreline. **Jardine Park** is bounded on three sides by a sloping sandy beach near the mouth of the Richibucto River. In the late 1800s, Richibucto's Liverpool Shipyard was one of eastern Canada's most productive.

ACCOMMODATION AND FOOD

Waterfront Point à Jacquot acreage surrounds **Le Vieux Presbytère de Bouctouche**, *157 ch. du Couvent, Bouctouche, NB E0A 1G0; tel: (506) 743-5568,* moderate, built in 1880s Acadian Gothic style as a priests' rectory. Chef de cuisine Michelle Albert excels with her *table d'hôte* specials in this auberge's moderate–pricey **Le Tire-bouchon** dining room. Elsewhere locally, budget–moderate **Bouctouche Bay Inn**, *Bouctouche, NB E0A 1G0; tel: (506) 743-2726,* has a gemütlich German-Canadian restaurant, along with 27 motel rooms. Each housekeeping unit at moderate **Les Chalets de Havre**, *York Point, Richibucto, NB E0A 2M0; tel: (506) 523-1570 or (800) 277-9037,* a vacation resort, includes two bedrooms and fully equipped kitchen for overnight or longer stays, moderate.

Indulge in the area's fresh shellfish at Bouctouche's bayside **McPhail's Lobster Haven**, *Dixon Point Rd; tel: (506) 743-8432.* In Cocagne, a short drive south, seafood is also the mainstay of budget–moderate **Le Pélican**, *Rte 134; tel: (506) 576-7001.*

SIGHTSEEING

You'll hear French and almost nothing else spoken at **Le Pays de la Sagouine**, *Bouctouche; tel: (506) 743-1400,* an imaginary island awash in Acadian music, story-telling and theatrics, open daily 1000–1800 (mid June–Sept), $6.50. Its moderate **L'Ordre du Bon Temps** restaurant menu is bilingual, listing such Acadian staples as *poutin râpée* pie and chicken *fricot.*

Irving Eco-Centre, *Rte 11, Bouctouche; tel: (506) 743-2600,* was developed to preserve and restore the sand barrier stretching 12 km across Bouctouche Bay. A boardwalk (with beach access) curves along an 1.8-km portion of the dune.

Near Richibucto, **Bonar Law Historic Site**, *Rte 116, Rexton; tel: (506) 523-7615,* preserves the birthplace and boyhood farm home of Andrew Bonar Law, the only British prime minister (1922–23) born outside the UK. Open daily 0930–1630 (late June–Aug), free.

SHEDIAC

Tourist Information: Shediac Visitor Centre, *Rotary Park, Rte 133, Shediac, NB E0A 3G0; tel: (506) 532-7788,* open daily 0800–2200 (June–mid Oct).

This is the self-proclaimed world's lobster capital. During the Pan Am Clipper era, Shediac was a refuelling stopover on the flying boats' transatlantic air route. A common and bandstand, 1900 train station (now police headquarters) and historical markers on numerous buildings add to Shediac's small-town charm. Ask at the Visitor Centre about walking tours and Shediac Bay cruises. Three km of golden sand alongside grassy dunes draw sun lovers to **Parlee Beach Provincial Park**, locale of July's annual **Lobster Festival**. A 7-km nature trail meanders from downtown to the park.

For eating and sleeping, choose between two turn-of-the-century heritage inns: **Auberge Belcourt**, *112 Main St, Shediac, NB E0A 3G0; tel: (506) 532-6098,* or **Chez Françoise**, *93 Main St, Shediac, NB E0A 3G0; tel: (506) 532-4233.* Accommodation moderate, dinner moderate–pricey at both. Same-category dinners, too, at budget–moderate **Hotel Shediac**, *Main St, Shediac, NB E0A 3G0; tel: (506) 532-4405,* hosting guests since 1853.

Crêpes, shrimp linguini, cioppino, mussels marinière – a seafood bonanza at classy, mostly moderate **Le Péché Mignon**, *15 Queen St; tel: (506) 532-6555.* Comparably moderate: **Le Quai du Homard** ('The Lobster Deck'), *118 Main St; tel: (506) 532-8787.* In nearby Shediac Bridge, dig your fork into fried clams at budget **Chez Leo**, *Rte 134; tel: (506) 532-4543.*

MONCTON–SAINT JOHN

Go city-to-city by way of a pastoral river valley noted for its inland marshes, along with covered bridges reached by occasional country-road detouring. Moreover, you'll be tempted to linger a while in several appealingly casual farm-market towns.

For a slower-going alternative, drive south towards Shepody Bay, then westward to Saint John along two separate portions of the Bay of Fundy's sometimes-fogbound shoreline, deluged twice daily by the world's highest tides.

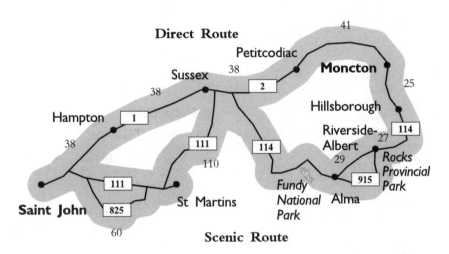

Direct Route

Scenic Route

DIRECT ROUTE: 155 KM

231

ROUTES

DIRECT ROUTE

From downtown Moncton, follow *Main St* onto *Foundry St* and cross Gunningsville Bridge into Riverview. Promptly turn right and follow signs for Rtes 112/106 west to Salisbury, 21 km from Moncton. A short distance beyond Salisbury, take the Trans-Canada (Hwy 2) south to **Petitcodiac** and another 38 km to **Sussex**, then Provincial Rte 1 for a 38-km drive via **Hampton** to Saint John. In all, the trip is 131 km.

Unless you're in a feverish hurry, we suggest a short stretch of countryside touring that closely parallels the end of the direct route. Beginning at **Norton**, take rural Rte 100 instead of Rte 1 through the tucked-in-valley hamlets of **Bloomfield**, **Lakeside**, **Nauwigewauk** and then south through the three posh suburbs of **Rothesay**, **Renforth** and **Kingshurst**. Return to Rte 1 for quick highway access into Saint John.

SCENIC ROUTE

To explore New Brunswick's scenic Fundy coast, follow the direct route to Riverside. Bear left onto Rte 114 and drive 17.5 km south along the tidal Petitcodiac River to **Hillsborough**. Continue toward Shepody Bay to **The Rocks Provincial Park**, then **Hopewell Hill** and **Riverside-Albert**. Bear left onto coastal Rte 915 for very scenic motoring 24 km to **Alma**.

From Alma, leave the coast by following Rte 114 through **Fundy National Park**. Beyond the park, the coastline remains roadless for 21.75 km, so continue north to Trans-Canada Hwy 2 and take it a short distance to **Sussex Corner**. Head south again on Rte 111 through **Hammondville** and **Hanford Brook**; you'll get back to the Fundy coast at **West Quaco** after about 55 km. There, drive west 2–3 km to visit **St Martins**. After returning to West Quaco, follow Rte 111 west until you spot a Rte 825 sign; follow that twisty, hilly road for a scenic drive through **Gardner Creek**, **Black River** and **Garnet Settlement** and eventually back to Rte 111. After passing the Saint John airport, take *Loch Lomond Dr.* to Rte 100 into Saint John.

BUSES

SMT run two buses daily via Sussex. Journey time: 2¾ hrs. See OTT table 236.

PETITCODIAC

Nothing's fast in this town, anchored by its 19th-century United Baptist church and providing meagre but useful opportunities for petrol fill-up and modest shopping needs. Local ambience is epitomised by the cheap–budget **Cozy Café**, *233 Old Post Rd; tel: (506) 756-1917*, good home cooking. **Petitcodiac Valley Golf & Country**

Club, *Glenvale Rd; tel: (506) 758-8129*, is open to the public; club rentals available.

SUSSEX

Tourist Information: Kings County Tourism Association, *P.O. Box 2214, Sussex, NB E0E 1P0; tel: (506) 433-1845*. For seasonal walk-in information, there's a visitors centre in Sussex's 1913 railroad station, *Broad St*, open daily 1000–1900 (May–Aug).

Accessible on both the direct and scenic routes, this is one of south-eastern New Brunswick's most appealing communities (population 4100), known province-wide as 'Dairy Capital of the Maritimes' and maker of superior-quality King Cole tea. Ask about escorted or self-guided walking tours; they include the 1883 brick Town Hall and six exemplary heritage homes of pre-World War I Victorian vintage.

ACCOMMODATION

The local 54-room *QI* has an indoor swimming pool. For centrally located lodgings, both moderate, try **All Seasons Inn**, *1019 Main St, Sussex, NB E0E 1P0; tel: (506) 433-2220* or *(800) 452-1616* (toll-free); or **Amsterdam Inn**, *143 Main St, Sussex, NB E0E 1P0; tel: (506) 432-5050* or *(800) 468-2828*. Off-highway **Timberland Motor Inn**, *Sussex (Penobquis), NB E0E 1P0; tel: (506) 433-2480*, also moderate, is 6 km east of downtown. If you'd rather snooze in a neighbourhood Bed and Breakfast, we suggest Stark's **Hillside Bed and Breakfast**, *RR4, Waterford/Sussex, NB E0E 1P0; tel: (506) 433-3764*.

EATING AND DRINKING

It's the rare, finicky food critic who hasn't heaped praise on the virtually perfect **Broadway Café**, *73 Broad St; tel: (506) 433-5414*, where lunch or dinner consists of sautéed Digby scallops, California quiche, chicken Dijonnaise or curry-spiced beef kebab; moderate. Linger on the streetfront deck or in the backyard garden patio. Still hungry? Purchase a warm-from-the-oven take-away at nearby **Cream Puff Bakery**, *27 Broad St; tel: (506) 433-4979.*

EVENTS

Sussex's sky bursts into colour during the annual **Atlantic Balloon Fiesta**, *tel: (506) 432-9444* (plus a craft fair, classic automobile show and bandstand music), mid Sept in Princess Louise Park. The park, incidentally, has picnic tables amidst the birch trees alongside Trout Creek.

OUT OF TOWN

Nine of Kings County's numerous **covered bridges** dating from the early 20th century are scattered amidst Sussex's agricultural outskirts. Pick up a locator map at the rail station Tourist Office. Look for a 1992 Canadian dime in your pocket change; it depicts the 1910 Oldfield Bridge, spanning Smiths Creek in **Newtown**, 12 km north-east of Sussex.

KENNEBECASIS RIVER VALLEY

Enjoy driving through very pretty farm country flanked by wooded hillsides and steep sedimentary rock formations. Small-town **Norton** looks big when compared with a succession of lazy villages south from there along seldom busy Rte 100.

Overnight in a 150-year-old farmhouse furnished with heirloom antiques, **Evelyn's Bed & Breakfast**, *Bloomfield, NB E0G 1J0; tel: (506) 832-4450*, moderate. Same locale for tours of the property's **OxBow Farm** dairy- and beef-cattle acreage (your chance to feed calves, even milk Cloe the docile cow), $12, $25 per family.

HAMPTON

Tourist Information: Hampton Tourist Bureau, *P.O. Box 329, Main St, Hampton, NB E0B 2Z0; tel: (506) 832-5720*, open daily 0900–2000 (mid June–Sept).

Befitting its stature as the shire town of Kings County, Hampton (population 3600) sports an 1870s court house. Imposing residences line streets shaded by emblematic Canadian maple trees. Some of these officially designated heritage houses were built during settlement of the area by United Empire Loyalists in the late 18th century.

Kings County Museum, *Centennial Building; tel: (506) 832-6009*, behind the court house, contains photos, documents, clothing, early furniture and pioneer household and farm items – mostly connected with the early Loyalist period, open Mon–Fri 1000–1700 (mid June–Sept), $2. Additional displays are in the adjacent **Old Kings County Gaol**.

The **Hampton-Kennebecasis Marsh**, spread over 5000 riverside acres at the foot of 'Sleeping Princess' hills, comprises one of New Brunswick's most extensive and diverse freshwater marsh systems, protected habitat for ducks, herons, ospreys, salmon and brook trout.

Built in 1876 by a local shipwright, moderate **Bamara Inn**, *998 Main St, Hampton, NB E0G 1Z0; tel: (506) 832-9099*, serves elegant, moderate–pricey dinners, in addition to welcoming overnight guests. Hamptonians mingle at Narda and Dave O'Donnells' three-meals-daily **Kozy Korner**, *1051 Main St; tel: (506) 832-3153*, cheap–budget.

KINGSTON PENINSULA

A major southward flow of rivers ultimately widens into parallel bays, thus forming this unique inland peninsula. During your Rte 100 drive along the south (Kennebecasis Bay) side of the peninsula – identified on some maps as the Long Reach of the Saint John River – you'll pass marshy wetlands, ferry boat docks, fishing piers, pleasure boat marinas, roadside farm stands and Englishy cottages with flower gardens. The short toll-free cable-ferry crossing over to **Gondola Point** is worthwhile, for this genteel suburb

233

of Saint John has historic buildings – among them an imposing Georgian church.

Upon reaching **Nauwigewauk**, watch for a sign pointing towards the 1914 Darlings Island covered bridge, 1 km off Rte 100. For up-close waterway viewing, **River Marsh Tours**, *Darlings Island; tel: (506) 832-1990*, offers daily summertime cruises, which include the Hampton-Kennebecasis Marsh. This outfitter has canoe and kayak rentals available for independent sightseeing.

MONCTON TO HILLSBOROUGH

Tourist Information: Moncton's Visitor Centres (see p.260) provide assistance for scenic-route touring down towards the Fundy coast. **Hillsborough Tourism**, *40 Mill St, Hillsborough, NB E0A 1X0; tel: (506) 734-2172*, staffed in the town's 1812 William Henry Steeves house, is open daily 0900–1700 (June–Aug).

The road between Moncton/Riverview and Hillsborough reaches high enough altitudes for valley panoramics of the Petitcodiac River. Depending upon the timing of your drive, you're liable to see it at high tide, or with broad mudflats exposed during ebb-tide hours.

An hour-long ride on the clickety-clack **Salem & Hillsborough Railroad**, *Main St; tel: (506) 734-3195*, is an easygoing way to view the river valley's maple-forested scenery. Boarded in Hillsborough, excursions run mid June–mid Oct, $7.50, $23 family fare. The old-fashioned station is also the admittance office for a fairly sizeable **Railroad Museum**, open daily 1000–1800 (late June–Aug), $1.50.

THE ROCKS PROVINCIAL PARK

New Brunswick's most photographed natural attraction? No contest: the park's **Flower Pot Rocks**, soft sandstone columns with balsam fir and dwarf black spruce growing on top in **The Rocks Provincial Park**,

off Rte 114; tel: (506) 734-3429, open daily 0800–2100 (mid May–Oct), $4 per vehicle.

These odd formations, each approximating the height of a four-storey building, were carved by ceaseless tidal action against Hopewell Cape's cliffsides. The sea stacks become offshore islands when the water level rises. At low tide during the twice-daily gravitational cycle, visitors clamber over the Bay of Fundy's stony bottom to explore caves, tunnels and mini-beaches. Due to the angle of the light, morning is the best time for picture-taking.

An interpretive centre and a budget restaurant/snack bar are on-site. So is **Baymount Outdoor Adventures** outfitter, in case you'd like to go sea-kayaking beyond the rocks. Landlubbers' low-tide access to the 'Flower Pots' is via wooden stairway or, for less vigorous individuals, an elevator due to be completed in 1999.

For something more substantial (and less hectic) than the park's eatery, mostly moderate **Log Cabin Restaurant**, *Rte 114; tel: (506) 734-2110*, with next-door barn chock full of crafts, is nearby in Hopewell Cape. Also in the immediate vicinity: **Hopewell Rocks Motel & Country Inn**, *Hopewell Cape, NB E0A 1Y0; tel: (506) 734-2975*, budget–moderate.

South of the park in Hopewell Hill, **Woodworth General Store**, quintessentially countryish, includes the village post office. For rustic overnighting (expensive, but full breakfast and dinner included) and/or horseback trail riding, pull into **Broadleaf Guest Ranch**, *Rte 114, Hopewell Hill, NB E0A 1Z0; tel: (506) 882-2349* or *(800) 226-5405*.

MARYS POINT AND CAPE ENRAGE

Tourist Information: Riverside-Albert Tourism Office, *Rte 114, Riverside-Albert, NB E0A 2R0; tel: (506) 882-2015*, open daily 0900–1800 (June–late Sept).

In Riverside-Albert, detour off Rte 114

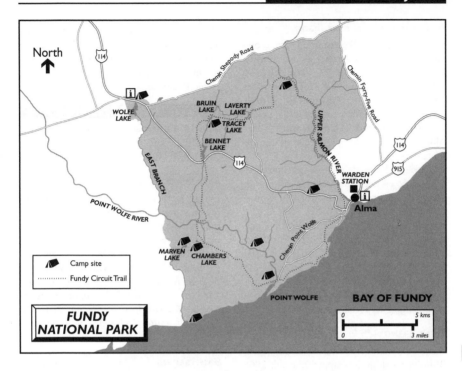

North ↑

WOLFE LAKE

BRUIN LAKE
LAVERTY LAKE
TRACEY LAKE
BENNET LAKE

EAST BRANCH

UPPER SALMON RIVER

Chemin Shepody Road

Chemin Forty-Five Road

WARDEN STATION

POINT WOLFE RIVER

Alma

MARVEN LAKE
CHAMBERS LAKE

Chemin Point Wolfe

🔺 Camp site
········· Fundy Circuit Trail

POINT WOLFE

BAY OF FUNDY

FUNDY NATIONAL PARK

0 _____ 5 kms
0 _____ 3 miles

235

for a 2-km drive up to **Crooked Creek Lookout Park** for, upper altitude lookouts, plus a short woodland walking trail. Then, soon after returning to the highway, views of the Calhoun Marsh and dramatic seascapes are yours by opting for a turn onto remote Rte 915 – occasionally very steep, unpaved over some stretches, but well worth the gear-shifting, dust and bumpiness. Make a side-road loop to reach the **Marys Point Waterfowl Sanctuary**. On any single day between mid July and mid Aug, as many as 250,000 sandpipers and other shore birds can be seen, pecking and diving for food during their migratory flight to Colombia and Venezuela.

Further west along the coast, scrounge for driftwood washed by Chignecto Bay tides onto sandy **Dennis Beach** and **Waterside Beach**; they're separated by a solitary tall sea-stack called Red Head. You'll drive past fields of wild purple fireweed, summertime's

Far Out ice-cream stand, artsy-craftsy studios selling pottery and stained glass, as well as the Ha Ha Cemetery (no fooling: that's the name of this 1800 burial ground outside **New Horton**). The lonesome lighthouse high atop **Cape Enrage**, a rocky headland, has been 'adopted' and restored by Moncton High School students. They serve budget meals in the **Keeper's Lunchroom**; *tel: (506) 887-2273.*

All this plus accommodation in an 1860 heritage inn, **Florentine Manor**, *Rte 915, Harvey, NB E0A 1A0; tel: (506) 882-2271 or (800) 665-2271,* moderate. Full breakfast in the Victorian dining room; reservation-required dinners, too.

FUNDY NATIONAL PARK

Tourist Information: *P.O. Box 40, Alma, NB E0A 1B0; tel: (506) 887-6000,* park open year round, $4 per adult, $7 per family (charged mid May–mid Oct, otherwise free).

Accommodation and Food

Seawinds Dining Room, moderate, is on-site, along with moderately priced **Fundy Park Chalets**, *P.O. Box 72, Alma, NB E0A 1B0; tel: (506) 887-2808.* Five campsites serve park visitors. **Chignecto North Campground**, with a total of 264 pitches, and **Headquarters Campground**, near Alma, both have RV hook-ups; others are for tenters only.

Alma, right beside the east-gate entrance, fills additional needs for lodging and eating. Moderate **Captain's Inn**, *Main St, Alma, NB E0A 1B0; tel: (506) 887-2017,* is a homely Bed and Breakfast. It's across the street from moderate, motel-type **Parkland Village Inn**, *Alma, NB E0A 1B0; tel: (506) 887-2313.* At lunch or dinnertime in the inn's restaurant (also moderate), try for bay-view window seating to watch humming-birds feasting at specially set-up feeders.

Sightseeing

236

Much of what's so alluring about New Brunswick's shore is wrapped into this 206-square-km spread, where natural beauty and recreational opportunities coexist. Sloping inland from coastline forests of red spruce and balsam fir, hills rise to a plateau cut by deep valleys and streams tumbling through wildflower meadows. The park has 110 km of coastal, forest, waterfall and lakeside trails, plus a heated saltwater swimming pool, beach at Point Wolfe, public golf course, tennis courts, even a lawn bowling green.

Both the Information Centre at the park entrance and the exhibits posted along the scenic turnout at **Herring Cove** are good places to learn more about those amazing Bay of Fundy tides, which often reach peak levels of 14–16m. Each 12½ hours, 100 billion tons of seawater roll in and out of the bay – equalling the daily discharge of all the world's rivers.

After leaving the park, follow Rte 114 to

Hwy 2; you can follow this portion of the Trans-Canada to Sussex (see p.232) and on toward Saint John along the Direct Route, or turn off at Rte 111 to get back to the scenic Fundy coast.

ST MARTINS

Tourist Information Centre: *St Martins, NB E0G 2Z0; tel: (506) 833-2209,* open 0900–1800 (July–Sept).

Accommodation and Food

Despite its small size, St Martins has a trio of inviting past-century lodgings, all serving moderate–expensive dinners along with inclusive breakfasts. **Quaco Inn**, *16 Beach St, St Martins, NB E0G 2Z0; tel: (506) 833-4772,* and hilltop **St Martins Country Inn**, *St Martins, NB E0G 2Z0; tel: (506) 833-4534* or *(800) 565-5257,* have moderate rooms. **Weslan Inn**, *St Martins, NB E0G 2Z0; tel: (506) 833-2351,* is moderate–expensive.

Sightseeing

St Martins' photogenic elements include two covered bridges, Quaco Head and Bicentennial lighthouses, the Old Pepjepscot fishing-boat wharf, community park, in-town marshfields, a Victorian gift shop, Hutges General Merchandise store (picnic supplies available) and stately residences on substantial spreads of lawn. On the village's eastern end, low tide at **Mac's Beach** reveals sea caves in the red-rock cliffs. For communing with nature and bird-watching here and in the vicinity, call local **Fundy Hiking and Nature Tours**, *tel: (506) 833-2534.*

Beyond **West Quaco**, the coastline ramble along Rte 825 through **Gardner Creek** and **Black River** includes a 'covered-bridge encore' – the 1927 oldie spanning Tynemouth Creek – shortly before you come to metro Saint John.

SAINT JOHN

Atlantic Canada's third largest city (population 125,000), after Halifax and St John's, Newfoundland, has the economic advantage of an ice-free, deep-water harbour. Its waterfront is the centrepiece of downtown rejuvenation, with skywalks and pedestrian tunnels linking hotels to Brunswick Square and Market Square shopping malls.

Samuel de Champlain dropped anchor here on St John the Baptist's feast day in 1604, hence the name (always Saint, never abbreviated). Permanent settlement, however, didn't occur until some 3000 United Empire Loyalists set sail from colonial America after the USA's War of Independence ended in 1783. Two years later, Saint John became Canada's first incorporated city.

TOURIST INFORMATION

Saint John Visitor & Convention Bureau, City Hall, King St, Saint John, NB E2L 4L1; tel: (506) 658-2990 or (888) 364-4444 (toll-free), open Mon–Fri 0900–1800 year round. Three walk-in **Tourist Information Centres** open the same daily hours: Market Sq. (main level, access from St Patrick St); tel: (506) 658-2855, open year round. Also, Reversing Falls lookout; tel: (505) 658-2937, and Rte 1, Island View Heights; tel: (506) 658-2940, both open mid May–mid Oct.

ARRIVING AND DEPARTING

By Air
Saint John is New Brunswick's hub. Air Canada-affiliated Air Nova; tel: (506) 632-1500, and Canadian Airlines' Air Atlantic; tel: (506) 657-3860, fly here from numerous Canadian cities, also US gateways, including Boston and New York.

Saint John Airport is 25 km east of the city centre. Flat-rate fare from or to the airport is $23; call **Diamond Taxi**; tel: (506) 648-8888 or 8889. Avis, Budget, Hertz and Tilden/National have car-rental counters at the airport.

By Car
From either east or west, make Rte 1 your access highway into Saint John. From Fredericton, take Rte 7, then connect onto Rte 1; crossing the **Harbour Bridge** to reach downtown entails $0.25 toll.

By Boat
The M/V Princess of Acadia makes 2½- to 3-hr Bay of Fundy crossings between Saint John and Digby, Nova Scotia; three-times daily summer service, reduced schedule other seasons. One-way summertime fares: $50 per auto, $23 per adult. Operated by **Bay Ferries**; tel: (506) 649-7777 in Saint John, (902) 245-2116 in Digby, or (888) 249-SAIL. The ferry terminal is at the end of Lancaster St in west-side Saint John.

GETTING AROUND

Public Transport
Saint John Transit (SJT) buses travel city-wide routes; exact-change fare is $1.45; tel: (506) 658-4700.

Driving in Saint John
Nothing's bewildering about the city centre grid layout. Union, King and Princess are the main thoroughfares; watch for one-way signs

237

on many side streets. On-street meters are prevalent downtown, but you can park free Mon–Fri after 1800, Sat after 1300 and Sun all day. Also free parking on outdoor lots Mon–Fri after 1800, all day Sat–Sun. Saint John's two downtown shopping malls include indoor garages. The 24-hr rate at **Brunswick Square**: $8.80; at **Market Square**: $8.60.

Communications
The main post office is far from the city centre. Rely instead upon a branch facility on *Brunswick Square*'s lower level, at the rear of Lawton's Pharmacy; *tel: (506) 652-7100.*

Accommodation
Chains include *CI, HJ* and *Kd.* For four-star pizzazz at a downtown waterfront location: moderate–expensive **Saint John Hilton**, *One Market Sq., Saint John, NB E2L 4Z6; tel: (506) 693-8484 or (800) 561-8282* (toll-free) – plus *Brunswick Sq.'s* **Delta Brunswick Hotel**, *39 King St, Saint John, NB E2L 4W3; tel: (506) 648-1981 or (800) 268-1133,* comparable price range and atmosphere along with close-to-everything convenience. Moderate **Hotel Courtney Bay**, *350 Haymarket Sq., Saint John, NB E2L 3P1; tel: (506) 657-3610 or (800) 563-2489,* with its free guest parking lot, is near the eastern edge of the walkable downtown area.

Dating from 1904 and in an upper-crust neighbourhood, **Red Rose Mansion**, *112 Mount Pleasant Ave; Saint John, NB E2K 3V1; tel: (506) 649-0913 or (888) 711-5151,* was built for the owner of the Red Rose Tea Company; moderate–expensive. Also in that price range is **Homeport**, *80 Douglas Ave, Saint John, NB E2K 1E4; tel: (506) 672-7255 or (888) 678-7678,* west of downtown. On the west side's shore, moderate–expensive **Inn on the Cove**, *1371 Sand Cove Rd, Saint John, NB E2M 4X7; tel: (506) 672-7799,* overlooks Saint John's harbour.

Guests get gourmet morning meals at each of these Bed and Breakfasts.

If you're seeking motor lodgings instead, moderate **Park Plaza Motel**, *607 Rothesay Ave, Saint John, NB E2H 2G9; tel: (506) 633-4100 or (800) 561-9022,* is less than 2 km east of downtown. Other such accommodations line Rte 1 in the east-suburban **Rothesay** vicinity. And that moneyed town has an elegant Victorian mansion with a cordon bleu chef's extravaganzas for evening meals: moderate–expensive **Shadow Lawn Inn**, *3180 Rothesay Rd (Rte 100), Rothesay, NB E2E 5A3; tel: (506) 847-7539 or (800) 561-4166.*

Eating and Drinking
Best for harbourfront seafood or steak, upstairs or out on the terrace, is moderate–pricey **Grannan's**, *1 Market Sq.; tel: (506) 634-1555.* Next door, same address, Canadian ice-hockey photos and regalia set the sporty tone at moderate **Don Cherry's Grapevine**; *tel: (506) 635-7870.* **Tapp's** is a brewpub-steakhouse, *78 King St; tel: (506) 634-1937.* In the Old City Market, **Billy's Seafood Company** has a classic oyster bar, *49–51 Charlotte St; tel: (506) 672-3474.*

The Trinity Royal historic district's moderate **Incredible Edibles**, *42 Princess St; tel: (506) 633-7554,* excels with such entrées as garlic roasted game hen and almond-crusted fillet of salmon. Saloon atmospherics are enhanced by an old-time bar and pressed-tin ceiling at moderate **Chizzler's**, *89 Prince William St; tel: (506) 652-1331.* You'll find a varied menu at moderate **Beatty and the Bistro**, *60 Charlotte St; tel: (506) 652-3888,* a chic Euro-type café. Want Italian? Consider moderate–pricey **Il Fornello**, *33 Canterbury St; tel: (506) 648-2377.*

Across the Harbour Bridge in Saint John West, **The Falls**, *200 Bridge Rd; tel: (506) 635-1999,* is OK for mostly moderate meals, great for views from high above the Reversing Falls (see Sightseeing, p. 240). On

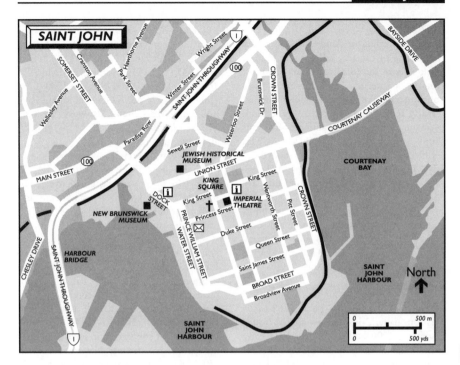

the same side of town for pricey cuisine, is **Dufferin Inn**, *357 Dufferin Row, Saint John, NB E2M 2J7; tel: (506) 635-5968,* which doubles as a Bed and Breakfast.

ENTERTAINMENT

The *Times Globe,* Saint John's evening newspaper, has what's-going-on updates in its Entertainment section. Listings and reviews are also in Sat morning's *Telegraph Journal.*

Nightlife

High-decibel rock reverberates at **Pillar's**, *125 Prince William St; tel: (506) 635-4444,* inside the former 1826 Bank of New Brunswick. In Atlantic Canada's biggest per-capita Irish city, there's bound to be an **O'Leary's Pub**, *43 Princess St; tel: (506) 634-7135,* for Celtic and Maritime folk music, whilst **Nipper's Pub**, *43 Princess St; tel: (506) 635-8829,* usually features blues combos.

Performing Arts

Restored to its 1913 splendour, the **Imperial Theatre,** *King Sq. S.; tel: (506) 633-9494,* is Saint John's prime performing arts venue for symphony, opera, drama and musicals, open, too, for July–Aug tours.

Spectator Sports

Wager on harness racing at Saint John East's **Exhibition Park Raceway,** *McAllister Dr.; tel: (506) 653-2020.* Hockey is a nationwide Canadian passion, so watch 'em slap the puck at downtown's **Harbour Station**, home ice of the Saint John Flames, *tel: (506) 657-1234* or *(800) 267-2800.*

Events

Mid July's **Loyalist Days** recalls the 18th-century emigration of US Loyalists to Saint John; *tel: (506) 634-8123.* **Festival by the Sea** is the big local happening mid Aug; *tel: (506) 674-4100* or *(800) 323-7469.*

SHOPPING

Since the malling of America has spawned the malling of Canada, side-by-side **Brunswick Square** and **Market Square** shouldn't come as a surprise. They house the usual conglomeration of stores and budget eateries. **Trinity Royal** shuns look-alike retail chains in favour of independent antiques and crafts shops, especially along *Prince William St.* This six-block historic enclave is bounded by *King, Charlotte, Duke* and *Water Sts.* Price-savvy Saint Johners rely upon the **Old City Market**, *between Germain and Charlotte Sts*; *tel: (506) 658-2820,* for their produce, meats and take-home seafood. Browse for craft items and souvenirs in this rafter-ceilinged hall, doing business since 1876. Open Mon–Thur, Sat 0830–1730, Fri 0830–2100.

SIGHTSEEING

Special SJT 'Site Seeing' buses take passengers on daily 2-hr driver-narrated tours, beginning 1200 and 1445, late June–early Oct, $12; *tel: (506) 658-4700.* For self-guided sightseeing, Tourist Information Centre staffers have mapped brochures detailing *The Loyalist Trail, A Victorian Stroll* and *Prince William's Walk.*

After cascading through a narrow chasm, the Saint John River runs into the tidal Bay of Fundy with such watery impact that its downstream flow changes direction. Result: splashing rapids and whirlpools twice daily at **The Reversing Falls**, *off Chesley Dr./Bridge Rd (Rte 100), Saint John W.; tel: (506) 658-2937, or (506) 635-1999* off season. If just watching that phenomenon is too tame for you, shoot the rapids via **Reversing Falls Jet Boat**, *Fallsview Ave; tel: (506) 634-8987,* a 20-min thriller for $20.

Waterfront **Barbour's General Store** is a touristy, reproduced 19th-century store-barbershop-schoolhouse, open daily 0900–1900 mid May–mid Oct. Free guided walking tours leave here, daily 1000 and 1400, (July–Aug). Also downtown, costumed guides welcome visitors to **Loyalist House**, *120 Union St; tel: (506) 652-3590,* a Georgian manse completed in 1817 for a United Empire Loyalist from New York, open Sat–Sun 1000–1700 (June and Sept), Mon–Fri 1000–1900, Sat 1000–1700, Sun 1300–1700 (July and Aug), $3. Tours and tastings cost nothing at **Moosehead Brewery**, *89 Main St W.; tel: (506) 635-7000,* Mon–Fri 0930 and 1400 (mid June–late Aug).

Carleton Martello Tower, *Corner Fundy Dr. and Whipple St, Saint John W.; tel: (506) 636-4011,* standing guard over Saint John since 1815, is an ideal perch for city and harbour panoramics, open daily 0900–1700 (early June–mid Oct), $2.50.

Canada's biggest municipal greenspace wholly inside city borders, **Rockwood Park**; *tel: (506) 658-2883,* contains lakes for swimming, all-seasons trails, an arboretum, picnic nooks, 18-hole golf course, campsite and children's animal farm – plus **Cherry Brook Zoo**; *tel: (506) 634-1440.* An exemplary result of corporate and environmentalists' partnership, **Irving Nature Park**; *tel: (506) 653-7367,* covers Fundy bayside marshland west of the city centre. Tamarack pathways attract bird-watchers and amateur botanists; hike the 3.7-km Seal Trail to observe harbour seals and, perhaps, porpoises.

Amongst numerous attention-getters at the **New Brunswick Museum**, *Market Sq.; tel: (506) 643-2300,* are the complete skeletal specimen of a North American right whale, nautical memorabilia, a geological time line and decorative and fine arts galleries, open Mon–Fri 0900–2100, Sat 1000–1800, Sun 1200–1700, $6. Saint John's **Jewish Historical Museum**, *29 Wellington Row; tel: (506) 633-1833,* includes a Hebrew school, chapel and Judaic art, open Mon–Fri 1000–1600, Sun 1300–1600 (mid May–Sept); free. Atlantic Canada's first municipal gallery, in the **Aitken Bicentennial Exhibition Centre**, *20 Hazen Ave; tel: (506) 633-4870,* showcases art and science, open Tues–Sun 1000–1700 (early June–late Aug), 1130–1630 off season, free.

SAINT JOHN–ST STEPHEN

Southern New Brunswick has always been a 'pass-through' zone for travellers hurrying from Maine to Nova Scotia, which is a shame. Just off Hwy 1 is the historic and beautiful seaside town of St Andrews, and short ferry rides open up a cluster of charming islands, including Grand Manan, with its dramatic sea cliffs and easygoing way of life.

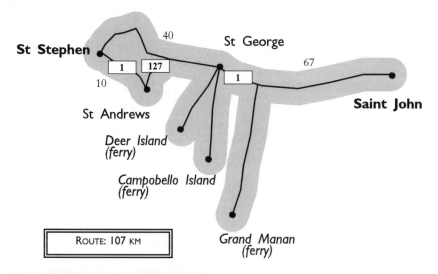

St Stephen

40

St George

67

| 1 | 127 |

1

10

St Andrews

Saint John

Deer Island
(ferry)

Campobello Island
(ferry)

ROUTE: 107 KM

Grand Manan
(ferry)

241

ROUTE

Follow Hwy 1 from Saint John, through **St George**. Rte 127 takes a scenic loop south into **St Andrews** and rejoins Hwy 1 into **St Stephen**. Saint John direct to St Stephen is 107 km, via St Andrews 127 km. Allow about one hour to either town.

BUSES

SMT operate a daily service, taking 1½ hrs. See OTT table 236.

SAINT JOHN TO
ST ANDREWS

Follow Hwy 1 from Saint John to **Penfield**, where the side track to **Grand Manan** leaves on Rte 776 to **Blacks Harbour** and the ferry. The side track to **Deer Island** and **Campobello** begins at **St George**, where Rte 772 leads to the ferry in **Letete**. About 8 km after St George, look for signs for **Oven Head Salmon Smokers**, *Oven Head Rd; tel: (506) 755-8333,* open daily 0800–2100, where you can tour the smoke-house and sample maple-smoked salmon.

 **SIDE TRACK
TO GRAND MANAN**
Tourist Information: Grand Manan Tourism Association, *P.O. Box 193, North Head, NB E0G 2M0; tel: (506) 662-3442.*

ARRIVING AND DEPARTING

Ferries from Blacks Harbour to Grand Manan are operated year round by **Coastal Transport Ltd**; *tel: (506) 662-3724*, six return trips daily (July–Aug), three daily (Sept–June), $25.50 automobiles, $8.50 adult, $4.25 age 5–12. Reserve only for the first morning ferry leaving Grand Manan.

GETTING AROUND

One main road runs the length of the island, with a few others leading to coves and headlands. Roads and drivers are bike-friendly. Rent bikes from **Adventure High**, *tel: (506) 662-3563.*

ACCOMMODATION AND FOOD

Make a reservation before you arrive, since summer occupancy is high. **Shore Crest Lodge Country Inn**, *North Head, Grand Manan, NB E0G 2M0; tel: (506) 662-3216 or (410) 247-8310* (Nov–Apr), open May–Oct, moderate, is just what you imagined an island inn to be, with bright rooms, white wicker chairs and a wrap-around porch. The restaurant, budget–moderate, serves the day's catch. So does the **Compass Rose**, *North Head, Grand Manan, NB, E0G 2M0; tel: (506) 662-8570 or (514) 458-2607* (Nov–Apr), open May–Oct, moderate, a hospitable inn in two vintage houses. Afternoon tea is served here and at **Aristotle's Lantern**, *North Head; tel: (506) 662-3788*, which has a full restaurant. Make dinner reservations early anywhere.

On its own cove, **The Inn at Whale Cove Cottages**, *North Head, Grand Manan, NB, E0G 2M0; tel: (506) 662-3181*, moderate, has rooms and cottages, plus an exceptional dining room. Further south, **McLaughlin's Wharf Inn**, *Seal Cove, Grand Manan, NB E0G 2M0; tel: (506) 662-8760*, moderate, overlooks the harbour with a restaurant serving lobster (by reservation) and other entrées.

Camp along the clifftops or at less heady heights at **Hole in the Wall Park Campground**, *North Head, Grand Manan, NB E0G 2M0; tel: (506) 662-3152*, where the genial staff includes a naturalist. **Anchorage Provincial Park**, *Rte 776; tel: (506) 662-3215*, has a beach (unsupervised), tent pitches and hook-ups.

SIGHTSEEING

The best way to see whales and the island's 250 avian species is from the sea by kayak or whale-watch tour. Hiking trails lead to **Hole-in-the-Wall** stone arch, **Swallowtail Light**, **Ross Island** (at low tide) and to glacial boulders called **Flock of Sheep**. **Adventure High Sea Kayaking**, *North Head; tel: (506) 662-3563*, daily (May–Oct), from $35, $50 with dinner, can take you to explore Hole-in-the-Wall and other coastal formations (with instruction for beginners), or on a sunset paddle that can include lobster dinner on the beach.

Sail among whales aboard the schooner *D'Sonoqua* with **Sea-Land Adventures**, *Castalia; tel: (506) 662-8997*, $70 full day including lunch, with a naturalist. Ask your innkeeper's advice before booking conventional whale-watches, since some cancel arbitrarily, too late to re-book elsewhere.

Grand Manan Museum, *Grand Harbour; tel: (506) 662-3524*, open Mon–Sat 1030–1630, Sun 1400–1700 (mid June–Sept), free, shows the island's unique geology, history (it was once part of the USA) and birdlife.

> ## SIDE TRACK
> ## TO DEER ISLAND AND CAMPOBELLO ISLAND
> **Tourist Information: Provincial Information Centre, International Bridge**, *tel: (506) 752-7043*, open daily 0900–1900 (May–mid Oct), or **Campobello Chamber of Commerce**,

242

Welshpool, Campobello, NB E0G 3H0; tel: (506) 752-2233.

From Letete, 13 km from St George via Rte 772, a ferry takes cars to **Deer Island**, daily every half hour 0700–2200 (July–Aug), 0700–2100 (Sept–June), free. From there, **East Coast Ferries**, *tel: (506) 747-2159*, continues to **Campobello Island**, seven return crossings daily (July–Aug), six daily (June, Sept), $11 car and driver, $2 passengers, $16 maximum. From there, a bridge crosses to **Lubec, Maine** and US Rte 1 (via Rte 189).

On the ferry between Deer Island and Campobello, you may pass **The Old Sow**, the world's largest tidal whirlpool, which you can also view from a tent pitch at **Deer Island Point Camping Park**, *tel: (506) 747-2423*. Campobello Island is best known for **Roosevelt Campobello International Park**, *Rte 774; tel: (506) 752-2922*, open daily 1000–1800 (May–mid Oct), free, last tour 1645. US President Franklin Roosevelt spent childhood summers at this large rustic cottage, set in splendid gardens.

Drive to **East Quoddy Head Lighthouse**, the most photographed in eastern Canada, and look for whales from its high cliffs. **Cline Marine**, *tel: (506) 747-0114*, departs Head Harbour daily 1000 and 1500 (mid June–Sept), for whale-watch cruises, $38 adult, $15 child. ▣

ST ANDREWS

Tourist Information: St Andrews Welcome Centre, *46 Reed Ave, St Andrews, NB E0G 2X0; tel: (506) 529-3000*, open daily 0900–2000 (July–Aug), 0900–1800 (May, Sept). Advance information on the entire route: **Quoddy Coastal Tourism Association**, *P.O. Box 446, St Andrews, NB E0G 2X0; tel: (506) 529-4677*.

ACCOMMODATION

St Andrews has been a resort since the Canadian Pacific Railroad connected it to the rest of Canada and built the elegant **Algonquin Hotel**, *184 Adolphus St, St Andrews, NB E0G 2X0; tel: (506) 529-8823* or *(800) 563-4299*, expensive. The full-service resort offers two golf courses, outdoor heated pool, tennis, lawn croquet, a health club and a dining room, expensive.

The remarkable restoration of the nearly-in-ruins **Hiram Walker Estate Heritage Inn**, *109 Reed Ave, St Andrews, NB E0G 2X0; tel: (506) 529-4210*, moderate–expensive, into one of Canada's showpiece inns is a story you'll want to hear over afternoon tea (with lemon bars). Its rooms are tasteful and classy. Don't miss dinner, by reservation only.

For well kept budget–moderate rooms, stop at **Picket Fence Motel**, *102 Reed Ave (P.O. Box 424), St Andrews, NB E0G 2X0; tel: (506) 529-8985*, open May–Oct. In the centre of town, at **Treadwell Inn**, *129 Water St, St Andrews, NB E0G 2X0; tel: (506) 529-1011*, moderate, you can overlook the harbour from antique-furnished rooms. Caravan or tent at **Passamaquoddy Park**, *P.O. Box 116, St Andrews, NB E0G 2X0; tel: (506) 529-3439*.

EATING AND DRINKING

Chef's Cafe, *180 Water St; tel: (506) 529-8888*, open 24 hrs daily (June–Aug), moderate, Canada's oldest restaurant, makes terrific fish and chips. For lobster, overflowing fisherman's platter and harbour views, choose **Lighthouse Restaurant**, *Water St; tel: (506) 529-3082*, moderate. **L'Europe**, *48 King St, tel: (506) 529-3818*, open May–Sept, moderate, has a German/continental menu.

SHOPPING

One of the pleasures of St Andrews is browsing in studios and shops on *Water St* and Market Wharf, where you'll find **Cottage Craft Ltd**, *tel: (506) 529-3190*, selling handmade cardigans, jumpers and traditional Fundy fisherman guernseys made by local knitters. **Katy's Cottage**, *171 Water St;*

243

tel: (506) 529-4770, carries home décor items, including table linens.

SIGHTSEEING

At least two of the homes that line the trim streets were disassembled and brought on ships from Maine by Loyalists. Find these with *A Guide to Historic St Andrews*, free at the Welcome Centre. **Heritage Discovery Tours**, *Town Wharf; tel: (506) 529-4011*, $15, conducts lively history tours of the town and nature tours of the intertidal shore.

Choose boat tours at kiosks along Market Wharf or reserve at the Welcome Centre. Sail aboard the classic yacht *Cory, tel: (506) 529-8116*, or conventional tour boat with **Quoddy Link Marine**, *tel: (506) 529-2600*. **Fundy Tide Runners**, *tel: (506) 529-4481*, watches bird and marine life up close, on a high-speed Zodiac.

St Andrews Blockhouse National Historic Site, *Water St; no tel*, open daily 0900–2000 (June–Aug), 0900–1700 (early Sept), adults $1, children free, is among 12 built along the coast in the War of 1812. **Ross Memorial Museum**, *188 Montague St; tel: (506) 529-1824*, open Tues–Sat 1000–1600 and Sun 1330–1600 (July–Aug), Tues–Sat 1000–1630 (late May–June, Sept–mid Oct), donation, is filled with antiques and decorative arts. **Sheriff Andrews House**, *King and Queen Sts; tel: (506) 529-5080*, open daily 0930–1630 (July–mid Oct), free, restored to 1820, has period rooms and beehive ovens.

Ministers Island Historic Site, *Bar Rd; tel: (506) 529-5081*, open daily at low tide (June–mid Oct), open by tour only, $2.50–5, is across a sand-bar, which is under 3 m of sea at high tide. Sir William Van Horne, whose summer home, huge barn and stone bathhouse are seen, was president of the Canadian Pacific Railway.

Meet the King of Fish eye-to-eye at the **Atlantic Salmon Centre**, *Rte 127; tel: (506) 529-1084)*, open daily 1000–1800 (June–Aug), Thur–Mon 1000–1700 (Sept),

$1. The **Huntsman Aquarium Museum**, *Brandy Cove Rd; tel: (506) 529-1202*, open daily 1000–1800 (July–Aug), shorter hours other seasons, $2.50–3.50, $10 family, has a 'Please Touch' aquarium, with starfish and lobsters; feeding time for the seals is at 1100 and 1600.

Katy's Cove has a beach in a protected bay, and the Algonquin's heated pool is open to the public, as is the **Algonquin Golf Club**, *tel: (506) 529-3062*, $36–40. **Seascape Kayak Tours**, *tel: (506) 529-4866*, rents equipment and runs guided trips with full instruction. Sign up for deep-sea fishing with **St Andrews Bay Sport Fishing**, *Market Wharf; tel: (506) 529-8196 or (888) 808-FISH*, three trips daily, $50 adult, $30 under age 16.

ST STEPHEN

Tourist Information: Provincial Information Centre, *Rte 1, St Stephen, NB E3L 2W9; tel: (506) 466-7390*, daily 0800–2100 (May–Aug), 0900–1900 (Sept–mid Oct).

St Stephen faces Calais, Maine, across the St Croix River, so close they seem like one town. They celebrate their long-standing friendship early each Aug with an **International Festival**. **Ganong Chocolate Factory Store**, *73 Milltown Blvd; tel: (506) 465-5611*, sells 100 kinds of chocolates, with 'blems' at bargain prices.

At **Crocker Hill Studios**, *Ledge Rd; tel: (506) 466-4251*, open daily 1000–1500 (mid May–mid Oct), free, stroll in terraced herb gardens overlooking the river, where eagles, ospreys and hummingbirds are common.

Blair House, *38 Prince William St (P.O. Box 112), St Stephen, NB E3L 2W9; tel: (506) 466-2233*, includes full English breakfast in the budget–moderate range. Outdoor enthusiasts appreciate **Loon Bay Lodge**, *Rte 745 (P.O. Box 101), St Stephen, NB E3L 2W9; tel: (506) 466-1240 or (888) LOON-BAY*, high moderate, overlooking the St Croix River, with canoeing, fishing, trails and wildlife.

ST STEPHEN–
BAR HARBOR/ACADIA

Most travellers quickly drive the 136 miles between Calais and Bar Harbor to reach the scenery and attractions of Acadia National Park on the 108-square-mile Mt Desert (pronounced 'dessert' by the locals) Island, the third largest island on the US Atlantic coast.

Mt Desert Island gives fresh meaning to the hoary tourism phrase, 'the rocky coast of Maine'. The island is shaped like a lobster claw divided by Somes Sound, the only natural fjord on the US East Coast. It is a region of great natural beauty with occasional enclaves of human activity. The eastern half includes Bar Harbor, the major shopping, dining and lodging town, as well as Northeast Harbor, where the rich rebuilt their 'cottages' after the apocalyptic fire of 1947. The 'quiet side' is west of the sound, anchored by Southwest Harbor, which struggles to maintain its fishing village identity. More than 1 million people visit the 41,000-acre Acadia National Park each year. From Bar Harbor, it is an easy six-hour ride by car ferry to Yarmouth, Nova Scotia.

245

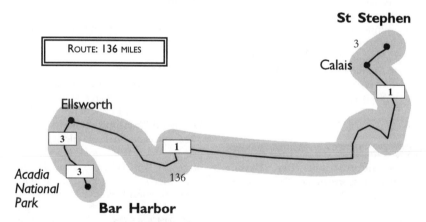

ROUTE: 136 MILES

St Stephen

Calais

Ellsworth

Acadia National Park

Bar Harbor

ROUTE

From Rte 3 in St Stephen, cross through Customs to Rte 1 in Calais, Maine, USA. Continue south on Rte 1 for 116 miles through Machias, Jonesport and Gouldsboro to Ellsworth, where a well-marked left turn connects to Rte 3 south to Bar Harbor, 20 miles.

BUSES

There is no direct service from St Stephen to Bar Harbor, but SMT make two trips a week from St Stephen to Bangor. Journey time: 2 hrs. Vermont Transit operate a seasonal service from Bangor to Bar Harbor. See OTT table 517.

CALAIS TO BAR HARBOR

This drive along the Passamaquoddy Bay recapitulates views from the Canadian side, then passes through spruce and blueberry barrens as the road turns inland at Perry, en route to **Machias**, where the first naval battle of the American Revolution took place in 1775.

The **Burnham Tavern Museum**, *Main St, Machias; tel: (207) 255-4432*, open 0900–1700 Mon–Fri (mid June–Sept), US$2, chronicles the encounter amid Revolutionary-era furnishings. On the third weekend of Aug, the **Machias Blueberry Festival** combines a craft fair with athletic, artistic and blueberry-baking and eating events.

Continue 6 miles to **Jonesport** and **Beals Island**, fishing communities picturesque in their authenticity; they stonily ignore tourists and have almost no amenities. In **Gouldsboro**, a half-mile turnout leads to a tour and tasting of fruit and honey wines at **Bartlett Maine Estate Winery**; *tel: (207) 546-2408*, open Sat 1000–1700 and Sun 1200–1700 (May), Tues–Sat 1000–1700, Sun 1200–1700 (June–mid Oct). Rte 3 intersects Rte 1 in 23 miles.

BAR HARBOR

Tourist Information: Bar Harbor Chamber of Commerce, *93 Cottage St, P.O. Box 158, Bar Harbor, ME 04609; tel: (207) 288-5103*, open daily 0800–1700 (mid May–mid Oct), 0800–1630 (mid Oct–mid May); **information booth**, *Marine Atlantic Terminal, Bar Harbor; tel: (207) 288-2404*, open 0900–2300.

WEATHER

July–Aug daytime highs reach the low–mid 80°sF, evenings cool to mid 50°s and

lower. Autumn temperatures range into the 60°s for daytime highs, the low 40°s at night. Radio station WDEA (1370 AM) broadcasts marine weather every half hour and provides a weather phone; *tel: (207) 667-8910*.

ARRIVING AND DEPARTING

By Air
Hancock County Airport; *tel: (207) 874-8300*, is 12 miles from Bar Harbor. **Colgan Air**; *tel: (207) 667-7171 or (800) 272-5488*, provides daily service between Bar Harbor and Boston.

By Ferry
Bay Ferries, *Hull Cove Terminal, 121 Eden St, Bar Harbor; tel: (207) 288-3395*, operates a car and passenger ferry that makes the 6-hr cruise to Yarmouth, Nova Scotia (see p. 307), which saves 1017 km of driving. For fares and departure times, see p. 308.

By Bus
Bar Harbor is served mid June–early Sept from Boston by **Greyhound/Vermont Transit**; *tel: (207) 772-6587*.

GETTING AROUND

Bar Harbor is best navigated on foot, as parking, while free, is scarce (June–Oct). RV parking is allowed only in designated areas. **Downeast Transportation**; *tel: (207) 667-5796*, provides free shuttle bus service (late June–early Sept) from Agarmont Park in central Bar Harbor to Sieur de Monts, Sand Beach and Blackwoods campsite in Acadia National Park.

ACCOMMODATION

Chain hotels: *BW, DI, HI, Ma, QI*. Bar Harbor has the largest concentration and greatest variety of lodgings on Mt Desert Island. Motels along Rte 3 have the lowest rates. Prices range from the (barely) budget to the outlandishly pricey, with most inns, larger motels and Bed and Breakfasts at the dividing line between moderate and expensive. Many places require a three-day minimum stay (July–Aug); reservations essential. Most lodgings close mid Oct–mid May.

About a 15-min walk north of town, **Edenbrook Motel**, *Rte 3, 96 Eden St, Bar Harbor, ME 04609; tel: (207) 288-4975* or *(800) 323-7819*, was the first motel in Bar Harbor (1953) and is well-kept with modern amenities, moderate. Almost adjacent, **The Atlantic Eyrie**, *Highbrook Rd, Bar Harbor, ME 04069; tel: (207) 288-9786* or *(800) HABA-VUE*, has an eagle's-eye view of Frenchman Bay and offers some self-catering suites, expensive.

Within a 5-min walk south of town are **Cadillac Motor Inn**, *336 Main St, Bar Harbor, ME 04609; tel: (207) 288-3831;* and **Cromwell Harbor Motel**, *359 Main St, Bar Harbor, ME 04609; tel: (207) 288-3201* or *(800) 544-3201*. *Holland Ave*, a side street at the edge of town, offers other moderate options: **Aurora Motel**, *51 Holland Ave, Bar Harbor, ME 04069; tel: (207) 288-3771* or *(800) 841-8925;* and **Higgins Holiday Motel**, *43 Holland Ave, Bar Harbor, ME 04069; tel: (207) 288-3829* or *(800) 345-0305*.

Bed and Breakfasts occupy the remaining grand cottages built by the wealthy in the late 19th century along *West St* and *Mt Desert St*, including **Kedge**, *112 West St, Bar Harbor, ME 04069; tel: (207) 288-5180* or *(800) 597-8306*, expensive; **Manor House Inn**, *106 West St, Bar Harbor, ME 04069; tel: (207) 288-3759* or *(800) 437-0088*, moderate–expensive; and **Mira Monte Inn**, *69 Mt Desert St, Bar Harbor, ME 04609; tel: (207) 288-4263* or *(800) 543-7842*, expensive, with its grand overgrown gardens. The Victorian showpiece **Holbrook House**, *74 Mt Desert St, Bar Harbor, ME 04069; tel: (207) 288-4970*, features the perfect porch on which to enjoy a summer day and breakfast in a delightful sun room, moderate–expensive.

Close to the Acadia Visitors Centre is **Bar Harbor Campground**, *RFD#1, Box 1125 (Rte 3), Bar Harbor, ME 04609; tel: (207) 288-5185.*

EATING AND DRINKING

Bar Harbor has the widest selection of dining. **Acadia Restaurant**, *62 Main St; tel: (207) 288-4881*, has sandwiches and locally favoured fish chowder in low-rent ambience, budget. **Jordan's**, *80 Cottage St; tel: (207) 288-3586*, serves breakfast 0500–1400. Excellent breakfasts and good casual food are the order at **Cottage Street Bakery and Deli**, *59 Cottage St; tel: (207) 288-3010.*

Locals favour **West Street Café**, *West and Rodick Sts; tel: (207) 288-5242*, for a quintessential Downeast meal of fish chowder, french fries, lobster and blueberry pie; budget–moderate. Simple seafood fried or steamed is the strength of **Fisherman's Landing**, *West St dock; no tel;* dine inside a protected area or out on the waterfront deck.

Lompoc Café & Brewpub, *36 Rodick St; tel: (207) 288-9392*, has homemade beers and British ales on tap along with slightly pretentious bar food; budget–moderate. For more conventional pub grub and good beers made on the premises, try **Maine Coast Brewing Company Tap Room & Grill**, *21A Cottage St; tel: (207) 288-4914*, budget. For bold cooking, the best bet is the moderate **Porcupine Grill**, *123 Cottage St; tel: (207) 288-3884*. For perhaps too much of a good thing, sample the lobster ice-cream at **Ben & Bill's Chocolate Emporium**, *80 Main St; tel: (207) 288-3281.*

Markets are readily available. **Don's Shop'n'Save**, *86 Cottage St, Bar Harbor; tel: (207) 288-3621*, is the island's most complete food centre. For gourmet groceries and excellent sandwiches, try the **J.H. Butterfield Co.** market, *152 Main St, Bar Harbor; tel: (207) 288-3386.*

Communications

The main post office in Bar Harbor is at *55 Cottage St*, open Mon–Fri 0800–1700, Sat 0900–1200; *tel: (207) 288-3122.*

247

ENTERTAINMENT

Acadia Weekly is a free guide to Acadia National Park schedules, entertainment, activities and events throughout Mt Desert Island.

Criterion Theatre, *35 Cottage St; tel: (207) 288-3441*, has been restored to its 1932 art deco elegance – but with a Dolby Stereo Surroundsound system for films; rainy day matinees at 1400. **Acadia Repertory Theatre** performs in summer and winter in *Masonic Hall, Rte 102, Somesville; tel: (207) 244-7260*. **Bar Harbor Music Festival**, *The Rodick Building, 59 Cottage St, Bar Harbor; tel: (207) 288-5744*, performs recitals, chamber music, pops and orchestral concerts (early July–early Aug).

Outdoor Activities

A state licence is required for freshwater fishing – available at town offices in Bar Harbor and other communities and at most hardware stores. Saltwater fishing requires no licence. Originally established for croquet, **Kebo Valley Golf Club**, *Eagle Lake Rd; tel: (207) 288-5000*, is more than 100 years old; the 18-hole PGA championship course is open to the public.

The **Shore Walk** is an under-utilised mile-long pathway along the edge of Frenchman Bay and past some grand summer cottages in Bar Harbor; the path begins near Agarmont Park at the town pier. **Bar Island** lies about a quarter of a mile off shore from Bar Harbor, but is accessible for two hours before and after low tide at the foot of *Bridge St (Bridge* and *West Sts)* via the sandbar that gave the town its name.

Bar Harbor Bicycle Shop, *141 Cottage St; tel: (207) 288-3886*, rents mountain bikes and accessories. **Acadia Outfitters**, *106 Cottage St; tel: (207) 288-8118*, rents bicycles, canoes and sea kayaks and offers guided sea kayak tours. **Acadia Bike & Coastal Kayaking**, *48 Cottage St; tel: (207) 288-9605* or *(800) 526-8615*, rents mountain bikes, Old Town canoes (the local brand)

and touring kayaks; they also offer a guided sunrise bicycle descent of Cadillac Mountain and guided sea kayak tours. **National Park Sea Kayak Tours**, *137 Cottage St; tel: (207) 288-0342*, offers half-day tandem kayak tours. **Harbor Boat Rentals**, *1 West St; tel: (207) 288-3757*, provides 13- and 17-ft Boston whalers.

Bird-watching tours at different proficiency levels can be booked with **Down East Nature Tours**; *tel: (207) 288-8128*.

SHOPPING

Souvenir shops of all levels of taste (or lack thereof) line *Cottage* and *Main Sts*. **The Blueberry Patch**, *7 Main St; tel: (207) 288-2131*, has locally made gifts and souvenirs a cut above the usual. Some galleries and craft shops feature local artists, including **Island Artisans**, *99 Main St; tel: (207) 288-4214*. **Sherman's Book & Stationery Store**, *56 Main St; tel: (207) 288-3161*, proffers a good selection of books of local interest. Superb estate jewellery and other artefacts of the art nouveau and art deco periods are offered at **Albert Meadow Antiques**, *10 Albert Meadow; tel: (207) 288-9456*, open daily June–Sept. A full and well-priced line of outdoor gear is found at **Acadia Outdoors**, *45 Main St; tel: (207) 288-5592*.

SIGHTSEEING

Narrated tour buses jockey for parking along *Main St* near the Bar Harbor Town Pier, including **Jolly Roger's Trolley**, US$10, which passes some of the mansions and takes in Cadillac Mountain summit in one hour, and the 2½-hr **National Park Bus Tour**, US$15. Tickets are sold at Testa's Restaurant, *53 Main St*.

A better and less expensive choice for more autonomous touring is the **Acadia Tape Tour**, with directions covering a 56-mile driving tour of *Park Loop Rd* and Northeast Harbor, available at Hulls Cove Visitor Centre; US$9.95 rental, US$12.95 purchase. **A Step Back in Time**: A

Walking Tour of Victorian Bar Harbor; *tel: (207) 288-9605,* offers an alternative approach to the wealthy village, US$10.

Wildlife-watching cruises – for whales, seals and puffins – leave from the Holiday Inn Marina, the Bluenose Ferry Terminal and the Town Pier, with prices ranging US$15–30. **Frenchman Bay Company**, *1 West St; tel: (207) 288-3322,* offers a wide variety. For graceful windjammer sail or motor yacht cruising, contact **Historic Vessels**, *27 Main St; tel: (207) 288-4585* or *(207) 288-2373,* US$16–20. **Coastal Cruises**, *137 Cottage St; tel: (207) 288-3886,* offers 2-hr sail cruises on a Friendship sloop; US$20.

Natural History Museum, *College of the Atlantic, Turrets Building, Rte 3; tel: (207) 288-5015,* open daily 0900–1700 (mid June–early Sept), 1000–1600 (early Sept–mid Oct), has exhibits of plant and animal life on the island and a self-guided nature trail, US$2.50. Visit **St Saviour's Church**, *41 Mt Desert St; tel: (207) 288-4215,* to see the magnificent collection of 42 stained-glass windows, including ten by Tiffany.

ACADIA NATIONAL PARK

Tourist Information: Acadia National Park Headquarters, *Rte 233, near northern edge of Eagle Lake, P.O. Box 177, Bar Harbor, ME 04609; tel: (207) 288-3338,* serves as the park's Visitor Centre (Nov–Apr). **Hulls Cove Visitor Center**, *just off Rte 3 at head of Park Loop Rd,* open 0800–1630 (May–June, Sept–Oct), 0800–1800 (July–Aug), has an introductory film, maps of roads and trails and a schedule of ranger-led programmes. General park information; *tel: (207) 288-3338;* for naturalist activities and reservations; *tel: (207) 288-5262.* Admission to Acadia National Park: automobile pass 1 day US$5, 4 days US$10, annual pass US$20, foot or bicycle pass 4 days US$3.

ACCOMMODATION

There are more than 500 woodland camp pitches in Acadia National Park, but no RV utility hook-ups. **Blackwoods Campground**, *6 miles east of Bar Harbor on Rte 3,* has 310 pitches, which must be reserved in advance (mid June–mid Sept) by telephone only: **Destinet**; *tel: (800) 365-2267.* **Seawall Campground**, 4 miles south of Southwest Harbor on Rte 102A, has more than 200 pitches on a first-come, first-served basis.

Jordan Pond House, *Park Loop Rd, Acadia National Park (near Seal Harbor); tel: (207) 276-3316,* is renowned for afternoon tea on the lawn; dinner is budget–moderate.

GETTING AROUND

Acadia National Park covers much of Mt Desert Island, touching on every municipality. The most-used route, however, is the **Park Loop Rd**, a 27-mile scenic road through the most visited areas of Acadia on the eastern lobe of the island. Another 57 miles of carriage roads wander through the eastern section of Acadia. The carriage roads are open to hikers, horse riders and (except in privately owned sections) bicyclists. Autos are banned. Roads and carriage roads are open to cross-country skiing in the winter (skiers must share park roads with snowmobiles).

SIGHTSEEING

Horse-drawn carriage tours of Acadia's carriage roads – a superior alternative to narrated bus tours – are available from **Carriages in the Park**, *Wildwood Stable, Acadia National Park; tel: (207) 276-3622,* US$12–15.

Park Loop Rd offers a sampler of the coast and interior of Mt Desert Island and is the most accessible way to visit. Highlights include: **Sieur de Monts Spring**, with a Nature Centre and wildflower gardens; **Sand Beach**, swimming beach with 54°F water (at its warmest); **Thunder Hole**, where wave motion and hollow rocks create thunderclaps at a three-quarter rising tide with rough seas,

249

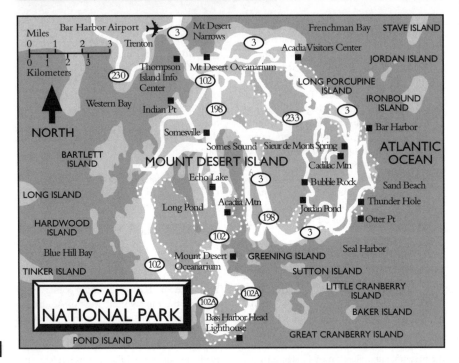

Miles
0   1   2   3

0   1   2   3
Kilometers

Bar Harbor Airport ✈
Mt Desert Narrows
Frenchman Bay   STAVE ISLAND
Trenton   (3)
(3)
Acadia Visitors Center
JORDAN ISLAND
Thompson   Mt Desert Oceanarium
(230)   Island Info   (102)
Center
LONG PORCUPINE ISLAND
Western Bay   Indian Pt   (198)
IRONBOUND ISLAND
(233)   (3)
NORTH
Somesville ■   ■ Bar Harbor
BARTLETT ISLAND
Somes Sound   Sieur de Monts Spring ■   **ATLANTIC OCEAN**
MOUNT DESERT ISLAND   Cadillac Mtn
Echo Lake   (3)   ■ Bubble Rock   Sand Beach
LONG ISLAND   Long Pond   Acadia Mtn   Jordan Pond   ■ Thunder Hole
(198)   (3)   ■ Otter Pt
HARDWOOD ISLAND   (102)
Blue Hill Bay   (102)   Mount Desert ■   GREENING ISLAND   Seal Harbor
TINKER ISLAND   Oceanarium
SUTTON ISLAND
ACADIA NATIONAL PARK   (102A)   (102A)   LITTLE CRANBERRY ISLAND
Bass Harbor Head   BAKER ISLAND
Lighthouse
POND ISLAND ■   GREAT CRANBERRY ISLAND

250

but otherwise much ado about nothing; **Otter Cliff**, with pounding surf and wonderful waves; **Otter Point**, with superb tidepooling at low tide; **Jordan Pond House**, once a farm, now a tea house and beautiful gardens; and **Bubble Pond** and the **Bubble Erratics**, easy hiking from the 'Bubbles' parking lot or difficult climbing from Jordan Pond to see geological anomalies.

Cadillac Mountain, at the end of a 3.5-mile road, is the island's highest peak with 360-degree views. **Blue Hill Parking Lot** is a great vantage for sunsets. **Champlain Mountain** is where peregrine falcons nest (May–Aug).

Park Loop Rd will not satisfy those seeking uncrowded wilderness experiences. But Acadia has more than 120 miles of hiking trails, which radiate from strategically placed parking lots and scenic overlooks. The western side of Acadia is less visited and also has

outstanding hiking, especially the **Acadia Mountain loop hike**, 2.5 easy miles overlooking Somes Sound and small islands. Park on the west side of Rte 102 at Echo Lake, 3 miles south of Somesville, and pick up the trailhead across the road.

To experience Acadia in greater depth, take advantage of the broad variety of free ranger-led programmes, which include natural history walks and the exceptionally good series of photographic workshops and hikes led by a Kodak representative. See the *Beaver Log* handout at the Visitors Centre for schedule.

Abbe Museum, *Sieur de Monts Spring, Acadia National Park; tel: (207) 288-2179,* open 1000–1600 (May–June and Sept–Oct), 0900–1700 (July–Aug), has exhibits and artefacts of Maine Amerindians, US$2. An auxiliary location on *Mt Desert St, Bar Harbor,* is planned for opening in mid 1999.

SAINT JOHN– FREDERICTON

Three routes lead from Saint John to Fredericton, one direct and uninspiring, one along the scenic west bank of the wide Saint John River and a third across a series of long bays and almost-islands by ferry before crossing the main river and continuing up its western bank to Fredericton. The latter routes are filled with rolling green landscapes set against wide expanses of water, and both pass through the attractive old riverside settlement of Gagetown. The province's capital, Fredericton, is a lively, comfortable city with a wealth of historic attractions.

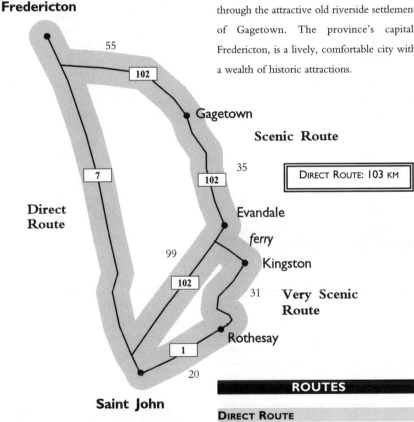

Fredericton

55

102

Gagetown

Scenic Route

DIRECT ROUTE: 103 KM

35

102

7

Direct Route

Evandale

ferry

99

Kingston

102

31 **Very Scenic Route**

Rothesay

1

20

Saint John

ROUTES

DIRECT ROUTE

Depart Saint John on Hwy 1 west, turning north onto Hwy 7, about 7 km from the bridge toll station. Follow

Hwy 7 all the way to **Fredericton**, a distance of 103 km, about one hour.

SCENIC ROUTE

▪▪▪▶ For the land route along the western bank of the Saint John River, follow the direct route onto Hwy 7, leaving it at Westfield (Exit 80). Follow Rte 102 through **Gagetown** to Fredericton.

VERY SCENIC ROUTE

▪▪▪▶ The ferry route leaves Saint John on Hwy 1 heading east to **Rothesay** (if you begin this route at the Saint John Airport in Loch Lomond, go directly to Rothesay on Rte 111). Go west to **Gondola Point**, following Rte 100, then Rte 119. Cross Kennebecasis Bay on the ferry, following Rte 845 east to **Kingston**, and Rte 850 to the ferry over Belleisle Bay. Rte 124 leads to the third ferry, to **Evandale** on Rte 102, where you head north to **Gagetown** and on to **Fredericton**. These free ferries shuttle back and forth, so waiting times are minimal.

BUSES

SMT operate a service along the direct route twice daily. Journey time: 1½ hrs. See OTT table 235.

SAINT JOHN TO GAGETOWN

If you begin at the Saint John Airport or wish to stay outside the city, **Shadow Lawn Country Inn**, *3180 Rothesay Rd (P.O. Box 41), Rothesay, NB E2E 5A3; tel: (506) 847-7539 or (800) 561-1466*, high moderate, is right on the way. Stylish rooms are matched by the excellent menu in its restaurant, moderate. Rothesay, still a wealthy community, is filled with other fine Victorian mansions.

Rte 845 snakes up and down the rolling hills of the peninsula to **Kingston**, settled by Loyalists during the American Revolution. The **Anglican Church** and **Rectory** are two of several fine examples of architecture from the late 1700s. Surrounding the

Kingston Peninsula are the Long Reach of the Saint John River, its tributary the Kennebecasis and Grand Bay, where they come together.

After the third ferry, Rte 102 follows the broad river past fertile farmlands, orchards and tiny riverport communities to the largest of these, Gagetown.

GAGETOWN

Tourist Information: Gagetown Tourist Office, *Front St; tel: (506) 488-3306*, open Wed–Sun 0900–1900 (mid June–mid Sept).

You find a record of Gagetown's colonial past and its days as an important stop for the river steamers that were once the lifeblood of the province at **Queen's County Tilley House Museum**, *tel: (506) 488-2966*, open daily 1000–1700 (mid June–mid Sept), Sat–Sun 1300–1700 (mid Sept–mid Oct), adults $1, children $0.25, and at **Queens County Courthouse** (1836), same hours. More fine 19th-century architecture lines the streets. Reserve ahead for a **Village of Gagetown Walking Tour**, *tel: (506) 488-2903*.

Gagetown is filled with craft studios and art galleries. Stop at **Acacia Gallery**, *Front St; tel: (506) 488-1119*, open daily 1100–1800 (mid May–mid Oct), which represents more than 20 artists, and at **Loomscrofters**, *tel: (506) 482-400*, open Mon–Sat 1000–1700, Sun 1400–1700 (May–Oct), in a 1761 trading post, for hand-woven clothing.

Steamers Stop Inn, *Front St (P.O. Box 155), Village of Gagetown, NB E0G 1V0; tel: (506) 488-2903*, moderate, blends the atmosphere of its riverboat days with modern conveniences. Antiques vie for attention with riverfront views, and canoes, kayaks and a dock are for guests' use. The dining room, moderate, serves old-fashioned favourites and contemporary seafood, by reservation only.

FREDERICTON

Tourist Information: City Hall Visitor Information Centre, *397 Queen St (P.O. Box 130), Fredericton, NB E3B 4Y7; tel: (506)*

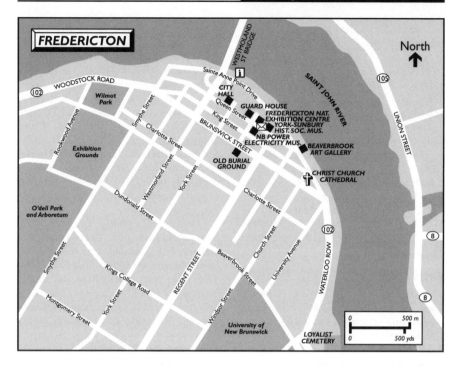

452-9508, open daily 0800–2000 (mid June–Aug), daily 0800–1630 (mid May–mid June, Sept–mid Oct), Mon–Fri 0815–1630 (Oct–May), or **Visitor Information Centre**, *Hwy 2, near Exit 289 (Hanwell Rd); tel: (506) 458-8331 or (506) 458-8332,* open daily 0800–2000 (July–Aug), 0900–1700 (mid May–June, Sept–mid Oct).

ACCOMMODATION

As the capital city, Fredericton has plenty of rooms, including *BW, CI, HJ, Kd* and *Sh.* Most centrally located is the **Lord Beaverbrook Hotel**, *659 Queen St (P.O. Box 545), Fredericton, NB E3B 5A6; tel: (506) 455-3371 or (800) 561-7666,* high moderate, overlooks the river in the centre of the business district. The Terrace, budget–moderate, serves well-prepared dependables, and the pricey Governor's Room serves a smart new menu. There is a large indoor swimming pool, with Jacuzzi, sauna and games room.

Carriage House Inn, *230 University Ave, Fredericton, NB E3B 4H7; tel: (506) 452-9924 or (800) 267-6068,* low moderate, is on a street lined with elegant homes. Antiques and a hearty breakfast add to its appeal. Convenient to Trans-Canada Hwy 2, the **City Motel**, *1216 Regent St, Fredericton, NB E3B 3Z4; tel: (506) 450-9900,* low budget, has nicely furnished rooms. **York House Youth Hostel**, *193 York St, Fredericton, NB E3B 5A6; tel: (506) 454-1233,* open July–Aug, low budget, also downtown, is a dormitory, with a kitchen and cheap meals available.

EATING AND DRINKING

For special occasions, Frederictonians choose the terrace bistro at the **Sheraton Inn**, *225 Woodstock Rd; tel: (506) 457-7000,* with up-to-date entrées and decadent desserts.

Cafe du Monde, *610 Queen St; tel: (506) 457-5534,* budget–moderate, serves pastas and well-styled seafood in a contemporary atmosphere; open for three meals daily. In the next block, **The Barn**, *540 Queen St; tel: (506) 455-2742*, budget–moderate, serves traditional Acadian and continental French dishes, plus seafood. Almost next door is **Schade's**, *536 Queen St; (506) 450-3340*, budget–moderate, with a German and middle European menu.

The Diplomat, *253 Woodstock Rd; tel: (506) 454-2400*, budget–moderate, serves Canadian and Chinese dishes 24 hours daily and a Chinese buffet at lunch and dinner.

Go to **Boyce Farmers' Market**, *George St (between Regent and St John Sts); tel: (506) 451-1815*, open Sat 0600–1300, for picnic provisions, or lunch.

ENTERTAINMENT

The **Theatre New Brunswick**, *Playhouse, Queen St; tel: (506) 458-8344*, is the city's resident stage company (Aug and Oct–May). **Calithumpians**, *Officers Sq.; tel: (506) 452-9616*, Mon–Fri 1230, Sat–Sun 1400, free, blend history with humour in an outdoor theatre. **Band concerts**, Tues and Thur at 1930 in *Officers Sq.*, free, include marching, military or pipe bands. **Maritime music concerts** are held at the adjacent lighthouse.

SIGHTSEEING

Older than the province itself, Fredericton was settled three centuries ago, growing quickly with the arrival of Loyalists fleeing American colonies. Its long history and riverside setting give it an air of gentility; its residents make it one of Canada's most hospitable cities. The detailed *Fredericton Visitor Guide* includes a self-guided walking tour; while in the Visitor Centre, get a free Tourist Parking Pass. Also free are guided historical walking tours by costumed **Calithumpians**, *City Hall; tel: (506) 452-9616*. River tours on the *Bradside, tel: (506) 461-0633*, give good views of the lovely riverside mansions.

In the centre of everything is **Officers Square**, *Queen St*, once the military parade ground, where **Changing of the Guard** takes place, Tues–Sat 1100 and 1900 (July–Aug). **York-Sunbury Historical Society Museum**, *tel: (506) 455-6041*, is in the 1839 officers quarters for the British garrison. Open Mon–Sat 1000–1800 and Sun 1200–1800 (May–early Sept), Mon and Fri until 2100, Sun 1200–1800 (July–Aug), shorter hours other seasons, $0.50–1, $2.50 family. **Soldiers' Barracks and Guard House**, *Queen and Carleton Sts; tel: (506) 453-3747*, open daily 1000–1800 (June–Aug), free, has a room restored to its 1827 origins and a military history museum.

Salvador Dali's *Santiago El Grande* is the most famous piece in the **Beaverbrook Art Gallery**, *703 Queen St; tel: (506) 458-8545*, open Mon–Fri 0900–1800, Sat–Sun 1000–1700 (July–Aug), closed Mon and shorter hours rest of year, $1–3, but it has respectable collections that include paintings by Gainsborough, Reynolds, Constable and Turner and prominent Canadian artists, and period rooms from the 1500s–1800s.

Follow the **River Walk** from downtown to **Christ Church Cathedral**, *Brunswick St; tel: (506) 450-8500*, open Mon–Fri 0900–2000, Sat 1000–1700, Sun 1300–1700, tours free, built in 1845, one of the continent's best examples of decorated Gothic style, and the first new cathedral founded on British soil since 1066. The fine façades of **Waterloo Row** mansions face the river just beyond.

An arboretum of native trees, some over 400 years old, is located in **Odell Park**, *Rookwood Ave; tel: (506) 452-9500*, open daily 0700–2200, free, and reached by a 2.8-km walking trail with interpretive signs. For hikers, the park offers 16 km of trails. The adjacent **Fredericton Botanic Garden**, *Prospect St W.*, has nature trails through its emerging gardens. You can rent bicycles at **Radical Edge**, *Queen St; (506) 459-3478*, rent kayaks or canoes to explore the river at **Small Craft Aquatic Centre**, *Woodstock Rd; tel: (506) 462-6021*, where you can also take lessons or join a tour.

254

FREDERICTON–
RIVIÈRE-DU-LOUP

The Saint John River Valley cuts a swath through New Brunswick from the Maine and Québec borders to the Bay of Fundy. On the way, it flows under the world's longest covered bridge, over jagged cliffs at Grand Falls and through a gorge below. Downstream it widens out, passing the open-air historical museum at King's Landing before reaching Fredericton. This route follows it upstream, past wide vistas of growing vegetables and yellow grains on the low hills above its banks.

Rivière-Du-Loup

108

185

St-Jacques

65

2

11

New Denmark

Grand Falls

24

Plaster Rock

40

109

37

Perth-Andover

ROUTE: 398 KM

60

Hartland

2

25

Woodstock

Campbellton–
Moncton
p. 227

100

Fredericton

255

ROUTE

Leave Fredericton via *Regent St* or *Hanwell Rd*, travelling west on Hwy 2 (the Trans-Canada Hwy) to the Québec border at **St-Jacques**. There the route number changes to 185 to **Rivière-du-Loup**. From Fredericton to **Grand Falls**, Hwy 2 mainly follows the western bank, crossing when the river becomes the international boundary between the USA and Canada. At **Perth-Andover**, an optional side track travels through wooded highlands to **Plaster Rock** and **New Denmark**, rejoining Hwy 2 and the river at Grand Falls.

An alternative, Rte 105, leaves Fredericton on the opposite shore, which it follows as far as Grand Falls; you can skip back and forth across bridges evenly spaced along the way. The scenery is about equal, with longer vistas from the higher Hwy 2 and closer, more intimate river scenes from Rte 105.

The distance from Fredericton to the Québec border is 290 km; Rivière-du-Loup (see p.252) is 108 km further on.

BUSES

SMT operate one trip a day (at 0350) from Fredericton to Rivière-du-Loup, via Woodstock, Hartland, Grand Falls and Edmundston. Journey time: 7 hrs 10 mins. There is also a daily service at 1120, which stops at Woodstock and Edmundston. Journey time: 6 hrs. See OTT tables 235 and 227.

FREDERICTON TO HARTLAND

Mactaquac Hydro Generating Station, and the dam that created its headpond, are directly responsible for several attractions west of Fredericton. The **Generating Station**, *tel: (506) 363-3071,* open 0900–1600 (mid May–Aug), free, outfits visitors in hard hats and goggles to see the turbines at work. At the **Mactaquac Fish Culture Station**, *tel: (506) 363-3021,* open daily 0900–1600 (tours mid May–Aug), free, you can see live salmon being sorted into breeding pools and learn about their migrations.

Mactaquac Provincial Park, *Rte 105 (Trans-Canada Exit 274), Mactaquac, NB E0H 1N0; tel: (506) 363-3011,* open daily 0800–dusk (mid May–mid Oct), admission $3.50 per car, stretches along the dam's vast impound. Not surprisingly, water sports

are its speciality, with two supervised beaches, a marina and fishing. Nature trails, 0.3–2.4 km in length, explore marshland, forests and a beaver pond; some have interpretive maps. An 18-hole golf course offers equipment rental; three campsites provide over 300 tent pitches and caravan sites, usually full, since this is among the most heavily used parks in the province. A restaurant is in the *BW,* inside the park.

Woolastook Park, *5171 Trans-Canada Hwy 2, Upper Kinsclear, NB E3E 1P9, tel: (506) 363-5410,* open daily 0900–2100 (July–Aug), 0900–1700 (mid May–June and Sept), beach admission $2, also has a large campsite and a restaurant, plus beach, amusement park, water slides and a miniature golf course.

King's Landing Historical Settlement, *Hwy 2 Exit 259; tel: (506) 363-5090,* open daily 1000–1700 (June–mid Oct, admission $5.50–8.75, $23 family, is another spin-off from the dam. Before the rising waters submerged the vast area of riverside settlements, historians chose the best examples of each architectural style and assembled them at this open-air museum.

These original buildings span the period 1790–1910. Interpreters 'live' in the houses and work in the water-powered saw and grist mills and in the Sash and Door Factory (where a vintage 'one-lung' motor operates machinery from 1909). You will need a day to see everything here, but half a day allows time for the highlights: the **Jones House** with stencilled floors, the **Ingraham House** and its stunning garden, the **Victorian Perley House** and the **Joslin Farm** with its back-bred livestock. Demonstrations of early crafts and skills are regular fare. At the **King's Head Inn**, moderate, you can lunch on corn chowder and other traditional foods, and you'll find quality souvenirs and books at the well-stocked museum shop.

Chicadee Lodge, *Prince William, NB E0H 1S0; tel: (506) 363-2759* (May–Nov) or *(506) 363-2288* (Dec–Apr), budget–low moderate, is a log-built Bed and Breakfast in manicured lawns overlooking the river, which guests can explore in the lodge's canoes.

While Hwy 2 swings away from the river, Rte 105 stays close to its shore, through **Woodstock**, whose tree-shaded streets of Victorian buildings you can tour with a map from the **Visitors Centre**, *220 King St (at the bridge), Woodstock, NB E7M 1Z8; tel: (506) 325-9049,* open daily 0900–2000 (late June–Aug). The **Old Carleton County Court House**, *19 Court St, Upper Woodstock; tel: (506) 328-9706,* open daily 0900–1200, 1300–1800 (July–Aug), admission by donation, is a museum of historic crafts, including needlework.

Stiles Motel and Hometown Restaurant, *827 Main St, Woodstock, NB E0J 2B0; tel: (506) 328-6671,* both moderate, offer well-kept rooms and a menu filled with home-style dishes, well prepared. They are rightly known for their home-baked breads and pies. To see inside one of the fine homes, opt for **The Queen Victoria Bed & Breakfast**, *133 Chapel St, Woodstock, NB E0J 2B0; tel: (506) 328-8382,* low moderate, where rooms are furnished in Victorian antiques and bric-a-brac.

(Rte 95 leaves Hwy 2 here for the border crossing into Houlton, Maine, USA.)

HARTLAND TO GRAND FALLS

At **Hartland**, leave Hwy 2 and drive down (it seems straight down) to the **Hartland Covered Bridge**, the world's longest at an amazing 391m, which you can cross. The highway also crosses the river here, and you can rejoin it on the other side. A 33.5-km walking trail has river views and benches.

Along both sides of the river, rich, rolling farmlands stretch to the horizon in neat rows of potatoes, waves of ripening grain and green hillsides studded with weathered barns and grazing cattle. To learn more about this way of life, stay in the homely farmhouse at

Campbell's Bed & Breakfast, *Rte 105 north (R.R. 1), Hartland, NB E0J 1N0; tel: (506) 375-4775,* budget, where beds are covered in handmade quilts (more are for sale) and guests prepare their own breakfasts from a selection of farm-fresh provisions. North of **Florenceville**, in an idyllic riverbank setting, **River Country Campground**, *R.R. 2, Florenceville, NB E0J 1K0; tel: (506) 278-3700,* has tent pitches and caravan sites on an open grassy bank shaded by white birches; open May–Sept, $15–17. The beach, canoe rentals and river tours are open to the public.

Perth-Andover stretches along the riverbank, with a promenade and small shops, including **Mary's Bakery**, a good stop for raspberry pie or fresh-from-the-oven tea biscuits. On the opposite bank, a **Farmers' Market**, *tel: (506) 273-4939,* open Sat 0900–1700 (June–Sept), sells local produce and crafts. Take Hwy 2 or, for river views, Rte 105; it's 35 km by either road to **Grand Falls**.

The name says it all; through the middle of town the river drops over jagged rocks that whip it into a white froth, then rushes down through a rocky gorge where it has worn giant potholes. Two viewing platforms, a trail and stairs to the potholes give different perspectives of the river's dramatic descent, or you can take a **boat tour** of the gorge, *La Rochelle Visitor Centre, Centennial Park; tel: (506) 475-7788,* late May–mid Oct, $4–8. There is a *BW* in Grand Falls.

257

⤺ SIDE TRACK
TO PLASTER ROCK

Just north of Perth-Andover, the Tobique River joins the Saint John, and Rte 109 follows this famous fishing river into the mountains to **Plaster Rock**. The road immediately begins its steady climb through thick forests, with frequent glimpses down onto the river.

Plaster Rock is a centre for fishing and other outdoor activities, and you can get information on these at the **Tourist Park**, *Box 129, Plaster Rock, NB E0J 1W0; tel: (506) 356-6077*, open daily 0900–2000 (mid June–Aug), where there is also a campsite, $12–14, pool and trails around a small lake. You can easily recognise it by the giant fiddlehead fern (a local delicacy in spring) and the wooden lumberman in his canoe.

Next to the Tourist Park are the modern cottages of **Settler's Inn**, *141 Main St, Plaster Rock, NB E0J 1W0; tel: (506) 356-9000*, moderate, with full kitchens, screened porches, laundry and free swimming and tennis. The coffee shop serves light meals. **Tobique River Tours**, *Riley Brook; tel: (506) 356-2111*, rents canoes and provides transportation for canoeists.

From Plaster Rock, Rte 108 leads back to Hwy 2 and **Grand Falls** via **New Denmark**, the largest Danish colony in North America, set in the heart of scenic farmland. You can learn about the history of the community at **New Denmark Memorial Museum**; *tel: (506) 553-6724*, variable hours, which has a collection of tools, dolls and Danish porcelain, as well as an immigrant house.

Nyborg's Bed & Breakfast, *Foley Brook Rd, New Denmark, NB E0J 1T0; tel: (506) 553-6490*, budget, is less than 1 km from Rte 108. This area is particularly brilliant in the fall, when the foliage turns red and orange. 🔺

GRAND FALLS TO ST-JACQUES

At the falls, the river becomes the international boundary, and Hwy 2 moves to the east bank until **Edmundston**. The free **Musée du Madawaska**, with excellent displays of local history and culture, includes the **Tourist Information Centre**, *Blvd Hebert (Trans-Canada Hwy 2 Exit 18), Edmundston, NB E3V 1J6; tel: (506) 737-5064*, open daily, 0800–2000 (June–Aug). Lodgings

here include *CI* and *HJ*, and the outstanding **Auberge La Fief**, *87 Church St, Edmundston, NB E3V 1J6; tel: (506) 735-0400, fax: (506) 735-0401*, moderate, with beautifully furnished rooms and a dining room serving elegant French dinners.

The **Edmundston Golf Club**, *Victoria St; tel: (506) 735-4831*, open 0700–1800 (mid June–mid Oct), $65, is an 18-hole course in the heart of the city. **Eagle Valley Adventures**, *tel: (506) 992-2827* or *(888) 26-CANOE*, open June–Sept, from $60, operates 4-hr nature and historical tours in motorised canoes.

(In the centre of Edmundston, a bridge crosses into Madawaska, Maine, USA, and another border point at nearby **Clair** leads to Fort Kent, Maine.)

In **St-Jacques**, 7 km north, stop at **The New Brunswick Botanical Garden**, *Trans-Canada Hwy 2 Exit 8; tel: (506) 735-3074*, open daily 0900–dusk (June–mid Oct), $2.25–4.75, where over 7 hectares of themed gardens include collections of roses, lilies and alpine plants, as well as water and shade gardens. A café, **L'Oasis**, serves budget lunches on a terrace overlooking the gardens.

ST-JACQUES TO RIVIÈRE-DU-LOUP

At the Québec border, Trans-Canada Hwy 2 changes to Rte 185. On the right is **Tourisme Québec**, *1373 Rte 185, Dégelis; tel: (514) 873-2015* or *(800) 363-7777*, open daily 0800–1900 (late June–Aug), 0900–1700 (late May–late June, Sept–mid Oct), where you should get the very useful *Bas-St-Laurent Tourist Guide* with a fold-out map.

Rte 185 travels along scenic Lac Temiscouata, where a stop in **Cabano** is interesting for **Fort Ingall**, *81 Rue Caldwell; tel: (418) 854-2375*, open daily 0930–1800 (June–Oct), $3–6, built by the British in 1839 to protect the Portage Trail from the St Lawrence River. Adjacent to the reconstructed fort is **Roseraie du Temiscouata**, with over 250 rose varieties.

MONCTON–
CHARLOTTETOWN

Prior to mid 1997, travelling the direct route distance between these two cities necessitated a 45-min car-ferry crossing of the Northumberland Strait. Now you go zippity-zip via the world's longest continuous multi-span bridge, Prince Edward Island's first roadway link to mainland Canada. Same bridge, same convenience if you opt for a scenic alternative through Acadian meadows and wetlands in south-eastern New Brunswick, followed by portions of Prince Edward Island's coastal Blue Heron Drive.

Direct Route

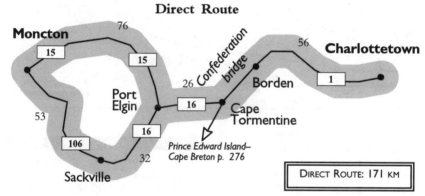

Moncton 76
15
15
26 *Confederation bridge*
56 **Charlottetown**
Borden 1
Port Elgin
16
Cape Tormentine
53
16
106
32 *Prince Edward Island–Cape Breton p. 276*
Sackville

DIRECT ROUTE: 171 KM

259

Scenic Route

ROUTES

DIRECT ROUTE

From downtown Moncton, head east on Rte 15 past **Dieppe** and the airport. You'll soon be driving through **Robichaud, Cap–Pelé, Shemogue** and **Murray Corner**, followed by a short inland swing south to **Port Elgin**, where Rte 15 meets the Trans-Canada Hwy (also connecting with PEI–Cape Breton, see p. 276). Take it eastbound to **Cape Tormentine**, 102 km from Moncton, for access onto the 12.9-km **Confederation Bridge**, thus crossing the strait and arriving at **Borden-Carleton** on

Prince Edward Island. Crossing the bridge into PEI is toll-free. Taking the bridge *back* to New Brunswick costs $35.50.

Continue 56 km west on the Trans-Canada Hwy, passing Crapaud and Cornwall and into PEI's capital city.

SCENIC ROUTE

Add about 20 km to the New Brunswick portion of your drive by taking Rte 106 south from Moncton through francophone **Chartersville, Saint-Anselme** and **Fox Creek** along the Petitcodiac River. This roadway brings you to **Memramcook** and **Saint-Joseph** in the Memramcook

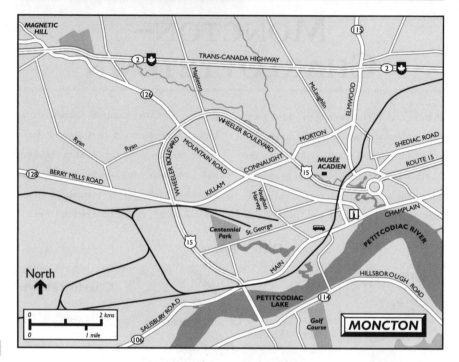

MAGNETIC HILL

TRANS-CANADA HIGHWAY

Mapleton

Ryan

Ryan

WHEELER BOULEVARD

MOUNTAIN ROAD

WHEELER BOULEVARD

BERRY MILLS ROAD

KILLAM

CONNAUGHT

Vaughan Harvey

MORTON

MUSÉE ACADIEN

McLaughlin

ELMWOOD

SHEDIAC ROAD

ROUTE 15

CHAMPLAIN

Centennial Park

St. George

PETITCODIAC RIVER

North

MAIN

HILLSBOROUGH ROAD

SALISBURY ROAD

PETITCODIAC LAKE

Golf Course

MONCTON

0   2 kms
0   1 mile

Valley. From there, via **Dorchester** and **Frosty Hollow**, traversing the Tantramar Marshes and passing Acadian-made *aboiteaux* dikes, you reach **Sackville**, 53 km from Moncton. Connect onto the Trans-Canada Hwy for a 58-km drive via **Aulac** to **Cape Tormentine** and the bridge.

Promptly after departing **Borden**, exit the Trans-Canada Hwy for some PEI shoreline motoring on the sign-posted Blue Heron Drive – first on Rte 10 via **Cape Traverse** to **Tryon**, then Rte 116 to **Victoria**, from there on Rtes 19-19A through **Argyle Shore**, **Canoe Cove** and **New Dominion**. You'll get back to the highway at **Cornwall**, 10 or so km west of the capital.

BUSES

SMT run a daily afternoon service from Moncton to Charlottetown and a morning service on Fri, Sat and Sun. Journey time: 3 hrs. See OTT table 230.

MONCTON

Tourist Information: Moncton Visitor Information Centre, *City Hall, 655 Main St, Moncton, NB E1C 1E8; tel: (506) 853-3590*, open daily 0900–1700 (extended hours mid May–early Sept). The city is on the **VIA Rail** network.

ACCOMMODATION AND FOOD

Chains in metro Moncton/Dieppe include *BW, CI, EL, Hd* and *TL*, plus *CP*'s expensive, centrally located **Hotel Beauséjour**, *750 Main St, Moncton, NB E1C 1E6; tel: (506) 854-4344* or *(800) 441-1414* (toll-free). Also central, but moderate and with historic ambience: **Canadiana Inn**, *46 Archibald St, Moncton, NB E1C 5H9; tel: (506) 382-1054*. Five-room **Bonnacord House**, *250 Bonnacord St, Moncton NB E1C M56; tel: (506) 388-1535*, and **Victoria Bed & Breakfast**, *71 Park St, Moncton, NB E1C*

2B2; tel: (506) 389-8296, are two of several moderate, in-town Bed and Breakfasts.

Moncton's best for Canadian/Acadian cuisine is **Le Chateau à Pape**, 2 Steadman St; tel: (506) 855-7273, moderate–pricey. Meals are moderate in an amiable setting at **Garden Breeze Restaurant**, 502 Kennedy Dr.; tel: (506) 855-0564. In nearby Cap-Pelé, **Fred's** is budget–moderate and family-style, Cap-Pelé; tel: (506) 577-4269.

SIGHTSEEING

Just off the Trans-Canada Hwy (or north-west from downtown via Mountain Rd), **Magnetic Hill** is Canada's third most visited natural attraction. Turn off your vehicle's motor, put the gearshift in neutral, take your foot off the brake and roll backward uphill by some mystical (i.e. illusionary) force; $2 per car. This is part of a family amusement layout, including mini-golf, 'water theme park' and Wharf Village shops, tel: (506) 853-3516, open daily 1000–1700 (June–early Oct).

The twice-daily 25-ft rise of the Petit-codiac River's water level is connected to the **Tidal Bore**, an incoming river-wide wave generated by the Bay of Fundy's tides – the world's highest. It's a slow-motion, hour-long occurrence; get each day's tide schedule from the Visitor Centre. View from Bore Park, King/Main St intersection.

Le Musée Acadien, Université de Moncton, Wheeler Blvd; tel: (506) 858-4088, is a key to appreciating Moncton's historic importance as a centre of Acadian culture (35% of New Brunswickers have this French heritage). Quotidian Acadian life is presented in themes: kitchen, textiles, carpentry, folk art, blacksmithing, fishing, agriculture, open Mon–Fri 1000–1700, Sat–Sun 1300–1700 (June–Sept), shorter off-season hours, free.

MONCTON TO CAPE TORMENTINE

If it's summertime and you've decided upon the direct route from Moncton to Cape Tormentine, **Cap-Pelé** has a sandy beach off

Rte 15: **Plage L'Aboiteau** – and in **Murray Corner** you can work on a suntan at larger **Murray Beach Provincial Park**.

SACKVILLE

Tourist Information: Sackville Information Centre, 6 King St, Sackville, NB E0A 3C0; tel: (506) 364-0431, daily 0800–2000 (July–Aug), 0830–1630 (Sept–Dec).

ACCOMMODATION AND FOOD

Marshlands Inn, 59 Bridge St, Sackville, NB E0A 3C0; tel: (506) 536-0170, one of New Brunswick's best, exudes 19th-century grace and charm, moderate. For a budget Bed and Breakfast: **The Harbourmaster's House**, 30 Squire St, Sackville, NB E0A 3C0; tel: (506) 536-0452. East of town and recommendable for its waterfront site and German-style meals is **Little Shemogue Country Inn**, RR2, Hwy 955, Port Elgin, NB E0A 2K0; tel: (506) 538-2320, moderate, .

Borden's Restaurant, 100 Bridge St; tel: (506) 536-1066, is appealing for breakfast, lunch or dinner. Also moderate and with an outdoor patio is **Vienna Coffee House & Restaurant**, 32 York St; tel: (506) 536-0409.

SIGHTSEEING

Stroll on the nature trail and elevated board-walk in Sackville's 55-acre **Waterfowl Park**, East Main St. It extends 3 km into the Tantramar Marsh's habitat for geese, ducks and other feathered friends. The park's flora and fauna is covered in an illustrated pamphlet, free from the information centre.

Outside Aulac, **Fort Beauséjour**, Trans-Canada Hwy Exit 550A; tel: (506) 536-0720, was a French stronghold during the Seven Years War, culminating in the 1759 fall of Québec City and British dominance in North America. Four years previously, this star-shaped citadel's defenders surrendered to Redcoats under the command of Lt Col Robert Monckton, explaining why the region's biggest city is called Moncton; open daily 0900–1700 (early May–mid Oct), $1.

261

BORDEN TO CHARLOTTETOWN

Tourist Information: Borden-Carleton Gateway Village, at the northern end of the bridge, is a well-stocked information centre, open daily 0800–2200 during early summer, 0900–2100 (mid Aug–early Sept), 0900–1700 other periods. For advance planning, contact **Tourism PEI**, *P.O. Box 940, Charlottetown, PEI C1A 7M5; tel: (902) 368-4444* or *(888) 734-7529.*

ACCOMMODATION AND FOOD

If you forgo much of the Trans-Canada Hwy in favour of the Blue Heron Drive en route to Charlottetown, staying awhile on the southerly shore might be tempting. Consider the moderate **Orient Hotel**, *Main St, Victoria, PEI C0A 2G0; tel: (902) 658-2503* or *(800) 565-ORIENT*, a heritage inn, including **Mrs Proffitt's Tea Room** (lunch and dinner in addition to traditional mid-afternoon 'cuppa'). Also moderate is the **Victoria Village Inn**, *P.O. Box 1, Victoria, PEI C0A 2G0; tel: (902) 658-2483*, with its budget–moderate **Artist's Retreat Café**.

Victoria's **Sea Winds**, *tel: (902) 658-2200*, is a steak and seafood restaurant overlooking the Northumberland Strait. Home cooking makes the village's **Landmark Café**, *Main St; tel: (902) 658-2286*, a pleasing choice for lunch or dinner. Both moderate. Cappuccino and desserts are served at **Island Chocolates Company**, *Main St; tel: (902) 658-2320*, a maker of Belgian-type chocolate goodies.

Moderate weekly rates pertain to 1-, 2- and 3-bedroom housekeeping lodgings with Amherst Cove frontage at **Ferryview Beach Cottages**, *RR 1, Borden-Carleton (Cape Traverse), PEI C0B 1X0; tel: (902) 437-6061* or *(800) 244-5935*. Daily and weekly rates are moderate too at **Amy-Don Cottages**, *RR 1, DeSable (Argyle Shore), PEI C0A 1C0; tel: (902) 675-4737.*

Further inland, atop away-from-it-all Camelot Hill, **Strathgartney Country Inn**, *Bonshaw, PEI C0A 1C0; tel: (902) 675-4711* or *(800) 267-4407*, is an 1860s homestead turned into a Bed and Breakfast augmented by a dining room for evening meals. Cornwall, west of Charlottetown, abounds in budget–moderate lodgings, as well as shops, fast-food chains and petrol stations.

SIGHTSEEING

Victoria Playhouse stages summertime repertory productions in the village's circa-1912 community hall; *Main St; tel: (902) 658-2025* or *(800) 925-2025.*

Westmoreland's Emporium, *On the Wharf, Victoria; tel: (902) 658-2288*, stocks PEI crafts, books, preserves, souvenirs and whatnot, open daily (mid June–mid Sept). **Pottery by the Sea**, *Main St; tel: (902) 658-2653*, produces fine porcelain and stoneware pottery, open daily (May–Sept).

The **International House of Dolls**, *Trans-Canada Hwy, DeSable; tel: (902) 658-2449*, exhibits over 1500 of the cuties in national costumes and as nursery-rhyme characters. VIP doll: a wax damsel made by Madame Tussaud and dressed by royal collectress Queen Mary, open daily 1000–1630, Sun 1300–1630 (mid June–early Sept), adults $4, children under 18 $2.50, 12 and under $1.50; free admittance Tues, Thur.

The **Car Life Museum**, *Bonshaw; tel: (902) 675-3555*, is a collection of old farm machinery, carriages and automobiles, highlighted by a 1959 pink Cadillac once owned by Elvis Presley, open daily 0900–1900 (July–Aug), 1000–1700 (May and Sept), $4.

An operating lighthouse doubles as the **Victoria Seaport Lighthouse Museum**, *Water St, Victoria; tel: (902) 658-2602*, tracing this tidy village's nautical yesteryears. Harbour views are worth a climb to the top, open daily, except Mon, 1000–1700 (early July–early Sept), free.

Two south coastal public lands for picnics and swimming are **Victoria Provincial Park** and larger **Argyle Shore Provincial Park**.

CHARLOTTETOWN

Canada's smallest province has a proportionately small capital, where the central-city population barely nudges 16,000. But this low-key waterfront town played a big role in early national history. The 1864 Charlottetown Conference was the first time that delegates formally discussed the idea of uniting present-day Nova Scotia, New Brunswick, Ontario and Québec. Their talks and debates laid the groundwork for confederation three years later – bringing those four provinces together as the Dominion of Canada. (Independent-minded islanders didn't join in until 1873.)

This pint-size capital is also Prince Edward Island's cultural, commercial, culinary and entertainment hub. Settled as a fortified French outpost called Port La Joye in 1720, the city was named after George III's consort Queen Charlotte after France ceded the island to Britain under terms of the 1763 Treaty of Paris, which ended the French and Indian War in North America.

TOURIST INFORMATION

Charlottetown Visitor Information at *City Hall, 199 Queen St, Charlottetown, PEI C1A 4B7; tel: (902) 629-4116*, open daily 0800–1700 (July–Aug), 0830–1700 off season. For all-province information: **PEI Visitor Information Centre,** *Water St, Charlottetown, PEI C1A 7M5; tel: (902) 368-4444*, open daily 0800–2200 (July–Aug), 0930–1700 off season.

WEATHER

Expect July and Aug temperatures to reach 22°–24°C during daytime, occasionally climbing past 29°–32°C for a blast of mid-summer heat without excessive humidity. It averages a comfortable 8°–22°C from May to June, also throughout the autumn, with colourful foliage. In winter, expect windchill and snowfall; average -9° to -4°C readings might plunge to -11°C.

ARRIVING AND DEPARTING

By Air
PEI's airport is on Charlottetown's northern outskirts; *tel: (902) 566-7997*. It's a gateway for daily summer Air Canada flights from Toronto. Air Nova, Air Atlantic and Air Alliance fly to Charlottetown from various locales in Canada, also from the USA (usually via Halifax). The airport is 5–6 km from downtown; figure on about $6.75 for taxi fare.

By Boat
Northumberland Ferries Ltd., *P.O. Box 634, Charlottetown, PEI C1A 7L3; tel: (902) 962-2016* or *(888) 249-7245* (toll-free), operates a daily schedule of frequent 75-min car-ferry crossings between Wood Islands, PEI (61 km south-east of Charlottetown), and Caribou, Nova Scotia (early May–mid Dec). Fare each way is $35.50 per auto, plus $9.50 per passenger age 13–64, $5 for each child 5–12, under 5 free.

GETTING AROUND

Public Transport
Charlottetown Transit buses cover city-wide routes for $1.50 fare, with a $7 six-ticket book available; *tel: (902) 566-5664*.

263

Driving in Charlottetown

Reaching PEI's capital from New Brunswick entails crossing the **Confederation Bridge**, then continuing 56 km east from Borden-Carleton (see Moncton to Charlottetown, p. 259).

If you've already driven in Montréal or Toronto, Charlottetown's traffic will seem virtually invisible by comparison. The Trans-Canada Hwy (Rte 1) traverses the city via bridges spanning North and Hillsborough Rivers at the west and east edges of town.

Direct route driving distances to Charlottetown are 1199 km from Montréal, 1389 km from Ottawa. Perhaps surprisingly, the drive from Boston is shorter: 999 km.

If you plan on renting a car upon arrival, Avis, Budget, Hertz and Tilden InterRent have counters at the airport. Parking meters consume coins at the rate of $0.10 each 10 mins or $0.25 for 30 mins. Unmetered parking on side streets is usually plentiful. For long sojourns, consider a downtown garage: **Queen Parkade**, *Queen St* ($4.50 for 24 hrs), or **Pownal Parkade**, *Pownal St between Grafton and Richmond Sts* ($3.60 for 24 hrs).

Bicycles

Bike (and in-line skate) rentals are available hourly, daily or weekly at **Smooth Cycle**, *172 Prince St; tel: (902) 566-5530*. Also at **Fun on Wheels**, *Peake's Wharf; tel: (902) 368-7161*, which rents kayaks, too.

STAYING IN CHARLOTTETOWN

Accommodation

Chains in town and nearby are *BW, CI, HJ, QI* and *TL*. Also, on Coast Guard Wharf, *CP*'s slick and expensive–pricey **Prince Edward Hotel**, *18 Queen St, Charlottetown, PEI C1A 8B9; tel: (902) 566-2222 or (800) 441-1414*. Two nothing-fancy, moderate alternatives are **The Charlottetown**, *Kent and Pownal Sts, Charlottetown, PEI C1A 7K4; tel: (902) 894-7371 or (800) 565-RODD*, and **The Islander Motor Lodge**, *146–148*

Pownal St, Charlottetown, PEI C1A 7N4; tel: (902) 892-1217.

Several 19th-century heritage houses have been reborn as moderate–expensive Bed and Breakfasts, such as **Hillhurst Inn**, *181 Fitzroy St, Charlottetown, PEI C1A 1S3; tel: (902) 894-8004*. Nearby is the 1860s **Shipwright Inn**, *51 Fitzroy St, Charlottetown, PEI C1A 1R4; tel: (902) 368-1905*. In the National Historic District is a row of five Georgian-style buildings, now **The Inns on Great George**, *58 Great George St, Charlottetown, PEI C1A 4K3; tel: (902) 892-0606*.

For travellers touring PEI via camper vehicle, **Southport RV Park**, *20 Stratford Rd, Charlottetown (Stratford), PEI C1A 7B7; tel: (902) 569-2287 or (800) 565-5586*, has 85 sites alongside the Hillsborough River.

Eating and Drinking

Moderately priced seafood is inevitable on a maritime island. Choose the fish platter at **The Claddagh Room**, *131 Sydney St; tel: (902) 892-9661*, or chowder at **Kelly's**, *136 Richmond St; tel: (902) 628-6569*.

Meals are also moderate but more varied at French-influenced **Café Soleil**, *52 University Ave; tel: (902) 368-8098*, **Piece a Cake**, *119 Grafton St; tel: (902) 894-4585*, and **Off Broadway**, *125 Sydney St; tel: (902) 566-4620* (great crêpes; open for Sun brunch). Even picky eaters will like **Primrose**, *186 Prince St; tel: (902) 892-3257*, a budget–moderate family restaurant. **Peake's Quay Restaurant & Lounge**; *tel: (902) 368-1330*, is budget–moderate, too, and features waterfront panoramas from an upstairs deck. For Italian cuisine, try **Sirenella Ristorante**, *83 Water St; (902) 628-2271*.

Best for coffee and pastry on an umbrella-festooned terrace is **Café Diem**, *130 Richmond St; tel: (902) 892-0494*. Another central coffee-break choice is **Grabba jabba**, *137B Kent St; tel: (902) 892-3362*. Fatten up on Charlottetown's very own **Cows ice-cream**, *150 Queen St; tel: (902) 892-6969*, purveyed in a recycled 1810

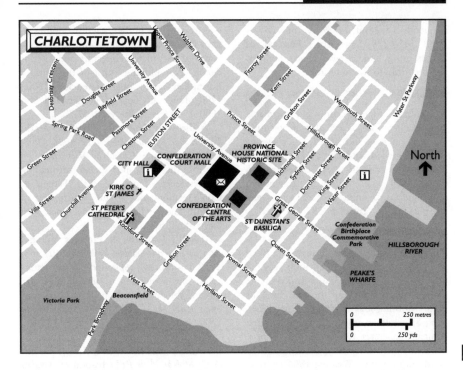

apothecary, where equally irresistible 'Cow-riginal' T-shirts and sweatshirts are for sale.

Communications

Charlottetown's central post office is at *135 Kent St; tel: (902) 628-4400.*

ENTERTAINMENT

Refer to the daily *Guardian* newspaper for what's-going-on updates; more of that is covered in the free *Buzz* tabloid. Numerous in-town eateries feature live jazz, blues, Celtic music, twangy Maritime country tunes and stand-up comedy. Two such venues are **Piazza Joe's Italian Bistro**, *189 Kent St; tel: (902) 894-4291*, and the **Island Rock Café**, *132 Richmond St; tel: (902) 892-2222*. **The Arts Guild**, *111 Queen St; tel: (902) 368-4417*, stages cabaret evenings. So does **Myron's** (which also has a billiard parlour), *151 Kent St; tel: (902) 892-4375*.

Dinner-theatre productions have caught on in PEI – locally at the **Charlottetown Hotel**; *tel: (902) 894-7371*.

Avant-garde movies are shown at **City Cinema**, *64 King St; tel: (902) 368-3669*. Harness racing is a century-old island passion: **Charlottetown Driving Park**, 2 km from downtown, *Kensington Rd; tel: (902) 892-6823*, $2, June–Sept.

Events

The **Charlottetown Festival** has been Atlantic Canada's standout event since its 1965 inception. The annual showpiece (mid June–early Sept) is a musical-comedy adaptation of Lucy Maud Montgomery's PEI classic *Anne of Green Gables,* in the Mainstage Theatre at the **Confederation Centre of the Arts**. There are also children's theatricals, choral music, outdoor concerts and CCA art exhibitions, plus a smaller-stage drama or musical in next-door **MacKenzie Theatre**. Reserve in advance for *Anne,* frequently a sell-out; *tel: (902) 566-1267* or *(800) 565-0278*. Late June's **Festival of Lights** brings buskers, musical acts, concerts and fireworks to the waterfront.

SHOPPING

Souvenirs, antiques, crafts, and inevitable *Anne of Green Gables* keepsakes are plentiful in shops on *Kent* and *Queen Sts, University Ave* and pedestrian-only *Richmond Row*. Stores galore cram tri-level **Confederation Court Mall**, entered from four downtown thoroughfares. Be mindful of PEI's 10% sales tax, plus the 7% Canadian GST (see p. 31).

SIGHTSEEING

Abegweit Sightseeing Tours; *tel: (902) 894-9966*, provides city orientation via a red double-decker London bus, boarded at the Confederation Centre of the Arts for 1-hr rides. Morning and afternoon tours June–Sept; $8, children under 12 $1. (The same company operates full-day North Shore/Anne of Green Gables excursions and 6-hr South Shore tours.) Wearing 1864-era outfits, members of the Confederation Players troupe conduct $2 one-hour **walking tours** through the city's historic centre; daily 1000, 1300 and 1500 (July–Aug). **Peake's Wharf Boat Cruises**, *Peake's Wharf; tel: (902) 566-4458*, gets landlubbers acquainted with Charlottetown's waterways and offers afternoon seal-watching tours; June–Sept.

Province House National Historic Site, *between Great George St and University Ave; tel: (902) 566-7626*, is the prime 'must-see' attraction. Charlottetown Conference attendees did their historic thing in this colonnaded structure, built in 1847, centred upon *Queen Sq.*, and still the seat of PEI's legislative government. Period furnishings embellish the Confederation Chamber and other rooms. Open daily 0900–2000 (July–Aug), 0900–1800 (June and Sept–mid Oct), Mon–Fri 0900–1700 rest of year, free.

Beaconsfield, *2 Kent St; tel: (902) 368-6600*, was constructed on a shipbuilder's

riverfront estate in 1877; worth visiting to see a mint-condition North American adaptation of Victorian architecture and interior décor exemplifying turn-of-the-century Edwardian tastes, open Tues–Sun 1000–1700 (June–early Sept), Tues–Fri and Sun 1300–1700 (rest of the year), $2.50.

Ardgowan National Historic Park, *Mt Edward Rd and Palmers Lane; tel: (902) 566-7050*. More Canadian Victoriana, in this case the landscaped spread surrounding the residence of one of PEI's 'Fathers of Confederation', due to his participation in the you-know-what conference. Open daily dawn–dusk, free.

Jewell's Gardens & Pioneer Village, *Hwy 25 in north-suburban York; tel: (902) 368-2538*, is a touristy, replicated pioneer settlement, plus a museum of antique glass and gardens abloom with fuchsias and begonias, open daily 0900–1800 (July–Aug), 0900–1700 (June and Sept), $3.75, under 13 free.

Three churches are in the city centre. **St Dunstan's Basilica**, *Great George St; tel: (902) 894-3486*, is PEI's bastion of Roman Catholicism, with fan vaulting and a rose window crafted in Germany. Presbyterian **Kirk of St James**, *Fitzroy and Pownal Sts; tel: (902) 892-2839*, has stained-glass windows from Scottish Iona, an early Christian site. Island architect William Critchlow Harris and his artist brother Robert collaborated on Victorian Gothic Revival-style All Souls' Chapel in Anglican **St Peter's Cathedral**, *Rochford St; tel: (902) 566-2101*.

OUT OF TOWN

Drive south from downtown to reach the **Fort Amherst/Port-La-Joye National Historic Site** overlooking Hillsborough Bay; *tel: (902) 672-6350*. The French established their outpost on this peninsular. Then came the larger English fort (surviving earthworks hint at its dimensions). Interpretive displays and a film presentation cover colonial yesteryears. Visitor Centre open daily 0900–1700 (mid June–early Sept), free.

EASTERN PRINCE EDWARD ISLAND LOOP

A signposted purple crown marks the Kings Byway Drive, following the contours of Queens and Kings counties. Attractions here include waterfront provincial parks and lighthouses, uncrowded sandy beaches, golf courses, clifftop lookouts and a long portion of the island's Confederation Trail pathway. Iron in PEI's soft sandstone produces rusty-reddish topsoil, backroads, rock formations and cliffsides.

You could make a curving, 456-km loop during a rushed day trip. Slower-paced vacationers prefer dividing their excursion into 'Sou'east' and 'Nor'east' segments.

267

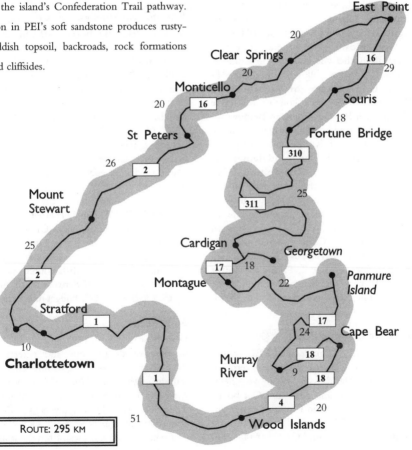

ROUTE: 295 KM

ROUTE

Cross the Trans-Canada Hwy bridge spanning the Hillsborough River on Charlottetown's east side. Zip through suburban **Stratford**. You'll soon be in south-coastal Queens County, where the Trans-Canada is signposted the Kings Byway Drive to **Wood Islands**, 61 km east of the capital. From that PEI/New Brunswick car-ferry town (for ferry details, see p. 263), continue 29 km on the scenic drive (now Rte 18 entering Kings County) that winds around the peninsula at **Cape Bear** (where, in 1912, the first distress signal telegraphed from the *Titanic* was heard), taking you westward to **Murray River**. Then head northbound via Rte 17 to **Panmure Island** to crossroads at **Montague**. If the mood strikes, detour 18 km east to **Georgetown** near the end of another peninsula. Otherwise choose Rte 4 directly out of Montague, followed by a Rte 311 swing to **Cardigan, St Georges** and **Dundas**, where you'll connect onto Rte 310 to reach Rte 2 at **Fortune Bridge**.

Cross the sand-bar causeway into **Souris**, where ferries cruise between PEI and Québec's **Îles de la Madeleine**; the distance from Souris to **East Point** is 29 km via Rte 16. Along the way, take in the sweeping sea vistas; watch for lupins growing wild in roadside gullies. Two-lane Rte 16 continues 60 km along PEI's north-eastern flank through **Clear Springs** and **Monticello** to bayside **St Peters**, where you'll 'rediscover' Rte 2. Take it to **Mount Stewart**, near the Kings County/Queens County line; stay southward for a 25-km drive back to Charlottetown.

TOURIST INFORMATION

Avail yourself of three coastal **PEI Visitor Information Centres**. At the ferry terminal in **Wood Islands**, *tel: (902) 962-2015*, phone ahead for mid May–mid Oct hours. On the eastern shore in **Pooles Corner**, *tel: (902) 838-0670*, open daily 0930–1700 (June and Sept–mid Oct), 0900–1900

(July–Aug). And further north on Rte 2 in **Souris**, *tel: (902) 687-7030*, open daily 0930–1700 (June, early Sept–mid Oct), 0900–1900 (July–Aug).

CHARLOTTETOWN TO MURRAY RIVER

Nearly the entire Kings Byway Drive along this stretch runs close enough to shore for panoramics encompassing coastal meadows, the Northumberland Strait and, on clear days, far-distant Nova Scotian promontories. Inland views are sure to include PEI potato patches and, at summer's height, 'U-pick' strawberry fields.

ACCOMMODATION AND FOOD

Artsy, moderate **Bayberry Cliff Inn**, *Rte 4, Little Sands, PEI C0A 1W0; tel: (902) 962-3395*, nestles amidst bayberry bushes at south-coastal cliff's edge. Budget–moderate farm stays can be prearranged in various parts of PEI, for instance **Wood's Farm Bed & Breakfast**, *RR 2, Orwell, PEI C0A 2E0; tel: (902) 651-2620*. Watch for vacancy signs outside cottages and Bed and Breakfasts. Especially attractive ones are in the Murray Harbour vicinity and on Point Prim's pastoral finger of land.

Rub shoulders with the locals at **Brehaut's**, *Rte 18, Murray Harbour; tel: (902) 962-3141*, budget–moderate. Or splurge in that village's moderate–pricey eatery, **Terrace Heights**, *Rte 348; tel: (902) 962-2465*. In Murray River, herb-flavoured potato soup is a must at **The Primrose Path**, *Main St; tel: (902) 962-3793*, budget–moderate.

SIGHTSEEING

Learn how folks in an 1895 agricultural community got things done and entertained themselves at **Orwell Corner Historic Village**, *Orwell; tel: (902) 651-2013*, open Mon–Fri 1000–1500 (mid May–mid June), Tues–Sun 0900–1700 (July–Aug), Tues–Sun 1000–1500 (early Sept–late Oct), $3.

Attain knockout views of terrain around

Hillsborough Bay by clambering to the lantern room inside 1895 **Point Prim Lighthouse**, PEI's oldest, *tel: (902) 659-2312*, open daily 0900–2000 (July–Aug), free (there's a budget chowder house just around the bend). PEI has craft shops like Australia has kangaroos. Island-made products fill **Wood Islands Handcraft Co-Op**, *Main St; tel: (962-3539)*. Same folksy bounty, plus Maritime artists' paintings, in Murray River's **Old General Store**, *Main St; tel: (902) 962-2459*.

Wine tasting in Atlantic Canada? Sure, at **Rossignol Estate Winery** on a Northumberland Strait headland, *Little Sands; tel: (902) 962-4193*, open Mon–Sat 1000–1700 (June–Oct). Murray River's wharf is the port for mid May–early Sept excursions featuring a harbour-seal colony, bird-watching and close-ups of mussel farms, with **Captain Garry's**, *Mill St, Murray River; tel: (902) 962-2494* or *(800) 561-2494*.

MONTAGUE AND GEORGETOWN

Tourist Information: The Station Hospitality Centre, *Station St, Montague, PEI C0A 1B0; tel: (902) 838-4778*, open daily 0900–1800 (early June–late Sept).

With stores, banks, post office, a fast-food hangout and the Down East Mall, Montague (population 2000) is Kings County's commercial hub. But the take-your-time island lifestyle prevails, and the harbour – deep inside an inlet – is a photo op.

ACCOMMODATION AND FOOD

For upmarket ambience, nothing beats **Rodd Brudenell River Resort**, *P.O. Box 67, Roseneath, PEI C0A 1G0; tel: (902) 652-2332* or *(800) 565-RODD*, in the riverbank park, which offers pro-calibre golf plus other activities, moderate–expensive. In town, try moderate **Windows on the Water Inn**, *106 Sackville St, Montague, PEI C0A 1R0; tel: (902) 838-2080*, a three-room harbourside property. Lunches and dinners are served in a

café with a wraparound deck. Also combining lodgings and three-meals-daily restaurant is the **Whim Inn**, *Pooles Corner, PEI C0A 1G0; tel: (902) 838-3838*, moderate.

SIGHTSEEING

For $15 you can go seal-watching from Montague as well as Murray River, here via **Cruise Manada**, *Montague Marina; tel: (902) 838-3444* or *(800) 986-3444*. Central Montague's **Garden of the Gulf Museum**, *2 Main St; tel: (902) 838-2467*, an 1887 sandstone landmark, chronicles local history, open Mon–Sat 1000–1700, Sun 1300–1700 (mid July–late Sept), $2.50. A Georgetown detour is worth the extra kilometres, thanks to the delightful **Georgetown Theatre Festival** (mid July–mid Sept); *tel: (902) 652-2053* or *(800) 803-1421*.

CARDIGAN TO EAST POINT

Take your pick of PEI's absolutely best beaches – particularly **Little Harbour**, **Basin Head**, **Red Point** and **South Lake**. Points of land poke into numerous bays that shelter little here-and-there fishing harbours.

269

ACCOMMODATION AND FOOD

Flowery gardens and stupendous country breakfasts characterise moderate **Woodlands Country Inn**, *Rte 311, Woodville Mills, PEI C0A 1G0; tel: (902) 583-2275* or *(800) 380-1562*. This part of the coast's niftiest full-fledged resort, including haute-cuisine dining, is moderate–expensive **Inn at Bay Fortune**, *Rte 310, Bay Fortune (Souris), PEI C0A 2B0; tel: (902) 687-3745*, in winter *(860) 296-1348*. All-day meal service, too, at the seaside **Ark Inn**, *Little Pond (Souris), PEI C0A 2B0; tel: (902) 583-2400*, moderate. The moderate **Platter House** eatery overlooks Souris's causeway and Colville Bay, *Rte 2; tel: (902) 687-2764*.

SIGHTSEEING

Upper Kings County's vital inshore fishing livelihood gets its due at the **Basin Head**

Fisheries Museum, *off Rte 16 from Kingsboro; tel: (902) 357-2966*, open Mon–Fri 1000–1500, Sat–Sun 1000–1900 (mid June–Sept), $3. The boardwalk stairway descends to sublime Singing Sands Beach. **East Point Lighthouse** blinks atop a bluff at PEI's northeastern-most extremity, where tides of the Northumberland Strait and Gulf of St Lawrence meet. For nature-trekking, set foot on the **Trails at Spry Point** (map obtainable at the Ark Inn) and/or **Sailor's Hope Bog**, accessed from Howe Bay. Villagers hoot 'n' holler during their **Rollo Bay Fiddle Festival**, (mid July).

SIDE TRACK TO MAGDALEN ISLANDS (ÎLES-DE-LA-MADELEINE)
Tourist Information: Association Touristique des Îles-de-la-Madeleine, *C.P. 1028, Cap-aux-Meules, Îles-de-la-Madeleine, PQ G0B 1B0; tel: (418) 986-2245.*

CTMA car ferries make 5-hr crossings between Souris and Cap-aux-Meules, (Apr–Jan); *tel: (902) 687-2181* (Souris), *tel: (418) 986-6600* (Cap-aux-Meules), adults $33 one-way, children 5–12 $16.50, under 5 free.

This off-shore tidbit of Québec province, 134 km from Souris's ferry terminal, is an archipelago consisting mainly of six islands in the Gulf of St Lawrence, interconnected by sand dunes. It became controversial for the late Feb hunting of newborn, adorably white-coated harp seal pups. But the 15,000 Madelinot islanders have much to offer in other seasons, including their scenically undulating landscape, bird-watching, close-to-nature recreation and Acadian-influenced cuisine. Their 'trademark' dish is *pot-en-pot,* flaky-crusted seafood pie.

Make tiny **Cap-aux-Meules** your base; the archipelago's attractions are easily reachable by car or bicycle. A terrific beach, **Grande-Échouerie**, is on

Grosse-Île; another is **Dune de la Sud** on **Île du Havre aux Maisons**. **L'Étang-du-Nord** is a picture-postcard fishing port on the western shore of **Île du Cap aux Meules**. **La Grave** has handicraft boutiques and a summer theatre.

NORTH COAST

Tourist Information: Bays and Dunes Tourist Association, *Rte 2, Morell; tel: (902) 961-3323*, open Mon–Sat 0900–2100, Sun 1100–1900 (mid June–mid Aug).

Commercial and chartered fishing boats chugging out of North Lake haul in bluefin tuna, often exceeding 1000 pounds. White buoys sprinkled over St Peters Bay mark the 'mesh stockings' where millions of PEI's prized blue mussels mature. North along the bay, vegetation and wildlife thrive amidst the Greenwich Dunes. And PEI's biggest marshlands ecosystem fringes the Hillsborough River's headwaters at Mount Stewart.

ACCOMMODATION AND FOOD

Though choices are rather scant up this way, you'll pass the usual cottages and Bed and Breakfasts – also an occasional motel – around the Morell, Cable Beach, Naufrage, North Lake and Savage Harbour townships. Slim pickin's restaurant-wise, too. One stellar exception is the pinewood-decorated, organic-devoted **Carousel**, *Rte 16, Clear Springs; tel: (902) 687-4100*, moderate.

SIGHTSEEING

For more than a century, the Prince Edward Island Railway connected 121 stations across the province. That vanished clickety-clacking is remembered in the **Elmira Railway Museum**, *Rte 16A, Elmira; tel: (902) 357-2481*, open daily 0900–1700 (mid June–early Sept), $1.50. The trackbeds have been redeveloped as the **Confederation Trail**. One 69-km stretch, ideal for bicycling (snowmobiling, too), runs from Elmira south to Mount Stewart. **Cycle East** rentals are available at the museum.

270

WESTERN PRINCE EDWARD ISLAND LOOPS

Much can be covered unhurriedly on an island measuring only 5656 square km, slightly smaller than Devonshire or Delaware. From Charlottetown, a series of leisurely loops – offering opportunities to tailor your explorations – lead you through the rural countryside of PEI's central Queens and western Prince counties.

Prince County Route

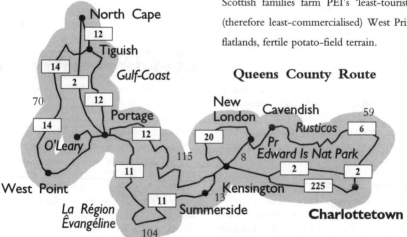

The first loop dallies along the Gulf of St Lawrence shore and Blue Heron Drive, a signposted scenic drive, with bay and estuary indentations, boat docks, Prince Edward Island National Park and various sites connected with *Anne of Green Gables* creator Lucy Maud Montgomery. Further west, Acadian influences are apparent, especially along windswept coastlines carved out of red sandstone cliffs. Ancestral Acadian, Irish and Scottish families farm PEI's 'least-touristed' (therefore least-commercialised) West Prince flatlands, fertile potato-field terrain.

271

Queens County Route

ROUTES

QUEENS COUNTY ROUTE

From Charlottetown, go 18 km north on Rte 2 to **Tracadie Cross**; turn onto narrower Rte 219 for a westward drive past

Donaldston, **Corran Ban** and **Grand Tracadie**, thus reaching the east-end access to **Prince Edward Island National Park**. Visit it now or bypass it by heading onto Rte 6 (you'll come upon five additional park entrances). Opting for Rte 6 brings you to **Brackley Beach** after 13 km, then across the wooden **Wheately River Bridge** to reach **The Rusticos**, followed by 5 km to intensely touristed **Cavendish**, and another 13 km via **Stanley Bridge** to **New London**. Add 14 km by switching from Rte 6 to Rte 20 for further-west coastal motoring through **French River**, **Park Corner**, **Darnley** and finally into **Malpeque**. Curve south on short Rte 104 via **Hamilton** and **Indian River**, after which you'll reconnect with Rte 20 to reach crossroads at landlocked **Kensington**, handy for petrol fill-up.

Take Rte 2 eastbound for a 48-km return to Charlottetown. Time allowing, turn off at **Pleasant Valley** for a scenic drive along Rte 227 and rollercoaster-hilly Rte 225 in the central heartland before reaching the Trans-Canada Hwy on Charlottetown's western outskirts.

PRINCE COUNTY ROUTES

Make Kensington your jumping-off point for a longer excursion by driving 13 km from there to **Summerside** via Rtes 2, 1A and 11. Following Rte 11 reaches a succession of Acadian communities along part of west-coast PEI's 288-km Lady Slipper Drive – notably **Mont-Carmel**, **Cap Egmont**, **Abram-Village** and **Baie Egmont**. Rte 11 intersects with Rte 2 at **Mount Pleasant**; take the latter highway to **Portage**, where you have the option of a longer loop west and north or finishing up the shorter one east and south.

For the longer loop, drive 18 km past Portage to **Carleton**. Turn left onto Rte 14 for a coast-hugging jaunt to **West Point**, **West Cape**, **Campbellton**, **Miminegash** and far-north **Christopher Cross** – then do some careful road-junction sign-reading in the **Tignish** vicinity, aimed at reaching **North Cape Lighthouse** via Rte 12 to land's end. Same route number for more Lady Slipper driving, south to **Kildare Capes**, **Jacques Cartier Provincial Park**, **Alberton** and tiny **Cascumpec**. After 21 km from Alberton, you're back on Rte 2

at **Portage**. From there, conclude the Lady Slipper swing – Rte 12 again – to east-shore **Foxley River**, **Tyne Valley** and **Grand River**, bringing you to the Rte 2 junction at **Miscouche**. Close the east–west Prince County loop by driving 18 km from that Acadian town back to Kensington – or turn off onto Rte 1A at **Sherbrooke**, either to leave PEI via the Confederation Bridge or to join the Moncton to Charlottetown route (see pp. 259–262).

(The direct route distance from Charlottetown to Tignish, via Rte 2, is 153 km.)

TOURIST INFORMATION

Nine **PEI Visitor Information Centres** are located throughout the province. On the north coast: *Rte 13, Cavendish; tel: (902) 963-7380,* open daily 0900–2100 (summer), 0930–1700 (early Sept–mid Oct). Another is further west at midpoint in Prince County, *Rte 2, Portage; tel: (902) 859-8796,* open daily 0900–1900 summertime, otherwise 1000–1800.

PRINCE EDWARD ISLAND NATIONAL PARK

Tourist Information: Information Centre, *Rtes 6 and 13, Cavendish.* (Mail address: **PEI National Park**, *Parks Canada, 2 Palmers Lane, Charlottetown, PEI C1A 5V6; tel: (902) 672-6350.*)

This recreational and ecological treasure covers 40 km of shorefront, featuring beaches washed by the warmest ocean waters north of the US Carolinas – plus dunes, red sandstone cliffs, salt marshes, freshwater ponds, spruce and birch woodlands, campsites, nature trails and birdlife, including migratory blue heron and endangered piping plover. Open year-round; full-day $3, $6.50 per family.

Expensive–pricey **Dalvay-by-the-Sea**, *P.O. Box 8, Little York, PEI C0A 1P0; tel: (902) 672-2048,* inside the park's eastern section, has beach frontage, tennis courts and a top-calibre dining room. On a peninsula just outside southern access to the park, the 1860 **Shaw's Hotel**, *Winslow RR 9, Brackley Beach, PEI C1E 1Z3; tel: (902) 672-2022*, is a family-friendly country inn, expensive, but full breakfast and dinner included. Also on the park's perimeter, facing Covehead Bay: the moderate–expensive **Stanhope-by-the-Sea**, *Rte 25 (Bayshore Rd), Little York, PEI C0A 1P0; tel: (902) 672-2407 or (888) 999-5155 (toll-free)*.

THE RUSTICOS

Five boat-harbour communities settled by Acadians in the 1790s have 'Rustico' as part of their names. All are on Rustico Bay, sheltered by causeway-connected Rustico Island, part of the national park.

ACCOMMODATION AND FOOD

Beach cottages, tourist homes, motels and Bed and Breakfasts are plentiful. Same for snack stands, bakeshops and big and small seafood restaurants. For salty atmosphere in minimal space, squeeze into the harbourside **Blue Mussel Café**, *N. Rustico; tel: (902) 675-2501*, budget. Or, same town: **Idle Oars**, *tel: (902) 963-2534*, moderate.

SIGHTSEEING

With their anchored craft and stacked-up lobster traps, the harbours are photogenic. Focus on the busiest one at **North Rustico** from a waterfront boardwalk. Your reward for Rte 242 side-tracking beyond **South Rustico** to **Cymbria** is a close-up view of square-towered **St Augustine's**, built in 1838, PEI's oldest Catholic church.

For sea-kayaking, rely upon **Outside Expeditions**, *N. Rustico Harbour; tel: (902) 892-5425*. The **Rustico Resort Golf & Country Club**, *Rte 242, S. Rustico; tel: (902) 963-2357*, has an 18-hole course.

CAVENDISH AND NEW LONDON

Tourist Information: The **PEI Visitor Information Centre** in Cavendish (see

p.272) is essential for sorting things out. Also, **New London Tourist Association**, *Rte 6, New London, PEI C0B 1M0; tel: (902) 886-2315*, open daily 0900–1900 (late June–early Sept), Sat only 1100–1900 (late Mar–May).

Fair warning: attractions related directly or remotely to *Anne of Green Gables* entice a heavy influx of visitors, arriving by carload and busload. So come prepared for traffic and crowds, fun parks, a wax museum and other kitschy hotspots.

ACCOMMODATION AND FOOD

Inexpensive places to stay seem limitless, but be mindful of the mid-year tourism crunch by reserving ahead. Try for **Shining Waters Inn**, *Rte 13, Cavendish, PEI C0A 1N0; tel: (902) 963-2251*, with swimming pool and sun deck, moderate. Or **Kindred Spirits Country Inn & Cottages**, *Rte 6, Cavendish, PEI C0A 1N0; tel: (902) 963-2434*, moderate. Cavendish's **The Friendly Fisherman**, *Rte 6; tel: (902) 963-2234*, lays out a heaping buffet. Near New London, **Spot o' Tea**, *Rte 6, Stanley Bridge; tel: (902) 886-3346*, is especially worthwhile for fishcakes.

Community-hall lobster suppers, initially conceived as church fund-raisers, have become PEI traditions. The oldest (since 1964) and best-known is 6 km from Stanley Bridge, at the church in **St Ann**, *Rte 224; tel: (902) 621-0635*. Served twice daily except Sun, early June–mid Oct, suppers consist of lobster, plus chowder, soup, mussels, salad, rolls, dessert and beverage for $22.95 or $26.95, depending upon preferred lobster size.

SIGHTSEEING

Parks Canada's domain encompasses **Green Gables House**, *Rte 6, Cavendish; tel: (902) 672-6350*, on the farm site owned in the 1890s by cousins of Lucy Maud Montgomery's grandfather, inspiring her very popular *Anne of Green Gables*. Homespun Victorian, it's a veritable literary shrine for some 350,000 visitors yearly, open daily

0900–2000 (mid June–Aug), 0900–1700 (mid May–mid June, early Sept–Oct), $2.50.

Built in the mid 1800s, the **Lucy Maud Montgomery Birthplace**, *Rte 20, New London (Clifton Corner); tel: (902) 886-2099,* is filled with the belongings of PEI's most famous person. A craft/gift shop and tea room are on the premises, open daily 0900–1900 (July–Aug), 0900–1700 (late May–June, early Sept–mid Oct), $2, children under 12 $0.50.

EASTERN MALPEQUE BAY

West of Cape Tryon's dramatically high cliffs, the cool-water coves and estuaries of sizable Malpeque Bay produce famously fat, gourmet-class Malpeque oysters. Sightsee at the harbour; swim and commune with nature at **Cabot Beach Provincial Park**, open mid June–early Sept, free. Savour the oysters at local **Cabot's Reach Restaurant**, *Cabot Park Rd; tel: (902) 836-5596,* or nearby Darnley's **Blue Dolphin Restaurant**, *Rte 20; tel: (902) 836-4730.*

Vistas of the bay and Darnley Basin are splendid from **Keir Memorial Museum**, *Rte 20, Malpeque; tel: (902) 836-3054,* a repository of Acadian and Scottish family heirlooms with old-time oyster-gathering implements, open Mon–Fri 0900–1700, Sat–Sun 1300–1700 (June–Sept), $1.50. Driving south from there, it's impossible to miss hilltop **St Mary's Catholic Church**, *Rte 104, Indian River*, PEI's largest wooden ecclesiastical structure, and the vaulted-ceilinged venue for the **Indian River Classical Music Festival**, (July–Aug).

KENSINGTON

Tourist Information: Kensington Area Tourist Association, *Broadway, Kensington, PEI C0B 1M0; tel: (902) 836-3031,* open 0900–2100 (June–early Sept).

Crossroads Kensington meets travellers' needs for petrol, meals, etc. A few kilometres north, **Woodleigh Replicas & Gardens**, *Rte 101, Burlington; tel: (902) 836-3401,* has

30 scale replicas of British landmarks, including a mini-St Paul's Cathedral and Dunvegan Castle, open daily 0900–1700 (June–mid Oct), 0900–1900 (July–Aug), $6.80.

SUMMERSIDE

Tourist Information: Spinnakers' Landing Visitor Information Centre, *Harbour Dr., Summerside, PEI C1N 5R1; tel: (902) 436-6692,* in a lighthouse overlooking Bedeque Bay, open daily 0930–2130 (mid June–early Sept).

Summerside (population 7500) flourished briefly as the centre of PEI's silver-fox industry early this century. Hence the 'fox house' mansions on residential streets.

There's a local *QI* and, more central, **Loyalist Country Inn**, *195 Harbour Dr., Summerside, PEI C1N 5R1; tel: (902) 436-3333* or *(800) 361-2668,* moderate. In the Spinnakers' Landing waterfront complex, meals are budget–moderate at the **Deckhouse**, *tel: (902) 436-0660.*

Arrange bay cruising and bicycle rentals at Spinnakers' Landing. Adjacent **Harbourfront Jubilee Theatre** is a handsome performing-arts centre; *tel: (902) 888-2500* or *(800) 708-6505.* Summersiders and visitors whoop it up during mid July's **Lobster Festival**. Learn about the fox-breeding heyday at the **International Fox Museum & Hall of Fame**, *286 Fitzroy St; tel: (902) 436-2400,* open Mon–Sat 0900–1700 (May–Sept), $1.

LA RÉGION ÉVANGÉLINE

This indicates West Prince's south-coastal stretch of Acadian country, where tri-colour/yellow star flags flap on many poles. Delve into the culture at **Le Musée Acadien**, *Rte 2, Miscouche; tel: (902) 432-2880,* open daily 0930–1700 (late June–Sept), Mon–Fri off season. Then sample home-cooked *râpure* or *fricot au poulet* across the street at **Mémé Jane's**; *tel: (902) 436-9600,* moderate.

Le Village, *Rte 11, Mont-Carmel; tel:*

274

(902) 854-2227, replicates an 1820s settlement, open daily 0900–1900 (June–mid Sept), $3.50. Same locale and phone number for Acadian cuisine at moderate–expensive **Étoile de Mer.** Recycler Édouard Arsenault's outbuildings consist of 25,000-plus bottles, hence the weirdly fascinating **Bottle Houses,** *Rte 11, Cap-Egmont; tel: (902) 854-2987.* Call for June–Sept days, hours, $3.25.

⚡ SIDE TRACK TO O'LEARY

After veering north from shoreline Rte 14, you'll see neatly furrowed potato fields, white-blossomed in summer. Half the crop, 120 varieties overall, grows in West Prince County, where **O'Leary** reigns as 'Spud Capital'. What better place for a late-July **Potato Blossom Festival?** Ditto for Canada's only **Potato Museum,** *22 Parkview Dr.; tel: (902) 859-2039,* open Mon–Sat 0900–1700, Sun 1400–1700 (June–mid Oct), $2.50. ⬆

WEST POINT TO NORTH CAPE

Tourist Information: West Prince Tourism Association, *RR 1, Alberton, PEI C0B 1B0; tel: (800) 565-2299.*

Crashing waves have pounded sea caves and arches out of PEI's bleak western headlands; such as off-shore **Elephant Rock** up near North Cape. Islanders call purplish seaweed Irish Moss, marketable because extracted Carrageenan gum becomes an emulsifier for ice-cream and toothpaste.

You've come this far west for serenity, so don't fret about places to stay and eat being far apart. For memorable quirkiness (Room 10 is *in* the lighthouse), overnight at **West Point Lighthouse,** *Rte 14 (to reserve: RR 2, O'Leary, PEI C0B 1V0); tel: (902) 859-3605* or *(800) 764-6854,* moderate. Same locale for chowder or full menu. Up north, an historic convent is now comfortable **Tignish Heritage Inn,** *Box 398, Tignish, PEI C0B 2B0; tel: (902) 882-2491,* moderate.

Burton, Nail Pond and **Seacow Pond** have budget–moderate lodgings.

Everything you never knew about seaweed harvesting gets answered at the **Irish Moss Interpretive Centre,** *Rte 14, Miminegash; tel: (902) 882-4313,* open Mon–Sat 1000–1800, Sun 1200–2000, (Aug–Sept), $1. Carageenan is an ingredient in the on-site **Seaweed Pie Café's** dessert speciality. **North Cape Lighthouse** shares its perch on North America's longest rock reef with wind-energy generators at the **Atlantic Wind Test Site** and its Visitor Centre; *tel: (902) 882-2991,* open daily 0900–2000 (July–Aug), 1000–1800 (June and Sept), $2. Meals are also offered here at **Wind & Reef;** *tel: (902) 882-3535.* Towering over Tignish is **Sts Simon & Jude Church,** known PEI-wide for its immense pipe organ. Summer recitals; *tel: (902) 882-2488.*

GULF-COAST PRINCE COUNTY

Swerving south alongside the Gulf of St Lawrence, feast your eyes on the **Kildare Capes,** a segment of steep, craggy, sandstone seaside cliffs. **Jacques Cartier Provincial Park,** *tel: (902) 853-8632,* reputed to be where explorer Cartier first came ashore in 1534, features nature trails, a beach on the Gulf of St Lawrence and campsite, open mid June–early Sept. Epicures praise Cascumpec Bay's mussels and soft-shell clams.

Budget–moderate **Hunter House,** *RR 2, Alberton, PEI C0B 1B0; tel: (902) 853-4027* or *(888) 853-4027* (toll-free), is a villagey Bed and Breakfast (luncheon, tea room, too). Comparable price hospitality at **Doctor's Inn,** *P.O. Box 92, Tyne Valley, PEI C0B 2C0; tel: (902) 831-3057,* also serving critically acclaimed dinners. Reaching Tyne Valley, furthermore, means you're back in the realm of Malpeque Bay oyster farming. On shore is East Prince's **Green Park Shipbuilding Museum,** *Rte 12, Port Hill; tel: (902) 831-7947,* open daily 0900–1700 (mid June–early Sept), $3.50.

PRINCE EDWARD ISLAND– CAPE BRETON ISLAND

The northern shore of Nova Scotia is washed by the Northumberland Strait, which laps the sandy beaches with some of the warmest salt-water in the Atlantic provinces. The scenery is open, sometimes gently rolling shore and farmland, with small fishing villages, beaches and wetlands. The route travels through the heart of the province's Scottish bastion.

There are two ways to drive from Prince Edward Island into Nova Scotia. You can backtrack across the Confederation Bridge to New Brunswick then turn east, or take the ferry from Wood Islands to Caribou, which joins the scenic route halfway across Nova Scotia's northern shore.

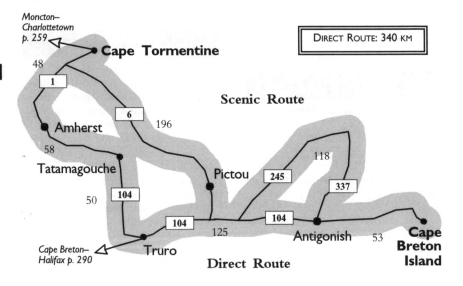

Moncton–
Charlottetown
p. 259

Cape Tormentine

48

1

DIRECT ROUTE: 340 KM

Scenic Route

6

196

Amherst

58

118

Tatamagouche

Pictou

245

337

50

104

104

104

125

Antigonish 53

Cape Breton Island

Cape Breton–
Halifax p. 290

Truro

Direct Route

ROUTES

DIRECT ROUTE

From the bridge at Cape Tormentine, NB, take Hwy 1 (Trans-Canada) south to Hwy 104 near Sackville, NB. Follow Hwy 104 east past Amherst, NS, and all the

way to Auld's Cove for the Canso Causeway to Cape Breton. You can get off the highway in Amherst, Truro, Pictou and Antigonish to explore local sights, or (except at Truro) to follow portions of the scenic route. From the bridge to Hwy 104 is about 55 km; from there to the causeway is another 338 km.

For travellers coming from the Wood Islands ferry landing at Caribou, NS, follow Hwy 106 past Pictou, meeting Hwy 104 near New Glasgow and on to the Canso Causeway, a total of 128 km.

SCENIC ROUTE

➡ Travellers coming from the bridge at Cape Tormentine follow Hwy 1 (Trans-Canada) to the left turn onto an unnumbered road marked **Tidnish**, where you turn left again (east) onto Rte 366. At **Port Howe**, the route joins Rte 6. At **Pictou** take Hwy 106 south to Hwy 104 at **New Glasgow**. Follow Hwy 104 east to Exit 27, and take Rte 245 north. The route number soon changes to Rte 337, continuing to **Antigonish**, where you rejoin Hwy 104 east to the Canso Causeway onto Cape Breton.

Travellers coming from the **ferry landing** at Caribou follow Hwy 106 to Pictou and continue on to the intersection with Rte 104 to join the scenic route.

TOURIST INFORMATION

Tourist information for the entire area is available from **Central Nova Scotia Tourist Association**, Box 1761, Truro, NS B2N 5Z5; tel: (902) 893-8782, fax: (902) 897-6641.

AMHERST

Tourist Information: Amherst Tourist Bureau, *Laplanche St, Amherst, NS B4H 3Z5; tel: (902) 667-0696*, open daily 0900–1800, (mid May–Oct).

ACCOMMODATION

Several budget–moderate inns and motels are off Rte 104, including *CI* and *WL;* **Victoria Garden Bed & Breakfast**, *196 Victoria St E.; tel: (902) 667-2278*, is in a fine Victorian home with unique architectural detail.

SIGHTSEEING

Above the **Tantramar Marsh**, which fills the Chignecto Isthmus with space so open and bright that it spawned an entire school of art, Amherst's compact main street is lined by brick buildings.

The home of R. B. Dickey, a Father of Confederation (one of four from Amherst) is now the **Cumberland County Museum**, *Grove Cottage, 150 Church St; tel: (902) 667-2561*, open Mon–Sat 0900–1700, Sun 1400–1700 (June–Aug), other seasons shorter hours, which emphasises the area's human and natural history; $1.

The annual **Blueberry Harvest Festival** is held the first week of Aug; in Sept is the ten-day **Four Fathers Festival**.

TRURO

Tourist Information: Truro Tourist Bureau, *Victoria Sq., Truro, NS B2N 5Z5; tel: (902) 893-2922*, open daily 0900–1750 (mid May–Oct).

ACCOMMODATION

Chain hotels include *BW, CI, HJ* and *Kd*. Or try the locally run **Palliser Hotel**, *Tidal Bore Rd* (Rte 102 Exit 14, 2 exits south of Exit 15 on Rte 104), *Box 821, Truro, NS B2N 5G6; tel: (902) 893-8951*; moderate, buffet breakfast included. They have a lighted viewing of the tidal bore.

EATING AND DRINKING

The **Palliser Restaurant** is known for good food and for windows that overlook the Salmon River and tidal bore. Moderate, traditional cuisine.

SIGHTSEEING

Located along two direct routes (see p. 290), Truro is the largest city you will encounter when travelling from New Brunswick or PEI to Cape Breton and Halifax. Known as *Cobequid* to the Indians, it was settled by Acadians and then Loyalists.

In the late 19th century, it became the

277

railway hub of the province, and the train still stops here.

At **Howe Falls** in the 1000-acre **Victoria Park**, a stream falls from high among the rocks of a deep gorge that cuts through the park. The **tidal bore**, a rushing wall of water several feet high, races up Salmon River from the Bay of Fundy. Check the tide table and go to **Tidal Bore Park** just before high tide.

At **Shubenacadie Provincial Wildlife Park**, *Rte 2 (Exit 9 or 11 off Rte 102); tel: (902) 758-2040*, open daily 0900–1900 (mid May–mid Oct), ducks, swans, reindeer, moose, cougar and Sable Island horses are among the species you'll see. There is an environmental centre and a picnic area for outings.

TIDNISH TO TATAMAGOUCHE

For those on the scenic route, the road hugs the coast, passing Tidnish's smooth, sandy beaches and a picnic area at **Tidnish Dock Provincial Park**, as well as other warm water beaches at **Northport** and **Port Howe** before rejoining Rte 6. In **Pugwash**, an annual Gathering of the Clans in early July is held on land donated by the financier Cyrus Eaton, a native of this little fishing and shipping village. **Gulf Shore Park**, 5 km north of Pugwash, has long sandy beaches. All along this route you will find excellent beaches, with soft, white sand, gentle surf and warm water for swimming.

More than 150 species of birds have been identified at **Wallace Bay National Wildlife Area**, *off Rte 366, no tel.* Close by, on the Malagash Peninsula, follow signs to **Jost Vineyards**, *tel: (902) 257-2636 or (800) 565-4567*, which produces wines and offers tastings and tours of the cellars. They rent bicycles as well. A bit further east along Rte 6 are remains of **Acadian dikes**, irrigation systems built between 1716–55.

The **Jubilee Cottage Country Inn**, *Rte 6, off Exit 1 or 3 from Rte 104; tel: (902) 257-*

2432 or *(800) 481-9915,* specialises in five-course candelight dinners and maple sugar planked salmon.

TATAMAGOUCHE

On Tatamagouche Bay, almost enclosed by two small peninsulas, Tatamagouche is a small, but convenient centre.

ACCOMMODATION AND FOOD

Balmoral Motel, *Rte 6 (Box 178), Tatamagouche, NS B0K 1V0; tel: (902) 657-2000,* has clean motel-style rooms at moderate prices. Their dining room, **The Mill Room**, budget, overlooks the bay and serves seafood and German specialities, with hot oatcakes at breakfast. At the end of Tatamagouche Bay, **Nelson Memorial Park and Campground**; *RR3, Tatamagouche, NS B0K 1V0; tel: (902) 657-2730,* offers open and wooded tent pitches, sporting activities and hiking trails. Budget, open mid May–mid Sept.

SIGHTSEEING

In the **Fraser Culture Centre**, *Main St; tel: (902) 657-3285,* open daily 0900–2000 (May–Oct), a collection of important local materials helps preserve the historical culture of the area. They also have a display about Anna Swan, a local giant, as well as a nature trail.

Nearby, the **Sunrise Trail Museum**, *Main St,* open Sat and Sun 1000–1600 (June and Sept), daily (July–Aug) illustrates Micmac and Acadian cultures and the ship-building and agricultural lives of settlers; $1.

TATAMAGOUCHE TO PICTOU

The road skirts the shores of Tatamagouche Bay, and a short detour south takes you to the **Balmoral Grist Mill**, *off Rte 311; tel: (902) 657-3016,* open Mon–Sat 0930–1730, Sun 1300–1730 (June–mid Oct), a fascinating water-powered grist mill remaining from the last century. Interpreters demonstrate how the mill works, and they sell oats, bread and oatcakes in their shop.

In **River John**, community lobster suppers are held May–July. Shortly beyond are **Waterside** and **Caribou Provincial Parks**, sandy beaches with the warm waters of the Northumberland Strait. Both these beaches are a short distance north of Rte 6, on an unnumbered but well-marked road that follows the shore to Caribou. If you follow this scenic side road, you can connect to Hwy 106 at the ferry landing in Caribou and go directly into Pictou.

PICTOU

Tourist Information: Nova Scotia Tourist Office, *junction of Rte 6 and Rte 106, just off the rotary*, open daily 0800–2000 (mid May–mid Oct).

On Rte 104, there is a **tourist information cabin** 30 km south of town, open 0800–2000 daily in summer. **Pictou County Tourist Association**, *980 East River Rd, New Glasgow, NS B2H 3S5; tel: (902) 755-5180, fax (902) 775-2848.*

ACCOMMODATION

The Braeside Inn, *126 Front St, Pictou, NS B0K 1H0; tel: (902) 485-5046 or (800) 565-0000 (toll-free), fax: (902) 485-1701*, is a genteel and comfortable traditional hotel with hospitable owners. Moderate. The **Consulate Inn**, *115 Water St, Pictou, NS B0K 1H0; tel: (902) 485-4554*, has rooms and housekeeping units in a stone building that was the US consulate in 1865. These and a neighbouring cottage are attractive and comfortable budget–moderate lodgings, continental breakfast included.

Pictou Lodge Resort, *PO Box 1539, Pictou, NS B0K 1H0; tel: (902) 485-4322 or (800) 495-6343, fax: (902) 485-4945*, a cabin resort by the sea, was built in the 1920s for Canadian Pacific Railway executives. The rustic cabins are in good repair and occupy a secluded spot on the ocean, 4 km from the PEI ferry. Moderate. Sport facilities

and a budget–moderate dining room are in the main lodge. Moderate rates include continental breakfast at **Walker Inn**, *34 Coleraine St, Pictou, NS B0K 1H0; tel: (902) 485-1433*, an 1865 townhouse in the town centre. Rooms are quiet, comfortable and beautifully furnished. A three-course dinner is served by reservation only.

EATING AND DRINKING

Reservations are suggested at **Braeside Inn**'s casual-elegant dining room overlooking the harbour. The budget–moderate menu includes filet mignon, salmon, lamb and lobster. Less formal **Stone House Café**, *13 Water St; tel: (902) 485-6885*, has cheap–budget seafood, sandwiches, pizza and German specialities. Another option for burgers, fish and chips and sandwiches is the pub-like **Press Room**, *50 Water St; tel: (902) 485-4041*, cheap. Sat brunch includes steak or bacon and eggs.

SIGHTSEEING

279

Settled by a few colonists from Philadelphia in 1767, the town grew with Scottish immigrants who arrived after a harrowing ten-week voyage on the *Hector* in 1773. Many more Scots followed.

The story of *Hector*'s voyage is told at the **Hector Heritage Quay**, *29–33 Caladh Ave; tel: (902) 485-8028*, open Mon–Sat 1000–1700, Sun 1100–1700 (June–mid Oct) and occasional longer hours. A full-size replica of the ship is being built on the site; visit the carpentry and blacksmith shops. The five-day **Hector Festival** is held in mid Aug.

McCulloch House & Hector National Exhibit Centre and Archive, *Old Halliburton Rd; tel: (902) 485-4563*, open Mon–Sat 0930–1730, Sun 1300–1730 (June–mid Oct), includes an 1806 house, with original furniture and artefacts from Pictou's early history and a highly prized ornithology collection. There is also an archive with a genealogical centre and library. **Grohmann Knife Factory**, *116 Water St, tel: (902) 485-6775,* has tours and an outlet store that sells kitchen knives, chef sets and pocket-knives.

The **Pictou Golf and Country Club**, *Beeches Rd; tel: (902) 485-4435,* is on the shore and open to the public. Bicycle tours are operated by **Pictou County Cycling Club**, *tel: (902) 755-2704* or *752-8904,* and visitors are invited to join.

PICTOU TO ANTIGONISH

Hwys 106 and 104 are uneventful, a quick way of getting to Exit 27 and the headland of Cape George. Rte 245 follows the shore closely, through the village of **Merigonish** to **Arisaig**, with its fossil-filled cliffs at **Arisaig Provincial Park**. Along with fossil-hunting on the shore, the park has a boardwalk to a lovely beach and hiking trails along the shore.

As you approach the tip of **Cape George**, the road climbs the headland, where scenic overlooks provide views over the water and along the coast. A lighthouse marks the highest point, and you can see the western shore of Cape Breton Island from its lookout. The tiny village of **Ballantyne's Cove** has fish-and-chip stands along its wharf. Rte 338 continues to Antigonish, a centre for Scottish culture.

ANTIGONISH

Tourist Information: Nova Scotia Tourist Office, *56 West St (Exit 32 off Rte 104); tel: (902) 863-4921* or *(800) 565-0000,* opens daily 0800–2000 (July–Aug), 0800–1700 (June and Sept). **Antigonish/Eastern Shore Tourist Association**, *Musquodoboit Harbour, NS B0J 2L0; tel: (902) 889-2362, fax: (902) 889-2101.*

ACCOMMODATION

There are several choices of lodging, including *BW* and *WL*, but if you plan to attend the Highland Games, book months ahead. Avoid graduation week in mid May.

Old Manse Inn, *5 Tigo Park, Antigonish, NS B2G 1M7, tel: (902) 863-5696, (902) 863-5259* off season, is budget–moderate, including full breakfast. In an 1874 Victorian house with character on a hill, it's a 5-min walk from downtown. (Driving directions: take Exit 32 from Rte 104 to the Government Building, turn left on *Hawthorne St* and then the second left, onto Tigo Park.)

EATING AND DRINKING

Sunshine Cafe, *332 Main St, tel: (902) 863-5851,* has a chef trained in French classical cuisine, who adapts that style using local fresh vegetables, grains, fruits, cheeses, meats and seafoods. Breakfast, lunch and dinner, cheap–moderate.

SIGHTSEEING

Antigonish is an attractive small city known for its Scottish connection. The annual **Highland Games** in early July are popular with devotees of Scottish sports, bagpipes and dances. Held annually since 1863, the games feature concerts, youth competitions, clan gatherings, Celtic workshops, ceilidhs and many other pre-games festivities held at Columbus Field. There are Highland dancers, athletes racing, hammer throwing, broadjumping and 'tossing the caber', while pipe bands march and skirl in between rounds. At the end, there are massed bands with hundreds of players; contact **Antigonish Highland Society**, *274 Main St, Antigonish, NS B2G 2C4; tel: (902) 863-4275.*

Festival Antigonish, *tel: (902) 867-3954* or *(800) 563-7529,* has professional theatre, drama, musicals, revues and children's theatre in July and Aug at the Bauer Theatre on the university campus.

CAPE BRETON ISLAND

Scenery and a world-class historic reconstruction beckon travellers to this island, attached to mainland Nova Scotia by a slender thread of causeway. Cape Breton Highlands National Park offers some of Canada's best coastline vistas, sea and mountain views that, combined with the Cabot Trail's precipitous hairpin turns, will quite literally take your breath away.

Louisbourg, a French colonial city rebuilt on its original foundations, is the largest historical reconstruction in North America. Not far away, Bras d'Or, one of the world's largest saltwater lakes, home to the continent's largest bald eagle population, cuts the island almost in half.

TOURIST INFORMATION

If you want information in advance, you can contact either **Nova Scotia Tourism**, *P.O. Box 130, Halifax, NS B3J 2M7; tel: (902) 425-5781* or *(800) 565-0000* (toll-free), or **Enterprise Cape Breton**, *P.O. Box 1448, Sydney, NS B1P 6R7; tel: (800) 565-9464.*

Just off the Canso Causeway, the **Nova Scotia Visitor Information Centre**, *Port Hastings; tel: (902) 625-4201,* is open daily 0900–2100 (July–Aug), 0900–1900 (mid May–June, Sept–mid Oct).

Local tourist centres are open part or all of the summer season at the following locations: Baddeck, Cheticamp, Louisbourg, Margaree, North Sydney, Port Hood, and others.

WEATHER

Cape Breton's weather is much like the rest of Nova Scotia, but a bit cooler, with summer daytime temperatures averaging 20°–25°C, nights 10°–20°C. Spring and fall days are around 10°–15°C.

ARRIVING AND DEPARTING

By Air
Air Nova and Air Atlantic operate four flights a day between Sydney and Halifax. The Sydney airport is off Hwy 4 halfway between Sydney and Glace Bay.

By Car
Hwy 104 connects Cape Breton Island to mainland Nova Scotia via the Canso Causeway.

By Ferry
Ferries to Newfoundland arrive and depart from North Sydney, operated by **Marine Atlantic**, *355 Purves St, N. Sydney, NS B2A 3V2; tel: (902) 794-5254* or *(800) 341-7981, fax: (902) 564-7480.*

The shortest route (5 hrs) is to **Port aux Basques** (see p. 332), departing each way at least once a day all year; fares $19 adult, $9.50 ages 5–12, $13 berth, $42–90 cabin, $59 autos. The trip to **Argentia** (see p. 322) takes 14 hrs and is offered seasonally, three times weekly (late June–early Sept), and is fully booked months in advance; fares $52.50 adult, $26.25 ages 5–12, $20 berth, $100–125 cabin, $118 autos.

It is important to make reservations and to arrive one hour ahead to claim them. Also, be sure your vehicle's fuel tank is no more than three-quarters full. On the ferry are restaurants, lounges, live entertainment, cinema and children's play areas.

281

By Bus

Acadian Lines, *tel: (902) 454-9321*, operates between Halifax and Sydney; buses stop opposite the ferry terminal in North Sydney and at the Sydney bus station, *Terminal Row, off Prince St.*

GETTING AROUND

A glance at the map shows three natural divisions in Cape Breton Island, reached by a series of Scenic Trails. As you drive over the Canso Causeway, you arrive in the western section, separated from the eastern by the huge Bras d'Or Lake. To the north is Cape Breton Highlands National Park, circled by the justly famous Cabot Trail.

Often listed among the world's great scenic drives, the Cabot Trail loops around the peninsula from **Margaree**, through **Cheticamp** to **Cape North**, then back south via **Ingonish** to **St Ann's Bay**. Views from the road are most spectacular if you go clockwise, beginning on the west.

The area east of Bras d'Or Lake is connected to the Canso Causeway by Hwy 105, leading to the island's only dual carriageway, Hwy 125, around **Sydney** and **North Sydney**. Hwy 105 winds along the northern shore of the lake, through the resort town of **Baddeck**. To reach **Fortress Louisbourg**, follow Rte 22 from Hwy 125, at Sydney. To return along the lake's scenic southern shore, follow Rte 4 from **Sydney River**, through **St Peter's**.

To tour the western part of the island, follow Rte 19 to **Mabou, Inverness** and **Margaree Forks**. Or take Hwy 105 through **Whycocomagh** and follow Cabot Trail signs north to Margaree Forks. Another un-numbered route, part of the Bras d'Or Scenic Trail, travels along the western shore of the lake from St Peter's to **Orangedale**.

WESTERN CAPE BRETON

Along the western coast, the **Mabou Highlands** are cliffs and headlands reached only by spectacular hiking trails. This, and the inland area around **Lake Ainslie**, is Scottish country; **Isle Madame**, islands off the southern shore, are as intensely French.

STAYING IN WESTERN CAPE BRETON

Accommodation

Kd and *TL* are in Port Hastings; neighbouring Port Hawkesbury, almost the same town, has *WL* and **MacPuffin Motel**, *Rte 4 (P.O. Box 558), Port Hawkesbury, NS B0E 2V0; tel: (902) 625-0621*, moderate, with modern rooms, an indoor swimming pool, exercise room and laundry. A dining room serves breakfast and dinner.

Close to the 1854 St Peter's Canal, **Bras d'Or Lakes Inn**, *General Delivery, St Peter's, NS B0E 3B0; tel: (902) 535-2200* or *(800) 818-5885*, moderate, has attractive cedar-panelled rooms and custom-built furniture. The dining room serves home-style meals. With a more inn-like atmosphere, the newly built **L'Auberge Acadienne**, *P.O. Box 59, Arichat, NS B0E 1A0; tel: (902) 226-2200*, moderate, has large guest rooms and a dining room, on Isle Madame.

Overlooking Barra Straits, next to the Highland Village Museum, **Highland Heights Inn**, *Rte 223, P.O. Box 19, Iona, NS B0A 1L0; tel: (902) 725-2360*, moderate, is a motel with the hospitality of an inn. The dining room serves country cooking, with home-made breads and pastries.

For lodging rich in luxury and hospitality, reserve one of the large, custom-furnished rooms at **Duncreigan Country Inn**, *Rte 19 (P.O. Box 59), Mabou, NS B0E 1X0; tel: (902) 945-2207*, moderate. The outstanding dining room, where the best local produce, lamb and superb salmon, are prepared with sophistication and style, is no secret, so dinner reservations are wise. **Glenora Inn**, *Rte 19 (P.O. Box 181), Mabou, NS B0E 1X0; tel: (902) 258-2662* or *(800) 565-0000* in Canada, has modern guest rooms at a single malt whiskey distillery. The

282

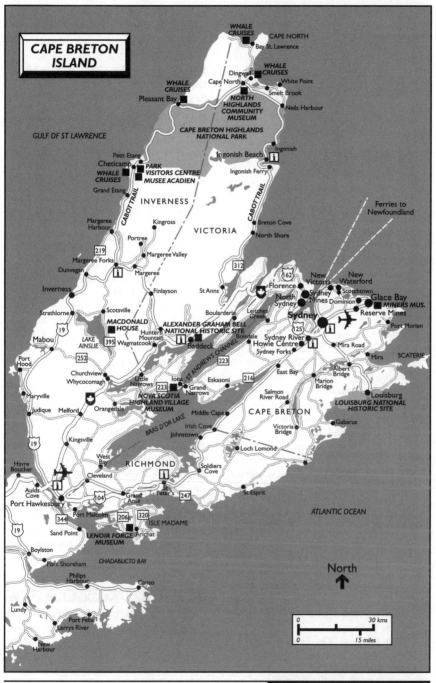

CAPE BRETON
ISLAND

WHALE
CRUISES · CAPE NORTH
Bay St. Lawrence

WHALE
CRUISES
Dingwall · White Point
Cape North
Smelt Brook
WHALE
CRUISES
Pleasant Bay · Neils Harbour
NORTH
HIGHLANDS
COMMUNITY
MUSEUM

GULF OF ST LAWRENCE

CAPE BRETON HIGHLANDS
NATIONAL PARK

Petit Etang
Cheticamp · Ingonish
Ingonish Beach
PARK
WHALE · VISITORS CENTRE · Ingonish Ferry
CRUISES · MUSEE ACADIEN
Grand Etang

INVERNESS

Ferries to
Newfoundland

Margaree · Kingross · Breton Cove
Harbour
Portree · VICTORIA · North Shore

219
Margaree Forks · Margaree Valley
Dunvegan · 312
Margaree · New New
Victoria Waterford
Inverness · Finlayson · St Anns · 162 · Florence · Sydney Scotchtown
Mines
North · Dominion · Glace Bay
Scotsville · Boularderie · Sydney · MINERS MUS.
Strathlorne · Leitches · Reserve Mines
MACDONALD · Creek · Sydney · Port Morien
HOUSE · ALEXANDER GRAHAM BELL
19 · Hunters · NATIONAL HISTORIC SITE · 125
LAKE · Mountain · Boisdale
Mabou · 395 Wagmatcook · Baddeck · Sydney River
AINSLIE · Howie Centre · Mira Road
Port · 252 · ST ANDREWS CHANNEL · Sydney Forks · Mira
Hood · 223 · SCATERIE
Churchview · Little · Eskasoni · East Bay · Albert
Whycocomagh · Narrows · 216 · Bridge
Maryville · 223 · Grand · Marion · Louisburg
Judique · Melford · Orangedale · NOVA SCOTIA · Narrows · Salmon · Bridge · LOUISBURG NATIONAL
HIGHLAND VILLAGE · River Road · HISTORIC SITE
MUSEUM
19 · Middle Cape · CAPE BRETON · Gabarus
Kingsville · BRAS D'OR LAKE · Irish Cove
Johnstown · Victoria
Havre · West · Bridge
Boucher · Bay · RICHMOND · Loch Lomond
Cleveland · Soldiers
Cove
Auids · Grand · Peter's
Cove · Anse · 247 · St Esprit
Port Hawkesbury · 104
344 · Port Malcolm · ATLANTIC OCEAN
19 · Sand Point · 206 320
ISLE MADAME
Boylston · LENOIR FORGE · Arichat
MUSEUM
Port Shoreham · CHADABUCTO BAY
Philips
Harbour · Canso
North
Lundy
Port Felix
Larrys River
New
Harbour

0 ———— 30 kms
0 ———— 15 miles

283

moderate–pricey dining room has a varied menu with occasional Scottish dishes.

Normaway Inn, *Egypt Rd (Box 100), Margaree Valley, B0E 2C0; tel: (902) 248-2987 or (800) 565-9463,* open May–Nov, moderate, has bright airy guest rooms in the main lodge, plus one- and two-bedroom cabins. Dinner, pricey, is also served to the public; almost nightly musical entertainment.

Eating and Drinking

Most hotels near the causeway have their own dining rooms. For basic family dining with large servings, try the inaccurately named **La Cuisine Acadiene**, *Louisdale; tel: (902) 345-2817,* budget, where they serve Italian, Chinese and seafood. On Isle Madame, **Claire's Cafe**, *D'Ecousse; tel: (902) 226-1432,* budget, offers home-cooked meals and conversation with Claire, who'll show you an album of photos of the town way back when. **Au Bord de la Mer**, *Petit de Grat; tel: (902) 226-0011,* moderate, also on Isle Madame, serves healthy lunches and light dinners until 2030.

Further north, stop at **Mull Cafe**, *Rte 19, Mabou; tel: (902) 945-2244,* moderate, for a meal or for high quality deli to supply a picnic. Dinner features scallops and chicken dishes. **Crossroads Restaurant**, *Rte 19, Belle Cote; tel: (902) 235-2888,* budget–moderate, has home-style meals. At the beach in Inverness, **The Casual Gourmet**, *off Rte 19; tel: (902) 258-3839,* moderate, serves seafood, vegetarian dishes, traditional oatcakes and porridge bread (June–Oct).

SIGHTSEEING

Some of the most picturesque fishing harbours in all Nova Scotia are on Isle Madame and its small adjacent islands. Possibly the best of these are on **Petit-de-Grat**, where natural rock formations and the assemblage of small boats create good views no matter where you look.

On Isle Madame, **The Island Forge** is a traditional blacksmith shop operating at

LeNoir Forge Museum, *Waterfront, Arichat; tel: (902) 226-9364,* open daily 1000–1800 (May–Sept), an historic forge where ironwork has been done for ships built there since the 1700s. Along with the tools and equipment for blacksmithing – and hand-forged pieces for sale – the museum has relics of the town's past.

On highland meadows overlooking the lake, **Nova Scotia Highland Village Museum**, *4119 Rte 223, Iona; tel: (902) 725-2272,* open Mon–Sat 0900–1700, Sun 1000–1800 (June–Sept), admission $4, family $8, recreates the sense of homeland brought by early Scottish immigrants. Along with homes of several periods, a school, carding mill, blacksmith shop and general store, the village has the continent's only example of a 'black house', the traditional cottage of the Hebrides Islands.

MacDonald House, *Rte 395, Lake Ainslie; tel: (902) 258-3317,* open daily 0900–2100 (mid June–mid Sept), admission $2, family $4, is a 150-year-old furnished Victorian Gothic farmhouse, showing home and farm life in that era, with exhibits of farming tools, spinning and weaving.

Visitors to **Glenora Distillery**, *Rte 19, Mabou, tel: (902) 258-2662,* open daily 0900–1700 (June–Oct), tours $4, see the process of creating North America's only single malt whiskey, with a guide who explains the still and the Mash House. The first single malt will be ready in the year 2000, but you can sample their rums. The **Margaree Salmon Museum**, *N.E. Margaree; tel: (902) 248-2848,* open daily 0900–1700 (mid June–mid Oct), $0.50, shows off the Margaree River's most famous residents, with an aquarium of young trout and salmon and fishing exhibits.

NORTHERN CAPE BRETON

Cape Breton Highlands National Park paints a stripe across the map of the northern peninsula, cutting off the towns at its tip from the rest of the island. To stop anywhere inside the park as you drive through, even to look at a view, requires an entry permit, $3.50 adult, $8 family per day.

STAYING IN NORTHERN CAPE BRETON

Accommodation

The only accommodation in the park, the toney (and pricey) **Keltic Lodge**, *Middle Head Peninsula, Ingonish Beach, NS B0C 1L0; tel: (902) 285-2880 or (800) 565-0444*, has a setting nothing short of spectacular, on its own peninsula above the sea. All the luxuries are there: a large pool, tennis courts, private lake, golf course and two dining rooms. The ultra-pricey **Purple Thistle** has a stylish continental menu and the more informal **Atlantic Restaurant**, moderate, serves heartier fare.

Other accommodations are close to all the park's borders. **Cheticamp**, the largest town on the west shore, has the most.

Laurie's Motor Inn, *Rte 19 (P.O. Box 1), Cheticamp, NS B0E 1H0; tel: (902) 224-2400 or (800) 959-4253*, is high moderate, is a modern motel with a variety of rooms, some with balconies, and a dining room serving seafood and Acadian specialities. In an 1870 home facing the harbour, **The Laurence Guest House**, *Rte 19 (P.O. Box 820), Cheticamp, NS B0E 1H0; tel: (902) 224-2184*, open May–Oct, budget, offers Bed and Breakfast, and fine views of this coast's famous sunsets.

At the top of the peninsula, **Oakwood Manor Bed & Breakfast**, *North Side Road, Cape North, NS B0C 1G0; tel/fax: (902) 383-2317*, open May–Oct, budget, is a farm with gardens and orchards. **Highlands By the Sea**, *St Margaret's Village, NS B0C 1R0; tel: (902) 383-2537*, open mid June–Oct, budget, also a Bed and Breakfast, was built a century ago as the church rectory, in a small fishing village with mountains as a backdrop.

The Markland, *Box 62 Dingwall, NS B0C 1G0; tel: (902) 383-2246 or (800) 872-*

6084, is a classy moderate–expensive resort overlooking the sea. Large pine-panelled rooms and self-catering cabins are nicely furnished; canoes and bikes are provided. Their pricey dining room (open to the public by reservation) offers a sophisticated menu (scallops sautéed with leeks) and creditable wine list.

Sleepy Hollow Cottages, *Snow Rd (Box 175), Ingonish, NS B0C 1K0; tel: (902) 285-2227*, open mid June–mid Oct, high moderate, are spacious and fully equipped, right down to bathrobes and hairdryers. You can walk to a secluded cove beach. Six **campsites** in the national park have tent pitches and full caravan hook-ups, $14–20. No reservations, but the park never turns campers away. Latecomers camp in overflow sites and have first choice of spaces the next day.

Eating and Drinking

Chez Renee Cafe, *Rte 19, Grand Etang; tel: (902) 244-1446*, budget, south of Cheticamp, features a nice blend of Acadian and French cuisine, from hearty stews and meat pies to Coquilles St-Jacques and ratatouille. **Restaurant Acadien**, *774 Main St, Cheticamp; tel: (902) 224-3207*, open June–Oct, budget, serves Acadian dishes common in homes, but hard for travellers to sample. The chicken fricot (a hearty stew) is outstanding, as is gingerbread. **Le Gabriel Restaurant**, *Rte 19, Cheticamp; tel: (902) 224-3685*, budget–moderate, is easy to spot with it's lighthouse-like entrance. Seafood and some Acadian dishes are specialities. The **Harbour Restaurant**, *Le Quai Mathieu, Rte 19, Cheticamp; tel: (902) 224-2042*, moderate, overlooks the busy fishing harbour and serves, not surprisingly, seafood.

After Cheticamp, the next oasis is Pleasant Bay, at the northern park boundary. **The Rusty Anchor**, *Rte 19; tel: (902) 224-1313*, moderate, is known for its salad bar and seafood, while **The Black Whale**, *Rte 19; tel: (902) 224-2185*, budget–moderate, has an oyster and mussel bar and plentiful seafood caught locally.

Morrison's Pioneer Restaurant, *Rte 19 at Bay St Lawrence Rd, North Cape; tel: (902) 383-2051*, moderate, is next to the North Highlands Museum, serving seafood in a relaxed setting.

SIGHTSEEING

It's not surprising that some of the best vantage points for viewing the water-surrounded highlands are from the sea. Since whales are plentiful most of the summer, boat trips combine sightseeing and whale-watching, for pilot, fin, humpback and minke whales. Cruises offer two or three trips daily (May–Oct), $20–25 adult, $10–15 children.

Cheticamp's harbour has kiosks where you can sign on, or you can (wisely) reserve ahead with **Acadian Whale Cruise**, *tel: (902) 224-1088;* **L'Escaoette Whale Cruise**, *tel: (902) 224-1959*, which also runs shorter harbour cruises; or **Whale Cruises, Ltd**, *tel: (902) 224-3376 or (800) 813-3376*.

Pleasant Bay Whale and Seal Tours, *tel: (902) 224-1315*, and **Highland Coastal Tours & Charters**, *tel: (902) 224-1825*, sail from the tiny west coast harbour at Pleasant Bay. East, near Dingwall, spot whales with **Captain Cox's Whale Watch**, *Bay St Lawrence; tel: (902) 383-2981*, **Highlander Whale Watch**, *Bay St Lawrence; tel: (902) 383-2287*, or **White Point Whale Cruise and Nature Tour**, *White Point; tel: (902) 383-2817*.

CAPE BRETON HIGHLANDS NATIONAL PARK

Tourist Information: Cape Breton Highlands National Park, *Ingonish Beach, NS B0C 1L0; tel: (902) 224-2306, fax: (902) 285-2866*. On-site information is available at the **Park Visitors Centre**, *Rte 19, Cheticamp*, open daily 0800–2000 (July–Aug), 0900–1500 (Sept–June).

One of the wonders of this 950 square km

of protected land is its topography, a slice of mountain range cast adrift in the sea. The Cabot Trail, skirting its dramatic perimeter, brings motorists to its most outstanding scenery, while miles of hiking trails open its interior to walkers.

From Cheticamp, where you first enter, to Ingonish, where you leave, it is 113 km. It can be travelled, with lookout stops and a few side trips, in a day, but a two-day visit allows time for hikes and whale-watching. Stop at the Cheticamp entrance for a map and trail descriptions, and to pay the fee.

Most hiking trails are on the west, while most recreation facilities – golf, tennis and beaches – are on the east. Among the western highlights, clearly labelled with roadside signs, are **Le Buttereau**, a 2-km headland loop with good bird sitings; **Corney Brook**, a longer (8 km return) hike past a gorge to a waterfall; **Bog Trail**, a 0.6-km boardwalk past insect-eating pitcher plants; and **MacIntosh Brook**, a 2.8-km trail through hardwood forest to a waterfall.

Lone Shieling is a short (0.8 km return) easy trail to a replica of a Scottish crofter's hut, built as a visual link between the original settlers and the highland life they left. Nearby is the road to the high **Beulach Ban Falls**, a rushing torrent in the spring or after rain.

On the eastern shore, the **Coastal Trail** is a long hike, at 11 km return, but offers fine views along the granite headlands, passing a narrow cove where surf makes weird noises. A much shorter (0.4-km) trail at **Green Cove** leads to another rocky headland. Just before the park border at Ingonish, a road leads to **Mary Ann Falls**, a half-hour side trip, which has a swimming hole and picnic area.

Ingonish Beach is one of the province's best, with white sand and clear, cold ocean water or a warmer freshwater lake. **Highlands Links Golf Course**, *Keltic Lodge, Ingonish Beach; tel: (902) 285-2600*, open daily 0600–2100 (late May–mid Oct), 18 holes $36, has such a beautiful setting that it's hard to concentrate on the game. No carts allowed.

Historic Sites and Museums

Musee Acadien, 774 *Main St, Cheticamp; tel: (902) 224-2170*, open daily 0800–2100 (mid June–Sept), 0900–1800 (mid May–mid June, Oct), free, records the past of an Acadian fishing town, and offers a chance to try your hands at rug hooking, so popular here that Cheticamp is called the 'Hooked Rug Capital of the World'. You'll believe it upstairs, in the **Cooperative Artisanale**, where hooked rugs and other handwork is sold.

At **North Highlands Community Museum**, *Rte 19, Cape North; no tel*, open daily 1000–1800 (mid June–mid Oct), free, you'll encounter the early Gaelic settlers and learn of their isolated lives in these northern ports. Relics from the 1761 wreck of the *Auguste,* and memorabilia from World War II, when this was an important observation station, are also displayed.

Outdoor Activities

South Harbour is a broad cove almost completely separated from the Atlantic by a long sandbar, perfect for paddlers. **Eagle North Canoe and Kayak Rentals**, *299 Shore Rd, South Harbour; tel: (902) 383-2552*, $30 half-day, even rents binoculars to help you observe the loons and eagles. **Sea Spray Cycle Center**, *Dingwall; tel: (902) 383-2732*, open daily 0900–1700, rents bicycles, including car racks, and provides maps of coastal trails.

Deep-sea fishing for cod and mackerel centres at **Bay St Lawrence**, on the tip of the peninsula. **Captain Burton**, *tel: (902) 383-2268*, three trips daily (June–Oct), $12–25, guarantees that you will catch fish, or your money back. **Fan-A-Sea VI Adventures**, *tel: (902) 383-2680*, three trips daily (June–Oct), $12.50–25, also does charter diving trips.

EASTERN CAPE BRETON AND BRAS D'OR LAKE

Encompassing all the waters of Bras d'Or, as well as several long channels and St Anns Bay, this region has almost as much water as land. If you have time, follow any road along the scenic shores of these giant lakes, where you are quite likely to see eagles.

STAYING IN EASTERN CAPE BRETON

Accommodation

Lodgings are most abundant in the old lakeside resort town of **Baddeck**, and around **Sydney** and **North Sydney**, where you will find *BW, CI, De* and *Hd.*

Auberge Gisele, *387 Shore Rd (P.O. Box 132), Baddeck, NS B0E 1B0; tel: (902) 295-2849*, open mid May–Oct, high moderate, has rooms in a modern annex or the original inn. Extras include a whirlpool, sauna and solarium. The dining room has a continental flair. **Telegraph House**, *Chebucto St (P.O. Box 8), Baddeck, NS B0E 1B0, tel: (902) 295-9988*, moderate, is big and warm and lovable, filled with hospitality. Rooms in the main house are reached by two flights of stairs; those in the newer motel annex are easier, but more expensive.

West along the lake, **Castle Moffett**, *Box 678, Baddeck, NS B0E 1B0; tel: (902) 756-9070*, expensive–pricey, is unique in Atlantic Canada. The Moffetts' home is indeed their castle, complete with crenelated stonework, astride a brook on their hillside estate. Inside, the great hall is impressive, but very comfortable, with a wee library and cosy corners. All luxury suites, with a licensed lounge for guests only.

The **Gowrie House Country Inn**, *139 Shore Rd, Sydney Mines, NS B1V 1A6; tel: (902) 544-1050*, open Apr–Oct, moderate–expensive, is filled with fine antiques and set in stunning gardens. Some guest rooms share baths. Multi-course dinners are served by reservation in the dining room (pricey). It's 5 mins from the Newfoundland ferries.

287

Close to the fortress at Louisbourg, **Cranberry Cove Inn**, *17 Wolfe St, Louisbourg, NS B0A 1M0; tel: (902) 733-2171,* moderate, has rooms and suites with Jacuzzis, but keeps its Victorian charm for all its modern amenities. Antiques mix tastefully with modern furnishings. The dining room, open to the public, serves innovative entrées, such as oysters sautéed in champagne.

North of St Anns Bay, **The Stephen's Bed and Breakfast**, *Murray Rd, North River (RR#1, Baddeck, NS B0E 1B0); tel: (902) 929-2860,* budget, offers beautifully appointed rooms and warm hospitality overlooking a tidal estuary, within walking distance of North River Kayaking.

Eating and Drinking
Bell Buoy, *Chebucto St, Baddeck; tel: (902) 295-2581,* moderate, has three things going for it: the seafood, the view and the genuine hospitality of its lively staff. The **Baddeck Fish Company Restaurant**, *Chebucto St, Baddeck; tel: (902) 295-1238,* budget–moderate, serves fresh seafood that is never deep fried; the atmosphere is informal. **Baddeck Lobster Suppers**, *Ross St, Baddeck; tel: (902) 295-3307,* daily 1600–2100, moderate, are served 'in the rough' accompanied by unlimited seafood chowder and steamed mussels. Lunch includes lobster rolls.

The Grubstake, *Louisbourg; tel: (902) 733-2308,* moderate, serves its seafood poached or sautéed, with subtle seasoning. On the south shore of Bras d'Or Lake, **Cookies Chowder House**, *Johnstown; tel: (902) 535-2442,* offers traditional chowders, sandwiches and teatime treats.

SIGHTSEEING
Perhaps the best way to tour Bras d'Or Lake is by boat, from which you can usually spot the resident eagles. **Amoeba Sailing Tours**, *Government Wharf, Baddeck; tel: (902) 295-2481 or 295-1426,* four departures daily (June–Sept), $8–16, sail the lake aboard the schooner *Amoeba*. On the southern shore, **Super Natural Sailing Tours**, *Johnstown; tel: (902) 535-3371 or (800) 903-3371,* two tours daily (mid June–mid Oct), $12–26, conducts nature tours on a catamaran.

Bird Islands, 2 km off the coast near St Anns Bay, are nesting grounds for puffin, razorbill, black guillemot and other sea birds. **Bird Island Boat Tours**, *Big Bras d'Or (off Hwy 105); tel: (902 674-2384 or (800) 661-6680),* four tours daily (July–Aug), two daily (June), one daily (late May), $10–24, tours the islands, where seals are also often spotted.

Historic Sites and Museums
The primary historic re-creation in Atlantic Canada is the **Fortress of Louisbourg National Historic Site**, *Louisbourg; tel: (902) 733-2280,* open daily 0900–1900 (July–Aug), 0930–1700 (May–June, Sept–Oct, with limited facilities May and Oct), admission $5.50–11, $27.50 family. Access is limited by the free shuttle bus from the Visitor Centre to the site, with the shortest waits in early morning or early afternoon.

When the reconstruction began several decades ago, little more than a few crumbling foundations of the massive outer walls remained of the prosperous fortified city built here by the French in the early 1700s and blown up in 1758. Two centuries later it has risen to life, inhabited in the summer by costumed interpreters engaged in the daily life of a thriving commercial outpost. You can join them in homes, shops, gardens,

Colour section (i): Province House, Charlottetown (p. 266); St Mary's Church, Indian River, PEI (p. 274).
(ii): Nova Scotia: Halifax at sunset (pp. 294–299); Lunenberg (p. 310).
(iii): Cape Breton coastline; Annapolis Royal Historic Gardens (p. 304).
(iv): Newfoundland dories and lobster pots; Quidi Vidi Harbour (p. 318); inset: icebergs near St Anthony (p. 338).

Scottish Fiddle Music

The most popular – with tourists and locals alike – evening activities on Cape Breton involve fiddle music, as accompaniment to dancing or part of a *Ceilidh* (pronounced KAY-lee), a community get-together featuring Celtic music and dance. **Square dances** with local fiddlers are held in **West Mabou** every Sat night year round, and in **Glencoe**, near Mabou, every Thur in the summer. You are welcome to dance, learn or watch.

On Wed (July–Aug) and Fri (June, Sept), **The Normaway Inn**, *Egypt Rd, Margaree; tel: (902) 248-2412*, admission $6, has fiddle concerts followed by a barn dance. Ceilidhs are held by the Gaelic College; *tel: (902) 295-3411*, admission $7, Wed evenings (July–Aug) at the **Englishtown Community Hall**. Each Tues and Fri evening and Sun afternoon, **Music on the Boardwalk**, brings free concerts of Acadian music to the Cheticamp dock. The **Savoy**, *Lower Union St, Glace Bay; tel: (902) 849-1999*, a 1920s theatre, frequently features top Nova Scotia performers.

bakery, tavern or guard house, sampling their foods and learning about their lives.

The **Alexander Graham Bell National Historic Site**, *Chebucto St, Baddeck; tel: (902) 295-2069*, open daily 0900–2000 (July–Aug), 0900–1900 (June, Sept), 0900–1700 (Oct–May), $2–3.75, is a large modern museum showing Bell's experiments with *Silver Dart*, an early airplane, and a prototype hydrofoil. His family life and his love for Cape Breton are captured in a play and slide shows.

Grittier history is recorded at the **Miners' Museum**, *42 Birkley St, Glace Bay; tel: (902) 849-4522*, open daily 1000–1800 (mid June–mid Sept), Mon–Fri 0900–1600 (mid Sept–mid June), $3–6 admission includes a film and tour of the mine led by retired miners. Wear sturdy shoes and dress warmly. In **Miner's Village** are homes, the company store and a budget–moderate restaurant.

The **Gaelic College of Celtic Folk Arts**, *St Anns; tel: (902) 295-3411*, offers summer courses in Gaelic language, music, bagpipe, Scottish and Cape Breton step dancing, weaving and kilt making, and, in early Aug, the **Gaelic Mod**, a Scottish festival. The **Hall of Clans**, open daily 0800–2000 (July–Aug), Mon–Fri 0800–1700 (mid May–June, Aug–mid Dec), $2,

has exhibits on Scottish traditional dress, history and bagpipes, and on Angus MacAskell, who, at nearly 2.5 m in height, was known as 'The Cape Breton Giant'. The shop has kilts and tartans, and excellent book and music selections.

Outdoor Activities

The protected waters of the lake, channels and deep estuaries are prime for sea kayaking. **North River Kayak Tours**, *Murray Rd, North River Bridge; tel: (902) 567-2322*, $35–85, teaches the basics in a 2½-hour course on the quiet waters of North River estuary, and leads half- or full-day paddles, rich in local lore, history and nature experiences. Or you can combine one day of kayaking with a full-day hike to the 30-m North River Falls. If you're there during the full moon, sign up for the unforgettable Full Moon Paddle. On the southern shore of Bras d'Or, near Dundee, **Kayak Cape Breton**, *Roberta; tel: (902) 535-3060*, $175–490, conducts multi-day kayak and camping tours, and one-day river kayaking courses, $80, in the spring.

To bicycle along the rolling lake shores, you can rent equipment at **Island Eco-Adventures**, *16 Chebucto St, Baddeck; tel: (902) 295-3303*.

289

CAPE BRETON–HALIFAX

The coastal route from the Canso Causeway to Halifax, called the Marine Drive, is one of the least visited of the province's scenic trails, although it offers uncrowded beaches, small fishing harbours, an outstanding historic village restoration, wildlife and a low rocky shoreline of deep inlets and islands.

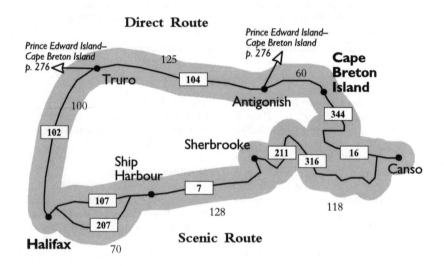

DIRECT ROUTE: 285 KM

DIRECT ROUTE

From the Canso Causeway, follow Rte 104 to **Antigonish** (see p.280), bypassing **New Glasgow**, to **Truro** (p. 277). Turn onto Rte 102 south, which will take you straight into **Halifax**, a distance of about 285 km. Driving time is about 4½ hours.

SCENIC ROUTE

At the end of the causeway take Rte 344 south along the shore of the Strait of Canso. At **Boylston**, Rte 344 ends at Rte 16, which you take south along Chedabucto Bay. Just past **Philips Harbour** is an intersection with Rte 316, but continue on Rte 16 for a short diversion into the village of **Canso**, then return to the intersection. Rte

316 cuts south to the Atlantic shore, to **Isaacs Harbour North**, where it intersects Rte 211. Follow Rte 211 and signs to the **Country Harbour Ferry**. After crossing, continue on to the intersection with Rte 7, where you turn left into **Sherbrooke**. Stay on Rte 7 through **Port Dufferin, Sheet Harbour, Ship Harbour** and **Jedore**. A short distance beyond **Musquodoboit Harbour**, you have the option of continuing on Rte 7, taking a fast route (Hwy 107) into **Halifax**, or, one last coastal circuit following Rte 207. Throughout the entire route, until this last option, follow signs for the Marine Drive.

BUSES

Acadian Lines operate services to and from Cape Breton Island. Leaving Sydney twice daily at 0700 and 1630, the service follows the direct route via Antigonish. In addition, there is an 0830 service via Big Pond. See OTT table 232.

TOURIST INFORMATION

Tourist Bureau, *Whitman House, 1297 Union St, Canso, NS B0H 1H0; tel: (902) 366-2170,* open daily 0900–1800 (late May– Sept), or **Guysborough County Tourism**, *P.O. Box 49, Guysborough, NS B0H 1N0; tel: (902) 533-3731.*

CANSO CAUSEWAY TO SHERBROOKE

Rte 344 hugs the shore of the Strait of Canso, with views across to Cape Breton and Isle Madame. **Mulgrave** was the ferry connection to Cape Breton before the causeway was built in 1955, and it remains an important seaport. The road continues through rough wooded countryside along the highlands of **Chebucto Bay**.

At **Port Shoreham**, the **Port Shoreham Beach Provincial Park** (no phone) provides a chance to enjoy the bay, with picnic tables and a swimming beach. This is a day-use park, but tent pitches and caravan

sites are available at **Boylston Provincial Park**; *tel: (902) 533-3326,* open mid June– Sept, $10.

Take Rte 16 to **Guysborough**, stopping at the **Old Court House Museum**, *Main St; tel: (902) 533-4008,* erected in 1843 and now serving as a local history and genealogical centre; open daily 0900–1700, June–Sept, free. **Mulgrave Road Theatre**, *68 Main St; tel: (902) 533-2092,* is a professional touring company with performances here on a varying schedule. Two km south, at the intersection of Rtes 16 and 401, is parking for the 3.7-km **Guysborough Nature Trail** along a gravel former rail bed.

Rte 16 continues along Chebucto Bay; at the intersection with Rte 316, carry on a short distance to the town of **Canso**, occupied in the 1500s and permanently settled in 1605. **Grassy Island National Historic Site**, off shore, is accessible by boat. Get current schedules at the **Visitor Centre** in **Whitman House Museum**, *1297 Union St, Canso; tel: (902) 366-2170,* open daily 0900–1800 (June–Sept), free. Grassy Island was an early and important fishing centre. There is an interpretive trail around the island, and the Visitor Centre has a diorama, artefacts and a video explaining the lives of the early inhabitants.

Retrace your route back to Rte 316 and turn south along the coast, past wilderness inland and a succession of sea views on the other side. **Sea Wind Landing Country Inn**, *RR2, Charlos Cove, NS B0H 1T0; tel: (902) 525-2108 or (800) 563-INNS,* is a destination in itself, offering moderate modern lodgings and outdoor activity. Their **Sugar Island Life Excursion** on a 30-ft cruiser finds views of herds of seals and other wildlife. They also provide directions for nature explorations on the inn's lands and beaches and directions for nearby hikes.

At **Isaacs Harbour North**, Rte 316 turns inland. Take Rte 211, following signs to the ferry across Country Harbour. This short cable ferry shuttle saves miles of driving. Look for the mussel farm off the opposite shore. Rte 211 passes through a few villages before ending at Rte 7, where you turn left into Sherbrooke.

SHERBROOKE

Although settled in the 18th century, the town's heyday came in the 1860s when gold was found in great quantity, more gold in fact than in the Klondike. With gold mining, the town prospered until 1906, when the last mine closed.

In the 1960s, **Sherbrooke Village**, *tel: (902) 522-2400,* a living museum, was created in the original buildings; open daily 0930–1730 (June–mid Oct), admission $2– 4, $12 family. Twenty of the 80 restored buildings are open for viewing; the others are still private residences restored to the period 1860–early 1900s. You can tour several homes, a general store, restored tailor and blacksmith shops and even an authentic Ambrotype photographic studio, where you can have your portrait taken in period costume.

Be sure to see the MacDonald Brothers up-and-down water-powered sawmill and lumber camp near the museum grounds, open same hours, free. The old **Sherbrooke Hotel** is the museum's restaurant serving lunches and teas of sandwiches and traditional Nova Scotia dishes.

The museum entrance building has a full range of **tourist information**, *tel: (902) 522-2400,* and can help with lodging. For bicycle, canoe and kayak rentals, contact **Camtech**, *tel: (902) 522-2192.* Sherbrooke, apart from the restoration, has few tourist services, but **Bright House Restaurant**, *Main St; tel: (902) 522-2691,* open daily (June–Oct), moderate, is in a large square colonial home and offers luncheon and dinners of traditional fare, especially seafood dishes, such as scallops in Pernod. Behind the restaurant is their bakery, where you can buy cakes, tea, biscuits and bread fresh from the oven.

SHERBROOKE TO SHIP HARBOUR

From Sherbrooke, Rte 7 clings closely to the coast almost all the way to Ship Harbour. There are myriad short peninsulas to explore and towns with names that tinkle in the ear, like Ecum Secum, Port Dufferin, Mushaboom and Spry Bay.

At **Liscomb Mills**, the province operates **Liscomb Lodge**, *Rte 7, Liscomb Mills, NS B0J 2A0; tel: (902) 779-2307 or (800) 665-6343,* moderate–expensive, a full service destination resort with bicycles, canoe, tennis and a variety of other activities and tour packages available. The **Riverside Room**, moderate–expensive, is open to the public and specialises in planked salmon served overlooking the river.

At the bridge over the **Liscomb River**, where you should look upstream to see the stair-stepped **Liscomb Falls**, are **hiking trails** around and through the Mayflower Peninsula, an area that was filled with homes, shops and lumbering operations until the early 1900s. Today, little remains but the forests which have reclaimed all. These are rough trails, best hiked in heavy shoes. A few kilometres on, the **English Garden Tearoom**, *Moser; tel: (902) 347-2870,* budget, is a good place to stop for tea, and they have a full breakfast menu, hot and cold sandwiches, fish and chips and fixed menu dinners.

Port Dufferin has two good choices for lodging and dining. **Marquis of Dufferin Seaside Motel**, *RR1, Rte 7, Port Dufferin, NS B0J 2R0; tel: (902) 654-2696,* budget-moderate, has motel-style rooms, but the warmth of an inn, with a fine dining room serving innovative and interesting continental dishes. Outdoor dining in the summer overlooks the water; they also have bicycles and a dock on the bay with canoes. **Black Duck Seaside Inn**, *25245 Rte 7, Port Dufferin, NS B0J 2R0; tel/fax: (902) 885-2813,* moderate, has the look and atmosphere of a fine old Victorian mansion, but the building is brand new. The dining room serves creative dinners, such as fisherman's lasagne with scallops and haddock. They also have a floating dock.

At **Spry Bay**, visit **Taylor Head Provincial Park**, *off Rte 7 between Mushaboom and Spry Harbour*, open all year, services (mid May–mid Oct), free, on **Mushaboom Harbour**. Outstanding interpretive signs describe the opposing syncline and anticline geological pressures that continue to form the area, the changing face of the land and its ecosystems and the life forms along the intertidal zone. Four hiking trails, from 2–6 km, pass beaches, seashore barrens and bluffs. A long swimming beach of white sand, picnic tables and a canteen are also available.

Beyond, **Coastal Adventures**, *P.O. Box 77, Tangier, NS B0J 3H0, tel/fax: (902) 772-2774*, specialises in **kayaking**, and the owner, Scott Cunningham, literally wrote the book on the sport in the province. Novices are welcome. They offer trips among the neighbouring islands and longer expeditions to prime locations elsewhere in Atlantic Canada. Nearby, **J. Willy Krauch & Sons Smokehouse**, *Tangier (look for the signs); tel: (902) 772-2188 or (800) 758-4412*, sells salmon, eel and mackerel woodsmoked in the old-fashioned Danish way, a favourite of the British royal family. You can take a short tour through the curing rooms.

When passing through **Murphy's Cove**, notice **St Peter's Church** high above its well-kept churchyard. Although the name might not attract you, **Family Fries**, *Rte 7, Ship Harbour, no tel*, budget, is good for a fast meal, offering fish and chips, fried clams and lobster salad.

SHIP HARBOUR TO HALIFAX

This coast was settled and occupied by fishermen, and one fisherman's home and docks have been restored as a memorial and museum. **The Fisherman's Life Museum**, *off Rte 7, Jedore Oyster Ponds; tel (902) 889-*

2053, open Mon–Sat 0930–1730, Sun 1300–1730 (June–mid Oct), free, interprets the daily lives of several generations of a fishing and farming family, one of whom raised 13 daughters in this tiny house. It's an inspiring and enjoyable stop, and there's always something fresh from the oven to sample.

Rte 7 goes along the heads of a number of bays formed by long peninsulas. Each of these points has a road to the end, and they make scenic side trips. The **Musquodoboit Railway Museum and Tourist Information Centre**, *Rte 7, P.O. Box 303, Musquodoboit Harbour, NS B0J 2L0; tel: (902) 889-2689*, open daily 0900–1700 (July–Aug), 0900–1600 (June and Sept–mid Oct), free, has a large collection of memorabilia inside the Victorian station house and a collection of passenger and freight cars outside. **Camelot Inn**, *c/o P.M. Holgate, Musquodoboit Harbour, NS B0J 2L0; tel: (902) 889-2198*, low moderate, is in an attractive Victorian cottage on five acres overlooking the river rapids, near a salmon pool. At the end of the peninsula, **Martinique Beach Provincial Park** has swimming, picnic facilities and a bird sanctuary.

Just beyond **Musquodoboit Harbour**, *Rte 207 and the Marine Drive*, turn to the left. Here you have three options: taking a short cut directly into Halifax via Hwy 107, following the Marine Drive for more shore scenery through **Lawrencetown**, or continuing on Rte 7. The latter leads to **Porter's Lake Provincial Park**, *West Porter's Lake Rd, Porter's Lake, NS B0J 2S0; tel: (902) 827-2250*, offering camping, swimming and picnic areas, and **The Old Hall Wilderness Heritage Centre**, *4694 Rte 7, Porter's Lake; tel: (902) 827-2364*, dedicated to the appreciation and preservation of the natural environment, it has exhibits on natural history and the relationship of people to the surrounding wilderness.

From Porter's Lake, you can join Hwy 107 at Exit 19 and continue into Halifax.

293

HALIFAX

It's easy to feel at home in compact, un-pretentious Halifax. At 115,000 residents, it's large enough to have the sophistication of good restaurants, lively nightlife and quality entertainment, but it never seems crowded, nor does it suffer from the urban sprawl of many other cities.

Instead, its tidy centre of historic buildings – under the stern eye of an impressive early 19th-century Citadel – gives way smoothly (and quickly) to tree-shaded streets lined with gracious Victorian homes. These quiet neighbourhoods are as good for a summer evening stroll as the lively waterfront, where you may hear the sounds of experimental jazz or the alternatively hearty and haunting maritime music, drifting out of stone warehouses built in the 1700s. Halifax wears its present as smartly as its past.

TOURIST INFORMATION

The **Nova Scotia Tourist Information Centre**, *P.O. Box 130, Halifax, NS B3J 2M7; tel: (902) 424-4247*, is on the waterfront in an old **Historic Properties** building, open daily 0830–1900 (June–mid Sept), Mon–Fri 0830–1630 (Sept–May). Along with a cheerful staff, they have a selection of books, including walking and nature guides. Another office is at **Halifax International Airport**; *tel: (902) 873-1223*, and a third at the airport interchange of Hwy 102; *tel: (902) 873-3608*.

Tourism Halifax, *P.O. 1749, Halifax,* *NS B3J 3A5; tel: (902) 421-8736; fax: (902) 421-6897,* is in the **Old City Hall** on *Duke St,* open daily in summer 0830–1800 (to 2000 Thur–Fri), and Mon–Fri 0900–1630 the rest of the year. Their bulletin board lists current events. A seasonal kiosk in the **Public Gardens** is open daily 0900–1700 (June–Aug).

WEATHER

The sea brings cooling breezes year round and warming currents which make heavy snow rare. Prepare for occasional fog and rain, and for cool summer evenings mid May until mid Sept, when daytime temperatures average 20°–25°C. Expect winter temperatures to average -3° to 1°C. For a weather report; *tel: (902) 426-9090.*

ARRIVING AND DEPARTING

Airport
Halifax International Airport is on Hwy 102, about 40 km (45 mins) north of the city centre. **Aerocoach City Shuttle**; *tel: (902) 468-1258,* provides transport to downtown hotels ($11, $18 return). The terminal has currency exchange, car rentals, visitor information and a bookstore with a good selection on the province. Rental cars are parked opposite the exit nearest to arrival and departure gates.

By Train
VIA Rail, *1161 Hollis St.; tel: (800) 561-3949* (toll-free). Trains arrive once daily (except Wed) from Montréal, with stops in New Brunswick. The ticket window is open daily 0900–1730.

By Bus
Buses arrive and depart from a station at

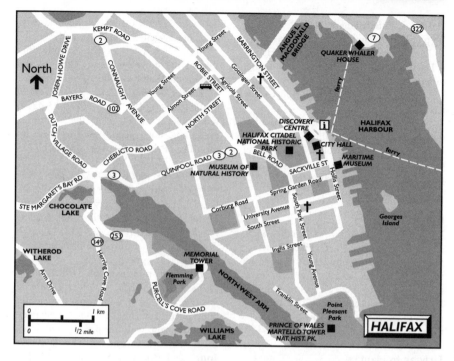

6040 Alton St. **Acadian Lines**, tel: (902) 454-8279 Mon–Fri 0900–1700, (902) 454-9321 other hours, runs to and from Amherst, connecting with SMT buses to New Brunswick (SMT connects to Voyageur to Montréal and Greyhound throughout Canada and the USA). Acadian also connects with lines to Cape Breton Island and Newfoundland ferries. **McKenzie Bus Lines**, tel: (902) 543-2491 or 742-5011, runs daily to Yarmouth and the South Shore.

By Car

From Truro and other points north, Hwy 102 brings traffic to Halifax. From Yarmouth, at Nova Scotia's south-east tip, follow Hwy 103 east to the outskirts of Halifax, where it joins Hwy 102 to enter on *Bayers Rd*. If you use a map to locate your destination in relation to the harbour and Signal Hill, you will find driving in Halifax easy.

GETTING AROUND

Halifax is almost entirely surrounded by water. Its historic centre lies in today's compact grid of downtown streets, between the waterfront and the **Citadel**, the star-shaped fortress that still commands the best view from above the town.

You always have visual landmarks: walking downhill, you are going east to the harbour; uphill, west to the Citadel. Since the slope is always apparent, you can hardly get lost in the ten-or-so blocks where hotels, restaurants and activities are clustered. Detailed free city maps are available from Tourist Offices, hotels and from roving street ambassadors.

Tourism Halifax maps a self-guided walking tour in its free *Visitor Guide*. In imperfect weather you can make your way via indoor walkways (pedways) from the waterfront to Citadel Hill, with help from the map in

Where (see Entertainment, p. 297), also free. Be prepared to climb some steep streets.

Directly across the harbour from Halifax is **Dartmouth**, where you will find dining, shopping and a restored canal to stroll along. It is reached by the MacDonald Bridge or by ferry.

Taxi ranks are at the airport, rail and bus stations, major hotels and throughout downtown. You won't have trouble hailing one of the 800-plus licenced cabs, but any company, including **Aero Cab**; *tel: (902) 445-3333,* will send one to pick you up.

Public Transport

Local buses; *tel: (902) 421-6600* ($1.30 adults, $0.95 seniors, $0.80 children) include transfers for the Dartmouth ferry ($1.10); ask for one when you board. The ferry leaves from the easy-to-spot waterfront terminal. Hours vary seasonally, so be sure to check return times. A trolleybus (fare $0.25) circles the downtown area.

Driving in Halifax

Halifax drivers are courteous, and the streets well marked. Pedestrians have the right of way, so stop whenever one steps off a kerb. Metered parking is $0.25 for 15 mins, usually with a 2-hr maximum; it is free before 0800 and after 1800 weekdays, and all day Sat, Sun and holidays. Be sure to feed your meter, since a parking ticket costs $12. Park RVs in lots along *Lower Water St.* All-day parking in the garage at Purdy's Wharf costs $4.50. The only confusing roundabout is the Armdale Rotary, where roads from Peggy's Cove meet two highways and two major streets into the city. Finding your way *in* is easy, but you may have to go round twice to get *out.*

STAYING IN HALIFAX

Accommodation

In-town lodgings represent everything from small inns to large full-service hotels, with all the major chains represented. Advance booking is almost essential in July and early Aug, and suggested at any time of year.

Most larger hotels are conveniently situated in the downtown area. Close to the waterfront, **Hotel Halifax**, *1990 Barrington St, Halifax, NS B3J 1P2; tel: (902) 425-6700 or (800) 441-1414, fax: (902) 425-6214,* moderate–expensive, is in the centre of everything, but especially easy to reach by car. The **Prince George Hotel**, *1725 Market St, Halifax, NS B3J 3N9; tel: (902) 425-1986 or (800) 565-1567; fax: (902) 429-6048,* also with fine views, faces the Citadel. Expensive. Nearby is **Lord Nelson Hotel**, *South Park St, PO Box 700, Halifax, NS B3J 2T3; tel: (902) 423-6331 or (800) 565-2020,* with a stunning lobby and plain, but moderately priced, rooms.

Halliburton House Inn, *5184 Morris St, Halifax, NS B3J 1B3; tel: (902) 420-0658; fax: (902) 423-2324,* is luxurious with an inn atmosphere and free parking, moderate–expensive. Also with free parking, and funky in its Victorian excesses, is **The Waverly Inn**, *1266 Barrington St, Halifax, NS B3J 1Y5; tel: (902) 423-9346 or (800) 565-9346* (toll-free) in the Maritimes; *fax: (902) 425-0167.* Oscar Wilde once stayed there.

Bed and Breakfasts are a few blocks further on, still within an easy walk of attractions – and close to *Spring Garden Rd* restaurants. These include **The Garden Inn**, *1263 South Park St, Halifax, NS B3J 2K8; tel: (902) 492-8577 or (800) 565-0000,* has free parking; budget–moderate. Without breakfast (available nearby), but in a home filled with fine Canadian art and antiques, is **Queen Street Inn Tourist Home**, *1266 Queen St, Halifax, NS B3J 2H4; tel: (902) 422-9828,* moderate.

Across the harbour, a 10-min walk from the Halifax ferry, **Stearns Mansion**, *17 Tulip St, Dartmouth, NS B3A 2S5; tel: (902) 465-7414; fax (902) 466-8832,* includes a four-course breakfast with five rooms furnished in Victorian antiques. Two (at a higher rate) have large Jacuzzis. Moderate.

Budget choices downtown include the clean **Heritage House Hostel**, *1253 Barrington St, Halifax, NS B3J 1Y2; tel/fax: (902) 422-3863*, with group, private and family rooms, and the **YMCA**, *1565 S. Park St, Halifax, NS B3J 2L2; tel: (902) 423-9622, fax: (902) 425-0155*, opposite the public garden, open to men and women over 18; rates include use of many of the facilities. The **YWCA**, *1239 Barrington St, Halifax, NS B3J 1Y3; tel: (902) 423-6162, fax: (902) 423-7761*, houses women only. All have shared baths.

City-run **Shubie Park**, *Jaybee Dr., off Rte 318*, has a campsite near a lake; mailing address: *Box 817, Dartmouth, NS B2Y 3Z3; tel. (902) 435-8328* (mid May–Sept), *(902) 464-2121* other times. **Juniper Park**, *near Exit 4 on Hwy 103*, has wooded tent pitches on a lake; mailing address: *Box 6, Site 15, RR 3, Armdale, NS B3L 4J3; tel: (902) 876-2814*.

Eating and Drinking

Dining out is popular with Haligonians, so restaurants have the steady clientele that encourages excellence. They are open quite late. Buy picnic fare in any shopping complex, or at the food court in **Maritime Mall**, *1505 Barrington St*, or at **Spring Garden Grocery**, *5640 Spring Garden Rd*, near the Public Gardens.

For restaurants at all prices, head for *Upper* and *Lower Water Sts*. On the top floor of **Privateer's Warehouse**, once filled with booty from rebellious American colonies, the moderate–pricey **Upper Deck Restaurant**, *Historic Properties; tel: (902) 422-1501*, serves an innovative menu strong in seafood dishes, such as Atlantic seafood stew. Below, in the **Middle Deck**; *tel: (902) 425-1500*, pasta is the speciality, at lower prices. **Lower Deck**; *tel: (902) 422-1289*, at street level, is a pub ringing with Maritime music, where you can get fish and chips, bangers and kraut or sandwiches. Budget, with $2–3 cover for music Wed–Sun.

Sweet Basil Bistro, *1866 Upper Water*

St; tel: (902) 425-2133, serves nouvelle Italian in a colourful trattoria atmosphere, budget–moderate. **Salty's on the Waterfront**, *1869 Lower Water St; tel: (902) 423-6818*, overlooks the harbour, serving fresh Atlantic seafood, with light meals on an outdoor deck. Moderate–pricey. In a reclaimed brick fire station, **McKelvie's**, *1680 Lower Water St; tel: (902) 421-6161*, also offers seafood, often with a foreign flair. Moderate.

The other prime neighbourhood for dining is up the hill on *Spring Garden Rd*. **Il Mercato**, *5475 Spring Garden Rd; tel: (902) 422-2866*, budget–moderate, has a smart Tuscan piazza décor with a fountain, as well as quality pasta, focaccia and not-your-average pizzas,. A block away on a side street is **Paloma**, *1463 Brenton St; tel: (902) 429-2425*, with paellas, Basque dishes and live Spanish guitar weekends. Budget–moderate.

Granite Brewery, *1222 Barrington St; tel: (902) 423-5660*, has pub fare with three good ales of their own, plus British brews. Budget. Nearby, the stately **Halliburton House**, *5184 Morris St; tel: (902) 420-0658*, specialises in game, which may include wild Arctic musk-ox. Pricey. Take the ferry to Dartmouth for inspired Italian dishes at **La Perla**, *opposite the Ferry Terminal; tel: (902) 469-4231*. Moderate–pricey.

Communications

Halifax Main Post Office, *1680 Bedford Row, B3J 3J5; tel: (902) 494-4734*, is open Mon–Fri 0730–1715.

Money

Exchange facilities are at the **International Visitor Centre**, *1595 Barrington St; tel: (902) 423-3392*.

ENTERTAINMENT

For its size, Halifax offers a lively night scene. For current performance schedules, pick up a free copy of *Where*, the Thursday entertainment section in the *Halifax Chronicle-Herald*, or read the bulletin board at City Hall.

297

Theatre

Good for comedy and drama, the **Neptune Theatre**, *5216 Sackville St (at Argyle); tel: (902) 429-7070*, is open Oct–May (senior/student discounts Sun–Thur). **Grafton St Dinner Theatre**, *1741 Grafton St; tel: (902) 425-1961)* presents musical comedies over dinners of prime rib, salmon or chicken, Tues–Sun evenings (about $30). For the same tariff, you can watch a lively dinner show set in Halifax's past at **Historic Feast Co**, *Historic Properties; tel: (902) 420-1840.*

Music

Symphony Nova Scotia; *tel: (902) 421-1300*, presents concerts (which may be Maritime or blues, as well as classical) at various locations (Sept–May), and **Saint Cecilia Concert Series**; *tel: (902) 466-3697*, features classical works at St. Andrew's United Church. The downtown **Metro Centre**, *5284 Duke St; tel: (902) 451-1221* for tickets, *(902) 451-1202* for recorded schedule, hosts big names such as Bob Dylan and Garth Brooks. Much of Halifax's music is in clubs, where you may hear locals or the hottest touring group. Check newspapers, or call the following venues. **Lower Deck Pub**, *in Privateers' Warehouse, Historic Properties; tel: (902) 425-1501*, is *the* place to hear live Maritime music, Mon–Sat from 1730. **Birmingham Grill**, *5657 Spring Garden Rd; tel: (902) 420-9622*, has live jazz nightly. For free summer noon-time concerts, usually Wed–Fri, go to the **Grand Parade** at *George* and *Argyle Sts.*

Clubs

The New Palace, *1721 Brunswick St; tel: (902) 429-5959*, has live bands 2200–0330, and **The Entertainment Dome**, *1740 Argyle St; tel: (902) 422-5453*, offers a variety of bands. **Split Crow**, *1855 Granville St; tel: (902) 422-4366*, has live Maritime music, and a sidewalk café in the summer.

Guppy's, *Prince George Hotel, Grafton and George Sts; tel: (902) 425-1986*, has disco

dancing for all ages, as do many other bars. Euphemistically called 'lounges', bars are plentiful and busy. Look in the streets surrounding the Grand Parade for the trendiest.

Sports

Hockey reigns supreme; you can watch games of the semi-pro Halifax Mooseheads at the **Metro Centre**, *5284 Duke St; tel: (902) 451-1221* for tickets, *(902) 451-1202* for recorded schedule.

Events

The Scotia Festival of Music, in late May, is followed by **The International Tattoo**; *tel: (902) 451-1221* (for tickets), bringing bands from all over the piping world in early July and overlapping with the **Metro Scottish Festival**. Public performances are held in the Grand Parade. Later in the month, the **Atlantic Jazz Festival** fills a week, and in late Aug is the **Buskers International Street Performers Festival**.

SHOPPING

Indoor shopping malls abound in Halifax, some connected to hotels by indoor 'pedways'. **Scotia Square**, *Barrington at Duke St*, has two levels of shops, mostly of interest to locals. Across the street, **Barrington Place**, *1903 Barrington St*, has more fashionable shops, including **Micmac Heritage Gallery** for native Indian crafts. **Maritime Centre**, *1505 Barrington (at Spring Garden Rd)*, is smaller and good for everyday items.

The waterfront blocks of old **Historic Properties** buildings have smart shops selling crafts, crystal and gourmet foods, as well as the expected souvenirs. For local folk arts, go to the shop at **Art Gallery of Nova Scotia**, *1741 Hollis St.*

On *Spring Garden Rd*, beyond the striking statue of Sir Winston Churchill at the Public Library, shops mix with restaurants in a lively, less tourist-filled atmosphere. **Park Lane**, *5657 Spring Garden Rd at Dresden Row*, is a fashionable complex.

SIGHTSEEING

Walking Tour

The short distance between major sights invites walking. Begin at the **Tourist Centre** – in **Historic Properties**, an area that includes some of North America's best Victorian Italianate façades – and walk through Canada's oldest surviving waterfront warehouses and along the wharves, where you will pass the Ferry Terminal and the **historic ships** moored behind the **Maritime Museum**. At **Sackville Landing Park**, the **Atlantic Marine Pavillion** offers an up-close look at sea life. Turn right and head up *Sackville St* to Hollis. After crossing *Prince St,* you will walk between the Georgian **Province House**, Canada's oldest legislative building, on your left, and the ornate façade of the **Art Gallery of Nova Scotia**.

Turn left and climb *George St,* through the **Grand Parade**, Halifax's original military parade. To your left is **St Paul's Church**, Canada's oldest Anglican church, and the city's oldest building (tour brochures are just inside). Facing it is **City Hall**, Victorian architecture at its height. Continue up *George St,* facing the **Town Clock**, built under the direction of Queen Victoria's father, Prince Edward, who commanded the fortress above it. Beside the clock, steps lead to the **Citadel**; *tel: (902) 426-5080,* a fine example of a mid 19th-century bastioned fort, open daily 0900–1800 (June–Aug), 1000–1700 (Sept–May); $2 summer only; seniors and children free. In summer, a kilted regiment of **78th Highlanders** parade, and guided tours are available. To return to the waterfront, take any street downhill.

Guided Tours

A two-hour **Double Decker Tour**; *tel: (902) 420-1155,* and one operated by **Acadian Lines**; *tel: (902) 454-9321,* daily in summer, cost about $15. You can combine the latter with a harbour tour for $25.

The best harbour tour, however, is aboard *Bluenose II,* a replica of the famous fishing schooner, when it is in port; *tel: (902) 422-2678* in July and Aug, *(902) 424-5000* year round. For other harbour tours, contact **Murphy's on the Water**, *Cable Wharf; tel: (902) 420-1015.*

Alexander Keith's Brewery gives free horse-drawn wagon tours; book ahead at any Information Office. **DTours**; *tel: (902) 429-6415,* offer 90-min walking tours at $3.

Top museum choice in this seafaring city is the **Maritime Museum of the Atlantic**, *1675 Lower Water St; tel: (902) 424-7490,* open Mon–Sat 0900–1730, Sun 1300–1730 and Tues until 2000 (June–mid Oct); slightly different hours, closed Mon (mid Oct–May); $4.50, under age 16 $1. It contains the deckhouse from a schooner, Queen Victoria's barge and flotsam from the *Titanic* (survivors were brought to Halifax). Samuel Cunard and his shipping line are featured, as is the devastating explosion of 1917. Admission includes **CSS Acadia**, moored outside, the hydrographic ship that was used to chart the North Atlantic. The adjacent **HMCS Sackville**; *tel: (902) 429-5600,* is open free Mon–Sat 1000–1700, Sun 1200–1700 (Oct–May). Built in 1941, it is the only remaining of the World War II corvettes built here as Royal Canadian Navy convoy escorts.

The **Nova Scotia Museum of Natural History**, *1747 Summer St (near Bell Rd); tel: (902) 424-7353,* opens Mon–Sat 0930–1730, Sun 1300–1730 and Wed until 2000 (June–mid Oct); closed Mon and at 1700 (mid Oct–May); $3, family $6.50, free Wed 1730–2000. Native Indian and local wildlife and marine species are the highlights.

The finest Victorian **Public Gardens** on the continent are on *Sackville St* past the Citadel. Open daily 0800–sunset, free, they are filled with brilliant flower displays. The elegant bandstand features free concerts. **Point Pleasant Park**, south of downtown, has one of the few Martello towers outside Great Britain. The park is open year-round, the tower 1000–1800 (July–Aug).

299

HALIFAX–YARMOUTH

The Evangeline Trail, named after the heroine of Henry Wadsworth Longfellow's romantic poem, will lead you through the original land of the Acadians. Tidy French towns and villages, each with its church of wood or stone, line Hwy 1, alternating with stately towns built in British colonial style.

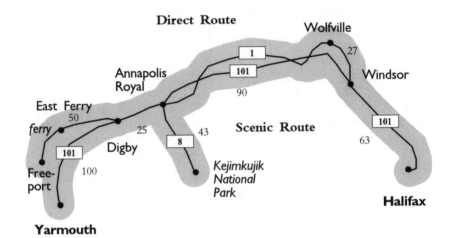

300

101 in **Lower Sackville**. Follow Hwy 101 all the way to Yarmouth, a distance of 340 km, stopping in **Wolfville** and **Annapolis Royal**. The driving time from Halifax to Yarmouth is 5 hrs.

DIRECT ROUTE: 340 KM

ROUTES

DIRECT ROUTE

Leave Halifax by following *Barrington St* to Hwy 111 over the bridge, then take Rte 7 *(Dartmouth Rd)* at Exit 2 to the Bedford Bypass, which becomes Hwy

SCENIC ROUTE

Follow the direct route from Halifax through **Lower Sackville** to **Windsor**, leaving Hwy 101 there to follow Rte 1 through **Grand Pré** and **Wolfville**, and along the Annapolis Valley to **Annapolis Royal**. Here you can take a side track to **Kejimkujik National Park** along Rte 8 (which continues to **Liverpool** on Nova Scotia's southern shore, see p. 306). From

Annapolis Royal, Rte 1 continues to **Digby** and **Digby Neck**, then on to **Yarmouth**.

BUSES

Acadian Lines operate a bus service from Halifax to Yarmouth four times a week. (journey time: 5½ hrs), and three times a week to Digby (journey time: 4 hrs). See OTT table 232.

TOURIST INFORMATION

Travel information on the entire route is available from **Evangeline Trail Tourism Association and Welcome Centre**, *5518 Prospect Rd, New Minas, NS B4N 3K8; tel: (902) 681-1645 or (800) 565-ETTA (toll-free), fax: (902) 681-2747.*

HALIFAX TO WOLFVILLE

A good spot for relaxing after a flight into Halifax is **Inn on the Lake**, *P.O. Box 29, Waverley, NS B0N 2S0; tel: (902) 861-3480, fax: (902) 861-4883,* close to the airport via Rte 102 at exit 5 (not 5A), a full service moderate resort, set in well-kept grounds. The restaurant, open daily until 2200, moderate, specialises in salmon fillet baked on a cedar plank. To join the Scenic or Direct Route from here or the airport, follow Hwy 102 south to Exit 4, onto Hwy 101.

At **Windsor**, home of the Canadian national winter sport of hockey, which originated here in 1800, visit the oldest original blockhouse in Canada, built in 1755, and the elegant **Shand House**, *Avon St; tel: (902) 798-8213,* open Mon–Sat 0930–1730, Sun 1300–1730 (June–mid Oct), free. Built in 1890, it featured every modern convenience – indoor plumbing, central heating and electric lighting. The interior panelling is superb.

The best place to see the famous **tidal bore** is along the Meander River, which flows into the Avon nearby. Twice daily, the tides force a wall of water back into the estuary, a dramatic sight, for which the **Visitor Centre**, *21 Colonial Rd; tel: (902) 789-2690,* can provide a schedule.

North on Rte 1, **Grand Pré National Historic Site**, *Grand Pré; tel: (902) 542-3631,* chapel open daily 0900–1500 (mid May–mid Oct), free, commemorates the forced deportation of French settlers who refused to swear allegiance to England after Nova Scotia became a British possession. A statue of Longfellow's fictional heroine of the poem *Evangeline,* a symbol of the Acadian expulsion, and a small stone church with exhibits about the events are set in a garden.

WOLFVILLE

Tourist Information: Wolfville Visitor Centre, *Willow Park, Main St (Rte 1), Wolfville, NS B0P 1X0; tel: (902) 542-7000,* open daily 0900–1900 (July–Aug), 0900–1700 (mid May–Oct).

ACCOMMODATION

During July and Aug, theatre-goers fill local inns (except Mon evenings), so early reservations are wise. **Blomiden Inn**, *127 Main St (P.O. Box 839), Wolfville, NS B0P 1X0; tel: (902) 542-2291 or (800) 565-2291, fax: (902) 542-7461,* moderate–expensive, is a fine Victorian mansion set in well-kept gardens. Public rooms are rich in exotic woods. Afternoon tea is included. A few doors away, **Garden House Bed & Breakfast**, *150 Main St, Wolfville, NS B0P 1X0; tel: (902) 542-1703,* budget, is a cosy 1830 home in a cottage garden overlooking the water and Cape Blomiden. Breakfasts are bounteous.

Gingerbread House Inn, *8 Robie Tufts Dr. (P.O. Box 819), Wolfville, NS B0P 1X0; tel: (902) 542-1458,* moderate, will trick you into believing it was built at the height of the Victorian era, but it's really quite new. Inside, it's filled with guest-pampering details. Next door, **Victoria's Historic Inn and Carriage House**, *416 Main St (P.O. Box 308), Wolfville, NS B0P 1X0; tel: (902) 542-5744 or (800) 556-5744, fax: (902) 542-7794,* moderate, is the real thing, with impeccably maintained period rooms and suites with Jacuzzis in the main house and

301

nicely appointed modern rooms in the adjoining coachmen's quarters.

In the same neighbourhood, **Tattingstone Inn**, *434 Main St, Wolfville, NS B0P 1X0; tel: (902) 542-7696 or (800) 565-7696, fax: (902) 542-4427*, moderate, is also in a restored Victorian mansion, with tennis courts and swimming pool in the gardens.

About 7 km away, **Planters' Barracks Country Inn**, *1468 Starr's Point Rd, R.R. 1, Port Williams, NS B0P 1T0; tel: (902) 542-7879 or (800) 661-7879, fax: (902) 542-4442*, moderate, occupies one of the area's oldest buildings, built in 1758 after the Acadian deportation. Spool beds, hand-stitched quilts and wing chairs furnish the large rooms; bicycles for guest use are free.

EATING AND DRINKING

You'll go a long way to find a better dinner than you'll get at **Chez La Vigne**, *17 Front St; tel: (902) 542-5077*, open until 2400, moderate. The cuisine is French, with Nova Scotia touches made from the finest local seafood and garden produce (the chef grows the herbs himself). Early and late, it is filled with theatre-goers, but mid evening you should be able to get reservations. The lunch menu of lighter entrées is served all day. The cuisine is also French at **Victoria's Historic Inn**, *416 Main St; tel: (902) 542-5744*, where you need to reserve for three-course *table d'hôte* dinners in the period dining room. For lunch or afternoon tea, drive to **The Acacia Croft Tearoom**, *1468 Starr's Point Rd, Port Williams; tel: (902) 542-7879*, where they serve scones and clotted cream and Ploughman's lunch, on the patio in summer, budget. **The Coffee Merchant**, *334 Main St; tel: (902) 542-4315*, serves sandwiches and bagels, along with coffees, teas and ice-cream, while **Joe's Food Emporium**, *Main St; (902) 542-3033*, is a big, casual place for steaks or pizzas.

ENTERTAINMENT

Atlantic Theatre Festival, *356 Main St,*

P.O. Box 1441, Wolfville, NS B0P 1X0, (902) 542-4242 or (800) 337-6661, performances Tues–Sun (mid June–early Sept), tickets $20–28, produces three major works each summer, from Shakespeare to modern dramatists. Audiences come from all over eastern Canada, so reserve well ahead.

SIGHTSEEING

Ask at the Visitor Centre for the *Self-Guided Walking Tour*. Among the earliest Georgian houses is **Randall House**, *171 Main St; tel: (902) 542-9775*, open Mon–Sat 1000–1700, Sun 1400–1700 (mid June–mid Sept), free, built in 1808 and furnished to the style of a century later. If you have energy after admiring the architecture and browsing in the art galleries and boutiques, follow the **walking trail** across *Main St* from the Blomiden Inn to the shore.

At early dusk, the **Robie Tufts Nature Centre**, *Front St*, late May–late Aug, located in an old chimney, is the scene of an aeronautical display by masses of **chimney swifts** returning in formation to roost. Informative displays tell about the birds and the history of this unique site.

Cape Blomiden is a short distance north of town along Rte 358 (which leaves Rte 1 in neighbouring **Greenwich**), one of the area's most scenic coastal roads. It passes through green farmlands reclaimed from the bay through a system of dykes built by early Acadian settlers. Stop at **The Lookoff** for sweeping views of Annapolis Valley and Minas Basin. At the end is **Blomiden Provincial Park**,; *tel: (902) 582-7319*, open daily 0800–dusk (mid May–mid Oct), free, with campsites and picnic area, plus walking trails along the high headland and beaches where rockhounds gather agates and amethyst.

WOLFVILLE TO ANNAPOLIS ROYAL

Rte 1 continues to parallel Hwy 101 through the gently rolling lush farmlands of the Annapolis Valley, past fields of produce destined for tables all over eastern Canada. At **Kentville**, stop at the Sat **Farmers Market** to provision a picnic at **The Ravine**, a woodland waterfall, or go for a walk through the dykelands along the tidal Cornwallis River. In **Aylesford** is the **Oaklawn Farm Zoo**, *tel: (902) 847-9790*, with farm and native animals to pet and feed, plus exotics including lions, tigers, zebras and gibbons.

ANNAPOLIS ROYAL

Tourist Information: Annapolis Royal and Area Information Centre, *Annapolis Tidal Power Project, Rte 1, Annapolis Royal, NS B0S 1A0; tel: (902) 532-5454,* open daily 0900–1900 (mid May–mid Oct).

ACCOMMODATION

Bread and Roses Country Inn, *82 Victoria St (P.O. Box 177), Annapolis Royal, NS B0S 1A0; tel: (902) 532-5727,* moderate, is a brick Queen Anne mansion, covered in vines. Inside, antique features are nicely balanced by Inuit and contemporary Canadian art. **Garrison House Inn**, *350 St George St (P.O. Box 108), Annapolis Royal, NS B0S 1A0; tel: (902) 532-5750, fax: (902) 532-5501,* overlooks Fort Anne and the gardens, which seem to have overflowed into the vases that fill the public rooms. Close by, **Queen Anne Inn**, *494 Upper St George St (P.O. Box 218), Annapolis Royal, NS B0S 1A0; tel: (902) 532-7850,* moderate, is a real head-turner, a three-storey Victorian building beautifully restored. Rooms are large, bright and tastefully decorated in a mix of antiques and contemporary pieces, all with the guests' comfort clearly in mind. Good-humoured hosts keep it feeling like a home. **The Hillsdale House**, in garden-filled grounds across the street, also moderate and owned by the same people, is less formal in its architecture, but just as impeccably furnished in antiques, and with the same hospitable atmosphere.

Across the Annapolis River, **Nightingale's Landing**, *P.O. Box 30, Granville Ferry, NS B0S 1K0; tel: (902) 532-7615,* budget–low moderate, is restored 1870 Victorian with ornate trim, owned by a folk artist whose work is for sale. Afternoon tea is served to guests.

EATING AND DRINKING

Newman's, *218 St George St; tel: (902) 532-5502,* open May–Oct, moderate, presents an innovative menu strong in fresh local ingredients. The charcoal-grilled gravlax is a new take on the ubiquitous salmon. Shortcakes come in mammoth portions.

Leo's Cafe, *222 St George St; tel: (902) 532-7424,* budget–moderate, has lighter fare, three meals daily, with impressive sandwiches and pasta dishes. **Garrison House Inn**, *350 St George St; tel: (902) 532-5750,* moderate, has a first-rate dining room, with several health-conscious grilled entrées, some inspired by exotic cuisines; try the Acadian jambalaya.

Secret Garden Restaurant, *Historic Gardens, St George St; tel: (902) 532-2200,* budget, is no secret; its courtyard overlooks the herb garden, serving lunches of delectable pastas, sandwiches and soups.

SIGHTSEEING

Annapolis Royal is filled with stunning Victorian buildings, which makes it a good place to explore on foot, wandering through its tree-shaded neighbourhoods to admire the restored homes and gardens. *Footprints with Footnotes* is a free walking tour brochure at the Information Centre, or take a 30-min guided **Stroll Through the Centuries**, *The Lighthouse, Lower St George St,* daily 1000–1700 (July–Aug), $3. Costumed guides lead lantern-light tours of the **Old Military Cemetery**, Thur, Sun 2130 (July–Aug), $3, site of Canada's oldest English epitaph, dated 1720.

Fort Anne National Historic Site, *St George St: tel: (902) 532-2321,* open daily except holidays 0900–1700 (mid May–mid Oct), $1–2.50, was built by the French in the

303

early 1700s and heavily used in both battles and sieges. Its high 1702 earthworks are intact, as are powder magazines. In the next block are the **Annapolis Royal Historic Gardens**, *441 St George St; tel: (902) 532-7018,* open daily 0900–dusk (May–Oct), admission $3–3.50, $9.75 family, which can be enjoyed as a remarkably accurate representation of garden styles throughout the three centuries of the valley's history, or as one of the loveliest places to stroll in all Canada. Particularly outstanding are the roses, the Acadian potager and farmhouse, and the Victorian Garden, almost florid in its exuberance.

The **O'Dell House Museum**, *136 Lower St George St; 532-2041,* open Mon–Sat 0930–1700, Sun 1300–1700 (June–Sept), free, is a restored 1860s stagecoach inn, with 15 rooms illustrating life of that period: a Victorian kitchen, a mourning room, ship building tools and ship models are the highlights. The **Sinclair Inn Museum**, *220 St George St; tel: (902) 532-7754,* open varying hours (July–Aug), free, is one of Canada's oldest buildings (1710), interesting for its demonstration of the building techniques of the last three centuries.

Less than 2 km across the river, **North Hills Museum**, *Granville Ferry; tel: (902) 532-2168,* open Mon–Sat 0930–1730, Sun 1300–1730 (June–midOct), free, is a 1764 farmhouse restored by a foremost collector of Georgian furniture, glass, silver, china and paintings as a museum for displaying these. Seven km further on is **Port Royal Habitation National Historic Site**, *Granville Ferry; tel: (902) 532-2898,* open daily 0900–1800 (early May–late Oct), $1.25–2.50, founded in 1605 by explorer Samuel de Champlain and the first permanent European settlement north of Florida. Destroyed a century later, it was reconstructed from its archaeological evidence. Costumed guides show the bunkrooms, kitchens, storerooms, chapel and the governor's quarters.

304

SIDE TRACK TO KEJIMKUJIK NATIONAL PARK

From Annapolis Royal, Rte 8 heads south through the wooded interior to Liverpool, where it connects with Hwy 103, providing a shorter route back to Halifax. It is also the route to **Kejimkujik National Park**, *Box 36A, Maitland Bridge, NS B0T 1N0; tel: (902) 682-2772,* halfway between the coasts.

The park's main attraction is its comparative wilderness of lakes, streams and woodlands, and the wildlife they support; admission free. It has hundreds of tent pitches and caravan sites in thickly wooded campsites. Swimming, a picnic area and bicycle and canoe rentals are available; walking trails are detailed on a map available from the Visitors Centre.

The Whitman Inn, *RR #2, Caledonia, NS B0T 1B0; tel: (902) 682-2226, fax (902) 682-3171,* moderate, just south of the park, is a good base for this area, with attractive country-style rooms and an indoor pool and sauna. Dining by reservation only.

ANNAPOLIS ROYAL TO DIGBY

Six km west on Rte 1 is the government-owned amusement park, **Upper Clements Park**, *Upper Clements; tel: (902) 532-7557* or *(800) 565-PARK,* open daily 1100– 2000 (late June–Aug), Sat–Sun 1100–2000 (early June, Sept), admission $2.30, rides pass $10, and the adjacent **Upper Clements Wildlife Park**, *tel: (902) 532-5924,* open daily 0900–1900 (mid May–mid Oct), admission included with amusement park, home to 25 species of native wild animals, including Sable Island ponies, moose, red deer and bald eagle.

DIGBY AND DIGBY NECK

Tourist Information: Evangeline Trail Visitor Information, *Montague Row, (P.O. Box 579), Digby, NS B0V 1A0; tel: (902)*

245-5714), open 0900–2030 (June–Aug), 0900–1700 (late May, Sept–late Oct).

The *M/V Princess of Acadia,* operated by **Bay Ferries**; *tel: (902) 245-2116,* makes 2½–3-hr Bay of Fundy crossings between Digby and Saint John, NB (see p. 237).

ACCOMMODATION AND FOOD

Rte 1 into Digby is lined with several motels. In town is **Admiral Digby Inn**, *Shore Rd (P.O. Box 608), Digby, NS B0V 1A0; tel: (902) 245-2531 or (800) 465-6262,* moderate, with motel-style rooms, a heated indoor swimming pool and budget–moderate dining room. **Coastal Kingfisher Motel**, *130 Warwick St, Digby, NS B0V 1A0; tel: (902) 245-4747 or (800) 665-7829,* low moderate, also has motel rooms and a restaurant. **Brier Island Lodge**, *Box 1197, Westport, NS B0V 1H0; tel: (902) 839-2300 or (800) 662-8355, fax (902) 839-2006,* moderate, has nicely furnished rooms, some with sea view and Jacuzzis, and a restaurant, budget–moderate, serving well-prepared seafood dishes.

While here, don't miss the town's most famous catch, Digby scallops, which you can eat overlooking the harbour and scallop fleet at **Fundy Restaurant**, *34 Water St; tel: (902) 245-4950,* moderate. **Red Raven Pub**, *100 Water St; tel: (902) 245-5533,* budget, serves a standard selection of deep-fried seafood, chowder and steaks, with a children's menu.

SIGHTSEEING

The main activities in Digby are whale-watching and exploring Digby Neck, the long tail of land extending into the Bay of Fundy, with two islands at its end. There's no choice of route, since it's barely wide enough for the one road, Rte 217, that runs its length.

At **East Ferry**, a ferry leaves for **Long Island** hourly on the half hour, $2; from **Freeport**, at the far end of Long Island, the ferry leaves hourly on the hour, $2, for **Brier Island**. To lessen the wait for the next Brier

Island ferry, go directly between them without stopping. Or you can just explore Long Island, especially its unique **Balancing Rock**, which you reach from Rte 217 by a well-marked trail.

Several whale- and seabird-watching cruises leave from the neck and islands; reservations are advised. Most run June–Oct, about $35. The Bay of Fundy's environment is especially hospitable for sea life, so both birds and whales are a common sight and the major reason people visit the islands. Opposite East Ferry at Tiverton, on Long Island, **Pirate's Cove Whale and Seabird Cruises**, *tel: (902) 839-2242,* runs 3-hr trips at 0800, 1300 and, often, a 1730 sunset cruise. **Mariner Cruises**, *tel: (902) 839-2346,* also has three cruises daily. On Brier Island, close to the ferry landing, both **Westport Whale Watch**, *tel: (902) 839-2467,* and **Brier Island Whale and Seabird Cruises Ltd**, *tel: (902) 839-2995,* are particularly popular for the well-regarded naturalists that guide all their cruises.

305

DIGBY TO YARMOUTH

Rte 1 travels close to the shore of St Marys Bay, often atop sand bluffs with views out toward Digby Neck. Imposing **St Bernard Church**, in the village of St Bernard, was built by parishioners, one course of granite blocks each year from 1910 to 1942, all cut and dressed by hand. You can go inside it and **St Mary's Church**, *Church Point; tel: (902) 769-2832,* the largest and tallest wooden church in North America, with a 56.3-m spire. Tours June–mid Oct, free.

A good stopping point is **Bayshore Bed and Breakfast**, *Rte 1 (P.O. Box 176), Saulnierville, NS B0W 2Z0; tel: (902) 769-3671,* budget, in an early 1800s cottage overlooking the bay. Further south, a marked road at Mavilette points to the nearly deserted white-sand **Mavilette Beach**, almost beneath the **Cape View Motel**, *PO Box 9, Salmon River, NS B0W 2Y0, tel: (902) 645-2258.*

YARMOUTH–HALIFAX

Quintessential Nova Scotia, this route along the southern shore, known as the Lighthouse Route, has all the familiar scenes from the travel brochures, but in real life: tiny fishing harbours, curving white sand beaches, off-shore islands, wharves stacked with lobster traps, turquoise water with sailboats scutting about, and, of course, lighthouses.

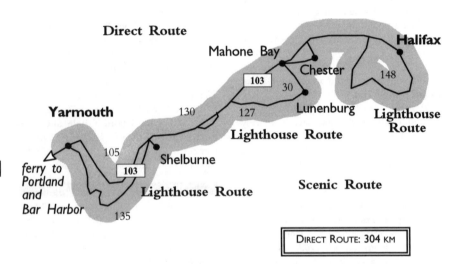

306

DIRECT ROUTE: 304 KM

ROUTES

DIRECT ROUTE

Hwy 103 is the fastest way from Yarmouth to Halifax, a distance of 304 km, which takes about 4½ hours to drive. Historic **Shelburne** and the attractive town of **Chester**, just off the highway, are convenient meal stops and worth seeing.

SCENIC ROUTE

Never far from Hwy 103, and often joining it, the scenic route follows the well-signposted Lighthouse Route, Nova Scotia's most popular scenic trail. Leaving Yarmouth, it follows Rte 3, paralleling Hwy 103 as far as **Pubnico**, where it drops south to continue along the irregular coast, with short diversions on Rte 334 to **Wedgeport** and Rte 330 to **Cape Sable Island** and **Barrington Passage**. There, the well-marked Lighthouse Route continues along winding shore roads through tiny villages, to **Shelburne**.

After a loop around the point south of Shelburne, it joins the direct route on Hwy 103 to **Summerville Centre**. Here Rte 3 parallels the highway through **Liverpool**, and rejoins it briefly, until **East Medway**, where the Lighthouse Route follows Rte 331 to **Le Have**. Cross the ferry to **East Le Have** and follow Rte 332 to **Lunenburg**. Take Rte 3 through **Mahone Bay** and **Chester**, following Lighthouse Route signs at **East River** onto Rte 329, rejoining Rte 3 in **Hubbards** and following it to **Upper Tantallon**. There, follow Lighthouse Route signs onto Rte 333 to **Peggy's Cove** and Halifax.

At almost any point along the way, you can shorten the route by returning to Hwy 103.

BUSES

Mackenzie Bus Line operates one trip a day via Mahone Bay and Lunenburg. Journey time: 5¾ hrs. See OTT table 237.

TOURIST INFORMATION

Travel information on the entire route is available from **South Shore Tourism Association**, *P.O. Box 380, Mahone Bay, NS B0J 2E0; tel: (902) 624-6466, fax: (902) 624-9734.*

YARMOUTH

Tourist Information: Yarmouth County Tourist Association, *P.O. Box 477, Yarmouth, NS B5A 4B4; tel/fax: (902) 742-5355.* **Visitor Information Centre**, *342 Main St (at the ferry docks); tel: (902) 742-6639,* open daily 0900–1900 (July–early Sept), 0900–1800 (June and early Sept–early Oct), 0900–1700 (May, Oct).

ACCOMMODATION AND FOOD

Because Yarmouth is the entry point for two ferry lines, lodging is plentiful, but for the same reason it is often filled to capacity, so reservations are important.

BW and *CI* have properties here. **Rodd Grand Hotel**, *417 Main St, Yarmouth, NS B5A 4B2; tel: (902) 742-2446 or (800) 565-RODD* (toll-free), *fax: (902) 742-4645,* moderate, is aimed at the convention trade,

but is a quality, full service hotel for tourists as well. **Murray Manor**, *225 Main St, Yarmouth, NS B5A 1C6; tel/fax: (902) 742-9625,* low moderate, is a Bed and Breakfast in a restored cottage Gothic home, a 3-min walk from the ferry. Hosts pay attention to the smallest detail of guest comfort, and afternoon tea is served.

Victorian Vogue Bed and Breakfast, *109 Brunswick St, Yarmouth, NS B5A 2H2; tel: (902) 742-6398,* low moderate, is a classic of Queen Anne architecture, with a turret and light wood interior. Guests and the public can enjoy desserts in the parlour on summer afternoons. **Loomer's Camper's Haven**, *Arcadia (Box 6245, RR4), Yarmouth, NS B5A 4A8; tel: (902) 742-4848,* open mid May–mid Oct, from $15, has wooded and open tent pitches and caravan hook-ups, on a lake, with swimming, fishing and boat rental.

Captain Kelley's Restaurant, *577 Main St, tel: (902) 742-9191,* budget–moderate, specialises in seafood, particularly lobster. **The Queen Molly**, *96 Water St; tel: (902) 742-6008,* a brew pub and restaurant in an historic harbourfront building, attracts a lively crowd to sample ales and lagers brewed on site, with more intimate dining upstairs.

307

SIGHTSEEING

As one of the major sailing ports in the Maritimes, Yarmouth was home to captains and merchants who brought goods and styles from all over the world. It shows in the wealth of fine buildings that remain today; even their hedged gardens reflect English styles popular then. You can tour the architecture and gardens of Yarmouth with the help of two handy free brochures available at the Visitor Centre.

Yarmouth County Museum and Archives, *22 Collins St; tel: (902) 742-5539,* open Mon–Sat 0900–1700, Sun 1400–1700 (June–midOct), Tues–Sun 1400–1700 (mid Oct–May), $1–2.50, family $5, depicts Yarmouth history through collections of ship models and paintings, period rooms (including a Victorian parlour and kitchen), costumes and a blacksmith shop. **Firefighters Museum of Nova Scotia**, *451 Main St, tel: (902) 742-5525,* open Mon–Sat 0900–2100, Sun 1000–1700 (July–Aug), Mon–Sat 0900–1700 (June and Sept), Mon–Fri 1000–1200 and 1400–1600 (Oct–May), $2 adults, $4 families, shows firefighting methods since the early 1800s, with horse-drawn equipment, an 1880 steamer and a 1930s ladder truck.

Yarmouth Light, *Rte 304, Cape Forchu; tel: (902) 742-1433,* would be interesting enough, but the route to it is even more picturesque, past a breakwater lined with fishing boats, sheds and lobster traps.

SIDE TRACK
TO PORTLAND AND BAR HARBOR, MAINE (USA)

A ferry operated by **Prince of Fundy Cruises**, *International Terminal, 468 Commercial St, Portland, ME 04101 USA; tel: (207) 775-5616 or (800) 482-0955* in Maine, *(902) 742-6460 or (800) 341-7540* in Canada, connects Yarmouth with **Portland, Maine** (see p. 197), saving 1375 km of driving.

The *MS Scotia Prince* leaves Yarmouth daily at 1000, arriving in Portland at 2000. Northbound crossings are overnight, departing Portland at 2100 and arriving in Yarmouth at 0900 the next morning. Single fares are US$78 adult, US$39 child, US$98 auto, US$32–95 cabin (mid June–mid Sept). Low-season fares are US$58 adult, US$29 child, US$80 auto, US$20–60 cabin (May–mid June, mid Sept–Oct). Packages with lodging and meals are available. Reservations are essential. The ferry has restaurants, snack service, shopping and entertainment on board.

The ferry to **Bar Harbor, Maine** (p. 246) is operated by **Bay Ferries**, *P.O. Box 634, Charlottetown, PEI C1A 7L3, tel: (902) 566-3838 or (888) 249-SAIL*

(toll-free). The *MV Bluenose* leaves Yarmouth daily at 1630, arriving 2130 in Bar Harbor, saving 1017 km of driving. Departure from Bar Harbor is daily at 0800, arriving in Yarmouth at 1500.

Single fares are US$41.50 adult, US$20.75 age 5–12, US$37.25 senior, US$55 auto (late June–early Sept). Low-season fares are US$27.25 adult, US$24.50 senior, US$13.75 age 5–12, US$50 auto (early–late June and early Sept–mid Oct). Reservations are essential and the *Bluenose* has dining, shopping, cinema and children's play area.

YARMOUTH TO SHELBURNE

Not far from Yarmouth, Rte 3 passes through **Arcadia**, where a short diversion onto Rte 334 leads to **Wedgeport**, debarkation point for **Tusket Island Cruises**; *tel: (800) 566-TUNA*, daily (June–mid Sept), adults $40, children 5–12 $15, 4-hr narrated excursions to the **Tusket Islands**, where fishing shanties line tiny wooden wharves. The cruise fare includes a clam-bake with lobsters.

Just past **Doctor's Cove**, Rte 330 leaves Rte 3 for a short trip to scenic **Cape Sable Island**, where the wharves at **West Head** and **Cripple Creek** are lined with colourful Cape Island boats, which originated here. The boat and its role in local maritime history are shown, along with shipwrecks and the seafaring life at the **Archelaus Smith Museum**, *Centreville; tel: (902) 745-3361,* open Mon–Sat 0930–1530, Sun 1330–1530 (mid June– late Sept), free.

In **Barrington**, where Rte 3 rejoins Hwy 103, **Barrington Woolen Mill**, *2402 Hwy 3; tel: (902) 637-2185,* open Mon–Sat 0930–1730, Sun 1300–1730 (mid June–Sept), free, opened in 1884, displays how woollen fabrics were made locally in the early days of industrialisation. Needleworkers will enjoy the tapestry mural. In the same complex are the 1765 **Old Meeting House Museum**, with costumed interpreters, the

Cape Sable Historical Society Centre, with more local history exhibits, and Seal Island Light Museum, inside a reconstructed lighthouse, all free and with the same hours.

Sand Hills Beach, along the eastern shore of Barrington Bay, is really two adjoining white sand swimming beaches, with boardwalk access over the beautiful dunes that give it its name. A good lunch or snack stop is at the Old School House Restaurant, *Barrington Passage; tel: (902) 637-3770*, budget–moderate, where you can get lobster, sandwiches or char-broiled fish and chips in a renovated village schoolhouse.

SHELBURNE

Tourist Information: *King St (at Dock St), Shelburne, NS B0T 1W0; tel: (902) 875-4547*, open daily 0900–2000 (July–Aug), 1000–1800 (mid May–June, Sept–mid Oct).

ACCOMMODATION AND FOOD

Cooper's Inn & Restaurant, *36 Dock St (P.O. Box 959), Shelburne, NS B0T 1W0; tel: (902) 875-4656 or (800) 608-2011*, open Apr–Oct, moderate, is among the finest historic inns in Atlantic Canada, housed in a 1785 New England house, disassembled, carried here by ship and rebuilt by Loyalists fleeing the American Revolution. Rooms are large, bright and beautifully furnished. It's also the area's premier dining room, moderate, serving impeccably prepared fresh local seafood and other dishes; the desserts are legendary.

MacKenzie's Motel and Cottages, *260 Water St (P.O. Box 225), Shelburne, NS B0T 1W0; tel: (902) 875-2842*, open Mar–Nov, budget, has both attractive motel rooms and one- and two-bedroom cottages, with a heated outdoor swimming pool. Charlotte Lane Cafe, *13 Charlotte Lane; tel: (902) 875-3314*, open May–Sept, moderate, has a Swiss-trained owner/chef and an innovative menu, with outdoor garden dining in the summer. German-owned Shelburne

Pastry Shop, *Water St; tel: (902) 875-1168*, budget, bakes giant loaves of bread and delicious pastries. In good weather, the café expands into an outdoor patio.

SIGHTSEEING

McNutt's Island, a 20-min boat ride from Shelburne, is a naturalist's paradise, with rare birds, ferns growing like orchids from the trees and a birch tree over 5 m in circumference, documented to be over 1500 years old. Add some human history – World War II emplacements with the guns still intact, an abandoned lighthouse and inscriptions believed to be Carthaginian – and a lobster cookout, and you have a fascinating adventure with McNutt's Island Coastal Encounters, *RR#1, Shelburne; tel: (902) 875-4269, fax: (902) 875-2294*, half day $50, full day $100, (June–Oct).

Birders should ask for the outstanding brochure *Birding on the Lighthouse Route in Shelburne County* for maps, siting lists and other details on this prime birding region.

A useful annotated walking tour map will help you identify the dozen or so Loyalist homes still standing in the town, as well as find the historic attractions.

These include the Shelburne County Museum, *8 Maiden Lane; tel: (902) 875-3219*, which records the history of this town that was once one of the major ports of eastern North America, with its shipbuilding and Loyalist past, open daily 0930–1730 (mid May–mid Oct), Mon–Sat 0930–1200, 1400–1700 (mid Oct–mid May), admission $2 (a combined ticket with the two following sites is $4). The Ross-Thomson House and Store Museum, *Charlotte Lane; tel: (902) 875-3141*, open daily 0930–1730 (June–mid Oct), $2, is a rare original, a completely stocked 1700s store; the home illustrates the life of Loyalist families. On the wharf, the Dory Shop, *tel: (902) 875-3219*, open daily 0930–1730 (June–mid Sept), $2, an active business until 1971, is now a living museum where wooden dory builders create these

309

sleek rugged craft that were the mainstay of the schooner fishing industry. A film and informative tour give visitors the boat's history.

Stop by **Tottie's Crafts**, *10A Anne St; tel: (902) 875-3219*, open Mon–Sat 0930–1700 (mid June–mid Sept) for quality Nova Scotia handwork, the proceeds from which go to maintain these historic sites.

SHELBURNE TO LUNENBURG

Tourist Information: Queens County Tourism, *P.O. Box 1264, Liverpool, NS B0T 1K0; tel: (902) 354-5741 or (800) 655-5741.*

Following *Water St* and Lighthouse Route signs out of Shelburne for a short loop south, past **Sandy Point Lighthouse**, take Rte 3 to **Lockeport**, best known for its historic houses and five white sand beaches. From its wharves, you can see two lighthouses.

The next large town is **Liverpool**, where Hwy 8 joins from **Kejimkujik National Park** (see p. 304). Liverpool was home port to several privateers who made their fortunes harassing ships of the American colonies during the Revolution, and you can still see their fine homes here. **Rossignol Surf Shop**, *216 Main St; tel: (902) 354-3733* (weekdays), *(902) 683-2530* (evenings and weekends), rents sea kayaks and surfboards and conducts kayaking tours.

If you choose to stay on Rte 103, through **Bridgewater**, on your way to Lunenburg, stop at the **DesBrisay Museum**, *130 Jubilee Rd; tel: (902) 543-4033*, open Mon–Sat 0900–1700, Sun 1300–1500 (mid May–Sept), Tues–Sun 1300–1700 (Oct–mid May), with varied historical collections, including a remarkable cradle decorated in porcupine quillwork, a traditional craft of the Native Americans.

LUNENBURG

Tourist Information: Lunenburg Tourist Bureau, *Blockhouse Hill Road,* Lunenburg, NS B0J 2C0; tel: (902) 634-8100, open 0900–2100 (July–Aug), 0900–1900 (June and Sept), 0900–1500 (May and Oct).

ACCOMMODATION AND FOOD

Bluenose Lodge Country Inn, *Falkland and Dufferin Sts (P.O. Box 399), Lunenburg, NS B0J 2C0; tel: (902) 634-8851 or (800) 565-8851*, moderate, includes a pair of mansions – one a glamorous Victorian restoration – and the Carriage House, suitable for families or groups travelling together. The inn's dining room, **Solomon Gundy's**, moderate–expensive, features seafood and is open to the public. **Compass Rose Inn**, *15 King St (P.O. Box 1267), Lunenburg, NS B0J 2C0; tel: (902) 634-8509 or (800) 565-8509*, moderate, fills a restored Georgian home. Antiques blend comfortably with more modern pieces, and in-room tea and coffee is a welcome amenity. The dining room, open to the public, serves imaginative fare along with traditional favourites such as Finnan Haddie. A sister Bed and Breakfast, **The Lion Inn** (same mailing address and telephone) is another restored Georgian, two blocks away.

Kaulbach House Historic Inn, *75 Pelham St (P.O. Box 1348), Lunenburg, NS B0J 2C0; tel: (902) 634-8818 or (800) 568-8818*, moderate, is in a restored 1880s mansion. Three-course breakfasts are memorable (such as crêpes with peaches and cream), and rooms are furnished with antiques. **The Lunenburg Inn**, *26 Dufferin St (P.O. Box 1407), Lunenberg, NS B0J 2C0; tel: (902) 634-3963 or (800) 565-3963*, moderate, a Bed and Breakfast also in a restored Victorian building, invites lingering on its wide verandahs.

Topmast Motel, *76 Masons Beach Rd (P.O. Box 958), Lunenburg, NS B0J 2C0; tel: (902) 634-4661*, low moderate, is a good choice for families, with housekeeping units as well as standard rooms. The fine view over town and harbour is free.

Several seafood restaurants are along the

waterfront, including **The Old Fish Factory**, *Fisheries Museum, Waterfront; tel: (902) 634-3333*, open mid May–mid Oct, moderate. Their seafood is seldom deep fried, and they have pasta and chicken, too. **The Knot Pub**, *4 Dufferin St; tel: (902) 634-3334*, budget–moderate, is tiny, but big on food. Pub fare includes fish and chips.

SIGHTSEEING

Begin with a map and walking tour brochure pointing out Lunenburg's outstanding architecture, free from Tourist Information, and stroll the streets that rise in terraces from the harbour. So many fine buildings fill the downtown that the entire area was proclaimed a UNESCO World Heritage Site. Look especially for Canada's second oldest church, **St John's Anglican Church**, a fine building whose timbers came from Boston by ship. Or walk with an informed and entertaining guide on **Lunenburg Town Walking Tours**; *tel: (902) 634-3848 or (902) 527-8555*, $6. **Lunenburg Whale Watching Tours**, *tel: (902) 527-7175*, trips daily at 0900, 1100 and 1400, usually turn up seals, puffins and other birds along with the whales.

Fisheries Museum of the Atlantic, *Waterfront; tel: (902) 634-4794*, open daily 0930–1730 (June–mid Oct), Mon–Fri 0830–1630 (mid Oct–May), $7 adult, $2 age 6–17, $17 family, includes, along with indoor displays on the fisheries and ships, the schooner *Theresa E. Connor*, the trawler *Cape Sable*, and *Royal Wave*, a scallop dragger, tied at the wharf and open for tours. An aquarium, theatre and active dory shop complete the complex. Next to the museum is a busy **wharf**, where an assortment of sailing and working scallop draggers may be moored, along with *Bluenose II*, which, like its namesake, the legendary racing ship, *Bluenose*, was built at the adjacent shipyard. When it's in port, you can usually go aboard.

The **Ovens Natural Park**, *Feltzen Park, off Rte 332, Riverport; tel: (902) 766-4621,*

open mid June–early Sept, admission $3–5, is a series of sea caves cut in cliffs. You can climb down the cliff trail or take a boat tour into the caves, $7–12.50. The site of a gold rush in the 1860s, the park rents equipment for gold panning on the beach, and has a small museum about the gold mining here.

Rent bicycles from **Lunenburg Bicycle Barn** at the **Blue Rocks Road B&B**, *RR #1, Garden Lots, Lunenburg, NS B0J 2C0; tel: (902) 634-3426*, low moderate, where you're likely to meet other cyclists over a bountiful breakfast. Rentals $8 half-day, $15 full day, $90 week. **Blue Rocks**, a charming string of tiny rocky harbours, is a short, level ride from Lunenburg's centre.

MAHONE BAY

Tourist Information: Visitor Information Centre, *165 Edgewater St, Mahone Bay, NS B0J 2E0; tel: (902) 624-6151 or (888) 624-6161*, open daily 0900–1930 (July–Aug), 0900–1800 (June, Sept), 1000–1700 (May, Oct).

ACCOMMODATION AND FOOD

Sou'wester Inn, *788 Main St (P.O. Box 146), Mahone Bay, NS B0J 2E0; tel: (902) 624-9296*, moderate, a fine, welcoming Victorian mansion with a verandah overlooking the bay, a few steps from the wharf and shops. **Amber Rose Inn**, *319 West Main St (P.O. Box 397), Mahone Bay, NS B0J 2E0; tel/fax: (902) 624-1060*, moderate, offers abundant luxuries, with whirlpool baths, hairdryers, bathrobes and coffee makers.

The Innlet Café, *Edgewater St; tel: (902) 624-6363*, moderate, has a menu brimming full of seafood dishes, but there's meat, too, and a good mixed grill. At **Mimi's Ocean Grill**, *664 Main St; tel: (902) 624-1349*, moderate, you'll find an eclectic menu full of happy surprises, as well as more mainstream dishes. A tad out of town, but perfect for lunch or a cream tea, is **Tingle Bridge Tea House**, *Rte 3, west of Mahone Bay; tel: (902)*

624-9770, open Wed–Sun 1200–1800 (May–Nov), moderate, reservations are recommended.

SIGHTSEEING

The town itself, with its relaxed atmosphere and fine collection of historic wooden boats displayed on the wharf, is the attraction. Boutiques and shops showing fine Nova Scotia crafts line the single street along the edge of the usually glassy bay.

The **Settlers Museum**, *578 Main St; tel: (902) 624-6263,* open Tues–Sat 1000–1700, Sun 1300–1700 (May–Sept), has antiques, including a major ceramics collection, plus information on the town's wooden boat industry.

Mahone Bay Adventures, *618 Main St; tel: (902) 624-6632,* rents kayaks and canoes, gives lessons and leads paddling tours. Kayaks $15 for 2 hours, $40 per day. **Bright Sea Charters**, *Mahone Bay Wharf; tel: (902) 624-1074,* $19.50 adult, $12 child, offers two-hour sailing cruises.

CHESTER

Tourist Information: Chester Visitor Information Centre, *Hwy 3, Chester, NS B0J 1J0; tel: (902) 275-4616,* open daily 0900–1800 (June–Sept).

ACCOMMODATION

The Visitor Centre has photographs of the local inns and lodgings, including the guest rooms and menus from the restaurants. **Mecklenburgh Inn**, *78 Queen St (P.O. Box 350), Chester, NS B0J 1J0; tel: (902) 275-4638,* open June–Oct, moderate, is a cheery, welcoming inn with large bright rooms, two opening onto a large upstairs porch. Antique furnishings, handmade quilts and memorable breakfasts add to its appeal. **Stoney Brook Bed & Breakfast**, *Rte 3 (P.O. Box 716), Chester, NS B0J 1J0; tel: (902) 275-2342,* open May–mid Oct, low moderate, is a heritage home, set in flower gardens.

Captain's House Inn, *129 Central St*

(P.O. Box 538), Chester, NS B0J 1J0: tel: (902) 275-3501, fax: (902) 272-3502, moderate, has four nicely furnished rooms enhanced by a fine art collection. The pricey dining room, for which the inn is best known, has a view over the yacht basin that matches its seafood menu and impeccable service.

EATING AND DRINKING

Campbell House, *Lacey Mines Rd, Chester Basin; tel: (902) 275-5655,* moderate, has an eclectic menu – try duck in black rum pecan glaze. **Seaside Shanty**, *Rte 3, Chester Basin; tel: (902) 275-2246,* moderate, has excellent chowders and seafood dishes, none deep fried. **Julien's Pastry Shop Bakery & Tearoom**, *43 Queen St, Chester; tel: (902) 275-2324,* has outstanding French pastries, breads and sandwiches.

SIGHTSEEING

The map of Chester, free at the Visitor Centre, has a **walking tour** of the historic streets of this town, founded in the mid 1700s. There are no sites you must visit here; the town is strictly for strolling, with attractive shops to detain you. A ferry (schedule in Visitor Centre) goes to **Big Tancook Island**, four return trips daily, $1, where there are walking trails and picnic tables.

Chester Playhouse, *22 Pleasant St; tel: (902) 275-3933* or *(800) 363-7529,* open July–Aug, Dec–Feb, $14–16, presents plays and musicals. In mid Aug, **Chester Race Week**, is a colourful keelboat sailing regatta, one of Canada's largest.

CHESTER TO HALIFAX

Rte 333 hugs an irregular, rocky coast that becomes even rockier at the best known and most photographed fishing village in the province, **Peggy's Cove**. You will have to park in the lot outside of town with the tour buses and walk around the quaint harbour, with its tidily painted little boats and fishing shacks hung with buoys.

ST JOHN'S

Newfoundland is the part of North America closest to Europe, both geographically and historically. A British colony until 1949, it joined Canada only by a close vote, and it kept the Union Jack as its flag until the 1980s. The ties are strongest in St John's, the first place settled in the New World, in 1528, only 31 years after John Cabot first sailed into St John's secure harbour.

Visitors today won't see much of the settlement of five centuries ago in St John's steep streets with a distinctly Victorian air. Instead, they'll see an unpretentious, unsophisticated and undeniably provincial seaport, filled with foreign ships and 172,000 genial, genuine and jovial residents.

TOURIST INFORMATION

St John's Economic Development and Tourism Division, *P.O. Box 908, St John's, NF A1C 5M2; tel: (709) 576-8106, fax: (709) 576-8246,* open Mon–Fri 0900–1630, is located at **City Hall**, *Gower St.* Handier are the **information desk** at the airport or their easy-to-spot **railway car** on *Harbour Dr.; tel: (709) 576-8514,* open daily 0900–1730 (June–Aug).

WEATHER

Warm Gulf Stream currents keep temperatures moderate in St John's and the east coast, but when the icy Arctic Stream from the north meets these, the area is blanketed in fog. Daytime temperatures are kept warm in the summer by long hours of bright sunlight,

but nights take on a chill, even in midsummer (July average 11°–21°C). Winter (Jan average -7°–0°C) is not nearly as cold here as inland. For weather information, *tel: (709) 772-5534.*

ARRIVING AND DEPARTING

By Air
The compact, well-organised **St John's International Airport** is 6 km north of the city centre. Several flights a day arrive from London, even more from Canadian cities. **Co-op Taxi**; *tel: (709) 726-6666,* and **Bugden's**; *tel: (709) 726-4400,* provide transportation to hotels for about $12, plus $2 for each additional passenger. There is no public transport.

All services are clearly visible from the arrival gate, with tourist information and rental car desks straight ahead. If you pick up a rental car at the airport, follow signs to the city centre via *Portugal Cove Rd* to *Rennies Mill Rd.*

By Bus
DLR Coachlines brings passengers to St John's from the ferries at Port aux Basques; *tel: (709) 737-5912,* and **Newhook's Transportation**; *tel: (709) 726-4876,* connects with the Argentia ferries. There is no train service.

By Car
Travelling east, Hwy 1 (Trans-Canada Hwy) becomes *Kenmount Rd* at the edge of the city, then changes names to *Freshwater, Pennywell* and *Long's Hill Rd* before intersecting with *Gower St* in the city centre. The harbour will be downhill to your right.

Approaching St John's on Rte 10 from the southern Avalon Peninsula, enter the city

313

on Rte 2 *(Memorial Dr.)* which becomes *New Gower St* after crossing the river at the end of the harbour.

GETTING AROUND

The steep drop to the harbour makes for some breathtaking hills to climb, but also makes orientation very easy. The centre lies between the Hotel Newfoundland, at the eastern end, and the City Hall at its western end. Between them run *Harbour Dr.*, at the base of the hill, and the parallel *Water, Duckworth, Gower* and *Bond Sts* in ascending order. *Military Rd* is even higher up the hill, defining the northern edge of the downtown area.

Central Area

Taxi ranks are at the airport, Hotel Newfoundland and other major hotels; in the city centre, you can hail a cruising cab.

Public Transport

314

Metrobus; *tel: (709) 722-9400* ($1.50 adults and seniors, $1 children) connects the city centre with major hotels and the malls on the outskirts, passing many of the city's sights along the way.

Driving in St John's

Since several of the most interesting sights are slightly out of town, and not on bus lines, a car is handy here. (If you don't have one, **Co-op Taxi**; *tel: (709) 726-6666*, offers tours for up to five people.) Drivers are courteous and rarely seem to be in a hurry. Be careful of streets which become one-way unexpectedly. Parking is metered ($0.25 for 15 mins) and a parking garage is located on *Harbour Dr.*

STAYING IN ST JOHN'S

Accommodation

Chain hotels include *De* and *QI* downtown, *BW* on Hwy 1 and *Hd* near the airport. Bed and Breakfasts are scattered throughout

residential neighbourhoods, most in Victorian houses. The grandest lodging is the modern **Hotel Newfoundland**, *Cavendish Sq., St John's, NF A1C 5W8; tel: (709) 726-4980* or *(800) 268-9411* (toll-free) in Canada, *(800) 828-7447* in the USA, *fax (709) 726-2025*, expensive. Posh rooms, most with harbour views, are all stylishly furnished; swimming pool and fitness facilities.

Less convenient, about a mile from downtown, **The Battery Hotel and Suites**, *100 Signal Rd, St John's, NF A1A 1B3; tel: (709) 576-0040* or *(800) 563-8181, fax: (709) 576-6943*, moderate, has full guest services and a pool. The 29-room, plain **Captain's Quarters Hotel**, *2 King's Bridge Rd, St John's, NF A1C 3K3; tel: (709) 576-7468, fax: (709) 738-2002*, offers free continental breakfast; some of its budget-moderate rooms share baths.

Bed and Breakfast homes, all moderately priced, include **Kincora Hospitality Home**, *36 King's Bridge Rd (at Empire Ave), St John's, NF A1C 3K6; tel: (709) 576-7415*, a showplace furnished in dramatic antiques serving a full hot breakfast on fine china. Equally classy, and also in a fine Victorian mansion, is **Waterford Manor**, *185 Waterford Bridge Rd, St John's, NF A1E 1C7; tel: (709) 754-4139, fax (709) 754-4155*. Guest rooms are skilfully fitted into unique spaces (the house has three turrets) and beautifully furnished in antiques.

The Roses, *9 Military Rd, St John's, NF A1C 2C3; tel: (709) 726-3336*, is comfortably furnished, in a downtown location. **Compton House**, *26 Waterford Bridge Rd, St John's, NF A1E 1C6; tel: (709) 739-5789*, is a freshly renovated 1919 mansion with spacious rooms and suites, some with whirlpool baths, several with working fireplaces. **Monkstown Manor**, *51 Monkstown Rd, St John's, NF A1C 3T4; tel: (709) 754-7324, fax: (709) 722-8557*, has large, bright airy rooms and shared baths with double whirlpool tubs.

On the *Marine Dr.*, about 15 mins north

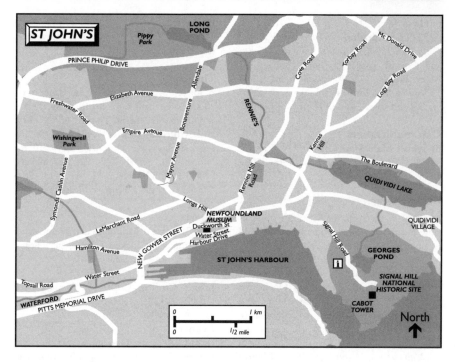

of the airport, **The Tides Inn**, *407 Windgap Rd, Flatrock, NF A1K 1C4; tel: (709) 437-1456*, has nicely furnished budget–moderate non-smoking rooms overlooking a bay where icebergs and whales are common. The glassed-in porch is a tea room.

In a park close on the northern edge of the city is **Pippy Park Trailer Park**, *Nagles Pl., St John's, NF A1B 3T2; tel: (709) 737-3669, fax: (709) 737-3303*, a campsite with tent pitches and caravan hook-ups, open May–Sept.

Eating and Drinking

St John's lacks the number and variety of gourmet restaurants that you find in Halifax, but you will be well fed and get good value for your dollar. The classiest menu is at **Stone House**, *8 Kennas Hill; tel: (709) 753-2380*, which specialises in wild game and prepares it skilfully and innovatively, moderate–pricey. In the **Hotel Newfoundland**,

the moderate–pricey, upmarket **Cabot Club** serves a frequently changing menu of classic dishes, and **The Outport** is an informal buffet of traditional local dishes at moderate prices.

For the most eclectic, innovative menu in town, served in intimate surroundings, step down into **The Cellar**, *Baird's Cove (off Water St); tel: (709) 579-8900*, moderate–pricey. Look to **Stella's**, *183 Duckworth St; tel: (709) 753-9625*, for vegetarian fare, seafood and smashing desserts, all moderate. **Cavendish Café**, *73 Duckworth St; tel: (709) 579-8024*, serves budget soups and sandwiches inside or on a patio. **Zachary's**, next door at *71 Duckworth St; tel: (709) 579-8050*, is a family restaurant with a varied moderate menu that includes a lot of local dishes. For 24-hr service and local seafood dishes, **Classic Café**, *364 Duckworth St; tel: (709) 579-4444)*, serves budget foods and local beers. For espresso, cappuccino or lunch, go to **Hava Java**, *216 Water St; tel: (709) 753-5282*. **The Ship Inn**, *265 Duckworth St; tel: (709) 753-3870*, is a pub serving sandwiches and Cornish pasties at lunch, budget. At **Mary Jane's**, *377 Duckworth St; tel: (709) 753-8466*, look for fresh bakery goods, sandwiches and salads, a good choice for picnics.

Communications
St John's Main Post Office, *354 Water St; tel: (800) 267-1177*, is open Mon–Fri 0800–1715.

ENTERTAINMENT
Music is at the heart of St John's spirit. It rings out in restaurants, pours from pubs and is sung on the streets. Folk music is a living art, and you'll hear songs of the sea, fiddle music and Celtic ballads wherever you go.

Newfoundland Symphony Orchestra plays at the Arts and Culture Centre, and often features well-known guest musicians. Choirs and other groups perform at **Cochrane St United Church**, *Cochrane St at Military Rd; (709) 729-3900*. **Pigeon Cove Productions** has weekly events at various pubs and local halls, featuring traditional Newfoundland music and dance (including instruction in local folk dancing); *tel: (907) 754-7324*.

Pick up a free copy of *What's Happening* for monthly calendar of performances and a listing of clubs.

Clubs and Pubs
Irish music plays at **Erin's Pub**, *184 Water St; tel: (709) 722-1916*; blues Thur at **Lottie's Place**, *3 George St; tel: (709) 745-3020*; dance music at **Junctions**, *208 Water St; tel: (709) 579-2557*; and traditional Newfoundland folk music at **Yellow Dory**, *6 George St; tel: (709) 579-2101*. The charge, if there is one, is never over $3. The free newspaper called *Signal* lists all the pubs and their music schedule for the current week.

For friendly bars, go to **Nautical Nellies**, *201 Water St; tel: (709) 726-0460*, and

Breezeway Bar; *tel: (709) 737-7464*, in the Thompson Student Centre at the university, where drinks are only $2.

Theatre
A variety of theatre, music and dance productions are held both in the main theatre and in the Basement Theatre of the **Arts and Culture Centre**, *Allandale Rd and Prince Phillip Dr.; tel: (709) 729-3650* for information, *(709) 729-3900* for tickets. **LSPU Hall Theatre**, *3 Victoria St; tel: (709) 753-4531*, is the alternative theatre venue.

Sports
The **St John's Maple Leafs**, members of the American Hockey League, play home games at *Memorial Stadium, King's Bridge Rd at Lake Ave; tel: (709) 576-7688*. The **St John's Curling Club**, *135 Mayor St; tel: (709) 722-3291*, welcomes drop-ins.

Events
In early Aug, the **George Street Festival** features five nights of top Newfoundland bands; *tel: (709) 576-8455*, at the same time as the **Newfoundland and Labrador Folk Festival**, in Bannerman Park, which preserves the arts of storytelling, dancing and traditional music; *tel: (709) 526-8508*. Immediately following these is the annual **Royal St John's Regatta**, North America's oldest continuing sporting event, at Quidi Vidi Lake.

In July and Aug, the **Signal Hill Tattoo** is scheduled on Wed, Thur, Sat and Sun, 1500 and 1900 at Signal Hill.

SHOPPING
People have been shopping on *Water St* for more than 400 years, earning it the title of the continent's oldest commercial street. That and *Duckworth St* are where you'll find shops today.

Newfoundland Weavery, *177 Water St; tel: (709) 753-0496*, sells handcrafts, including handknit sweaters and hooked mats. **The Cod Jigger**, *250 Duckworth St;* *(709) 726-7422*, is an artisans co-operative selling handknits, weaving, duffel coats, quilts, woodcarvings and model boats. **James Baird Gallery**, *221 Duckworth St; tel: (709) 726-4723*, sells Newfoundland fine arts, including prints and sculpture. For Newfoundland music, **O'Brien's Music Store**, *278 Water St; tel: (709) 753-6958*, sells CDs and tapes. For fine art and handcrafts, visit **Devon House Craft Centre**, *59 Duckworth St (opposite the Hotel Newfoundland); tel: (709) 753-2749*, where you will find glass, wood inlay, caribou antler jewellry, and handknit clothing.

Walking Tour
Newfoundland began at St John's Harbour, and so should you, starting at the **Tourist Information Rail Car** and walking west along *Harbour Dr.*, past ships from the far corners of the world, into the **Murray Premises**, a restored mercantile building from 1846, the oldest surviving in the city.

Out the opposite side of the premises is **Water St**, a block north of *Harbour Dr.*, once a pathway for early explorers and settlers. Continue to your right on *Water St*, past blocks of Victorian commercial buildings to the granite **Court House**, and climb **Church Hill**, which rises steeply behind it. Along it are fine wooden Victorian rowhouses, most restored and painted in their original lively colours. Here you will pass the city's major churches, each in a different architectural style. Stop to admire the stained-glass windows in the Gothic revival Anglican **Cathedral of St John the Baptist**, rebuilt after the great fire of 1892. Free tours are given by reservation 1030–1630 (late May–mid Oct). At the top of the hill is the Roman Catholic **Basilica of St John the Baptist**, whose towers have guided ships since 1841, when it was built.

Walk along *Military Rd*, past the Basilica,

to the **Colonial Building**; *tel: (709) 729-3065*, where the first legislature met. The painted decorations in the legislative chambers are well worth a stop, open Mon–Fri 0900–1615 and Wed–Thur 1430–2145.

Further along *Military Rd* is the 1836 **St Thomas Church**, Newfoundland's second oldest place of worship. When you reach *Cavendish Sq.*, turn hard right and return along *Gower St*, which has a fine group of Victorian houses. At *King's Rd*, turn left downhill to the **War Memorial**, on the spot where, in 1583, Newfoundland was claimed as a territory under the British Crown, making it Britain's first colony. A walk through **Harbourside Park** will bring you back to your starting point.

Guided Tours
Three-hour **Double Decker Bus Tours**; *tel: (709) 738-8687*, cover the downtown area before going to Signal Hill and Quidi Vidi Village. Buses pick up passengers at the Hotel Newfoundland, Delta and Holiday Inn. **St John's Historic Walking Tours**, *3 Fitzpatrick Ave; tel: (709) 738-3781*, delve into the 500 years of the city's history as they explore its streets on foot. During the summer, **Adventure Tours of Newfoundland**, *Pier 7; tel: (709) 726-5000* or *(800) 77-WHALE*, takes passengers on the schooner *Scademia* on a 2-hr sail through the harbour and the Narrows to Cape Spear, $20. **J&B Schooner Tours**, *Pier 7; tel: (709) 682-6585*, also offers daily cruises; evening and sunset cruises.

McCarthy's Party, *Topsail, Conception Bay; tel: (709) 781-2244, fax (709) 781-2233*, conducts bus tours of St John's and the area for $25.

Bird Island Charters and Humpback Whale Tours, *150 Old Topsail Rd; tel: (709) 753-4850*, runs boat excursions to see the bird sanctuary in the islands of Witless Bay. Expect whales here early July–early Aug. A shuttle bus ($10 extra) picks up passengers at hotels; costs are $28–35.

317

Wildland Tours, *124 Water St; tel: (709) 722-3335*, takes full-day trips to the bird islands, continuing on to see the caribou herds of the southern Avalon Peninsula or to Cape St Mary's to see gannets.

Museums

The permanent exhibits of the **Newfoundland Museum**, *285 Duckworth St; tel: (709) 729-2329*, open daily 0900–1630 (July–Aug), other seasons slightly shorter, centre around Native peoples of Newfoundland and on 19th-century daily life of its settlers. Collections include rural furnishings and toys, a schoolroom, cooperage, fishing stage and grocery store. Admission is free.

On the shore of Long Pond, the **Fluvarium**, *Pippy Park; tel: (709) 754-FISH*, open daily 0900–1700 (July–Aug), slightly shorter hours other seasons, provides a close-up perspective of the insects, plants and fish that live under the water and, in winter, beneath the ice.

Commissariat House, *King's Bridge Rd; tel: (709) 729-6730*, open daily 1000–1730 (June–mid Oct), is a beautiful Georgian building, furnished to show life in the early days of a British colony. Admission is free.

The Newfoundland Transport Museum, *212 Mount Scio Rd; tel: (709) 722-7224*, open daily 1000–1800 (July–Aug), has indoor exhibits featuring a different transportation theme each year. Outdoor exhibits, open daily during daylight hours (mid May–mid Nov), include a growing collection of railway passenger cars, a locomotive and ship-related artefacts. Admission is by donation.

Parks

North-west of the city centre, **Pippy Park**, *Mount Scio Rd*, has an 18-hole golf course, swimming, walking trails and a campsite. Adjoining the park is the **Botanical Garden**, *tel: (709) 737-8590*, with extensive native plant collections and display beds of perennials and annuals. **Bowring Park**, *Waterford Bridge Rd*, is a few miles from the centre, with tennis courts, ponds, gardens and walking and cycling paths through the woods between two streams. Scattered through are statues: *The Fighting Newfoundlander*, *Peter Pan* (a copy of the one in London's Kensington Gardens) and *The Caribou*.

Signal Hill National Historic Park, *at the entrance to St John's Harbour; tel: (709) 772-5367*, commands the best view in town, even better from **Cabot Tower**, built to commemorate Queen Victoria's jubilee and the 400th anniversary of John Cabot's landing in 1497. Here, Marconi received the first transatlantic wireless broadcast from England in 1901. A hiking path runs along the tops of the sea cliffs to **Quidi Vidi Battery**, another defensive position, and to the picturesque old fishing harbour of **Quidi Vidi Village**.

OUT OF TOWN

Marine Dr. makes a loop via Rtes 20 and 21, north of the city to Pouch Cove and Cape St Francis. The coastal road past Logy Bay to Outer Cove and Torbay consists of deep-cut coves, backed by towering headlands. At **Flat Rock**, where you can stop for tea at **Tides Inn**, the shore is a series of low flat ledges that invite walking. At **Cape St Francis**, at the very tip and approached over the hills via an unpaved road, is a lighthouse and more spectacular views.

South, and only 7 km from downtown, is **Cape Spear**, the most easterly point in North America. At **Cape Spear National Historic Site**; *tel: (709) 772-5367*, a Visitor Reception Centre explains the history of the 1836 lighthouse and the defensive batteries and underground passages that surround it. The area is covered with scenic walking trails.

AVALON PENINSULA LOOP

At the easternmost point of Canada, the Avalon Peninsula was the first part of Newfoundland to be settled and is the most densely populated, but it is a microcosm of the whole island in many ways. From the urban centre of St John's to the tundra barrens of the Avalon Wilderness Reserve, one encounters old pioneer civilisation, wild landscapes and seascapes and the open welcome of Newfoundland's people.

As with much of the island, the direct route is also the scenic route. While you could travel this route in two days, plan on three or more to follow side routes along the way.

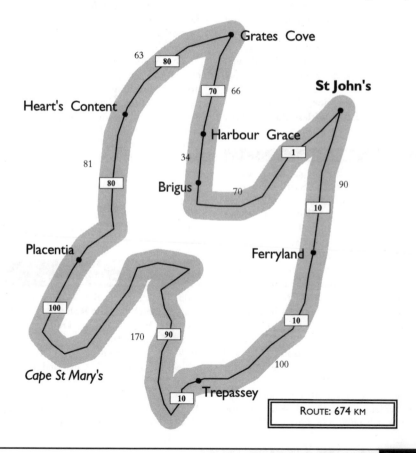

Grates Cove

63 | 80

70 | 66

St John's

Heart's Content

Harbour Grace

1

34

81

80

Brigus

70

90

10

Placentia

Ferryland

100

10

170 | 90

100

Cape St Mary's

Trepassey

10

ROUTE: 674 KM

ROUTE

From downtown St John's, take *Long's Hill Rd* (which will turn into *Pennywell*, then *Freshwater Rd*) west onto Hwy 1 (Trans-Canada), which soon travels through open countryside, past small, deep blue lakes. Turn north to **Avondale**, taking Rte 60 north to **Brigus**. The road goes along the west shore of **Conception Bay**; roads to the right go to small outport villages tucked into little coves. At **Grates Cove**, at the north end of the peninsula, follow Rte 80 south and back to the Trans-Canada Hwy. Only 1 km west, take Rte 100 south toward **Placentia**.

From Placentia, Rte 100 follows the coast to the end of the peninsula at **St Bride's**, then travels north to Rte 91 in **Colinet**. Follow Rte 91 to **Salmonier**, where you have the option of returning to St John's via Rte 90 north or taking it south toward **St Mary's**. Just past the village of **Peter's River**, the road designation mysteriously changes to Rte 10, a number it keeps through **Trepassey**, along the Atlantic shore through **Ferryland**, **Witless Bay** and back into St John's.

BRIGUS

North St Café, *North St; (no phone)*, budget, is a good place for lunch, serving soups, meat pies and sandwiches. They also have scones for tea. **Brittoner**, *12 Water St, P.O. Box 163, Brigus, NF A0A 1K0; tel: (709) 528-3412*, has Bed and Breakfast accommodations in a restored Victorian home on the waterfront and serves a full breakfast, budget–moderate. **Skipper Ben's B&B**, *Box 76, Cupids, NF A0A 2B0; tel: (709) 528-4436*, budget–moderate, is in a big old home overlooking Cupids Harbour.

Brigus was the home town of Capt. Robert A. Bartlett, fisherman, sealer and Arctic explorer. Captain of the ships for Robert E. Peary's 1898, 1905 and 1908 expeditions, he made 16 other arctic voyages. Bartlett's home, **Hawthorne Cottage**, *Main St; tel: (709) 528-4004 or 753-9262*,

Screech

You won't be long in Newfoundland before you hear about its infamous rum called **Screech**. The name probably originated with the first sound that follows a drink of it. There is a tradition of being 'screeched in', which refers to your first encounter with the deadly stuff, which most visitors wisely choose to forgo.

open daily 1000–1800 (June–Aug), $2.50, is a museum with his family's memorabilia. **Brigus Museum**, *4 Magistrate's Hill; tel: (709) 528-3298*, open Mon–Fri 1000–1800, Sat–Sun 1000–2000 (mid June–Aug), $1, in a restored small stone barn, has historic photographs, artefacts and Bartlett materials.

The Walk, a large stone outcrop, was pierced by a tunnel in 1860 to provide access from the town to the harbour. Walk through for a view of the harbour. You can visit the formal flower beds of **Wilcox Gardens** along the river bank. Take a short side trip to **Cupids**, where the first English settlement was made in 1610. An archaeological excavation of that plantation is ongoing in summer, and items recovered are in the **Cupids Museum**, *Main Rd; tel: (709) 528-3477 or 596-1906*, open Mon–Fri 1130–1630, Sat–Sun noon–1700 (mid June–mid Sept), free.

BRIGUS TO HARBOUR GRACE

From Brigus, follow Rte 70 north through Clarke's Beach to **Bay Roberts**. The **Bay Roberts East Walking Trail**, *tel: (709) 786-3482*, meanders through the remaining walls and foundations of the town's earliest settlements at Juggler's Cove and French's Cove.

Continue on Rte 70 north to **Spaniard's Bay**, then follow the road to the left through **Tilton** before heading north again to

Harbour Grace. At Spaniard's Bay you can travel straight ahead or to the right around the scenic peninsula through **Upper Island Cove**.

HARBOUR GRACE

Tourist Information: Harbour Grace Tourist Information Office, *Rte 70, Harbour Grace, NF A0A 2M0; tel: (709) 596-5561,* open daily 0900–1800 (May–Oct).

Across from the Conception Bay Museum (see below), elegant lodging is available at **Garrison House,** *Water St, Harbour Grace, NF A0A 2M0; tel: (709) 596-3658,* moderate. It's in a restored 19th-century home with fine details. They serve full breakfasts, as well as special dinners by reservation.

You will know you've reached Harbour Grace when you see the ship *Kyle.* An important passenger and freight link to Labrador and Newfoundland ports in the early 20th century, she has long lain derelict in the harbour. Just up Rte 70, at the Tourist Information kiosk, a restored DC-3 aircraft, the *Spirit of Harbour Grace,* is preserved as a memorial to aviation pioneers.

About 8 km from the DC-3, take *Bannerman Lake Rd* west to the **Harbour Grace Airstrip.** When the paved road ends, go right, avoiding smaller side roads and staying to the larger road. This primitive field is where Amelia Earhart started her solo transatlantic flight on 20 May 1932. Learn the stories of the many who used this field at **Conception Bay Museum,** *Water St; tel: (709) 596-1309,* open daily 1000–1800 (June–Sept), free, via pictures and a logbook with their signatures and flight plans. Ask for the free guide map to a **walking tour** of historic buildings.

HARBOUR GRACE TO GRATES COVE

Carbonear, 5 km north on Rte 70, had residents prior to 1600 and has been a fishing, sealing and commercial harbour ever since. It was also the home of the legendary Sheila Na Geira, an Irish princess captured by pirates. **Keneally Manor,** *8 Patrick St, Carbonear, NF A0A 1T0; tel: (709) 596-1221,* originally a double mansard home built in 1839 by two schooner captain brothers, is now a fine moderate Bed and Breakfast furnished with period antiques. For dining, locals chose **Fong's Restaurant,** *143 Columbus Dr.; tel: (709) 596-5114,* featuring Chinese and Canadian dishes, moderate.

Rte 70 continues to **Victoria,** home to the **Victoria Lifestyles Museum,** *tel: (709) 596-1004,* with an active cooper, blacksmith, sawmill and more. If you don't want to go north to the end of the peninsula, take Rte 74 west to **Heart's Content** (see p. 322) on the east shore of Trinity Bay. To see the scenic treasures of this peninsula, however, follow Rte 70 north, along the often soaring rocky shore of Conception Bay.

The 20-odd towns along this shore give a good view of fishing coves and harbour communities, as well as some striking views. You'll pass **Blow Me Down, Salmon Cove, Broad Cove** and **Blackhead** before reaching **Ochre Pit Cove** and **Burnt Point.** Continue on Rte 70 north to **Red Head Cove** (the name refers to the colour of the rock), **Bay de Verte** (the colour of the water) and **Grates Cove.**

Until the mid 1960s, there was a rock here carved by John Cabot verifying his landing. It was stolen, chiselled off the rock by people claiming to be engaged in research. The **Grates Cove Rock Wall National Historic Site,** *Rte 70; tel: (709) 587-2326,* encompasses many unusual stone-walled gardens and pens scattered about the hillsides, and a number of **walking trails.** Follow the road to the head of land and **Land's End Restaurant** *(no phone)* for some of the best food on the peninsula, with traditional dishes that are hard to find elsewhere, and the best craft shop, as well. The view over the town is good, too.

WESTERN SHORE

Return to Rte 80, following it to **Heart's Content**. **Heart's Content Cable Station**, *Rte 80; tel: (709) 729-2460 or 583-2160,* free, is a museum at the site where the first transatlantic telegraph cable came ashore from the *Great Eastern* in 1866, serving as the major communications connection between Europe and North America until the 1960s.

From **Heart's Content**, Rte 80 goes through **Heart's Desire** and **Heart's Delight**, a trio of towns whose names reflect the sentiments of their early settlers.

Just beyond, in the village of **Dildo**, the **Dildo Interpretive Center**, *Rte 80 (12 km from the Trans-Canada Hwy); tel: (709) 582-3339 or 3327,* is interesting for its aquariums and exhibits (many based upon nearby excavations) showing the vitality of the Maritime Archaic, Dorset and Beothuk native cultures. **Dildo Tours**, *P.O. Box 6, Dildo, Trinity Bay, NF A0B 1P0; tel: (709) 582-2687,* combines whale-watching with learning about the history of the area's fisheries and Indians. **The Lookout B&B**, *P.O. Box 4, Dildo, NF A0B 1P0; tel: (709) 582-2630,* has two rooms with shared bath in a modern cottage, budget.

CAPE ST MARY'S

From Dildo, follow Rte 80 to Hwy 1 and take it west about 1 km to Rte 100 south, through interior woodlands and tundra to **Placentia**, the French capital of the island from 1622–92.

In 1941, British prime minister Winston Churchill and US President Franklin Roosevelt met aboard a warship off shore and enunciated the Atlantic Charter. You can see the town's strategic importance from **Castle Hill National Historic Site**, *off Rte 100; tel: (709) 227-2401,* open daily 0830–2000 (mid June–Aug), 0830–1630 (Sept–mid June), on the north side of the bay and get a splendid view as well. The **Harold Motel**, *P.O. Box 142, Placentia, NF A0B 2Y0; tel: (709) 227-2107 or 2108,* has

budget–moderate rooms and a free guide to the area's attractions.

Nearby, inside a protected harbour, **Argentia** is the northern terminus of the ferry from **North Sydney, Nova Scotia** (see p. 281). To the south, Rte 100 parallels the coast, through towns sited where rivers run into the sea. **Little Barasway** and **Great Barasway** are names for the *barrachois* (protective sandbars) along the shore. Along the way are ocean views. About 30 km south, **Gooseberry Cove Provincial Park** has a picnic area and sandy beach, but wave action is too strong for swimming.

About 35 km south of Placentia, Rte 100 turns east, and just beyond St Bride's a gravel road leads south to **Cape St Mary's Ecological Reserve**, *tel: (709) 729-2431,* open daily, daylight hours (May–Oct), free, which has the second largest nesting gannet colony in North America, as well as significant colonies of black-legged kittiwakes, Atlantic murres and northern razorbills. There is an interpretive centre and a half-mile walk along the cliffs to a bird-encrusted sea stack just off shore.

CAPE ST MARY'S TO TREPASSEY BAY

Follow Rte 100 as it turns north along the west coast of St Mary's Bay from **Branch**, where the road is re-designated as Rte 92, to **Colinet** at the north end of the Bay. Just before the turn east to Colinet, Rte 92 ends and Rte 91 begins. Take it west about 3 km to **Cataracts Provincial Park** *(no phone)*, a set of waterfalls and cascades in a gorge, accessible by walkways. Return to Rte 91 and continue through Colinet, where there is a **salmon ladder**, *tel: (709) 521-2719,* open daily 0900–1700 (July–mid Nov), free. The best time to watch the salmon heading upstream to spawn is during the spring run.

At this point you can return to St John's via Rte 90 through the central Avalon wilderness to Hwy 1. On the way, stop at the **Salmonier Nature Park**, *Holyrood; tel:*

(709) 729-6974, open Thur–Mon, 1200–1900 (June–mid Oct), free. Along a 3-km nature walk, indigenous animals are displayed in enclosures designed to maintain the natural habitat of each.

To continue around the Avalon, turn south onto Rte 90 along the waters of **Salmonier Arm** to **St Joseph**, where the road cuts inland across more wooded wilderness before emerging on the shore again at **Gulch**. At **Point La Haye** is a fine overlook of St Mary's Bay from the **lighthouse**, originally established in 1883. The beach here was used by early Basque fishermen to dry their catch, and is a good spot for collecting shells and driftwood.

Rte 90 then follows **Holyrood Pond**, a long brooding arm of the sea that runs 25 km inland. The south end, at **St Vincent's**, is protected from the sea by a large sand and cobble seawall and beach. Stop here, especially in the spring and early summer, to see humpback whales cavorting just off shore. **Fleming's Little Ocean Discovery Boat Tours**, *P.O. Box 145, St Vincent's, NF A0B 3C0; tel: (709) 525-2943,* has guided cruises of the pond on a stable pontoon boat. The highway passes over the beach and on to **Peter's River**, where it becomes Rte 10.

From this point you are in **caribou** country. There are so many here that you are almost certain to see them as they graze and cross this highway through moorlands. About 10 km from Peter's River is the road to **St Shott's**. The province is building a **Caribou Interpretation Center** near this intersection. St Shott's is on an unpaved go-and-return road to a fishing and peat gathering community, and a side road leads to **Cape Pine Lighthouse**, built of cast iron in 1821. This whole area is highly prone to fog, so be cautious.

TREPASSEY TO FERRYLAND

Trepassey is an old fishing town now in transition with the loss of the fisheries. **Trepassey Museum**, *Main St; tel: (709)*

438-2044, open Mon–Sat 1000–1700, Sun 1300–1700 (July–Aug), admission $1, has, in addition to furniture, glass, china and local historical items, photos of Amelia Earhart as she left here as a passenger to become the first woman to cross the Atlantic by air. Trepassey was an important early flying boat base.

Trepassey Motel and Restaurant, *P.O. Box 22, Trepassey, NF A0A 4B0; (709) 438-2934,* open all year, budget–moderate, is like an inn with comfortable rooms and the best dining in the area. **Northwest Bed & Breakfast**, *Box 5, Site 14, Trepassey, NF A0A 4B0; (709) 438-2888,* budget, offers privacy and quiet, with a shared bath.

From Trepassey, continue along Rte 10 to **Portugal Cove**, a small fishing village, where a 21-km unpaved road leads to **Cape Race Lighthouse** alone (except for grazing sheep) on a point known as the graveyard of the Atlantic because of the numerous shipwrecks there. The very scenic route crosses moors and travels over high rocky headlands.

Beyond Portugal Cove, Rte 10 cuts inland across the wilderness, passing **Chance Cove Provincial Park**, *off Rte 10; (no phone),* with a fine beach; you can see grey and harbour seals and it's on the Atlantic flyway for migrating waterfowl. There are also 25 free tent pitches. **Renew**, on a small ocean inlet, was a reprovisioning stop for the Pilgrims aboard the *Mayflower* in 1620. The road passes through several small fishing villages, offering fine views of their docks, with lines of fishing shacks on piers, boats moored below them.

FERRYLAND TO ST JOHN'S

Ferryland was the site of a settlement in 1621 by Lord Baltimore. He moved on to found the Maryland colony, and the village he left here is being excavated. You can watch the dig in progress during the summer and see its artefacts at the **Colony of Avalon Archaeology Project**, *Ferryland; tel: (709) 432-2767* summer, *(709) 432-2820* year round, open daily 0900–1900 (mid

323

Newfy Foods

The variety of foods found in Newfoundland is much more limited than elsewhere in Eastern Canada. Seafood is the mainstay, and it's usually fried. **Cod tongues,** deep-fried or sautéed, are on most menus. **Salmon** is also common, and is sometimes the basis of a **fish chowder**, a combination of fish, potatoes, onions and cream.

Newfoundland's most traditional dish is **fish and brewis**, salt-cod cooked with a hard, fine-textured bread, served with **scrunchions**, crisp bits of rendered saltpork.

Pea soup here (unlike Québec or New Brunswick) is a thin pease porridge made with Swedes and carrots, often served with a dumpling, especially at Saturday lunch.

Jiggs Dinner is boiled corned beef with vegetables, often found at church suppers. Another entrée is **fries with the works**, a plateful of chips covered by minced beef in gravy, usually with peas and carrots.

Newfoundland is particularly adept at using **partridgeberries** (similar to Scandinavia's lingonberry) and **blueberries** in tarts and pies. Orange **bakeapples** are seedy berries with a sweet, smokey flavour. They are known elsewhere as cloudberries.

Toutons are disks of fried bread dough, served hot with optional dark treacle. Soft ice-cream cones are known as **custard cones**.

June–mid Oct), which re-creates their historical context very well. Admission $2, family $5. You can also visit the lab upstairs where artefacts are sorted, cleaned and identified. The museum shop is almost a museum, too, with fine Newfoundland art and craft work.

Southern Shore Eco Adventures, *P.O. Box 125, Ferryland, NF A0A 2H0; tel: (709) 432-2659,* provides guided walking trips and nature explorations throughout Avalon. They also have sea kayaking and diving tours. **The Downs Inn,** *Rte 10 (P.O. Box 15), Ferryland, NF A0A 2H0; tel: (709) 432-2808 or 2163,* budget, in a converted convent, has comfortable rooms overlooking the harbour, with private or shared baths. It also has traditional afternoon tea, as well as lunches in its tea room.

La Manche Provincial Park, *Department of Tourism & Culture, P.O. Box 8700, St John's, NF A1B 4J6,* has a campsite for tents and caravans. They also have a swimming pond and hiking trails, including to the site of a fishing village destroyed by a storm in 1966. More than 50 species of birds have been seen here.

Witless Bay Ecological Reserve encompasses the area between Great Island and Gull Island, the breeding ground of millions of rare water birds, including puffin, storm petrel, gannet, murre and auk. To see them, and the whales, seals and icebergs, take a boat tour, $25–35: **O'Brien's Whale and Bird Tours,** *Bay Bulls, NF A0A 1C0; tel: (709) 753-4850 or (709) 334-3140,* daily 0930, 1100, 1400, 1700 and 1830 (June–Sept); **Capt. Murphy's Bird Island and Whale Tours,** *P.O. Box 149, Puffin Cove, Witless Bay, NF A0A 4K0; tel: (709) 334-2002 or (888) 783-3467* (toll-free), daily 1030, 1300, 1400, 1600, 1700 and 1900 (late June–early Sept); **Humpback Whale Tours,** *Bay Bulls, NF A0A 1C0; tel: (709) 753-4850 or (709) 334-2355,* daily 0930, 1100, 1400 and 1700 (Apr–Oct).

Rte 10 returns you to St John's, with a stop at **Admiralty House Museum and Archive,** *23 Old Placentia Rd, Mount Pearl; tel: (709) 748-1124,* which was built as a wireless station in 1915 to monitor German maritime radio traffic in the North Atlantic. In addition to the military and broadcasting museums, there is an English country garden.

ST JOHN'S– PORT AUX BASQUES

A trip across Newfoundland from its eastern to its western edge reveals the island's many landscapes: soaring sea cliffs, rock-bound fishing villages, a coastline of long points and deep coves, tree-surrounded lakes, high plateaus and many miles of spruce and fir forest. You may see moose or caribou and, even in summer, icebergs where the road travels near the shore.

Distances between towns are long, but petrol stations with simple restaurants are spaced along the Trans-Canada Hwy (Hwy 1). Across the centre of the province, Hwy 1 is the only road, and three scenic diversions travel north and south to the coasts.

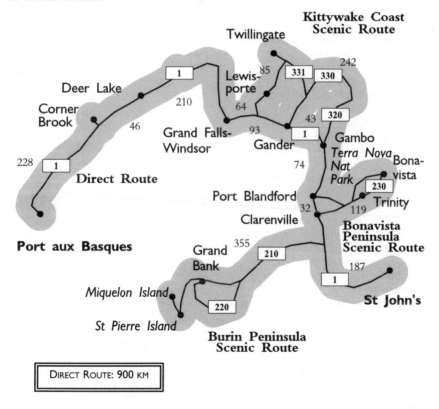

Kittywake Coast Scenic Route

Twillingate

Lewisporte

Deer Lake

Corner Brook

1

210

242

331 **330**

85

64

43 **320**

Grand Falls-Windsor

Gander

93

1

Gambo

228 **1**

46

Direct Route

74

Terra Nova Nat Park

Bona-vista

230

Port Blandford

32

119

Trinity

Clarenville

Bonavista Peninsula Scenic Route

Port aux Basques

Grand Bank

355

210

187

1

Miquelon Island

220

St John's

St Pierre Island

Burin Peninsula Scenic Route

DIRECT ROUTE: 900 KM

ROUTES

DIRECT ROUTE

➡ From *Gower St* in central St John's, follow *Long's Hill Rd*, which turns into *Pennywell*, then *Freshwater Rd*, before reaching the edge of the city and becoming the limited access Trans-Canada Hwy 1, which takes you to Port aux Basques. Stopovers are easy at **Terra Nova National Park**, **Gander** and **Corner Brook** to visit local sights. St John's to Port aux Basques is about 900 km; Gander is about one-third of the way and Corner Brook just over two-thirds.

SCENIC ROUTES

➡ Three scenic diversions take you off the Trans-Canada Hwy for explorations along the coast.

Burin Peninsula: From St John's, follow Hwy 1 as described above until you reach Rte 210, about 8 km north of the Sunnyside Exit (signposted 'Burin Peninsula'), for a 200-km drive to **Grand Bank**. Drive south to **Fortune** for a ferry side track to the French islands of **St-Pierre and Miquelon**. Rte 220 loops around the end of the peninsula, then rejoins Rte 210 to return to Hwy 1.

Bonavista Peninsula: Continue north on Hwy 1 to Rte 230A in **Clarenville**, then follow it north to Rte 230 through **Trinity** along the eastern shore of the **Bonavista Peninsula** to **Catalina**. There you follow Rte 238 to the town of **Bonavista**, returning along the western shore on Rte 235, joining Rte 230 in **Southern Bay**. In **Lethbridge**, only a few kilometres further on, take Rte 233 west until it rejoins Hwy 1 at **Port Blanford**.

Kittywake Coast: Continue north on Hwy 1 through **Terra Nova National Park** to **Gambo**, where you take Rte 320 north to Rte 330, which travels along the shore of Hamilton Sound. Follow this road inland to **Gander** and Hwy 1, or continue along the coast on Rte 331 (with a short diversion to **Twillingate** on Rte 340), then

along Rte 340 south via **Lewisporte** to Hwy 1.

BUSES

DRL Bus Lines operate one trip a day from St John's to Port aux Basques, which leaves at 0745. Journey time: 13 hrs. See OTT table 246.

TOURIST INFORMATION

Information is available in the very useful annual *Newfoundland and Labrador Travel Guide*, which you can get from the **Department of Tourism, Culture and Recreation**, *P.O. Box 8730, St John's, NF A1B 4K2; tel: (709) 729-2830* or *(800) 563-6353* (toll-free).

ST JOHN'S TO SUNNYSIDE

Not long after leaving the suburbs of St John's, Hwy 1 passes through a high, rolling area of low growth scattered with glacial boulders. **Butterpot Provincial Park**, *Rte 1 (13 km west of Holyrood); tel: (709) 580-7573* or *(800) 866-CAMP*, lies along the north side of the highway, with 126 tent pitches, walking and hiking trails, swimming and nature programmes. You pass several routes into the Avalon Peninsula (see pp. 319–324) before reaching the narrow isthmus that connects the Avalon to the rest of Newfoundland.

BURIN PENINSULA

Tourist Information: Marystown Visitor Information Center, *Rte 210, north of town* (mail address: *P.O. Box 757, Marystown, NF A0E 2M0); tel: (709) 279-1211,* open daily 0900–1800 (mid June–Aug).

Rte 210 leaves Hwy 1 about 13 km north of Sunnyside and travels through wilderness barrens, high bogs and scrubby forest, with a few side roads leading to tiny fishing villages, until it reaches **Marystown**, 145 km later. Continue on Rte 210 (better labelled on road signs than it is on the Newfoundland highway map) to **Grand Bank**.

On the way from Marystown to Grand Bank, the route passes **Frenchman's Cove Provincial Park**, *Rte 213, Frenchman's Cove; tel: (709) 826-2753*, where 76 tent pitches are set in low woodlands along a beach.

At **Grand Bank**, just beyond, you will find old-fashioned rooms in a sea captain's house at **The Thorndyke**, *33 Water St, Grand Bank, NF A0E 1WO; tel: (709) 832-0820*, budget, or a comfortable motel and restaurant at **Granny's Motor Inn**, *Grand Bank Hwy Bypass, Grand Bank, NL A0E 1OW; tel: (709) 832-2180, fax: (709) 832-0009*, budget–moderate.

In Grand Bank, the **Southern Newfoundland Seamen's Museum**, *Marine Dr.; tel: (709) 832-1484*, has ship models and photos of Banks fishing, open Mon–Fri 0900–1200 and 1300–1700, Sat–Sun 1400–1700, free. The **George Harris House Museum of Local History**, *16 Water St; tel: (709) 832-1574*, open daily 1000–1600 (July–Aug), free, is one of the many Queen Anne-style buildings dating from the early 1900s, all described in the free *Heritage Walk* brochure available at the museum.

SIDE TRACK
TO ST-PIERRE AND MIQUELON
Tourist Information: Agence Regionale du Tourisme, *Place du General de Gaulle, BP 4274-97500, St-Pierre; tel: (508) 41 22 22* or *(800) 565-5118*, open daily 0900–1800 (June–Aug) Mon–Fri 0900–1200 and 1400–1800 (Sept–May).

Bring your passport and be prepared to clear Customs for a visit to these tiny islands: they are not Canadian but French soil, remnants of a colonial presence that ended in 1763. Attractions include French food and wines, shopping, sea scenery, wild horses, and the very French villages.

The passenger ferry *L'Anahitra* departs from the village of **Fortune**, just south of Grand Bank, for the 70-min crossing to St-Pierre, daily 0900, return 1630 (July–Aug), less frequent other months, adults $47, children $27–37. Reservations are essential, and preference is given to those who make hotel reservations on the island at the same time; contact **St-Pierre Tours**; *tel: (709) 832-0429* (in Fortune) or *(709) 722-3892* (in St John's).

While you cannot take a car to St-Pierre, you can hire bicycles or use the buses or taxis to tour the island. Ferries operate from St-Pierre to the island of Miquelon and the smaller islands.

In St-Pierre, you'll find comfortable lodgings at **Hotel Robert**, *10 r. du 11 Novembre, BP 4329; tel: (508) 41 24 19, fax: (508) 41 28 79* (or book through St-Pierre Tours), moderate, and at **Chez Marcel Helene**, *15 r. Beaussant, BP 1081 97500; tel: (508) 41 31 08*, budget–moderate. Both have restaurants (Chez Marcel Helene by reservation only), or you can eat at one of the several restaurants which are, for many, the reason for going there. Most are moderate–expensive; they are listed, with hours and prices, in the informative booklet the Tourist Office will send you.

327

The drive around the Burin Peninsula follows the shore closely through colourful fishing villages, with excellent views of the French islands and striking coastal scenery. In **St Lawrence**, the **Miner's Museum**, *Rte 220; tel: (709) 873-2222*, open daily 1000–1800 (July–Aug), illustrates both early mining and modern methods used in Canada's only fluorspar mine.

Few towns have a more scenic setting than **Burin**, off Rte 220 about 5 km south of Salt Pond, with its rocky hills dropping into the harbour. **Heritage Square** is a complex including **Burin Heritage House**, *tel: (709) 891-2217*, open Mon–Fri 0900–1700, Sat–Sun 1300–2030 (May–Oct), free. In the restored home are exhibits on daily life, schools, fishing and local history, which you can browse through alone or with a guide who adds life to the displays with local stories. A park has picnic tables and a stage for weekend programmes. Across the street, in another restored building, is **Heritage Square B&B**, *37 Seaview Dr., Burin, NF A0E 1E0; tel: (709) 891-1353,* with fine views and elegant weekend breakfasts.

Follow Rte 210 back through Marystown and on to Hwy 1.

Tourist Information: Interpretation Center, *Rte 239, Trinity; tel: (709) 464-2042,* open daily 0900–1800 (mid June–mid Oct). (Note: Trinity has no street addresses; send all mail *c/o General Delivery, Trinity, NF A0C 2H0.*)

From the Rte 210 intersection, follow Hwy 1 about 25 km north to Clarenville, then take Rte 230A to Rte 230 and the well restored town of **Trinity**. When the fisheries and commerce that had built and supported it for four centuries died, Trinity re-created itself as an historic attraction.

It is not a theme park, but a living restoration, where people live in the houses and welcome visitors to learn about Trinity's distinguished past in museums, restored buildings and the unique **Trinity Pageant**; *tel: (709) 464-3232,* a dramatic production that moves through the town as it moves through its history; held Wed, Sat–Sun at 1400 in July and Aug, $5.

ACCOMMODATION AND FOOD

Campbell House; *tel: (709) 464-3377* (off season mailing address: *24 Circular Rd, St John's, NF A1C 2Z1; tel: (709) 753-8945),* open late May–mid Oct, moderate, provides luxuries in a meticulously restored 1840 home set in fine gardens overlooking the sea. You can rent mountain bikes. **Peace Cove Inn**, *Trinity East; tel: (709) 454-3738* or *(709) 464-3419* (off season in St John's *(709) 781-2255),* open late May–mid Oct, is a

cosy turn-of-the-century home, moderate. It also serves moderate family-style meals to guests. **Riverside Lodge**, *Box 9, Trouty, NF A0C 2S0; tel: (709) 464-3780,* open Apr–Oct, budget, overlooks the harbour in a tiny fishing village only 6 km from Trinity, offering homely rooms and homecooked meals of cod or salmon, daily at 1900.

Old Trinity Cookery, *Trinity; tel: (709) 464-3615,* serves three meals a day, specialising in local dishes, including pea soup and baked apples with blueberry filling, moderate. **Dock Marina Restaurant**, *Trinity Wharf; tel: (709) 464-2133,* moderate, serves char-broiled steak, along with seafood that is *not* deep fried.

SIGHTSEEING

Hiscock House, *tel: (709) 464-2042,* open daily 1000–1730 (June–mid Oct), free, restored to 1910, shows everyday family life. The 200-year-old **Green Family Forge**, *tel: (709) 464-3720,* open daily 1000–1730 (mid June–mid Sept), $2, and the beautifully reconstructed **Lester-Garland House and Premises**; *tel: (709) 464-2042,* open daily 1000–1800 (mid June–mid Oct), free, illustrate the life and business of the wealthy commercial class. All three adjoin the Interpretation Center.

To see whales up close, join **Atlantic Adventures**, *Trinity Wharf; tel: (709) 464-3738,* for a nature cruise aboard a sailboat.

Rte 230 continues on to **Bonavista** at the top of the peninsula; go via **Little Catalina** and **Maberley**, an 8-km detour, to see Arch Rock and other dramatic cliffs. In Bonavista, **Cape Bonavista Lighthouse**, *tel: (709) 468-7444,* open daily 1000–1730 (mid June–mid Oct), free, built in 1843, is one of Canada's oldest, with historic displays and more fine views. On the waterfront is **Ryan Premises National Historic Site**, *Old Catalina Rd; tel: (709) 772-5364,* open daily

1000–1800 (mid June–mid Oct), free, with a restored 19th-century residence, shop, fish shed, store and carriage shed.

Follow Rtes 235, 230 and 233 to Port Blanford and Hwy 1. Near the intersection is **Terra Nova Hospitality Home and Cabins**, *Hwy 1, Port Blanford, NF A0C 2G0; tel: (709) 543-2260, fax: (709) 543-2241,* moderate, with upmarket rooms and home-cooked meals, or modern, well-appointed self-catering cabins.

TERRA NOVA NATIONAL PARK

The next 50 km of the Trans-Canada Hwy go through **Terra Nova National Park**; *tel: (709) 533-2801,* headquarters open daily 1000–2000 (mid May–mid Oct), admission $3.25 one day, $9.25 four days, family $6.50 and $19.50. (You must pay this fee in order to leave Hwy 1 anywhere in the park.)

The emphasis in this park is recreation, with a golf course, resort hotel, supervised beaches, playgrounds, interpretive boat tours, hiking and bicycling paths, and an outdoor theatre.

A **Marine Interpretation Centre**, *Saltons Day Use Area,* open daily 0900–2100 (June–Aug), reduced hours Sept–Oct, $1.25, uses interactive displays to explain the sea and its creatures. **Ocean Watch Tours**, *Saltons Wharf; tel: (709) 533-6024,* several tours daily (mid May–Oct), $19–26, combines sightseeing, whale-watching, fishing and watching for icebergs and bald eagles. **Twin Rivers Golf Course**, *Port Blanford; tel: (709) 543-2626,* open daily May–Oct, greens fee $27–34, is considered one of the finest in Atlantic Canada.

In the park, **Newman Sound Campground** has 417 tent and RV pitches, and the more rustic **Malady Head Campground** has 153 tent pitches. For a more luxurious but moderately priced lodging, **Terra Nova Park Lodge**, *Port Blanford, NF A0C 2G0; tel: (709) 543-2535* reservations, *543-2525* for information, is a modern resort alongside

the golf course, with golf packages and events and well-furnished family-sized rooms. **Mulligan's Pub** serves light meals, and a dining room serves lunches and dinners.

Reached from the northern end of the park via Rte 310, is **Eastport Peninsula**, rich in coastal scenery, secluded beaches (go to Sandy Cove), hiking trails to abandoned towns, and charming fishing villages, such as **Salvage**, with its **Fisherman's Museum**, *tel: (709) 677-2609,* open daily 0900–1930 (mid June–Aug), $1. The **Burnside Project** is excavating an early Paleo-Eskimo site, rare in Newfoundland, already uncovering over 2000 artefacts. At Burnside a small **museum** interprets the site; *tel: (709) 677-2474,* open Mon–Fri 1000–2000, Sat–Sun 1200–1800 (June–Aug), free, or you can take a boat there at 1300 when the dig is in progress.

One of the loveliest Bed and Breakfast homes in the entire province is **Laurel Cottage**, *41 Bank Rd, Eastport, NF A0G 1Z0; tel: (709) 677-3138,* budget–moderate, where a full breakfast with home-baked breads is served on fine china. **Pingent Bed and Breakfast**, *17 Church St, Eastport, NF A0G 1Z0; tel: (709) 677-3021,* budget, is also spotless and comfortable, with an art studio. Eat at **Little Dernier Restaurant**; *tel: (709) 677-3663,* for well-prepared dishes and genial service, budget.

GANDER

Tourist Information: Visitors Center, *109 Trans-Canada Hwy, Gander, NF A1V 1P6; tel: (709) 256-7110.*

The entrance to **Gander International Airport** is 2 km east of the Visitor Centre. Despite its name, the airport now offers flights to Deer Lake and St John's only. You cna get there from town by taxi.

ACCOMMODATION AND FOOD

Gander's location as one of the few cities with good tourist services in central Newfoundland makes it a favourite stopover, offering *CI* as well as **Hotel Gander**, *100*

329

Trans-Canada Hwy, Gander, NF A1V 1P5; tel: (709) 256-3931, fax: (709) 651-2641, moderate, with modern rooms and a number of extra services, and **Sinbad's Motel**, Bennet Dr. (P.O. Box 450), Gander, NF A1V 1W8; tel: (709) 651-2678 or (800) 563-4900, moderate. This attractive modern hotel has a good dining room, moderate, the best choice in town.

Cape Cod Bed and Breakfast, 66 Bennett Dr., Gander, NF A1V 1M9; tel: (709) 651-2269, budget–moderate, has luxurious details and décor in a modern home, with elegant breakfasts.

As the closest fog-free spot to England, Gander was chosen for a British airfield that proved to be a vital supply link and refuelling point for nearly all Europe-bound military flights in World War II. That role continued into the 1990s for a diminishing number of commercial airlines. The wartime settlement is a ghost-town now, young forest replacing the military housing that once lined the streets. Gander was moved a short distance west about 50 years ago, but you can drive or walk down memory lane by taking Garret and Circular Rds, near the airport entrance.

Today's Gander has vintage aircraft decorating its parks, and the **North Atlantic Aviation Museum**, Trans-Canada Hwy 1; tel: (709) 256-2923, has aircraft and exhibits, plus the chance to climb into the cockpit of a DC-3; open daily 0900–2100 (mid May–early Sept), 0830–1630 (Sept–mid May), $3, youth/senior $2.

More old aircraft assemble here in early Aug for the **Festival of Flight**. North America's only **Commonwealth War Graves**, Trans-Canada Hwy 1; tel: (709) 651-2930, also from the war era, are 3.5 km east of the town.

KITTYWAKE COAST

Tourist Information: Kittywake Coast Tourism Association, 109 Trans-Canada

Hwy, Gander, NF A1V 1P6; tel: (709) 256-5070.

The coastline of **Hamilton Bay** is lower and less dramatic than other areas, but equally lovely, with beaches, picturesque harbours and sand dunes. At **Gambo**, 24 km west along Hwy 1 from Terra Nova National Park's northern border (and 40 km before Gander), take Rte 320 north to **Wesleyville**, where the **Regional Museum**; tel: (709) 536-2077, open daily 1300–1800, longer Tues–Wed (July–Aug), $2, is worth a stop for its re-creations of early household life and displays on the methods of the fisheries.

In **Newtown**, an attractive port set on low, rocky islands connected by bridges, the **Barbour Heritage Site**; tel: (709) 536-2441, open daily 1000–2000 (late June–early Sept), $5, students $3, centres around two heritage homes, filled with the everyday lives of different generations. Costumed guides, a small theatre, tea room and art gallery complete the experience.

From Newtown, Rte 330 follows the coast past **Deadman's Bay Natural Sanctuary**, where dunes and beaches, overlook waters that icebergs frequent. At **Musgrave Harbour** is a small **Fishermen's Museum**, Marine Dr.; tel: (709) 655-2119, open 1000–2000 (July–Sept), $1.

At the village of Gander Bay, Rte 330 leads 40 km south to Gander and the Trans-Canada Hwy. To continue instead along the scenic loop, Rte 331 heads north to **Boyd's Cove**, stopping at **Beothuk Interpretation Centre**, tel: (709) 656-3114, open daily 1000–1800 (June–Sept), free, to learn about this native tribe which became extinct in 1829 as a result of contact with European settlers. A short walk with interpretive signs leads to the archaeological site where a Beothuk village has been excavated.

TWILLINGATE

Rte 340 diverges at Boyd's Cove, leading to Twillingate, a harbour town with scenery, services and history.

To understand the latter, head for the **Twillingate Museum**, *North Island; tel: (709) 884-2825*, open daily 1000–2100 (late May–Sept), $1, showing the town's past as a fishing industry hub in the 1700s and 1800s. Look here, too, in the shop, for high quality Newfoundland crafts.

Twillingate is the centre for whale- and iceberg-watching, with tours leaving daily: **Twillingate Island Boat Tours**, *The Iceberg Shop; tel: (709) 884-2242* or *(800) 611-BERG*, or **Twillingate Adventure Tours**, *tel: (709) 884-5999* or *(888) 447-TOUR*. Both operate May–Sept.

Crewe's Heritage Bed and Breakfast, *33 Main St, Twillingate, NF A0G 4M0; tel: (709) 884-2723*, open June–Sept, budget, is right on the waterfront in the centre of town. **Anchor Inn**, *P.O. Box 550, Twillingate, NF A0G 4M0; tel: (709) 884-2777*, moderate, has modern rooms and a dining room that serves a varied menu; try Fisherman's Brewis, a traditional dish that's especially good here.

In a scenic setting nearby, **Beach Rock Bed and Breakfast**, *P.O. Box 350, RR 1, Little Harbour, NF A0G 4M0; tel: (709) 884-2292*, budget, serves seafood dinners by advance reservation.

Rte 340 returns to Hwy 1 via Lewisporte, the southern landing for ferries to Labrador (see p. 340). Its location, in a protected bay filled with tiny islands, makes it a favourite yachting centre.

Spinning Wheel Crafts and Bye the Bay Museum, *Main St; tel: (709) 535-2844*, is a co-operative with varied crafts, especially hand-knit sweaters and mittens; open daily 0900–2100 (July–Aug), Tues–Sat 0900–1700 (June, Sept–Dec), admission to museum $0.50. **Northgate Bed and Breakfast**, *106 Main St, Lewisporte, NF A0G 3A0; tel: (709) 535-2258*, has charming budget rooms in a hospitable setting, plus hearty full breakfasts. They also do boat tours

and lobster cookouts, visiting abandoned island communities in the bay. **Brittany Inns**, *Rte 341 (P.O. Box 730), Lewisporte, NF A0G 3A0; tel: (709) 535-2533*, moderate, has a dining room, also moderate.

The Scenic Route rejoins the Direct Route at Notre Dame Junction, and Hwy 1 continues to **Grand Falls-Windsor**, where more Beothuck culture is shown at the **Mary March Regional Museum**, *Cromer Ave; tel: (709) 489-7331*, open Mon–Fri 0900–1200, 1300–1700, Sat–Sun 1400–1700, closed holidays, admission free. Behind the museum is **Beothuk Village**, *tel: (709) 489-3559*, open same hours (late May–early Sept), $2, with replicas of the Beothuk homes. A good lunch stop in Grand Falls is the **Valley Restaurant**, *Exploits Valley Mall, Harris Ave; tel: (709) 489-5961*, budget.

Hwy 1 travels through largely unsettled land for the next 200 km, with few reasons to stop, except for **Woodland Kettle Bed & Breakfast and Tea Room**, *19 Church St, Badger, NF A0H 1A0; tel: (709) 539-2588* or *(888) 539-2588*, open May–Sept, budget–moderate, with well-decorated rooms, hot tea and biscuits on arrival, and nicely prepared breakfasts. Near South Brook, **Fort Birchy Campgrounds**, *Hwy 1 (P.O. Box 1440), Springdale, NF A0J 1T0; tel: (709) 551-1318*, has tent and caravan pitches, and a bakery and restaurant with home-style Newfoundland dishes, budget.

A short distance beyond, Rtes 390 and 391 make a short detour to **Kings Point** and **Rattling Brook Falls**, thundering during spring runoff, but impressive for its height any time of year. In Kings Point, **Budgell's Motel**, *P.O. Box 76, King's Point, NF A0J 1H0; tel: (709) 268-3364*, budget, has a good budget restaurant with a bit more variety than most.

Turn off at **Deer Lake** (p. 339) for Gros Morne National Park and the Viking Trail.

331

CORNER BROOK

Tourist Information: Tourist Chalet, *West Valley Rd (just off Hwy 1), Corner Brook, NF A2H 6E6; tel: (709) 639-9792,* open daily 0900–2100.

Newfoundland's second largest city, Corner Brook is set on the steep banks of the Humber Arm as it rises to the Blow Me Down Mountains.

ACCOMMODATION AND FOOD

Along with *BW, CI* and *HI,* Corner Brook has the historic **Glynmill Inn**, *1 Cobb Lane (P.O. Box 550), Corner Brook, NF A2H 6E6; tel: (709) 634-5181 or (800) 563-4400, fax: (709) 634-5106,* moderate, a hotel rich in gracious atmosphere, set in park-like grounds. Dine in their **Carriage Room**, moderate–pricey, or **The Wine Cellar**, downstairs, a steakhouse in a stone-walled room.

Mamateek Inn, *64 Maple Valley Rd (P.O. Box 787), Corner Brook, NF A2H 6G7; tel: (709) 639-8901 or (800) 563-8600, fax: (709) 639-7567,* moderate, also has a dining room, overlooking the city, moderate–pricey. **Thirteen West**, *13 West St; tel: (709) 634-1300,* moderate, serves an innovative and eclectic menu. Bread and pastas are made right there.

SIGHTSEEING

The Humber River and Arm provide a lot of water-based activities, including sightseeing cruises to see a variety of wildlife. You can go by sail boat, canoe or motor – the latter with **Teaco Boat Tours**, *Steady Brook; tel: (709) 639-1538,* adults $20, children $10–15.

The scenic Rte 450 leads along the Humber Arm to nearby **Blow Me Down Provincial Park**, *Lark Harbour; tel: (709) 570-7573 or (800) 866-CAMP* (mid May–Aug), with tent and caravan pitches and hiking trails, and to **Bottle Cove**, which is almost completely enclosed by rocky headlands.

CORNER BROOK TO PORT AUX BASQUES

Hwy 1 travels south-west, past several short roads leading to scenic coastal villages, and into the Codroy Mountains, where snow patches linger on the slopes into mid July, melting into waterfalls that drop in silver ribbons down the mountainsides.

A good stop along this scenic route is **Chignic Lodge**, *Trans-Canada Hwy 1, Doyles; tel: (709) 955-2880,* cheap–budget, a spotless restaurant serving three meals daily. **Grand Codroy Provincial Park**, *Doyles, NF A0N 1J0; tel: (709) 570-7573 or (800) 866-CAMP* (mid May–Aug), has tent and caravan pitches and swimming.

PORT AUX BASQUES

Tourist Information: Port aux Basques Information Centre, *Hwy 1, Port aux Basques, NF A0N 1K0; tel: (709) 695-2262,* open Mon, Tues, Thur, Sat 0600–2300, Wed, Fri, Sun 0600–2130 (June–Oct).

Port aux Basques crowns a rocky knob overlooking the harbour and an endless stretch of sea. It is the major ferry terminal, with several arrivals a day in summer from North Sydney, Nova Scotia (see p. 281).

Heritage Home, *11 Caribou Road (P.O. Box 1187), Port aux Basques, NF A0M 1C0; tel: (709) 695-3240,* is a budget Bed and Breakfast next to the ferry terminal. **St Christopher's Hotel**, *Caribou Road (P.O. Box 2049), Port aux Basques, NF A0M 1C0; tel: (709) 695-7034, fax: (709) 695-9841,* is a moderate motel-style property with a dining room.

Gulf Museum, *118 Main St; tel: (709) 695-3408,* has maritime artefacts, including a 17th-century astrolabe found on the shore and a working print shop; open daily 1000–1800 (June–Aug). J.T. **Cheeseman Provincial Park**, *Cape Ray; tel: (709) 695-7222 or (800) 866-CAMP* (mid May–Aug), on the Cape Ray Barrens, is a prime birding site with sandy beaches for swimming, walking trails and tent pitches.

332

DEER LAKE–
L'ANSE AUX MEADOWS

It would be hard to find a piece of Newfoundland coast without a view that ranges from photogenic to simply spectacular. But the shoreline of this Great Northern Peninsula, the route known as the Viking Trail, outshines them all.

L'Anse aux Meadows

St Barbe

430

125

36

St Anthony

55

Port au Choix

8

DIRECT ROUTE: 445 KM

Hawke's Bay

430

158

Rocky Harbour

Gros Morne National Park

430

29

431

Woody Point

55

Wiltondale

34

Deer Lake

333

Gros Morne National Park, which encompasses the fjord-cut coastline where the last thrust of the Appalachian Mountains fall off into the sea, is perhaps Canada's most memorable national park, yet it is one of its least visited. Among its wonders is a geological phenomenon, the Tablelands, so unusual that it has been named a UNESCO World Heritage Site.

But it would be a shame to go no further than Gros Morne; the entire route to the far northern tip is scenic, and the reward for the journey is the only known Viking settlement in the New World. Icebergs are such a common sight along the Strait of Belle Isle, which washes the northern shore of the peninsula, that it is known as Iceberg Alley.

ROUTE

Only one road, Rte 430, travels the 445 km from the Trans-Canada (Hwy 1) at Deer Lake to **St Anthony**, at the northern tip of the peninsula. Rte 430 hugs the shore nearly all the way, and few roads branch off to the sides. Rte 431 leaves it in **Gros Morne National Park** to reach the southern shore of Bonne Bay, while Rte 432 in the north travels across to the peninsula's eastern shore. Only at the far end, close to St Anthony, do a few short roads reach out like fingers to clusters of tiny outports. At **St Barbe**, in the north, you can take a ferry across the Strait of Belle Isle to **Labrador** (p. 340).

The shortest possible time you should schedule for the entire route, without a side trip to Labrador, is three days; five would allow you to see and do more.

Tourist information on the entire route is available in the *Newfoundland and Labrador Travel Guide*, which can be obtained free from the **Department of Tourism, Culture and Recreation**, *P.O. Box 8730, St John's, NF A1B 4K2; tel: (709) 729-2830* or *(800) 563-6353* (toll-free), and from the **Viking Trail Tourism Association**, *P.O. Box 430, St Anthony, NF A0K 4S0; tel: (709) 454-8888*. When you arrive, pick up a free copy of *Where It's At* from any Tourist Office along the Viking Trail. This magazine is filled with articles on places, events, people and activities in the area.

BUSES

Viking Express operate a service from St Anthony to Deer Lake three times a week. Journey time: 7 hrs. See OTT table 242.

DEER LAKE

Tourist Information: Tourist Information Chalet, *Trans-Canada Hwy 1; tel: (709) 635-2202*, open daily 0900–2100 (June–Aug), 1000–1700 (May and Sept).

ACCOMMODATION AND FOOD

Deer Lake Motel, *Trans-Canada Hwy 1*

(P.O. Box 820), Deer Lake, NF A0K 2E0; tel: (709) 635-2108, fax: (709) 635-3842, moderate, offers, in addition to modern rooms, a small shop, take-away food and the **Cormack Dining Room**, moderate.

SIGHTSEEING

Deer Lake marks the turn-off for Rte 430, leading to **Gros Morne National Park** (see below). **Roy Whalen Regional Heritage Centre**, *tel: (709) 635-4440*, open 0900–2100 (mid June–mid Sept), $2, at the intersection, next to the Tourist Chalet, shows life from the early settlement of the Humber Valley. Its shop, **Valley Crafts**, sells hand-knit sweaters and mittens, moose hide slippers and local woodcarvings. **Deer Lake Municipal Park**, *133 Nicholsville Rd; tel: (709) 635-5885*, day admission $1, has a sandy swimming beach and lakefront tent pitches.

DEER LAKE TO GROS MORNE

The Viking Trail begins in Deer Lake, at the intersection of Trans-Canada Hwy 1 and Rte 430, and its signs will guide you throughout the entire route. The first town is **Wiltondale**, just south of the entrance to the national park.

Wiltondale Pioneer Village, *Rte 430; tel: (709) 453-2464*, open daily 1000–1800 (mid June–mid Sept), $3, family $6, is a reconstruction of an early 20th-century town, with a home, school, church, general store and **Aunt Nellie's Tea Room and Bakery**, *tel: (709) 453-2464*, which serves traditional Newfoundland dishes and pastries.

No matter which road you take from Wiltondale, you will soon come to the entrance to Gros Morne National Park.

GROS MORNE NATIONAL PARK

Tourist Information: Gros Morne Visitor's Centre, *Rte 430, north of Wiltondale (mailing address: P.O. Box 130, Rocky*

Harbour, NF A0K 4N0); tel: (709) 458-2066, open daily 0900–2200 (late June–early Aug), 0900–1600 other seasons. Be sure to see the short film, *A Wonderful Fine Coast*, for an introduction to the park's geology and wildlife. Park headquarters is in **Norris Point**; *tel: (709) 458-2417,* open daily 1000–2000 (mid May–mid Oct).

Admission to the park is $3.25 one day, $9.25 four days, family $6.50 one day, $19.50 four days. Note that you must pay this fee in order to leave the highway anywhere in the park, even to stop at a lookout point. (Passes are not sold at the entrance to the park's southern section on Rte 431; buy them at the park entrance on Rte 430.)

SOUTHERN SECTION

Rte 431 turns west in **Wiltondale**, leading to the southern section of Gros Morne, which is almost completely divided by the long East Arm of **Bonne Bay**. Although a ferry no longer connects the two sections across the bay, you should not miss this part of the park, even though it means returning to Wiltondale on the same road. This is the section of the park that earned it a UNESCO World Heritage Site designation, and some of the finest of its scenery is here.

Rte 431 goes west to the fishing village of **Woody Point**, on the steep bank of South Arm. The scenery gets better and better, mountainsides rising more precipitously from the water as you drive west.

Accommodation and Food

Trout River Campground, *no phone, but the Woody Point Visitors Center has radio contact; tel: (709) 458-2417 and ask for the Visitors Center,* has well-spaced tent pitches overlooking the lake, $8 daily fee. Trout River sits around its fishing harbour at the mouth of the river, between rocky headlands.

The town is outside the park borders, and it is in these little islands of private land that you will find lodging and dining. **Victorian Manor**, *Main St (P.O. Box 165), Woody*

Point, NF A0K 1P0; tel: (709) 453-2485, is a moderate family-run inn with rooms, self-catering units and two adjunct Bed and Breakfast homes. **Crockers Bed and Breakfast**, *P.O. Box 165, Woody Point, NF A0K 1P0; tel: (709) 451-5220,* budget, offers the warmth of a family home, with a kitchen available for guest use. **Seaside Restaurant**, *Trout River; tel: (709) 451-3461,* moderate, overlooks the beach and waters, where you can watch whales as you dine on fresh fish.

Sightseeing

The road continues to **Trout River**, along the **Tablelands**, a barren red landscape of crumbling rock that is actually a piece of the earth's mantle, usually a mile or more beneath the surface, but forced to the surface here 450 million years ago as Europe and North America moved closer. Geologists come from all over to study this rare sample of the earth's interior. **Tablelands Lookout** has interpretive signs with diagrams.

At Trout River, you can learn more about the fascinating geology on a boat tour into the land-locked fjord that lies between this upthrust and the grey cliffs of the neighbouring mountain. **Tablelands Boat Tour**, *Trout River; tel: (709) 451-2101,* offers tours daily. 0930, 1300 and 1600 (July and Aug), 1300 (late June and early Sept), $30. A hiking trail leads from Rte 431 to **Green Gardens**, an area of highland meadow along a coast marked by sea stacks and caves. To explore the waters of Bonne Bay, where whales and eagles are not unusual sights, take a cruise with **Gros Morne Boat Tours**, *Norris Point; tel: (709) 458-2871,* daily 1300 (late June–mid Sept), $25.

NORTHERN SECTION

The **Long Range Mountains**, at the end of the Appalachian chain, form the spine of Gros Morne, but are a mere shadow of their former selves. Worn and ground by glaciers, which scraped them bare of vegetation and left their summits a rocky jumble, their

335

slopes are matted with a dense, impenetrable coniferous scrub called Tuckamore. Along with scouring their tops, the glaciers left behind them the deep slashes of fjords, some of which have become land-locked as long narrow lakes cutting between sheer cliffs, like Trout River Pond.

Accommodation and Food

Sugar Hill Inn, *P.O. Box 100, Norris Point, NF A0K 3V0; tel: (709) 458-2147, fax: (709) 458-2147*, moderate, has four guest rooms with queen-size beds, as well as a dining room serving expensive–pricey dinners by reservation. **Gros Morne Cabins**, *P.O. Box 151, Rocky Harbour, NF A0K 4N0; tel: (709) 458-2020, fax (709) 458-2882*, off season reservations *(709) 458-2525*, moderate, is a group of 22 self-catering log cabins, each with television, carpeting and full kitchens, and each overlooking the water. Picnic tables and barbecue grill are on the lawn. **Ocean View Motel**, *Rte 430 (P.O. Box 129), Rocky Harbour, NF A0K 4N0; tel: (709) 458-2730, fax (709) 458-2841*, moderate, is handily located on the harbour. Its **Ocean Room**, moderate, serves three meals daily.

Fisherman's Landing, *Rte 430, Rocky Harbour; tel: (709) 458-2060*, moderate, serves three meals daily, year round. In summer it's open until 2300, breads are home-made. The bread, scones and other pastries are also home-baked at **Aunt Polly's**, *Rte 430, Sally's Cove, no phone*, a bakery with two tables, open daily 0800–2400.

Inside the national park, the major northern campsites are at **Berry Hill**, **Trout River**, **Green Point** and **Shallow Bay**, with tent and caravan pitches, but no electrical hook-ups. None accept reservations; rates are $10–14. The privately operated **Juniper Campground**, *Pond Road, Rocky Harbour, NF A0K 4NO; tel: (709) 458-2917*, has 54 tent pitches.

Sightseeing

Park naturalists lead nature walks and evening slide programmes, listed on a schedule available at the Visitor's Centre. Be sure also to get a free copy of *Tuckamore*, a magazine-style publication listing the many hiking trails throughout the park, which range from short flat walks to full-day challenging climbs to the summits. A short and easy trail goes to **Southeast Brook Falls**, its entrance clearly marked on Rte 430. A longer trail leads from Berry Brook Campground to **Baker's Brook Falls**. Also accessible only by trail is **Broom Point**, where an isolated fishing settlement has been restored, with local fishermen available to discuss the fisheries.

In a park where dramatic scenery is almost commonplace, **Western Brook Pond** stands out as the signature view. Access is by a 3-km walk on a boardwalk over peatbogs carpeted in wildflowers, and through low woodlands, with tantalising views of the fjord rising ahead. Interpretive signs explain the plant life and geology. The trail ends at the shore of an intensely blue lake, so deep its temperature never rises far above freezing, which extends out of sight between the straight 650-m high walls of the land-locked 16-km long fjord. To tour deeper into the fjord, where waterfalls drop hundreds of feet from the cliffs, reserve space on one of the boats operated by **Bontour Cruises**, *Ocean View Motel, Rocky Harbour; tel: (709) 458-2730*, daily 1000, 1300 and 1600 (late June–early Sept), 1300 (June and Sept), $25. Allow an hour to walk to the boat.

North of Western Brook Pond, you can tour **St Paul's Inlet**, where seals sun on the rocks and terns and eagles soar, with **Seal Island Boat Tours**, *P.O. Box 11, St Pauls; tel: (709) 243-2376 or 2278*, daily 1000, 1300, 1600 and 1900 (mid June–Sept) 1000, 1300, 1600 (late May–mid June), $20. Visit **Cow Head Lighthouse**, *Cow Head; tel: (709) 243-2446*, free, and the nearby **Tete de Vache Museum and Craft Shop**, *tel: (709) 243-2023*, open daily 1000–1700 (late June–Sept), donation requested, a small

336

community museum with mittens and other locally made crafts for sale in its shop. The adjacent beaches are back on park land, in **Shallow Bay**, reached by a boardwalk across the dunes.

GROS MORNE TO HAWKE'S BAY

Tourist Information: Tourist Chalet, *Torrent River Bridge, Hawke's Bay, NF A0K 3B0; tel: (709) 248-5344,* open daily 1000–1800 (July–Aug), *tel: (709) 248-5225* (Sept–June).

The scenery is less dramatic north of the national park, where Rte 430 hugs a more gentle coastline of low headlands interspersed with coves. Whales and icebergs keep the sea vistas interesting, while small villages perched along the sea and lighthouses and fishing harbours mark the foreground.

Not far beyond the park boundary, **The Arches** is a formation worn by the waves in a huge outcrop of white dolomite standing in the edge of the sea. **River of Ponds Provincial Park** has rustic wooded tent pitches, plus picnic tables and swimming. It's a major trout fishing area.

At **Hawke's Bay**, along the banks of the Torrent River, **Torrent River Nature Park** provides a boardwalk and stairs through bogs and woodlands, past gorges and rapids, to a waterfall. A **salmon ladder** has been constructed here to make the waters upstream available to spawning salmon, which had previously not been able to jump the falls. The trail into the park begins at the Tourist Chalet.

Maynard's Motel, *Rte 430 (P.O. Box 59), Hawke's Bay, NF A0K 3B0; tel: (709) 248-5225 or (800) 563-8811, fax: (709) 248-5363,* has rooms, self-catering units and a restaurant, all moderate.

PORT AU CHOIX TO ST ANTHONY

Just off Rte 430, on Ingornachoix Bay, **Port au Choix** is the centre of the northern

shrimp fleet, and in mid July they celebrate with a **Shrimp Festival and Blessing of the Fleet,** *tel: (709) 861-3911.* You can see the boats come in around dusk each evening from May through July, when the docks are abuzz with activity.

An important archaeological dig at **Port au Choix National Historic Site** continues to yield evidence of North America's southernmost Eskimo settlement. Tools, implements and skeletons have been unearthed in cemeteries, revealing previously unknown information about the Maritime Archaic people, who lived here over 4000 years ago, and much later cultures of the Dorset and Groswater Paleo Eskimos who followed them. Enter at the new **Visitor Center,** *tel: (709) 861-3522* (mid June–mid Sept), *(709) 623-2608* (winter), open daily 0900–1900 (mid June–Aug), $2.75. The sites are a short distance farther on at **Philip's Garden**, overlooking the sea. **Point Richie Lighthouse** is at the end of the road.

Close to it is **Point Richie Inn,** *32 Point Richie Rd, Port au Choix, NF A0K 4C0; tel: (709) 861-3773 or 861-2112,* budget, where sweeping sea views accompany breakfast. **Sea Echo Motel,** *P.O. Box 179, Port au Choix, NF A0K 4C0; tel: (709) 861-3777,* low moderate, has comfortable rooms with television and phones. The nearby **Anchor Café,** *tel: (709) 861-3665,* serves three meals daily until 2400, with plentiful seafood plus Italian, vegetarian and low-fat choices.

Archaeologists have long thought that other aboriginal sites must exist in the area, and, quite recently, finds at **Bird Cove**, 60 km north of Port au Choix, seem to prove the theory. A dig is in progress, and visitors are welcome to visit it and to see the artefacts recovered so far, displayed in the Community Center.

At **St Barbe**, a ferry is operated by **Northern Cruiser Ltd,** *tel: (709) 931-2309,* across the Strait of Belle Isle to Labrador; two round trips daily (May–Dec), passengers $9, automobiles $18.50. Roads do

337

not connect this small coastal area to the rest of Labrador, so this is the best way to see it. Ferry schedules vary daily, but in midsummer allow a same-day return trip, with about 5 hours there. You can often see Labrador across the strait, and you can see icebergs in its currents well into July.

At **Eddie's Cove**, Rte 430 turns east across a wild, unsettled interior, emerging briefly on Pistolet Bay before reaching the coast.

ST ANTHONY

Tourist Information: Tourism Association, *Rte 430 (P.O. Box 430), St Anthony, NF A0K 4S0; tel: (709) 454-3077* (July–Aug), *(709) 454-8888* (Sept–June).

The coast becomes high and craggy again at this northern tip of Newfoundland that faces the open Atlantic Ocean. Icebergs broken away from their moorings in Greenland's glaciers drift past, and whales follow schools of fish south in the spring. In June or July, you are almost certain to see both from vantage points high above the sea on rocky headlands.

ACCOMMODATION AND FOOD

For those who prefer a hotel atmosphere, **St Anthony Haven Inn**, *Goose Cove Rd (P.O. Box 419), St Anthony, NF A0K 4S0; tel: (709) 454-1900, fax: (709) 454-2270,* moderate, has rooms and suites, all freshly renovated, as well as a dining room.

The Lightkeeper's Café, *Fishing Point, St Anthony; tel: (709) 454-4900,* budget–moderate, serves three meals daily, but its prime location and view make reservations a good idea in the evening.

SIGHTSEEING

Having come so far, it would be a shame to miss any of the tiny harbour villages or headland views at the ends of the few roads in this remote corner, so follow any one of them; it won't go far until it finds the sea. St Anthony is the only large town, its harbour well pro-

tected from the heavy seas. It grew as a reprovisioning port for Labrador-bound fishing boats.

You can learn a lot about these fisheries, as well as St Anthony's own history, at **Grenfell House**, *Rte 430, St Anthony; tel: (709) 454-3333,* open daily 1000–2000 (late May–early Sept), $2. Wilfred Grenfell founded the Grenfell Medical Mission in 1894 to provide the Labrador fishing settlements with medical care. He built nursing stations and hospitals there, financed by Grenfell Crafts, which made parkas from a specially designed weatherproof material. Local people were employed to make and embroider designs on the coats. The Grenfells' home has been restored to it's 1900 origins.

The rest of the story is told at the **Dockhouse Museum**, *Rte 430, St Anthony; tel: (709) 454-2281,* open daily 1000–2000 (June–Aug), free, a restored drydock and slipway that shows life and work in the fisheries. You can buy the handmade coats, jackets and snowsuits in Grenfell cloth, as well as knit sweaters, mittens and other apparel, at **Grenfell Handcrafts**, *Rte 430, St Anthony; tel: (709) 454-3576,* open Mon–Fri 0900–2100, Sat 0900–1800, Sun 1300–1800.

While in that neighbourhood, stop to see the **Jordi Bonet Murals** in the rotunda of the Memorial Hospital, which capture the spirit of the people of Newfoundland and Labrador. A good spot for whale- and iceberg-spotting is at the far end of St Anthony, on **Fishing Point**, near the 1889 lighthouse, where viewing platforms overlook the sea and harbour. Trails climb along the high cliffs.

L'ANSE AUX MEADOWS

The second site in the Great Northern Peninsula that UNESCO has proclaimed as world class is **L'Anse aux Meadows National Historic Site**, *Rte 436, L'Anse aux Meadows; tel: (709) 623-2608,* open daily 0900–2000, $2.50. Its discovery and excavation in the 1960s finally answered the question of where the Vikings settled on their trips to the New World.

Dating from AD 1000, it is the only Viking settlement in North America yet discovered, and the first known European colony in the Americas. The exceptional museum in the Visitor Centre explains its history, as well as the Vikings who lived there. The village site is a short walk away, with clearly visible foundation lines and nearby reconstructions of a sod home and workshop built of peat.

To complete the Viking experience and get the best view of the rocky coast and islands, reserve space aboard an authentic replica of a Viking ship with **Viking Boat Tours**, *P.O. Box 45, St Lunaire; tel: (709) 623-2100, fax (709) 623-2098,* tours daily 1030, 1300, 1530 and 1830 (late June–Aug), two daily tours (late May–late June), $26. Advance reservations are highly recommended. *The Viking Saga* is a knaar, a working ship much like those which brought Norse settlers to L'Anse aux Meadows.

Coast Guard rules prohibit carrying passengers under sail on this boat, but the crew demonstrate the sail and explain the boat's authentic construction. The crew explains the wildlife you'll see and the area's history during a close-up visit to a shipwreck; there's a sea view of the Viking settlement and encounters with whales and icebergs among the bay's scenic islands.

Facing L'Anse aux Meadows across the island- and iceberg-filled bay, **Tickle Inn**, *R.R. 1 (Box 62), Cape Onion, NF A0K 4J0; tel: (709) 452-4321* (June–Sept) or *(709) 739-5503* (Oct–May), budget–moderate, sits in a cove between two tall promontories. Whale-watching is as easy as looking out of a window in this historic island home. Dinners (which you shouldn't miss) are served by reservation, and use local specialities, such as wild berries. **Marilyn's Hospitality Home**, *P.O. Box 5, Hay Cove, NF A0K 2X0; tel: (709) 623-2811,* budget, 2 km from the Viking site and boat trips, is a true Bed and Breakfast, where you share the family's home.

Close to the Viking site, **Smith's Restaurant**, *Rte 436, St Lunaire-Griquet; tel: (709) 623-2539,* budget, serves traditional local dishes, topped off with wild berry pies and parfaits, until 2400 daily. **Norsemen Gallery and Cafe**, *Harbourfront, L'Anse aux Meadows; tel: (709) 623-2018,* moderate, serves Newfoundland specialities with a personal flair, amid a collection of local art.

339

LABRADOR

There are several ways to get to Labrador – by car, train, air or boat – but no way to get around all of it by land. The easiest route takes you to the string of communities along the Strait of Belle Isle, a pleasant and manageable taste of a wildly beautiful place with a long, long history. Labrador's Indian culture reaches back at least eight millennia, and its Inuit (Eskimo) culture four. The Vikings were newcomers in 1010, leaving traces along the coast closest to Newfoundland.

Labrador is decidedly not for everyone. Settlements are remote, services few and nightlife almost non-existent. But the people, who live in the close-knit communities born of severe winters and isolation, are among the friendliest and most welcoming on earth.

TOURIST INFORMATION

Department of Tourism, Culture and Recreation, *P.O. Box 8730, St. John's, NF A1B 4K2; tel: (709) 729-2830 or (800) 563-6353* (toll-free). **Destination Labrador**, *118 Humphrey Rd, Bruno Plaza, Labrador City, NF A2V 2J8; tel: (709) 944-7788 or (800) 563-6353.*

GETTING THERE

From St Barbe, Newfoundland (see p. 334) a ferry operated by **Northern Cruiser Ltd**, *tel: (709) 931-2309* (May–Dec), makes two daily trips across the Strait of Belle Isle to Blanc Sablon, Québec, at the border of Labrador; passengers $9, automobiles $18.50.

From there, the paved Rte 510 travels

65 km to Red Bay. Roads do not connect to the rest of Labrador, but this coast has vestiges of much of Labrador's early history in a small area, easily reached by car.

Ferry schedules vary daily, but in midsummer they allow enough time for a same-day return trip. An overnight stay is preferable, since in the 5 hours between ferries you will not be able to linger anywhere to enjoy the easy humour and warm hospitality that will greet you.

SOUTHERN COAST

Tourist Information: Gateway to the Straits Visitor Information Centre, *St Andrews Church, L'Anse au Clair, Labrador, NF A0K 2K0; tel: (709) 931-2013*, open 1000–1800 (June–Aug). Along with information, the centre has displays about the history and culture of the region.

The ferry arrives in **Blanc Sablon, Québec**, a 5-km drive south of **L'Anse au Clair**, on the provincial border. The area's only road connects eight outport towns between L'Anse au Clair and Red Bay, 65 km away, with no side roads. Population is sparse, clustered into tight villages right along the strait. Like the road on the opposite shore, Rte 510 provides good views of the icebergs that earn the Strait of Belle Isle the title of 'Iceberg Alley.' Whales are also a fairly common sight. Vegetation is low, with wildflowers in the spring and summer, and the rich colours of bog foliage in the fall punctuated by white tufts of cotton grass.

ACCOMMODATION AND FOOD

The largest hotel in the area is the **Northern Lights Inn**, *P.O. Box 92, L'Anse au Clair, Labrador, NF A0K 2K0; tel: (709) 931-2332, fax (709) 931-2708*, moderate. Along with 35 rooms and self-catering units, they have a restaurant (moderate) and coffee shop. **Sea-View Motel and Restaurant**, *35 Main St, Forteau, Labrador, NF A0K 2P0; tel: (709) 931-2840*, moderate, has four motel rooms at their restaurant, budget–moderate, along with a bakery.

For a more personal experience, stay in any of the following hospitality homes (Bed and Breakfasts). **Beachside Hospitality Home**, *9 Lodge Rd, L'Anse au Clair, Labrador, NF A0K 3K0; tel: (709) 931-2662* or *(800) 563-8999*, budget. Home-cooked meals are served by reservation, or guests can use the kitchen or grill. **Davis Bed & Breakfast**, *L'Anse Amour, Labrador, NF A0K 3J0; tel: (709) 927-5690*, budget, with a trail to the lighthouse. **Grenfell Louie A. Hall Bed & Breakfast**, *4 Willow Ave (P.O. Box 137), Forteau, Labrador, NF A0K 2P0; tel: (709) 931-2916*, budget, in an historic Grenfell Nursing Station.

SIGHTSEEING

While you are in the Visitor Centre, ask for directions to the 'fairy holes', the local name for the holes in the shoreline rocks thought to have been left by Vikings, who tied their ships to stakes driven into them.

Moore's Handicrafts, Ltd, *8 Country Rd, L'Anse au Clair (just off Rte 510); tel: (709) 931-2022, fax: (709) 931-2054*, open daily 1000–2200 (year round), carries handmade winter coats and parkas, knitted sweaters and mittens, and home-made wild berry jams. The traditional cassocks (anoraks) have embroidered designs, and if you choose a design as you head north, you can pick up your finished coat on your return the same day.

At **L'Anse Amour** is the oldest dated **burial mound** in the Americas, where in 1973 archaeologists discovered a pit with the 7500-year-old remains of a young Maritime Archaic Indian boy, at the edge of an ancient campsite. The mound is identified by a monument on the road to the **Point Amour Lighthouse**, *tel: (709) 927-5826*, open daily 0800–1700 (June–mid Oct), free, built in 1857 and the tallest in eastern Canada. You can climb the 120 steps to the top, and the keeper's cottage has been restored to its mid 19th-century origins. Exhibits there portray the history of the lighthouse and area; a craft shop is in a nearby building. The **Labrador Straits Museum**, *L'Anse Amour; tel: (709) 931-2067*, open daily 1000–1800 (July–mid Sept), $1.50, shows the changes in local life over the past 150 years, especially the role of women in these coastal communities. The museum craft shop offers coats, knit sweaters and mittens, and hooked work.

L'Anse au Loup has an annual **Bakeapple Festival**, *tel: (709) 931-2920*, in early Aug, in honour of the cloudberry, which grows only in the far north.

The land becomes noticeably greener and the trees a bit taller as the road parallels the Pinware River before coming to **Pinware Provincial Park**, *tel: (800) 866-CAMP*, open mid May–Aug, with a beach, picnic area, hiking trails and 15 tent pitches. Although the Pinware is not a very long river, it is well known for its salmon fishing.

Red Bay is at the end of the road; a snowmobile trail is the only route to the coastal communities further north. **Red Bay National Historic Site**, *Rte 510; tel: (709) 920-2197*, open Mon–Sat 0800–2000, Sun 1300–2000 (mid June–Sept), free, has an Interpretation Centre for **Saddle Island**, where in the late 1500s Basque whalers established the largest whaling port of its day. Models of a cooperage and the tryworks, where blubber was rendered to make oil, and a one-hour film on the settlement's history are at the centre. Boats take visitors to the island, 0900–1600 (Mon–Sat), free. As many as 2000 whalers were here at its height, and the remains of the station, including their cemetery, are still there.

REMOTE AREAS

Because the major regions are not connected by a land route, many travellers arrive by air.

Whales and Icebergs

Belle Isle Strait is called 'Iceberg Alley' for good reason: in the spring and early summer, you will almost certainly see these icy giants as you drive along the Labrador shore. They are carried south by the Labrador Current after 'calving' from the glaciers of Greenland and Baffin Island, travelling several years to reach these waters.

You may think ice is ice, but an iceberg is quite different from winter ice in coves and bays. Protected waters have a lower salt content than the ocean, so their ice freezes at a higher temperature. These slabs and 'slob ice' from the Labrador Sea even look different from icebergs, which are distinguished by their blue-green colour.

Icebergs change shape as they drift, melting and often developing towers and arches. This increased surface melts more quickly, eventually breaking the iceberg in two. When they melt unevenly, their weight becomes unbalanced and they topple over, sometimes turning upside-down. Small icebergs, those about the size of your house, are called '**bergy-bits**'.

It's no coincidence that the best time to see icebergs — mid May through mid July – is also the best time to spot **whales**. An iceberg creates its own wildlife eco-system. Meltwater around them makes an ideal habitat for plankton. This attracts species of fish, sea birds and whales that thrive on plankton, as well as those whales and sea birds that feed on the smaller fish.

Other whale species follow the capelin, small silver fish that run in enormous schools from mid June to mid July. Where whales follow the capelin and other small fish in their annual migrations, as they do here, you are likely to see whales quite near the shore, so a driving tour quickly becomes a whale-watch.

In June or July, when as many as 20 species may breach and spout wherever the water is deep enough for them, often swimming among icebergs, it's difficult to remember to watch the road. Even the locals, who have seen this annual spectacle all their lives, stop to watch.

It's easy to see why the Basque whalers working these waters early in the 1500s built whaling stations all along the shores. But today, with whaling outlawed in all North American waters, the whales swim in peace.

Services to and between regions is provided by **Air Labrador**, tel: (709) 896-3387 or (800) 563-3042 in Newfoundland, with scheduled flights between St Anthony and the Labrador coast and Goose Bay, as well as charter air service by float-, ski- and wheel-landing planes. **Air Nova (Air Canada)**, tel: (800) 776-3000 in the USA, (800) 4-CANADA in Canada, (800) 563-5151 in Newfoundland, 081-759-2636 in Britain, flies into Goose Bay and Wabush from Halifax, Nova Scotia, and St John's, Newfoundland.

Ferry service along coastal areas is provided by **Marine Atlantic**, *Marine Atlantic Reservations Bureau, 355 North Purves St, North Sydney, NF B2A 3V2; tel: (902) 794-5700 or (800) 341-7981, fax (902) 564-7480.*

EASTERN AND NORTHERN COASTS

Happy Valley–Goose Bay, at the end of the deep Hamilton Inlet, is connected to Labrador City, in the west, by the mostly unpaved Rte 500, still quite rough east of Churchill Falls.

From the east, the only access to Goose Bay and the towns along the Atlantic coast is by ferry. **Marine Atlantic** operates the ferry from Lewisporte, in central Newfoundland (p. 331), twice weekly July–Aug, weekly June and early Sept; fares are $48–97, berth $37-75, automobile $160. The non-stop crossing to Goose Bay takes 38 hours, longer for those stopping in Cartwright.

The only way to reach the scenic **Atlantic Coast** and its outport towns is by a coastal ferry that leaves St Anthony, Newfoundland (p. 338), semi-weekly for 12-day 'cruises' that reach as far north as Nain, Labrador's northernmost permanent settlement, departing July–Oct, fares from $1800. These are also operated by Marine Atlantic.

WESTERN LABRADOR

Tourist Information: Labrador West Tourism Development Association, *tel: (709) 282-3337,* or **Mehihek Nordic Ski Club**, *Labrador City; tel: (709) 944-5842.*

A rail line serves the route between Sept-Isles, Québec and **Labrador City**, operated by **Québec, North Shore and Labrador Railway**; *tel: (418) 968-7805 in Québec, (709) 944-8205* in Newfoundland and Labrador, northbound departures Mon, Tues, Thur, southbound Tues, Wed, Fri (June–early Sept).

Rte 389, a mostly paved road with some gravel surfaced sections, connects Baie Comeau, on the St Lawrence River in Québec, to Labrador City, a 600-km trip, largely through wilderness. Allow a minimum of 8 hours to drive it.

Western Labrador comes into its own in late March, when the winter days have begun to lengthen, but the snow cover is still deep enough for enjoying all winter's outdoor sports. **The Labrador 400**, a 400-mile sled-dog race, the East's answer to Alaska's Iditarod, as well as ski races provide spectator sports, while the **Polar Bear Dip** and the **Great Labrador Loppet** are events anyone can join in.

FISHING EXCURSIONS

Tourist Information: Department of Tourism, Culture and Recreation, *P.O. Box 8730, St John's, NF A1B 4K2; tel: (709) 729-2830* or *(800) 563-6353*, ask for the publication *Hunting and Fishing Guide*.

More than two dozen outfitters take guests into the remote regions of northern Labrador to fish in rivers whose wildlife populations have been protected by limited access and isolation. The numbers, varieties and sizes of fish are staggering, providing a fishing experience few destinations can match. Brook trout, Atlantic salmon, lake trout, white fish, Arctic char, ouananiche and northern pike provide both challenge and reward.

The experience can be as rustic or as pampered as you choose. Some outfitters provide suites with bed linens, hot showers, all the comforts of a hotel, others expect you to bring your own sleeping bag to use in rustic cabins. Each outfitter describes the experience fully in advance, so you can choose your own style and comfort level. Be warned, however, that no amount of pampering can protect you from the voracious blackflies, so prepare to stock up on quantities of 'bug dope'.

Most trips include all transportation, often by float plane or helicopter, meals, lodging, guide, smoke house, and fish cleaning. Costs per person range $1000–3000 a week. The *Hunting and Fishing Guide* lists fishing outfitters, or you can try the following: **Big River Camps**, *c/o R. W. Skinner, P.O. Box 250, Pasadena, NF A0L 1K0; tel: (709) 686-2242, fax: (709) 686-5244*; **Drover's Labrador Adventures**, *P.O. Box 121, Labrador City, Labrador, NF A2V 2K3; tel/fax: (709) 944-6947*, **Park Lake Lodge**; *c/o D.L. Hollett, P.O. Box 332, Station C, Happy Valley-Goose Bay, Labrador, NF A0P 1C0; tel: (709) 896-3301.*

343

WEBSITES AND EMAIL ADDRESSES

Prices, opening hours and other details change as quickly in Eastern Canada as they do anywhere else in the world. Details in this volume were checked just before publication, but you can still expect to find changes that came too late for inclusion. For the absolutely latest updates, nothing beats the World Wide Web and Email. If the idea or attraction you're looking for isn't listed, a few moments with your favourite search engine may turn up a new website. For details of **Thomas Cook** and its services around the world, visit their website on *http://www.thomascook.com*. (VCB=Visitor and Convention Bureau; CC=Chamber of Commerce; CVB=Convention and Visitor Bureau; CVA=Convention and Visitor Association.) All the websites below and most other relevant sites can be accessed via links provided on the Canadian Tourism Commission's **Canadian Tourism Information Network**: *http://info.ic.gc.ca/tourism/* or *www.travelcanada.ca*

Air Canada: *http://www.aircanada.ca*

Canada Post: *http://www.mailposte.ca*

Canadian Airlines: *http://www.cdnair.ca*

Cape Breton Island: *http://www.cbisland.com*

Greater Halifax Visitor Guide:
http://ttg.sba.dal.ca/nstour/halifax/

Greater Québec Area Tourism and Convention Bureau:
http://www.quebec-region.cuq.qc.ca

Greater Montréal CVB:
http://www.tourism-montreal.org

Greyhound of Canada Transportation Corp.: *http://www.greyhound.ca*

Kingston, Ontario:
http://www.kingstonarea.on.ca

Moncton Visitor Information Centre:
http://www.greater.moncton.nb.ca.

National Gallery of Canada (Ottawa):
http://national.gallery.ca Email: info@gallery.ca

Newfoundland Dept of Tourism, Culture and Recreation:
http://www.gov.nf.ca/tourism
Email: info@tourism.gov.nf.ca

Niagara Falls Canada:
http://tourismniagara.com
Email: nfcvcb@tourismniagara.com

Niagara Falls, NY, USA:
http://www.niagara-usa.com

Niagara-on-the-Lake CC:
http://www.niagaraonthelake.com

Nova Scotia Tourism: *http://explore.gov.ns.ca*

Ontario Tourism: *http://www.travelinx.com*

Ottawa Tourism & Convention Authority: *http://www.tourottawa.org*

Parks Canada: *http://parkscanada.pch.gc.ca*

Revenue Canada: *http://www.rc.gc.ca*

Royal Ontario Museum:
http://www.rom.on.ca

Saint John (New Brunswick) VCB:
http://www.city.saint-john.nb.ca

St John's, Newfoundland:
http://www.city.st-johns.nf.ca

Shaw Festival: *http://shawfest.sympatico.ca*

Toronto Bed and Breakfast:
Email: bed@torontobandb.com

London, Ontario: *http://www.city.london.on.ca*

Tourism New Brunswick:
http://www.cybersmith.net/nbtour
Email: NBTOURISM@gov.nb.ca

Tourism PEI: *http://www.gov.pe.ca.*

Tourisme Québec:
http://www.gouv.qc.ca/tourisme/

Tourism Toronto/Metropolitan Toronto CVA: *http://www.tourism-toronto.com*

VIA Rail: *http://www.viarail.ca*

Wine Council of Ontario:
http://www.wineroute.com

HOTEL CODES
AND CENTRAL BOOKING NUMBERS

The following abbreviations have been used throughout the book to show which chains are represented in a particular town. Central booking numbers are shown in bold – use these numbers whilst in North America to make reservations at any hotel in the chain. Where available, numbers that can be called in your own country are also noted. (Aus=Australia, Can=Canada, Ire=Ireland, NZ= New Zealand, SA =South Africa, UK=United Kingdom, WW=Worldwide number).

BI	**Budgetel Inn**	Hd	**Holiday Inn**	Rd	**Radisson**
	(800) 428 3438		**(800) 465 4329**		**(800) 333 3333**
BW	**Best Western**		Aus *(800) 221 066*		Ire *(800) 557 474*
	(800) 528 1234		Ire *(800) 553 155*		NZ *(800) 443 333*
	Aus *(1 800) 222 422*		NZ *(0800) 442 222*		UK *(800) 191991*
	Ire *(800) 709 101*		SA *(011) 482 3500*	RI	**Residence Inn**
	NZ *(09) 520 5418*		UK *(0800) 897121*		**(800) 331 3131**
	SA *(011) 339 4865*	HG	**Hotel des Gouverneurs**		Aus *(800) 251 259*
	UK *(0800) 393130*		**(888) 910 1111**		Ire *(800) 409929*
Ch	**Choice**	HI	**Hostelling International**		NZ *(800) 441035*
	See Comfort Inn, Quality		**(800) 444 6111**	Rm	**Ramada**
	and Clarion		UK *(0171) 248 6547*		**(800) 854 7854**
CI	**Comfort Inn**	HJ	**Howard Johnson**		UK *(800) 181 737*
	(800) 228 5150		**(800) 654 2000**	Ro	**Rodeway Inn**
	Aus *(008) 090 600*		Aus *02 262 4918*		**(800) 228 2000**
	Can *(800) 888 4747*		UK *(0181) 688 1418*	Sh	**Sheraton**
	Ire *(800) 500 600*	Hn	**Hilton**		**(800) 325 3535** or
	NZ *(800) 8686 888*		**(800) 445 8667**		*(800) 325 1717*
	UK *(0800) 444 444*		Aus *(800) 222 255*		(hearing impaired)
Cr	**Clarion**		NZ *(800) 448 002*		Aus *(008) 073 535*
	(800) CLARION		SA *(011) 880 3108*		Ire *(800) 535 353*
CP	**Canadian Pacific**		UK *(0345) 581595*		NZ *(0800) 443 535*
	(800) 441 1414	IC	**Inter-Continental**		UK *(0800) 353535*
De	**Delta**		**(800) 327 0200**	Su	**Susse Chalet**
	(800) 268 1133		UK *(0345) 581 237*		**(800) 524 2538**
DI	**Days Inn**	Kd	**Keddy**	S8	**Super 8**
	(800) 325 2525		**(800) 561 7666**		WW *(800) 800 8000*
	UK *(01483) 440470*	Ke	**Kempinski**	TL	**Travelodge**
DT	**DoubleTree Inn**		**(800) 426 3135**		**(800) 578 7878**
	(800) 222 8733	Ma	**Marriott**		Aus *(800) 622 240*
EL	**Econolodge**		**(800) 228 9290**		Ire *(800) 409 040*
	(800) 424 6423		Aus *(800) 251 259*		NZ *(800) 801 111*
	WW *(800) 221 2222*		NZ *(800) 441 035*		SA *(011) 442 9201*
ES	**Embassy Suites**		UK *(800) 221222*		UK *(0345) 404040*
	(800) 362 2779	Nv	**Novotel**	Ve	**Venture Inn**
	Aus *02 959 3922*		**(800) NOVOTEL**		**(888) 483 6887**
	Can *416 626 3974*	QI	**Quality Inn**	We	**Westin**
	NZ *09 623 4294*		**(800) 228 5151**		**(800) 228 3000**
	SA *11 789 6706*	QS	**Quality Suites**	WI	**Wandlyn Inns**
	UK *(01992) 441517*		**(800) 228 5151**		**(800) 561 0000**

345

DRIVING TIMES AND DISTANCES

Approximate distances from major cities to surrounding places and main centres are given following the most direct routes. Driving times are meant as an average indication only, allowing for the nature of the roads but not for traffic conditions, which can be very variable (see the route descriptions throughout the book). They do not include allowance for stops or breaks en route. The journey times of the main ferry crossings are also shown.

Charlottetown to ...	Kilometres	Hours
Cape Breton (road)	462	5½
(road/ferry)	200	3
Halifax (road/ferry)	262	5
Moncton	181	2½
Saint John	334	5
Tignish	153	2
Wood Islands	65	1

Halifax to ...	Kilometres	Hours
Cape Breton	340	4½
Charlottetown	262	5
Digby	230	2¾
Moncton	282	3
N. Sydney	473	5¾
Saint John (road)	435	5
(road and ferry)	230	5¾
Yarmouth	308	4½

Montréal to ...	Kilometres	Hours
Mont-Tremblant	194	2½
Ottawa	203	2½
Québec City	260	3½
Toronto	486	6

Ottawa to ...	Kilometres	Hours
Algonquin Park	246	3
Kenora	1976	26
Montréal	203	2½
Sudbury	494	6
Toronto	486	5¼

Québec City to ...	Kilometres	Hours
Chicoutimi	225	3
Fredericton	605	7
Gaspé	709	9¼
Portland, Maine	270	3½
Rivière-du-Loup	214	2½

Saint John to ...	Kilometres	Hours
Campbellton	490	6
Cape Breton	500	5½
Charlottetown	334	5
Fredericton	103	1¼
Halifax	435	5
Moncton	152	2

St John's to ...	Kilometres	Hours
Gros Morne	708	9
L'Anse aux Meadows	1088	14
Port aux Basques	905	14

Toronto to ...	Kilometres	Hours
Kenora	1902	24
London	188	2½
Montréal	486	6
Niagara Falls	128	1½
Ottawa	445	5½
Sudbury	469	6

346

CONVERSION TABLES

DISTANCES (approx. conversions)
1 kilometre (km) = 1000 metres (m) 1 metre = 100 centimetres (cm)

Metric	Imperial/US	Metric		Imperial/US	Metric	Imperial/US
1 cm	3/8 in	9 m	(10 yd)	29 ft	0.75 km	½ mile
1 m 0 cm	3 ft 3 in	10 m	(11 yd)	33 ft	1 km	5/8 mile
2 m 0 cm	6 ft 6 in	20 m	(22 yd)	66 ft	5 km	3 miles
3 m 0 cm	10 ft 0 in	50 m	(54 yd)	164 ft	10 km	6 miles
4 m 0 cm	13 ft 0 in	100 m	(110 yd)	330 ft	20 km	12½ miles
5 m 0 cm	16 ft 6 in	200 m	(220 yd)	660 ft	30 km	18½ miles
6 m 0 cm	19 ft 6 in	250 m	(275 yd)	820 ft	50 km	31 miles
7 m 0 cm	23 ft 0 in	300 m	(330 yd)	984 ft	75 km	46 miles
8 m 0 cm	26 ft 0 in	500 m	(550 yd)	1640 ft	100 km	62 miles

24-HOUR CLOCK
(examples)

0000 = Midnight	1200 = Noon	1800 = 6.00 p.m.
0600 = 6.00 a.m.	1300 = 1.00 p.m.	2000 = 8.00 p.m.
0715 = 7.15 a.m.	1415 = 2.15 p.m.	2110 = 9.10 p.m.
0930 = 9.30 a.m.	1645 = 4.45 p.m.	2345 = 11.45 p.m.

TEMPERATURE
Conversion Formula: $°C \times 9 \div 5 + 32 = °F$

°C	°F	°C	°F	°C	°F	°C	°F
-20	-4	-5	23	10	50	25	77
-15	5	0	32	15	59	30	86
-10	14	5	41	20	68	35	95

WEIGHT
1 kg = 1000 g 100 g = 3½ oz

Kg	Pounds	Kg	Pounds	Kg	Pounds
1	2¼	5	11	25	55
2	4½	10	22	50	110
3	6½	15	33	75	165
4	9	20	45	100	220

FLUID MEASURES
1 litre(l) = 0.88 Imperial quarts = 1.06 US quarts

Litres	Imp.gal.	US gal.	Litres	Imp.gal.	US gal.
5	1.1	1.3	30	6.6	7.8
10	2.2	2.6	35	7.7	9.1
15	3.3	3.9	40	8.8	10.4
20	4.4	5.2	45	9.9	11.7

MEN'S CLOTHES

UK	Europe	US
36	46	36
38	48	38
40	50	40
42	52	42
44	54	44
46	56	46

MENS' SHOES

UK	Europe	US
6	40	7
7	41	8
8	42	9
9	43	10
10	44	11
11	45	12

LADIES' CLOTHES

UK	France	Italy	Rest of Europe	US
10	36	38	34	8
12	38	40	36	10
14	40	42	38	12
16	42	44	40	14
18	44	46	42	16
20	46	48	44	18

MEN'S SHIRTS

UK	Europe	US
14	36	14
15	38	15
15½	39	15½
16	41	16
16½	42	16½
17	43	17

LADIES' SHOES

UK	Europe	US
3	36	4½
4	37	5½
5	38	6½
6	39	7½
7	40	8½
8	41	9½

AREAS
1 hectare = 2.471 acres

1 hectare = 10,000 sq metres

1 acre = 0.4 hectares

INDEX

References are to page numbers. **Bold** numbers refer to the grid squares on the planning maps at the end of the book.

349

350

READER SURVEY

If you enjoyed using this book, or even if you didn't, please help us improve future editions by taking part in our reader survey. Every returned form will be acknowledged, and to show our appreciation we will give you £1 off your next purchase of a Thomas Cook guidebook. Just take a few minutes to complete and return this form to us.

When did you buy this book? _____

_____

Where did you buy it? (Please give town/city and if possible name of retailer)

_____

When did you/do you intend to travel in Eastern Canada?

    For how long (approx.)? _____
    How many people in your party? _____

Which cities, towns, parks and other locations did you/do you intend mainly to visit?

_____

_____

_____

Did you/will you:
    ☐ Make all your travel arrangements independently?
    ☐ Travel on a fly-drive package?
Please give brief details: _____

_____

Did you/do you intend to use this book:
    ☐ For planning your trip?
    ☐ During the trip itself?
    ☐ Both?

Did you/do you intend also to purchase any of the following travel publications for your trip?

    A road map/atlas (please specify) _____
    Other guidebooks (please specify) _____

_____

Have you used any other Thomas Cook guidebooks in the past? If so, which?

_____

Please rate the following features of Touring Eastern Canada for their value to you (Circle VU for 'very useful', U for 'useful', NU for 'little or no use'):

The 'Travel Essentials' section on pages 15–39	VU	U	NU
The 'Driving in Eastern Canada' section on pages 41–48	VU	U	NU
The 'Touring Itineraries' on pages 56–61	VU	U	NU
The recommended driving routes throughout the book	VU	U	NU
Information on towns and cities, National Parks, etc	VU	U	NU
The maps of towns and cities, parks, etc	VU	U	NU
The colour planning map	VU	U	NU

Please use this space to tell us about any features that in your opinion could be changed, improved, or added in future editions of the book, or any other comments you would like to make concerning the book:

_____

_____

_____

_____

_____

_____

_____

352

_____

_____

Your age category: ☐ 21-30 ☐ 31-40 ☐ 41–50 ☐ over 50

Your name: Mr/Mrs/Miss/Ms
(First name or initials) _____
(Last name) _____

Your full address: (Please include postal or zip code)

_____

_____

_____

_____

Your daytime telephone number: _____

Please detach this page and send it to: The Project Editor, Touring Eastern Canada, Thomas Cook Publishing, PO Box 227, Peterborough PE3 6PU, United Kingdom.

We will be pleased to send you details of how to claim your discount upon receipt of this questionnaire.

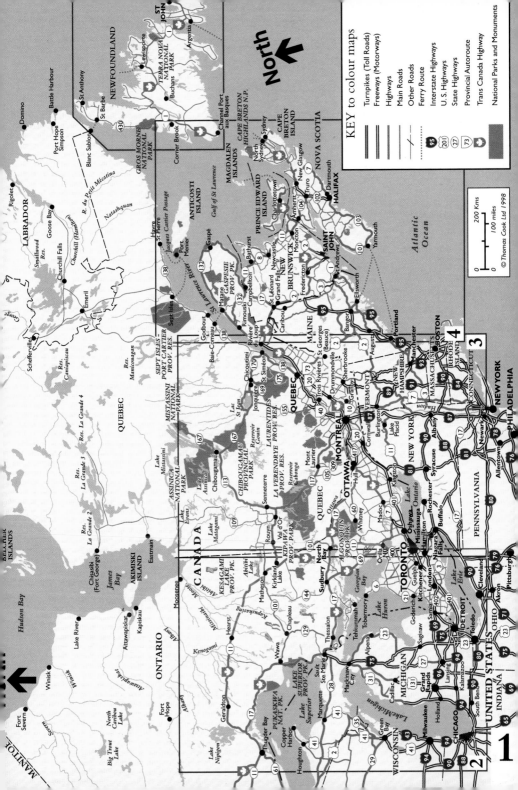

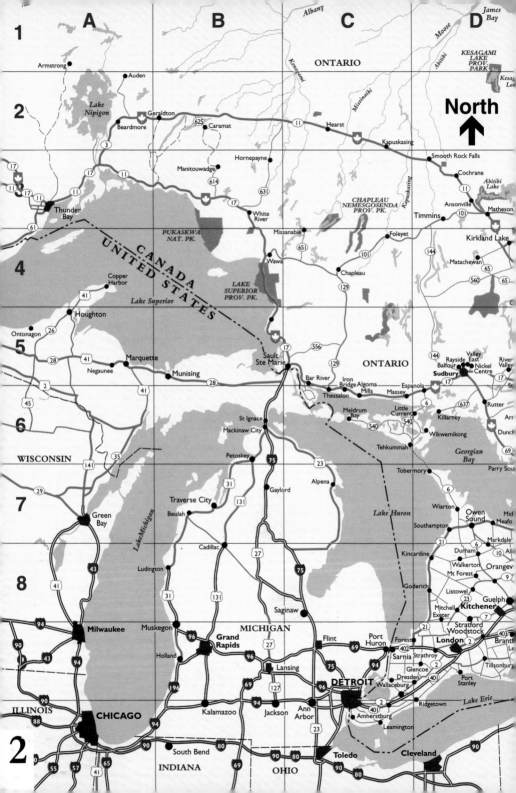

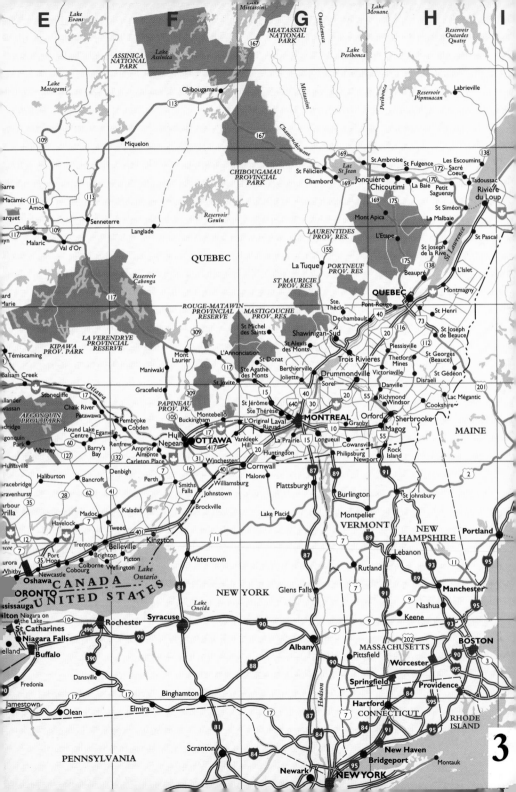